The Affirmative Action Empire

Nations and Nationalism in the Soviet Union, 1923–1939

TERRY MARTIN

Cornell University Press   ITHACA AND LONDON

First published 2001 by Cornell University Press
First printing, Cornell Paperbacks, 2001

Printed in the United States of America
Martin, Terry (Terry Dean)
   The affirmative action empire : nations and nationalism in the Soviet
Union, 1923–1939 / Terry Martin.
      p.   cm. — (The Wilder House series in politics, history, and
culture)
   Includes bibliographical references and index.
   ISBN 0-8014-3813-6 (cloth : alk. paper) — ISBN 0-8014-8677-7
(pbk. : alk. paper)
   1. Minorities—Soviet Union.   2. Nationalism and socialism—Soviet
Union.   I. Title.   II. Series.
   JN6520.M5 M27 2001
   947.084'2—dc21   2001003232

Cloth printing   10 9 8 7 6 5 4 3 2 1

Paperback printing   10 9 8 7 6 5 4 3 2 1

To Sally and Eli

Contents

Tables and Maps

Maps

Acknowledgments

My maternal grandmother, Margaret Horst, spent a summer with me a decade ago recalling her experiences as a young Mennonite girl growing up in prerevolutionary Dagestan with Kumyk Tatars as neighbors. She later experienced the ferocious assault of Makhno's peasant bands on the wealthy south Ukrainian Mennonite community during the revolution and civil war, before finally leaving the Soviet Union in 1924 to join the Russian Mennonite diaspora in Canada. Her stories first forced me to grapple with the fascinating problem of ethnicity. I've never been able to provide an adequate answer to a simple question that I'm always asked when I visit Russia or Ukraine: "What's your nationality?" Mennonite or Canadian, the only answers with any meaning to me, never satisfy anyone. One is a religion and the other is just citizenship, I am told. One might say that this book is an extended explanation as to why I, only two generations removed from Russia and Ukraine, can no longer provide a satisfactory answer to this seemingly straightforward Soviet question.

This book began as a dissertation at the University of Chicago, where I have never felt more intellectually at home. My dissertation committee was a true "dream team": Richard Hellie, who provided basic training in Russian history after I dropped my planned dissertation on seventeenth-century English religious poetry; Ron Suny, who shared his encyclopedic knowledge of the nationalities question as well as his good cheer and personal kindness; and David Laitin, whose crystal-clear intellect and commitment to comparative and interdisciplinary work broadened my horizons immensely. My greatest debt is to my adviser, Sheila Fitzpatrick, who taught me the craft of history, offered a model of integrity and discipline, and provided moral support when needed, but always gave me complete intellectual freedom.

Thanks also to my friends at Chicago—Matt Payne, James Harris, Josh Sanborn, Golfo Alexopolous, Jon Bone, and John McCannon—who made the writing ordeal endurable and occasionally even fun. Special thanks to Julie Hessler, not only for the weekly bridge games and cheap Chianti, but also for reading the entire manuscript and providing the crucial advice that allowed me finally to find the right structure for the book, and to Matt Lenoe, whose ideas had a fundamental influence on my conception of Soviet history.

In addition to those already mentioned, I received helpful comments from Joerg Baberowski, Peter Blitstein, David Brandenberger, John Bushnell, Andrea Graziosi, Peter Holquist, Hiroaki Kuromiya, Douglas Northrop, Gabor Rittersporn, Yuri Slezkine, Roman Szporluk, James Urry, Lynne Viola, and Mark Von Hagen. In Moscow, I am indebted to Aleksandr Livshin, Oleg Khlevniuk, Lidiia Kosheleva, Aleksandr Kvashenkin, Dina Nokhotovich, and Larisa Rogovaia. In Kyiv, I am particularly indebted to Ruslan Pyrih for his enlightened policy of archival openness and to my good friend Iurii Shapoval, for sharing freely his inexhaustible knowledge of Ukrainian history and archives. Finally, I would like to thank William Exley, Robert Huschka, Michael Murrin, Malcolm Gladwell, Bruce Headlam, and the entire Martin clan, and above all my parents, Lloyd and Delphine Martin.

The research for this book was supported by the International Research and Exchanges Board (IREX), the Social Sciences and Humanities Research Council (SSHRC) of Canada, the MacArthur Foundation's CASPIC program, and the C. Boyden Gray fund for junior faculty research in Harvard's history department. Parts of Chapter 2 were published as "Borders and Ethnic Conflict: The Soviet Experiment in Ethno-Territorial Proliferation," *Jahrbücher für Geschichte Osteuropas* 47 (September 1999): 538–555. An earlier version of Chapter 8 was published as "The Origins of Soviet Ethnic Cleansing," *Journal of Modern History* 70 (December 1998): 813–61. Parts of Chapter 10 were published as "The Russification of the RSFSR," *Cahiers du monde russe* 39, nos. 1–2 (1998): 99–118. The author thanks the publishers for permission to reprint this material.

This book is dedicated to Sally, without whose love and extraordinary tolerance it could never have been written, and to Eli, who appeared in the middle of the project and made it all much more fun.

T.M.

Cambridge, Massachusetts

Footnote Abbreviations

The following footnote format, with one exception, is used throughout the book: ARCHIVE *fond/opis'/delo* (date): *listy*. For protocols of Communist Party meetings, the following format is used: ARCHIVE *fond/opis'/delo* (date): *protokol/punkt*. For the Harvard Interview Project, the citation HIP A26, 43 means Harvard Interview Project, "A" Interview Series, Respondent #26, page 43.

BFORC	British Foreign Office: Russia Correspondence
CGM	Captured German Materials
GARF	Gosudarstvennyi Arkhiv Rossiiskoi Federatsii
GARF (TsGA)	Gosudarstvennyi Arkhiv Rossiiskoi Federatsii [formerly TsGA RSFSR]
HIP	Harvard Interview Project
PSS	*Polnoe sobranie sochineniia*
RGAE	*Rossiiskii gosudarstvennyi arkhiv ekonomiki*
RGVA	*Rossiiskii gosudarstvennyi voennyi arkhiv*
RTsKhIDNI	*Rossiiskii Tsentr Khraneniia i Izucheniia Dokumentov Noveishei Istorii*
SU	*Sobranie uzakonenii i rasporiazhenii*
SZ	*Sobranie zakonov i rasporiazhenii*
TsDAHOU	*Tsentral'nyi derzhavnyi arkhiv hromads'kykh ob'ednan' Ukrainy*
TsDAVOU	*Tsentral'nyi derzhavnyi arkhiv vykonnykh orhaniv Ukrainy*
TsKhSD	*Tsentr khraneniia sovremennoi dokumentatsii*

A Note on Style

I used the Library of Congress transliteration system for Russian, Ukrainian, and Belorussian, suppressing soft signs in proper names and with the usual exceptions for well-known names such as Trotsky. The cast of characters and places in this book covers dozens of languages, and it would be impossible to accurately name all non-Russians in their native languages. Therefore, I have used Russian names throughout for individuals' and place names, with the sole exception of several well-known Ukrainians. I have also used the contemporary place names rather than the emerging new ones, such as Kirgizia not Kyrgyzstan.

The Affirmative Action Empire

I

The Soviet Affirmative
Action Empire

The Soviet Union was the world's first Affirmative Action Empire. Russia's new revolutionary government was the first of the old European multiethnic states to confront the rising tide of nationalism and respond by systematically promoting the national consciousness of its ethnic minorities and establishing for them many of the characteristic institutional forms of the nation-state.[1] The Bolshevik strategy was to assume leadership over what now appeared to be the inevitable process of decolonization and carry it out in a manner that would preserve the territorial integrity of the old Russian empire. To that end, the Soviet state created not just a dozen large national republics, but tens of thousands of national territories scattered across the entire expanse of the Soviet Union. New national elites were trained and promoted to leadership positions in the government, schools, and industrial enterprises of these newly formed territories. In each territory, the national language was declared the official language of government. In dozens of cases, this necessitated the creation of a written language where one did not yet exist. The Soviet state financed the mass production of books, journals, newspapers, movies, operas,

---

[1] The Austro-Hungarian empire was the first of the old European empires to see its existence threatened by separatist nationalism. After 1867, the Hungarian half of the empire pursued a strategy of building a Hungarian nation-state through assimilation, whereas the Austrian half of the empire pioneered many of the strategies later adopted by the Soviet Union. Their policy, however, was primarily a defensive strategy of granting concessions to nationalist demands, whereas the Soviets pursued an active, prophylactic strategy of promoting non-Russian nation-building to prevent the growth of nationalism. On the policies of the Austro-Hungarian empire, see Adam Wandruszka and Peter Urbanitsch, eds., *Die Habsburgermonarchie, 1848–1918. Band III. Die Völker des Reiches* (Vienna, 1980).

museums, folk music ensembles, and other cultural output in the non-Russian languages. Nothing comparable to it had been attempted before, and, with the possible exception of India, no multiethnic state has subsequently matched the scope of Soviet Affirmative Action. This book is devoted to an analysis of this novel and fascinating experiment in governing a multiethnic state.

The Logic of the Affirmative Action Empire

Why did the Bolsheviks adopt this radical strategy? When they seized power in October 1917, they did not yet possess a coherent nationalities policy. They had a powerful slogan, which they shared with Woodrow Wilson, of the right of nations to self-determination. This slogan, however, was designed to recruit ethnic support for the revolution, not to provide a model for the governing of a multiethnic state. Although Lenin always took the nationalities question seriously, the unexpected strength of nationalism as a mobilizing force during the revolution and civil war nevertheless greatly surprised and disturbed him. The Bolsheviks expected nationalism in Poland and Finland, but the numerous nationalist movements that sprang up across most of the former Russian empire were not expected. The strong nationalist movement in Ukraine was particularly unnerving. This direct confrontation with nationalism compelled the Bolsheviks to formulate a new nationalities policy.[2]

This did not occur without contestation. On the one side were the nation-builders, led by Lenin and Stalin; on the other side were the internationalists, led by Georgii Piatakov and Nikolai Bukharin. At the Eighth Party Congress in March 1919, the two sides clashed over the question of the right of national self-determination.[3] Piatakov argued that "during a sufficiently large and torturous experience in the borderlands, the slogan of the right of nations to self-determination has shown itself in practice, during the social revolution, as a slogan uniting all counterrevolutionary forces."[4] Once the proletariat had seized power, Piatakov maintained, national self-determination became irrelevant: "It's just a diplomatic game, or worse than a game if we take it seriously."[5] Piatakov was supported by Bukharin, who argued that the right to self-determination could only be invested in the proletariat, not in "some fictitious so-called 'national will.'"[6]

[2] Richard Pipes, *The Formation of the Soviet Union* (rev. ed., Cambridge, Mass., 1964); Ronald Grigor Suny, *The Revenge of the Past* (Stanford, Calif., 1993); Andrea Graziosi, *Bol'sheviki i krest'iane na Ukraine, 1918–1919 gody* (Moscow, 1997); Jeremy Smith, *The Bolsheviks and the National Question, 1917–1923* (London, 1999); Yuri Slezkine, "The USSR as a Communal Apartment, or How a Socialist State Promoted Ethnic Particularism," *Slavic Review* 53 (Summer 1994): 414–452. Francine Hirsch, "Empire of Nations: Colonial Technologies and the Making of the Soviet Union, 1917–1939" (Ph.D. diss., Princeton University, 1998).

[3] For a good background discussion, see Smith, *The Bolsheviks and the National Question*, 7–28.

[4] *Vos'moi s"ezd RKP/b/. Protokoly* (Moscow, 1933): 79–80.

[5] Ibid., 82.

[6] Ibid., 48–49. This position was briefly supported by Stalin as well in December 1917 and January 1918. I. V. Stalin, "Otvet tovarishcham Ukraintsam v tylu i na fronte," *Sochineniia* 4 (Moscow, 1953–1955): 8; "Vystupleniia na III vserossiiskom s"ezde sovetov R., S. i K. D.," 4: 31–32.

Lenin had clashed with Piatakov and others on this issue before and during the revolution.[7] He now answered this renewed challenge with characteristic vigor. Nationalism had united all counterrevolutionary forces, Lenin readily agreed, but it had also attracted the Bolsheviks' class allies. The Finnish bourgeoisie had successfully "deceived the working masses that the Muscovites [*Moskvaly*], chauvinists, Great Russians want[ed] to oppress the Finns." Arguments such as Piatakov's served to increase that fear and therefore strengthen national resistance. It was only "thanks to our acknowledgement of [the Finns'] right to self-determination, that the process of [class] differentiation was eased there." Nationalism was fueled by historic distrust: "The working masses of other nations are full of distrust [*nedoverie*] towards Great Russia, as a kulak and oppressor nation." Only the right to self-determination could overcome that distrust, Lenin argued, but Piatakov's policy would instead make the party the heir to Tsarist chauvinism: "Scratch any Communist and you find a Great Russian chauvinist. . . . He sits in many of us and we must fight him."[8]

The congress supported Lenin and retained a qualified right of national self-determination.[9] Of course, the majority of the former Russian empire's nationalities were forced to exercise that right within the confines of the Soviet Union. The period from 1919 to 1923, therefore, was devoted to working out what exactly non-Russian "national self-determination" could mean in the context of a unitary Soviet state. The final result was the Affirmative Action Empire: a strategy aimed at disarming nationalism by granting what were called the "forms" of nationhood. This policy was based on a diagnosis of nationalism worked out largely by Lenin and Stalin. Lenin had addressed the national question repeatedly from 1912 to 1916, when he formulated and defended the slogan of self-determination, and again from 1919 to 1922, after the alarming success of nationalist movements during the civil war.[10] Stalin was the Bolsheviks' acknowledged "master of the nationalities question"[11]: author of the standard prerevolutionary text *Marxism and the Nationalities Question*, Commissar of Nationalities from 1917 to 1924, and official spokesman on the national question

---

[7] Lenin's two major prerevolutionary attacks on Piatakov's position, whose major exponent was Rosa Luxemburg, were "O prave natsii na samoopredelenie" (1914) in V. I. Lenin, *PSS* 25 (Moscow, 1975–1977): 255–320, and "Sotsialisticheskaia revoliutsii i pravo natsii na samoopredelenie" (1916) *PSS* 27: 151–166. He also debated Piatakov at the party's seventh conference in April 1917; see *Natsional'nyi vopros na perekrestke mnenii* (Moscow, 1992): 11–27.

[8] *Vos'moi s"ezd*, 54–55, 107–108.

[9] Ibid., 387. Smith, *The Bolsheviks and the National Question*, 21.

[10] For the period 1912 to 1916, in addition to the works cited above, see "Tezisy po natsional'nomu voprosu" (1913) *PSS* 23: 314–322; "Kriticheskie zametki po natsional'nomu voprosu" (1913) *PSS* 24: 113–150; "Itogi diskussii o samoopredelenii" (1916) *PSS* 30: 17–58. For the period 1919 to 1922, see "Pis'mo k rabochim i krest'ianam Ukrainy . . ." (1919) *PSS* 40: 41–47; "Ob obrazovanii SSSR" (1922) *PSS* 45: 211–213; "K voprosu o natsional'nostiakh ili ob 'avtonomizatsii'" (1922) *PSS* 45: 356–362.

[11] "Iz istorii obrazovaniia SSSR. Stenogramma zasedaniia sektsii 12 s"ezda RKP/b/ po natsional'nomu voprosu 25.04.23" *Izvestiia TsK KPSS*, no. 3 (1991): 169.

at party congresses.[12] Lenin and Stalin were in fundamental agreement on both the logical rationale and the essential aspects of this new policy, although they came into conflict in 1922 over important issues of implementation. Their diagnosis of the nationalities problem rested on the following three premises.

The Marxist Premise

First, the point on which Piatakov and Lenin agreed, nationalism was a uniquely dangerous mobilizing ideology because it had the potential to forge an above-class alliance in pursuit of national goals. Lenin called nationalism a "bourgeois trick"[13] but recognized that, like the hedgehog's, it was a good one. It worked because it presented legitimate social grievances in a national form. At the Twelfth Party Congress in 1923, Bukharin, by then a fervid defender of the party's nationalities policy, noted that "when we tax [the non-Russian peasantry] their discontent takes on a national form, is given a national interpretation, which is then exploited by our opponents."[14] Ernest Gellner has parodied this argument as the "wrong-address theory" of nationalism: "Just as extreme Shi'ite Muslims hold that Archangel Gabriel made a mistake, delivering the Message to Mohammed when it was intended for Ali, so Marxists basically like to think that the spirit of history or human consciousness made a terrible boob. The wakening message was intended for *classes*, but by some terrible postal error was delivered to *nations*."[15]

The Bolsheviks viewed nationalism, then, as a masking ideology. Masking metaphors recur again and again in their discourse about nationality. Stalin was particularly fond of them: "The national flag is sewn on only to deceive the masses, as a popular flag, a convenience for covering up [*dlia prykrytiia*] the counter-revolutionary plans of the national bourgeoisie." "If bourgeois circles attempt to give a national tint [*natsional'naia okraska*] to [our] conflicts, then only because it is convenient to hide their battle for power behind a national costume."[16] This interpretation of nationalism as a masking ideology helps explain why the Bolsheviks remained highly suspicious of national self-expression, even after they adopted a policy explicitly designed to encourage it. For example, in justifying a wave of national repression carried out in 1933, Stalin characteristically invoked a masking metaphor: "The remnants of capitalism in the people's consciousness are much more dynamic in the sphere of nationality than in any other area. This is because they can mask themselves so well in a national costume."[17]

---

[12] Stalin's articles and speeches are collected in I. Stalin, *Marksizm i natsional'no-kolonial'nyi vopros* (Moscow, 1934).

[13] Lenin, "Kak Episkop Nikon zashchishchaet Ukraintsev?" (1913) *PSS* 24: 9.

[14] *Dvenadtsatyi s"ezd RKP/b/. Stenograficheskii otchet* (Moscow, 1968): 612.

[15] Ernest Gellner, *Nations and Nationalism* (Ithaca, N.Y., 1983): 129.

[16] Stalin, "Politika sovetskoi vlasti po natsional'nomu voprosu v Rossii" (1918), in *Marksizm*, 54; "Vystupleniia na III vserossiiskom s"ezde," 31.

[17] *XVII s"ezd VKP/b/. Stenograficheskii otchet* (Moscow, 1934): 31.

This understanding of nationalism led Piatakov to support the only apparently logical response: attack nationalism as a counterrevolutionary ideology and nationality itself as a reactionary remnant of the capitalist era. Lenin and Stalin, however, drew the exact opposite conclusion. They reasoned as follows. By granting the forms of nationhood, the Soviet state could split the above-class national alliance for statehood. Class divisions, then, would naturally emerge, which would allow the Soviet government to recruit proletarian and peasant support for their socialist agenda. Lenin argued that Finnish independence had intensified, not reduced, class conflict.[18] National self-determination would have the same consequences within the Soviet Union. Likewise, Stalin insisted it was "necessary to 'take' autonomy away from [the national bourgeoisie], having first cleansed it of its bourgeois filth and transformed it from bourgeois into Soviet autonomy."[19] A belief gradually emerged, then, that the above-class appeal of nationalism could be disarmed by granting the forms of nationhood. This was the Marxist premise.

The Modernization Premise

This conclusion was buttressed by a second premise: national consciousness was an unavoidable historic phase that all peoples must pass through on the way to internationalism. In their prerevolutionary writings, Lenin and Stalin argued that nationality emerged only with the onset of capitalism and was itself a consequence of capitalist production.[20] It was not an essential or permanent attribute of mankind. Piatakov understandably interpreted this as meaning that nationality would be irrelevant under socialism and therefore should be granted no special status. Both Lenin and Stalin insisted, however, that nationality would persist for a long time even under socialism.[21] In fact, national self-awareness would initially increase. Already in 1916, Lenin stated that "mankind can proceed towards the inevitable fusion [*sliianie*] of nations only through a transitional period of the complete freedom of all oppressed nations."[22] Stalin later explicated this paradox as follows: "We are undertaking the maximum development of national culture, so that it will exhaust itself completely and thereby create the base for the organization of international socialist culture."[23]

Two factors appear to have combined to create this sense of the inevitability of a national stage of development. First, the collapse of the Austro-Hungarian empire and the surprisingly strong nationalist movements within the former Russian empire greatly increased the Bolsheviks' respect for the power and

[18] In his prerevolutionary writings, Lenin repeatedly cited Sweden's granting Norway independence in 1905 as having sped the emergence of class conflict in both countries. Lenin, "O prave natsii," 289; "Sotsialisticheskaia revoliutsiia," 253.

[19] Stalin, "Odna iz ocherednykh zadach" (1918) *Sochineniia* 4: 75.

[20] Stalin, *Marksizm*, 4–15; Lenin, "O prave natsii," 255–271.

[21] On Lenin, see *Tainy natsional'noi politiki TsK RKP. Stenograficheskii otchet sekretnogo IV soveshchaniia TsK RKP, 1923 g.* (Moscow, 1992): 30–31; on Stalin, see *Marksizm*, 155–165.

[22] Lenin, "Sotsialisticheskaia revoliutsiia," 256.

[23] *RTsKhIDNI* 558/1/4490 (1929): 9.

ubiquity of nationalism. Stalin was particularly impressed by the process of national succession in the formerly German cities of Austro-Hungary. At the 1921 party congress, he pointed out that just fifty years earlier all cities in Hungary were predominantly German, but had now become Hungarian. Likewise, he maintained, all Russian cities in Ukraine and Belorussia would "inevitably" be nationalized. Opposing this was futile: "It is impossible to go against history."[24] Elsewhere Stalin called this pattern "a general law of national development in the entire world."[25] National consolidation, then, was unavoidable even under socialism.

Moreover, this national stage of development took on a more positive connotation as it became associated not only with capitalism but also with modernization in general. In his rebuttal of Piatakov and Bukharin, citing the example of the Bashkirs, Lenin had stated that "one must wait the development of a given nation, the differentiation of proletariat from bourgeois elements, which is unavoidable . . . the path from the medieval to bourgeois democracy, or from bourgeois to proletarian democracy. This is an absolutely unavoidable path."[26] As Lenin focused Bolshevik attention on the Soviet Union's eastern "backward" nationalities, the consolidation of nationhood became associated with historical developmental progress. This trend reached its climax during the cultural revolution, when Soviet propaganda would boast that in the far north, the thousand-year process of national formation had been telescoped into a mere decade.[27] The formation of nations, then, came to be seen as both an unavoidable and positive stage in the modernization of the Soviet Union. This was the modernization premise.

The Colonial Premise and the Greatest-Danger Principle

A third and final premise asserted that non-Russian nationalism was primarily a response to Tsarist oppression and was motivated by a historically justifiable distrust (*nedoverie*) of the Great Russians. This argument was pressed most forcefully by Lenin, who already in 1914 had attacked Rosa Luxemburg's denial of the right of self-determination as "objectively aiding the Black Hundred Great Russians. . . . Absorbed by the fight with nationalism in Poland, Rosa Luxemburg forgot about the nationalism of the Great Russians, though it is exactly this nationalism that is the most dangerous of all." The nationalism of the oppressed, Lenin maintained, had a "democratic content" that must be supported, whereas the nationalism of the oppressor had no redeeming value. He ended with the slogan "Fight against all nationalisms and, first of all, against Great Russian nationalism."[28]

---

[24] *Desiatyi s"ezd RKP/b/. Protokoly* (Moscow, 1933): 216.

[25] *RTsKhIDNI* 558/1/4490 (1929): 16.

[26] *Vos'moi s"ezd*, 55.

[27] *II sessiia VTsIK XV sozyva. Stenograficheskii otchet* (Moscow, 1931), 16. Yuri Slezkine, *Arctic Mirrors* (Ithaca, N.Y., 1994).

[28] Lenin, "O prave natsii," 277, 275–276, 319.

Bolshevik conduct between 1917 and 1919 convinced Lenin that the all-Russian Communist party had inherited the psychology of great-power chauvinism from the Tsarist regime. In non-Russian regions, the Bolshevik party, relying almost exclusively on the minority Russian proletariat and agricultural colonists, had frequently adopted an overtly chauvinist attitude toward the local population.[29] This attitude alarmed Lenin, and his harsh attack on Piatakov was partly motivated by the latter's anti-Ukrainian policy in Kiev. In December 1919, Lenin again launched a fierce denunciation of Bolshevik chauvinism in Ukraine.[30] His anger climaxed during the notorious Georgian affair of 1922, when he denounced Dzerzhinskii, Stalin, and Ordzhonikidze as Great Russian chauvinists (russified natives, he maintained, were often the worst chauvinists).[31] Such Bolshevik chauvinism inspired Lenin to coin the term *rusotiapstvo* (mindless Russian chauvinism), which then entered the Bolshevik lexicon and became an invaluable weapon in the rhetorical arsenals of the national republics.[32]

Lenin's concern over Great Russian chauvinism led to the establishment of a crucial principle of the Soviet nationalities policy. In December 1922, he reiterated his 1914 attack on Great Russian chauvinism with the added admonition that one must "distinguish between the nationalism of oppressor nations and the nationalism of oppressed nations, the nationalism of large nations and the nationalism of small nations. . . . [I]n relation to the second nationalism, in almost all historical practice, we nationals of the large nations are guilty, because of an infinite amount of violence [committed]."[33] This concept entered formulaic Bolshevik rhetoric as the distinction between offensive (*nastupatel'nyi*) great-power nationalism and defensive (*oboronitel'nyi*) local nationalism, the latter being viewed as a justifiable response to the former. This belief in turn led to the establishment of the important "greatest-danger principle": namely, that great-power (or sometimes Great Russian) chauvinism was a greater danger than local nationalism.[34] This was the colonial premise.

Lenin's extreme formulation of this principle led to one of his two differences of opinion with Stalin over nationalities policy in late 1922.[35] Stalin had supported the greatest-danger principle before 1922–1923, reiterated his support in 1923, and from April 1923 to December 1932 supervised a nationalities policy based on that principle. Nevertheless, Stalin was uncomfortable with the insistence that *all* local nationalism could be explained as a response to great-power chauvinism. Based on his experience in Georgia, Stalin insisted that Georgian nationalism was also characterized by great-power exploitation of

[29] *Desiatyi s"ezd*, 195–209. Pipes, *The Formation*, 126–154, 172–183.

[30] Richard Pipes, ed., *The Unknown Lenin* (New Haven, Conn., 1996): 76–77.

[31] Lenin, "K voprosu o natsional'nostiakh," 356–362.

[32] At the 1921 party congress, Zatonskyi attributes this term to Lenin. *Desiatyi s"ezd*, 207.

[33] Lenin, "K voprosu o natsional'nostiakh," 359.

[34] *Dvenadtsatyi s"ezd*, 693–695.

[35] Their second difference of opinion came over the structure of the Soviet Union and in particular the place of Russia within the Soviet Union. This is discussed in Chapter 10.

their Ossetine and Abkhaz minorities. Stalin therefore always paired his attacks on Great Russian chauvinism with a complementary attack on the lesser danger of local nationalism.[36] This difference in emphasis led Stalin, in September 1922, to accuse Lenin jocularly of "national liberalism."[37] This difference of emphasis was also evident in Lenin's and Stalin's terminologies. Lenin typically referred to Russian nationalism as great-power chauvinism, which distinguished it from other nationalisms, whereas Stalin preferred the term Great Russian chauvinism. Despite these differences in emphasis, Stalin consistently supported the greatest-danger principle.

The Marxist, modernization, and colonial premises, then, combined to form the theoretical rationale for the nationalities policy that Lenin and Stalin successfully imposed on a reluctant Bolshevik Party through a series of resolutions at the 1919, 1921, and 1923 party congresses.[38] Their reasoning can be summarized as follows. Nationalism is a masking ideology that leads legitimate class interests to be expressed, not in an appropriate class-based socialist movement, but rather in the form of an above-class national movement. National identity is not a primordial quality, but rather an unavoidable by-product of the modern capitalist *and* early socialist world, which must be passed through before a mature international socialist world can come into being. Since national identity *is* a real phenomenon in the modern world, the nationalism of the oppressed non-Russian peoples expresses not only masked class protest, but also legitimate national grievances against the oppressive great-power chauvinism of the dominant Russian nationality. Therefore, neither nationalism nor national identity can be unequivocally condemned as reactionary. *Some* national claims—those confined to the realm of national "form"—are in fact legitimate and must be granted to split the above-class national alliance. Such a policy will speed the emergence of class cleavages and so allow the party to recruit non-Russian proletarian and peasant support for its socialist agenda. Nationalism will be disarmed by granting the forms of nationhood.

The Piedmont Principle

The intersection between nationalities and foreign policy was a fourth factor influencing the formation of the Affirmative Action Empire. Already in November 1917, Lenin and Stalin issued an "Appeal to all Muslim Toilers of Russia and the East," which promised to end imperial exploitation within the former Russian empire and called on Muslims outside Russia to overthrow their colonial masters.[39] This linkage between domestic nationalities policy and foreign policy goals in the east was quite common during the civil war period. After

---

[36] *Dvenadtsatyi s"ezd*, 487–490.

[37] "Iz istorii obrazovaniia SSSR," no. 9 (1989): 16.

[38] The key resolutions are found in *Vos'moi s"ezd*, 387; *Desiatyi s"ezd*, 573–583; *Dvenadtsatyi s"ezd*, 691–697; *Tainy natsional'noi politiki*, 282–286.

[39] I. Lazovskii and I. Bibin, *Sovetskaia politika za 10 let po natsional'nomu voprosu v RSFSR* (Moscow-Leningrad, 1928): 2–3.

the 1921 Treaty of Riga included millions of Ukrainians and Belorussians within the borders of Poland, Soviet attention shifted westward. The Soviet Union's western border now cut through the ethnographic territory of Finns, Belorussians, Ukrainians, and Rumanians. It was hoped that an ostentatiously generous treatment of those nationalities within the Soviet Union would attract their ethnic brethren in Poland, Finland, and Romania.

The attraction and eventual annexation of Poland's large Ukrainian population was the most important object of this strategy. In April 1924, Soviet Ukraine's major newspaper gave expression to this desire[40]:

> There was a time when Galicia served as the "Piedmont" for Ukrainian culture. Now, when Ukrainian culture is suffocating in "cultured," "European" Poland, its center has naturally shifted to the Ukrainian SSR.

In Ukrainian political discourse of the 1920s, Soviet Ukraine was seen as a twentieth-century Piedmont that would serve as the center to unite, first culturally and then politically, the divided Ukrainian populations of Poland, Czechoslovakia, and Romania.[41] Therefore, I refer to the Soviet attempt to exploit cross-border ethnic ties to project political influence into neighboring states as the Piedmont Principle. It should be emphasized, however, that this foreign policy goal was never the primary motivation of the Soviet nationalities policy. It was seen as an exploitable benefit of a domestically driven policy that affected the intensity of implementation in sensitive regions, but not the content of the policy itself. The Piedmont Principle would, however, play a crucial role in the revision of that policy in late 1932.

The Content of the Affirmative Action Empire

An authoritative account of the content of the Soviet nationalities policy was finally delineated in resolutions passed at the Twelfth Party Congress in April 1923 and at a special Central Committee (TsK) conference on nationalities policy in June 1923. These two resolutions, along with Stalin's speeches in their defense, became the standard Bolshevik proof texts for nationalities policy and remained so throughout the Stalinist era.[42] Before April 1923, nationalities policy had been debated repeatedly at important party meetings. After June 1923, this public debate ceased.[43] The 1923 resolutions affirmed that the Soviet state would maximally support those "forms" of nationhood that did not conflict with a

---

[40] "Ukrains'ka kul'tura v 'kul'turnii' Pol'shchi," *Visti VUTsIK*, no. 87 (17.04.24): 1.

[41] See, for instance, "The Ukrainian SSR—Piedmont of the Ukrainian Laboring Masses," by Mykola Skrypnyk, in *Statti i promovy. Natsional'ne pytannia*, vol. 2, part 2 (Kharkov, 1931): 153–159.

[42] These proof texts were collected in periodic editions of Stalin's *Marksizm i natsional'no-kolonialnyi vopros*.

[43] After June 1923, the content of the Soviet nationalities policy was not discussed again in higher party bodies, with the sole exception of a Politburo commission on RSFSR affairs in

unitary central state. This meant a commitment to support the following four national forms: national territories, national languages, national elites, and national cultures.

National Territories

By June 1923, national territories had in fact already been formed for most of the large Soviet nationalities.[44] The 1923 resolutions merely reaffirmed their existence and denounced all plans to abolish them. There still remained, however, the problem of territorially dispersed national minorities. Soviet policy opposed their assimilation. It also opposed the Austro-Marxist solution of extraterritorial national–cultural autonomy.[45] Both were considered likely to increase nationalism and exacerbate ethnic conflict. The solution hit on by the Bolsheviks in the mid-1920s was characteristically radical. Their national–territorial system would be extended downward into smaller and smaller national territories (national districts, village soviets, collective farms) until the system merged seamlessly with the personal nationality of each Soviet citizen. The result was a grandiose pyramid of national soviets consisting of thousands of national territories.

National Languages and Elites

The primary focus of the 1923 resolutions were the twin policies of promoting national languages and national elites. In each national territory, the language of the titular nationality was to be established as the official state language. National elites were to be trained and promoted into positions of leadership in the party, government, industry, and schools of each national territory. While these policies had been articulated as early as 1920, and officially sanctioned at the 1921 party congress, virtually nothing had been done yet to implement them.[46] The two 1923 decrees condemned this inactivity and demanded immediate action. These two policies were soon referred to as *korenizatsiia* and became the centerpiece of the Soviet nationalities policy.

Korenizatsiia is best translated as indigenization. It is not derived directly from the stem *koren-* ("root"—with the meaning "rooting"), but from its

---

1926–1927, whose deliberations proved fruitless (see Chapter 10). Issues of implementation were periodically discussed, but from 1925 to 1936, nationalities policy was never an agenda point at a party congress or a TsK plenum.

[44] By June 1923, there were already two federal republics, five union republics, twelve autonomous republics, and eleven autonomous oblasts. The delimitation of Central Asia in 1924 would complete the process of forming national territories. For an overview of the establishment of national territories in this period, see the special issue of *Zhizn' natsional'nostei*, no. 1 (1923); also, Smith, *The Bolsheviks and the National Question*, 29–107.

[45] Tim Bottomore and Patrick Goode, eds., *Austro-Marxism* (Oxford, 1978).

[46] This policy was not yet articulated in the 1919 party congress resolution. For early statements, see S. Dimanshtein, "Eshche malo opyta," *Zhizn' natsional'nostei*, no. 33 (31.08.19): 1; Stalin, "Politika sovetskoi vlasti po natsional'nomu voprosu v Rossii," in *Marksizm*, 58–64.

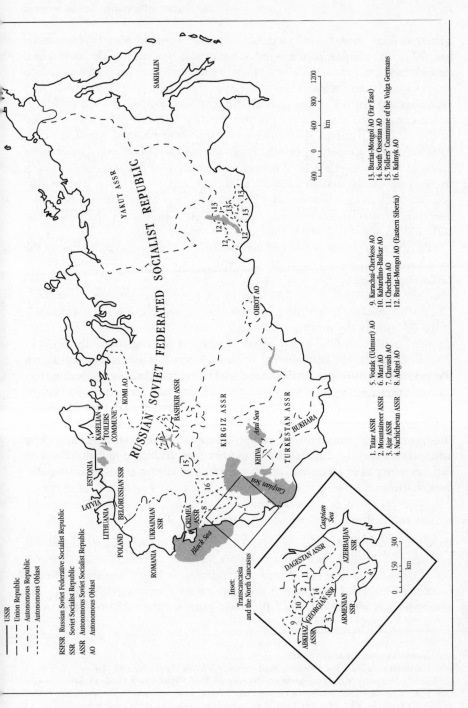

Map 1. Federal Structure of the USSR, December 1922

USSR
—— Union Republic
— — Autonomous Republic
- - - - Autonomous Oblast

RSFSR Russian Soviet Federative Socialist Republic
SSR   Soviet Socialist Republic
ASSR   Autonomous Soviet Socialist Republic
AO   Autonomous Oblast

1. Tatar ASSR
2. Mountaineer ASSR
3. Ajar ASSR
4. Nachichevan ASSR

5. Votiak (Udmurt) AO
6. Mari AO
7. Chuvash AO
8. Adigei AO

9. Karachai-Cherkess AO
10. Kabardino-Balkar AO
11. Chechen AO
12. Buriat-Mongol AO (Eastern Siberia)

13. Buriat-Mongol AO (Far East)
14. South Ossetian AO
15. Tollers' Commune of the Volga Germans
16. Kalmyk AO

RUSSIAN SOVIET FEDERATED SOCIALIST REPUBLIC

YAKUT ASSR

SAKHALIN

KARELIAN TOILERS' COMMUNE

KOMI AO

BASHKIR ASSR

KIRGIZ ASSR

OIROT AO

TURKESTAN ASSR

BUKHARA

KHIVA

Aral Sea

Caspian Sea

Black Sea

CRIMEA ASSR

UKRAINIAN SSR

BELORUSSIAN SSR

ESTONIA

LATVIA

LITHUANIA

POLAND

ROMANIA

km
400 0 400 800 1200

Inset:
Transcaucasia
and the North Caucasus

Caspian Sea

DAGESTAN ASSR

AZERBAIJAN SSR

GEORGIAN SSR

ARMENIAN SSR

ABKHAZ ASSR

Black Sea

km
0 150 300

adjectival form *korennoi*, as used in the phrase *korennoi narod* ("indigenous people"). The coining of the word *korenizatsiia* was part of the Bolsheviks' decolonizing rhetoric, which systematically favored the claims of indigenous peoples over "newly arrived elements" (*prishlye elementy*). In 1923, however, *korenizatsiia* was not yet in use. Instead, the term *natsionalizatsiia* was preferred, which emphasized the project of nation-building.[47] This emphasis was echoed in the national republics where the policy was simply named after the titular nationality: *Ukrainizatsiia, Uzbekizatsiia, Oirotizatsiia*. The term *korenizatsiia* emerged later from the central nationalities policy bureaucracy, which primarily serviced extraterritorial national minorities and so preferred a term that referred to all indigenous (*korennye*) peoples, not just titular nationalities. *Korenizatsiia* gradually emerged as the preferred term to describe this policy, but it should be noted that Stalin always used *natsionalizatsiia*.[48]

The 1923 resolutions established *korenizatsiia* as the most urgent item on the Soviet nationalities policy agenda. In keeping with Lenin's and Stalin's highly psychological interpretation of nationalism, the subjective effects of *korenizatsiia* were emphasized. It would make Soviet power seem "native" (*rodnaia*), "intimate" (*blizkaia*), "popular" (*narodnaia*), "comprehensible" (*poniatnaia*). It would address the positive psychological needs of nationalism: "The [non-Russian] masses would see that Soviet power and her organs are the affair of their own efforts, the embodiment of their desires." It would likewise disarm the negative psychological anxiety associated with the perception of foreign rule: "Soviet power, which up to the present time [April 1923] has remained Russian power, [would be made] not only Russian but international, and become native [*rodnaia*] for the peasantry of the formerly oppressed nationalities." Native languages would make Soviet power comprehensible. Native cadres, who understood "the way of life, customs, and habits of the local population," would make Soviet power seem indigenous rather than an external Russian imperial imposition.[49]

National Culture

Finally, the resolutions also reiterated the party's recognition of distinct national cultures and pledged central state support for their maximum development.[50] Stalin famously defined Soviet national cultures as being "national in form, socialist in content," but did not elaborate on what exactly this meant.[51] The ambiguity was intentional, since Bolshevik plans for the social transformation

---

[47] *Tainy natsional'noi politiki*, 284.

[48] For instance, *XVI s"ezd VKP/b/. Stenograficheskii otchet* (Moscow, 1930): 54.

[49] Stalin, *Marksizm*, 62; *Tainy natsional'noi politiki*, 102; *Dvenadtsatyi s"ezd*, 481–482.

[50] The more important statement on national culture, however, was a 1925 speech by Stalin. Stalin, "O politicheskikh zadachakh universiteta narodov vostoka," in *Marksizm*, 155–165.

[51] Stalin, "O politicheskikh zadachakh universiteta narodov vostoka," *Marksizm*, 158. Stalin's original formulation was actually "proletarian in content." In June 1930, he shifted to the canonical "socialist in content." *Marksizm*, 194.

of the country did not allow for any fundamentally distinctive religious, legal, ideological, or customary features.[52] The translation that best captures the meaning of Stalin's *natsional'naia kul'tura* is not "national culture," but "national identity" or "symbolic ethnicity."[53]

Soviet policy did systematically promote the distinctive national identity and national self-consciousness of its non-Russian populations. It did this not only through the formation of national territories staffed by national elites using their own national languages, but also through the aggressive promotion of symbolic markers of national identity: national folklore, museums, dress, food, costumes, opera, poets, progressive historical events, and classic literary works. The long-term goal was that distinctive national identities would coexist peacefully with an emerging all-union socialist culture that would supersede the preexisting national cultures. National identity would be depoliticized through an ostentatious show of respect for the national identities of the non-Russians.

Federation

The major positive features of the Soviet nationalities policy, then, were the promotion of national territories, languages, elites, and identities. It is also important to understand what that policy did not involve. Above all, it did not involve federation, if this term means anything more than the mere formation of administrative territories along national lines. At the April and June 1923 gatherings, the Ukrainian delegation, led by Khristian Rakovskii, pressed very aggressively for the devolution of meaningful federal powers to the national republics. Stalin rebuffed Rakovskii's proposals scornfully and mendaciously labeled his goal as confederation.[54] Although the 1922–1923 constitutional settlement was called a federation, it in fact concentrated all decision-making power in the center. National republics were granted no more powers than Russian provinces.[55] Prior to June 1917, both Lenin and Stalin denounced federation and advocated a unitary state with oblast autonomy for national regions. This meant the formation of national administrative units and the selective use of national languages in government and education.[56] In June 1917, Lenin abruptly

---

[52] For an account of Soviet attacks on such customs, see Gregory J. Massell, *The Surrogate Proletariat: Moslem Women and Revolutionary Strategies in Soviet Central Asia, 1919–1929* (Princeton, N.J., 1974). Douglas Northrop, "Uzbek Women and the Veil: Gender and Power in Stalinist Central Asia" (Ph.D. diss., Stanford University, 1999).

[53] Herbert Gans, "Symbolic Ethnicity: The Future of Ethnic Groups and Cultures in America," *Ethnic and Racial Studies* 2 (1979): 9–17.

[54] "Iz istorii obrazovaniia SSSR," *Izvestiia TsK KPSS*, no. 9 (1989): 18–19; "Iz istorii obrazovaniia SSSR. Stenogramma," no. 3 (1991): 170–172; no. 5 (1991): 154–176; *Dvenadtsatyi s"ezd*, 576–582; *Tainy natsional'noi politiki*, 107–110; *Natsional'nyi vopros na perekrestke mnenii*, 86–91; 97–100.

[55] They were granted different governmental structures, however, including their own Sovnarkom, several independent commissariats, and, in Ukraine, even their own Politburo.

[56] Stalin, *Marksizm*, 42–43, 48–49; "Protiv federatsii" (1917) *Sochineniia* 3: 23–28; Lenin, "Proekt platformy k 4s"ezdu sots-dem latyshskogo kraia" (1913) *PSS* 23: 209–210; "Tezisy po natsional'nomu voprosu," 317–320.

rehabilitated the term federation, but he used it to describe what amounted to a much more ambitious version of oblast autonomy. As Stalin noted coyly in 1924, federation "turned out to be not so nearly in contradiction with the goal of economic unification as it might have seemed earlier."[57] Soviet federation did not mean devolution of political or economic power.

Economic Equalization

Economic equalization occupied a much more ambiguous place in the Soviet nationalities policy. The 1923 nationalities policy decrees called for measures to overcome "the real economic and cultural inequality of the Soviet Union's nationalities." One economic measure proposed was transferring factories from the Russian heartland to eastern national regions.[58] This policy was in fact adopted but then almost immediately discontinued. This proved typical of economic equalization programs. In contrast to the commitment to cultural and national equalization, through Affirmative Action in education and hiring, the Soviet commitment to economic equalization was never institutionalized. Attempts by the "culturally backward" republics to obtain an annual budget line for a program designed to combat their "backwardness" failed. The economic commissariats were consistently hostile to the Soviet nationalities policy. On the other hand, national republics could and often did use the 1923 resolutions and their "backward" national status to lobby all-union agencies for privileged economic investment.[59] However, they could make no absolute claim to investment based on their national status. Gerhard Simon concludes, only a little too strongly, that "Soviet economic policy has never made overcoming the rift between economically underdeveloped national territories a high-priority issue. Wherever economic equalization occurred, it was only a side effect of other planning priorities, such as development of new resources, increasing regional economic specialization and primarily military-strategic conceptions."[60]

Migration

One issue that was not prominently discussed during the 1923 nationalities policy debates was control over migration into the non-Russian republics. The Soviet nationalities policy called for the formation of national territories. Did it also sanction measures to preserve (or create) national majorities in those republics? Initially the answer appeared to be yes. In Kazakhstan and Kirgizia,

---

[57] "Protiv federatsii," 31.

[58] *Dvenadtsatyi s"ezd*, 694; *Tainy natsional'noi politiki*, 285.

[59] Matthew Payne, "Turksib. The Building of the Turkestano-Siberian Railroad and the Politics of Production during the Cultural Revolution, 1926–1931" (Ph.D. diss., University of Chicago, 1995).

[60] Gerhard Simon, *Nationalism and Policy Towards the Nationalities in the Soviet Union* (Boulder, Colo., 1991), 297. On this issue, see Alec Nove and J. A. Newth, *The Soviet Middle East: A Model for Development?* (London, 1967). Donna Bahry, *Outside Moscow: Power, Politics, and Budgetary Policy in the Soviet Republics* (New York, 1987).

central authorities even sanctioned the expulsion of illegal Slavic agricultural settlers as a decolonization measure. In the early 1920s, the Soviet Union's eastern national territories were closed to agricultural colonization. However, by 1927 all-union economic interests had again prevailed over local national concerns and all restrictions on migration were removed.

An Affirmative Action Empire

The Soviet Union was not a federation and certainly not a nation-state. Its distinctive feature was the systematic support of national forms: territory, culture, language, and elites. Of course, these were hardly novel choices. They are the primary domestic concerns of most newly formed nation-states. In Georgia and Armenia, for instance, the Soviet government did not repudiate the nation-building efforts of the Menshevik and *Dashnaktsutiun* governments that it deposed in 1920–1921, but rather boasted that Soviet power had deepened the national work begun by them.[61] Soviet policy was original in that it supported the national forms of minorities rather than majorities. It decisively rejected the model of the nation-state and replaced it with a plurality of nation-like republics. The Bolsheviks attempted to fuse the nationalists' demand for national territory, culture, language, and elites with the socialists' demand for an economically and politically unitary state. In this sense, we might call the Bolsheviks internationalist nationalists or, better yet, Affirmative Action nationalists.

To develop this idea, I will compare Soviet practice with Miroslav Hroch's famous three-phase model for the development of nationalism among the "small" stateless peoples of Eastern Europe: first, elite nonpolitical interest in folklore and popular culture (Phase A); second, the consolidation of a nationalist elite committed to the formation of a nation-state (Phase B); third, the emergence of a nationalist movement with mass popular support (Phase C).[62] Hroch largely ignored the existing multiethnic state, reflexively assuming it would oppose these developments. The Soviet state instead literally seized leadership over all three phases: the articulation of a national culture, the formation of national elites, and the propagation of mass national consciousness. It went still further and initiated even "Phase D" (my term now, not Hroch's) measures typical of newly formed nation-states: establishing a new language of state and a new governing elite. To use more familiar Bolshevik terminology, the party became the vanguard of non-Russian nationalism. Just as party leadership was needed to lead the proletariat beyond trade union consciousness to revolution, the party could also guide national movements beyond bourgeois primordial nationalism to Soviet international nationalism.

---

[61] *Tainy natsional'noi politiki*, 141–156. *Natsional'nyi vopros na perekrestke mnenii*, 141–150.
[62] Miroslav Hroch, *Social Preconditions of National Revival in Europe* (Cambridge UK, 1985).

This policy represented a dramatic shift from 1913, when Lenin had argued that the party should condemn all national discrimination but warned that "the proletariat cannot go further [than this] in the support of nationalism, for going further means the 'positive' [*pozitivnaia*] affirmative action [*polozhitel'naia deiatel'nost'*] of the bourgeoisie which aims at strengthening nationalism."[63] In the same spirit, Zinoviev told a Ukrainian audience in 1920 "that languages should develop freely. In the end, after a period of years, the language with the greater roots, greater life and greater culture will triumph."[64] Dmitrii Lebed, Secretary of the Ukrainian TsK, called this theory "The Battle of Two Cultures," in which "given a party policy of neutrality, the victory of the Russian language will be guaranteed due to its historic role in the epoch of capitalism."[65]

By the 1923 party congress, neutrality had become anathema. Zinoviev himself now stated: "We should first of all reject the 'theory' of neutralism. We cannot adopt the point of view of neutralism . . . we should help [the non-Russians] create their own schools, should help them create their own administration in their native languages. . . . Communists [should not] stand to the side and think up the clever phrase 'neutrality.'" Neutrality, Zinoviev insisted, was simply a cover for Great Russian chauvinism.[66] The 1923 resolutions supported this position. Not only was Piatakov's call for a positive fight against nationalism denounced as great-power chauvinism, but so was Lenin's prerevolutionary policy of neutrality. Lebed's "Battle of Two Cultures" was condemned in 1923, as was a similar "leftist" position in Tatarstan and Crimea.[67]

The Communist party had now embraced the "positive affirmative action of the bourgeoisie" that Lenin had criticized in 1913. However, as the Hroch comparison illustrates, Soviet affirmative action supported national minorities, not majorities. The Bolsheviks now scorned bourgeois governments for supporting only formal "legal equality" instead of taking positive action to achieve "actual [*fakticheskoe*] equality."[68] This extreme suspicion of neutrality explains one of the most striking features of the Soviet nationalities policy: its resolute hostility to even voluntary assimilation. In this new model, neutrality would inevitably lead to voluntary assimilation due to the historic strength of Russian national culture. Positive action, therefore, was needed to defend non-Russian national culture against this unjust fate. No one denounced neutrality and assimilation more categorically than Stalin[69]:

We are undertaking a policy of the maximum development of national culture . . . It would be an error if anyone thought that in relation to the development of the national cultures of the backward nationalities, central workers should

[63] Lenin, "Kriticheskie zametki," 132.
[64] *RTsKhIDNI* 374/27s/1709 (1929): 50.
[65] D. Lebed, *Sovetskaia Ukraina i natsional'nyi vopros za piat' let* (Kharkov, 1924): 50.
[66] *Dvenadtsatyi s"ezd*, 604.
[67] *Tainy natsional'noi politiki*, 83–84.
[68] *Dvenadtsatyi s"ezd*, 694.
[69] *RTsKhIDNI* 558/1/4490 (1929): 9.

maintain a policy of neutrality—"O.K., fine, national culture is developing, let it develop, that's not our business." Such a point of view would be incorrect. We stand for an affirmative [*pokrovitel'stvennaia politika*] policy in relation to the development of the national cultures of the backward nationalities. I emphasize this so that [it will] be understood that we are not indifferent, but actively supporting [*pokrovitel'stvuiushchie*] the development of national culture.

Of course, positive action on behalf of one nationality implies negative action toward others.

In the Soviet case, where all non-Russians were to be favored, Russians alone bore the brunt of positive discrimination. Bukharin stated this fact bluntly: "As the former Great Power nation, we should indulge the nationalist aspirations [of the non-Russians] and place ourselves in an unequal position, in the sense of making still greater concessions to the national current. Only by such a policy, when we place ourselves artificially in a position lower in comparisons with others, only by such a price can we purchase for ourselves the trust of the formerly oppressed nations."[70] Stalin, who was more sensitive to Russian feelings, rebuked Bukharin for the crudeness of his statement but did not and could not dispute its content.[71] Soviet policy did indeed call for Russian sacrifice in the realm of nationalities policy: majority Russian territory was assigned to non-Russian republics; Russians had to accept ambitious Affirmative Action programs for non-Russians; they were asked to learn non-Russian languages; and traditional Russian culture was stigmatized as a culture of oppression.[72]

New phenomena merit new terminology. As a national entity, the Soviet Union can best be described as an Affirmative Action Empire. I am, of course, borrowing the contemporary American term for policies that give preference to members of ethnic groups that have suffered from past discrimination. Such policies are common internationally and go by various names: compensatory discrimination, preferential policies, positive action, affirmative discrimination.[73] They often accompany decolonization. I prefer the term Affirmative Action because, as the above paragraphs have shown, it describes precisely the Soviet policy choice: affirmative action (*polozhitel'naia deiatel'nost'*) instead of neutrality. The Soviet Union was the first country in world history to establish

[70] *Dvenadtsatyi s"ezd*, 613.

[71] Ibid., 651. In fact, in a follow-up note to Bukharin, Stalin claimed that Bukharin had misunderstood him: "I never said that the battle with anti-Russian nationalism was as important; on the contrary, I said that the battle with Russian nationalism was more important . . . I even went further and talked about the need to recruit even the most minimally loyal [native] elements (up to and including even Octobrists)." RTsKhIDNI 558/11/708 (1923): 10.

[72] This does not mean Russians were discriminated against in any other aspect. All nationalities had equal legal rights. The expression of national hatred was punished. Moreover, as individuals, Russians were often in a better position, since the central government worked in Russian, as did the best universities.

[73] Marc Galanter, *Competing Equalities* (Delhi, 1991); Thomas Sowell, *Preferential Policies* (New York, 1990); Nathan Glazer, *Affirmative Discrimination* (Cambridge, Mass., 1975); Donald Horowitz, *Ethnic Groups in Conflict* (Berkeley, Calif., 1985): 653–680.

Affirmative Action programs for national minorities, and no country has yet approached the vast scale of Soviet Affirmative Action.[74] The Soviet Union also adopted even more extensive class-based Affirmative Action programs and considerably less-assertive gender-based programs.[75] As a result, the vast majority of Soviet citizens were eligible for some sort of preferential treatment. Affirmative Action permeated the early Soviet Union and was one of its defining features.

However, the existence of such programs alone does not justify calling the Soviet Union an Affirmative Action Empire, since I am proposing this term as an ideal-type to distinguish the Soviet Union *as a national entity* from alternative ideal-types: nation-state, city-state, federation, confederation, empire. *Affirmative Action* refers here not only to programs on behalf of members of a given ethnic group, but primarily to Soviet state support for the national territories, languages, elites, and identities of those ethnic groups. As noted in the Hroch comparison, above, the Communist Party assumed leadership over the usual process of national formation and took positive action to construct Soviet international nations (nations in form, not in content) that would accept the formation of a unitary, centralized Soviet state. Positive support of the forms of nationhood was the essence of Soviet nationalities policy. The formation of the Soviet Union in 1922–1923 established the territorial form of nationhood rather than a federation of autonomous national territories.

I will therefore refer to the Affirmative Action Empire as the national constitution of the Soviet Union. I am using the word *constitution* here in the British sense of a set of fundamental rules that structure the political life of a state. I add the adjective *national*, as I am concerned exclusively with how the Soviet Union was structured as a national or nationlike entity, that is, with regard to the problem of nationality. It was not the Soviet Union's formal written constitution of December 1922 that constituted the Soviet Union as a national entity, but rather the nationalities policy articulated in 1923. It was Affirmative Action, in the broad sense that I have defined it, that structured the Soviet Union as a multiethnic state.

The term *Affirmative Action Empire* represents an attempt to capture the paradoxical nature of the multiethnic Soviet state: an extraordinarily invasive, centralized, and violent state formally structured as a federation of sovereign nations; the successor state to the collapsed Russian empire that successfully reconquered most of its former national borderlands but then set out to

---

[74] India is usually credited with having invented Affirmative Action, but Indian Affirmative Action programs for national minorities (the Scheduled Tribes) began in 1951. Galanter, *Competing Equalities*, 18–40.

[75] Sheila Fitzpatrick, *Education and Social Mobility in the Soviet Union, 1921–1934* (Cambridge UK, 1979); Wendy Z. Goldman, *Women, the State, and Revolution. Soviet Family Policy and Social Life, 1917–1936* (Cambridge, UK, 1993): 109–118. These Soviet programs were established at the same time as the first caste-based Affirmative Action programs in pre-independence India, which were adopted in the 1920s and 1930s. Galanter, *Competing Equalities*, 18–40.

systematically build and strengthen its non-Russian nations, even where they barely existed. In 1967, Alec Nove and J. A. Newth puzzled over a state that seemed to privilege its eastern periphery while simultaneously holding it in subjugation: "Therefore, if we do not call the present relationship colonialism, we ought to invent a new name to describe something which represents subordination and yet is genuinely different from the imperialism of the past."[76]

The Affirmative Action Empire was not a traditional empire. I am not aligning myself with those who now argue that the Soviet Union, as a result of its shared characteristics with other empires, can be classified in objective social science terms as an "empire."[77] On the contrary, I am emphasizing its novelty. Mark Beissinger has pointed out that prior to the collapse of the Soviet Union, by and large only hostile observers called it an empire.[78] Supporters and neutral scholars called it a state. Beissinger likewise has noted the circularity of the currently popular argument that the Soviet Union collapsed, like the Habsburg and Ottoman empires before it, because it was an empire: In the modern world, empires collapse along national lines; the Soviet Union collapsed along national lines; therefore, the Soviet Union was an empire; therefore, as an empire, the Soviet Union was bound to collapse along national lines.[79] However, Beissinger goes on to argue that because of the widespread assumption that in the modern world empires are doomed, empire is a very important subjective category. To the extent that citizens perceive their state as an empire (and themselves as subjects), its long-term viability is gravely compromised.

Lenin and Stalin understood very well the danger of being labeled an empire in the age of nationalism. In fact, here lies the real connection between the Soviet Union's national constitution and the collapse of the Habsburg and Ottoman empires. The nationalities crisis and final collapse of the Habsburg empire made an enormous impression on Lenin and Stalin, who viewed it as an object lesson in the danger of being perceived by their population as an empire. As a result, the Soviet Union became the first multiethnic state in world history to define itself as an anti-imperial state. They were not indifferent to the word "empire." They rejected it explicitly.

Indeed, the Affirmative Action Empire was a strategy designed to avoid the perception of empire. The greatest-danger principle was based on the belief that non-Russian nationalism was a defensive response to the experience of Russian great-power or imperial chauvinism. Because the Bolsheviks intended to rule dictatorially and to promote major social transformation, their actions

---

[76] Nove and Newth, *The Soviet Middle East*, 122.

[77] Karen Dawisha and Bruce Parrot, eds., *The End of Empire? The Transformation of the USSR in Comparative Perspective* (Armonk, N.Y., 1997). Karen Barkey and Mark Von Hagen, eds., *After Empire. Multiethnic Societies and Nation-Building. The Soviet Union and the Russian, Ottoman and Habsburg Empires* (Boulder, Colo., 1997).

[78] Mark Beissinger, "The Persisting Ambiguity of Empire," *Post-Soviet Affairs* 11 (1995): 149–151.

[79] Ibid., 154–158.

were likely to be perceived as Russian imperialism. To avoid this perception, the central state would not be identified as Russian. Russian national self-expression would be downplayed. Ironically, this preserved the national structure of the old empire. The Soviet Union explicitly renounced the idea of a state-bearing people. Despite this fact, in an important sense the Russians did remain the Soviet Union's state-bearing people. Only the Russians were not granted their own territory and their own Communist Party. Instead, the party asked the Russians to accept a formally unequal *national* status to further the cohesion of the multinational state. The hierarchical distinction between state-bearing and colonial peoples was thus reproduced, but reversed, as the new distinction between the formerly oppressed nationalities and the former great-power nation. As the state-bearing people, Russians were now literally asked to bear the burden of empire by suppressing their national interests and identifying with a non-national affirmative action empire. Had Lenin lived to write a theoretical account of his creation, he might have called it *The Soviet Union, as the Highest Stage of Imperialism.*[80]

The Party and the Affirmative Action Empire

The Affirmative Action Empire was never an independent Bolshevik goal. It was instead a strategy to prevent the emergence of a potentially dangerous obstacle, non-Russian nationalism, to the accomplishment of other core Bolshevik goals: industrialization, nationalization of the means of production, abolition of the market, collectivization of agriculture, and the creation of socialism and its export abroad. For most rank-and-file Bolsheviks, promoting internationalism rather than separate national identities was the core Bolshevik task. Therefore, almost all observers agreed that the majority of party members received the Soviet nationalities policy with incomprehension. In 1919 Stanislav Pestkovskii, Stalin's deputy at the Commissariat of Nationalities, bluntly stated: "Among the majority of Old Bolsheviks the conviction reigns that revolutionary Marxists should not support the 'spreading' of national culture. 'We internationalists,' they say 'are aware that division into nationalities prevents the proletariat of all countries from uniting.'"[81] In 1923, Zinoviev insisted that many party members still expressed the same sentiment: "Isn't it written somewhere in the Communist Manifesto that the proletariat has no fatherland, workers of the world unite, etc.?"[82] The new nationalities policy was widely seen as "a temporary, if necessary, evil." It was assimilated as one of the many unpleasant "short-term" (*kratkovremennaia*) "concessions" (*ustupki*) associated with the New Economic Policy (NEP). This view was so prevalent that the Tatar Communist Said-Galiev requested and received a formal

---

[80] Lenin, "Imperializm, kak vysshaia stadiia kapitalisma" (1916), *PSS* 27: 299–426.

[81] S. Pestkovskii, "Natsional'naia kul'tura," *Zhizn' natsional'nostei*, no. 21: 1.

[82] *Dvenadtsatyi s"ezd*, 225.

refutation from Lenin, who stated that national republics would continue to exist "for a long time."[83]

The party leadership was well aware that a majority of Russian party members disliked the new nationalities policy and viewed it as no more than a temporary "concession." This unpopularity had an important impact on policy implementation as it led to ongoing active and passive resistance. Nor did this sentiment disappear after 1923. On the contrary, in 1929 Stalin publicly remarked that he frequently received letters that "hint that the existence of national governments and national republics with national governments is not our goal, but rather a tactic—if you will, a kind of limited short-term concession [*ustupka*]."[84] Stalin felt this opinion was still sufficiently widespread in 1929 to warrant refuting it on three separate occasions.[85]

The Hard and the Soft Line

The party leadership did not place their nationalities policy into a Bolshevik/non-Bolshevik framework, but rather one of hard-line and soft-line policies. Hard-line policies were the core Bolshevik tasks, whereas soft-line policies were designed to make those policies palatable to the larger population. *Korenizatsiia* was a quintessential soft-line policy, although, as we shall see, local efforts were occasionally made to upgrade its status.[86] This did not mean that the policy was insincere or purely decorative, but simply that it was a secondary consideration and would be implemented only to the extent it did not conflict with hard-line policy goals.

The Soviet bureaucracy was likewise divided into soft-line and hard-line institutions.[87] A given policy sphere was typically dealt with by both institutions. Soft-line institutions dealt openly with the Soviet public, and their job was to present Soviet policy in as attractive a light as possible. Typical soft-line tasks were receiving petitions and petitioners, correcting excesses (*peregiby*), restoring rights, bestowing awards, and providing a forum for mass participation in elections and soviets. Hard-line institutions, on the other hand, specialized in maintaining Bolshevik vigilance and ensuring the implementation and preservation of core Bolshevik policies and values. Typical hard-line activities were unmasking enemies, promoting vigilance, receiving denunciations, and arresting and deporting enemies.

[83] Stalin, "Politika sovetskoi vlasti," 62; "Iz istorii obrazovaniia SSSR," no. 9 (1989): 18; *Natsional'nyi vopros na perekrestke mnenii*, 127; *Dvenadtsatyi s"ezd*, 496; "Iz istorii obrazovaniia," no. 3 (1991): 168–169; *Tainy natsional'noi politiki*, 30–31.

[84] *RTsKhIDNI* 558/1/4490 (1929): 2.

[85] Ibid., 2; Stalin, "Natsional'nyi vopros i leninizm. Otvet tovarishcham Meshkovu, Koval'chuku i drugim" (1929) *Sochineniia* 9: 333–355; Stalin, *Marksizm*, 191–198.

[86] Chapter 3.

[87] For a more detailed analysis of this distinction, as well as a discussion of the source-base for this book, see Terry Martin, "Interpreting the New Archival Signals: Nationalities Policy and the Nature of the Soviet Bureaucracy," *Cahiers du monde russe* 40 (1999): 113–124.

The Bolshevik leadership assigned primary responsibility for the implementation of *korenizatsiia* to its soft-line bureaucracies: the Central Executive Committee (TsIK), and its Soviet of Nationalities; the Russian Federated Republic's (RSFSR) Central Executive Committee (VTsIK), and its Nationalities Department; and the Commissariat of Education (*Narkompros RSFSR*) and its Nationalities Committee (*Komnats*). Supervision of their work, as well as the repression of "nationalist" deviations, was assigned to hard-line bureaucracies: the Soviet political police (OGPU-NKVD); the Central Control Committee (TsKK), and the Party's Central Committee (TsK), including its Nationalities Subdepartment, Cadres Department (*orgraspred otdel*), Orgburo, and Politburo.

An exclusive emphasis on the activities of either the soft-line or hard-line institutions can easily lead to historical misinterpretations. In nationalities policy, the job of soft-line institutions was almost exclusively positive: to service, increase, and celebrate the number of national territories, schools, newspapers, theaters, written languages, museums, folk music ensembles, and so forth. The job of hard-line institutions was much more negative: to engage in surveillance over the implementation of nationalities policy and, when necessary, to take measures to prevent the intended development of national self-consciousness from evolving into an undesired growth of separatist nationalism. Although there were oscillations between the hard-line and soft-line institutions over time, the more striking fact is that the two policy lines coexisted. Indeed, this division of bureaucratic responsibility was often so stark that the records of soft-line institutions do not even mention actions being simultaneously undertaken by hard-line institutions.[88]

For instance, from 1935 to 1937, the hard-line party and NKVD were supervising the ethnic cleansing and mass arrest of the Soviet Union's diaspora nationalities.[89] At the exact same time, the Soviet of Nationalities was making the continued improvement of the national institutions of these same nationalities a major priority. Moreover, in the internal records of the Soviet of Nationalities, there are absolutely no references to the deportations and arrests, although its leadership clearly knew of them. This was not bureaucratic conflict. The weak Soviet of Nationalities was never rebuked by the Politburo. If it had received a signal of displeasure, it would have backed off immediately. It did not and so it continued its job of promoting the Soviet nationalities policy maximally. This was an admittedly extreme example of the common bureaucratic division of labor. The official sanctioning of coexisting and contradictory policy lines meant that the true policy line emerged from a dialogue between them. The historian, like the local party official, has to learn to read the center's signals.

---

[88] This was very much the case in religious policy. Martin, "Interpreting the New Archival Signals," 117.

[89] Ibid., 121–122.

Terror as a System of Signaling

The most important central signaling device was the terror campaign. Local officials were constantly being asked to fulfill an unrealistic number of often contradictory assignments. They therefore had to read central signals to determine which policies were high priority and must be implemented and which could be deferred or ignored with impunity. Terror was the most important signal marking a policy as hard-line and mandatory. For instance, in Ukraine from 1928 to 1930, the official policy line called for an intensification of Ukrainization in keeping with the new increased tempos of socialist construction. At the same time, a terror campaign was launched against Ukrainian "bourgeois nationalists." The terror campaign undermined the stated policy as officials decided that implementing the policy was more dangerous than ignoring it.

The evolution of the Soviet nationalities policy cannot be properly understood without integrating the effects of Soviet terror campaigns. In three successive major waves (1928–1930, 1932–1933, and 1937–1938), terror was employed asymmetrically against bourgeois nationalists rather than great-power chauvinists in violation of the greatest-danger principle. This pattern frustrated national communists, such as Ukraine's Mykola Skrypnyk, who understood that it was undermining *korenizatsiia*. What explained this odd pattern? Terror campaigns accompanied a turn toward the hard-line and the pursuit of core Bolshevik policies. In nationalities policy, the hard-line emphasized the threat of separatist "bourgeois nationalism," in particular the threat of counter-revolutionary penetration through cross-border ethnic ties. As a result, "bourgeois nationalists" were targeted, which in turn had the effect of undermining the Soviet nationalities policy.

The Geography of the Affirmative Action Empire

East and West

The Affirmative Action Empire and the policy of *korenizatsiia* were highly theorized and coherent. They applied to all non-Russians. Nevertheless, the Soviet government did divide its population into two broad and traditional categories: eastern and western nationalities. The dichotomy was not so much geographic as developmental. The Affirmative Action Empire provided two justifications for preferential treatment. One was indigenousness (*korennost'*), which was available to all non-Russians. The second was "cultural backwardness" (*kul'turno-otstalost'*), which was available only to those considered developmentally backward. After considerable debate, the vast majority of Soviet nationalities were judged culturally backward. Of the Soviet Union's large titular nationalities, only the Russians, Ukrainians, Georgians, Armenians, Jews, and Germans were deemed "advanced" and were grouped together as western nationalities.

The same policies applied in both the Soviet east and west, but there were important differences in implementation. In the east, the major problem was a lack of literate, educated titular nationals and so the policy emphasis was on affirmative action in education and hiring to create national elites. Only after their creation would linguistic *korenizatsiia* be possible. The training of cadres required money and so the eastern republics were more dependent on central financial aid. Such aid was more forthcoming during the first five-year plan (1928–1932), which was accompanied by a strong developmentalist ideology. As a result, the greatest progress in *korenizatsiia* was achieved during this time period. In the Soviet West, literate and educated titular nationals were plentiful and could be promoted with little difficulty. Therefore, the main policy emphasis was on linguistic *korenizatsiia*, that is, on establishing the national language as the official state language. Progress was more rapid during NEP (1923–1928) because the terror campaigns and increased centralization of the first five-year plan undermined linguistic *korenizatsiia*.

The Ukrainian Question

Ukraine occupied the central role in the evolution of the Soviet nationalities policy throughout the Stalinist period. The Ukrainian question took over the role played by the Polish question in prerevolutionary Russia. This was partly a matter of sheer size. Ukrainians made up 21.3 percent of the Soviet population in 1926, the next largest nationality being the Belorussians at 3.2 percent.[90] Ukrainians, in fact, composed just under half (45.6 percent) of the entire Soviet non-Russian population. The Ukrainians were not only the largest titular nationality, they were also twice as large as any other national minority in the RSFSR. Ukraine also had an extremely strong cadre of experienced national communists. It was located along the crucial Soviet–Polish border. Its cross-border ethnic ties to Poland's large Ukrainian population were considered an important foreign policy benefit in the 1920s and a threat in the 1930s. Ukraine was both a crucial agricultural and industrial region. For all these reasons, Ukraine played a large role in determining the course of the Soviet nationalities policy, a role that is reflected in the attention devoted to Ukraine in this book.

The Russian Question

Still more important, however, was the Russian question. The Russians were also a Soviet nationality, although the Soviet state initially downplayed this inconvenient fact. The Russian question—that is, the role and status of the Russian people, language, and culture within the Soviet Union—lies at the heart of my book, just as it lay at the heart of Lenin's and Stalin's thought on the nationalities question. The Russian question cannot be understood separate from the non-Russian question. Policy toward the non-Russians determined

[90] *Natsional'naia politika v tsifrakh* (Moscow, 1930): 36–38.

policy toward the Russians. To take only the most obvious example, Affirmative Action for all non-Russians necessarily implied reverse discrimination against Russians. The most important single change in the Soviet nationalities policy would be the rehabilitation of the Russians after 1933. Soviet history cannot be divided into Russian and non-Russian history. The two are inextricably intertwined. Soviet history can be fully understood only as the history of a multiethnic state and a multiethnic society.

The Chronology of the Affirmative Action Empire

A major concern of this book is to analyze the evolution of the Affirmative Action Empire from its inauguration with the 1923 nationalities policy decrees through to the completion of a fundamental policy revision at the height of the Great Terror in 1938. The periodization of nationalities policy developments follows the conventional Soviet periodization: New Economic Policy (NEP) (1923–1928), Socialist Offensive/Cultural Revolution (1928–1932), the Great Retreat (1933–1938). The distinctive feature of nationalities policy was the important policy impact of the Great Terror.

New Economic Policy, 1923–1928

The period from 1923 to 1928 witnessed an initial working out of the consequences of the 1923 nationalities policy decrees. Two controversial questions, whether national republics would be able to control migration into their territories and whether titular nationals could be granted preferential access to agricultural land, were both answered in the negative. The problem of extraterritorial national minorities was addressed through the formation of thousands of small national territories, which formed a pyramid of national soviets extending down from the large union republics to small national districts and finally merging seamlessly with the individual's personal nationality. The introduction of these territories inadvertently increased ethnic conflict and national consciousness as ethnic groups mobilized to avoid becoming a national minority in another group's national territory. In both the Soviet east and west, the Russian question emerged. In Ukraine, there was a debate, ultimately answered in the positive, over whether Russians, as the former great-power nationality, could be recognized as a national minority. In the Soviet east, the issue was the attempt to drive recent Russian settlers out of Kazakhstan, Kirgizia, and other high ethnic conflict areas. In the Soviet west, linguistic *korenizatsiia* made considerable progress while in the east *korenizatsiia* stalled due primarily to financial problems.

The Socialist Offensive—Cultural Revolution, 1928–1932

In 1928, Stalin launched his Socialist Offensive, which involved forced industrialization, collectivization, the abolition of the market, increased centralization, and terror against "bourgeois" population categories. Initially, the combination of this violence against "former people" (*byvshie*) and the utopian cultural revolutionary mood that accompanied the socialist offensive led militant Bolsheviks to assume that the Affirmative Action Empire would be abolished, national differences declared irrelevant, and a unified Soviet nationality created. Stalin rejected this interpretation of cultural revolution and instead turned these utopian energies in a developmentalist direction with his declaration that cultural revolution would mean the flowering of nations. This developmentalism led to rapid progress on *korenizatsiia* in the eastern national regions, though the problem of training technical cadres remained unsolved. Educated titular nationals were directed into leadership positions or the cultural sphere, above all primary school education.

In the Soviet west, the socialist offensive had the opposite effect. The violence against the non-Russian intelligentsia, who were closely associated with *korenizatsiia*, signaled a retreat from that policy. The centralization that accompanied the new changes strengthened the resistance of all-union economic trusts and commissariats to linguistic *korenizatsiia*. As a result, the attempt to create a hegemonic linguistic environment in Belorussia and Ukraine failed and a bilingual public sphere emerged. More importantly, an anti-*korenizatsiia* hard-line stance emerged as central authorities grew increasingly concerned that *korenizatsiia* was abetting rather than disarming nationalism. These suspicions were nurtured by the putative defection of national communists, such as Ukraine's Oleksandr Shumskyi and Mykola Khvylovyi, to nationalism under the cross-border influence of west Ukrainian nationalists.

The December 1932 Politburo Decrees

A number of factors converged in December 1932 to lead the Politburo to issue two decrees criticizing Ukrainization, decrees that would usher in a fundamental revision of the Affirmative Action Empire. First, collectivization had been resisted more violently in the non-Russian periphery, and many diaspora nationalities had responded to the new campaign by disloyally seeking to emigrate to their "home" nations. Second, Ukrainian efforts to annex majority Ukrainian territory from the RSFSR and to act as patrons for the large RSFSR Ukrainian community strengthened the growing anti-*korenizatsiia* hard-line stance. Finally, the grain requisitions crisis of the fall of 1932 was partially attributed to the failings of Ukrainization. This led to the Politburo decrees and a subsequent terror wave in Ukraine and Belorussia against "bourgeois nationalists."

The Great Retreat, 1933–1938

The Politburo decrees and the terror campaign initiated a far-reaching revision of the Affirmative Action Empire, a revision that would proceed gradually and culminate with a series of decisive central decrees at the height of the Great Terror in 1937–1938. The Piedmont Principle was abandoned and a defensive foreign policy stance adopted. This led eventually to ethnic cleansing and mass arrests and executions among the Soviet Union's diaspora nationalities who were now assumed to be disloyal because of their national identity alone. *Korenizatsiia* was scaled back, although not abandoned, and implemented silently so as not to offend Russian sensibilities. Most dramatically, the Russian nationality and Russian national culture were rehabilitated. The Russians and Russian culture were now made the unifying force in a newly imagined Friendship of the Peoples.

PART ONE

IMPLEMENTING THE
AFFIRMATIVE ACTION EMPIRE

2

Borders and Ethnic Conflict

The Soviet nationalities policy began with the formation of national territories. Already in March 1918, the intention to form a Tatar-Bashkir republic was announced. Two months later, a similar promise was made for the Turkestan region. Because of the exigencies of civil war, the first national republic (the Bashkir ASSR) was not actually formed until March 1919, but it was swiftly followed by a flood of autonomous republics, autonomous oblasts, and workers' communes. The 1922 Soviet constitution added the formerly independent republics of Ukraine, Belorussia, Georgia, Armenia, and Azerbaijan. With the national delimitation of Central Asia in 1924, the formation of the large Soviet national republics was completed, and the Soviet Union consisted of two federal republics, eight union republics, seventeen autonomous republics, and thirteen autonomous oblasts.[1] Thirty-eight new national majorities had been formed, and the 1923 nationalities decrees had articulated policies to indigenize these new national territories.[2] It seemed that the territorialization of ethnicity had been accomplished.

---

[1] Daniel Schafer, "Building Nations and Building States: The Tatar-Bashkir Question in Revolutionary Russia, 1917–1920" (Ph.D. diss., University of Michigan, 1995): 159–226, 345–393; Jeremy Smith, *The Bolsheviks and the National Question, 1917–1923* (London, 1999): 29–65; Robert Kaiser, *The Geography of Nationalism in Russia and the Soviet Union* (Princeton, N.J., 1994): 409–413. Francine Hirsch, "Toward an Empire of Nations: Border-Making and the Formation of Soviet National Identities," *Russian Review* 59 (2000): 201–226.

[2] Thirty-eight, not forty, since the Transcaucasus federation was not a national republic and the RSFSR counted as both a non-national federation and a union republic, with the Russians as a majority.

However, national majorities imply national minorities, and a complex network of forty national territories implied an equally complex national minorities problem. There were two contemporary models available for dealing with territorially dispersed national minorities, both of which were rejected by the Bolsheviks. The first was assimilation, the solution associated with the nation-state. In this model, nontitular national minorities would be expected, in the long run, to assimilate with the majority population. They would therefore be provided with no special national institutions or rights. One of the most striking aspects of the Soviet nationalities policy in the 1920s was its uncompromising hostility to assimilation, even if such assimilation was completely voluntary. The Affirmative Action Empire was premised on the belief that Tsarist colonialism had systematically advanced Russian culture and repressed non-Russian culture and that a position of state neutrality—of allowing voluntary assimilation—was both unjust and dangerous: unjust because the deck had been stacked in favor of the Russians, and dangerous because such assimilation would provoke a fearful, defensive nationalism among the remaining unassimilated group members. Instead, the Affirmative Action Empire strategy called for the strengthening of national identity and even measures of derussification.

Given this hostility to assimilation and support for national identity, the Bolsheviks might have embraced a second contemporary model for defusing nationalism: the strategy of extraterritorial national-cultural autonomy. This strategy was formulated by the Austrian Marxists, above all Otto Bauer and Karl Renner, as a potential solution to the Austro-Hungarian empire's extraordinarily complex national minorities problem. In brief, this policy called for non-national administrative territories and for special representative bodies, elected by all members of a given nationality throughout the empire, that would be granted exclusive jurisdiction over cultural policy toward their own nationality.[3] The Treaty of Versailles provided a half-hearted and ultimately inadequate version of this policy in its system of extraterritorial protection for national minorities in the new nation-states of Central and Eastern Europe.[4] This policy had been adopted by the Bund in 1901, which led it to claim the right to be the sole representative of the Jewish proletariat within the Russian Social Democratic movement. This challenge eventually prompted Lenin to commission Stalin's famous 1913 pamphlet, *Marxism and the Nationalities Question*, which argued for a strictly territorial definition of nationality and so rejected extraterritorial autonomy.[5] The rejection of both assimilation and extraterritorial nationality left the Bolsheviks with a gaping hole in their strategy for governing their multinational state. The formation of republics and autonomous oblasts did not solve the problem of national minorities. It

---

[3] Otto Bauer, *Die Nationalitätenfrage und die Sozialdemokratie* (Vienna, 1907). Tim Bottomore and Patrick Goode, eds., *Austro-Marxism* (Oxford, 1978).

[4] C. A. Macartney, *National States and National Minorities* (London, 1934).

[5] I. Stalin, "Marksizm i natsional'nyi vopros" (1913), in *Marksizm i natsional'no-kolonial'nyi vopros* (Moscow, 1934): 3–45.

only submerged it. The national majorities of those territorial units still implied national minorities.

To phrase this problem in a different form, the tension between a territorial and personal definition of nationality was one of the central dilemmas of the Soviet nationalities policy.[6] An Uzbek living in the Uzbek SSR both had the right to express his personal nationality (within the limits prescribed by Soviet policy) and was provided with an environment (through policies supporting the Uzbek language and culture) within which he could express it. An Uzbek living outside Uzbekistan, however, lacked this environment, and Soviet policy opposed the establishment of extraterritorial organizations to provide that environment.[7] Yet, this Uzbek was neither expected nor encouraged to assimilate. The problem, then, was how to find an adequate supportive environment for territorially dispersed national minorities.

This chapter analyzes the Soviet Union's historically unique response to that problem: the strategy of ethno-territorial proliferation. The Soviet solution was to extend their system of national-territorial units downward into smaller and smaller territories, the smallest being the size of a single village. The great era of the territorialization of ethnicity did not end in 1924, but began in that year. The Soviet government hoped that these small national soviets would resolve their national minorities problem. Territorially dispersed nationalities would no longer be threatened with assimilation, and therefore, according to Soviet theory, the potential for defensive nationalism and the resulting ethnic conflict would be defused. As one nationalities policy specialist put it: "The organization of national soviets is, above all, the precondition for overcoming national hostility, alienation and prejudice."[8]

That was the theory. In practice, the opposite occurred. Drawing tens of thousands of national borders forced every village and every individual to declare a national loyalty. It mobilized ethnic groups to forestall the possibility of becoming a national minority after those borders had been drawn. For these and other reasons, national soviets in fact called forth an enormous increase in ethnic mobilization, as well as a considerable growth in ethnic conflict. In this chapter, I first trace the emergence of the strategy of ethno-territorial proliferation in Ukraine and its subsequent spread across the entire Soviet Union, and then analyze the social consequences of this unprecedented policy.

The Emergence of National Soviets in Ukraine

National soviets developed as an unintended consequence of the regionalization (*raionirovanie*) movement. *Raionirovanie* began as a purely economic

---

[6] On this question, see Rogers Brubaker, *Nationalism Reframed* (Oxford, 1996): 23–54.

[7] In principle, that is. In practice, national schools were provided extraterritorially as were some other cultural services, such as national clubs and reading rooms.

[8] *Prakticheskoe razreshenie natsional'nogo voprosa v Belorusskoi SSR.* vol. 2 (Minsk, 1928): 100.

endeavor, an effort to create larger economic units that would better reflect the economic realities of the Soviet Union and better suit the needs of central economic planners. The first proposal was presented to the Eighth Congress of Soviets in December 1920 and published by the State Planning Committee (Gosplan) in 1921.[9] This proposal enraged the non-Russian republics because it subordinated all small autonomous oblasts and republics to the new large economic oblasts without granting them any special national status. It also divided Ukraine and Kazakhstan into several smaller economic oblasts, thereby compromising the territorial integrity of those republics. Gosplan's 1921 publication led to a variety of national counterproposals. Tatarstan proposed uniting the national territories of the middle Volga into their own oblast. Komi leaders insisted on forming a separate economic oblast.[10] The response of the national republics to economic *raionirovanie* plans led TsIK Secretary Avel Enukidze to call "the conjunction of economic and national *raionirovanie*" the most difficult nationalities problem facing TsIK.[11] In this case, the economic organs quickly backed down and the ultimate *raionirovanie* plans respected national differences. However, as we shall see, the central economic bureaucracies would periodically propose grand *raionirovanie* plans, invariably hostile to nationalities interests, and the nationalities would then lobby intensively to blunt the impact of those proposals or to manipulate them to their own advantage.

National soviets emerged out of a creative manipulation of *raionirovanie*. *Raionirovanie* consisted of two processes: macro-*raionirovanie*, the formation of large economic oblasts, and micro-*raionirovanie* (*nizovoe raionirovanie*), the simplification of the existing four-step administrative system (village soviet-*volost'-uezd-guberniia*) into a three-step system (village soviet-district-*okrug*).[12] Macro-*raionirovanie* was centrally administered, whereas micro-*raionirovanie* was assigned to local organs, who carried out the first stage of the process between 1923 and 1926.[13] Micro-*raionirovanie* initially had no nationalities content, but it ended up producing a major innovation in the Soviet nationalities policy: national soviets.

---

[9] I. G. Aleksandrov, *Ekonomicheskoe raionirovanie Rossii* (Moscow, 1921). Smith, *The Bolsheviks*, 172–175.

[10] I. Trainin, "Ekonomicheskoe raionirovanie i natsional'naia politika," *Zhizn' natsional'nostei*, no. 21 (1921): 1; S. N., "Ekonomicheskoe raionirovanie i problemy avtonomno-federativnogo stroitel'stva," no. 26 (1921): 1; "Administrativnoe delenie RSFSR v primenenii k ekonomicheskomu raionirovaniiu," *Vlast' sovetov*, no. 3 (1922): 25–37; *Kazan'-tsentr Volzhsko-Kamskoi oblasti* (Kazan, 1923); "Avtonomnaia oblast' Komi v voprose o raionirovanii severa," *Komi mu—Zyrianskii krai*, nos. 3–4 (1925): 2–30.

[11] A. Enukidze, "Natsional'naia problema v sovetskom stroitel'stve," *Sovetskoe stroitel'stvo. Sbornik 1* (Moscow, 1925): 189–190.

[12] Given the set of two different territorial terms, it is impossible to find equivalents. Therefore, I use the Russian terms with two exceptions: I follow conventional usage in translating *raion* as district and *sel'sovet* as village soviet.

[13] L. L. Nikitin, "Raionirovanie za piat' let," *Planovoe khoziaistvo*, no. 3 (1926): 197–202.

The first region to establish a complete system of functioning national soviets was Ukraine.[14] The Ukrainian system of national *raionirovanie* called for the creation of the maximum possible number of national soviets, which would include in each soviet the maximum possible percentage of each national minority. To this end, national soviets could be formed with a smaller minimum population than ordinary soviets. This practice meant not simply taking into account national interests alongside economic ones, but in giving them an absolute priority. Within the national soviets themselves, the entire array of Soviet nationality policies was to be implemented: use of the national language, formation of national cadres, promotion of the national culture. In short, *korenizatsiia* was extended downward to the village level. Ukraine offered this system as a model to the rest of the Soviet Union.[15] In this, they were ultimately successful.

There were a number of reasons why Ukraine played this pioneering role. First, Ukraine had unusually demanding national minorities. As Ukraine's first party secretary, Lazar Kaganovich, noted in May 1926: "Our national minorities are not like those in some province in Russia. We have solid, compactly settled national minorities, who are presenting their demands to us. It is enough to quote the GPU's data to draw a clear enough picture in that regard."[16] Kaganovich was referring to the peoples that Soviet terminology categorized as "western national minorities": Poles, Germans, Bulgarians, Greeks.[17] These national minorities were typically more prosperous and more educated than the Ukrainian majority, they frequently lived in territorially compact settlements, and they had well-developed prerevolutionary traditions of local self-government. Both their greater prosperity and their greater religiosity made the Soviet authorities particularly suspicious of them.[18] The distrust was often mutual. The most dramatic instance of national minority discontent was the mass emigration movement among the Mennonites, a prosperous German Protestant confession, that caused the Ukrainian government considerable concern throughout the 1920s.[19]

In addition to Germans and Poles, the other significant non-Russian national minority in Ukraine were Jews. Although Jews benefited from the abolition of previous political restrictions and so were often initially pro-Soviet, the Soviet

---

[14] The first region to conduct a national *raionirovanie* appears to have been Saratov *guberniia*, which in late 1923 formed ten Ukrainian, eight Mordvinian, and eight Tatar national *volosti*, but these appear to have existed largely on paper and the Saratov project had no further influence. S. Chugunov, "Raionirovanie Saratovskoi gubernii," *Vlast' sovetov*, no. 10 (1923): 61; K. Stasevich, "Po natsional'nym men'shinstvam," *Zhizn' natsional'nostei*, no. 5 (1923): 120; *GARF* 1235/122/47 (1927–1928): 49–50.

[15] *GARF* 3316/20/153 (1927): 97, 103, 122, 133.

[16] *TsDAHOU* 1/6/102 (12.05.26): 44.

[17] *GARF* 3316/23/1360 (1930). Other major "western national minorities" living outside Ukraine were Finns, Estonians, Latvians, and Lithuanians.

[18] See the GPU reports in *TsDAHOU* 1/16/2 (1926): 133–134; 1/16/34 (1928): 92–106.

[19] *RTsKhIDNI* 17/26/17 (17.05.27): 82/2. *GARF* 3316/20/153 (1927): 162.

government's economic policies led to the devastation of the Jewish shtetls. The Ukrainian government felt that this economic distress was the main reason for the popularity of Zionism and the large numbers of extremely active Zionist groups in Ukraine in the early 1920s. The Ukrainian government took the Zionist threat very seriously.[20]

Foreign policy goals also added to general Soviet concerns over the discontent of their German, Polish, and Jewish minorities. Soviet foreign policy attached great importance to the goal of turning Poland's large Ukrainian and Belorussian populations against the Polish government. The transfer of large stretches of territory from the RSFSR to Belorussia in 1924, for instance, was explicitly linked to this foreign policy goal. The establishment of a Moldavian ASSR was likewise designed to advance the Soviet claim to Romanian-occupied Bessarabia.[21] The Treaty of Versailles had already established national minority policy as an international concern. In order to join the League of Nations, sixteen East European and Middle Eastern states, most newly formed, were required to sign treaties in which they guaranteed to protect the legal and cultural rights of their national minorities.[22] The Soviet Union wanted its national minority policy to appear more generous than these treaty requirements. National territorial units, which Poland resolutely refused to grant its minorities, were one means to that end.

However, the Bolsheviks were at least as concerned about the reverse process: the influence of Poland and Germany on Soviet Poles and Germans. They were aware of the support given by Ukrainian Germans to the German occupation army in 1918, and by Ukrainian Poles during the brief Polish occupation of right-bank Ukraine in 1920.[23] Moreover, Ukrainian GPU reports in the mid-1920s emphasized the strong influence of the German and Polish governments, through their consuls and through religious leaders, on their respective minorities.[24] This was not just Soviet paranoia. In the post-Versailles era of politicized ethnicity, both Germany and Poland did maintain a lively interest in the condition of their respective nationalities.[25] The granting of national soviets was seen as a step toward reducing national discontent and thereby reducing the potential influence of Germany and Poland.

Finally, the most important reason the status of Ukraine's national minorities became controversial was the policy of Ukrainization, which involved the promotion of the Ukrainian language and culture, as well as the creation of a

---

[20] On Zionism, see *RTsKhIDNI* 17/16/1396 (30.10.25): 94/8; 17/26/3 (08.01.26): 4/4. *TsDAHOU* 1/16/1 (22.08.24): 101.

[21] The internal discussion on the formation of the Moldavian ASSR makes the primacy of the foreign policy concern evident. *TsDAHOU* 1/16/1 (1924): 90, 93, 116–119, 130.

[22] Macartney, *National States and National Minorities*, 212–369.

[23] *Itogi raboty sredi natsional'nykh men'shinstv na Ukraine* (Kharkov, 1927): 5–6.

[24] *TsDAHOU* 1/16/2 (1926): 117–123; 133–134.

[25] On Germany, see Meir Buchsweiler, *Volksdeutsche in der Ukraine am Vorabend und Beginn des Zweiten Weltkriegs—ein Fall doppelter Loyalität?* (Gerlingen, 1984); on Poland, see Mikolaj Iwanow, *Pierwszy narod ukarany. Polacy v zviazku radzieckim, 1921–1939* (Warsaw, 1991).

Ukrainian governing elite. This policy was very unpopular among many Bolshe-viks in Ukraine and Russia, but since it enjoyed consistent support from the Politburo and Stalin himself, attacks on Ukrainization tended to be indirect and to focus on the mistreatment of national minorities. From 1925 to 1927, for example, Iurii Larin launched a series of provocative attacks on Ukraine's treat-ment of their national minorities.[26] The Ukrainian government responded by developing the most systematic policy promoting national minorities' rights in the Soviet Union and then aggressively advocating this policy as a model for others.[27]

Ukraine's national minorities problem emerged in early 1924, just as the first serious Ukrainization efforts were being undertaken. Ukraine had, in fact, undertaken one of the Soviet Union's first micro-*raionirovanie* projects in 1923, a project that had ignored the national principle entirely.[28] In May 1924, at the Eighth Ukrainian Party Congress, Ukraine's first party secretary, Emanuel Kviring, condemned this policy:

> The chief error, comrades, was that in all our *gubernii* where national minori-ties live compactly, an incorrect policy was carried out during *raionirovanie*. Instead of uniting those regions where national minorities live compactly into one compact district, they attempted to disunite them . . . individual national villages were attached to the nearest Russian or Ukrainian district.

Kviring noted that these decisions did follow the correct class line: "This policy was based largely on the fact that these compact groups of national minorities make up richer groups than the surrounding peasantry."[29]

However, in this instance, Kviring maintained that the national principle should have been given precedence over the class principle[30]:

> Therefore, although these comrades wanted to maintain the correct Soviet policy in these villages, in fact they only deepened the anti-Soviet mood, and pushed these groups away from us. And when [the Ukrainian] TsK looked at this ques-tion, it declared this line incorrect and ordered our Central Administrative Com-mission and our *guberniia* commissions to review all these incorrect divisions and to try to unite these national minorities into national districts, so that they will be given the possibility to develop their national culture.

[26] See Larin's speeches at the Third Congress of Soviets and the April 1926 session of TsIK. *III s"ezd sovetov SSSR. Stenograficheskii otchet* (Moscow, 1925): 277–281; *2 sessiia TsIK SSSR 3 sozyva. Stenograficheskii otchet* (Moscow, 1926): 458–468; and his article, "Ob izvrashcheniiakh pri provedenii natsional'noi politiki," *Bol'shevik*, nos. 23–24 (1926): 50–58; no. 1 (1927): 59–69.

[27] See in particular the articles in *Vlast' sovetov*, no. 9 (1924): 41–43; no. 12 (1925): 3–4; no. 19 (1926): 2–4. *Sovetskoe stroitel'stvo*, nos. 3–4 (1926): 120–128; no. 1 (1927): 79–85; no. 4 (1928): 89–93. A. Butsenko, *Sovetskoe stroitel'stvo i natsmen'shinstva na Ukraine* (Kharkov, 1926); see also *Itogi raboty sredi natsional'nykh men'shinstv*.

[28] A. Butsenko, "Itogi raionirovaniia USSR," *Vlast' sovetov*, no. 15 (1926): 3–4.

[29] *Biulleten' VIII-i vseukrainskoi konferentsii KP/b/ Ukrainy. Stenogramma* (Kharkov, 1924): biull. 2: 94.

[30] Ibid., 2: 94.

Despite Kviring's comments, Ukraine was still singled out for criticism at the Thirteenth Party Congress in Moscow the following week. In the official Central Committee report, Zinoviev criticized the treatment of national minorities and in particular singled out Ukraine's treatment of their Poles and Germans.[31] No Ukrainians spoke in the ensuing discussion, but evidently they complained to Zinoviev privately, since in his concluding remarks he again addressed this issue[32]:

> Evidently I spoke too politely. Well then, I'll say it more frankly. The fact is that, for instance in Ukraine, where the question of Ukrainization is moving forward rapidly, they need to guarantee properly the rights of Germans, Poles, Moldavians, Jews, and so forth.

The remarks of Kviring and Zinoviev led to immediate action. On July 7, the first two German districts, Prishib and Molochansk, were formed.[33] On August 29, the Ukrainian Sovnarkom passed a decree reducing the mandatory number of residents needed to form a national district from 25,000 to 10,000, and from 1000 to 500 for a national village soviet.[34] This decree led to the gradual development of an extensive network of national soviets. Special ethnographic expeditions were undertaken to determine the exact ethnic composition of each potential soviet, so that the network could be maximally expanded. There was a striking emphasis on maximum ethnic segregation. Already in 1927, Ukrainian authorities boasted that 92.1 percent of Bulgarians, 85.8 percent of Greeks, 67.8 percent of Germans, and 100 percent of Swedes lived in their own national soviets.[35]

Before its national minority system could be completed, the Ukrainians had to confront an exceptionally important and fundamental question: Were the Russians a national minority in Ukraine? Most Russians and non-Russians, Bolsheviks and non-Bolsheviks, considered this notion absurd. How could the "great-power" nationality be a national minority? In the early 1920s, non-Russians and national minority (*natsmen*) were essentially synonyms. Prior to 1926, no criticism of Ukraine's nationalities policy mentioned Russians, nor did the Ukrainians treat Russians as a national minority. Iurii Larin broke the silence on this issue at an April 1926 session of TsIK, when he provocatively addressed "that part of the nationalities question, which one must name the Russian question in Ukraine, for regrettably such a question does exist."[36] Larin attacked several policies designed to promote the Ukrainian language: forced subscriptions to Ukrainian newspapers, mandatory Ukrainian-language signs, requiring

---

[31] *Trinadtsatyi s"ezd RKP/b/. Stenograficheskii otchet* (Moscow, 1963): 43.

[32] Ibid., 242.

[33] Butsenko, *Sovetskoe stroitel'stvo*, 17.

[34] *Itogi raboty*, 19.

[35] *Itogi raboty*, 21; S. Vlasenko, "O X vseukrainskom s"ezde sovetov," *Sovetskoe stroitel'stvo*, no. 5 (1927): 103–104.

[36] *2 sessiia TsIK SSSR 3 sozyva*, 460.

russified Ukrainians to attend Ukrainian-language schools. He noted that Russians were not treated as a national minority and so were denied national soviets. The stenogram recorded prolonged applause after Larin's speech.[37]

Larin had violated the great taboo of the Affirmative Action Empire. He had addressed the Russian Question. His speech provoked some discord in the usually united Ukrainian delegation. Grigorii Petrovskii called Larin's speech "dangerous," especially as it received "a certain sympathy" from the audience. Volodymyr Zatonskyi stated the conventional view that, given the strength of Russian culture, "it is impossible to behave towards the Russians in Ukraine as a national minority." Hrihoryii Hrynko seconded this sentiment. Mykola Skrypnyk, Ukraine's most influential nationalities policy specialist, defended Ukraine's treatment of Russians but surprised his delegation by agreeing that Russians should be treated as a national minority.[38]

Larin received support from only one, but important, speaker, the secretary of TsIK Avel Enukidze, who argued that Ukrainization was being hurried and the role of Russian culture slighted: "The study of the Russian language and culture is necessary in the building of our culture, and we will succeed in nothing without the mastering of the Russian language and culture."[39] Enukidze repeated those concerns in a subsequent article.[40] Larin also reworked his criticisms into an influential article in the party's theoretical journal, Bol'shevik.[41] The Russian question had been launched.

These attacks forced the Ukrainians to rethink the status of Russians. As seen in the TsIK debate, there were two schools of thought. One position, represented by Zatonskyi, argued that as the former ruling nationality, Russians had too strong a cultural position to warrant additional protection as a national minority.[42] A second position, represented by Skrypnyk, argued that with the growing success of Ukrainization, Russians had "become a national minority."[43] In both cases, Ukrainians were granted the status of national majority, but Skrypnyk's position had the advantage of granting Russians a formal standing and thereby addressing Larin's criticism.

Skrypnyk's position, therefore, was adopted with one exception. Everyone agreed that urban Russians could not be granted the right to form national soviets. Otherwise important Ukrainian cities like Kharkov (Ukraine's capital city) and Odessa would become official Russian cities with Russian city soviets.[44] Beginning in late 1926, the formation of Russian national soviets

---

[37] Ibid., 460–468.

[38] Ibid., 499, 515, 474, 532–536.

[39] Ibid., 500.

[40] A. Enukidze, "K voprosu o natsional'nykh iazykakh," *Sovetskoe stroitel'stvo*, no. 1 (1926): 39–53.

[41] Larin, "Ob izvrashcheniiakh."

[42] *RTsKhIDNI* 17/113/336 (07.10.27): 54–55.

[43] A. Butsenko, "Natsional'ni menshosti Ukrainy," *Bil'shovyk Ukrainy*, no. 12 (1928): 69.

[44] Butsenko did discuss the possibility of forming urban Russian districts but nothing came of this; see *Pervoe vseukrainskoe soveshchanie po rabote sredi natsional'nykh men'shinstv. Stenografich-eskii otchet* (Kharkov, 1927): 44.

Table 1. National Soviets in Ukraine, 1924–1929

National Districts	1924	1925	1926	1927	1928	1929
Russian	—	—	—	9	9	9
German	5	5	5	7	7	7
Bulgarian	1	3	3	4	4	4
Greek	—	—	—	—	3	3
Polish	—	—	1	1	1	1
Jewish	—	—	1	1	1	2
Total	6	8	10	22	25	26
National Village Soviets						
Russian	—	69	122	292	388	408
German	98	117	221	237	251	253
Polish	15	61	129	139	143	150
Jewish	19	19	34	56	77	92
Moldavian	—	9	57	57	57	90
Bulgarian	25	28	43	42	42	45
Greek	26	27	27	30	30	30
Czech	5	13	13	13	13	13
Albanian	—	—	—	3	3	3
Belorussian	—	1	1	2	2	4
Swedish	—	—	1	1	1	1
Total	188	344	648	872	1007	1089
National Town Soviets						
Russian	—	—	—	—	39	41
Jewish	—	19	52	52	53	66
Total	—	19	52	52	92	107

M. V., "Itogi nizovogo raionirovaniia Ukrainy," *Sovetskoe stroitel'stvo*, no. 12 (1929): 61; *Ot s"ezda k s"ezdu: Materialy k otchetu pravitel'stva na V s"ezde sovetov SSSR* (Moscow, 1929): 120. The 69 Russian village soviets in 1925 represent a retrospective inclusion of village soviets that were not granted official national soviet status until 1926.

began. Zatonskyi remained skeptical but gradually warmed to the thesis of the gradual emergence of a Russian national minority: "A Russian national minority does not yet exist. But exactly because we have now gone rather far along the path of Ukrainization, it is time to introduce special national minority workers [to service Russians]."[45] With the status of Russians clarified, the Ukrainian national minorities network grew rapidly (see Table 1).

What was the social impact of Ukraine's national minorities system? The official goal of this policy was to preempt the emergence of an above-class national movement in pursuit of common national goals and thereby to reduce the level of ethnic conflict. As one Belorussian authority put it: "National soviets create the possibility to politically strengthen and organize the national

[45] Ibid., 16.

minority poor peasants in their battle with the kulaks, which will bring forth significant fissures in the existing national unity." Class conflict would replace ethnic conflict: "The organization of national soviets is above all the basis for the overcoming of national antagonism and alienation."[46] This was the theory.

In practice, the opposite occurred. An April 1926 report from Sazonov, the head of the Ukrainian Central Committee's Information Department, revealed that the formation of national soviets had actually intensified ethnic conflict. Sazonov noted that this electoral campaign coincided with "the mass formation of independent national village soviets," and that although the electoral instructions called for pre-electoral meetings to discuss various economic and class issues:[47]

> Despite the uncontested importance of these questions . . . they did not make up the chief content of the campaigns. The core question which throughout the whole campaign drew the attention of the national minority population (and in mixed villages, the entire population) was the question of forming independent national village soviets.

The formation of national soviets actually spurred ethnic conflict. National minorities "with stubbornness and resolution" insisted on the formation of national soviets: "moreover, this effort underlay the observable antagonism between the national minority population and the remaining population, which clearly revealed itself in the process of forming national village soviets." "Almost everywhere, national minorities voted for independent national village soviets, and Ukrainians against." Communities divided along ethnic lines. In one German village, the Russians proposed a list with one Russian candidate, "and that list was of course refused." In another case, "Poles disrupted an election meeting with a demonstrative departure after a Pole was not elected to the village soviet."[48]

Sazonov was particularly disturbed by a tendency to understand national soviets extraterritorially: "For instance, in one okrug, Jews living in villages were attached to the town soviet, and Ukrainians living in town were attached to the village soviet." In another case, the assistant director of a local factory was excluded from the electoral lists as a Ukrainian. Most strikingly, the secretary of a local party committee told Sazonov: "I won't go and vote in the elections of the town soviet, when I don't understand the Jews and they don't understand me. It's better if I go and vote in the nearest village."[49]

These anecdotes illustrate the difference between the official government conception of national soviets and the popular understanding. Despite the tendency toward ethnic segregation inherent in the formation of minute national

[46] *Prakticheskoe razreshenie*, vol. 2, 100.
[47] *TsDAHOU* 1/20/2534 (1926): 740b.
[48] Ibid., 740b, 76, 75, 740b.
[49] Ibid., 750b.

territories, the official government line stressed that national soviets should not be ethnically homogeneous units. Ukrainians in a German village soviet did not forfeit their national rights. National soviets existed to help national minorities preserve their culture and to use their native language in daily life.

The popular conception saw national soviets as their territory. As one Jewish Bolshevik argued, "in Jewish national soviets, the Jewish masses feel life, manifest their full capacities, and in other soviets they often feel like foreigners [chuzhie]."[50] Once even the small number of villages composing a village soviet were granted a formal ethnic status, minorities were almost inevitably viewed as a foreign presence. This could and did lead to demands for expulsion. The Ukrainian GPU reported that during the 1926 census in Zhitomir, "in connection with rumors that Ukrainians were to be expelled from Polish village soviets, there were cases when Ukrainians hid their true national identity and told the census-taker that they were Poles."[51] In the eastern national regions, as we shall see, such popular ethnic expulsions became surprisingly common.

The formation of national soviets, then, established a crucial connection between ethnic identity and administrative control of territory. Unsurprisingly, these two elements became further entwined with a third category: land ownership. As Kviring noted, prior to 1924 a class-based approach to raionirovanie had prevailed, in which more prosperous peasants were combined administratively with less prosperous peasants to facilitate economic leveling. In practice, this meant combining German and Polish villages with Ukrainian and Russian ones. When this policy was suddenly reversed in 1924 and the national principle elevated above the class principle in forming local soviets, this naturally led to anger among the Russian and Ukrainian peasantry. As Sazonov reported: "Especially energetic resistance was encountered from the Ukrainian population in Polish and German villages. In these villages, because the Party's nationalities policy was unclear to the villagers, the formation of national village soviets was identified with the restoration of that economic strength and those privileges, which the German and Polish colonists enjoyed in the pre-revolutionary era."[52] The reference to prerevolutionary privileges adds the fourth category that I see as combining to create the conditions for serious ethnic conflict: namely, differences in prerevolutionary estate (soslovie) status. In this case, Russians and Ukrainians had belonged to the peasant estate, whereas Germans had belonged to a higher "colonist" estate, and Poles were popularly stereotyped as belonging to the nobility (though in reality few Polish former nobles remained in the Soviet Union).

Moreover, the local peasantry was not inventing this linkage between land ownership, ethnicity, and administrative territory. In November 1925, a Ukrainian TsK decree, noting widespread German discontent over previous land confiscations, authorized a 20 percent increase in land holdings for all German

[50] GARF 3316/20/153 (1927): 87.
[51] TsDAHOU 1/20/2524 (1927): 2.
[52] TsDAHOU 1/20/2534 (1926): 1750b.

colonists with fewer than 32 *dessiatina* (86.4 acres).[53] It was estimated that this would require 50,000 *dessiatina*. To satisfy these needs, it was decreed that "colonial land funds located in existing or projected German districts and village soviets should be reserved in first order for German colonist settlers."[54] In other words, wherever Germans were settled compactly they would form national territories, and any free land located within those territories would be reserved not only for local Germans, but also for any Ukrainian Germans who wanted to settle there.

This connection between ethnicity, territory, and land ownership was particularly evident in Soviet Jewish policy. The Jewish question represented an unusual dilemma for the Bolsheviks. The Bolsheviks firmly opposed anti-Semitism, both as one of their favored symbols of Tsarist depravity and because the large numbers of Jews in the Soviet government made anti-Semitism a proxy for anti-Bolshevism. The Bolsheviks' economic and class policies, however, with their hostility both to trade and to former traders, led to the economic annihilation of the Jewish shtetls and the stigmatizing of a majority of their inhabitants as *lishentsy* (those deprived of their electoral rights).[55] This situation greatly embarrassed the Bolsheviks.[56] It was also considered to be dangerous, for it provided a social base for Zionism, which was the Ukrainian government's largest national minority concern.[57] This problem was addressed through a massive program for the compact settlement of Jews in agricultural communities. This program aimed not only to rehabilitate former Jewish small traders through honest agricultural labor, but also to establish a base for the creation of Jewish national territorial units.[58] At a 1926 Jewish conference, Kalinin highlighted these national goals[59]:

> I should say that if we ideologically approach this question from the national point of view, then I would allow that hidden behind the [economic] motive is a national one. It seems to me that this phenomenon represents an attempt at national self-preservation [*samosokhranenie natsional'nosti*]. In opposition to assimilation and the elimination of the national character, which threatens every small people deprived of national development,—in the Jewish masses developed a feeling of self-preservation, a battle for nationality [*bor'ba za natsional'nost'*].

Kalinin's remarkable comment illustrated the extent to which Soviet nationalities policy opposed assimilation and supported the preservation of nationality,

---

[53] *TsDAHOU* 1/20/2019 (1925): 174.

[54] Ibid., 171. See also, "VUTsIK USSR," *Sovetskoe stroitel'stvo*, nos. 5–6 (1928): 218–219.

[55] Iurii Larin, *Evrei i antisemitizm v SSSR* (Moscow, 1929).

[56] See Kalinin's comments in *Pervyi vsesoiuznyi s"ezd "Ozet" v Moskve. Stenograficheskii otchet* (Moscow, 1927): 64.

[57] On the GPU's assessment of the danger of Zionism, see *TsDAHOU* 1/20/2019 (1925): 50.

[58] On this program, see I. Kantor, *Natsional'noe stroitel'stvo sredi evreev v SSSR* (Moscow, 1934); I. Gol'de, *Evrei zemledel'tsy v Krymu* (Moscow, 1932).

[59] *Pervyi vsesoiuznyi s"ezd "Ozet,"* 65–66.

and how Soviet policy linked that preservation to the establishment of national soviets.

Jewish agricultural settlement initially focused on south Ukraine and Crimea, where by 1931 four national districts and 127 national village soviets had been formed.[60] The formation of Jewish national soviets provoked even greater ethnic hostility than the creation of German and Polish soviets. Kalinin received so many letters of complaint that he felt compelled to publish one such letter in *Izvestiia* and respond to it.[61] The head of the Ukrainian GPU, V. A. Balitskii, reported that such peasant discontent was widespread.[62] In an April 1926 letter to the Politburo, A. Smirnov warned of peasant resentment[63]:

> Innumerable attempts to create exceptionally favorable conditions for Jewish agricultural settlement, to the detriment of the interests of the broad mass of Soviet agriculturalists, has called forth from the latter a sharply heightened anti-Jewish mood.

The conflict over Jewish settlement illustrates perhaps the most important single aspect of the formation of national soviets. The combination of ethnicity, control of territory, and land ownership led to a politicization of ethnicity. Competing national leaders, in this case prominent communists, publicly mobilized ethnic support for and against the formation of national soviets.

The Jewish example also illustrates the connection between the formation of national soviets and the transfer of national populations. This policy was not confined to Jews. An organization was also formed to settle Roma (gypsies), resulting in the formation of one Roma national village soviet and 23 Roma collective farms. Similarly, the small territorially dispersed Assyrian population was settled compactly to form a single Assyrian village soviet.[64] In 1933, the North Caucasus administration transferred 300 extraterritorial Kalmyks into the North Caucasus' lone Kalmyk national district, so that they could be properly serviced as nationalities.[65] Ukraine reserved land in German and Polish districts for ethnic Germans and Poles as well.[66] Moreover, there was an all-union policy that in the process of agricultural resettlement, national groups should be settled compactly.[67] This policy deepened the feeling among national minorities that they did not belong and so should move to a territory where they formed the national majority. Most importantly, it reinforced the belief of national majorities that minorities did not belong and should be expelled. This sentiment would prove of particular importance in the Soviet

---

[60] Kantor, *Natsional'noe stroitel'stvo sredi evreev v SSSR*, 23–28.

[61] M. I. Kalinin, *Evrei-zemledel'tsy v soiuze narodov SSSR* (Moscow, 1927): 24–40.

[62] *TsDAHOU* 1/20/2019 (1925): 86.

[63] *RTsKhIDNI* 17/113/193 (10.05.26): 188.

[64] *GARF* 1235/128/2 (1933): 110; 166.

[65] *GARF* 1235/141/1531 (1933): 103. "Khronika," *Revoliutsiia i gorets*, no. 8 (1933): 79–80.

[66] "VUTsIK USSR," *Sovetskoe stroitel'stvo*, nos. 5–6 (1928): 218.

[67] "V sovete natsional'nostei SSSR," *Revoliutsiia i natsional'nosti*, no. 1 (1930): 111.

Union's eastern national regions, where ethnic relations were much more strained.

I have now outlined the emergence of the Ukrainian national minorities system and some of its most important consequences. The larger significance of this system can be highlighted by contrasting the positions of its major opponent and proponent: Avel Enukidze and Mykola Skrypnyk. Enukidze criticized the Ukrainians publicly at the April 1926 TsIK session and in a subsequent article. However, he expressed his most severe criticism in response to a report on the Ukrainian national minorities policy during a closed session of the Presidium of the Soviet of Nationalities on June 24, 1927. At that meeting, Enukidze took aim at the core principle of the Ukrainian system: its hostility to assimilation. He criticized the Ukrainian policy of conducting all correspondence with each national soviet in the national language of that soviet:

Our task is to unite around some general culture the whole population of the Ukrainian republic, including all national minorities; by a policy of enclosing [*zamykanie*] each nationality within the confines of their own language, conducting all correspondence with them in their own language, we differentiate the whole Ukrainian republic into separate nationalities. Is that necessary? It isn't necessary.

Enukidze was then interrupted with astonishment, "Is our goal assimilation?" Enukidze answered:

Where we can assimilate, we should assimilate . . . one must comprehend that not every group of the population is a nation. We call compact masses nations, and we form these masses into autonomous republics or oblasts; and small groups of the population, which for instance in the RSFSR are territorially dispersed, we assimilate with Russian culture.

Enukidze maintained contemptuously that the Ukrainian policy led to the creation of a series of "little islands."[68]

Enukidze's tone was generally mocking, but it could take on a threatening edge. In response to complaints of mistreatment from a Jewish spokesperson, Enukidze snapped[69]:

You are exhibiting separatist pretensions, and these should not exist. I fear that the Ukrainian policy towards small nationalities reflects that very psychology. Soon every Armenian and Greek will be making demands on us. Our task is, in an ascending line, to lead national minorities towards the basic culture of their republic. That is for union republics. With relation to the USSR as a whole, our

[68] *GARF* 3316/20/153 (1927): 122.
[69] Ibid., 119–120.

task is different. Russian culture and Russian language is the main axis, around which we should raise up all nationalities settling the USSR.

Enukidze finished his attack with a warning:

> We are creating closed [*zamknutye*] nationalities, not at all tied to one another, disassociated [*razobshchennye*] and enclosed [*zamykaiushchikhsia*] in the circle of their own culture, their own language; and this in a state which is building, and must build, socialism.

Enukidze's comments embodied the traditional view of the nation-state, in which the goal is the eventual triumph of a single culture within a single state. In Enukidze's view, the Soviet nationalities policy was a transitional strategy toward that goal. Each national minority should, "in an ascending line," assimilate with the national majority in their own republic, and then each of those majorities should eventually assimilate with Russian culture. This model eliminated the need for national soviets. Enukidze described them either contemptuously (*zamknutyi, obosoblennyi, malenkie ostrovki*) or sinisterly as the potential embodiment of "separatist pretensions." With the latter comment, Enukidze showed an appreciation of national soviets' potential for spurring, rather than defusing, ethnic mobilization and thereby exacerbating ethnic conflict.

Enukidze (who was Georgian, not Russian) was articulating the unspoken sentiments of the majority of party members, but it was unusual to air such sentiments in an official forum. As soon as Enukidze finished, Skrypnyk rose and expressed his pleasure that Enukidze had spoken his mind in the presence of a stenographer: "It is always useful to have such a line established. We feel it. It is represented in scattered speeches, but until now we lacked a theoretical grounding for this line." Skrypnyk correctly noted that Enukidze's speech reflected the opinion of many communists, but no one would state it openly since, as Skrypnyk also correctly noted and went on to demonstrate, "it is not the party's line." Enukidze was asked to retract his comments.[70] He declined, but he also never said anything remotely similar at a public forum.

Mykola Skrypnyk worked out most comprehensively the ideology of the Ukrainian national minorities system. In a 1931 speech, Skrypnyk made the following statement: "Our task is to arrange our work so that the laboring masses of every nationality can develop as widely as possible their national consciousness [*svoiu natsional'nu svidomist'*]."[71] As an illustration, Skrypnyk recounted a recent controversy in which several Polish spokesmen in Moscow had proposed the theory that Soviet Poles could not develop proletarian Polish culture by themselves because the Soviet Union lacked a Polish proletariat. Skrypnyk countered that Polish national soviets "are not only organs of

---

[70] Ibid., III, 83.
[71] Mykola Skrypnyk, "Perebudovnymy shliakhamy," *Bil'shovyk Ukrainy*, no. 12 (1931): 14.

self-government, they are not some organ of national personal autonomy, but organs of proletarian power [*sovetskaia vlast'*]."[72] This example linked the two principal components of Skrypnyk's national minorities policy: the promotion of ethnic self-consciousness and the formation of national soviets. National soviets existed to preserve and develop national culture.

Skrypnyk developed the Soviet definition of the term "national minority" to its logical conclusion. At a 1930 meeting of the presidium of the Soviet of Nationalities, he addressed the prevailing terminological confusion[73]:

> I think that we have developed a bad habit when speaking about national minorities. Each of the nationalities inhabiting our Union is a national minority—Ukrainians, Russians, Jews, Belorussians, and so forth. . . .

At this point, Semen Dimanshtein, a long-time nationalities specialist, interrupted, "Russians are not, Russians are 57% [of the total Soviet population]," to which Skrypnyk answered:

> No, that's not right, now the situation has changed . . . in every union republic there are substantial national minorities, but the *natsmen* of one republic are the national majority of a national district. In a Polish district, the Poles are the national majority; and in Ukraine, Ukrainians are the national majority, but in a Polish district they are the national minority . . . Therefore when we speak about national minorities, it is not clear which minority we are speaking about: the national minority of a republic or a district.

Skrypnyk made the terms "national majority" and "national minority" entirely relative. Everyone could be national majority or national minority, depending entirely on their place of residence.

Skrypnyk felt he had solved the contradiction between the Soviet Union's profession of both a territorial and personal nationality. The solution was to extend national territorial units down to the lowest level until they merged seamlessly with the individual's personal nationality. Thus, in 1930, Skrypnyk protested against the creation of international collective farms and called for the application of the nationality principle to this level as well.[74] The following pyramid of national territorial soviets resulted:

Soviet Union

Federal republic (RSFSR, ZSFSR)

Union republic (Ukraine, Belorussia, etc.)

Autonomous republic (Tatarstan, Moldavia, etc.)

Autonomous oblast (Komi, Chechen, etc.)

[72] Ibid., 22.
[73] *GARF* 3316/23/1318 (24.04.30): 11.
[74] Ibid., 10.

Autonomous okrug (Komi Perm, Nenets, etc.)
National district (Finnish, Polish, Korean, etc.)
National village soviet (Roma, Assyrian, etc.)
National kolkhoz (all nationalities)
Personal nationality (fixed in passport in 1932)

Enukidze saw this as a ladder of assimilation, in which the seventh through ninth rungs were unnecessary, and all but the first would eventually be discarded as well. Skrypnyk saw it as a permanent pyramid, in which each individual's nationality would be fixed and preserved. This was the model he and the Ukrainians proposed for the rest of the Soviet Union.

National Soviets in Belorussia and the RSFSR

The Ukrainian model rapidly gained support among the Soviet Union's central nationalities specialists. Ukraine's presentation of its policy to the presidium of the Soviet of Nationalities in 1927 drew lavish praise. Khatskevich, the secretary of Belorussia's TsIK, called Ukraine's work "colossal." Bashkiria's representative, Kushaev, maintained that Ukraine's work served as "a model for the rest of the union and autonomous republics."[75] Semen Dimanshtein, who as head of TsK's Nationalities Subdepartment, tended to have a rivalrous relationship with the Ukrainians, praised Ukraine's national minorities program on numerous occasions.[76] Most striking were the remarks of A. I. Dosov, head of VTsIK's Nationalities Department: "I have the impression that Ukraine's national minorities live better than our nationalities with autonomous territories."[77]

Belorussia was the first republic to follow Ukraine's example. This was no surprise because their situations were quite similar. Belorussia also had prosperous and demanding western national minorities: Poles and Latvians.[78] They had a large and influential Jewish population. Their Russian population was smaller, but after the 1926 annexation of Gomel *guberniia*, Belorussia also faced an unhappy Russian minority.[79] The same foreign policy pressures applied in Belorussia as in Ukraine. Finally, the surprisingly rapid progress of Belorussization also made the protection of the rights of national minorities a politically sensitive topic.

As in Ukraine, Belorussia first completed a micro-*raionirovanie* that ignored nationality and then, in late 1924, began a program of forming national soviets.

[75] *GARF* 3316/20/153 (1927): 133; 103.
[76] *RTsKhIDNI* 17/113/336 (07.10.27): 68. *Soveshchanie upolnomochennykh po rabote sredi natsional'nykh men'shinstv. Stenograficheskii otchet* (Moscow, 1928): 104.
[77] *GARF* 3316/20/153 (1927): 97.
[78] On Latvian demands, see *RTsKhIDNI* 17/32/100 (1927): 35. *GARF* 3316/16a/271 (1927): 21.
[79] *GARF* 3316/16/206 (1923–1924).

Table 2. National Soviets in Belorussia, 1924–1933

National Village Soviets	1924	1925	1926	1927	1928	1933
Polish	—	2	13	23	19	40
Jewish	7	11	18	22	23	24
Russian	—	1	1	2	16	15
Latvian	2	5	4	5	5	5
German	—	1	2	2	2	2
Ukrainian	—	—	—	—	2	6
Lithuanian	—	—	—	—	—	1
Total	9	20	38	54	67	93

Prakticheskoe razreshenie, 96; *GARF* 3316/20/211 (1928): 115; *GARF* 3316/29/631 (1936): 33.

The right to form national soviets was even included in their constitution. Belorussia likewise initially denied Russians national minority status but changed their stance after Ukraine had shifted its policy on this question.[80] Table 2 illustrates the growth of Belorussia's national minorities network. Unlike in Ukraine, foreign colonists had not been settled compactly in Belorussia, so it was possible to form only a single Polish national district.[81]

The RSFSR moved more slowly in establishing national soviets. Through 1925, with a few exceptions, the RSFSR served its national minorities primarily through native language schools. Pressure to create national soviets, ironically, emerged out of a Ukrainian-Jewish polemic, the author of which was once again Iurii Larin. In early 1925, Larin presented to the Politburo materials he had collected on violations of the rights of national minorities in Ukraine. In April 1925, the Politburo formed a commission, which included Larin and Kalinin, to investigate these charges and formulate a coherent all-union national minorities policy.[82] The commission's recommendations reflected the dual agenda of Larin and Kalinin, who both supported Jewish colonization and therefore Jewish national soviets, but also disapproved of measures to prevent the assimilation of urban Jews. In particular, they opposed the major effort undertaken by Ukrainians to send urban Jews to Yiddish schools (the rather transparent motive being to prevent the growth of the Russian urban population) when their parents were vehemently opposed.[83] The commission also condemned

[80] *GARF* 3316/20/211 (1928): 6, 111, 198; "Raionirovanie Belorussii," *Sovetskoe stroitel'stvo: zhurnal gosplana BSSR,* nos. 8–9 (1926): 131–132; A. Khatskevich, "Azhits'tsiaulen'ne leninskai natsiianal'nai palityki u Belaruskai SSR," *Bol'shevik Belarusi,* nos. 10–12 (1930): 25.

[81] And not until 1932. E. Prynts, "Natsyianal'na-kul'turnae budavnitstva pol'skaga nasel'nitstva BSSR," *Bol'shevik Belarusi,* no. 13 (1932): 43.

[82] *RTsKhIDNI* 17/3/497 (16.04.25): 57/25.

[83] The practice of sending all Jewish children to Yiddish schools created enormous protest and was soon abandoned. Volodymyr Zatonskyi sarcastically recounted how Yiddish-speaking children were "caught" and sent to Yiddish schools:

We receive information from Nikolaev, from Kiev, and from a series of other places, that during pre-enrollment examinations children "suspected of belonging to the Jewish nation", if it becomes

as national minority violations some measures found in the Ukrainization
program, such as forced subscription to Ukrainian newspapers.

The Ukrainians defended themselves by submitting to the commission a rival
proposal, which, adopting their usual strategy, offered still greater national
minority protection.[84] Larin's proposal had established a minimum national
minority population (at least one-sixth) in a local region before minorities
gained full language rights. Ukraine's proposal had no minimum. The Ukrainians provided much more detail on the scope of national minority language
rights. Larin and the Ukrainian delegation sparred over these issues at the Third
Congress of Soviets in May 1925. The congress' general resolution favored
the Ukrainians. It called for[85]:

> the introduction of national minority representatives into all elected soviet
> organs; when national minorities form the majority of the local population,
> separate soviets should be formed that use the language of those minorities,
> that schools and courts in the native language should also be formed, and
> so on. . . .

This resolution made the Ukrainian system of territorial national soviets
obligatory for the entire Soviet Union, without even indirectly criticizing any
Ukrainization measures.

Thus, a Ukrainian-Jewish polemic led to an all-union decree calling for the
formation of national soviets. The Politburo endorsed this decree and dissolved
the Larin commission.[86] With official Politburo sanction, the center's nationalities specialists, who were concentrated in the soft-line soviet organs of TsIK
and its Soviet of Nationalities, as well as VTsIK and its Nationalities Department, set out with great resolve to transfer the Ukrainian system of national
soviets to the rest of the Soviet Union.[87] In October 1925, the Soviet of Nationalities issued a circular demanding information from local authorities on their

---

clear that "these malefactors [*zloumyshlenniki*] know Yiddish", they are automatically sent to a
Yiddish school "for, you see, we give every nationality full possibilities in this respect,—so off you
go to a Yiddish school." The children don't want this and their parents instruct them not to
admit that they know Yiddish. And so, comrades, an exam is conducted in order to trick these
children—they speak with the child in Russian or Ukrainian, and then, when the child has calmed
down (they speak nicely with them), suddenly the examiner tells him in Yiddish to go home. The
child jewishly turns around and leaves [*po-evreiski povarachivaetsia i ukhodit*] [laughter]. "That
means you know Yiddish. We'll send you to a Yiddish school."
Pervoe vseukrainskoe soveshchanie, 14.
[84] Ibid., 10–11.
[85] *III s"ezd sovetov SSSR. Stenograficheskii otchet* (Moscow, 1925): 272–284; 290–294.
[86] *RTsKhIDNI* 17/3/507 (18.06.25): 67/26.
[87] Two of the three major party commissions on nationalities policy in the mid-1920s, the
1925 Orgburo Commission on Soviet Construction in National Republics and Oblasts and the
1926–1927 Orgburo Commission for the Examination of Nationalities Policy, both included a
point endorsing national soviets in their final resolutions. *RTsKhIDNI* 17/112/715 (30.11.25): 10;
17/113/336 (07.10.27): 94.

Table 3. National Soviets in Leningrad Oblast, 1929–1936

| | 1929 | | | 1936 | |
| | Village | | | Village | |
Nationality	Soviets	Districts	Kolkhozy	Soviets	Districts
Finns	67	2	580	62	2
Veps	24	—	137	27	1
Estonians	8	—	136	17	—
Saami	6	—	9	10	2
Latvians	5	—	33	3	—
Germans	2	—	24	2	—
Karelians	2	—	22	2	—
Izhemtsy-Zyriane	2	—	2	2	—
Izhor	1	—	52	7	—
Norwegians	1	—	1	1	—
Jewish	—	—	1	—	—
Chinese	—	—	1	—	—
Total	118	2	998	133	5

Natsional'nye men'shinstva leningradskoi oblasti (Leningrad, 1929); P. M. Ianson, *Ot ugneteniia i bespraviia—k schastlivoi zhizni* (Leningrad, 1936).

implementation of the third congress' decree on national minorities.[88] The next month, VTsIK established a network of plenipotentiaries on national minority affairs in all oblasts and *gubernii*, whose duty was to supervise the formation of national soviets.[89] At a special national minorities congress in 1926, a member of VTsIK's presidium, S. D. Asfendiarov (a Kazakh), asserted that the formation of national soviets was now "our most serious concern."[90]

Due to the size and diversity of the RSFSR, the process of forming national soviets proceeded unevenly. In regions such as Leningrad, whose prosperous western national minorities resembled those of Ukraine and Belorussia, it occurred quite quickly.[91] In 1925, Leningrad oblast already had a Finnish district, in which all twenty Finnish village soviets conducted government business in Finnish.[92] As Table 3 shows, Leningrad eventually developed a national soviet network comparable to Ukraine and Belorussia. Few RSFSR oblasts, even those with much larger national minority populations, developed a network comparable to that of Leningrad.

The great complexity of the RSFSR's national-territorial structure complicated and politicized the formation of national soviets. National soviets were often seen as a threat to Russian *gubernii*. For instance, if a Russian *guberniia*

[88] *GARF* 3316/16a/175 (1925): 3.
[89] *SU RSFSR* (23.II.25): 85/628.
[90] *GARF* 1235/121/2 (1926): 76.
[91] *Soveshchanie upolnomochennykh*, 31.
[92] D. B., "Rabota sredi natsmen'shinstv," *Vlast' sovetov*, no. 42 (1925): 24–25.

formed a Tatar district adjacent to the Tatar ASSR, it would often serve as an invitation to annexation. On the other hand, refusal to form national soviets could be interpreted as national repression and likewise have serious repercussions. The Mordvinian question nicely illustrates this dilemma. The Mordvinians were the RSFSR's third most populous indigenous national minority. While the thirteen other most populous nationalities were all granted national territories prior to 1923, a Mordvinian autonomous oblast was not formed until 1929. The official reason was that the Mordvinians were too territorially dispersed to form a majority Mordvinian autonomous oblast. Mordvinian leaders noted that there were other minority autonomous republics (Karelia, Moldavia, Bashkiria, Crimea), but these all owed their existence to foreign policy or civil war–era tactical concerns. The Mordvinians were strategically insignificant, and their population was in fact so assimilated that it vigorously resisted native language education.[93]

Despite this extremely low level of national consciousness, in 1925 Mordvinian leaders succeeded in mobilizing street demonstrations in support of autonomy in several Mordvinian villages.[94] They did so by mobilizing economic arguments, correctly noting that financial support for "culturally backward" regions, representatives to the Soviet of Nationalities, reserved places in higher education for "backward" peoples, and other Soviet Affirmative Action benefits were all primarily dispersed to territorially organized nationalities.[95] The Mordvinian movement for autonomy is one of the best examples of how the Soviet national territorial system encouraged ethnic mobilization and greatly enhanced ethnic awareness. Central authorities attempted to placate the Mordvinian movement with national soviets. A special June 1925 VTsIK decree demanded the maximum formation of Mordvinian national soviets. Several Russian *gubernii* obeyed, and a few dozen Mordvinian districts and several hundred village soviets were formed. Others resisted, fearing this as the first step to a larger Mordvinian territory.[96] They proved prescient, because the formation of a Mordvinian autonomous oblast in 1929 was accompanied by the abolition of several Russian *gubernii* and the formation of a large multinational Middle Volga oblast.

If the Mordvinian question demonstrated the threat national soviets could pose to the Russian regions of the RSFSR, the politics surrounding the expansion of the Chuvash ASSR in 1925 illustrated how national soviets could serve as a spur to separatism. The Chuvash expansion was made possible by the general principle, again linked to the central logic of the Affirmative Action Empire, that the size of autonomous republics could be expanded beyond their ethnographic borders to strengthen them economically. This meant the annex-

[93] G. Ulianov, "Natsional'no-kul'turnaia problema v mordovskoi derevne," *Kommunisticheskoe prosveshchenie*, no. 19 (1931): 26–37.

[94] *RTsKhIDNI* 17/84/997 (1925): 20–21.

[95] *RTsKhIDNI* 17/113/781 (30.09.29): 78, 83–85; *GARF* 1235/142/3 (1925–1929): 4–16.

[96] I. Lazovskii and I. Bibin, eds., *Sovetskaia politika za 10 let po natsional'nomu voprosu v RSFSR* (Moscow, 1928): 157, 164; *GARF* 1235/121/2 (1926): 98; *Soveshchanie upolnomochennykh*, 87.

ation of majority Russian regions.[97] An expansion on these grounds in 1923 made Bashkiria a minority Bashkir republic.[98] An awareness of this principle led the Chuvash ASSR to claim all of Ulianovskaia *guberniia* (part of which was also simultaneously being claimed by the Mordvinians!), even though this would have reduced the Chuvash population within their own ASSR from 82 percent to 10 percent.[99] The larger claim failed, as the Chuvash surely knew it would, but as a consolation prize three districts with a sizable Chuvash *minority* were transferred to the Chuvash ASSR, which thereby reduced its Chuvash majority to 74 percent.[100]

These three districts contained sizable Russian, Mordvinian, and Tatar populations, all of whom resented the transfer because they suspected their rights would be subordinated to the Chuvash. OGPU reports noted ongoing difficulties in the new territories: "[There is] massive dissatisfaction over joining Alatyrskii district to the Chuvash ASSR. This dissatisfaction has grown into dissatisfaction with the very existence of the Chuvash ASSR."[101] Russians complained that after the territorial transfer, "the Chuvash fired all Russian workers, including even the chairman of the district." Mordvinians likewise maintained that "the Chuvash live much better than Mordvinians, because the government supports them and they themselves sit in positions of power." One Tatar complained evocatively: "We Tatars earlier were dependent on Ivan the Terrible, and now are dependent on the Chuvash and live under their yoke."[102] The OGPU still noted ongoing separatist sentiment in the new Chuvash territories two years after the transfer. Such separatist movements were the major source of ethnic mobilization in the 1920s. In December 1926, the OGPU reported that Greeks in the Karachai autonomous oblast had petitioned either to be granted their own autonomous territory or to be attached to an adjacent Russian region.[103] Such separatist agitation was often quite strategic. Another OGPU report noted the odd agitation of one German village in Kabardinia to join Ingushetia. The head of the German village was arguing that "in Ingushetia they have much lower taxes, and in general the Ingush would give them greater privileges."[104] These examples show how the establishment of a complex national territorial system and an openness to nationality-based claims for border revisions proved a recipe for ethnic mobilization.

Despite these difficulties, when VTsIK convened its second national minorities congress in 1928, it could report a much more extensive national soviet network than at its first congress in 1926. Perhaps more important was the

---

[97] *GARF* 3316/16a/177 (1924): 26.
[98] "K dekretu o bol'shoi Bashkirii," *Zhizn' natsional'nostei*, no. 13 (1922): 5.
[99] *GARF* 3316/16a/177 (1924): 27–28.
[100] *GARF* 1235/120/2 (1925): 248. Lazovskii and Bibin, *Sovetskaia politika*, 105–106.
[101] *RTsKhIDNI* 17/87/200a (1926): 2370b.
[102] *RTsKhIDNI* 17/87/201 (1927): 81.
[103] *RTsKhIDNIi* 17/87/200a (1926): 208.
[104] *RTsKhIDNI* 17/87/201 (1927): 134.

rhetorical shift. At the 1926 congress, Enukidze could still maintain: "We cannot tell every village, for instance those settled by Mordvinians, Chuvash, and so forth, that they should shift the bookkeeping in their village soviets to their native language, for they are sufficiently assimilated and know the Russian language."[105] In 1928, Kalinin, Enukidze's immediate superior, read a keynote address that sounded like Mykola Skrypnyk. Like Skrypnyk, Kalinin emphasized the relativity of the term national minority: "there is not one ethnic group, which does not form a minority in some republic, not excluding the Russian nationality."[106] He even repeated the Ukrainian argument that with the growing success of Ukrainization, Russians were in the process of becoming a national minority in Ukraine. Finally, he gave a striking endorsement of the value of national self-consciousness[107]:

> The first stage in true cultural development is the discovery of one's own nationality, that is the first step in cultural development and the first step in political self-determination. Therefore, I say that we will strive to protect nationalities, to create the prototype [*proobraz*] of a government, of the future communist government.

Enukidze had seen the future communist government as leading to the assimilation of nations. Kalinin, along with Skrypnyk, presented it as the proliferation of nations.

In a report on the work of VTsIK's Nationalities Department, its head Dosov (a Kazakh) noted considerable success in the construction of Kalinin's multinational prototype. He told the congress that an incomplete count gave an RSFSR-wide network of 2930 national village soviets, 110 national *volosti*, and 33 national districts.[108] Nevertheless, Dosov still complained that the network was incomplete. The congress agreed and declared the end of 1930 the deadline for completing the RSFSR's network of national soviets. Table 4 illustrates the substantial progress made in those two years.[109]

A complete network meant not only a maximum number of national soviets, but also a minimum number of mixed soviets. As in Ukraine, ethnic segregation was doggedly pursued and with considerable success. By 1931, in the RSFSR's nationally heterogeneous eleven autonomous republics and fifteen

---

[105] *GARF* 1235/121/2 (1926): 29.

[106] *Soveshchanie upolnomochennykh*, 1.

[107] Ibid., 3.

[108] Ibid., 6.

[109] P. Zaitsev, "Zadachi ukrepleniia apparata natsraionov v sviazi s likvidatsiei okrugov," *Revoliutsiia i natsional'nosti*, nos. 8–9 (1930): 48. The RSFSR had a much higher percentage of national minorities than Ukraine or Belorussia, which explains its high totals. The ZSFSR had a high percentage of national minorities but a weaker network of national soviets. These statistics do not include Russian national districts and village soviets in the RSFSR's autonomous republics and oblasts.

Table 4. National Soviets in the USSR, 1930

	DISTRICTS			VILLAGE SOVIETS		
Republic	Total	National	National as percent of Total	Total	National	National as percent of Total
Russian SFSR	2,017	127	6.3	52,844	4,264	8.0
Ukrainian SSR	494	27	5.8	10,880	1,085	9.9
Belorussian SSR	100	—	0.0	1,419	67	4.2
Transcaucasian SFSR	143	18	1.3	2,501	n/a	n/a

P. Zaitsev, "Zadachi ukrepleniia apparata natsraionov v sviazi s likvidatsiei okrugov," *Revoliutsiia i natsional'nosti*, nos. 8–9 (1930): 48. The RSFSR had a much higher percentage of national minorities than Ukraine or Belorussia, which explains its high totals. The ZSFSR had a high percentage of national minorities but a weaker network of national soviets. These statistics do not include Russian national districts and village soviets in the RSFSR's autonomous republics and oblasts.

autonomous oblasts, only 146 of 497 national districts (29.3 percent) were nationally mixed. More strikingly, only 851 of 12,766 national soviets (6.6 percent) were nationally mixed.[110] These statistics illustrate the extent to which the Ukrainian national minorities system was firmly adopted in the RSFSR as well as in Belorussia.

These statistics also illustrate that national soviets were not confined to the Russian regions of the RSFSR. As VTsIK Secretary A. S. Kiselev told the 1928 congress, however, national minorities policy faced unusual difficulties in the RSFSR's autonomous republics. In particular, Kiselev singled out Kazakhstan[111]:

They do not even consider Ukrainians and Russians national minorities, because in the Tsarist period, these were the peoples, to whom the autocracy assigned the role of colonizers. . . . Thus, quoting a whole series of reasons, [the Kazakh government] shows every kind of resistance to the formation of administrative-territorial units and refuses to realize party directives on this question.

For the past two years Kiselev had led a series of commissions to regulate the position of the Russian population in Kazakhstan and Kirgizia. He knew that the major national minority issue in the eastern republics was the status of Russians and that it was much more difficult for the eastern nationalities, many of whom had recently been subject to mass Russian colonization, to legitimate the presence of the former great-power nationality.

[110] B. Rodievich, "Korenizatsiia apparata v avtonomiakh i raionakh natsmen'shinstv RSFSR," *Revoliutsiia i natsional'nosti*, no. 12 (1931): 113. There was no exact definition of a nationally mixed soviet. Usually it meant about 20 to 50 percent national minority.

[111] *Soveshchanie upolnomochennykh*, 125.

National Soviets and Ethnic Conflict in the Soviet East

As we shall see in the following two chapters, the Soviet nationalities policy made a sharp distinction between eastern and western nationalities. The distinction was not geographic. Crimean Tatars were eastern and Armenians western. Rather, eastern nationalities were those labeled "culturally backward" (*kul'turno-otstalyi*). These represented the vast majority of Soviet nationalities. An official 1932 list established ninety-seven "culturally backward" nationalities (see Table 21) as eligible for preferential treatment in university admissions.[112] In general, only the western national minorities and Jews, Russians, Ukrainians, Belorussians, Georgians, and Armenians were not categorized as "culturally backward." When I refer to the Soviet east without quotations, I am following (but of course not endorsing) this Soviet terminology.

Ethnic conflict was generally more severe in the Soviet east. This is not surprising. Donald Horowitz's magisterial survey of ethnic conflict found that ethnic groups that had been popularly stereotyped as "backward" (often by former colonial authorities) were much more likely to initiate *violent* ethnic conflict.[113] Leaving aside the issue of popular stereotyping, Ted Gurr's massive "Minorities at Risk" database (covering post-1945 conflicts) found that violent ethnic conflict was much more common in poor countries (as measured by GDP per capita).[114] This same pattern can be found in the Soviet Union of the 1920s, not only between "western" and "eastern" national regions but within the Soviet east. In republics such as Tatarstan, Crimea, and Chuvashia, ethnic conflict was typically nonviolent and focused on access to white-collar jobs and linguistic politics. In republics such as Kazakhstan and Uzbekistan, conflict was more often violent and focused on control of agricultural land and administrative territory. However, one needs to consider factors other than relative poverty to understand the pattern of ethnic conflict in the Soviet east.

Thus far, my model for explaining ethnic conflict has included three main factors. First, the drawing of tens of thousands of borders to form tens of thousands of minute national territories led to an increase in ethnic conflict, as ethnic groups (whose ethnicity was now officially recognized and defined by the state) mobilized to avoid becoming a national minority in the newly formed national territories. Soviet policy politicized ethnicity by linking it to the control of administrative territory. Second, such ethnic contention tended to become more severe when this connection between ethnicity and administrative territory was further linked to control over agricultural land and when ethnic divisions coincided with former estate (*soslovie*) divisions. When invidious estate categories, such as *inorodtsy* or peasant, were identified in a given region with a single ethnic group, they served the function of Horowitz's negative stereotyping. Soviet

---

[112] "Ob udarnom kul'tobsluzhivanii otstalykh natsional'nostei," *Biulleten' narodnogo komissariata po prosveshcheniiu RSFSR*, no. 5 (1932): 13–14.

[113] Donald Horowitz, *Ethnic Groups in Conflict* (Berkeley, Calif., 1985): 141–185.

[114] Ted Robert Gurr and Barbara Harff, *Ethnic Conflict in World Politics* (Boulder, Colo., 1994).

policy often exacerbated this second factor by explicitly linking the formation of national soviets to control over agricultural land and by perpetuating some aspects of estate stereotyping through the formal category of "culturally backward" nationalities. Third, ethnic conflict was more likely to become violent in poorer regions. To complete my model, a crucial fourth factor needs to be added. Ethnic conflict was much more likely to become violent in regions where large-scale agricultural colonization had taken place in the recent past.

Using these four factors, we can construct a typology of ethnic conflict in the Soviet east that consists of three variants, which I will name after the largest representative of each type: the Tatar variant, the Kazakh variant, and the Uzbek variant. These are, of course, ideal-types, and each national example has its own specifics and some regions either do not fit the typology well or are mixed types. The following summarizes the main features of the three variants:

1. *The Tatar Variant.* In this situation, there is a large, but long established, Russian colonial presence. The region is relatively well developed and has, in comparison to other Soviet eastern regions, a well-developed national intelligentsia. Given the binational population, complete national control over the republic is impossible, and so the national intelligentsia focuses on furthering the Soviet policy of *korenizatsiia* (indigenization). In particular, they emphasize control over white-collar jobs and promotion of the national language. The national intelligentsia supports the formation of national soviets to divide the republic into Russian and national regions, so that the national language can at least be dominant at the subrepublican level. In this situation, elite ethnic contention is strong. However, given minimal conflict over land possession and no invidious historic estate divisions, popular ethnic conflict is weak and violent ethnic conflict entirely absent. Examples: Tatarstan, Crimea, Chuvashia, the Volga German republic.

2. *The Kazakh Variant.* In this situation, there has been a relatively recent and large-scale agricultural colonization that was predominantly Slavic (and perceived by the local population as Russian). The region is poor and the national movement is comparatively weak. National elites are less concerned about issues of *korenizatsiia*, although they of course support the policy, than about decolonization: the return of agricultural land to the native population and, ideally, the expulsion of "Russian" settlers. This agenda has strong popular support given the region's poverty, ethnic conflict over land possession, and deeply felt invidious estate divisions. In this situation, popular ethnic violence is widespread. Examples: Kazakhstan, Kirgizia, Bashkiria (eastern regions), Buriat-Mongolia, most North Caucasus Mountaineer (*gortsy*) regions.

3. *The Uzbek Variant.* In this situation, there is a low level of colonial settlement and a low level of development. The national movements are relatively weak and so issues of *korenizatsiia* are not particularly salient. There are, however, large non-Russian national minority populations, and conflicts over land ownership are widespread. As a result, the drawing of borders tends to lead to levels of popular ethnic conflict higher than in the Tatar variant but con-

siderably lower than in the Kazakh variant. Ethnic conflict occurs between non-Russians, not between natives and Russians. Examples: Uzbekistan, Turkmenistan, Tajikistan, Kirgizia (mixed Uzbek-Kirgiz regions).

Case studies of Tatarstan, Kazakhstan, and Central Asia illustrate the different patterns of rural ethnic conflict in the Soviet east.

The Tatar Variant

The Tatar national movement was among the strongest in the Soviet Union, and certainly the strongest in the Soviet east. The Tatar nationalist elite lobbied aggressively for and vigorously supported the Soviet policy of *korenizatsiia*: the formation of a Tatar republic, the promotion of Tatars into leadership positions, the use of the Tatar language in government and education, and support for Tatar national culture. However, this movement also faced formidable resistance. Tatars formed a narrow plurality in their own republic (48.7 percent Tatar and 43.1 percent Russian).[115] Kazan had been an important regional capital, an old university town and a center for Orthodox missionary activity, so there was a strongly entrenched Russian bureaucracy and intelligentsia. This situation led to perpetual political conflict along ethnic lines. In its first five years, Tatarstan went through six obkom secretaries. Tatarstan became famous in Moscow for its incessant internecine political strife. In this divided environment, it was impossible for Tatar national communists to follow the Ukrainian model and advocate Tatar cultural and linguistic hegemony within all of Tatarstan.

The solution found was to open up a space for Tatar linguistic hegemony at the regional, subrepublican level. Unlike Kazakh national communists, who vigorously resisted the formation of national soviets that they felt would legitimize an unwanted Russian presence in their republics, Tatarstan undertook a national *raionirovanie* already in 1924, just after the first Ukrainian efforts.[116] The primary goal was not the formation of national minority soviets as in Ukraine, but rather the administrative separation of the republic's two national majorities: Russians and Tatars. The explicit aim was to create nationally homogeneous Tatar districts, in which Tatar could be made the language of government: "it is necessary to undertake a general reorganization of the *volosti* of the Tatar republic on linguistic lines in order to create unilingual *volosti*, in which it will be easier to promote the Tatar language."[117] National *raionirovanie* did produce an impressive increase in ethnic separation, 74 Tatar and 52 Russian districts, in which 45 percent of the districts were almost purely

---

[115] *Natsional'naia politika VKP/b/ v tsifrakh* (Moscow, 1930): 45. (This figure combines the Tatars and Kryashen, the latter being Christian Tatars, 3.82 percent of whom declared Kryashen as their ethnicity.)

[116] *RTsKhIDNI* 17/33/443 (1925): 26–35; Chanyshev, "Proekt ukrupneniia volostei ATSSR," *Vlast' sovetov*, no. 1 (1924): 141–145.

[117] Chanyshev, 141.

unilingual (94 percent or higher). Only 8 percent of the Tatar rural population was now located in Russian districts.[118] The Tatar model was followed by the more developed autonomous republics and oblasts, such as Crimea, Chuvashia, and the Volga German republic, that wanted to pursue linguistic *korenizatsiia* aggressively but had a large and politically powerful Russian population.[119]

As in Ukraine and the RSFSR, the formation of national soviets in Tatarstan led to a mobilization of ethnic groups to avoid becoming national minorities. In response to Chuvash agitation, two Chuvash national districts were formed later in 1924. These districts immediately responded by petitioning to separate and join Samara *guberniia* "due to bad service from the Tatar republic."[120] This was a typical strategic response to national *raionirovanie*: playing off one potential majority host (the Samaran Russians) against one's existing national majority (the Tatars). Given their stormy *korenizatsiia* battles with the Russians, the Tatar leadership could not afford another enemy. In 1926, and again in 1930, they passed extremely generous national minority legislation explicitly designed to satisfy the Chuvash.[121]

Relations with the Russian peasantry were also momentarily strained when Tatar national communists, as a mild decolonization measure, succeeded in passing legislation giving Tatar peasants preferential access to desirable agricultural land along the railways and in the river valleys. Local Tatar authorities also started to tax Russian villages more highly on purely ethnic grounds.[122] Unsurprisingly, Russian peasants reacted with hostility to such measures. Attempts in 1923–1924 to remove Russian peasants from quality land along rivers and railways "almost went so far as to provoke an uprising." In the summer of 1925, "petitions to separate from the Tatar republic, even in non-border villages, took on a mass character." These complaints often referred to a sense of second-class status: "This isn't our republic, it's your republic."[123] In the face of these aggressive protests and threats, the Tatar government backed down and abolished these preferential policies for Tatar peasants. It was no coincidence that the two republics with the fiercest *korenizatsiia* wars, Tatarstan and Ukraine, produced the two most systematic examples of national minority legislation.

The Kazakh Variant

Since decolonization measures in Tatarstan were half-hearted and brief, ethnic contention was largely confined to the elite political sphere. The opposite was

---

[118] *RTsKhIDNI* 17/33/443 (1925): 27; Chanyshev, "Proekt ukrupneniia volostei ATSSR," 141.

[119] *GARF* 1235/122/47 (1928): 81–84; 102–103.

[120] *RTsKhIDNI* 17/69/60 (1926): 26; 46.

[121] *SU Tatarskoi respubliki* (1926): 15/101; (1926) 21/121; (1930) 26/249; (1930): 26/250.

[122] *RTsKhIDNI* 17/69/58 (1926): 210; *GARF* 3316/64/397a (1927): 13–15; *Stenograficheskii otchet zasedaniia XIII oblastnoi partiinoi konferentsii* (Kazan, 1927): 215, 229; *RTsKhIDNI* 17/87/196 (1925): 236–248.

[123] *RTsKhIDNI* 17/69/58 (1926): 210; 17/69/60 (1926): 290b; 17/113/305 (27.06.27): 54.

the case in Kazakhstan and Kirgizia. In these areas, Russian colonial settlement was recent and massive.[124] Both the 1916 Kazakh uprising and the civil war pitted Russian Cossacks and Slavic agricultural settlers against the local Kazakh and Kirgiz population.[125] With the possible exception of the North Caucasus, the demand for drastic decolonization measures was stronger in Kazakhstan and Kirgizia than anywhere else in the Soviet Union. In these republics, the central conflict was not over the rights of Russian settlers, but over their very presence.

In September 1920, the Ninth Turkestan Congress of Soviets issued a decree, with the support of central authorities in Moscow, that called for the removal of illegal settlers, the equalization of native and European land holdings, and the prohibition of future settlement from without Turkestan.[126] This decree reversed the Turkestan government's civil war affiliation with the local Russian population. Instead, it sought native support by promising to reverse the massive Russian land seizures of 1916 to 1920, which had taken place primarily in what would become, after 1924, southeast Kazakhstan and Kirgizia.[127]

The actual land reform took place from January 1921 to December 1922 and led to the mass expulsion of Slavic settlers and Cossacks.[128] From 1920 to 1922, Kazakhstan's Russian population dropped from approximately 2.7 to 2.2 million (about 20 percent) and its sewn area of crops from 3.3 to 1.6 million *dessiatina*. The OGPU reported that "this work was carried out by special punitive expeditionary missions." According to one report, in a single day, "the entire settlement of [Iurev], with 500 to 600 households, was driven out into the frost." The center quickly concluded that the process "took place with excessive cruelty, and took on the character of revenge." The Kazakh government, however, as late as 1927, called it the October Revolution in Kazakhstan and the foundation of Kazakh autonomy: "The Kazakh people interpret autonomy above all as the right to independently decide questions of land."[129]

An analogous process took place in the North Caucasus. During Tsarist rule, the indigenous mountain peoples (*gortsy*) had been progressively driven out of the more fertile Caucasian foothills and deeper into the mountains. Their land was granted first to Cossacks and then to Slavic settlers. As in Kazakhstan, the resulting ethnic tension led to brutal national conflict during the civil war. The first act of the newly formed Mountaineer ASSR in 1921, again with central authorization, was to redress this historical grievance: "For the satisfaction of

---

[124] George J. Demko, *The Russian Colonization of Kazakhstan, 1896–1916* (Bloomington, Ind., 1969).

[125] Richard Pipes, *The Formation of the Soviet Union* (rev. ed., Cambridge, Mass., 1964): 172–184.

[126] *S"ezdy sovetov SSSR, soiuznykh i avtonomnykh respublik*, vol. 1 (Moscow, 1959): 434–436.

[127] *GARF* 3316/64/220 (1926): 11–140b.

[128] Ibid., 110b. *RTsKhIDNI* 558/11/29 (28.06.22): 121; 558/11/30 (17.07.22): 28. See also, V. L. Genis, "Deportatsiia russkikh iz Turkestana v 1921 godu ('Delo Safarova')," *Voprosy istorii*, no. 1 (1998): 44–58.

[129] *GARF* 3316/16a/177 (1924): 28–31; 1235/140/127 (1926–1928): 39; 3316/64/220 (1926): 13; *RTsKhIDNI* 17/113/338 (31.10.27): 105.

the desperate needs of landless Mountaineers, immediately begin the planned expulsion of Cossack settlements beyond the borders of the Mountaineer ASSR."[130] In fact, on central orders the liquidation of nine Terek Cossack settlements and the deportation of approximately 15,000 Cossacks had already begun in 1920 and would be completed in 1921.[131] Their land was given to landless Mountaineers. These deportations punished the Cossacks for their role in the anti-Bolshevik White movement.[132] However, they were also a form of anticolonial reparation directly linked to the formation of a new Mountaineer national territory.

While the expulsions in Kazakhstan and the North Caucasus were both legally sanctioned actions, the center nevertheless viewed both of them as exceptional one-time measures and strongly condemned the punitive way in which the Kazakh expulsions were carried out. The Kazakh government, however, stubbornly attempted to preserve in law two cardinal principles from the 1921–1922 land reform: first, their right to continue expelling those settlers who had arrived without legal permission after the failed 1916 uprising; and second, the principle of "*ocherednost*'," which meant that Kazakhs were granted unconditional priority in the acquisition of all available agricultural land. Kazakhstan's agricultural commissar, Dzhandosov, summarized this position well: "Our current agricultural policy is based on the principle that, first of all, the interests of the Kazakh population should be satisfied, that they should receive land first of all."[133] While the Soviet nationalities policy supported a variety of privileges for titular nationalities, such a categorical priority in economic matters was not recognized. As the Central Committee secretary A. A. Andreev put it: "As soon as you speak of *ocherednost*', of advantages for the Kazakh population, you unavoidably slip away from a class position."[134] As a result, in August 1922, Moscow ended all expulsions and insisted on equal rights for all remaining Slavic settlers.[135] The Kazakh government, on the other hand, continued to insist on a policy of decolonization.[136]

The position of the Kazakh government created an environment that encouraged a variety of illegal measures against Russian settlers. From 1924 to 1927, central OGPU reports regularly cited the following actions against Russians in Kazakhstan and Kirgizia: punitive taxation, false arrest, cattle theft, armed seizures of land, the trampling of crops, and armed attacks with the goal of

---

[130] *S"ezdy sovetov SSSR*, vol. 1 (Moscow, 1959): 718.

[131] N. F. Bugai and A. M. Gonov, *Kavkaz: Narody v eshelonakh (20-60-e gody)* (Moscow, 1998): 83–87. N. F. Bugai, "20-40e gody: deportatsiia naseleniia s territorii evropeiskoi Rossii," *Otechestvennaia istoriia*, no. 4 (1992): 37–40. For documents, see N. F. Bugai, "Kazaki," *Shpion*, no. 1 (1993): 40–55.

[132] Peter Holquist, "'Conduct Merciless Mass Terror': Decossackization on the Don, 1919," *Cahiers du monde russe* 38 (1997): 127–162.

[133] *5-ia Vsekazakskaia konferentsiia RKP/b/. Stenograficheskii otchet* (Kzyl-Orda, 1925): biull. evening (05.12.25): 3.

[134] *6-ia vsekazakskaia konferentsiia VKP/b/. Stenograficheskii otchet* (Kzyl-Orda, 1927): 235.

[135] *GARF* 3316/64/220 (1926): 140b.

[136] *RTsKhIDNI* 17/85/105 (1926–1927): 750b.

driving the attacked from their homes.[137] Kazakhs and Kirgiz appointed to
govern Russian regions regularly refused to punish native wrongdoers. In
August 1925, armed Kazakhs seized a Russian pasture. When the Russians threatened to seek redress, the Kazakhs yelled, "we don't fear anyone, and above
all local authorities."[138] A Russian petition lamented that "there is nowhere to
go to complain: go to the militia—a Kirgiz, go to the GPU—Kirgiz, go to
the local soviet—Kirgiz."[139] In 1926, Iakov Peters, former head of the
OGPU's Eastern Department, called the Russians of Kazakhstan "eternally
persecuted."[140]

The OGPU closely monitored the mood of Russians in Kazakhstan. One
Russian response to their situation was to petition for land anywhere in Russia.
In 1923, there was even a mass petition from Russian settlers to the Turkestan
TsIK asking permission to move to western China.[141] There was an almost universal call for the establishment of Russian national soviets, preferably subordinated to the RSFSR, not Kazakhstan.[142] This internal separatism was matched
by external separatism among the Russians in north Kazakhstan, who petitioned
to have their territories transferred to the RSFSR.[143] In general, Russians keenly
felt their loss of status, a loss they viewed as especially unjust given their civil
war service. One communist was reported to have said, "how can it be, we
fought and fought, and all we got is that under Soviet power, you can't beat
the hell out of the Kirgiz." This feeling led to predictions of revenge. The
OGPU reported Russians "threatening to cut the throats of all the Kirgiz 'when
a better day arrives,'" or threatening "just wait, there will come a time, and it'll
be all over for you Kirgiz." Such sentiments led the head of the OGPU
in Central Asia to take seriously the possibility of a Russian uprising in
Kazakhstan.[144]

Faced with this potential threat, the center undertook a series of direct interventions beginning in late 1924. In November 1924, VTsIK's presidium formed
a "Commission on the Question of Regulating the Position of Russians in the
Autonomous Republics and Oblasts" under the chairmanship of Enukidze.[145]
In April 1925, a TsK plenum discussed the status of Cossacks and passed a

---

[137] There are literally hundreds of such incidents reported in the national OGPU reports for
1924 to 1927 in *RTsKhIDNI* 17/87/181–183, 196–198, 200, 200a, 201. For Kirgizia in 1927 and
1928, further numerous accounts can be found in the Central Asian OGPU monthly reports in
RTsKhIDNI 62/2/881–882, 1349–1352. Kazakhstan and Kirgizia are by far the most frequently
cited locations for violent ethnic conflict in the 1920s.

[138] *RTsKhIDNI* 17/87/196 (1925): 146.

[139] *RTsKhIDNI* 17/33/418 (1927): 50. In this and other quotations, Kazakhs are often referred
to as Kirgiz, since this was the common term among Russians in the Tsarist period. The Kirgiz
were then known as Kara-Kirgiz.

[140] *RTsKhIDNI* 17/87/196 (1925): 146; 17/33/418 (1927): 50; 17/113/229 (22.09.26): 38.

[141] *GARF* 3316/16a/176 (1926): 13.

[142] *RTsKhIDNI* 17/69/61 (1926): 40–41; 17/87/201 (1927): 520b; 17/87/200a (1926): 35.

[143] *RTsKhIDNI* 17/87/200 (1926): 147.

[144] *RTsKhIDNI* 17/112/686 (10.08.25): 29; 17/87/201 (1927): 380b; 17/87/196 (1925): 373;
GARF 1235/140/127 (1927): 200–201.

[145] *GARF* 1235/140/127 (1924): 1.

resolution improving their status.[146] In October 1924, VTsIK also formed a special commission headed by Serafimov and devoted exclusively to regulating land reform in south Kazakhstan and Kirgizia.[147] Finally, in 1925 TsK sent Kazakhstan a new kraikom secretary, F. I. Goloshchekin. The previous kraikom secretary, Khodzhanov, had unambiguously supported the Kazakh nationalist position. Goloshchekin played a mediating role between central demands and Kazakh goals, thereby weakening the previous Kazakh solidarity.

The formation of the Enukidze committee represented the first official acknowledgment of a Russian national minority question. It is striking that a Russian question arose first in the RSFSR, two years before Larin's incendiary speech at the April 1926 TsIK session. The Enukidze committee studied the Russian question in the three regions where relations between Russians and natives were considered worst: Kazakhstan and Kirgizia, eastern Bashkiria, and Buriat-Mongolia. In each case, the conflict was between Russian settlers and native nomads (or recently settled former nomads). The Agricultural Commissariat strongly argued for the protection of "cultured" Russian agriculture from "backward" nomadic practices. They noted that in the fertile Dzhetsuiskaia oblast of Kazakhstan the sewn grain crop had declined from 740,000 *dessiatina* in 1913 to 284,000 in 1924.[148] Their proposal was the now familiar one of ethnic segregation into separate national soviets. The Enukidze commission endorsed this recommendation in its final February 1926 resolution.[149]

The Cossack question was first raised in TsK at an October 1924 Politburo meeting, the same time VTsIK began to deal with the Russian question.[150] The reasons were similar. A TsK informational report on the Cossack mood reported that "one cannot exclude the threat that the Cossack nests could be transformed into a Russian 'Vendee.'"[151] The two Cossack regions that most worried TsK were those where the Cossack question and the Russian question combined: the North Caucasus and Kazakhstan/Kirgizia. In his report on the Cossack question at the April 1925 TsK plenum, Syrtsov emphasized this connection. While warning against illusions of Cossack autonomy, Syrtsov suggested that the formation of separate Cossack districts would "soften" Cossack anger at the Soviet nationalities policy.[152] A year later, Russian national soviets were in fact formed for the Cossack communities of North Ossetia and Chechnya.[153] The formation of Cossack soviets (even if they were called "Russian") in the North Caucasus intensified an already strong movement for Cossack autonomy in Kazakhstan and Kirgizia. There were identifiable leaders of this movement,

---

[146] *RTsKhIDNI* 17/2/172 (1925): 386–415; "Rezoliutsiia plenuma TsK po voprosu o kazachestve," *Izvestiia TsK RKP/b/*, nos. 17–18 (1925): 5.

[147] *GARF* 3316/64/220 (1926): 58.

[148] *GARF* 3316/16a/177 (1924): 31.

[149] Ibid., 1–7.

[150] *RTsKhIDNI* 17/3/470 (23.10.24): 30/9; 17/3/472 (20.10.24): 32/24.

[151] *RTsKhIDNI* 17/84/904 (1925): 82.

[152] *RTsKhIDNI* 17/2/172 (1925): 407–409.

[153] Lazovskii and Bibin, *Sovetskaia politika*, 160. *GARF* 1235/122/47 (1928): 46.

known as *avtonomisty*, who according to OGPU reports had even established contacts with the North Caucasus.[154] The two commissions working on the Cossack and Russian questions, then, converged on the same solution: national soviets.

VTsIK's Serafimov commission was assigned the job of supervising the formation of national soviets for Russians and Cossacks in Kazakhstan.[155] Serafimov proposed forming four Russian *okrugi* within this region, which would embrace 289,000 Russians and Ukrainians. These four *okrugi*, which were not contiguous, would be combined to form the Kalinin Autonomous Oblast, directly subordinate to VTsIK in political matters and to the RSFSR Agricultural Commissariat in agricultural matters. They would also form a base for future Russian agricultural settlement.[156] This plan was not realized, but it represented the type of thinking that stiffened the Kazakh leadership's resistance. Serafimov's plan linking Russian nationality, the possession of land, the regulation of immigration, and the political control of territory naturally threatened the Kazakh leadership's own principles, which linked the formation of a Kazakh republic with control over the land (*ocherednost'*) and control over immigration. The Serafimov proposal amounted to a right of secession for even territorially dispersed Russians. The Kazakh leadership viewed such separatism as a threat to the very existence of their republic. The head of the Kazakh Sovnarkom, N. N. Nurmakov, articulated this fear at a Kazakh party congress in 1925[157]:

> We cannot allow the separation of different regions of the Kazakh republic; one cannot do this, for that would mean dividing up [*razmezhevanie*] the Kazakh republic . . . it would be equivalent to the collapse of the Kazakh republic. . . . On this question the conference should firmly tell those comrades who are inclined to separate from us, *as well as those comrades from the center who, under the impression that the Kazakh population supposedly oppresses national minorities, aim at separating our border regions from the Kazakh republic* [*my emphasis*]. Under no circumstance can we allow this for, I repeat, allowing further separation would be the source of the collapse, the destruction of the Kazakh republic and all our accomplishments.

Therefore, the Kazakh leadership refused to cooperate with the VTsIK commission even after a special intervention by Kalinin.[158]

This stalemate created an environment of uncertainty that encouraged ethnic mobilization and ethnic conflict. The appearance of the Serafimov commission in Kazakhstan in 1925 alerted the local Russian population to the weakness of the Kazakh government, which prompted an increase in separatist agitation. Serafimov claimed to have received 1500 separate complaints from local

[154] *GARF* 1235/140/127 (1927): 2–5, 200; *RTsKhIDNI* 17/87/201 (1927): 76.
[155] *GARF* 1235/140/376 (1926): 3; 3316/64/220 (1926): 98.
[156] *GARF* 3316/64/220 (1926): 61–80.
[157] *5-ia vsekazakskaia konferentsiia*, 15.
[158] *GARF* 1235/140/376 (1926): 101–1010b.

Russians.[159] Local Kazakh and Kirgiz leaders, however, insisted that Serafimov had encouraged those complaints. The Kirgiz obkom secretary wrote to Stalin that Serafimov had engaged in "the purposeful collection and encouragement of complaints on local soviet organs and the local population."[160] Zelenskii, head of the Central Asian *Biuro*, agreed.[161] Asfendiarov, Kazakhstan's lone ally in VTsIK, presented VTsIK secretary Kiselev with a special collection of OGPU materials demonstrating the "fabrication" of "complaints literally flooding Kalinin's office."[162] Such charges did finally lead to the abolition of the Serafimov commission in April 1926. However, for an entire year both sides had attempted to enlist ethnic support, leading, in Zelenskii's words, to a "maximum nationalist outburst."[163]

It would be false, however, to claim that ethnic conflict was only a result of elite manipulation. On the contrary, popular conceptions of territorial exclusivity were at least as strong as elite ones. For instance, during the violent seizure of land from local Russians, a group of Kazakhs declared: "Russian immigrants have been our guests for thirty-five years, and now let them get the hell out of here to Russia and leave our land and pasture."[164] The sentiment could be put in still blunter terms: "Now power is in our Kirgiz hands [*teper vlast' nasha kirgizskaia*], therefore we do what we please."[165] The popular conception, then, maintained that assigning a territory to one nationality meant granting that nationality total control.

Allied to this conception was the belief that non-natives were guests and could be asked or forced to leave. OGPU reports, in the midst of conflicts, frequently noted taunts such as "it's time for all you Russians to get out of the Kirgiz republic." Nor did the Russian settlers find this concept alien. A Russian miller commented that "in the Kirgiz republic we won't be able to live, it'd be better if the government resettled us into our own [*svoiu*] republic." Russians keenly resented their role reversal: "Now the Kirgiz are the masters [*gospoda*]; they just lie around, drink kumys [fermented mare's milk], and Russians do half their field work for them."[166] These comments illustrated why so much conflict centered around the formation of national soviets. Each group strove to assert its status as national majority and so avoid becoming a national minority.

Popular and elite resistance to Russian national soviets prevented their formation through 1926 in all of the regions where the Kazakh variant prevailed. Only toward the end of 1926, due to considerable central pressure, did Kirgizia, Bashkiria, and the North Caucasus autonomous regions finally agree to

---

[159] *RTsKhIDNI* 17/85/105 (1926): 23.
[160] Ibid., 14.
[161] *GARF* 1235/140/127 (1927): 206–209.
[162] *GARF* 1235/140/127 (1926): 5.
[163] Ibid., 207.
[164] *RTsKhIDNI* 17/87/196 (1925): 6.
[165] Ibid., 199.
[166] *RTsKhIDNI* 17/87/196 (1925): 267; 214; 97.

form Russian soviets and therefore accept the permanence of the Russian presence.[167]

Kazakhstan continued to hold out because they feared that legitimizing the existing Russian colonial presence would leave them vulnerable to a massive influx of settlers, which could tilt the ethnic balance against them. The key issue in Kazakhstan remained the question as to whether the Soviet nationalities policy allowed the local republic to control internal migration and therefore control the ethnic demography of their republic.

In Tatarstan, local Russian pressure and central disapproval led to a rather swift abandonment of their decolonization policies. In Kazakhstan, a much greater degree of central pressure was required. In 1927, VTsIK formed yet another commission (its fourth in three years), headed now by its secretary Kiselev and with the unambiguous backing of TsK.[168] Its goal was to force the Kazakh government to give way on the principle of *ocherednost'* (Kazakh priority in acquiring land) and control of immigration. Russian national soviets were now a secondary goal. This central pressure finally split the native Kazakh leadership in 1927, allowing Goloshchekin to form a shaky majority in favor of concessions. Kazakhstan began forming Russian national soviets in late 1927.[169] By April 1928, Kazakhstan had unambiguously agreed to repeal *ocherednost'* and to open Kazakhstan to immigration.[170] This marked an important moment in the history of the Soviet nationalities policy as it determined that the policy of *korenizatsiia* did not mean that national majorities would be granted the right to preserve their demographic majority status.

This policy reversal in 1927–1928 did not lead to a cessation of ethnic conflict. It did, however, change the hierarchy of domination. The OGPU had long reported Russian threats to wreak vengeance on Kazakhs when the proper time came: "I'm waiting for the time when we will get to thrash the Kazakhs."[171] In the spring of 1928, the Russians of Semipalatinsk apparently felt their time had arrived. The implementation of a decree to seize the possessions of a few hundred wealthy *bai* households turned into a mass repression of Kazakhs. A Politburo decree removed Semipalatinsk's party secretary, Bekker, and yet again sent a commission (now the fifth in four years) headed by Kiselev to investi-

---

[167] I. A. Fat'ianov, "Itogi raionirovaniia Kirgizii," *Planovoe khoziaistvo*, no. 4 (1927): 247–254. *RTsKhIDNI* 17/32/III (1927): 23. Kirgizia formed 29 Kirgiz, 11 Russian, 1 Uzbek, and 11 mixed districts.

[168] *RTsKhIDNI* 17/113/338 (31.10.27): 151/4.

[169] *RTsKhIDNI* 62/2/972 (1927). On the center's unhappiness, see Kiselev's comments at *Soveshchanie upolnomochennykh*, 125.

[170] The details of this battle can be found in *RTsKhIDNI* 17/3/679 (29.03.28): 17/12; 17/113/229 (22.09.26): 58/1; 17/113/299 (06.06.27): 119/4; 17/113/338 (31.10.27): 151/4; *GARF* 1235/122/283 (1927); 1235/140/127 (1926–1928); 1235/140/376 (1925–1927); 3316/65/22 (1927): 11–26. *6-ia Vsekazakskaia konferentsiia*. To give a sense of what was at stake, in late 1927, the All-Union Resettlement Committee wrote the Andreev committee, a TsK committee formed to deal with Kazakh land politics, and argued that it was impossible to fulfill their ten-year goal of settling 5,200,000 souls without Kazakhstan. They set a goal of 3.6 million agricultural settlers. Ultimately Kazakhstan would become one of the major dumping grounds for dekulakized peasants and later for deported nationalities.

[171] *RTsKhIDNI* 17/87/200a (1926): 730b.

gate. Kiselev reported that over 17,000 Kazakh households had been repressed and that there had been "a mass flight into China."[172] A similar urban episode took place in May 1928 in Semipalatinsk. Unemployed workers who had arrived in Semipalatinsk to seek work on the Turksib railway construction project rioted. Among their targets was the city's small Kazakh population. A more substantial pogrom took place later in 1928 in the Cossack town of Sergiopol. Already in July 1926, the OGPU had noted among the Cossacks of north Kazakhstan "declarations about the need to unleash a Kirgiz pogrom."[173] In Sergiopol, this Cossack hostility to Kazakhs combined with working-class hostility. The OGPU reported an instance of this hostility from a Semipalatinsk Russian employee after an official meeting with local Kazakhs:

> What is the use of such meetings with the Kirgiz. I'd prefer not to meet them like this; I'd put up a machine-gun and meet them so that now they'd be carried away to a fraternal grave, and there I'd place a memorial with the inscription: "In memory from the Ridder enterprise."

On December 31, 1928 this hostility broke out into in a pogrom in which over four hundred Russian workers engaged in a mass beating of Kazakhs.[174]

The Uzbek Variant

I now conclude with a discussion of the Uzbek variant, prevalent throughout the rest of Central Asia, where the Russian population and Russian colonialism were minor factors in rural life and where substantial non-Russian national minorities led to ethnic conflict over territorial borders, both the borders between republics and national soviet borders within the republics. The republican-level borders of Central Asia were only established in 1924 in a "national delimitation" (*natsional'noe razmezhevanie*), which divided the Turkestan ASSR into an Uzbek SSR, Turkmen SSR, Kirgiz AO (within the RSFSR), and Tajik ASSR (within the Uzbek SSR).[175] The rationale put forward was the usual one, as officially expressed by the head of the Central Asian Biuro, Jan Rudzutak: "It was necessary to eliminate the moment of national hostility between the different peoples, and in doing so open up the possibility to lay bare class contradictions within each nationality."[176] Again, the opposite occurred.

---

[172] *RTsKhIDNI* 17/3/697 (26.07.28): 35/22; 94/1/1 (1928): 625–685.

[173] *RTsKhIDNI* 17/87/200a (1926): 11.

[174] Payne, "Turksib." The Building of the Turkestano-Siberian Railroad and the Politics of Production during the Cultural Revolution, 1926–1931 (Ph.D. diss, University of Chicago, 1995): 251–259.

[175] For a splendid acount of the national delimitation, see Adrienne Edgar, "The Creation of Soviet Turkmenistan, 1924–1938" (Ph.D. diss., University of California-Berkeley, 1999): 42–84. Steven Sabol, "The Creation of Soviet Central Asia: The 1924 National Delimitation," *Central Asian Survey* 14 (1995): 225–241. Kirgizia became an ASSR in 1926 and a union republic in 1936. Tajikistan became a union republic in 1929.

[176] *RTsKhIDNI* 17/2/153 (25–27.10.24): 125, 128.

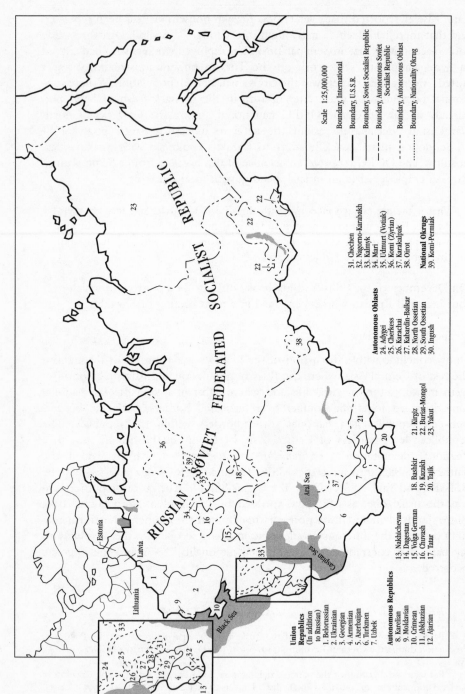

Map 2. Federal Structure of the USSR, 1926

Scale 1:25,000,000

Boundary, International
Boundary, U.S.S.R.
Boundary, Soviet Socialist Republic
Boundary, Autonomous Soviet Socialist Republic
Boundary, Autonomous Oblast
Boundary, Nationality Okrug

Union Republics
(In addition to Russian)
1. Belorussian
2. Ukrainian
3. Georgian
4. Armenian
5. Azerbaijan
6. Turkmen
7. Uzbek

Autonomous Republics
8. Karelian
9. Moldavian
10. Crimean
11. Abkhazian
12. Ajarian
13. Nakhichevan
14. Dagestan
15. Volga German
16. Chuvash
17. Tatar
18. Bashkir
19. Kazakh
20. Tajik
21. Kirgiz
22. Buriat-Mongol
23. Yakut

Autonomous Oblasts
24. Adygei
25. Cherkess
26. Karachai
27. Kabardin-Balkar
28. North Ossetian
29. South Ossetian
30. Ingush
31. Chechen
32. Nagorno-Karabakh
33. Kalmyk
34. Mari
35. Udmurt (Votiak)
36. Komi (Zyrian)
37. Karakalpak
38. Oirot

National Okrugs
39. Komi-Permiak

Almost all internal reports noted a massive increase in ethnic conflict.[177] In particular, the OGPU reported incessant border disputes, in which one nationality agitated "for the union of their district, which almost always has a mixed population, to one or other of the neighboring republics."[178] The formation of national republics not only increased ethnic conflict, but also turned local disputes, often with a clan or regional aspect, into national ones: "It is characteristic that groups which were in conflict within a given nationality before national division [razmezhevanie] have now been united by general national interests."[179] This was an extremely important development, as it meant that any ethnic conflict immediately drew the interest of that ethnic group's "home" republic. The national delimitation also left some ethnic groups isolated in the center of another republic. Already during the delimitation, this led to demands for Kazakh and Uzbek national soviets.[180]

The fact that most Central Asian national minorities had a "home" republic made it difficult to distinguish border disputes from demands for national soviets. Often a border district demanded either to be joined to an adjacent republic or to form a national soviet.[181] However, border disputes best illustrate the role played by government actors—at the local, republican, and all-union levels—in exacerbating ethnic conflict. There was a general agreement that local officials manipulated ethnic conflict strategically. A Central Asian Biuro report asserted: "Local party and Soviet officials not only do not want to solve one or another national question objectively from the point of view of the overall government interest, but usually they themselves take active part, often even the leading role in inflaming national antagonism."[182] Some officials solicited privileges from competing sides; others looked after their own economic interests. Most frequently, ethnic agitation was used in battles to take or maintain control in local soviets.[183] In one instance, this resulted in the competing ethnic elites attempting to arrest one another.[184]

Such strategic use of ethnic conflict by local officials was common elsewhere, although it would seem to have been most widespread in Central Asia. What was unique to Central Asia was the extent of the involvement of the republican-level leadership in exploiting ethnic conflict. These conflicts then drew in the all-union authorities as referees. Thus, throughout the 1920s, TsIK formed a series of commissions to regulate border disputes in Central Asia. An astute chairman of one such commission, Murza-Galiev, concluded that, "in the majority of cases, the border conflicts were initiated by the respective governments, sometimes through their agents at the local level, sometimes through

[177] RTsKhIDNI 17/69/59 (1926): 23; 62/2/535 (1926): 58; GARF 3316/64/46 (1925): 41–47.
[178] RTsKhIDNI 62/2/2245 (1925): 41.
[179] GARF 3316/64/46 (1925): 42–43.
[180] Ibid., 12–15.
[181] RTsKhIDNI 17/87/201 (1927): 75; 62/2/536 (1926): 13.
[182] RTsKhIDNI 62/2/945 (1926): 22.
[183] RTsKhIDNI 17/87/201 (1926): 52; 62/2/535 (1926): 3.
[184] RTsKhIDNI 62/2/536 (1926): 13; 62/2/593 (1926): 5.

the appropriate economic or administrative organs." He noted a tendency of each side to make as many claims as possible on the other side in the hope that some would stick: "These counter-claims, however, immediately became known to the local population who, naturally, began to harass the republican government with further requests to be joined to their kindred republic."[185] Thus, there was a reinforcing relationship between local and republican level manipulation.

Murza-Galiev was sufficiently self-aware to also note the negative role played by the center in these disputes[186]:

> Taking into consideration from where these declarations of the desire of one or another district to be united with a given national republic, and that these declarations arouse the local population to an extraordinary degree, and intensify national conflict, it would be best to forbid the [republican] organs of power (at least for the next three years) from petitioning the center, in particular the Presidium of TsIK and VTsIK, with border disputes.

Despite this lucid analysis, the central government did not cease reviewing border complaints regularly until around 1929, when Stalin himself rejected a Ukrainian proposal to annex neighboring RSFSR regions with the explanation: "We change our borders too often . . . we must be especially careful [about border changes], since such changes provoke enormous resistance from some Russians."[187]

Granted the ubiquity of these border disputes, one might have expected a conciliatory policy toward national minorities to forestall separatist agitation. Murza-Galiev noted that each republic was extremely eager to expand its territory, but "considering this fact, it is astounding how little interest they show to the national minority regions they already have."[188] Nevertheless, central pressure and ongoing agitation by national minorities for national soviets did lead the Central Asian republics all to undertake a national *raionirovanie* between 1926 and 1928. Table 5 reports the results. Most observers noted that these national soviets had less status than national soviets in the western republics.[189]

In fact, the formation of national soviets in Central Asia was often viewed with trepidation by the nationality for whom the soviet was being formed.[190] This seemingly odd reaction is explained by the violent resistance to national soviets on the part of national majorities. As in Kazakhstan, conflicts frequently led to the demand for minorities to return to their "home" republics. The OGPU reported Uzbeks screaming at Turkmen: "Get out of Uzbekistan, go

---

[185] *GARF* 1235/120/31 (1926): 358; 361.
[186] Ibid., 362.
[187] *RTsKhIDNI* 558/1/4490 (1929): 19–20.
[188] *GARF* 1235/120/31 (1926): 361.
[189] *GARF* 374/27s/1707 (1929): 71.
[190] *RTsKhIDNI* 17/87/196 (1925): 293.

Table 5. National Soviets in Central Asia, 1927–1928

	UZBEKISTAN		KIRGIZIA		TURKMENISTAN
Nationality	Village Soviets	Districts	Village Soviets	Districts	Village Soviets
Tajik	4	81	—	—	—
Kazakh	4	68	—	—	3
Kirgiz	1	25	—	—	—
Russian	1	20	11	91	10
Karakalpak	—	17	—	—	—
Turkmen	1	11	—	—	—
Uzbek	—	—	1	19	32
Arab	—	7	—	—	—
Uigur	—	6	—	—	1
Azerbaijani	—	4	—	—	—
Persian	—	2	—	—	1
Kurama	1	—	—	—	—
Dungan	—	—	—	1	—
Tatar	—	—	—	2	—
Bukharan	—	—	—	—	1
Beluchi	—	—	—	—	1
Djemshid	—	—	—	—	1
Total	12	241	12	113	50

RTsKhIDNI 62/2/945 (1927): 1–2; *GARF* 374/27s/1707 (1929): 72.

to your own [*svoi*] Turkmenistan." Tajiks seized Kirgiz land based on the argument "that the Kirgiz have their own republic, where they should go to get land." National minorities accepted this logic. Kirgiz in Uzbekistan argued that "the decrees of Uzbek authorities are not binding on us."[191] These sentiments did lead national minorities, under pressure of discrimination and often violence as well, to flee to their "home" republics.[192] In 1927, TsIK received a report that two hundred Uzbek families were preparing to flee Kirgizia and another 16,000 Uzbek might follow.[193]

If expulsion was one way to assert the majority's exclusive rights, assimilation was another. If flight was one national minority response to persecution, another was the masking of identity. The 1926 census provoked this behavior. Kurds in Turkmenistan declared themselves Turkmen out of fear they might lose their land. Kazakhs and Uzbeks did likewise out of a fear of repression. In Uzbekistan, Tajiks either masked their identity or were declared Uzbeks by the census-takers to such an extent that a Control Commission (Rabkrin) report declared the results meaningless.[194] In Samarkand, 1925 city data registered

[191] *RTsKhIDNI* 62/2/882 (1927): 274; 62/2/1808 (1929): 134; 62/2/1809 (1929): 3.
[192] *RTsKhIDNI* 62/2/535 (1926): 58.
[193] *GARF* 3316/64/411 (1927): 3.
[194] *RTsKhIDNI* 62/2/881 (1927): 27; 62/2/1279 (1928): 39; *GARF* 374/27s/1707 (1929): 64–65.

76,000 Tajiks, whereas the 1926 census counted only 10,000.[195] Uzbekistan, in fact, actively forced the assimilation of Tajiks. A 1929 Central Asian Biuro report described the Uzbek position: "The Tajiks are a disappearing ethnicity and there is nothing wrong with the fact that Tajiks are Uzbekifying, because the culture of the Uzbeks is higher."[196] In a 1929 report to the Orgburo, Uzbek First Party Secretary Ikramov admitted this policy: "Even [Tajik] Party members were afraid and hid their national origin and declared themselves Uzbeks."[197] As usual, the center opposed this process and instead favored ethnic separation: the formation of a Tajik union republic in 1929.

The Uzbek variant, then, was characterized by both an enormous increase in national self-consciousness and high levels of ethnic conflict. The hegemonic national identities established in the 1924 national division of Central Asia were adopted by the population with surprising vigor. The reason for this strong response was not simply the one-time division into four union republics, but the constant contestation over the borders of these republics, and over the formation of national minority soviets within them. This process led local and republican leaders to mobilize ethnic support for their positions. The center's willingness to consider border revisions again and again validated those mobilizing efforts. By bringing national borders down to the village level, the population's natural feelings of ethnic exclusiveness, previously expressed as often in kinship or clan terms, were recast in national terms. Outsiders now had a "home" republic to which they could be expected to return. Thus, the national division of Central Asia fulfilled its designers' goal to spur national self-consciousness, but frustrated their hopes at an increase in ethnic harmony.

Conclusion

The Soviet nationalities policy dilemma emerged from a simultaneous embrace of both an extraterritorial personal definition of nationality and a territorial one. The authorities were unwilling to accept extraterritorial organizations whose membership belonged exclusively to a single nationality, but they were equally unwilling to accept the principle of assimilation implied by a territorial definition of nationality. The Soviets believed they had solved this dilemma by establishing a pyramid of national territorial units, beginning at the top with the Soviet Union and extending downward to smaller and smaller national territorial units until these units merged seamlessly with the individual. In this way, a maximum number of individuals would live in their own national territory, which would allow them to preserve their nationality. Kalinin called this system the prototype for a future world communist government.

---

[195] *RTsKhIDNI* 62/2/2003 (1929): 1–2.
[196] Ibid., 2.
[197] *RTsKhIDNI* 17/113/725 (08.05.29): 44.

This system was based on the assumption that, to use Stalin's famous formulation, national territorial forms could be empty of national content, that if national territories were granted, national solidarity would crumble and class differentiation would become apparent. In practice, this ideal Bolshevik concept of national soviets conflicted with the popular notion of national sovereignty: that the national soviet was their own (*nash*). Language was a secondary concern, often not a concern at all. Theories of ethnic conflict emphasize the importance of borders. The larger the territory, and the more multinational its composition, the less intensely any one given ethnic group will feel its minority status. As the scale of territory is reduced and the number of ethnic groups drops to only two, the minority group becomes acutely aware of its minority status.[198] Drawing any national border creates ethnic conflict. The Soviet Union literally drew tens of thousands of national borders. As a result, every village, indeed every individual, had to declare an ethnic allegiance and fight to remain a national majority rather than a minority. It is difficult to conceive of any measure more likely to increase ethnic mobilization and ethnic conflict.

Moreover, in places such as Central Asia, where identities tended to be pre-national, the drawing of borders involved the consolidation of disparate local identities into a larger national identity. This had the effect of turning local ethnic conflicts into national conflicts on a local level. Thus, the Soviet system both increased local ethnic conflict and raised the level of its significance. This led national republican governments to manipulate local conflicts. I have noted this tendency in Central Asia, as well as in the concern of the central RSFSR government, especially VTsIK, over the fate of Russians in eastern national territories. In Chapter 7, we will see the Ukrainian government show a similar interest in extraterritorial Ukrainians. This tendency was exacerbated by the central government's willingness to repeatedly reconsider national borders at all levels. Therefore, thousands of national borders were not only drawn once, but repeatedly reconsidered and redrawn.

Moreover, the central government itself did not honor its commitment to contentless national territories. Instead, it repeatedly linked national soviets to the possession of land: the single most sensitive political issue of the 1920s. In the early 1920s, the central government authorized the expulsion of Russians from the new national territories in the North Caucasus and Kazakhstan to free up land for the native populations. Land was reserved in large compact masses for the Jewish population to allow them to form national soviets. Germans in Ukraine were given preferential access to free land within their national soviets. In Tatarstan and Kazakhstan, the native population was given land first. Later, separate Russian national soviets were formed in Kazakhstan, which served as bases for Russian agricultural settlement. Thus, nationality, possession of land, and the political control of a territory became intertwined.

---

[198] Horowitz, *Ethnic Groups in Conflict*, 66–73.

The entire system pointed toward increased ethnic segregation. This reinforced the popular conception of a national territory as their own, and the tendency to view national minorities, especially at the local level, as foreign and often unwelcome guests. This led to frequent taunts and threats directed at minorities that they should return to "their" (*svoi*) national territory. When this ethnic exclusivity combined with issues of land possession, though not only then, it resulted in a form of popular ethnic cleansing. The relations between Kazakhs and Russians were the most striking such instance. Overall, the pyramid of national soviets led not to the diminution of ethnic conflict but rather to its considerable intensification.

3

Linguistic Ukrainization, 1923–1932

On October 10, 1920, Stalin published an article in *Pravda* that for the first time authoritatively announced the Soviet policy of *korenizatsiia*: "It is necessary that all Soviet organs in the borderlands—the courts, the administration, the economic organs, organs of local power (as well as Party organs)—be composed to the greatest possible degree of people who know the customs, habits and language of the local population."[1] *Korenizatsiia*, as definitively formulated at party congresses in March 1921 and April 1923, consisted of two major tasks: the creation of national elites (Affirmative Action) and the promotion of local national languages to a dominant position in the non-Russian territories (linguistic *korenizatsiia*). Linguistic *korenizatsiia* would prove much more difficult to achieve. Between April 1923 and December 1932, central party and soviet organs issued dozens of resolutions urging the immediate implementation of linguistic *korenizatsiia*. Local republican and oblast authorities issued hundreds, if not thousands, of similar decrees. Nevertheless, linguistic *korenizatsiia* failed almost everywhere. Why?

I initially assumed that central authorities must have been sending mixed signals, publicly trumpeting the need for immediate *korenizatsiia* while privately letting it be known that this public rhetoric was largely for show. I was wrong. Not only did the soft-line soviet bureaucracies in charge of nationalities policy, such as TsIK's Soviet of Nationalities and VTsIK's Nationalities Department, vigilantly monitor the implementation of *korenizatsiia*, hard-line organs attached to the party's Central Committee were equally vigilant. The Orgburo

---

[1] I. Stalin, "Politika sovetskoi vlasti po natsional'nomu voprosu v Rossii" (1920), in *Marksizm i natsional'no-kolonial'nyi vopros* (Moscow, 1934): 62.

and TsK's influential Cadres Department frequently rebuked local party organizations for failing to implement *korenizatsiia*. In 1926–1927, the Orgburo
formed a special commission on *korenizatsiia*, chaired by the future Politburo
member A. A. Andreev, which likewise categorically demanded that this policy
be implemented. Finally, in 1929–1930, when lower party activists began to
attack the policy of *korenizatsiia* and to call for its elimination, Stalin publicly
and privately defended *korenizatsiia* and silenced its critics. Despite this sustained central support, linguistic *korenizatsiia* failed. Why?

Central officials were initially also baffled by this question. They viewed *korenizatsiia* as a popular policy designed to satisfy heartfelt national desires, not
as a threatening policy like collectivization. As a result, early *korenizatsiia*
resolutions allowed for absurdly short periods of time to implement the policy.
Korenizatsiia was generally popular with non-Russians, but it encountered
unexpectedly fierce resistance from a variety of influential groups: urban workers
(who were usually Russian-speakers), Russians and russified titular nationals in
the party and state bureaucracies, industrial specialists, and the filials of all-union
enterprises. These were all groups that the party leaders relied on and, if possible, preferred not to offend.

Still, such resistance alone cannot explain the failure of linguistic *korenizatsiia*. Fierce resistance did not prevent the Soviet state from deporting several
million peasants, expelling over one hundred thousand party members, terror-
izing tens of thousands of valued specialists, and abolishing all trade union
autonomy in pursuit of its twin goals of industrialization and collectivization.
In comparison with collectivization, the opposition to *korenizatsiia* was trivial:
bureaucratic non-cooperation rather than violent and desperate resistance. Yet,
Bolshevik values made it difficult for the state to justify the use of terror to force
the implementation of *korenizatsiia*. As we have seen, popular party opinion
never accepted *korenizatsiia* as a core Bolshevik project, like industrialization or
collectivization, but rather as a kind of concession. In Bolshevik vocabulary, it
was a soft-line rather than a hard-line policy.

Although the Soviet leadership did consistently and sincerely support *korenizatsiia*, it nevertheless also viewed its implementation as a secondary task,
an auxiliary rather than a core Bolshevik project, and therefore its support was
soft. Failure to implement *korenizatsiia* was censured, but unlike failure to meet
grain requisition quotas or industrialization targets, it rarely led to demotion
and never resulted in arrest or execution. Interestingly, this meant that local
conditions proved decisive. If a republic's leadership aggressively supported *korenizatsiia* and could overcome local resistance without soliciting punitive measures from the center, linguistic *korenizatsiia* could be and was achieved. If not,
it would fail. The center would not tolerate an open and demonstrative repudiation of *korenizatsiia*, but it would likewise not intervene decisively to correct
a lackluster performance.

In terms of linguistic *korenizatsiia*, the Soviet Union's non-Russian territories can be divided into three categories. For the vast majority, most of the
regions that the Soviets called their "culturally backward eastern national

territories," complete linguistic *korenizatsiia* was never seriously attempted. The national languages were promoted vigorously in the press and general education but made little progress in government, industry, and higher education. There were simply too few educated titular nationals. As a result, all efforts were devoted to the Affirmative Action component of *korenizatsiia*: the training and promotion of natives into positions of authority. I analyze these policies and their consequences in Chapter 4.

The opposing category, where local conditions were so favorable that linguistic *korenizatsiia* was achieved rapidly and with little difficulty, consisted of only two republics: Georgia and Armenia. The Georgian Menshevik and Armenian *Dashnaktsutiun* governments had already established their respective languages as state languages prior to the Soviet conquest.[2] More important, both republics had experienced Bolshevik cadres, who immediately assumed leadership positions in their respective republics. Soviet Armenia and Georgia were unique in having influential native speakers, such as Sergo Ordzhonikidze, who occupied the top party positions. Moreover, both republics had large native intelligentsias and insignificant Russian populations. As a result, the Georgian and Armenian languages quickly assumed a hegemonic position, and linguistic *korenizatsiia* simply was not a salient issue in the 1920s.[3]

Most interesting was the third category, those republics where the local forces backing and opposing linguistic *korenizatsiia* were in near equilibrium. This was most true of Ukraine, Belorussia, and Tatarstan. In Ukraine, there was both exceptionally strong support for and resistance to linguistic Ukrainization. Moreover, both support and resistance came from within the party. Nowhere else did the higher party leadership more consistently or more aggressively attempt to implement linguistic *korenizatsiia*. On the other hand, nowhere else did it face such entrenched opposition. In Belorussia, support for *korenizatsiia* was considerably weaker, although in contrast to contemporary stereotypes, it was not at all nonexistent. However, resistance to *korenizatsiia* in Belorussia was likewise weaker since there was no entrenched urban Russian and russified proletariat as in Ukraine, nor such a strong russified Old Bolshevik cadre. Tatarstan resembled Ukraine, with a very strong national movement encountering an even stronger and more entrenched Russian presence. The large and politically influential Russian population ultimately confined linguistic Tatarization to majority Tatar regions, where it was nevertheless pursued with great vigor.

In this chapter, I undertake a detailed case study of linguistic *korenizatsiia* in Ukraine in order to understand why, despite aggressive backing form Ukraine's higher leadership, linguistic Ukrainization nevertheless ultimately failed.

[2] Ronald Grigor Suny, *The Making of the Georgian Nation* (Bloomington, Ind., 1988): 185–208. Richard G. Hovannisian, *The Republic of Armenia*, 4 vols. (Berkeley, Calif., 1971–1996).

[3] On Armenia, see Mary Matoissian, *The Impact of Soviet Policies in Armenia* (Leiden, 1962). On the degree to which linguistic *korenizatsiia* was a non-issue in Georgia, see *IV s"ezd KP/b/ Gruzii. Stenograficheskii otchet* (Tbilisi, 1925). *V s"ezd KP/b/ Gruzii. Stenograficheskii otchet* (Tbilisi, 1927). *VI s"ezd KP/b/ Gruzii. Stenograficheskii otchet* (Tbilisi, 1929).

The Background to Ukrainization, 1919–1923

Throughout the 1920s, both the Ukrainian and central party leaderships remained under the influence of what Grigorii Petrovskii called "the cruel lesson of 1919."[4] Petrovskii was referring to the mass peasant uprisings led by Petliura that combined with Deniken's White army in 1919 to drive the Bolsheviks out of Ukraine for a second time. The lesson, reiterated by Ukrainian Bolsheviks again and again, with uncharacteristic candor, was that their own chauvinist behavior had provoked this mass peasant nationalist uprising. Volodymyr Zatonskyi, a prominent Ukrainian nationalities specialist, recalled how Bolshevik soldiers "almost shot me because of a Ukrainian newspaper they found in my pocket," though it was in fact a Bolshevik publication. This was typical, he argued, of the "sharp hostility of the city to all things Ukrainian in the years from 1917 to 1919."[5] Nor was this hostility confined to party members from Russia: "The mass of the proletariat was opposed to anything Ukrainian." Like Petrovskii, Zatonskyi maintained that it was this flawed Bolshevik policy and primal anti-Ukrainian hostility that caused "the village to rise up against the foreigners [chuzhintsov], that is against us."[6]

The "cruel lesson of 1919" was perhaps the most important of the many factors that pushed the central leadership, Lenin in particular, toward the policy of korenizatsiia. As we have seen, already in March 1919, Lenin had rebuked Piatakov, then leader of the Ukrainian party, for maintaining that the national question was irrelevant under socialism. By the end of 1919, Lenin was no longer in a mood to argue and instead forced the Ukrainian party to adopt a decree in support of Ukrainization.[7] A single decree, of course, could hardly change the psychology of the entire party. From 1919 to 1923, the majority of Ukrainian party members remained either hostile to or bewildered by the policy of Ukrainization.[8] High-ranking party members continued to oppose Ukrainization, often making arguments far more overtly chauvinist than Piatakov's principled internationalism. A typical example would be the 1921 statement by Khristian Rakovskii, then the top-ranking Bolshevik in Ukraine, that "the triumph of the Ukrainian language would mean the rule of the Ukrainian petit-bourgeois intelligentsia and the Ukrainian kulaks."[9]

These notions were formalized in 1923 by Dmitrii Lebed, the second-ranking Bolshevik in Ukraine, under the slogan of "The Battle of Two Cultures."[10] In an aggressive polemic leading up to the April 1923 all-union party congress,

---

[4] TsDAHOU 1/6/102 (12.05.26): 144.

[5] RTsKhIDNI 17/69/58 (1927): 165; 17/85/108 (1927): 65.

[6] V. Zatonskyi, "Pro pidsumky ukrainizatsii" (1926); in Budivnytstvo radians'koi Ukrainy vol. 1 (Kharkov, 1928): 9; RTsKhIDNI 17/85/108 (1927): 65.

[7] Jurij Borys, The Sovietization of Ukraine, 1917–1923 (Edmonton, 1980): 249–257.

[8] "Natsional'nyi vopros posle XII s"ezda partii (pis'mo iz Ekaterinoslava)" Pravda, no. 150 (07.07.23): 4.

[9] Quoted by N. N. Popov in RTsKhIDNI 17/26/1 (01–06.06.26): 135.

[10] Dmitrii Lebed, Sovetskaia Ukraina i natsional'nyi vopros za piat' let (Kharkov, 1924).

Lebed argued that Ukrainization was objectively "reactionary since national-ization—that is, the artificial introduction of the Ukrainian language into the Party and working class—given the current political, economic, and cultural relations between city and village means to stand on the side of the lower culture of the village, instead of the higher culture of the city. We know theoretically that a battle of two cultures is inevitable. In Ukraine, due to historical condi-tions, the culture of the city is Russian culture and the culture of the village is Ukrainian." Based on this analysis, Lebed argued that Ukrainian should be used only for "cultural enlightenment" in the village to prepare the peasantry for an eventual transition to the higher Russian culture. Under no circumstances should the Ukrainian language or culture be promoted in urban environments.[11] No repressive measures would be needed; official state neutrality would ensure the triumph of the superior Russian culture.

Lebed's polemic marked the last gasp of open resistance to Ukrainization, indeed to *korenizatsiia* as a whole, from within the party. Still, the fact that the number-two party figure in Ukraine could openly defend attitudes essentially identical to those blamed for the "cruel lesson of 1919"—namely, that a higher Russian, proletariat culture stood in opposition to an inferior Ukrainian, peasant culture—meant that progress on Ukrainization was impossible. Indeed, Mykola Skrypnyk, a strong partisan of Ukrainization, called the December 1919 decree "a lost manifesto."[12] The same was true of a February 1920 all-Ukrainian Central Executive Committee (VUTsIK) decree that gave Ukrainian equal status along-side Russian as an official state language in Ukraine.[13] The only substantive success occurred in primary school education, where by 1923 76 percent of schools taught in Ukrainian. This was possible since the prevailing ideology maintained that "primary schools can be in Ukrainian, but as for higher educa-tion, here one must retain the Russian language."[14] Even this limited progress made Lebed nervous: "The work of our education organs in the Ukrainian village has often produced negative results. The work of the Commissariat of Education has been used by Petliurite agronomists and nationalist teachers and other groups . . . there have been a series of incidents of forced Ukrainization."[15]

Ukrainization, 1923–1925

Lebed's defiant resistance presaged the difficulties Ukrainization would encounter after the decisive central resolutions in support of *korenizatsiia* at the

---

[11] D. Lebed, "Podgotovka partiinogo s"ezda. Nekotorye voprosy partiinogo s"ezda," *Kommunist*, no. 59 (17.03.23): 1. For documents surrounding this debate, see *TsDAHOU* 1/20/2255 (1923): 1–69.

[12] Quoted in N. Popov, "Natsional'nyi vopros na Ukraine," *Kommunist*, no. 75 (05.04.23): 3.

[13] V. N. Durdenevskii, *Ravnopravie iazykov v sovetskom stroe* (Moscow, 1927): 145.

[14] *Biulleten' VIII-i vseukrainskoi konferentsii KP/b/ Ukrainy. Stenogramma* (Kharkov, 1924): biul. 1: 27. See also the decrees in Durdenevskii, 145, 159–160.

[15] "VIII Kievskaia gubernskaia partiinaia konferentsiia," *Kommunist*, no. 65 (24.03.23): 3.

April 1923 party congress and June 1923 nationalities conference forced a second and more decisive turn toward Ukrainization. These events marked the defeat of Lebed's theory. On the eve of the April 1923 Ukrainian Party conference, an authoritative article by Nikolai Popov, then head of the all-union Agitprop Department, denounced Lebed's theory as "mindless Russian chauvinism (*rusotiapstvo*)", adding that "it is shameful to have to write about such elementary truths six years after the revolution."[16] At the conference itself, Lebed was further attacked by Frunze (then assistant head of Ukraine's Sovnarkom and the conference's official speaker on nationalities policy) and Rakovskii (who had converted to an extremely pro-Ukrainian stance), as well as by Lebed's long-standing rivals, Zatonskyi and Skrypnyk. The Ukrainian conference officially declared Lebed's theory to be "chauvinist" and "the inevitable development of Luxemburgist views."[17] This resolution marked a decisive rejection of Lebed's advocacy of state and party neutrality on the nationalities question.

The period from April 1923 to April 1925 was subsequently known as the era of "Ukrainization by decree," a pejorative reference to the flood of decrees issued and then largely ignored.[18] The first such decree, a July 27, 1923 resolution on the Ukrainization of education and culture, aimed to extend the Ukrainian language beyond rural primary schools.[19] Five days later, a landmark VUTsIK decree was issued: "On measures for guaranteeing the equality of languages and for aiding the development of the Ukrainian language." This decree declared that "the previously existing recognition of the formal equality of the two most widespread languages in Ukraine—Ukrainian and Russian—[was] insufficient [and would result in] the factual domination of the Russian language." Although the decree recognized both Ukrainian and Russian as official languages of Ukraine, it demanded "a variety of practical measures" to establish Ukrainian as the sole language of government in all central state organs, as well as all local organs in regions where ethnic Ukrainians formed a plurality.[20]

The August 1 decree marked a decisive break with the policy of linguistic neutrality. To drive home this point, Ukrainian first party secretary Emmanuel Kviring wrote a lead editorial, in which he reiterated the decree's assertion that "we cannot confine ourselves to recognizing the formal equality of nations, for this formal equality will lead to factual inequality."[21] Instead, the new task was "positive work on behalf of the development of [Ukrainian] national culture."[22]

---

[16] N. Popov, "Natsional'nyi vopros na Ukraine," *Kommunist*, no. 75 (05.04.23): 3.

[17] Andrii Khvylia, *Do rozv'iazannia natsional'noho pytannia na Ukraini* (Kharkov, 1930): 16.

[18] N. Kalizzhnyi, "Ukrainizatsiia i NKRSI," *Visti VUTsIK*, no. 124 (03.06.25): 1.

[19] P. Solodub, "Spravy ukrainizatsii," *Bil'shovyk*, no. 160 (18.07.24): 1.

[20] Andrii Khvylia, *Natsional'nyi vopros na Ukraine* (Kharkov, 1926): 115–121; 116.

[21] Kviring, "Praktychni zasoby v spravi natsional'nii," *Bil'shovyk*, no. 121 (03.06.23): 1.

[22] S. Shchupak, "Praktychne perevedenniia natsional'noi spravy na Kyivshchyni," *Bil'shovyk*, no. 131 (15.06.23): 1; the phrase "active *Ukrainizatsiia*" also came into use, "Postanova TsK KP/b/U shchodo ukrainizatsii," *Bil'shovyk*, no. 72 (30.03.24): 1.

The Ukrainian language and culture were now to be placed in "a privileged position."[23] The Affirmative Action nation-building policy endorsed by the center in 1923 had now finally been authoritatively articulated in Ukraine. The justification given, as always, was "the cruel lesson of 1919" when the Ukrainian village rose up against the alien Russian city. Ukrainization, it was argued, would overcome this urban/rural split and help form a link (*smychka*) between the Russian city and Ukrainian village.[24] Instead of the Ukrainian village learning Russian to be enlightened by the Russian city, as in Lebed's model, the city would learn Ukrainian in order to instruct the village. The August 1 decree was followed by a series of decrees on Ukrainization in the party, army, and trade unions.[25] Nor was Ukrainization confined to support of the Ukrainian language. Ethnic Ukrainians were also given preferential access to government jobs and entrance into the party.[26]

A broad agenda of Ukrainization had now been proposed. In practice, however, almost all attention focused on the implementation of the crucial August 1, 1923 VUTsIK decree, which had ambitiously called for the complete linguistic Ukrainization of the entire government bureaucracy at all levels in the course of one year.[27] In some regions, those bureaucratic institutions most closely linked to the countryside were required to shift to Ukrainian in only six months.[28] This absurdly short time-frame was typical of the utopianism of the early *korenizatsiia* decrees across the Soviet Union. To achieve this goal, the Education Commissariat set up three-month and nine-month courses of language study for all civil servants who could not demonstrate an adequate command of the Ukrainian language.[29] The sanctions for failing to learn Ukrainian were theoretically quite stiff. Beginning on August 1, 1923, no one could be hired by a state institution who did not know both Ukrainian and Russian. Those who already held a government job would be fired if they had not learned Ukrainian by August 1, 1924.[30]

This program immediately encountered the bane of all future Ukrainization programs: stubborn passive resistance. From specialists, who were considered both a bourgeois and highly russified element, such resistance was expected,

---

[23] Kviring, "Praktychni zasoby," 1. For the same phrase, see *TsDAHOU* 1/20/1978 (1926): 1; *Biulleten' VIII-i vseukrainskoi konferentsii*, biul. 1: 26; *Tainy natsional'noi politiki*, 108.

[24] "VII Vseukrainskaia partiinaia konferentsiia. Natsional'nyi vopros. Doklad tov. Frunze," *Kommunist*, no. 81 (13.04.23): 3; Kh. Rakovskii, "Natsional'nyi vopros," *Kommunist*, no. 78 (10.04.23): 3; Kviring, "Praktychni zasoby," 1; "Postanova TsK KP/b/U shchodo ukrainizatsii," 1.

[25] *TsDAHOU* 1/20/1978 (1926): 2–3.

[26] "Postanova TsK KP/b/U shchodo ukrainizatsii," 1; "Doklad tov. Lavrentiia pro robotu Kyivs'koho gubkomu KP/b/U," *Bil'shovyk*, no. 102 (07.05.24): 2.

[27] Khvylia, *Natsional'nyi vopros*, 117–118.

[28] Shchupak, "Praktychne perevedennia," 1.

[29] Khvylia, *Natsional'nyi vopros*, 121.

[30] Ibid., 120. Sovnarkom could specially exempt "exceptionally qualified individuals and those sent [to Ukraine] on special assignments."

and it was zealously denounced in the press.[31] However, to the great embarrassment of the party, the worst resistance to Ukrainization came from within
the party itself and, above all, from those in leadership positions.[32] This would
be typical of future Ukrainization efforts as well. One study found that among
government employees, 43.7 percent of non-party members had a good
knowledge of Ukrainian, whereas only 18.1 percent of party members did.[33]
Managerial "indifference" was blamed for widespread poor attendance at
Ukrainization courses, which frequently led to their complete collapse.[34] The
Ukrainian TsK concluded that managers viewed Ukrainization as "not a serious
policy" and adopted a "mocking" attitude that undermined it.[35] Even when
people knew Ukrainian well, they preferred to speak Russian. A Ukrainization
inspector reported that when he showed up to inspect an institution, everyone
would speak in Russian until they realized he was an inspector, and then they
quickly switched to fluent Ukrainian.[36] The party leadership responded with
resolutions at both the March 1924 TsK plenum and the May 1924 party
conference demanding that all party members learn Ukrainian, but with no
noticeable impact.[37]

Such resistance is hardly a surprise. As we have noted, *korenizatsiia* was
unpopular with the party rank-and-file in general, and this was even more so in
Ukraine due to its bitter civil war experience. Moreover, while most of the key
Ukrainian commissariats were now staffed by strong supporters of Ukrainization (Mykola Skrypnyk, Volodymyr Zatonskyi, Oleksandr Shumskyi, Hrihoryi
Hrynko), the party's leadership was not. First secretary Emmanuel Kviring came
from the Ukrainian Party's Katerynoslav faction, which was strongly opposed
to Ukrainization and in 1918 had even supported the secession of the Donbass
and Krivoi Rog regions of Ukraine.[38] Kviring's support of Ukrainization was
ambivalent even after 1923, as evidenced by his stated concern that "Communist" Ukrainization might degenerate into "Petliurian" Ukrainization.[39]
Ukraine's second secretary, Dmitrii Lebed, was a principled opponent of
Ukrainization who, after his defeat in 1923, was not required to recant his

[31] Hun'ko, "Do ukrainizatsii radaparatu," *Visti VUTsIK*, no. 100 (06.05.24): 2; M. Sulyma,
" 'Lapsus Inguae' v ukrainizatsii," no. 209 (14.09.24): 1; "Ukrainizatsiia ukrains'kykh ustanov,"
Bil'shovyk, no. 164 (24.07.24): 5.

[32] *TsDAHOU* 1/20/1977 (1925): 7, 148–152; "Postanova TsK KP/b/U shchodo ukrainizatsii,"
1; V. Chubar, "Pytannia ukrainizatsii," *Bil'shovyk*, no. 66 (24.03.24): 5; V. Chubar, "Ukrainizatsiia partii," no. 88 (18.04.25): 2.

[33] *TsDAHOU* 1/20/1977 (1925): 170.

[34] *TsDAHOU* 1/20/1977 (1925): 148–151; V. Dnystrenko, "Do ukrainizatsii nashykh ustanov,"
Visti VUTsIK, no. 114 (22.05.24); P. Kobyliats'kyi, "Do ukrainizatsii," no. 166 (24.07.24): 1; M.
Vaisfligel', "Pro ukrainizatsiiu radaparatu," no. 229 (08.10.24): 1; P. Solodub, "Spravy ukrainizat-
sii," *Bil'shovyk*, no. 160 (18.07.24): 1.

[35] *TsDAHOU* 1/20/1977 (1925): 148–151; Chubar, "Pytannia ukrainizatsii," 6.

[36] Vaisfligel', "Pro ukrainizatsiiu radaparatu," 1.

[37] TsDAHOU 1/20/1977 (1925): 7; 1/20/1978 (1925): 3; *Biulleten' VIII-oi vseukrainskoi konferentsii*, biul. 4: 205.

[38] Mykola Skrypnyk, "Donbas i Ukraina" (1920) in *Statti i Promovy*, vol. 2, part 1, 22–31.

[39] Kviring, "Praktychni zasoby," 1.

previous views and even published a more moderate version of them.[40] Lebed continued to try to slow down Ukrainization: "It seems to me that now is not the time to advocate the complete Ukrainization of our central organs. Local party organs should first do preparatory work."[41]

The ambivalence of the higher party leadership led to a largely unsupervised process. Narkompros was required to set up courses and to administer examinations, but, as frustrated proponents of Ukrainization noted, no one was assigned the task of enforcing attendance or monitoring Ukrainization at the workplace.[42] As a result, reliable data on the results of Ukrainization were few.[43] Indeed, the Ukrainian central archives hold virtually no data on Ukrainization prior to April 1925. Employees quickly realized they could free themselves from an unpleasant and onerous task.[44] University students could refuse to listen to Ukrainian lectures.[45] Government bureaucracies could freely hire whomever they wished even if they did not speak Ukrainian.[46] The threat to fire Ukrainization shirkers was not executed. Instead, the deadline for complete Ukrainization was twice deferred: first from August 1, 1924 to August 1, 1925, and then again to January 1, 1926.[47] All this reinforced the popular party opinion that Ukrainization was not a serious Bolshevik policy, but a propagandistic soft-line initiative that could safely be ignored.

Given the lack of reliable data, it is difficult to judge the effectiveness of this first two-year experiment in linguistic Ukrainization. By the standards of the August 1, 1923 decree (100 percent Ukrainization in one year), it was an abysmal failure. However, clearly some modest progress was made. One study found that only 11 to 15 percent of those enrolled in Ukrainization courses completed them; nevertheless, with some justice, the study concluded: "At least the courses did exist. True, only superficially and partially, but at least some progress was made on Ukrainization."[48] The number of Ukrainians in government and party work rose somewhat.[49] The Ukrainization of the press and

[40] Lebed, *Sovetskaia Ukraina i natsional'nyi vopros za piat' let* (Kharkov, 1924); for irritation at Lebed's immunity from self-criticism, see Skrypnyk, "Zlikviduvaty liuksemburgiianstvo," (1925) *Statti i promovy*, vol. 2, part 1, 68–76.

[41] *Biulleten' VIII-i vseukrainskoi konferentsii*, biul. 1: 87–88.

[42] P. Solodub, "Spravy ukrainizatsii," *Bil'shovyk*, no. 160 (18.07.24): 1; P. Kobiliats'kyi, "Do ukrainizatsii," *Visti VUTsIK*, no. 166 (24.07.24): 1.

[43] F. T., "Od formal'noho vykonannia dekreta—do ukrainizatsii," *Visti VUTsIK*, no. 176 (05.08.24): 1.

[44] Vaisfligel', "Pro ukrainizatsiiu radaparatu," 1.

[45] A. Sluts'kyi, "Ukrainizatsiia narodnoi osvity na Kyivshchyni," *Bil'shovyk*, no. 166 (26.07.23): 2; P. Pis'mennyi, "Vyshcha shkola i ukrainizatsiia," no. 188 (02.07.24): 1.

[46] P. Solodub, "Voprosy ukrainizatsii," *Kommunist*, no. 187 (17.08.24): 2.

[47] "Postanova radnarkomu USRR pro ukrainizatsiiu," *Bil'shovyk*, no. 10 (14.01.25): 3; RTsKhIDNI 17/16/1396 (26.02.25): 55/2.

[48] Vaisfligel', "Pro ukrainizatsiiu radaparatu," 1.

[49] *TsDAHOU* 1/20/1978 (1925): 10, 16. From January 1924 to January 1925, the number of Ukrainians in the party grew from 33.4 percent to 37.0 percent; from April 1924 to April 1925, the number of Ukrainians in the Komsomol grew from 48.3 percent to 58.1 percent.

primary schools continued.[50] By April 1925, approximately 20 percent of government work was being conducted in Ukrainian.[51]

However, this success was spread unevenly across Ukraine. The further one descended down the Soviet hierarchy, the greater the degree of Ukrainization. Only 10 to 15 percent of central Ukrainian government paperwork was conducted in Ukrainian.[52] Village soviets, on the other hand, were almost 100 percent Ukrainized.[53] Likewise, as one traveled eastward, the government organs became less and less Ukrainian. In the predominantly agricultural Kiev and Vinnitsa regions, a majority of government paperwork was being carried out in Ukrainian by April 1925.[54] In the Donbass, the level of Ukrainization hovered just above zero.[55] Thus, as one proponent of Ukrainization lamented, the divide between the Ukrainian village and the Russian city continued to grow.[56] The reversal of this trend was one of the major tasks facing Lazar Kaganovich when he arrived in Ukraine in April 1925 to take over the leadership of the Ukrainian Communist party from Emmanuel Kviring.

Kaganovich's Ukrainization, April 1925–June 1926

The all-union Politburo appointed Kaganovich first party secretary of Ukraine on March 26, 1925.[57] Kaganovich later confessed that he was extremely nervous at the prospect of taking over such a fractious and powerful organization, and how difficult he found his tenure in Ukraine.[58] It was a mark of Stalin's confidence in Kaganovich that he gave him this assignment, since Ukraine's loyalty was and would continue to be crucial in Stalin's struggle with Trotsky and the left opposition. Kaganovich arrived in Ukraine with a clear mandate to imple-

---

[50] Khvylia, *Natsional'nyi vopros*, 37–40; *GARF* 374/27s/1709 (1929): 100–102. Primary schools went from 50 percent Ukrainian language in 1922 to 77.8 percent in 1925. From the academic year 1923–1924 to 1924–1925, institutes went from 17.1 percent Ukrainian language to 24.0 percent; technicums from 16.3 percent to 30.5 percent, and *profshkoly* from 1.9 percent to 22.0 percent. Over the same period, Ukrainian-language books expanded from 31.0 percent to 40.2 percent of all books published in Ukraine, journals from 32.4 percent to 44.6 percent, and newspapers from 37.5 percent to 38.7 percent.

[51] *RTsKhIDNI* 17/85/4 (1926): 1; *TsDAHOU* 1/6/105 (19.03.26): 144; 1/6/102 (1926): 11; *Deviatyi s"ezd*, 526.

[52] *RTsKhIDNI* 17/85/4 (1926): 50.

[53] A. Butsenko, "Uzhvavyty ukrainizatsiiu," *Visti VUTsIK*, no. 77 (05.04.25): 1.

[54] *TsDAHOU* 1/20/1977 (1925): 151. "Dovershyty ukrainizatsiiu," *Visti VUTsIK*, no. 112 (20.05.25): 1. On the Kiev region's considerable successes, see "Pidsumky ukrainizatsii radians'kykh ustanov na Kyivshchyni," *Bil'shovyk*, no. 148 (02.07.24): 2; "Ukrainizatsiia ukrains'kykh ustanov," no. 164 (24.07.24): 5; "Ukrainizatsiia radians'kykh ustanov," no. 172 (31.07.24): 3.

[55] *TsDAHOU* 1/20/1977 (1925): 153, 170–171; "Ukrainizatsiia na pervomaishchine," *Kommunist*, no. 76 (04.04.25): 3.

[56] Solodub, "Voprosy ukrainizatsii," 2.

[57] *RTsKhIDNI* 17/3/494 (26.03.25): 54/2.

[58] Lazar Kaganovich, *Pamiatnye zapiski* (Moscow, 1996): 373–403.

ment Ukrainization. Only a few days after his appointment, on April 4, a Ukrainian TsK plenum heard Oleksandr Shumskyi's devastating critique of the progress that had been made thus far on Ukrainization. The plenum's resolutions echoed Shumskyi's condemnation and called for a renewed and broadened effort at Ukrainization.[59] The press, after several months of silence, was suddenly filled with articles on the urgent task of Ukrainization.[60] On April 30, VUTsIK passed a new decree on the linguistic Ukrainization of all government work, which superseded the unfulfilled August 1, 1923 decree.[61] Kaganovich's arrival in Ukraine, then, marked the third turn toward Ukrainization. This new and more decisive phase was marked by three major changes in policy, each of them a direct response to the failures of 1923 to 1925.

First, the party now assumed direct leadership over Ukrainization, instead of ceding that role to the state bureaucracy, and as part of that new leadership role, insisted on its own Ukrainization. This was a new development. A Ukrainian TsK study had argued that the 1923–1925 Ukrainization campaign had been fatally compromised by passive resistance from within the party.[62] As a result, the April 1925 plenum called for the comprehensive Ukrainization of the party: all major party publications, including the TsK newspaper *Kommunist*, were to be shifted to Ukrainian; the TsK apparat as well as all lower party apparats were to carry out all paperwork in Ukrainian; meetings were also to be conducted in Ukrainian; party schools were to be shifted to Ukrainian; finally, individual party members, including ordinary workers, were ordered to study Ukrainian. All these requirements were applied to the Komsomol as well.[63]

Kaganovich himself set a personal example. He had grown up in a Ukrainian village until age twelve and, in his words, "spoke Ukrainian with an added mixture of Belorussian words."[64] Despite his weak command of Ukrainian when he arrived in 1925, Kaganovich immediately met with representatives of the Ukrainian intelligentsia and spoke with them in Ukrainian. He also promised to study Ukrainian so that he could address the next party congress in Ukrainian, a promise he failed to fulfill in 1925 but did at the next congress in 1927. More importantly, in April 1925 he formed a Politburo committee on

[59] "Voprosy ukrainizatsii na plenume TsK," *Kommunist*, no. 74 (02.04.25): 1; H. Petrovs'kyi, "Pisdumky plenumu TsK KP/b/U," *Visti VUTsIK*, no. 81 (10.04.25): 1; *RTsKhIDNI* 17/16/1396 (17.04.25): 63/5, 65/1, 65/3, 154–155; "Postanova plenumu TsK KP/b/U pro ukrainizatsiiu," *Visti VUTsIK*, no. 103 (09.05.25): 3; Khvylia, *Natsional'nyi vopros*, 108–114.

[60] "Pro ukrainizatsiiu," *Bil'shovyk*, no. 77 (05.04.25): 1; S. Shchupak, "Ukrainizatsiia partii," no. 83 (12.04.25): 1; V. Chubar, "Ukrainizatsiia partii," no. 88 (18.04.25): 2; A. Butsenko, "Uzhvavyty ukrainizatsiiu," *Visti VUTsIK*, no. 77 (05.04.25): 1; L. Kahanovycha, "Cherhovi zavdannia partii," no. 81 (10.04.25): 3; "Pro ukrainizatsiiu partii," no. 87 (17.04.25): 1.

[61] Khvylia, *Natsional'nyi vopros*, 123–128.

[62] *TsDAHOU* 1/20/1977 (1925): 170–171.

[63] *RTsKhIDNI* 17/16/1396 (17.04.25): 63/5, 65/1, 65/3, l. 154–155; Khvylia, *Natsional'nyi vopros*, 108–114.

[64] *TsDAHOU* 1/6/102 (1926): 154.

Ukrainization to supervise all aspects of that policy. Every major Ukrainian leader was included in the committee, and Kaganovich was made chairman. Unlike many previous Ukrainization committees, this one met frequently, with Kaganovich himself participating actively.[65]

Second, Kaganovich recognized the importance of establishing control over the implementation of Ukrainization. To service the Politburo committee, the TsK Information Department was ordered to solicit regular reports from local party Ukrainization committees, which were now set up in every Ukrainian oblast and city.[66] More importantly, the Ukrainian Control Commission (TsKK-Rabkrin), with its enormous staff, was given official control over the implementation of Ukrainization, and it undertook several massive investigations.[67] Sovnarkom also formed a Ukrainization committee that supervised and collected information from the massive network of Ukrainization committees set up in all the commissariats, economic institutions, local soviets, and factories.[68] This committee was supplied with information from the extensive staff of the Education Commissariat's department for the liquidation of Ukrainian illiteracy.[69] Thus, a massive crosscutting network of informational sources was established to monitor the implementation of Ukrainization. The formation of this network alone testified to the seriousness of the new Ukrainization drive.

Third, again in response to widespread resistance to Ukrainization, the party now emphasized the need to use force. The April 1925 resolution noted that there had thus far been only "a natural, routine Ukrainization of the Soviet apparat most closely tied to the village and of the primary schools."[70] Further progress, the decree argued, would require the use of pressure (*nazhim*).[71] In a letter to Stalin, the Ukrainian Politburo would later boast of Kaganovich's "hard line" (*tverdo provodimoi liniei*) on Ukrainization: "Not one of the former political secretaries in Ukraine . . . used so much pressure [*nazhim*] in the implementation of Ukrainization."[72] This was certainly true. Pressure, in this case, meant primarily the threat of being fired, not arrested. A TsK report called for the use of "exemplary firings for sabotage" to overcome inertia and passive

[65] *RTsKhIDNI* 17/16/1396 (03.04.25): 63/5; (17.04.25): 65/4, (13.05.25): 78/8. The committee's protocols with materials are preserved in *TsDAHOU* 1/20/1976 (1925); 1/20/2247 (1926).

[66] *RTsKhIDNI* 17/26/1396 (17.04.25): 154.

[67] Khvylia, *Natsional'nyi vopros*, 127; N. Kaliuzhnyi, "Ukrainizatsiia i NKRSI," *Visti VUTsIK*, no. 124 (03.06.25): 1. See the studies cited below from the TsKK-Rabkrin archive. *TsDAVOU*, fond 539.

[68] *TsDAHOU* 1/20/1976 (1925): 180; Khvylia, *Natsional'nyi vopros*, 126.

[69] On the formation of this organ, see *TsDAHOU* 1/20/2455 (1927): 119; see also studies cited below from Narkompros archive. *TsDAVOU* fond 166.

[70] Khvylia, *Natsional'nyi vopros*, 110.

[71] *Nazhim* was the favored word used by Ukrainian party leaders to describe their policy. See, for instance, *RTsKhIDNI* 17/26/3 (19.03.26): 14/1, 66; 17/69/59 (1926): 162; 17/113/336 (07.10.27): 149/1, 55; *TsDAHOU* 1/6/102 (1926): 11.

[72] *RTsKhIDNI* 17/85/4 (1926): 3, 7.

resistance.[73] This threat was immediately publicized after the April 4 plenum.[74] Public statements against Ukrainization were no longer tolerated. As Zatonskyi noted a year later: "Our most important accomplishment is that in Ukraine, it is no longer considered acceptable for a Party member to openly speak out against Ukrainization."[75]

These three policy changes were part of Kaganovich's attempt to send an unambiguous signal that Ukrainization was now considered a legitimate hard-line Bolshevik policy. To that end, the attitude and action of the Ukrainian Party's Central Committee were crucial. As noted earlier, in the Soviet Union's bureaucratic division of labor, the party was paradigmatically associated with the hard line and the soviet bureaucracy headed by TsIK with the soft line. Economic, security, and military commissariats tended to be grouped with the party, whereas cultural, agricultural, and social welfare commissariats were aligned with TsIK. Women, peasants, religion, and nationalities were all examples of soft-line policy sectors and so were primarily dealt with by TsIK. Central supervision of nationalities policy was formally entrusted to TsIK's Soviet of Nationalities and VTsIK's Nationalities Department. This same soviet/party division was replicated at the republican level. With only a few exceptions (most notably Georgia and Armenia), first party secretaries were not titular nationals, whereas the heads of the republican TsIK and Sovnarkom invariably were. This was the case in Ukraine from 1923 to 1937. Likewise, prior to Kaganovich's arrival, *Visti VUTsIK* was a Ukrainian language newspaper, and the TsK paper *Kommunist* was published in Russian.

This same division manifested itself in the 1923–1925 attempt at Ukrainization. The primary focus was the government organs, in particular those dealing with backward peasants, but not the party organs dealing with progressive urban workers. Thus, Lebed's distinction between a higher Russian culture associated with the Bolsheviks and a lesser Ukrainian culture associated with the soft-line soviet bureaucracy survived the formal condemnation of Lebed's theory in 1923. It did so because it reflected the a priori assumptions of most Bolsheviks that nationalities policy was simply not a core Bolshevik concern. Kaganovich, with the zealous support of Ukrainian Bolsheviks such as Skrypnyk and Zatonskyi, set out to overcome this distinction. One part of this attempt was the conscious cultivation of a "hard-line" rhetoric of *nazhim*. Likewise, Ukrainization was now called "a revolutionary task," "a great endeavor," and "an arduous task" requiring "concentrated will-power."[76] In other words, it was not a concession or a tactic, but a core Bolshevik project.

These were Kaganovich's tactics for achieving Ukrainization. It was still necessary, however, to specify more exactly the final goal. The August 1923 decree

[73] *TsDAHOU* 1/20/1977 (1925): 176.
[74] A. Butsenko, "Uzhvavyty ukrainizatsiiu," 1.
[75] *RTsKhIDNI* 17/85/206 (1926): 71.
[76] Butsenko, "Uvzhavyty ukrainizatsiiu," 1; Petrovs'kyi, "Pisdumky plenumu," 1; "Pro ukrainizatsiiu partii," 1.

was vague. It spoke of the equality of Ukrainian and Russian, but also of special privileges for the Ukrainian language. In April 1925, this ambiguity was replaced with the ambitious goal of establishing Ukrainian linguistic hegemony.[77] Russian would remain Ukraine's link language with the center and therefore would continue to be a mandatory subject in all Ukrainian schools. Otherwise, Ukrainian was to be the exclusive language of the public sphere. This goal in turn also served as a tactic, as Ukraine's leaders promoted the creation of a total Ukrainian linguistic environment. A critic from the all-union Orgburo, B. P. Sheboldaev, described this strategy as follows[78]:

> There is a theory that one should create a certain environment, that affairs should be objectively organized so that urban residents, against their will, will be forced to learn Ukrainian—for instance, by shifting the telephonist to Ukrainian, the conductors and so forth.

This was a fair description of the policy. All public announcements, all signs, all official stamps and blanks were to be exclusively in Ukrainian. The same was true of movie subtitles. Newspapers and books were to be rapidly made predominantly Ukrainian.[79]

This strategy was justified, once again, by the need to overcome the dangerous chasm between the Ukrainian village and the Russian city and thereby, in Kaganovich's words, "preserve the hegemony and leadership of the proletariat over the village."[80] This strategy was frequently contested at central gatherings. At an April 1926 TsIK session, the Bolshevik gadfly Iurii Larin, to boisterous applause, compared it to Petliura's policies and claimed Russian national rights were being trampled.[81] Petrovskii responded angrily that until now peasants would come to Kharkov and Odessa, see exclusively Russian signs, and wonder: "Where is Ukraine? . . . We are making every effort so that every peasant will be able to read signs—from TsIK down to the lowest commissariat—in his native language, so that he will understand that this is his government."[82] Petrovskii's comments followed precisely Lenin's and Stalin's psychological interpretation of *korenizatsiia*, that peasants should *feel* the government was theirs. Kaganovich responded likewise to criticisms made at an Orgburo session on Odessa: "Odessa is of course primarily a non-Ukrainian city, there are very few Ukrainians, but the village is totally Ukrainian, almost totally Ukrainian. The city should lead the village, correct? . . . If the *okrugkom* conducted its work

[77] *RTsKhIDNI* 17/16/1396 (17.04.25): 63/5, 65/1, 65/3, l. 154–155; Khvylia, *Natsional'nyi vopros*, 108–114, 123–128.

[78] *RTsKhIDNI* 17/69/58 (1926): 141.

[79] *RTsKhIDNI* 17/69/58 (1926): 125; 17/16/1396 (17.04.25): 154–155; (03.04.25): 63/5. *TsDAHOU* 1/20/1976 (1925): 79–80, 186–187.

[80] "Cherhovi zavdannia partii. Doklad tov. Kahanovicha," *Visti VUTsIK*, no. 81 (10.04.25): 3.

[81] *II sessiia TsIK III sozyva. Stenograficheskii otchet* (Moscow, 1926): 458–468.

[82] Ibid., 302.

in Russian, the Ukrainian village would be untouched. This is why the question about Ukrainization is not so simple."[83]

The Ukrainian leadership was determined to take active measures to prevent its cities from becoming Russian urban islands. In response to yet another attack made on Ukrainization at the all-union Orgburo, Zatonskyi made this clear: "Take the question of signs and posters, which seems to be a petty anecdotal question. It is really an extremely serious question as it is tied to the question of whether we will form separate [Russian] administrative and cultural districts [*raiony*] in the cities. You say that Petliura also repainted signs and now we are doing the same thing. That's absolutely right. Like Petliura we are repainting signs, but this doesn't scare us . . . it used to be that the peasant came to the city and thought he was in a foreign [*chuzhoi*] city. We need to create an environment where the peasant gets used to seeing Ukrainian signs, announcements and posters."[84]

The total environment strategy of Ukrainization raised the extremely sensitive issue of assimilation. This strategy seemed quite clearly to have the goal of assimilating urban Russians to a Ukrainian identity. Yet, Soviet policy was unambiguously hostile to both forced and voluntary assimilation. As a result, Ukrainians divided this question into two issues: the status of russified Ukrainians and of Russians. "The re-Ukrainization of the russified masses" was an explicit goal of Ukrainization.[85] So long as this process was the gradual outcome of creating a comprehensive linguistic Ukrainian environment and not forced assimilation, it could be justified as a decolonizing measure to overcome the unjust assimilatory impact of the artificial hegemonic Russian urban environment introduced by Tsarist colonialism. Zatonskyi often noted with satisfaction that "some individuals are [now] defining themselves as Ukrainians since, as the dominant [*gospodstvuiushchaia*] nationality, this is advantageous in all respects."[86] A highly symbolic case was Grigorii Petrovskii (head of VUTsIK), who was born in a Ukrainian village but lived for decades in the russified Ukrainian cities of Kharkov and Ekaterinoslav (as well as in Moscow as a Bolshevik Duma deputy) and could speak Ukrainian only with great difficulty. Petrovskii initially identified himself on the ubiquitous Bolshevik forms as a Russian, but with the period of rapid Ukrainization recategorized himself as Ukrainian.[87] With regard to ethnic Russians, policy was intentionally vague. In 1926, Russian national village soviets and districts were formed. However, Russian urban national districts were prohibited. Although it was not emphasized, even Kaganovich expressed the hope that in the long run, a Ukrainian environment would lead to the eventual Ukrainization of even the ethnic Russian proletariat.[88]

[83] *RTsKhIDNI* 17/113/265 (14.02.27): 63.
[84] *RTsKhIDNI* 17/69/58 (1926): 172–173.
[85] "Do ukrainizatsiia robitnychoi masy," *Visti VUTsIK*, no. 273 (29.12.25): 1.
[86] *RTsKhIDNI* 17/85/206 (1927): 68; *TsDAHOU* 1/6/102 (1926): 22.
[87] *RTsKhIDNI* 17/85/206 (1927): 68–69.
[88] *TsDAHOU* 1/6/102 (1926): 52.

Finally, it should be noted that Kaganovich's new nationalities program was not confined to this aggressive promotion of linguistic Ukrainization, but also involved "the promotion of Ukrainian culture." This was a controversial policy. V. Vaganian, a member of the left opposition, wrote a scorching polemic in 1927, filled with examples from Ukraine, arguing that Bolshevik nationalities policy should involve no more than the promotion of international culture in national languages, since national culture was a purely bourgeois phenomenon.[89] Stalin, of course, had declared in a famous 1925 speech, which Vaganian critiqued, that the Soviet nationalities policy would promote cultures "proletarian in content, national in form."[90] Already in 1920, Stalin had justified *korenizatsiia* by the need to promote "people who know the customs, habits and language of the local population."[91] In Ukraine, as in other republics, the policy of promoting Ukrainian culture had led to the appointment of former Ukrainian nationalists to important positions in the republics' academic establishment. By April 1925, this in turn had led to a widespread fear that these intellectuals were assuming a decisive influence over the Ukrainian youth and peasantry.[92] Therefore, as the April 1925 decree stated, "The party must now devote its energy to the mastery and leadership of all cultural and social processes."[93]

This meant that party members not only had to learn the Ukrainian language, but Ukrainian culture as well. It involved obligatory "Ukrainian studies" (*ukrainovedenie*) classes for all government workers and party members.[94] These courses involved an ambitious program of study: the history of the Ukrainian language, the development of the Ukrainian economy, pre- and postrevolutionary Ukrainian literature, the Ukrainian revolutionary movement, Ukrainian geography and natural resources, the Ukrainian diaspora, and much more.[95] Theoretically, failing an exam on these subjects could lead to the loss of employment. Anecdotes abounded, such as the cleaning lady being asked to write an essay on the reflection of the 1905 revolution in Ukrainian literature.[96] The promotion of Ukrainian culture also meant considerable attention and money devoted to the development of Ukrainian opera, theater, film, literature, and so forth. Finally, it meant laying claim to classic Ukrainian culture, which above all meant Shevchenko. In the 1920s, a veritable Shevchenko cult was propagated in Ukraine. When an old Bolshevik on an investigation of Ukraine's nationalities policy expressed alarm at this

[89] V. Vaganian, *O natsional'noi kul'ture* (Moscow-Leningrad, 1927).
[90] Stalin, *Marksizm*, 158.
[91] I. Stalin, "Politika sovetskoi vlasti po natsional'nomu voprosu v Rossii," (1920) in *Marksizm*, 62.
[92] See, for instance, Kaganovich's speech in *Deviatyi s"ezd KP/b/ Ukrainy. Stenograficheskii otchet* (Kharkov, 1926): 52–55.
[93] Khvylia, *Natsional'nyi vopros*, 111.
[94] *TsDAHOU* 1/20/1976 (1925): 155–158.
[95] Ibid., 155–158.
[96] *RTsKhIDNI* 17/113/265 (14.02.27): 46.

cult, he was sternly informed that "the battle for Shevchenko" was crucial: "we fought [with the nationalists] for a revolutionary Shevchenko, to use Shevchenko for the revolutionary education of the masses."[97] Ukrainization involved not only stealing Petliura's nationalities policy, but also his national hero.

Ukrainian culture also meant, paradoxically, Affirmative Action. In Vaganian's model, anyone who spoke Ukrainian could govern the construction of international culture in Ukraine. In Stalin's model, where a distinct Ukrainian national culture existed and the party was required to master it, ethnic Ukrainians who knew that culture were required. Therefore, the April 1925 decrees called for a massive campaign to promote Ukrainians into the party and into government service. All unemployed Ukrainians were to be identified and given work.[98] The Ukrainian government petitioned Moscow to assign all Ukrainians finishing higher education in the RSFSR to work in Ukraine. Ukrainian professors were recruited from abroad. In the case of firings, Ukrainians had priority over non-Ukrainians.[99]

The April 1925 decrees, then, launched a new unprecedentedly ambitious phase of Ukrainization. How successful was this campaign? Thanks to Kaganovich's insistence on frequent inspections and reports, considerable data exist to answer that question. The Affirmative Action programs proved particularly easy to implement, since Ukrainians were not substantially less educated than Russians. From January 1925 to January 1926, party membership increased from 37.0 percent Ukrainian to 43.0 percent; Komsomol membership from 50.9 percent to 63.0 percent; TsK nomenklatura posts from 15.4 percent to 34.4 percent; okruzhkom membership from 38.8 percent to 42.4 percent; raikom membership from 38 percent to 50 percent.[100] Similar successes were registered in soviet organs. Ukrainians formed the majority in VUTsIK (56.5 percent), okrug executive committees (60.0 percent), district executive committees (79.2 percent), and village soviets (88.5 percent).[101] Ukrainian representation in the local party troika (secretary, head of the Cadres, and Agitprop Departments) increased from 31.3 percent to 37.3 percent.[102] The percentage of Ukrainians in higher education also improved substantially: in institutes from 36.3 percent to 43.9 percent and in technicums from 55.5 percent to 58.6 percent.[103] By the end of 1926, there was already a sense that

[97] TsDAHOU 1/20/2631 (1928): 22–23; see also, 1/7/120 (03.04.29): 59; "Shevchenko i natsional'ne vyzvolennia Ukrainy," Bil'shovyk, no. 57 (11.03.25): 1; "Rokovyna smerti T. H. Shevchenka," Visti VUTsIK, no. 57 (11.03.25): 1.

[98] TsDAHOU 1/20/1976 (1925): 35.

[99] RTsKhIDNI 17/112/678 (10.07.25): 92/8; 17/16/1396 (03.04.25): 63/5; (17.04.25): 65/3; TsDAHOU 1/20/1976 (1925): 81, 108.

[100] TsDAVOU 539/5/249 (1926–1928): 1–3; RTsKhIDNI 17/69/59 (1926–1927): 5; TsDAHOU 1/20/2534 (1926): 10–12; Desiatyi z'izd KP/b/ Ukrainy. Stenohrafichnyi zvit (Kharkov, 1928): 526–527.

[101] TsDAVOU 539/5/249 (1926–1928): 1.

[102] GARF 374/278/1709 (1929): 64.

[103] GARF 374/278/1710 (1929): 94–95.

Table 6. Ukrainization of the Print Media, 1923–1928 (Percentage of Media in Ukrainian Language)

Year	Newspapers	Journals	Books
1923–1924	37.5	32.4	31.0
1924–1925	38.7	44.6	40.2
1925–1926	60.2	53.5	43.7
1926–1927	60.0	65.0	48.9
1927–1928	63.5	66.4	54.0

GARF 374/27s/1709 (1929): 100–102.

the problem of promoting Ukrainians into positions of power was well on its way to being solved.

Rapid progress was also made on the Ukrainization of the public sphere. Signs and public announcements were shifted to Ukrainian. As Table 6 shows, the Ukrainization of the print media was being carried out gradually and systematically.

There were certain difficulties. The April 1925 decrees called for the Ukrainization of the TsK newspaper *Kommunist*, but resistance within the party delayed this action until June 1926.[104] Also, even with the vast expansion of Ukrainian-language publishing within Ukraine, due to imports from the RSFSR, Russian books still represented 70 to 75 percent of the Ukrainian book market.[105] The schools were also gradually being Ukrainized. By 1927, 80.7 percent of primary education was being carried out in Ukrainian, 61.8 percent for elementary school (*semiletki*), and 48.7 percent for professional schools.[106] Higher education remained a weak point. Only in mid-1925 was a five-year plan for the linguistic Ukrainization of higher education put forward.[107]

As with the August 1923 decree, the April 1925 decrees continued to stress the linguistic Ukrainization of the government bureaucracy. The Ukrainian leadership was most proud of its success in this realm. After two years of effort, in April 1925, only 20 percent of central government paperwork was conducted in Ukrainian. Eight months later, that figure had increased to 65 percent.[108] Unsurprisingly, the success was uneven. The Donbass and south Ukraine performed much worse. In fact, their Ukrainization was considered completely superficial, the product of hiring translators or using "impossibly bad Ukrainian."[109] Within the central government, the soft-line institutions

---

[104] *RTsKhIDNI* 17/26/3 (02.04.26): 17/3.

[105] *RTsKhIDNI* 17/26/3 (19/03.26): 14/1.

[106] *Deviatyi s"ezd*, 456.

[107] O. Lozovyi, "Ukrainizatsiia VUZiv," *Visti VUTsIK*, no. 178 (06.08.25): 1; *TsDAVOU*, 166/6/10843 (1927–1928): 1–5.

[108] *RTsKhIDNI*, 17/85/4 (1926): 1; *TsDAHOU* 1/6/105 (19.03.26): 144; 1/6/102 (1926): 11; *Deviatyi s"ezd*, 526.

[109] *TsDAHOU*, 1/20/2894 (1929):106; *TsDAVOU*, 166/8/287 (1928): 11–13, 18–21; A. Butsenko, "Ukrainizatsiia radians'koho aparatu," *Visti VUTsIK*, no. 242 (22.10.25): 1. Quotation from Zatonskyi in *TsDAHOU* 1/6/102 (1926): 11.

(VUTsIK—90 percent, Education Commissariat—80 percent) performed much better than the hard-line institutions (commissariats of finance—45 percent, internal affairs—25 percent, labor—25 percent).[110] The economic trusts, in particular all-union ones, performed still worse. In fact, most all-union trusts boycotted Ukrainization completely until the party put pressure on them in late 1925.[111]

The Ukrainization campaign was not confined, however, to Ukrainian paperwork. A further goal was that all Ukrainian government employees should have a good command of the oral Ukrainian language and to use it regularly in their daily work. To achieve this goal, a grandiose network of Ukrainian studies courses was set up that reached into each government institution in the center and in the regions. I was unable to determine exactly how many individuals took these courses, but it was certainly in the hundreds of thousands. For instance, through June 1926 the railways alone had put 45,096 employees through Ukrainian studies courses. The Odessa *okruzhkom* reported in 1926 that 15,000 employees had formally studied Ukrainian.[112] Table 7 reports the results of this massive campaign as reported by a January-February 1926 TsKK-RKI study.[113] All tested employees were assigned to one of three categories: first category—good command of Ukrainian; second category—weak command; third category—negligible or no knowledge (Table 7). Those in the third category were subject to firing.

As before, managers performed slightly worse. Only 11.3 percent were assigned to the first category and 21.8 percent to the second category. This was only slightly better than the class-enemy specialists (9.7 percent and 18.1 percent, respectively).[114] Despite the new hard-line pressure, party members were still reported to be performing worse than non-party members.[115] Still more disturbing, the Komsomol were performing worst of all.[116] Oral work remained almost exclusively in Russian.[117] This began at the top. As Petrovskii joked at a TsIK session, "We'll start a meeting in Ukrainian and end in

[110] I. Bulat, "Iak provodyt'sia ukrainizatsiia v radians'kykh ta gospodarchykh ustanovakh," *Visti VUTsIK*, no. 257 (11.11.25): 2.

[111] On the boycott, see Butsenko, "Ukrainizatsiia radians'koho aparatu," 1; for their worse performance, see Bulat, "Iak provodyt'sia," 1. For the campaign pressuring the economic trusts to fulfill Ukrainization, see the series of reports, "Ukrainizatsiia v hospodarchykh ustanovakh," *Visti VUTsIK*, no. 262 (17.11.25): 4; no. 263 (18.11.25): 4; no. 266 (21.11.25): 4; no. 268 (24.11.25): 3; no. 277 (04.12.25): 4; no. 290 (19.12.25): 5; no. 294 (24.12.25): 5; no. 298 (31.12.25): 6.

[112] *TsDAHOU* 1/20/2247 (1926): 37; *TsDAVOU* 539/4/1399 (1926): 277.

[113] The commissariat and trust statistics are based on a survey of 35 central commissariats, economic and trade institutions. The okrug statistics are based on a survey of 29 *okrugi*, which included industrial *okrugi*, but the presentation did not indicate which commissariats, trusts, and Okrugi were included. *TsDAHOU* 1/6/105 (19.03.26): 144–150.

[114] *TsDAHOU* 1/20/2247 (1926): 29.

[115] *RTsKhIDNI* 17/26/3 (19.03.26): 14/1; *TsDAHOU* 1/6/102 (1926): 16–18.

[116] *RTsKhIDNI* 17/26/3 (14.08.26): 38/7.

[117] *TsDAHOU* 1/20/1976 (1925): 165.

Table 7. Employee Knowledge of Ukrainian, February 1926 (Number and Percentage of Employees by Category)

	CATEGORY 1 (GOOD)		CATEGORY 2 (WEAK)		CATEGORY 3 (NONE)	
	Total	Percent	Total	Percent	Total	Percent
Central commissariats	1247	22.0	2,042	36.1	2,366	41.8
Central trusts	497	9.5	2,422	46.5	2,293	44.0
Okrug employees	9,799	22.4	20,641	47.2	13,249	30.3

TsDAHOU 1/6/105 (19.03.26): 144–150.

Russian."[118] The shifting of oral work to Ukrainian remained a task for the future.

Thus, despite Zatonskyi's boast that party pressure had silenced open opposition to Ukrainization, passive resistance remained a major problem. If tens of thousands of employees fluent in Russian failed to acquire even a weak command of Ukrainian, it could hardly be due to the difficulty of the task. Shumskyi noted he learned Polish in six months after being sent there as Ukraine's representative, "and if they send me to China, I'd learn Chinese in two years."[119] TsK reports continued to speak of a contemptuous attitude toward the Ukrainian language. The head of an okrug Education Department bluntly told a language inspector, "I don't know Ukrainian, I don't want to learn Ukrainian, but I can sing Ukrainian songs."[120] As mentioned earlier, all-union institutions refused to submit even formally to Ukrainization until the last moment and continued to hire those who did not speak Ukrainian.[121] Specialists realized their value and threatened to leave for the RSFSR if forced to study Ukrainian. The party responded by ordering the GPU to establish surveillance over specialist attitudes to Ukrainization, but ultimately backed down and extended the deadline for specialists by six months.[122] Even the Ukrainization of the TsK newspaper, *Kommunist*, encountered resistance. A month after it switched languages, its circulation had plummeted from 70,000 to 37,000.[123]

This ongoing passive resistance created a dilemma for the party leadership. Strict enforcement of their hard-line rhetoric was literally impossible. It would have meant firing tens of thousands, approximately 40 percent of all Ukraine's white collar workers. Already in July 1925 a confidential Rabkrin report to Kaganovich stated that the January 1 deadline could not be met, but it likewise

[118] *II sessiia TsIK III sozyva*, 500.
[119] *TsDAHOU* 1/6/102 (1926): 118.
[120] *TsDAHOU* 1/20/1976 (1925): 165.
[121] Ibid., 164; *TsDAHOU* 1/6/105 (19.03.26): 145; *TsDAVOU* 539/4/1399 (1925): 153.
[122] *TsDAHOU* 1/20/1976 (1925): 86, 170, 189; 1/6/102 (1926): 70.
[123] *RTsKhIDNI* 17/26/1 (03–04.26): 50–51.

reported a widespread belief "that 'the deadline will be extended again and so there's no reason to hurry.' Therefore we must officially consider the Ukrainization of the government apparat finished by January 1st 1926."[124] Kaganovich agreed, and at the ninth party congress in December 1925, he announced that the January 1 deadline would stand but only "malicious saboteurs, those who don't want to study, who ignore Ukrainization," will be fired.[125] Thus, Ukrainization was triumphantly declared finished on January 1.[126] Three months later, sixty-three malicious saboteurs were fired. The rest (tens of thousands strong) were given three more months, until June 1, 1926, to learn Ukrainian.[127] This deadline likewise passed unfulfilled, and selective exemplary sackings continued. By 1927, 263 central Ukrainian government employees had been fired.[128] There were also regional firings, though I have no exact figures on their numbers. The total number fired throughout Ukraine certainly exceeded five hundred and may have been as high as one thousand.

If the exemplary firing of "malicious saboteurs" effectively silenced publicly expressed opposition to Ukrainization, it also had a cost: widespread Russian resentment. This resentment found an outlet in letters of complaint. Iurii Larin relied on letters to *Pravda* for his attacks on Ukrainization.[129] Stalin also reported receiving letters of complaint, such as the following one[130]:

> You have a duty to smash the chauvinistic soul of the infected Ukrainian chauvinists. We students read the decree of the Ukrainian republic that only those knowing the Ukrainian language will be allowed into university. . . . We are many and fervid defenders of Communism. We allow the need to support the national needs of the Yakuts, but not the Ukrainians, who speak Russian excellently and Chubar and Petrovskii will open a session in Ukrainian and end in Russian— some of us have been eye-witnesses to such scenes. . . . We are all unhappy. Let the dominant slogan be 'All Proletarians Unite, let everyone approach the light and knowledge and enter the house of science without regard to national dialects [*narechie*]. . . . Do not kill the proletarian offspring. Down with the chauvinists!'

The Ukrainian TsK was aware of this sentiment and took it seriously. The following note was passed up to a member of the Politburo Ukrainization committee, Kaliuzhnii, during a speech in Odessa[131]:

> For you more than anyone it should be clear that the majority population of Odessa is Russian and Jewish. Why do you childishly behave as if it isn't?

---

[124] *TsDAHOU* 1/20/1977 (1925): 175–176.
[125] *Deviatyi s"ezd*, 148.
[126] S Kasianiv, "Zakinchyty ukrainizatsiiu," *Visti VUTsIK*, no. 6 (09.01.26): 1.
[127] *TsDAHOU* 1/6/105 (19.03.26): 145; *TsDAVOU* 166/6/10854 (1925): 3–4.
[128] *RTsKhIDNI* 17/85/106 (1927): 18–19.
[129] Larin, "Ob izvrashcheniiakh," nos. 23–24 (1926): 50.
[130] *RTsKhIDNI* 17/85/77 (1926): 164–165. For Stalin's comment about receiving letters, see *RTsKhIDNI* 558/1/4490 (12.02.29): 1.
[131] *TsDAHOU* 1/20/2247 (1926): 2–3.

The comprehensive Ukrainization of a majority non-Ukrainian population is
a violent action, typical of bourgeois colonial policy. You want to force all
non-Ukrainians, against their will, into an alien Ukrainian culture and language. This current line will lead to the artificial assimilation of the Russian
and Jewish population with the privileged Ukrainian nation. How does this
relate to the Party's nationalities policy? It doesn't. . . . You should at last
open your eyes and stop stifling the freedom of language in Ukraine. How
long will the Ukrainian TsK undertake forced Ukrainization and what will
this lead to?

   Kravchuk 10.01.26

Kaliuzhnii distributed this note to the next Politburo Ukrainization session as
a particularly vehement example of the many anti-Ukrainization notes that he
received.

In early 1926, then, there was considerable uncertainty about the future
course of Ukrainization. Officially, the January 1, 1926 deadline had been met
and the Ukrainization of the government bureaucracy completed. Unofficially,
everyone understood that this was not at all the case and that much work
remained to be done. However, should a renewed campaign of forced
Ukrainization be undertaken or a more measured long-term effort? Growing
Russian resentment in Ukraine and Moscow suggested the need for a more
gradual approach. The depth of resistance to Ukrainization, on the other hand,
seemed to necessitate an intensified hard-line Ukrainization.

This question about the pace of Ukrainization did in fact lead to a major
controversy within the Ukrainian Politburo in the first half of 1926. After a
brief hiatus from Ukrainization, the Ukrainian Politburo gathered in mid-
March to hear a report from Zatonskyi on the results of the past year's
Ukrainization campaign.[132] On this occasion and at a subsequent Politburo
meeting in late March, a simmering personal feud between Kaganovich and
the commissar of education, Oleksandr Shumskyi, exploded into public confrontation. Their fight in turn triggered a political scandal that lasted two whole
years, involved Stalin's personal intervention, triggered a Komintern crisis,
and finally led to the denunciation of a native Ukrainian communist deviation:
Shumskyism.

Here, it will be sufficient to note that the Shumskyi affair originated in a
dispute over the Ukrainization of the proletariat. In March 1926, Kaganovich
proposed the slogan that the party would not promote the forced Ukrainization of the proletariat. Shumskyi objected vehemently. Stalin sided with
Kaganovich, and Shumskyi's deviation was anathematized. It was no surprise
that a political controversy would center on the Ukrainization of the proletariat.
This was the one Russian "urban island," to use Zatonskyi's phrase, exempted
from the April 1925 Ukrainization decrees. Moreover, this exemption was
due to Stalin's personal intervention. The initial draft of the April 1925

[132] *RTsKhIDNI* 17/26/3 (19.03.26): 14/1.

Ukrainization decree included union representatives as those who must learn Ukrainian under the threat of being fired. The all-union Trade Council immediately protested to Stalin, who in turn forwarded their complaint to the Ukrainian TsK secretary, Kviring, for action.[133] Kviring then wrote Stalin and informed him that the law would be amended to exempt union officials from the threat of firing.[134] Thus, the proletariat and its representatives were excluded from the hard-line Ukrainization campaign initiated by the April 1925 decrees.

Not only was the proletariat exempted from linguistic Ukrainization, but Affirmative Action was also not applied to industrial workers. In fact, when lay-offs took place in Krivoi Rog, they were done by seniority, which meant that younger Ukrainian workers suffered disproportionately.[135] This situation contrasted completely with the Soviet Union's eastern republics, where aggressive Affirmative Action was practiced in industrial hiring. This difference was partially explained by Stalin's particular concern over ethnic resentment among the crucial Donbass proletariat. In his April 1926 letter to Kaganovich, Stalin worried that forced Ukrainization of the proletariat might "provoke in the non-Ukrainian part of the proletariat anti-Ukrainian chauvinism."[136] This caution may have been effective. Ethnic conflict in Ukrainian industry remained a minor concern throughout the 1920s and 1930s, especially in comparison to the frequent and violent ethnic conflict that occurred on industrial sites in the Soviet Union's eastern regions.[137]

This background helps explain why Shumskyi reacted so vigorously to Kaganovich's formula that there would be no forced Ukrainization of the proletariat. This was, after all, no more than a restatement of existing policy. Still, that policy had previously been implemented in silence. Shumskyi therefore interpreted Kaganovich's insertion of this phrase into the new TsK theses on Ukrainization as a new public signal that the party was not serious about the Ukrainization of Ukraine's industrial regions. Shumskyi complained it was "a slogan that might undermine the Ukrainization of the proletariat."[138] This was not an unreasonable interpretation. For instance, a large number of Ukrainian leaders reported that criticisms of Ukrainization made by Larin and Enukidze at the April 1926 TsIK session, which were in fact the result of unauthorized freelancing, had been interpreted by Ukrainian party activists in exactly this fashion.[139] For this reason, the Ukrainian party leadership placed an enormous premium on stifling all party criticism of Ukrainization.

---

[133] *RTsKhIDNI* 17/33/392 (1925): 95–96.

[134] *TsDAHOU* 1/20/1976 (1925): 8.

[135] *RTsKhIDNI* 17/85/206 (1927): 89.

[136] Stalin, *Marksizm*, 172.

[137] Of course, as Chapter 2 makes clear, Affirmative Action was not the primary cause of ethnic conflict.

[138] *RTsKhIDNI* 17/85/4 (1926): 10.

[139] *GARF* 3316/20/153 (1927): 133; *RTsKhIDNI* 17/26/9 (03–08.06.27): 22; 17/26/1 (01–06.06.26): 128–129; *TsDAHOU* 1/6/102 (12.05.26): 67.

In the short run, Shumskyi was a bad prophet. The June 1926 Ukrainian TsK plenum, which summarized the progress made in Ukrainization and delineated new goals, placed the trade unions and industrial urban centers at the top of its agenda.[140] More significantly, the plenum announced that Ukrainization was no longer just a way to achieve the rural-urban *smychka* or to gain control over the construction of Ukrainian culture, but "one of the means of building socialism."[141] This formula was an attempt to address the widespread belief that Ukrainization was not a core Bolshevik task, not a hard-line policy, since "building socialism" was the paradigmatic Bolshevik task. Moreover, as in April 1925, this resolution was immediately backed up by deeds: a party conference report by the trade union chairman with a resolution on the Ukrainization of the unions; Politburo resolutions on the Ukrainization of the party, Komsomol, and transport workers, with special emphasis on Ukraine's industrial regions; and renewed work by the Politburo Ukrainization commission, with Kaganovich as an active chairman.[142] Moreover, these Politburo resolutions specifically recommended the use of exemplary firings to speed up Ukrainization.[143] As mentioned earlier, centrally authorized firings increased from 63 in March 1926 to 263 by late 1927. Despite Shumskyi's fears, then, hard-line Ukrainization continued.

The Failure of Comprehensive Ukrainization, 1926–1932

The new campaign initiated by the June 1926 plenum aimed to complete the original April 1925 plan of comprehensive Ukrainization, that is, the establishment of Ukrainian as the dominant language in the entire public sphere of the Ukrainian SSR. Certain tasks received less emphasis now, as they were felt to have been largely achieved. Affirmative Action continued but as a lower priority, since Ukrainians already formed a majority in most important institutions. The party was content with a bare Ukrainian majority (50 to 60 percent) and did not require that Ukrainian representation be exactly proportionate to their share of the overall population (80.02 percent). The Ukrainization of primary education and the press had been largely accomplished, although, as we shall see, this process was extended still further after June 1926. Finally, considerable progress had been made in the linguistic Ukrainization of soviet and cultural institutions.

Instead, the new campaign focused on three problem areas: the Ukrainization of the industrial proletariat, higher education, and those government organs, particularly all-union economic institutions in Ukraine's eastern

---

[140] *Budivnytstvo*, 65.

[141] *RTsKhIDNI* 17/26/1 (1926): 136.

[142] *Persha vseukrains'ka konferentsiia KP/b/U. Stenografichnyi zvit* (Kharkov, 1926): 294–309, 384; *RTsKhIDNI* 17/26/3 (14.08.26): 38/7; (18.08.26): 39/4; (07.09.26): 43/6; *TsDAHOU* 1/20/2247 (1926): 6–149.

[143] *RTsKhIDNI* 17/26/3 (07.09.26): 143; (25.12.26): 216.

industrial regions, that had successfully resisted linguistic Ukrainization. As of June 1926, very little had been accomplished in any of these areas. For the next six years, the party devoted considerable, though gradually diminishing, efforts to achieving breakthroughs in these three areas. By 1932, despite some solid progress, it was clear that the goal of comprehensive Ukrainization had failed. A bilingual Russian-Ukrainian public sphere was already in the process of formation. Comprehensive Ukrainization, in fact, failed before December 1932, when a Politburo decree formally abandoned that goal. Therefore, the cause of that failure cannot be sought in that decree and the subsequent 1933 terror campaign, but must emerge from an analysis of the last six-year campaign to achieve comprehensive Ukrainization.

The Factory

As already noted, the Ukrainian party leadership was extremely concerned about the potential for ethnic conflict within the republic's nationally mixed proletariat. They never considered transferring the practice of forced linguistic Ukrainization, used on their government employees, to the proletariat. In any case, Stalin's April 1926 letter clearly forbade that strategy. There were no mandatory Ukrainian studies courses for workers, only a small number of token courses to demonstrate the workers' voluntary enthusiasm for Ukrainization.[144] Theoretically, party discipline required all party members, even proletarians, to learn Ukrainian. However, few party proletarians actually studied Ukrainian and even fewer were punished for failing to do so.

Trade union officials continued to be exempt from the April 1925 decrees. Trade unions with a majority Ukrainian membership were required to shift their bookkeeping to Ukrainian, but even here the government made this a much lower priority than the Ukrainization of the government bureaucracy. Affirmative Action was practiced in recruiting trade union officials, as there was a strong desire to have a Ukrainian majority in these positions, even when the relevant union was not majority Ukrainian.[145] As the trade union chairman Radchenko laconically put it, "in the apparat of our unions, Ukrainians have a larger place than in the working mass as a whole and this is, of course, correct."[146] However, Affirmative Action was never practiced in industrial hiring.

To sum up, for government officials, the party used a model of hierarchical discipline: follow orders or be fired. As we shall see, however, they ultimately balked at enforcing the party's model of military discipline: follow orders or be shot. For proletarians, the party instead used a model of exhortation. The decrees on the Ukrainization of the proletariat consistently emphasized the need to explain to the workers the necessity "to master the Ukrainian culture and take an active part in Ukrainization as one of the processes of socialist

---

[144] *TsDAHOU* 1/20/2894 (1929): 109; *TsDAVOU* 166/10/336 (1931): 54.
[145] *TsDAHOU* 1/7/125 (19.06.29): 102–104; 1/20/2455 (1927): 47; *TsDAVOU* 539/5/1250 (1928): 34–35.
[146] *Persha vseukrains'ka konferentsiia KP/b/U*, 296.

construction."[147] This, of course, required those workers who were of ethnic Ukrainian heritage, first, to accept that they were ethnic Ukrainians and, second, to value that ethnic identification. The different approaches to bureaucrats and workers can be clearly seen in the official response to policy implementation. With government bureaucrats, there was a consistent tendency to emphasize the failures of and resistance to Ukrainization, whereas with workers there was an opposing tendency to exaggerate all successes.

In keeping with the exhortative model, major emphasis was placed on cultural work in the Ukrainian language.[148] This strategy involved extending the attempt to create a total Ukrainian urban environment to the last Russian stronghold. Workers were to be surrounded by Ukrainian culture. They were to be provided with Ukrainian newspapers (republican, urban, factory, and wall-newspapers), Ukrainian journals, books, theaters (both urban and factory), excursions to Ukrainian museums, Ukrainian banners and slogans in the factory, popular lectures and readings in Ukrainian, and Ukrainian cultural "evenings."[149] This strategy was to be fully implemented only in majority Ukrainian workplaces and partially implemented where Ukrainians were in the minority.

The project of bringing Ukrainian culture to the proletariat began at a modest pace in 1926, then accelerated dramatically with the onset of the cultural revolution in 1928, which led to a shift in emphasis from the creation of a Ukrainian government bureaucracy and high culture to the cultivation of a modernized, industrial Ukrainian culture. The most grandiose cultural revolution event was the "Three-month Festival of Ukrainian Culture" from June to September 1929.[150] It aimed "to mobilize the attention and activity of the party, Komsomol and working masses to the task of national-cultural construction, to propagandize the achievements of Ukrainian culture and bring them to the masses." The festival's main propagandist described its methods: "cultural processions to the theater, movies, museums; meetings with writers, artists, scientists; evenings of Ukrainian culture—these are the new forms which embrace a great mass of people and unite them with Ukrainian culture. One must bring these new forms of work into the workers' regions and enterprises."[151] Famous writers and academicians, including even the disgraced nationalist Mykola Khvylovyi, traveled to Ukraine's industrial regions to read their works aloud and lecture on their specialties. A large number

[147] TsDAVOU 539/5/1250 (1928): 34.

[148] TsDAHOU 1/20/2631 (1928): 70; 1/20/2455 (1927): 48; TsDAVOU 539/5/1250 (1928): 34–35.

[149] RTsKhIDNI 17/26/3 (31.08.26): 42/11; TsDAHOU 17/125 (19.06.29): 102–104; 1/20/2631 (1928): 70; 1/20/2455 (1927): 48; TsDAVOU 539/5/1250 (1928): 34–35; "Stan Ukrainizatsii v promyslovykh okruhakh," in Hirchak, Natsional'ne pytannia, 151–158.

[150] Hirchak, Natsional'ne pytannia, 32–43; E. Hirchak, Zavdannia natsional'no-kul'turnoho budivnytstva. Do trymisiachnyka ukrains'koi kultury (Kharkov, 1929). M. Skrypnyk, "Dlia choho potribnyi tr'omisiachnyk ukrains'koi kul'tury u Donbasi," in Natsional'ne pytannia, vol. 2, 142–143.

[151] Hirchak, Zavdannia, 18; 34.

of smaller "one-month festivals" and cultural processions were held across Ukraine in 1929 and 1930, with a particular emphasis on the heavily russified Donbass.[152]

This cultural strategy of proletarian Ukrainization appears to have enjoyed some success in introducing the Ukrainian language to the monolithically russified Ukrainian factories. It is difficult to evaluate precisely the progress made, since the complete absence of Ukrainization efforts prior to June 1926 meant that studies had not been conducted and statistics not recorded. Still, a February 1927 study of five major Kharkov factories gives some sense of the general situation.[153] In three of the five factories, Ukrainians were a majority (80 percent, 55 percent, and 55 percent), in a fourth they were a plurality (45 percent), and in a fifth they were a minority (28 percent). In all five factories, oral work was carried out almost exclusively in Russian. The vast majority of newspaper subscriptions were to the Russian-language *Pravda* and *Proletarii*. Virtually no one subscribed to the Ukrainian-language workers' newspaper *Proletar* or the Komsomol paper *Komsomol Ukrainy*. At one plant, 14.8 percent (18 of 122) of journal subscriptions were Ukrainian language; at another, the number was 1.6 percent (22 of 1362). Factory wall newspapers were almost exclusively in Russian. The factory libraries ranged from a high of 3.0 percent Ukrainian books to a low of 0.4 percent (150 of 3400). The only positive finding was the popularity of Ukrainian-language drama and choir groups. A more general January 1927 survey estimated that 16.7 percent of all union-sponsored lectures and conversations were conducted in Ukrainian. In heavy industry unions this figure plummeted to 5.7 percent for coal workers and 7.9 percent for chemical industry workers.[154] Given that informal language use was even more russified, it seems fair to conclude that Ukraine's factories were almost entirely linguistically Russian.

As elsewhere in Ukraine, the swiftest and easiest progress was made through Affirmative Action programs. It was relatively uncomplicated to promote ethnic Ukrainians up the trade union hierarchy. Their numbers grew steadily after 1926. By 1932, ethnic Ukrainians were a majority at almost all levels of the trade union hierarchy.[155] More striking was the success made in introducing the Ukrainian language to the workplace, as this policy met resistance from factory officials, trade unionists, and many workers. Table 8 shows the progress made by June 1932 in four categories.

[152] Iurii Luts'kyi, *Vaplitians'kyi zbirnyk* (Oakville, Ont., 1977): 63–68; Khvylia, *Do rozv'iazannia*, 108, 136; *XI z'izd*, 280; M. N. "Misiachnyk ukrains'koi kul'tury," *Visti VUTsIK*, no. 127 (04.06.30): 7; "Mystetstvo-misiachnykovi ukrains'koi proletars'koi kul'tury," no. 149 (01.07.30): 10; "Misiachnyk ukrains'koi proletars'koi kul'tury pid zahrozoiu," no. 158 (11.07.30): 8; "Misiachnyk ukrains'koi kul'tury—pid vohon' proletars'koi samokrytyky," no. 169 (24.07.30): 6.

[153] *TsDAHOU* 1/20/2455 (1927): 54–63.

[154] *TsDAHOU* 1/20/2632 (1927): 600b.

[155] George O. Liber, *Soviet Nationality Policy, Urban Growth, and Identity Change in the Ukrainian SSR 1923–1934* (Cambridge, 1992), 67–86; *TsDAVOU* 2605/4/192 (1932): 152–153.

Table 8. Percentage of Union Activities in Ukrainian Language, June 1932

Union	Cultural Circles	Lectures/ Discussions	Cultural Evenings	Wall Newspapers
Industrial unions				
Coal workers	48.5	42.9	n/a	10.1
Miners	61.9	75.0	39.7	29.2
Machine building	62.6	66.6	n/a	67.7
Electrical/technical	21.2	6.9	3.1	48.3
Chemical	55.2	48.2	n/a	68.4
Print	86.9	67.1	91.0	n/a
Construction	61.5	48.0	n/a	n/a
Railways	65.9	68.6	3.0	n/a
Medicine	46.1	33.2	47.9	n/a
Arts	75.8	58.4	n/a	n/a
Agriculture	97.8	96.8	97.5	n/a

TsDAVOU 2605/4/192 (1932): 144–145.

These statistics are incomplete but do illustrate a significant penetration of the Ukrainian language into the cultural work of trade unions. Although heavy industry remained less Ukrainized, given the total russification of these industries, the progress made there was actually most striking.

The Ukrainian language was readily accepted in circumstances requiring only a passive knowledge of Ukrainian. Lectures were frequently conducted in Ukrainian. The percentage of Ukrainian-language theaters for workers increased from 25 percent in 1928 to 75 percent by 1931.[156] Concerts and exhibitions were held overwhelmingly in Ukrainian. Ukrainian-language books and newspapers were made increasingly more accessible. By 1931, 32 percent of books in trade union libraries were Ukrainian language, although for heavy industry unions the figures varied from 14.5 percent to 19.3 percent.[157] By 1933, the number of Ukrainian books in trade union libraries had increased to 38 percent. This dramatic growth occurred thanks to an April 1932 Narkompros decree that required that 85 percent of books sent to all libraries be in the Ukrainian language.[158] By the early 1930s, in many factories there were as many subscriptions to Ukrainian-language newspapers as to Russian ones.[159] Of course, there is no evidence these books and papers were being read. Of more importance, then, was that the percentage of Ukrainian-language factory newspapers also grew, since they were presumably of greater interest to workers. However, activities that required workers to speak, such as social evenings and political discussions, took place primarily in Russian.[160]

[156] *TsDAHOU* 1/20/4172 (1931): 31.
[157] *TsDAVOU* 2605/4/192 (1933): 31, 38.
[158] *TsDAVOU* 2605/4/192 (1933): 146–147, 182.
[159] *TsDAVOU* 2605/4/192 (1931): 112, 161; 2605/4/195 (1933): 5; "Mistse KhEMZ'u ne v khvosti a v pershykh lavakh," *Visti VUTsIK*, no. 136 (16.06.31): 3.
[160] *TsDAHOU* 1/20/4172 (1931): 24.

Of course, this cultural Ukrainization was only one means to achieve the political goal of creating a hegemonic Ukrainian environment in the factories. Cultural activities represented an insignificant portion of the total work experience. The first five-year plan made a larger contribution by greatly accelerating the influx of Ukrainian peasants into Ukraine's industrial cities and factories. The percentage of Ukrainians in the major industrial cities increased rapidly from 1923 to 1926 to 1933: Lugansk (21.0/43.0/60.0); Zaporozhe (28.0/47.0/56.0); Kharkov (37.9/38.9/50.0); Dnepropetrovsk (16.0/36.0/48.0); Stalino (7.0/26.0/31.0). Ethnic Ukrainians increased from 41.7 percent of the proletariat in industry and construction in 1926 to a solid majority of 56.1 percent in 1934.[161] According to Stalin's frequently repeated paradigm, this process should have guaranteed the eventual Ukrainization of Ukraine's cities, as had happened before in Riga, Prague, and Budapest. However, was this occurring? Were the Ukrainian peasants bringing Ukrainian culture into the factories, or was the first five-year plan only continuing the established pattern of turning Ukrainian peasants into urban Russians?

Studies of language use on the work floor conducted by the trade unions, TsKK, and TsK's Agitprop Department from 1928 to 1933 suggested that the Russian language remained dominant. Almost all studies found that the language used for workplace communication was Russian. This was also the case for general union meetings and mass political work.[162] Party reports tended to blame the factory management for this situation, since they conducted all their oral work (and increasingly written work as well) in Russian and so communicated with workers exclusively in Russian. In any case, newly arrived workers quickly adjusted to the prevailing Russian-language environment. A TsKK study of three Kharkov factories in 1929 concluded that ethnic Ukrainians "rapidly russify here."[163] A major survey of the results of Ukrainization conducted by Tsk's Agitprop Department in December 1931 found that Ukrainian peasants arriving in Donbass factories frequently spoke in Ukrainian initially but were mocked "and then gave up the Ukrainian language."[164] Most strikingly, a 1931 trade union report found that workers were giving up the Ukrainian language even in a majority Ukrainian factory in the Ukrainian cultural capital of Kiev.[165]

These reports also noted a second important subjective fact. Both workers and their superiors tended to view Russian and Ukrainian workers as one cultural category, the ethnic majority, and other workers (Germans, Poles, Tatars, and others) as national minorities.[166] This lack of a strong sense of cultural distance was one reason for the striking lack of ethnic conflict between

[161] Liber, *Soviet Nationality Policy*, 57, 197.
[162] *TsDAVOU* 539/6/1599 (1928): 17; 539/5/1250 (1928): 137; 178; 2605/4/192 (1933): 450b; 112; 2605/4/194 (1933): 25; *TsDAHOU* 1/20/4172 (1931): 21–29.
[163] *TsDAVOU* 539/5/1250 (1929): 177.
[164] *TsDAHOU* 1/20/4172 (1931): 28.
[165] *TsDAVOU* 2605/4/192 (1931): 58–59.
[166] *TsDAHOU* 1/20/2894 (1929): 107; *TsDAVOU* 2605/4/192 (1933): 91; 105.

Ukrainians and Russians in comparison with the rather severe conflict between Russians and titular nationals in other Soviet republics. The comprehensive December 1931 Agitprop report on Ukrainization could only find a few anecdotal cases of ethnic conflict, as when Russian miners harassed a new Ukrainian colleague: "You, *khokhol*, get out of our mine shaft, only Russians work here."[167] One reason for this lack of ethnic differentiation was the Ukrainian leadership's cautious refusal to force the pace of Ukrainization, to practice Affirmative Action in industrial hiring, or to divide Ukrainians and Russians into "separate sections" for union work. Trade union cultural work could be conducted in Russian, Ukrainian, or a mixture of the two, but a decree forbade the formation of separate Russian-language groups for Russian workers and Ukrainian-language groups for Ukrainian workers.[168]

Despite the dominance of the Russian language and the lack of strong ethnic differentiation, it would be inaccurate to claim that Soviet industrial culture merely perpetuated the prerevolutionary paradigm of turning peasants into Russians. A sense of Ukrainian identity was being assimilated. It would be more accurate to speak of both Ukrainian peasants and Russian workers becoming russified Ukrainian workers. The majority of russified Ukrainians did not embrace linguistic Ukrainization, but their resistance was fairly mild, typical of their attitude toward many Bolshevik campaigns: "Before there was God's law and now there is Ukrainization." According to one report, the majority opinion could be summed up in one phrase: "You won't re-educate us!" However, even in the Donbass, a minority of workers embraced the new Ukrainian identity: "Among certain Ukrainian workers a mood of peculiar national pride is being born . . . at the factory, October Revolution, when the financial inspector delivered his concluding remarks in Ukrainian, some of the workers insisted he speak in Russian, but some insisted he must speak in Ukrainian."[169] Other reports also noted the growth of a certain Ukrainian patriotism even among russified workers.[170]

It is impossible to make definitive conclusions from anecdotal data, but the following sentiments attributed to Lugansk workers in 1929 appear to have been typical: "The majority of workers, both Ukrainians and Russians who have lived in Ukraine for a long time think that it is wrong and unnecessary to Ukrainize adult workers, 'We need to study more essential and useful subjects. One should Ukrainize the children through the schools.'"[171] In this model, an evolving urban Ukrainian identity, for both ethnic Russians and Ukrainians, could include both a knowledge of the Ukrainian language, an identification with Ukrainian culture and the Ukrainian SSR, and the daily use of Russian in the workplace. In his memoirs, the famous Soviet defector Victor Kravchenko,

---

[167] *TsDAHOU* 1/20/4172 (1931): 33–35.
[168] *TsDAHOU* 1/20/2455 (1927): 47.
[169] *TsDAHOU* 1/20/2894 (1929): 108–109.
[170] Khvylia, *Do rozv'iazannia*, 92–118.
[171] Ibid., 108.

who came of age in the late 1920s and early 1930s, exhibited both a strong Ukrainian identity and patriotism together with an insistence that technical education should take place in Russian.[172]

To sum up, despite the massive influx of Ukrainians into the factories of Ukraine's industrial cities and the efforts of the authorities to promote the Ukrainian language in those factories, the factory remained an overwhelmingly Russian-language environment. Arriving Ukrainians responded accordingly and adopted Russian as their professional language. Comprehensive linguistic Ukrainization had not been achieved, which of course would have been impossible in a mere six years, but neither had meaningful movement in that direction. The project of promoting a Ukrainian ethnic identity and Ukrainian patriotism does appear to have been more successful, not only with newly arrived Ukrainian peasants, but also with Russified Ukrainians and many long-term ethnic Russian residents. The Ukrainization of the proletariat, then, appeared to be moving in the direction of a territorial Ukrainian identity that was bilingual and open to both ethnic Ukrainians and Russians.

Higher Education

Alongside the factory, the other major institution where individuals assimilated an urban communist identity was the university. It was therefore crucial for the project of comprehensive Ukrainization to transform higher education from another of Ukraine's russified urban islands into a linguistically Ukrainian environment. This was partly a matter of prestige. Ukrainian was stigmatized as a peasant language. Nothing could better counter that prejudice than establishing Ukrainian as a language of science. More importantly, the universities trained Ukraine's future government officials. It would obviously greatly ease the Ukrainization of the government bureaucracy if new officials arrived already fluent in Ukrainian and accustomed to an urban Ukrainian environment. Despite considerable resistance, much progress was achieved in the Ukrainization of higher education. One reason for this success was bureaucratic. Narkompros concentrated the most avid proponents of Ukrainization within its apparat. It possessed, therefore, both the means and desire to enforce Ukrainization. It also possessed, from February 1927 to February 1933, a commissar of education, Mykola Skrypnyk, who was the most passionate and influential of the higher leadership's proponents of Ukrainization.

Skrypnyk wanted to establish Ukraine as a model for the Bolshevik solution of the nationalities problem. To that end, higher education and scholarship were important to him. In May 1926, he convinced the Ukrainian Politburo to form a separate faculty for the study of the nationalities policy in the Ukrainian Institute of Marxism-Leninism, with Skrypnyk himself as chairman of the faculty.[173]

---

[172] Cited in Liber, *Soviet Nationality Policy*, 116–117.
[173] *RTsKhIDNI* 17/26/3 (22.05.26): 25/6; (03.06.26): 27/30; (11.06.26): 27/18; (09.07.26): 33/10.

This was the first body of its kind in the Soviet Union; the All-Union Communist Academy only formed a commission on nationalities policy in 1928.[174] In a keynote address, significantly entitled "The Nationalities Question as a Separate Scientific Discipline," Skrypnyk argued that Leninist theory rested on three pillars: the relationship between the party and the proletariat, between the proletariat and the peasantry, and between the proletariat of the advanced nations and the revolutionary movement of the colonial and half-colonial peoples. The first two relationships had been studied scientifically, but the latter, he argued, had been neglected and now needed particular attention, "above all in Ukraine."[175] Skrypnyk's faculty helped produce Ukraine's superabundance of nationalities policy specialists. It also trained the necessary teachers to staff another of Skrypnyk's innovations: a mandatory course on nationalities policy included in the curriculum of all Ukraine's Institutes of Higher Education (VUZy).[176] Ukrainian students not only had to study the Ukrainian language but also to understand why they were being forced to study it.

Skrypnyk proved ingenious in pioneering theoretical breakthroughs that furthered the cause of Ukrainization. One such theory removed a major obstacle blocking an expanded Ukrainization of primary and secondary school education. By June 1926, the network of Ukrainian-language primary and secondary schools already embraced almost all native Ukrainian speakers. This seemed to mean there could be no further growth of these schools, since Soviet educational policy firmly stated that all children must attend native-language schools. Skrypnyk firmly supported this principle, because it meant Ukrainian parents could not send their children to Russian-language schools even if this was their desire.[177] For some ethnic Ukrainians, however, there was a loophole.

A large number of ethnic Ukrainians spoke Russian as their native language. Skrypnyk frequently noted that in the 1926 census 1.3 million individuals claimed Ukrainian nationality but Russian as their native language, whereas 200,000 claimed the opposite. As he put it, the 1.3 million russified Ukrainians represented "the coefficient of the old Tsarist russificatory policy," and the other 200,000 represented "formerly russified Ukrainians, who are now derussifying. This represents the coefficient of our nationalities policy through 1926."[178] Skrypnyk clearly wanted to raise that coefficient by derus-

---

[174] "Kommissiia po izucheniiu natsional'nogo voprosa," *Vestnik kommunisticheskoi akademii*, no. 30 (1928): 261–162.

[175] Skrypnyk, *Statti i promovy* vol. II, part 1, 5–12.

[176] "Pro zavedennia do navch. planiv VISh'iv ta tex-miv kursu natspytannia," *Biuleten' NKO*, no. 42 (1930): 5. *TsDAVOU* 539/10/1128 (1932): 4. These courses were abolished in January 1933. *RTsKhIDNI* 17/26/68 (20.02.33): 102/28. "Postanova Narkoma Osvity USRR tov. Skrypnyka M. O.," *Biuleten' narodn'oho komisariat' osvity*, nos. 8–9 (1933): 3–4.

[177] *GARF* 374/27s/1709 (1929): 81–83; *TsDAVOU* 166/6/10841 (1927): 136–137; 166/6/10842 (1927): 1.

[178] M. Skrypnyk, "Zblyzhennia i zlyttia natsii za doby sotsiializmu," *Bil'shovyk Ukrainy*, no. 8 (1931): 35.

sifying the other 1.3 million russified Ukrainians, but he faced the obstacle of the native-language education principle. His solution was to argue that these russified Ukrainians really spoke "a mixed and broken language," which contained elements of Russian and Ukrainian, but the base of this mixed speech was nevertheless usually Ukrainian and therefore most of these children could be safely assigned to Ukrainian schools.[179] Skrypnyk was pleased with this solution to his dilemma and repeated the argument on numerous occasions.[180]

This argument allowed the network of Ukrainian-language schools to expand accordingly. By the 1929–1930 school year, Skrypnyk could report that 97.4 percent of all Ukrainian children attended Ukrainian-language schools, whereas only 81.7 percent of Russian children did.[181] Since many of the children who were considered ethnic Ukrainians had Russian as their mother tongue, it is clear that the primary and secondary educational system had gone beyond linguistic equality and was now actually biased in favor of the Ukrainian language. For instance, in Dnepropetrovsk, only 69 percent of Russian children studied in native-language schools.[182] Likewise, a 1932–1933 study found that in the Donbass region only 74.8 percent of ethnically Russian children, and 62.7 percent of native Russian speakers attended Russian-language schools.[183] Thus, even in the most russified regions of Ukraine, the primary and secondary school systems had become slightly biased in favor of the Ukrainian language. As noted earlier, many parents accepted these Ukrainian schools, although Skrypnyk did admit that his educational policy encountered the greatest resistance from russified Ukrainians.[184]

Primary and secondary school education, then, represented one of the greatest successes of the policy of comprehensive Ukrainization. The only other area of comparable success was in publishing. The growth of Ukrainian-language newspapers provides the best illustration. In keeping with the policy of establishing a Ukrainian urban environment, in 1929–1930 the party launched a campaign to Ukrainize the newspapers of almost all of Ukraine's major industrial cities.[185] At the eleventh Ukrainian party congress in June 1930, Kosior boasted that the newspapers in Krivoi Rog, Zinovev, Kremenchug, Odessa, and Kharkov had all been recently Ukrainized.[186] By the end of 1930, Stalino remained the only major Ukrainian city with a Russian-language daily, and its Komsomol paper had already been Ukrainized.[187] Table 9 illustrates

---

[179] Mykola Skrypnyk, "Perebudovnymy shliakhamy," *Bil'shovyk Ukrainy*, nos. 13–14 (1931): 32–34.

[180] *Desiatyi z'izd*, 525–526; Skrypnyk, *Stan ta perspektyvy kul'turnoho budivnytstva na Ukraini* (Kharkov, 1929): 53; Skrypnyk, *Natsional'ne pytannia*, part 2, 142.

[181] Skrypnyk, "Perebudovnymy shliakhamy," no. 12 (1931): 27.

[182] Ibid., 26.

[183] *TsDAVOU* 539/11/1121 (1933): 51–54.

[184] *GARF* 374/27s/1709 (1929): 85.

[185] *RTsKhIDNI* 17/26/35 (11.03.30): 155/21.

[186] *XI z'izd*, 278.

[187] Liber, *Soviet Nationality Policy*, 60–61.

Table 9. Newspaper Circulation in Ukraine, 1923–1932

	UKRAINIAN LANGUAGE		RUSSIAN LANGUAGE		
Year	Circulation	Percentage of Total Circulation	Circulation	Percentage of Total Circulation	Total Circulation
1923	14,373	12.5	100,440	87.8	114,827
1924	21,195	17.9	96,938	81.9	118,475
1925	n/a		n/a		n/a
1926	53,387	29.9	121,392	68.1	178,309
1927	72,745	36.7	119,953	60.5	198,199
1928	111,098	46.3	123,096	51.3	240,030
1929	208,080	62.5	113,935	34.2	332,933
1930	349,290	76.7	85,080	18.7	455,406
1931	464,642	88.9	37,448	7.2	522,919
1932	950,295	91.7	48,948	4.7	1,037,164

Calculated from Liber, *Soviet Nationality Policy*, 60.

the massive growth in Ukrainian-language newspapers through 1932 and the near extinction of the Russian-language press in Ukraine.

Similar Ukrainian-language hegemony was achieved in the publication of books and journals. By 1930, 84.7 percent of journals were being published in Ukrainian, and a TsK decree had called for the gradual Ukrainization of even technical and scientific journals. Likewise, 80 percent of all books (78.7 percent of the total print run) were being published in Ukrainian.[188] However, this publishing hegemony did not guarantee a hegemony of readership, due to the massive impact of central publications. We have already seen that most workers subscribed to all-union newspapers despite the efforts of Ukrainian authorities to discourage this. Likewise, in 1929 Skrypnyk complained bitterly that only 15 percent of the literature being sold in Ukraine was Ukrainian-language, whereas the other 85 percent was Russian-language literature imported from the RSFSR.[189] The accelerated centralization that accompanied the implementation of the first five-year plan intensified this Russian central influence and became a major factor in the failure of comprehensive Ukrainization.

Increased centralization was one of the factors that slowed the Ukrainization of higher education. According to the original 1924 Narkompros plans, all VUZy not servicing national minorities were to shift their first-year classes

[188] In June 1930, 84.8 percent of journals were being published in Ukrainian (278 of 328), and many of the others serviced non-Russian national minorities (Jews, Poles, Germans). A January 1930 TsK decree called for the gradual Ukrainization of even specialized scientific and technical journals. Ukrainian-language books grew from 54 percent of all books published in Ukraine in 1927–1928 to 80 percent in 1930. *XI z'izd*, 278. *RTsKhIDNI* 17/26/35 (26.01.30): 145/12. M. Potapchyk, "Robitnycha kliasa Ukrainy v natsional'no-kul'turnomu budivnytstvi," *Bil'shovyk Ukrainy*, nos. 5–6 (1932): 130.

[189] *GARF* 374/27s/1709 (1929): 84.

to Ukrainian by the 1927–1928 school year and complete Ukrainization by 1930–1931.[190] With the arrival of Kaganovich and the acceleration of Ukrainization, more ambitious plans were put forward. As with the Ukrainization of the government bureaucracy, these plans encountered considerable resistance. One Odessa professor even demonstratively answered all questions in Turkish that were addressed to him in Ukrainian.[191] Most professors simply attempted to defer Ukrainization with various excuses, such as the Dnepropetrovsk professor who was still claiming his research left him no time to learn Ukrainian as late as April 1931.[192] However, the Narkompros inspectors insisted on compliance with unusual vigor and backed up their demands with a credible threat of firing.[193] Judging from their repeated circulars, the inspectors also had considerable difficulty enforcing the rule that all students must pass a Ukrainian-language competency test both to enter any VUZ in Ukraine, whether it had been Ukrainized or not, and to graduate.[194]

It is nevertheless quite clear that by the early 1930s most university students in Ukraine would have been forced to develop a working knowledge of Ukrainian. Table 10 shows the solid progress made in Ukrainization through the 1928–1929 school year. By 1931, the Ukrainian TsK was claiming, perhaps optimistically, that 90 percent of instruction in institutes was conducted in the Ukrainian language as was 80 percent of instruction in technicums.[195] The industrial universities continued to be most resistant to Ukrainization and were the focus of the vast majority of Narkompros' energies. Nevertheless, a 1931 study could report that a narrow majority (51.21 percent) of instruction in Ukraine's industrial VUZy took place in Ukrainian.[196]

This impressive record of accomplishment was, however, threatened by the increased centralization associated with the first five-year plan. In 1929, a TsK decree transferred all VUZy from the exclusive control of Narkompros to their respective commissariats (medical VUZy to the commissariat of health, etc.). This meant that industrial VUZy were assigned to the Supreme Economic Council (VSNKh), an all-union authority, which immediately put in question whether they would or should remain Ukrainian-language. A number of Ukraine's industrial VUZy, without waiting for instructions, immediately announced the end of Ukrainization or simply quietly switched back to Russian-language instruction.[197] Skrypnyk reacted vigorously to this threat of "de-Ukrainization," which brought him into conflict with central authorities.

[190] TsDAVOU 166/6/10843 (1926): 1–5.

[191] TsDAVOU 166/9/784 (1930): 68.

[192] TsDAVOU 166/10/336 (1931): 104.

[193] TsDAVOU 539/5/1250 (1928): 63; 166/6/10843 (1928): 241.

[194] TsDAVOU 166/10/336 (1931): 119–120; 166/6/10841 (1928): 122; 166/6/10842 (1926): 292.

[195] TsDAHOU 1/20/4172 (1931): 2.

[196] TsDAVOU 166/9/784 (1930): 69; 166/10/336 (1931): 119–120; 166/9/784 (1930): 2; "Pro nehaine nadislannia vidomostei za stan Ukrainizatsii ind. VIShiv ta Tekhnikumiv," *Biuleten' narodn'oho komisariatu osvity*, no. 4 (1931): 7.

[197] TsDAVOU 166/9/784 (1930): 65–72.

Table 10. Percentage of Post-Secondary Instruction in Ukrainian, 1926–1929

| | INSTITUTES | | | TECHNICUMS | | |
Type of School	1926–1927	1927–1928	1928–1929	1926–1927	1927–1928	1928–1929
Industrial-technical	12.0	23.1	34.9	33.2	40.3	36.9
Agricultural	61.0	71.4	69.4	58.9	69.2	71.2
Social sciences	16.0	42.3	62.5	26.3	33.0	67.1
Pedagogical	56.8	75.0	70.1	67.8	82.7	76.0
Medical	10.5	28.3	54.9	33.3	43.2	56.4
Total	32.9	45.8	58.1	46.5	55.6	59.6

GARF 374/27s/1710 (1929): 2–3.

His noisiest confrontation occurred during a TsKK investigation of nationalities policy implementation in early 1929. The head of the investigating team,
Azatian, asked Skrypnyk why the Dnepropetrovsk Mining Institute was not
being allowed to conduct courses in Russian as it was now under VSNKh's
authority.[198] To Azatian's surprise, Skrypnyk became enraged and accused
Azatian of *smenovekhovstvo*, since his question implied that all-union institutions
ought naturally to be Russian-language.[199] Skrypnyk noted that he had received
assurances from the All-Union Politburo that the transfer of the Mining Institute would not lead to its russification.[200] Still angry about Azatian's question,
Skrypnyk complained further about the identification of central institutions and
Russian cultural interests: "I can point out to you a whole series of strange
affairs. All-union scientific and cultural institutions declare Russian institutions
all-union and in this way Russian culture in different realms develops by two
paths—on the budget of the RSFSR and on the budget of the entire Union.
Due to this [situation], the cultural scissors between Russian culture and
the culture of other nationalities is not reduced but grows even greater."[201]
Skrypnyk was coming dangerously close here to the "battle of two cultures"
theory that he himself had denounced when put forward by Lebed and Mykola
Khvylovyi. Azatian in turn was enraged that Skrypnyk was treating him as a
"mindless Russian chauvinist [*rusotiap*]," and accused Skrypnyk of nationalism
in his final TsKK report.[202] The Ukrainian Politburo backed Skrypnyk, however,
and so the charge had no immediate consequences.[203] Still, in March 1931,
Narkompros was still vainly ordering the mining institute to complete
Ukrainization by the 1931–1932 academic year.[204] The resistance of all-union

[198] *GARF* 374/27s/1709 (1929): 81–93.

[199] Ibid., 90. On non-Russian *smenovekhovstvo*, see Chapter 6.

[200] Ibid., 91.

[201] Ibid., 90–91. The *smena vekh* (changing signposts) movement was led by noncommunist
Russian nationalists who argued that the Bolshevik regime was serving Russian national goals and
therefore deserved support. On this movement, see Hilde Hardeman, *Coming to Terms with the
Soviet Regime* (DeKalb, 1994).

[202] *TsDAHOU* 1/20/2631 (1929): 14.

[203] *RTsKhIDNI* 17/26/25 (16.05.29): 74/13.

[204] *TsDAVOU* 166/10/498 (1931): 38–41.

Table 11. Ukrainians in Post-Secondary Education, 1924–1925 to 1930–1931 (Percentage of Total Student Population)

Academic Year	Institutes	Technicums	Rabfaks
1924–1925	30.5	56.9	45.3
1925–1926	36.3	55.5	42.7
1926–1927	43.9	58.6	57.8
1927–1928	50.9	58.7	58.0
1930–1931	56.0	66.0	n/a

GARF 374/27s/1710 (1929): 94–95; XI z'izd, 276.

organs was one of the major factors preventing the complete Ukrainization of Ukraine's industrial VUZy.

In addition to professorial and all-union resistance, Ukrainian party leaders were disappointed to find that youth in general and students in particular were unenthusiastic about Ukrainization. The Komsomol had rapidly expanded from 50.9 percent Ukrainian in January 1924 to 66.1 percent Ukrainian in October 1928.[205] Nevertheless, the Komsomol was criticized as being even more backward than the party in embracing Ukrainization and was particularly criticized for its failure "to understand the political importance [of Ukrainization]."[206] At a May 1928 speech to the seventh Ukrainian Komsomol conference, Kaganovich began his speech with criticism of the Komsomol's attitude toward Ukrainization. They ought to serve as the "advance-guard of youth," but instead had "fallen behind, fallen far behind . . . [due to] the light-minded attitude of many Komsomol and party members to a most significant historical process, the realization of the Leninist nationalities policy."[207]

The Ukrainian leadership was likewise disappointed in its students. Table 11 illustrates how, as with the Komsomol, ethnic Ukrainians had quickly become a majority in Ukraine's VUZy. By 1930–1931, even Ukraine's industrial technicums had a small Ukrainian majority (50.7 percent).[208] As with the urban proletariat, a Ukrainian majority had been achieved without the use of formal Affirmative Action programs. Also, as with Ukraine's factories, there was little evidence of ethnic conflict in the universities, again in vivid contrast to the eastern republics.

There was however also a corresponding lack of enthusiasm for Ukrainization. A minority of Ukrainian students, particularly those in the humanities, enthusiastically supported Ukrainization and passionately embraced Khvylovyi's calls to build a modern Ukrainian national identity. However, Narkompros complained that most students were passive and sometimes even openly hostile to

[205] GARF 374/27s/1709 (1929): 78.
[206] RTsKhIDNI 17/26/3 (14.08.26): 33/7.
[207] "Doklad tov. L. M. Kahanovycha na VII vseukrains'komu z'izdi LKSM," Visti, no. 103 (04.05.28): 2.
[208] From a low of 20 percent in 1923–1924. M. Potapchyk, "Robitnycha kliasa Ukrainy v natsional'no-kul'turnomu budivnytstvi," Bil'shovyk Ukrainy, nos. 5–6 (1932): 130.

Ukrainization. At the Odessa Naval Technicum, for instance, students heckled a professor until he switched back to lecturing in Russian.[209] As noted above, despite his Ukrainian patriotism, Victor Kravchenko recalled that both he and his fellow ethnic Ukrainian students at the Airplane Construction Institute in Kharkov opposed Ukrainization and privately mocked it as "opera bouffe nationalism."[210] A 1931 TsKK report found the same attitude in Odessa's VUZy: "one notes a light-hearted, petit-bourgeois attitude to Ukrainization, ironical and mocking, sometimes even openly hostile."[211] Skrypnyk was angry that when an Odessa professor called Ukrainization "an act of violence" and labeled colleagues who switched to teaching in Ukrainian "renegades," no students spoke out against him. Even the students' communist cell was silent.[212] With the onset of the socialist offensive, a widespread sentiment even emerged within the student body that the forced construction of socialism had rendered Ukrainization obsolete. Postyshev described their attitude as "the position of either *industrializatsiia* or *Ukrainizatsiia*."[213] In other words, after all Skrypnyk's propaganda, they still considered the Ukrainian and the modern as in fundamental opposition.

To sum up, then, the Ukrainization of higher education represented the most successful effort to Ukrainize a recalcitrant Russian urban island. This success was explained by two factors. First, unlike with the proletariat, coercion could be employed. Second, there was the tenacious leadership of Skrypnyk and his Narkompros colleagues. Because of all-union resistance, however, the fate of the industrial VUZy still remained undecided by 1933. Moreover, despite their exposure to the Ukrainian language and propaganda in favor of a Ukrainian cultural identities, the universities did not produce the shock troops of Ukrainization that Skrypnyk had hoped for. Instead, somewhat like the urban proletariat, Ukrainian students were attracted to a Ukrainian identity that did not exclude a professional use of the Russian language or a strong all-union Soviet identity.

All-Union Institutions and the Government Bureaucracy

By the end of the first round of hard-line Ukrainization in June 1926, little progress had been made in Ukraine's factories and in higher education, a situation that was substantially improved in the following six years. The opposite was the case with the government bureaucracy, which had been the primary focus of the 1925 forced Ukrainization campaign. By June 1926, 65 percent of government business was already being conducted in Ukrainian and a final deadline of January 1, 1927 had been declared.[214] However, further progress

---

[209] *TsDAVOU* 166/9/784 (1930): 68.
[210] Cited in Liber, *Soviet Nationality Policy*, 116–117.
[211] *TsDAVOU* 539/9/1399 (1931): 5.
[212] M. Skrypnyk, *Neprymyrennym shliakhom* (Kharkov, 1929): 82–85.
[213] *XVI s"ezd*, 108.
[214] *TsDAHOU* 1/20/2894 (1929): 39.

proved extremely difficult, and by 1932, a limited de-Ukrainization was already taking place. The primary reason was resistance from central all-union institutions. Their ultimately successful resistance in turn made it easier for local Ukrainian bureaucracies, particularly in the eastern industrial regions, to thwart Ukrainization.

The April 1925 Ukrainization targeted all state institutions on Ukrainian soil, whether they were filials of larger all-union institutions or exclusively Ukrainian. All-union institutions immediately insisted that these decrees were illegal. The referees in this dispute—TsIK, Sovnarkom, and the all-union Politburo—proved extremely reluctant to issue an unambiguous decision. As a result, this dispute continued for over seven years, and a final, authoritative decision had still not been made when the attack on Ukrainization in 1933 rendered the issue obsolete. This issue represented yet another example of Ukraine's exceptional position in the nationalities question, as they were the only republic to insist, and insist vigorously, on their legal right to force all-union institutions to use the local non-Russian language. This dispute can be divided into three questions: First, did filials of all-union institutions in Ukraine have to correspond with Ukrainian institutions in Ukrainian? Second, did all-union filials in Ukraine have to conduct their internal paperwork in Ukrainian? Third, did Ukrainian institutions, including all-union filials in Ukraine, have the right to correspond with all-union institutions in Moscow in Ukrainian? In practice, the second and third issues were the focus of the controversy.

The dispute began a month after the April 1925 Ukrainization decrees, when on May 5, 1925, VSNKh sent a protest to TsIK's presidium arguing that the April 1925 decrees exceeded republican rights and would be wastefully expensive.[215] The issue lingered until October 1925, when the Soviet of Nationalities, which served primarily as a lobbyist for non-Russian interests, surprisingly rejected Ukraine's opinion and sided unambiguously with VSNKh, one of the all-union bureaucracies most hostile to *korenizatsiia*. Their decree denied the right of any republic to dictate the internal working language of all-union institutions (the second issue). Their decision was forwarded to TsIK's presidium for confirmation. Ukraine immediately protested vigorously that this was a violation of the Soviet nationalities policy.[216] At the same time, VTsIK resolved that all papers sent to it from the RSFSR's autonomous republics must be written in Russian (the third issue).[217] This proved significant because Stalin intervened on behalf of the non-Russian republics and sent a letter to Kalinin on November 18, instructing VTsIK to reverse its decree[218]:

The members of the Politburo instructed me (on the evening of November 17) to inform you that your decree contradicts the party line in the nationalities

[215] *GARF* 3316/16a/177 (1925): 14.
[216] Ibid., 8, 20–21.
[217] *GARF* 3316/64/43 (1925): 1.
[218] Ibid., 1–2.

policy. It should be reviewed by the presidium and changed in the following
spirit so that, first, any papers may be sent to VTsIK by any nationality in
any language without any restriction and, second, a special corpus of translators
competent in all the languages of the RSFSR should be organized within
VTsIK.

Presumably this intervention quickly became known to TsIK, since it immediately reversed the Soviet of Nationalities' decision and asked Sovnarkom to pass
a decree supporting Ukraine's position.[219] Stalin's letter, although it addressed
only the third issue and not the second, nevertheless had an immediate practical effect. As noted earlier, from November to December 1925, all-union filials
in Ukraine finally grudgingly began to implement Ukrainization.

Stalin's intervention, then, would seem to have resolved the issue. However,
the proposed legislation supporting Ukraine's position stalled in Sovnarkom.
When in July 1926, the Commissariat of Trade asked whether their Ukrainian
filials were in fact legally required to shift to Ukrainian (as the Ukrainian
government continued to insist), TsIK's presidium could not give a definitive
answer. They could only appeal to Sovnarkom to produce a formal law. Sovnarkom, however, would only definitively state that the Soviet Army had an
exceptional status and could conduct its paperwork in Russian throughout the
Soviet Union.[220] This issue was again taken up in the center in March 1928,
when the newspaper *Izvestiia* complained to TsIK that the Ukrainian government was threatening to take legal action against their Kiev office if the
newspaper's workers did not take Ukrainian-language examinations. TsIK's
presidium appealed to the Ukrainians to grant *Izvestiia* an exemption, but the
Ukrainian government, which resented the way in which all-union newspapers
frustrated their strategy of creating a complete Ukrainian linguistic environment, stubbornly refused. TsIK's presidium then told *Izvestiia* they could do
nothing until the issue had been formally resolved by higher authorities.[221]
Three years passed and the second issue, whether all-union filials could be
required to work in the local language, still remained unresolved.

The question of what language Ukrainian institutions should use in correspondence with all-union institutions in Moscow (the third issue) also remained
open. An April 1924 TsIK decree had asked, though not demanded, that
in correspondence with all-union institutions, republican organs "along with
the text in the national language include a Russian translation."[222] Stalin's
November 1925 letter directly contradicted this resolution, but the law had never
been formally repealed. Therefore, throughout 1926, agencies such
as the Commissariat of Trade, the Supreme Court, and the OGPU complained
to TsIK that they received untranslated materials from union republics. A TsIK

[219] *GARF* 3316/16a/177 (1925): 22.
[220] *GARF* 3316/19/189 (1926): 1–7.
[221] *GARF* 3316/21/130 (1928): 3, 7–70b, 10–15; *GARF* 3316/16a/353 (1928): 7.
[222] *GARF* 3316/17/190 (1926): 12.

nationalities specialist advised the TsIK presidium that since the Soviet constitution recognized the languages of all-union republics as equal, it would
be unconstitutional to force the issue and best to deal with it informally. Therefore, TsIK secretary Avel Enukidze sent a "comradely letter" to the secretaries
of each republic, in which he admitted that it was constitutionally valid to
correspond with the center in republican languages, but requested that they
include a Russian translation. All of the republics, except Georgia and of course
Ukraine, reported that they already conducted all correspondence in Russian
and would continue to do so. Georgia responded, perhaps disingenuously, that
they lacked enough officials fluent in Russian and that, "not only due to constitutional reasons, but also due to these concerns," they could not send Russian
translations.[223] Ukraine reported (falsely) that they already did correspond in
Russian, but that they gave "great political significance to the right of each
union republic to use the language of their own territory," and so asked TsIK
to hire translators.[224]

Since the friendly approach had failed, the Commissariat of Trade, citing the
April 1924 TsIK decree, began to return Ukrainian-language correspondence
with notes like the following: "This cannot be used by us as it is written in
Ukrainian, and so [the commissariat] requests that you send copies of this material in Russian as all other labor organs do. Also we ask that in the future you
send all materials in the all-union language." This infuriated the Ukrainians,
who complained (correctly) to TsIK that according to the USSR constitution,
there was no "all-union language."[225] This was an important issue to the
Ukrainians because their entire project of comprehensive Ukrainization was
threatened by the *smenovekhovstvo* principle that all-union and Russian should
be treated as equivalent terms. The ever-vigilant Skrypnyk addressed this point
in a separate memo[226]:

> The official language in the Ukrainian SSR is Ukrainian, and Russian is the
> language of a national minority, despite its numerical significance, despite the
> fact it has behind it all of Russian culture, the language in which Lenin wrote
> and in which the basic communist work of TsK VKP/b/ is undertaken. Bilin-
> gualism was our policy until we adopted the line of the Ukrainization of the
> government apparat. [Bilingualism] was rejected after we adopted the policy
> of Ukrainization. The Russian language is recognized as the language of a very
> significant national minority.

TsIK once again requested that the Ukrainians voluntarily send materials in
Russian, and they were once again rebuffed by Ukraine.[227] Thus, language
policy in this realm also remained ambiguous.

[223] Ibid., 28–29, 43, 61–63.
[224] Ibid., 30, 37.
[225] Ibid., 8; 5.
[226] *TsDAHOU* 1/6/150 (18.05.28): 129–130.
[227] *GARF* 3316/17/190 (1927): 10–14.

This prolonged ambiguity finally culminated in the formation of an authoritative Politburo commission consisting of two representatives of Ukraine,
Kaganovich and Chubar, and one all-union representative, Ordzhonikidze, who
himself was the Politburo's unofficial Georgian specialist. From February to
May 1928, the issue was placed on the Politburo agenda six times and then officially deferred due to ongoing disagreements.[228] Finally, on May 17, 1928, the
following resolution was issued[229]:

1. Declare correct the decision of the Ukrainian government requiring the officials of all-union state and economic organs to study the Ukrainian language
   and to use the Ukrainian language in its correspondence with all Ukrainian
   organs and with the Ukrainian population.
2. Due to difficulties in finding qualified managerial cadres in the near future
   that know Ukrainian, the Politburo declares that the period required to introduce Ukrainian paperwork into all-union enterprises be lengthened.
3. Declare incorrect any interpretation of the law on studying the Ukrainian
   language that would forbid hiring those who do not know Ukrainian.
4. Declare that for the Red Army the current practice remains in effect [i.e., the
   use of Russian].

Once again the Ukrainians won a victory in principle but with considerable
ambiguities in practice. First, two and a half years had already passed since the
original Ukrainization deadline, and they were now asked to again extend the
deadline indefinitely. Second, the established, though frequently flouted, rule
that non-Ukrainian speakers could not be hired was now lost. Nevertheless,
official Politburo approval of their position had finally been attained.

The timing of this decision proved unfortunate. The two and a half years of
ambiguity had allowed all-union filials in Ukraine to stall on the implementation of Ukrainization. A January–February 1927 investigation found that only
27.0 percent of employees in all-union economic trusts spoke Ukrainian well
and 8.9 percent fell into the category of absolutely no knowledge. According
to the formal Ukrainian law, they should all have been fired. Moreover, 29.2
percent of these employees avoided even taking the test. On the other hand,
50.3 percent of employees in Ukrainian commissariats spoke Ukrainian well, and
only 2.2 percent had no knowledge of the language.[230] Still, by mid-1928, with
the Politburo decree, all-union organizations were no longer denying that
Ukrainization applied to them and some progress was being made.

The launching of Stalin's industrialization drive in 1928, however, once again
stiffened the backs of the all-union filials. As we have seen, the increased

---

[228] *RTsKhIDNI* 17/3/688 (24.05.28): 26/14; 17/3/672 (09.02.28): 9/28; 17/3/674 (23.02.28):
11/2; 17/3/675 (01.03.29): 12/1; 17/3/685 (03.05.28): 23/18; 17/3/686 (10.05.28): 24/1; 17/3/687
(17.05.28): 25/1. For Ukraine's rejection of a proposal by Kuibyshev in March 1928, see *TsDAHOU*
1/20/2632 (1928): 3.
[229] *RTsKhIDNI* 17/3/688 (24.05.28): 26/14.
[230] *TsDAHOU* 1/20/2455 (1927): 190–1900b.

centralization accompanying Stalin's revolution from above had hindered the Ukrainization of industrial VUZy. Many party members now felt the socialist offensive had rendered *korenizatsiia* and Ukrainization obsolete. This changing attitude had repercussions even in Georgia, where the status of the Georgian language had been so secure that it was rarely discussed during NEP. However, at the July 1929 Georgian TsK party congress, a maverick Georgian Communist, Zhgenti, launched a passionate attack on the growing influence of the Russian language.[231] He noted that the Georgian TsK increasingly worked in Russian and only then translated the final resolution into Georgian. Russian was also being used to send out circulars to the regions, where it was often poorly understood. At the recent Tiflis party congress, the presidium had received a note: "Why are you speaking in Georgian? Isn't this a right deviation?"[232] Zhgenti and his allies blamed the growing influence of the Transcaucasus *kraikom* for this development. In this instance, TsK sided with the Georgians.[233] During a rare appearance of Stalin at an Orgburo meeting on October 19, 1931, he censured the *kraikom* for excessive centralization and declared that they had violated the Soviet nationalities policy. After Stalin's intervention, the issue again disappeared.[234]

In Ukraine, where the status of the national language was much more precarious, the socialist offensive had an enormous impact. In 1928–1929, all-union institutions again began to flout Ukrainization.[235] For instance, the Commissariat of Trade brazenly informed the Ukrainian TsK that their bread inspectors were shifting back to Russian forms because they had little connection with Ukraine.[236] In response to the new political atmosphere, TsIK's presidium also changed its position. On November 3, 1929, they issued a decree that all-union filials should correspond with their central superiors in Russian and with republican authorities in the republican language. Internal paperwork could be in Russian (a contradiction of the 1928 Politburo decree) unless it was closely tied to relations with the republican authorities. The TsIK decree did specify that it did not free employees from any obligations to study republican languages. The Ukrainian Politburo naturally immediately protested this decree.[237] A stalemate once again ensued. The decree was not repealed but, in an amusing form of compromise, it was also not published. Thus, when in 1931 the all-union factory inspection asked TsIK in what language their inspectors should work, they were sent the unpublished November 1929 decree; but when

---

[231] *VI s"ezd KP/b/ Gruzii. Stenograficheskii otchet* (Tiflis, 1929): 95–101.

[232] Ibid., 98.

[233] *RTsKhIDNI* 17/18/29 (22.03.31): 33/25; "Postanovlenie TsK VKP/b/ po dokladam zakkraikoma, TsK Gruzii, TsK Azerbaidzhana i TsK Armenii," *Ivestiia TsK VKP/b/*, no. 23 (1931): 58–61.

[234] *RTsKhIDNI* 17/114/265 (19.10.31): 75–202; 17/18/34–39, 45–47 (1932–1934); *Vtoroi ob"edinennyi plenum TsK i TsKK KP/b/Gruzii. Iiun' 1932 g. Stenograficheskii otchet* (Tiflis, 1932); *IX s"ezd KP /b/ Gruzii. Stenograficheskii otchet* (Tiflis, 1935).

[235] *TsDAHOU* 1/7/125 (19.06.29): 102–104.

[236] *TsDAVOU* 539/6/1582 (1928): 10.

[237] *GARF* 3316/24/643 (1932): 6–8; *RTsKhIDNI* 17/26/25 (28.12.29): 99/7.

they asked permission to distribute the decree to their inspectors, TsIK refused authorization because the decree was secret. This remained the formal legal situation through the end of 1932.[238]

This stalemate, however, did not maintain the status quo. Ukrainization inspectors reported that "in practice, some employees understood [the November TsIK decree] as freeing them from all obligations to study the Ukrainian language. Moreover, this decree led all-union institutions to begin to eliminate all Ukrainization from their internal paperwork and employees ceased studying the language. The number of employees studying, especially in Kharkov, began to diminish."[239] In July 1930, the south-west railway administration sent out a circular calling for the 1929 TsIK resolution to be implemented, including the specification that the Ukrainian language must be learned. However, according to inspectors, the effect was that "among all employees and transport workers reigns the opinion that in the transportation sector, the Ukrainian language is forbidden."[240]

This opinion spread throughout all-union filials in Ukraine. The December 1931 Agitprop study on the state of Ukrainization described the entire transport industry in Ukraine as "conducting a russificatory policy." Most brazen was the removal of all Ukrainian signs at the railway station in the Ukrainian capital, Kharkov, and their replacement with Russian ones. The all-union trust, "Steel," shifted its paperwork back to Russian. The Black Sea Port authorities in Odessa, Nikolaev and Kherson, agreed to correspond in Russian.[241] Similar instances were encountered in other reports from 1931–1932.[242] In no case was the switch to Russian sanctioned by the Ukrainian authorities, but by 1932 they felt completely unable to affect the process. A July 1932 investigator reported with resignation that "all written work in institutions and enterprises of all-Union significance and in transport is being carried out overwhelmingly in Russian.[243] This was a fatal blow to the project of comprehensive Ukrainization, since all-union enterprises represented a massive presence in Ukraine, especially in the industrial east. Moreover, their behavior provided a corrupting example for local Ukrainian institutions. By the end of 1926, the Ukrainian leadership had felt the Ukrainization of written government work was almost completed. By 1932, this was no longer the case.

The successful resistance of all-union enterprises helped accelerate the gradual collapse of hard-line Ukrainization. As outlined above, hard-line Ukrainization consisted of two main aspects. First, the party itself would take charge of the process, along with other hard-line organizations like TsKK and Sovnarkom, instead of leaving nationalities policy to its traditional soft-line sponsors,

---

[238] GARF 3316/24/643 (1931–1932): 1–9.
[239] TsDAVOU 166/6/10854 (1930): 523.
[240] TsDAHOU 1/20/4171 (1931): 2–5.
[241] TsDAHOU 1/20/4172 (1931): 12–15.
[242] TsDAVOU 166/10/336 (1931): 37; 166/10/968 (1932): 31–33; 539/10/1128 (1932): 1; 539/9/1399 (1931): 27.
[243] TsDAVOU 166/10/968 (1932): 31.

Narkompros and VUTsIK. This would illustrate to a skeptical Bolshevik rank-and-file that nationalities policy was a legitimate core Bolshevik concern and not an expendable short-term strategy. It would overcome the stereotype that cultural issues and institutions were national, whereas economic and political institutions and issues were all-union and therefore implicitly Russian. The second aspect was the willingness to use force to back up the policy. Hard-line Ukrainization continued through Kaganovich's departure in mid-1928 and gradually eroded thereafter. By the beginning of 1932, it no longer existed.

Hard-line Ukrainization was guaranteed by the active involvement of TsK, which was both symbolized and substantiated by the Politburo commission on Ukrainization, with Kaganovich as an active chairman. The commission met regularly through June 1928. Although the commission continued to exist formally until at least January 1931, there is no evidence it did any work after mid-1928.[244] The commission, then, ceased active work at exactly the moment Stanislav Kosior replaced Kaganovich as Ukraine's first party secretary. The former *borot'bist*, Ivan Maistrenko, who was involved in Ukrainization throughout this period, noticed this connection: "Kosior did not push as obstinately for Ukrainization as Kaganovich." Kaganovich spoke Ukrainian adequately, whereas Kosior did not, which "impeded the Ukrainization of Party cadres."[245] Still, Kosior did actively support Ukrainization and vigorously defended it from widespread party attack in 1928. Moreover, as we have seen, the socialist offensive had an independent impact, drawing more and more of TsK's attention. As a result, Ukrainization was consigned to the much less influential Agitprop department, which had influence over the press and cultural affairs but not over the government and economic bureaucracy.[246] TsKK's attention to Ukrainization declined likewise. Through 1928, TsKK undertook several comprehensive investigations of Ukrainization. From 1929 to 1932, it undertook gradually fewer investigations, and these were only small scale and anecdotal.

The Politburo commission formed the summit of a hierarchy of commissions created in 1925, which included a Sovnarkom commission and also commissions in every okrug, city, and major factory designed to monitor policy implementation. The Sovnarkom commission was active during the initial wave of Ukrainization, but it met for its last time in late 1927.[247] Without any effective leadership, the local commissions also ceased functioning. By 1931, their existence was purely formal.[248] This situation was formally acknowledged in 1932 when the commissions were replaced with Narkompros "oblast Ukrainization

---

[244] *TsDAHOU* 1/20/2632 (1928): 1–66; *RTsKhIDNI* 17/26/40 (28.01.31): 28/38.

[245] Ivan Maistrenko, *Istoriia moho pokolinnia* (Edmonton, 1985), 227–228.

[246] Agitprop's only major study of Ukrainization was its December 1931 study, which did not even produce a TsK resolution. *RTsKhIDNI* 17/26/45 (10.12.31): 87/4.

[247] *RTsKhIDNI* 17/26/34 (15.04.30): 158/1.

[248] *TsDAVOU* 166/6/10854 (1930): 422; 166/8/287 (1928): 11; 539/10/1128 (1932): 1; *TsDAHOU* 1/20/4172 (1931): 2–9.

inspectors."[249] This act merely legalized a situation that had already existed for four years. From early 1928 to late 1932, Narkompros and its Department for the Liquidation of Ukrainian Illiteracy (Likuknep) had supervised the implementation of Ukrainization. As in 1925–1926, Likuknep's main two functions were to organize Ukrainian courses for government employees and to periodically test their knowledge. It did this with considerable vigor. Likuknep was busy preparing a new testing campaign, defiantly including all-union enterprises, in late 1932 on the eve of its destruction in the 1933 Ukrainian terror.[250]

Likuknep, however, lacked the necessary authority to enforce its agenda. The key to the hard line was the threat to fire those who refused to learn Ukrainian. As noted earlier, through 1927 several hundred had been fired. Likuknep continued to threaten firings through the end of 1932, but after 1927 actual dismissals became increasingly rare.[251] Likuknep also found it impossible to enforce the rule that no institution could hire a new employee who had not passed a Ukrainian-language test. In Odessa, a 1931 investigation found that those with a knowledge of Ukrainian were actually more likely to be fired.[252] Likuknep continued to enroll tens of thousands in Ukrainian studies courses, but the courses typically collapsed due to lack of attendance. In 1931–1932 in Kharkov, 170 courses were organized for ten thousand employees, but only thirty-five of the courses actually functioned.[253] Likuknep also continued to conduct periodic tests. From 1927 to 1930, comprehensive tests were organized for all employees, although increasingly large numbers simply failed to show up for the tests and did so with impunity.[254] Despite repeated attempts, Likuknep failed to organize a comprehensive test in either 1931 or 1932.[255]

In short, Ukrainization did continue from 1928 to 1932. Every year tens of thousands attended courses and were tested. However, unlike the period from 1925 to 1927, tens of thousands also refused to attend courses or be tested and did so with no fear of punishment. Moreover, Likuknep became increasingly concerned that no progress was being made due to "recidivism," as those who

---

[249] "Pro utvorennia posady obl. inspektora ukrainizatsii ta pro ioho funktsii," *Biuleten' NKO*, no. 38 (1932): 6–7.

[250] "Pro ispyty z ukrainskoi movy dlia sluzhbovtsiv usikh ustanov ta pidpryiemstv iak respublikans'koho, mistsevoho, tak i vsesouznoho znachennia ustanov transportu ta riznykh orhanizatsii," *Biuleten' NKO*, no. 59 (1932): 3–8.

[251] For the threat of firing, see TsDAVOU 166/6/10854 (1930): 528; 539/7/1192 (1929): 9. I only encountered one instance of firings after 1927. The Likuknep inspector in Kiev reported 26 firings as late as 1931. TsDAVOU 166/10/336 (1931): 13.

[252] TsDAVOU 166/6/10855 (1931): 1350b.

[253] TsDAVOU 166/10/336 (1931): 31–34; 90–91; 539/5/1250 (1929): 224–230; 539/10/1128 (1932): 10.

[254] On the tests from 1927 to 1930, see TsDAVOU 166/6/10854 (1930): 517–532. On mass refusal to attend tests, see TsDAVOU 166/10/336 (1931): 37.

[255] *Biuleten' NKO*, no. 27 (1931): 9–12; no. 40 (1931): 12–13; no. 39 (1932): 6–7; no. 59 (1932): 3–8.

Table 12. Okrug-Level Employee Knowledge of Ukrainian, 1927–1930 (Percentage of Employees)

	CATEGORY			Not Tested Due to	
Year	1 (Good)	2 (Weak)	3 (None)	Absent	Exemption*
1927	16.0	39.0	16.0	29.0	n/a
1928	25.0	37.0	13.0	25.0	n/a
1929	21.3	30.2	11.3	30.0	7.2
1930	21.3	32.4	10.8	28.2	7.3

TsDAVOU 166/6/10854 (1930): 518.
* Beginning in 1929, employees in menial positions, such as janitors and couriers, were exempted from testing. A disproportionately large number of these would have been in the third category.

had acquired a superficial knowledge of Ukrainian lost it due to lack of use at work.[256] Table 12 illustrates why Likuknep was concerned. It shows a growth in the knowledge of Ukrainian through 1928 and then a slight decline through 1930.

In the Donbass, the major focus of Ukrainization in this period, employee knowledge of Ukrainian rose from 5.7 percent in 1927 to 16.9 percent in 1928, but by 1930 it had fallen again to 8.5 percent. More significantly, the number that failed to show up for the test at all rose from 21.5 percent in 1927 to 56.7 percent in 1930.[257] By 1930 there was a sense, in the words of a *Visti* article, that "the level of Ukrainization of employees has worsened considerably."[258] Regional tests carried out in 1931–1932, which now judged only whether the employees did or did not know Ukrainian, confirmed these fears: in Kiev, 58 percent of those tested did not know Ukrainian; in Odessa, 50 percent; in Kharkov, 60 percent. This led Likuknep to send out an August 1932 circular with the message that the current state of Ukrainization was "completely unacceptable."[259]

An approximate description of government employee knowledge of Ukrainian, then, would be that it grew steadily from 1925 to 1928, then leveled off and began to decline from 1930 to 1932. In 1932, most republican-level institutions still conducted the majority of their paperwork in Ukrainian, although some economic organizations were still using Russian.[260] Of much greater importance was the fact, reiterated in numerous investigations, that Russian remained the spoken language of almost all institutions. The only exceptions were such soft-line institutions as the Education and Justice Commissariats,

[256] TsDAVOU 166/6/10854 (1930): 517; 539/7/1192 (1929): 13; 539/5/1250 (1928): 58.
[257] TsDAVOU 166/6/10854 (1930): 519.
[258] "Ukrainizatsiia radaparatu pidupala," *Visti VUTsIK*, no. 118 (1930): 3. See also *TsDAVOU* 166/6/10854 (1930): 527; "Natsional'no-kul'turne budivnytstvo—nevid'iemna chastyna sotsialistychnoho budivnytstva," *Visti VUTsIK*, no. 76 (03.04.30): 3.
[259] *Biuleten' NKO*, no. 39 (1932): 6–7.
[260] TsDAHOU 1/20/4172 (1931): 5.

VUTsIK, and the Union of Artists.[261] Moreover, Ukrainization inspectors reported a strong hostility to the use of Ukrainian. One inspector reported that at a Kharkov factory, "in response to my insistent questions in Ukrainian, they insistently answered in Russian."[262] Another inspector reported his experience in VSNKh: "When you address a comrade in Ukrainian, he stares at you for about three seconds, then understands what you want, gathers himself, and with great effort answers you in Ukrainian."[263] The hegemony of the spoken Russian language in the workplace began to seep into the official urban space as well. For instance, in 1931 all public announcements in the Mariupol town square were in Russian, something that would have been unthinkable during the early forced Ukrainization campaign.[264]

Conclusion

By 1932, the project of comprehensive linguistic Ukrainization had failed. The goal of this project had been to create a total linguistic urban environment that would compel both Ukrainians and Russians to adopt Ukrainian as the language of public life in Ukraine. However, the two most important arenas where Ukrainian residents assimilated an urban identity, the factory and the office, remained dominated by the Russian language. By 1932, the dominance of Russian was growing in the office and only marginally diminishing in the factory. In the university, the Ukrainian language had gained a stronger foothold, although its position was under threat in the important industrial and techni-cal VUZy. In short, a Ukrainian peasant arriving in a major Ukrainian city in 1932 would most likely be compelled to adopt Russian as his workplace language.

My analysis, therefore, contradicts the conclusions of the two scholars who have analyzed Ukrainization from a sociological perspective: Bohdan Kraw-chenko and George Liber.[265] Both Krawchenko and Liber argue that by 1932 the process of urban migration and state-sponsored Ukrainization was produc-ing a hegemonic Ukrainian identity in Ukraine's cities. They explain the Ukrain-ian terror of 1933, then, as primarily an alarmed response to this new social phenomenon. In Liber's metaphor, it was a "scorching of the urban harvest" of Ukrainization. However, a hegemonic Ukrainian urban environment was not coming into being in 1932. On the contrary, a bilingual atmosphere was emerg-

---

[261] *TsDAHOU* 1/20/2631 (1929): 10; 1/20/4172 (1931): 5; 1/20/4172 (1932): 5; *TsDAVOU* 166/10/336 (1932): 31; 166/8/267 (1929): 19; 539/5/1250 (1929): 172–180; *Biuleten' NKO*, no. 39 (1932): 6–7; no. 59 (1932): 3–8.

[262] *TsDAHOU* 539/5/1250 (1929): 175.

[263] *TsDAHOU* 1/20/4172 (1931): 10.

[264] Ibid., 6.

[265] Bohdan Krawchenko, *Social Change and National Consciousness in Twentieth-Century Ukraine* (London, 1985); Liber, *Soviet Nationality Policy*.

ing with a pronounced cultural/economic split. In this emerging environment, Russian would be the dominant language in the economic, industrial, and hard-line political spheres, whereas Ukrainian would predominate in the cultural, rural, and soft-line political spheres. This, of course, was exactly the situation that Ukrainization had been meant to overcome. There were signs that a territorial Ukrainian identity was emerging, but this was bilingual and open to adoption by ethnic Russians. It is true that for this new equilibrium to emerge fully, the dominance of Ukrainian in the press, education, and government paperwork would have had to be loosened. However, this would have occurred without the massive 1933 terror. The terror was a response to the political and not the social consequences of Ukrainization.

Why then did comprehensive Ukrainization fail? First, as we have seen, Ukrainization encountered considerable passive resistance and noncooperation from the Russian and russified Ukrainian urban population. It did not turn out to be, as the Bolsheviks had initially assumed, a relatively easy policy to implement. Still, the party under Kaganovich's leadership was more than willing to use force (*nazhim*) against ordinary Russian bureaucrats. However, it was not ordinary bureaucrats but party members and higher management who, at least partially because of the greater security of their positions, most demonstratively failed to comply with the demands of Ukrainization. The center did consistently support Ukrainization but its support was soft. Stalin authorized hard-line Ukrainization in April 1925 and sent Kaganovich to implement it. However, when confronted with a long process that was causing considerable unhappiness in the party and among the working class, the center counseled a more cautious approach. It did so in Stalin's April 1926 letter, in the resolutions of the Orgburo committee on *korenizatsiia* of 1926–1927, in the TsKK investigations of 1927 and 1929, and in TsIK and the Politburo's ambiguous support for the complete linguistic Ukrainization of all-union filials. The party was not responding to Russian public opinion, but rather to Russian party opinion.

The combination of ongoing passive noncooperation by party members and managers combined with the center's soft support gradually undermined the hard line on Ukrainization. And if the policy was struggling with hard-line support, it was doomed without it. The socialist offensive brought increased centralization and therefore a greater penetration of the Russian language as well as a new wave of ideological hostility to Ukrainization. This further undermined the hard line. Finally, for reasons to be discussed in Chapter 5, the wave of terror that accompanied the socialist offensive targeted Ukrainian nationalists but not Great-Russian chauvinists. No all-union factory director was ever prosecuted in a show trial and shot for failing to promote the Ukrainian language, whereas many intellectuals were shot or imprisoned for too actively supporting Ukrainization. Terror served as a marker of a hard-line policy, such as collectivization or industrialization, that must be implemented at all costs. Ukrainian officials drew the appropriate conclusions. They interpreted

Ukrainization as what they always thought it should be: a soft-line cultural policy to be promoted conditionally and cynically for propaganda purposes. It was not a core Bolshevik policy and therefore could be ignored by serious economic, industrial, and hard-line political organs. As one investigator lamented, "they are waiting for us to force them to Ukrainize."[266] But the force never came.

[266] TsDAVOU 539/5/1250 (1929): 70.

4

Affirmative Action in the Soviet East, 1923–1932

Today, when Edward Said has turned "orientalism" into a universally recognized term and the inspiration for a burgeoning scholarly industry, nothing seems to us more characteristic of colonialism than the division of humankind into the arbitrary, essentialized, and hierarchical categories of east and west. It therefore seems odd that the Soviet Union, whose nationalities policy was explicitly formulated as a decolonizing measure, would not reject those categories and instead affirm the unity of mankind. In one sense, they did. The Bolsheviks' Marxist sociology led them to repudiate east and west as racial categories and to deny any long-term differences in the economic, social, or political capacities of all nationalities. However, the east/west dichotomy was nevertheless preserved as a cultural distinction (one that could at times contain much of the content of the old racial divide). This was not, in fact, surprising. Indeed, nothing better illustrates the way in which the Affirmative Action Empire preserved imperial categories, while reversing their policy implications, than the maintenance and systematization of colonialism's east/west dichotomy. Since this division did in fact influence policy implementation, my analysis of *korenizatsiia* has likewise preserved this old dichotomy. In Chapter 3, I undertook a case study of linguistic *korenizatsiia* in Ukraine, which was the most important policy in the Soviet "west." In this chapter, I analyze the most important policy in the Soviet "east": Affirmative Action, the practice of granting preferences to non-Russians in admissions, hiring, and promotion in education, industry, and government.[1]

---

[1] The best case study on *korenizatsiia* in the Soviet east is Adrienne Edgar, "The Creation of Soviet Turkmenistan, 1924–1938" (Ph.D diss., University of California-Berkeley, 1999): 249–90.

East and West

Before that analysis is undertaken, however, a closer look at the basis of the
Soviet east/west dichotomy is warranted. The Soviet Affirmative Action Empire
provided two important rhetorical resources that non-Russians could (and did)
mobilize in pursuit of their national interests. The first and most fundamental
was, to use an unlovely English word, the rhetoric of indigenousness. This
rhetoric was available to all Soviet nationalities except the Russians (that is, until
the Russification of the RSFSR in the mid-1930s). As we have seen in Chapter
1, *korenizatsiia* (indigenization) was a prophylactic policy designed to defuse
and prevent the development of nationalism among the formerly oppressed
non-Russian colonial peoples through the provision of national territories, languages, elites, and cultures. Part of the decolonizing rhetoric of indigenousness
was a rhetoric of abuse that could be (and was) hurled at any Russian (or russified native) who was felt to be behaving in a colonial manner: namely, the
potent Leninist charges of great-power chauvinism and mindless Russian chauvinism (*rusotiapstvo*).

All non-Russians, then, could make individual or collective claims on the
center by referring to their special status as indigenous peoples. The second
rhetoric of cultural backwardness (*kul'turno-otstalost'*) was not available to all
non-Russians. The category of cultural backwardness was, like indigenousness,
related to the Bolshevik decolonization project, since Tsarist colonial oppression was said to have greatly exacerbated cultural backwardness.[2] However,
unlike indigenousness, cultural backwardness was even more closely linked to
the Bolshevik ideology of developmentalism. Like the modernization theorists
of the 1950s, the Bolsheviks believed there was one path to progress and that
various nations were located at different points along that path. The Bolsheviks
aimed to dramatically accelerate the modernization of the former Russian
empire, which for them meant industrialization, urbanization, secularization,
education, universal literacy, and territorial nationhood. It was clear to the
Bolsheviks that, using any of these indicators, many of their nationalities (especially the "eastern" ones) were "backward" (the cultural being added to avoid
any implication of a racist interpretation of backwardness). By this logic,
the modernization of the Soviet Union required special measures, which
were promised in the 1923 nationalities resolutions, to overcome "the real economic and cultural inequality" between the advanced and backward Soviet
nationalities.[3]

Who was culturally backward? This was initially unclear, and, as we shall
see, it was hotly contested, since the rhetoric of cultural backwardness promised
to be useful in making financial claims on the center. Culturally backward
with respect to whom? This was obvious: the Russians. Not that the Russians
were considered the most culturally advanced nationality in the Soviet Union.

---

[2] *Dvenadtsatyi s"ezd VKP/b/. Stenograficheskii otchet* (Moscow, 1963): 693–694.
[3] *Dvenadtsatyi s"ezd*, 694. *Tainy natsional'noi politiki* (Moscow, 1992): 285.

Table 13. Literacy Rates by Nationality, 1926

Western Nationalities (Percent)		Eastern Nationalities (Percent)			
Latvians	78.1	Tatars	33.6	Ingush	9.1
Estonians	72.4	Chuvash	32.2	Azerbaijani	8.1
Jews	72.3	Mari	26.6	Ajars	7.8
Lithuanians	70.5	Udmurts	25.6	Kazakhs	7.1
Germans	61.2	Bashkirs	24.3	Kabardinians	6.8
Poles	53.8	Buriats	23.2	Balkars	5.3
Russians	45.0	Mordvinians	22.9	Kirgiz	4.6
Ukrainians	41.3	Ossetians	21.2	Uzbeks	3.8
Georgians	39.5	Cherkess	16.9	Chechen	2.9
Belorussians	37.3	Abkhazy	11.3	Turkmen	2.3
Armenians	34.0	Kalmyk	10.9	Tajik	2.2
		Karachai	9.2	Kara-Kalpaks	1.3

Natsional'naia politika v tsifrakh (Moscow, 1930): 271–272. The category Tatars includes Volga and Crimean Tatars.

That status, as we have seen, was reserved for the "western national minorities" (Germans, Poles, Finns). Russians were generally grouped in the next category with the developmentally similar Belorussians, Ukrainians, Jews, Georgians, and Armenians (although the last two were sometimes considered "eastern" and "backward" when the topic was "feudal" customs). The remainder were generally categorized as culturally backward, a dividing line that perfectly matched the official 1926 literacy rates as reported in Table 13.[4]

Within the culturally backward category, the nomadic peoples formed a still less developed category, and the least developed of all were the small peoples of the North. The important division, however, was between advanced and culturally backward. An official boundary between the two categories was not provided until 1932 when, due to controversy over who was eligible to fill all-union university admissions quotas for culturally backward nationalities, the commissariat of education finally produced an official list of ninety-seven culturally backward Soviet nationalities (Table 21).[5] The division between eastern and western nationalities, then, was a shorthand (and a strikingly traditionalist one) for the Bolshevik categories of advanced and culturally backward nationalities.

There were two important consequences of the east/west divide for *korenizatsiia*. The first was a practical outgrowth of the real developmental differences between eastern and western republics as reflected in the literacy rates of Table 13. This difference was already noted by Enukidze at a 1927 Orgburo discussion of *korenizatsiia*: "We have one system in the European national republics and another in the Asiatic ones." The reason for this was,

[4] The category Tatars includes Volga and Crimean Tatars.
[5] "Ob udarnom kul'tobsluzhivanii otstalykh natsional'nostei," *Biulleten' narodnogo komissariata po prosveshcheniiu RSFSR*, no. 5 (1932): 13–14.

he argued, that whereas in Ukraine (or Belorussia) it was easy to train and promote Ukrainian (or Belorussian) cadres, low literacy rates in the east made this exceptionally difficult: "The task consists of beginning from below. Over a course of years, through the establishment of special courses, we will create a satisfactory [national] cadre."[6] Enukidze was correct. Although the eastern republics initially attempted to follow Ukraine's example, they ultimately had to focus almost exclusively on Affirmative Action, while Ukraine and Belorussia focused overwhelmingly on linguistic *korenizatsiia*. To this end, as we have just seen, Ukraine mobilized the rhetoric of indigenousness in an ultimately unsuccessful attempt to limit the interference of all-union institutions who were sabotaging Ukrainization.

In the Soviet east, the exact opposite situation prevailed. Since the training of native cadres and the general education of the population were expensive, and since the eastern national territories had few independent resources, they actively solicited all-union interference in the form of desperately needed financial assistance. To this end, they naturally relied on the rhetoric of "cultural backwardness" and the center's promise to help them catch up to the advanced Soviet nationalities. This meant that it was in the Soviet east where two crucial unresolved questions about the Soviet nationalities policy were settled during NEP. The first question was whether the eastern republics could reverse the effects of Tsarist colonialism by expelling Slavic settlers and granting categorical preferences to natives in land distribution. After a fierce fight in Kazakhstan, as we saw in Chapter 2, this right was denied to the non-Russian republics. The second question was whether the center's general commitment to financial and economic aid for the non-Russian republics could be transformed into a formal right to preferential assistance as manifested in a separate budget line for helping the culturally backward republics. This fight would be waged over the creation and institutionalization of a special "cultural fund" (the name itself echoing the official category of cultural backwardness) to help the non-Russian republics implement *korenizatsiia*.

I begin my analysis of Affirmative Action in the Soviet east with the failed attempt to establish a permanent "cultural fund." I then turn to the early attempts to implement *korenizatsiia* in the Soviet east and demonstrate how the attempt to follow the Ukrainian model of *korenizatsiia* created financial, political, and social problems that forced the eastern republics to scale back their ambitions and focus on a more modest policy of Affirmative Action that they called functional *korenizatsiia*. I then undertake two case studies of Affirmative Action among the industrial workforce and in higher education, which show how the severe rural ethnic conflict in the Soviet east during NEP, noted in Chapter 2, migrated to the urban environment. Finally, I look at the impact of the socialist offensive and cultural revolution on *korenizatsiia* in the Soviet east and show how the developmentalist ideology accompanying them meant that the same policies that undermined linguistic *korenizatsiia*

[6] *RTsKhIDNI* 17/113/336 (07.10.27): 33; 34.

in Ukraine and Belorussia considerably strengthened *korenizatsiia* in the Soviet east.

The Cultural Fund

The battle over the cultural fund, which took place from 1924 to 1926 in the newly formed Soviet of Nationalities, exposed the radically different priorities of the Soviet Union's eastern and western nationalities. In short, western republics focused on sovereignty; eastern republics on funding. During the debates over the formation of the Soviet Union, Ukraine even attempted to confine representation in the new Soviet of Nationalities to union republics, which would have left Azerbaijan as the only eastern republic.[7] Stalin instead successfully imposed a plan that gave each union and autonomous republic five representatives and each autonomous oblast one representative. This gave the eastern republics a majority of the delegates. Still, Ukraine used its superior influence and dominant personalities to direct the work of the Soviet of Nationalities toward Ukrainian priorities. The most influential member of the Soviet of Nationalities was its first chairman, Mykola Skrypnyk, who was also Ukraine's Commissar of Justice.[8] Skrypnyk devoted his considerable energies exclusively to defending the union republics' constitutional rights from central intrusions. At the October 1924 session alone, he questioned the center's rights in the supervision of sanitation, resorts, the collection of taxes, and the amendment of the criminal and civil legal codes. He even questioned the constitutionality of the All-union Supreme Court.[9] At a later session of TsIK, Skrypnyk's frequent adversary, Iurii Larin, gave an ironic description of his performances[10]:

> I know how at sessions of TsIK people regard comrade Skrypnyk's frequent addresses somewhat skeptically. When he mounts the podium, pulls out our legal code and begins to speak: "This is unconstitutional and that is unconstitutional. There is a violation of the rights of the Union republics, and look, here a problem has not been considered." And so on, such that one frequently blurts out: "Ah, isn't it all the same whether we put the comma here or there."

Larin's sketch drew appreciative applause. The eastern delegates often admired Skrypnyk's bravura performances, but their own interests lay elsewhere.

Specifically, they were concerned to extract as much funding from the center as possible. Already during the debates over the Soviet constitution in 1923,

---

[7] "Iz istorii obrazovaniia SSSR," *Izvestiia TsK KPSS*, no. 3 (1991): 170–172, 178–180; no. 4 (1991): 171–175; no. 5 (1991): 158–165; no. 9 (1991): 211–215; *Dvenadtsatyi s"ezd*, 576–582, 655–657.

[8] *1 sessiia TsIK SSSR 2 sozyva. Stenograficheskii otchet* (Moscow, 1924): 9.

[9] *2 sessiia TsIK SSSR 2 sozyva. Stenograficheskii otchet* (Moscow, 1924): 326–333, 424–428, 616–624; *GARF* 3316/16a/166 (1924): 1–6, 22–32.

[10] *2 sessiia TsIK SSSR 3 sozyva. Stenograficheskii otchet* (Moscow, 1926): 458.

the future First Party Secretary of Kazakhstan, K. S. Khodzhanov, noted that while a constitution was fine for Ukraine, the eastern republics' major concern was the reduction in central funding that accompanied the introduction of NEP. The 1923 decrees had promised the transfer of factories from central regions to the backward eastern republics, but financial pressures quickly aborted this policy.[11] By October 1924, the eastern representatives were in a sour mood. During TsIK's debate on the new budget, which required all cultural programs to be funded locally, Dagestan's bold representative, Takho-Godi, angrily invoked the promise of the 1923 decrees to "create real equality among nationalities" and pointed out that this required money. In Dagestan, he noted, there were currently 130 Soviet schools with 3000 students and 2000 Islamic schools with 40,000 students: "We are not able to wage battle on this front with local funding." Anger was, above all, directed at Ukraine and Skrypnyk who had, according to Kazakh's representative, Dosov, used his "loud voice" to steal twenty million rubles from the Kazakh budget.[12] The Yakut old Bolshevik, Amosov, stated the issue of funding in particularly stark terms: "If we do not offer real support now, then in ten or twenty-five years we will be able to say that such and such nationalities have been wiped from the face of the earth."[13]

The eastern representatives demanded that a special "cultural fund" be established by the Commissariat of Finance exclusively for the exceptional cultural needs of the "backward" eastern republics. This was in fact a call for renewing the exceptional outlay of 1,200,000 rubles that the Politburo had authorized for the 1923–1924 budget year alone as a "cultural fund" for the emergency needs of backward national regions.[14] After considerable lobbying, a five-million ruble cultural fund was allocated for the 1924–1925 budget year, specifically "in order to fulfill the needs of the culturally backward autonomous republics and oblasts."[15] Later, culturally backward union republics were also included. However, the fund was yet again presented as "an experiment for one budget year."[16]

The eastern republics, then, had successfully deployed the rhetoric of backwardness to secure special financial help. However, it still remained to decide which republics were eligible as culturally backward. The Volga Germans' representative argued, to considerable scorn, that the Volga Germans should be included since "in general all national minorities lag behind the Russian proletariat in their cultural level."[17] His petition was rejected. The Belorussians

[11] "Iz istorii obrazovaniia SSSR," no. 3 (1991): 175; Tainy natsional'noi politiki, 115–116, 285.
[12] 2 sessiia TsIK SSSR 2 sozyva, 353–355; 392.
[13] GARF 3316/16a/166 (1924): 39.
[14] RTsKhIDNI 17/3/414 (04.02.24): 66/15; 17/3/418 (14.02.24): 70/38; 17/3/420 (21.02.24): 72/10; 17/3/432 (10.04.24): 84/17; 17/112/513 (08.02.24): 69/9; 17/112/526 (24.03.24): 82/7; GARF 3316/64/61 (1925): 10.
[15] GARF 3316/16a/166 (1924): 29–30; 3316/17/489 (1924–1925): 1–54.
[16] GARF 3316/17/489 (1925): 46–48; 3316/16a/166 (1924): 65.
[17] GARF 3316/16a/166 (1924): 44.

likewise attempted, with equal success, to argue that they too were culturally backward.[18] The acknowledged eastern republics vied to assert their greater cultural backwardness and therefore their greater need. Azerbaijan declared itself "a comparatively backward republic . . . , lacking solid cultural traditions."[19] The Ingush petitioned for money from the cultural fund as "the most culturally and economically backward people of the North Caucasus," although local pride forced them to add: "except Chechnya." A Chuvash petition spoke of the "poverty of the Chuvash people, reduced to misery, darkness and ignorance."[20] A member of the Soviet of Nationalities' presidium, Eliava, finally suggested the calculation of "a coefficient of backwardness."[21] While the reification of cultural backwardness did not lead to a scientific coefficient, a special commission headed by A. A. Andreev did somehow find some criteria by which to divide the five million rubles among twenty-eight eastern republics and autonomous oblasts.[22]

Although the five million rubles were extremely welcome, the cultural fund itself was not the ultimate object of the eastern republics. Rather, it was to establish the principle that the Soviet Union's eastern nationalities, due to their cultural backwardness, had a *right* to preferential financial investment and that right should be embodied in the concrete form of a separate budget line. The ultimate goal would be to acquire a comparable fund for economic investment. This was not to be. The fund was again abolished in the 1925–1926 proposed budget and again resurrected at the same level for another year.[23] The next year it was abolished for good. Its passing was much regretted by the eastern republics both because of the lost funding but more so because of its "enormous political significance."[24]

The cultural fund represented the last time a separate program existed to direct financial investment exclusively to "culturally backward" national regions. The attempt of the eastern nationalities to make preferential economic investment a core part of the Affirmative Action Empire failed, just as the attempt to make control over the possession of agricultural land and migration had failed at the same time. In 1926, in a symbolically important action, VSNKh abolished its largely moribund Nationalities Department.[25] The Soviet of Nationalities increasingly found it difficult to even get a VSNKh representative to deliver a report on economic development in the national regions.[26] In general, both eastern and western nationalities felt the economic organs were fundamentally

[18] *3 sessiia TsIK SSSR 2 sozyva. Stenograficheskii otchet* (Moscow, 1925): 69; *2 sessiia TsIK SSSR 3 sozyva*, 230.

[19] *3 sessiia TsIK SSSR. 2 sozyva*, 130.

[20] *GARF* 3316/19/852 (1926): 114; 123.

[21] *3 sessiia TsIK SSSR 2 sozyva*, 84.

[22] *GARF* 3316/17/489 (1925): 60.

[23] *GARF* 3316/19/852 (1926): 114–134; *2 sessiia TsIK SSSR 3 sozyva*, 144–148, 151, 174. *Vlast' sovetov*, no. 8 (1925): 9–10.

[24] *3 sessiia TsIK SSSR 3 sozyva. Stenograficheskii otchet* (Moscow, 1927): 740.

[25] *GARF* 3316/19/845 (1926): 1–6.

[26] *GARF* 3316/20/216 (1928): 23.

hostile to *korenizatsiia*. This did not mean that nationality played no role in securing economic investment. It could be a factor in individual cases, but it was not the categorical right as implied in the 1923 nationalities policy decrees. The Kazakh government, for instance, successfully deployed both the rhetoric of indigenousness and backwardness in lobbying the center to construct the Turksib railway.[27] Moreover, with the first five-year plan, the center revived its rhetorical commitment to the construction of new industrial enterprises in "culturally backward regions," particularly Kazakhstan and Central Asia. However, economic historians agree that while industry did grow more rapidly in these regions (from an extremely low level), the pattern of central investment was overwhelmingly driven by all-union economic interests, with nationality playing little, if any, role.[28]

The center's reluctance to commit extensive financial resources for the implementation of its nationalities policy had an important impact on *korenizatsiia* in the Soviet east. Fifteen percent of the cultural fund had been earmarked directly for the implementation of *korenizatsiia*, and another 45 percent was set aside for the educational systems that would train future national cadres.[29] The eastern republics repeatedly complained that the center was not providing financial assistance for *korenizatsiia*.[30] A major cost-cutting reduction in the size of the government bureaucracies of the Soviet Union's autonomous republics and oblasts in the mid-1920s also inhibited *korenizatsiia*. As we shall see, the lack of funding to train qualified native cadres and to expand their bureaucracies led the eastern governments to give up on linguistic *korenizatsiia* and to engage in a crude form of Affirmative Action that often involved directly replacing Russians with titular nationals, a policy that exacerbated interethnic hostility.

Mechanical *Korenizatsiia*, 1923 to 1926

The early history of *korenizatsiia* in the Soviet east resembled the situation in Ukraine. There were a few token decrees, the first being passed by the always aggressive Tatar government in June 1921, but serious work began only after the April and June 1923 nationalities policy decrees.[31] In the immediate aftermath of the Twelfth party congress, virtually every republic and autonomous oblast passed *korenizatsiia* decrees, creating such exotic movements as *Zyrianizatsiia* and *Iakutizatsiia*.[32] In February 1924, VTsIK, which at

[27] Matthew Payne, "Turksib" (Ph.D. diss., University of Chicago, 1995).

[28] R. W. Davies, *Crisis and Progress in the Soviet Economy, 1931–1933* (London, 1996): 485–490.

[29] *GARF* 3316/17/489 (1925): 49–51.

[30] *GARF* 1235/118/1 (1924).

[31] Durdenevskii, *Ravnopravie iazykov v sovetskom stroe* (Moscow, 1927): 189–191, 200–201, 218–220; *GARF* 1235/118/1 (1923): 1–5, 69–70.

[32] N. Shakhov, "Zyrianizatsiia," *Komi mu—zyrianskii krai*, nos. 1–2 (1924): 65–73; *GARF* 1235/122/166 (1924): 2–28; Durdenevskii, *Ravnopravie iazykov*, 119–237.

that time had jurisdiction over all the Soviet Union's eastern republics outside the Transcaucasus, formed a special committee to supervise *korenizatsiia*. The committee's work resulted in an April 1924 decree and subsequent circular that provided central sanction and guidance for the implementation of *korenizatsiia*.[33]

This launched the period that subsequently became known pejoratively as the period of mechanical *korenizatsiia*, a reference to the crude Affirmative Action programs that involved firing Russians to make room for natives and the use of highly arbitrary quotas. The initial decrees, however, followed the Ukrainian pattern in highlighting the goal of linguistic *korenizatsiia*. This was true of Tatarstan's decrees, the stated goal of which was "the realization of the Tatar language," as well as of the general April 1924 VTsIK decree entitled, "On measures towards the shifting of paperwork of government organs in national oblasts and republics to local languages."[34] Like the July 1923 Ukrainian decree, but unlike the April 1925 one, the eastern republics' decrees did not assert the supremacy of the local language, only its equality with Russian. As noted in Chapter 2, in Tatarstan, where Tatars formed a narrow plurality (44.88 percent vs. 43.13 percent Russians), all regions with a Tatar plurality were to use the Tatar language. Central organs were to correspond with these regions in Tatar but otherwise use Russian in their daily work. Most other eastern republics followed the Tatar lead.[35] Only in republics with a small Russian minority, such as in Central Asia, Azerbaijan, Yakutia, and the Komi oblast, was the Tatar plan seen as only a short-term step toward the eventual long-term goal of comprehensive linguistic *korenizatsiia*.[36]

Just as in Ukraine, the difficulty of achieving linguistic *korenizatsiia* was almost comically underestimated and the proposed time frames for shifting to local languages utopian in the extreme. A November 1923 Kazakh decree called for completing the introduction of parallel paperwork in Kazakh in all central government organs in thirteen months (despite a 7.1 percent literacy rate). A December 1924 Uzbek decree called for the same shift at the oblast and central level to be undertaken immediately (3.8 percent literacy). By the end of the 1920s, neither republic could claim even 10 percent of paperwork being conducted in the local language.[37] Most eastern republics also followed Ukraine in creating courses for Russians to study the national language. Yakutia even passed a law, again modeled on that in Ukraine, which threatened to fire all government employees who did not learn the Yakut language.[38] However, these

[33] *GARF* 1235/118/1 (1924): 21–22, 27–60; Durdenevskii, *Ravnopravie iazykov*, 176–177.

[34] Durdenevskii, *Ravnopravie iazykov*, 176–177; 192–195.

[35] Durdenevskii, *Ravnopravie iazykov*, 119–241.

[36] On Uzbekistan and Kazakhstan, see Durdenevskii, *Ravnopravie iazykov*, 135–136; 201–202; On the Komi republic, see Shakhov, "Zyrianizatsiia"; on Yakutia, see *GARF* 1235/122/166 (1926): 34–38; on Central Asia, see *RTsKhIDNI* 62/1/220 (24–27.01.27): 2–52.

[37] Durdenevskii, *Ravnopravie iazykov*, 201–202; *GARF* 374/27s/1707 (1929): 112, 117. *7 vsekazakskaia partiinaia konferentsiia VKP/b/. Stenograficheskii otchet* (Alma-Ata, 1930): 254.

[38] *GARF* 1235/120/101 (1925): 26–260b, 54; 1235/118/1 (1924): 4; *RTsKhIDNI* 17/32/111 (1927): 17.

courses failed to have any impact anywhere, except for sowing a momentary panic among local Russians.[39]

It is difficult to present a reliable picture of the success of these early programs of linguistic *korenizatsiia* because statistics are mostly absent or highly suspect. However, a large number of anecdotal reports suggest that by the end of the 1920s, no eastern republic could boast more than the most minimal use of the national language at either the republican or the regional (oblast/okrug/kanton) level. In the more successful eastern republics—Tatarstan, Chuvashia, Azerbaijan, Kazakhstan, Uzbekistan—the national language was being used in the majority of government organs at the district and village soviet level.[40] Tatarstan undertook by far the most systematic and energetic *korenizatsiia* and for that reason also kept the most reliable statistics. In 1924, the Tatar language was being used in 82 percent of majority Tatar rural soviets and in 45.9 percent of majority Tatar districts. By 1927, these statistics had been improved to 90 percent and 76.9 percent, respectively.[41] Since Tatarstan had the most literate population and by far the most resolute government policy, it is unlikely that any other eastern republic achieved better results.

The pro-*korenizatsiia* forces within the eastern republics quickly realized that the only way to introduce the native language into central republican institutions was through the mass promotion of titular nationals into the central apparat. Therefore, throughout the 1920s and 1930s, Affirmative Action became the overwhelming priority of *korenizatsiia* in the Soviet east. It is important here to note that this focus was the result of the eastern republics' own experience and their judgment (quickly endorsed by the center) that this was the best way to proceed. The center did not force a different policy on the eastern republics. Quite the contrary, the April 1924 VTsIK decree was quite utopian in recommending the Ukrainian model for the Soviet east.

The search for the best strategy to implement Affirmative Action also resulted in a furious bout of experimentation. The first method, which relied on the center's brief period of financial largesse from 1924 to 1926, was a program of national *praktikanstvo* (apprenticeship). In this program, unqualified titular nationals were paid a full government salary while they served as apprentices for white-collar government jobs. The April 1924 VTsIK circular generously authorized national republics to increase their number of employees by up to 10 percent to accommodate these national *praktikanty*.[42] As a result, in 1924, 126 of Turkestan's 1288 central government employees (9.8 percent) were

---

[39] *GARF* 1235/118/1 (1924): 4; see also *RTsKhIDNI* 17/69/60 (1926): 24; 17/32/111 (1927): 17.

[40] On Chuvashia and Kazakhstan, see *GARF* 1235/120/102 (1926): 1–5; also on Kazakhstan, 3316/20/431 (1927): 90; on Azerbaijan, *RTsKhIDNI* 17/17/13 (1927): 144–148; on Uzbekistan, *GARF* 374/27s/1707 (1929): 110–112.

[41] *RTsKhIDNI* 17/33/443 (1925): 27; *GARF* 1235/122/166 (1927): 103–104. Between 1924 and 1927, Tatarstan switched from *volosti* to districts, which were larger. The latter statistic in 1927 is for district executive committees, not *volost'* executive committees.

[42] *GARF* 1235/118/1 (1924): 197.

national *praktikanty*. This made an immediate and massive contribution to *korenizatsiia*. In Turkestan, they represented 46.7 percent of all titular nationals in the Turkestan government. In addition, there were thousands of *praktikanty* at the regional and local levels.[43]

Praktikanty were extremely unpopular with all-union commissariats and economic enterprises since their salaries came out of these institutions' own budgets. According to Turkestan authorities, these enterprises initially "categorically refused to accept *praktikanty*." After they were ordered to do so, they continued to sabotage the program by making work conditions intolerable and treating the *praktikanty* "as a temporary phenomenon, alien, to be eliminated without question in the near future."[44] Russians apprenticing the *praktikanty* naturally resented them as an imminent threat to their jobs. Due primarily to its cost—in 1927, the program cost over a million rubles in Tatarstan—*praktikanstvo* began to be abolished in 1926, the same time the cultural fund was eliminated.[45] By late 1927, it had disappeared entirely.

The period of *praktikanstvo* represented the last time that the center was willing to finance an expansion of the government bureaucracy exclusively to further *korenizatsiia*. Since the government bureaucracy in most eastern republics either did not grow or was curtailed during NEP, *korenizatsiia* involved a direct competition for jobs between Russians and titular nationals. In this competition, the latter were given legal priority. The April 1924 VTsIK decree stated that "in hiring for government employment, when all other conditions are equivalent, preference should be given to persons knowing the local languages."[46] At the republican level, VTsIK's measured favoritism based on language was transformed into a categorical priority based on ethnicity rather than language. In a report on *korenizatsiia*, Kazakhstan boasted that "almost all commissariats, *krai* and *guberniia* institutions have established a rule that for every new opening in the apparat, a Kazakh should first be invited and only when that position cannot be filled by a Kazakh should it be given to a Russian."[47] The North Caucasus Mountaineer obkom gave a directive to all its institutions ordering them "not to accept non-Mountaineers for employment or to hire them only in extreme cases, when there is no qualified Mountaineer."[48] The same rule applied in the case of dismissals. The Turkestan TsIK decreed that during layoffs, natives should be given priority in retaining their jobs.[49]

It was one thing to give preference to local nationalities, but it was another to find even minimally qualified candidates. In the majority of eastern regions,

---

[43] Ibid., 144; *RTsKhIDNI* 17/69/59 (1927): 18.

[44] *RTsKhIDNI* 62/2/489 (1926): 30–31.

[45] *RTsKhIDNI* 17/69/59 (1927): 18, 106; 17/85/206 (1927): 12; 62/2/489 (1926): 44; *GARF* 3316/20/431 (1927): 39.

[46] Durdenevskii, *Ravnopravie iazykov*, 177.

[47] *GARF* 1235/120/101 (1925): 8.

[48] *RTsKhIDNI* 17/33/382 (1924): 1.

[49] *GARF* 1235/118/1 (1923): 137.

the literacy rate in 1926 (see Table 13) was in the single digits, and this figure included many Islamic religious leaders. In 1927, there were reportedly only 960 literate Kirgiz in the entire republic.[50] This desperate situation led Stalin in 1923 to recommend that all members of the national intelligentsia, "up to and including Octobrists," be recruited into the Soviet organs of the eastern republics.[51] In 1927, Zelenskii stated this principle bluntly: "Our chief task is to attract all cultural forces in [Central Asia], regardless of their class position, as long as they are loyal to Soviet power."[52] This was done. Already in 1927, Goloshchekin reported that he had "recruited into the party, soviet, union and economic apparat all the literate and half-literate Kazakhs that we have."[53]

The task of placing titular nationals in the government apparat and the industrial workforce often devolved onto a special *korenizatsiia* commission. Tatarstan again provided the model with its 1922 "Commission on the Realization of the Tatar Language."[54] These commissions were always attached to the republican TsIK and had filials in executive commissions down to the district level.[55] None of the eastern republics formed a party organ to supervise *korenizatsiia* along the Ukrainian model, so *korenizatsiia* remained anchored in soft-line institutions. Theoretically, the *korenizatsiia* commissions were to supervise linguistic *korenizatsiia*, but in practice they confined themselves to two tasks. First, they established yearly *korenizatsiia* plans, which consisted of the number of nationals each government organ must employ by year's end. This was referred to as the "reservation system" or "the method of percentage norms."[56]

Second, the commissions also helped to fulfill those plans by locating all available titular nationals and sending them to the appropriate job openings. One Uzbek official described their *korenizatsiia* commission as "in reality a labor market. Every day twenty to twenty-five comrades show up and ask for work."[57] A Tatar described the work of a local *korenizatsiia* commission as follows: "In our region, we have a representative of the [*korenizatsiia*] commission who goes around to enterprises and says: 'I have a typist. If you need one, take her. She's a Tatar.'"[58] This crude Affirmative Action made the commissions very unpopular. Zelenskii brutally criticized Central Asia's *korenizatsiia* commissions: "One must say, comrades, that there are no more irresponsible institutions than these commissions. It seems there isn't a person who hasn't cursed these commissions for working poorly, for preventing others from working, for a nationalist

[50] *RTsKhIDNI* 62/1/220 (24–27.01.27): 12.
[51] *Tainy natsional'noi politiki*, 102.
[52] *RTsKhIDNI* 62/1/220 (24–27.01.27): 14.
[53] *6-ia vsekazakskaia konferentsiia VKP/b/. Stenograficheskii otchet* (Kzyl-Orda, 1927).
[54] Durdenevskii, *Ravnopravie iazykov*, 190.
[55] For accounts of the Tatar system, see *GARF* 1235/118/1 (1924): 1–5; for the Kazakh system, 1235/120/101 (1925): 5–13; for the Uzbek system, 374/27s/1707 (1929): 110–119.
[56] *GARF* 1235/122/168 (1927): 1250b; *RTsKhIDNI* 17/69/58 (1927): 243; 17/85/206 (1927): 19; Durdenevskii, *Ravnopravie iazykov*, 176–177.
[57] *RTsKhIDNI* 62/3/207 (1927): 30.
[58] *RTsKhIDNI* 17/69/58 (1927): 41.

deviation. . . . Instead of working out ways to introduce local languages into government, when you ask any commission what they have done, they all answer that they sent 117 people [to work]."[59]

Zelenskii cursed the commissions for sending those 117 people, not only because many were unqualified, but because there frequently were no jobs open for those people. This practice, along with unrealistically high *korenizatsiia* quotas in a tight labor market, put pressure on institutions to replace Russians directly with titular nationals. Andreev's Orgburo commission found that such direct replacement of Russians with titular nationals, which it called "mechanical *natsionalizatsiia* by quota," was common in the Soviet east from 1923 to 1926.[60] The Kazakh *korenizatsiia* commission likewise reported in 1924 that "the method of direct replacement of Russian employees with Kazakhs was widely used." In late 1923, Turkestan published a law authorizing the replacement of Russians with qualified natives, stipulating only that the Russians receive the same benefits as those released due to reductions in government size. Buriat-Mongolia kept an identical law through June 1927, and other republics informally engaged in the same practice.[61]

Russians were naturally unhappy with Affirmative Action in general, but it was the direct replacement of Russians with natives that particularly poisoned ethnic relations. At an Azerbaijan party congress, one delegate reported that Russians were saying, "Why did they fire me and replace me with an Azeri? What makes him better than me?"[62] In Kazakhstan, it was reported that Russians were being given "a certificate that they were fired 'as a result of korenizatsiia' [and they] spread their understandable discontent among other employees."[63] Quite frequently Russians became upset because of the complete lack of tact used in implementing *korenizatsiia*. The OGPU reported that Russians were "upset about Tatarization" because the head of the Tatar department of the State Bank refused their applications with the answer that "we need Tatars first of all and can do without Russians."[64]

In Uzbekistan, the OGPU opened letters of Russians writing to their relatives in the RSFSR in order to monitor popular mood. Letters intercepted in February–March 1928 expressed resentment toward *korenizatsiia* and hatred toward Uzbeks[65]:

"I am poor and unemployed and it is difficult to find work. And when there is work, then it goes mostly to the indigenous population, that is the Uzbeks, and our brother, the European, although dying of hunger, gets paid no attention."

[59] *RTsKhIDNI* 62/1/220 (24–27.01.27): 32.
[60] *RTsKhIDNI* 17/113/336 (07.10.27): 149/1, 20.
[61] *GARF* 1235/120/101 (1924): 8; 1235/118/1 (1923): 137, 597; *RTsKhIDNI* 17/113/298 (03.06.27): 118/10, 103; 17/113/193 (10.05.26): 27/1, 48.
[62] *RTsKhIDNI* 17/17/13 (25.08–19.11.27): 185.
[63] *RTsKhIDNI* 17/69/61 (1927): 17.
[64] *RTsKhIDNI* 17/87/196 (1925): 288.
[65] *RTsKhIDNI* 62/2/1349 (1928): 103–107; 62/2/1350 (1928): 46–47.

"It's difficult to live here. All jobs are taken by the Uzbeks and it is difficult for Russians to find work."

"In Central Asia now, it is hard for Russians to get work and in two to three years it will be impossible. They are implementing complete *natsionalizatsiia*."

"They just passed a law on the firm implementation of *Uzbekizatsiia*, that is the replacement of Russian employees with native Uzbeks."

"I am living and working among Uzbeks for the first time and it is in general difficult. National hatred exists in a sharp form."

At the exact same time, in March 1928, a group of workers wrote a letter to the Central Asian Biuro, which was discussed at a meeting of its *korenizatsiia* commission[66]:

> In every republic "their letters" and "their language" are being introduced . . . so the question arises: "where will the Russians go? Where will Russians work?" . . . with the implementation of *Uzbekization* in our institutions, there is no question that all Russians will be replaced with Uzbeks—that is a fact . . . one often hears discontent among employees and workers who have been fired in large numbers in connection with *korenizatsiia* . . . there is no question that our government considers that all Russians, whether they want to or not, will have to go to Russia, in connection with *korenizatsiia* and Uzbekization, Russians will be forced to flee to Russia . . . already from Uzbeks one often hears "that this is our country, not yours."

The letter concluded by asking what measures the government was going to take and where all the Russians would go once Uzbekization was completed.

It is very instructive to compare these extreme sentiments with an investigation carried out by Rabkrin in 1929 on the implementation of Uzbekization. This investigation concluded that serious work on Uzbekization had not begun until late 1928 and that the series of decrees passed from 1923 to 1928 had largely "a declarative character."[67] As Table 14 illustrates, the investigation also found that from August 1925 to April 1928 the number of "major local nationalities" (Uzbeks, Turkmen, Kirgiz, Tajiks) in the central Uzbek government and economic organs dropped precipitously both in absolute terms and especially as a percentage of the total workforce. Given these statistics, how does one explain the widespread Russian anger and even panic over Uzbekization?

One could cite at least five factors that appear to have contributed to this situation and all are valid for other eastern republics as well. First, the Soviet government constantly promised much more than it could possibly deliver in its "declarative" *korenizatsiia* decrees. This helped sow panic. Second, a small

[66] *RTsKhIDNI* 62/2/1262 (1928): 2–3.
[67] *GARF* 374/27s/1707 (1929): 113.

Table 14. Major Local Nationalities (MLN) Employed in Central Uzbek Government and Economic Organs, 1925–1928

Date	Central Government Organs			Central Economic Organs		
	MLN Employees	Total Employees	MLN Percent of Total	MLN Employees	Total Employees	MLN Percent of Total
August 1925	238	1253	19.0	623	1844	33.8
February 1926	254	1412	18.0	392	1766	22.2
September 1927	195	1160	16.8	135	1047	12.9
March 1928	227	1414	16.1	199	1310	15.2
April 1928	211	1741	12.1	161	1064	15.1

GARF 374/27s/1707 (1929): 108–109.

number of tactless incidents involving the direct replacement of Russians with titular nationals helped poison ethnic relations. Third, Affirmative Action often causes a disproportionate degree of ethnic resentment. When one unqualified Uzbek received a job, hundreds of Russians felt themselves cheated although only one would have actually gotten the job. Fourth, many eastern nationalities did view *korenizatsiia* literally as decolonization and, as the intercepted letters indicated, began to treat Russians as a temporary and unwanted presence. As the former dominant nationality, Russians strongly resented their loss in status. Fifth, in most cases the local Russian population supported the Bolsheviks during the civil war, whereas the native population was at best neutral. Therefore, Russians felt they had been cheated when the fruits of the revolution went to the local population: "When we Russians fought and made our support known, the Buriats did nothing. Now they are given all the advantages."[68]

Functional *Korenizatsiia*, 1926 to 1928

The period from 1923 to 1926 marked an experimental period as the eastern republics shifted from linguistic *korenizatsiia* to *praktikanstvo*, then to the quota system, and even the direct replacement of Russians by titular nationals. The year 1926 marked the beginning of a reevaluation of these *korenizatsiia* strategies, both in the center and in the eastern republics. Central support did not waver. It was reiterated by the soft-line soviet organs, such as TsIK's Soviet of Nationalities and VTsIK's Nationalities Department, as well as by major hard-line party organs, such as TsK's Cadres Department and the Orgburo. From 1924 to 1929, the Orgburo repeatedly heard reports from the first party secretaries of various national regions, during which

[68] *RTsKhIDNI* 17/87/201 (1927): 140.

korenizatsiia was discussed. The resulting TsK resolutions consistently called for more rapid implementation of *korenizatsiia*.[69] I have already mentioned the 1926–1927 Orgburo *korenizatsiia* commission, which also unreservedly backed the policy and endorsed measures for its further implementation.[70] Moreover, both Kaganovich and Molotov, who along with Kosior chaired Orgburo sessions from 1924 to 1930, personally endorsed *korenizatsiia* during these sessions.[71]

Although the center consistently supported *korenizatsiia*, it was vague in its instructions on how to implement it: What level of local representation in government organs was sufficient? Should it be their percentage of the republic's total population? A simple majority? A significant visible presence? To what extent should national languages be utilized in government? Should the goal be comprehensive linguistic *korenizatsiia*, as in Ukraine, or only the use of native languages to service the local population, as in Tatarstan? In practice, aggressive republics such as Ukraine, Tatarstan, and Kazakhstan initiated programs to implement *korenizatsiia*, and the center contested these actions when their results displeased it. Although a certain degree of Russian resentment was accepted as necessary, this was the outcome that in general most displeased central authorities. Thus, while the center did not contest absolute preferences for nationals in hiring, it consistently rejected the firing of Russians in order to replace them with titular nationals. The Orgburo categorically denounced a Buriat law authorizing this practice. The Andreev commission likewise censured this practice, labeling it "mechanical" *korenizatsiia*.[72]

Russian resentment was a major concern of the 1926 reevaluation, but it was not the only one. In the Soviet Union, titular nationals did not encounter a "glass ceiling" that prevented them from reaching leadership positions; instead, as Table 15 shows, the problem was a "hole in the middle." This pattern disturbed both the Andreev commission and the leadership of the eastern republics, since titular nationals were most poorly represented in exactly those positions that processed government paperwork, which meant that linguistic *korenizatsiia* remained a distant goal. Also, many of the trained professionals

---

[69] *RTsKhIDNI* 17/112/531 (14.04.24): 87/3; 17/112/691 (31.08.25): 105/1; 105/2; 17/112/699 (28.09.25): 112/1; 112/2; 17/112/715 (30.11.25): 125/1; 17/113/193 (10.05.26): 27/1; 17/113/270 (04.03.27): 95/1; 17/113/301 (14.06.27): 121/1; 17/113/305 (27.06.27): 125/1; 17/113/656 (10.09.28): 63/2; 17/113/669 (15.10.28): 73/1; 17/113 (08.05.29): 117/1; 17/113/756 (22.07.29): 138/1.

[70] For the main materials of the Andreev commission, see *RTsKhIDNI* 17/69/58 (1926–1927); 17/85/206 (1926–1927): 17/114/336 (07.10.27): 6–148.

[71] For instance, during an August 1925 discussion of a report by the Crimean obkom secretary, Molotov said: "One cannot agree with comrade Kalinin's judgement that there has only been a technical improvement in the work of the Soviet apparat. In this area much has been done to attract new workers, to shift the language of government [to Tatar] in the local apparat. Here we have a definite plus in the work of the obkom." *RTsKhIDNI* 17/112/691 (31.08.25): 159. During an October 1928 discussion of a report by the Votskii obkom first secretary, Kaganovich remarked: "Let us take the nationalities policy . . . a leadership of local workers is more or less in place. This is an enormous accomplishment. But it is not enough. One must widen the cadres of local workers loyal to the Party and Soviet power." *RTsKhIDNI* 17/113/669 (15.10.28): 136.

[72] *RTsKhIDNI* 17/113/298 (03.06.27): 118/10; 17/113/336 (07.10.27): 20.

Table 15. Employment Pattern of Titular Nationals, 1925–1926
(Titular Nationalities as Percent of Total Employees)

Job Category	Tatarstan	Bashkiria	Uzbekistan
1. Leadership	19.6	14.8	35.0
2. Technical	13.7	5.0	13.0
3. Menial	21.9	5.4	26.0
4. Total	17.0	n/a	n/a

GARF 1235/122/166 (1927): 105; GARF 1235/122/168 (1927): 590b;
RTsKhIDNI 17/85/206 (1926): 9.

who had the most contact with the "national masses"—agronomists, surveyors, veterinarians, doctors—were overwhelmingly Russian.[73] This contradicted the principle that *korenizatsiia* should make the non-Russian masses feel that the Soviet government was their own.

This situation was partially blamed on the system of setting quotas for the percentage of titular nationals that must be employed in each institution but not specifying what jobs they should hold. Both Kazakh and Tatar officials maintained that institutions were fulfilling their quotas by hiring "cleaning women, doormen, guards and coachmen [*kuchery*]."[74] This led to the popular anecdote in Tatarstan that the government "was not carrying out *korenizatsiia* but *kucherizatsiia*."[75] Alongside the appointment of nationals to menial jobs, there was a corresponding tendency to place them in high-visibility leadership positions, especially electoral posts, as Table 16 demonstrates. Affirmative Action programs for elected positions were the easiest to fulfill because the job required no particular qualifications. Many republics set specific ethnic quotas for all their elections.[76]

The tendency to place titular nationals in leadership positions, where they supervised a largely Russian technical apparat, caused concern in the center for at least three reasons.[77] First, because many of the newly promoted nationals had little expertise, it would be easy for non-party specialists to control them. This was a particular concern in Uzbekistan, where, according to one report, in the Kokand oblast agricultural department both the head and deputy head were newly promoted Uzbeks: "However, it turned out that neither the head nor his deputy managed work. Neither of them even had a desk or chair where they could sit. . . . in reality, the boss of the state land fund was a non-Party specialist who directed all work."[78] Similarly, in an intercepted letter, a Russian

---

[73] RTsKhIDNI 17/69/59 (1926): 6; 17/69/61 (1926): 6–9; 17/69/60 (1926): 132–136; 17/17/12 (28–29.05.27): 148–149.

[74] RTsKhIDNI 17/69/61 (1926): 16; 17/69/60 (1926): 46.

[75] RTsKhIDNI 17/85/58 (1926): 36.

[76] *Stenograficheskii otchet zasedanii XI oblastnoi partiinoi konferentsii* (Kazan, 1925): 344.

[77] RTsKhIDNI 17/113/336 (07.10.27): 149/1, 19.

[78] RTsKhIDNI 62/2/489 (1926): 100b.

Table 16. Representation of Titular Nationals in Elected Soviet Organs, 1927

	Village	Volost'	Uezd	TsIK	Percent of Total Population
Bashkir ASSR	25.9	29.4	34.7	34.7	23.7
Buriat-Mongol ASSR	50.8	47.6	55.1	49.1	43.8
Dagestan ASSR	67.4	n/a	56.0	n/a	61.8
Kazakh ASSR	59.9	62.5	n/a	n/a	57.1
Karelian ASSR	49.6	45.0	38.7	36.4	37.4
Kirgiz ASSR	73.1	66.7	55.2	50.0	66.6
Crimean ASSR	37.4	n/a	n/a	29.3	25.1
Tatar ASSR	51.9	52.8	55.2	52.4	44.9
Chuvash ASSR	77.8	77.6	68.2	78.3	74.6
Yakut ASSR	92.9	81.2	71.1	69.4	85.1

Natsional'nyi sostav vybornykh organov vlasti RSFSR v 1927 g. (Moscow, 1928), 56–66.

author wrote: "Here the chairman and other managers are all Sarts [a pejorative term for Central Asians], but the specialists and all the technical workers are Russians, who understand more. So [the Central Asians] hide behind the Russians' backs and earn a good salary."[79] On the one hand, this was a national version of the traditional Red/expert problem. On the other hand, it also echoes a phenomenon found in other countries practicing Affirmative Action. For example, in Malaysia, where Malay-owned businesses receive preferential treatment, there are businesses known as Ali-Baba enterprises in which a Malay (Ali) is paid to front as the formal owner, but a Chinese (Baba) in reality owns and runs the enterprise.[80]

Another concern was the tendency of titular nationals to assert their positive right to leadership positions rather than accepting them in a spirit of proper gratitude and humility. Russians repeatedly complained that every national wanted to be a people's commissar (*narkom*): "As soon as a [national] gets a little education, now he considers he's ready to be a *narkom* and you can't assign him to bureaucratic work."[81] Local Georgians spoke the same way about the Ajars: "All Ajars want to become a *narkom*."[82] Comments such as these represented a popular prejudice that the eastern nationalities were lazy and spoiled and that they were exploiting *korenizatsiia* strategically rather than embracing it sincerely: "They know that they are Uzbeks, that they got their jobs through *korenizatsiia*, and therefore [they say:] 'I can make more mistakes and do less work than others.' A number of employees have this sense of irresponsibility." If challenged, they could respond like one Tatar who, when Russians

[79] *RTsKhIDNI* 62/2/1349 (1928): 300b.

[80] Donald L. Horowitz, *Ethnic Groups in Conflict* (Berkeley CA, 1985): 666.

[81] *RTsKhIDNI* 17/69/58 (1926): 25. For the same complaint in Azerbaijan, see *RTsKhIDNI* 17/17/12 (28–29.05.27): 173.

[82] *GARF* 374/27s/1483 (1929): 44.

threatened not to elect him, said "elect [me] or else you are a great power chauvinist."[83]

These were only the most cynical manifestations of the general phenomenon of strategic ethnicity. Non-Russians, many of whom lacked an education and were not literate in Russian, were mobilizing one of their only sources of social capital. Bolshevik authorities, however, tended to view this behavior as selfish or nationalist, even though it was their own policy that had provided the social capital. It was a rare and perceptive Bolshevik, such as the first party secretary of the Central Asian Biuro, Zelenskii, who in January 1927 could describe this process calmly and accurately[84]:

> Our local *intelligent* is less educated, has fewer cultural skills and is less well prepared for work in the government apparat. He wants to get ahead. If he is a Communist, he has an advantage and this explains to a large degree the movement of the [local] intelligentsia into our Party. But if he is not a Communist— how can he get ahead up the ladder of government service? Either he must work like a European, or he can bring up some other issue which will give him an advantage over the European. Therefore he puts forward the indigenous nationalities issue. This source of nationalism is only beginning to appear and the more we have a [local] intelligentsia, the stronger this source will begin to pressure us.

However, while accurately understanding the phenomenon, even Zelenskii interpreted this strategic use of ethnicity as a form of nationalism. As we shall see in Chapter 6, Kaganovich came to a similar conclusion at the same time in Ukraine. This growing interpretation of *korenizatsiia* as strengthening both nationalism and interethnic conflict would gradually undermine support for the policy.

Finally, in addition to this vague concern about the growth of nationalism, the center was also worried about the use of *korenizatsiia* in local factional struggles within the Communist Party. Factionalism was much worse in the national republics than in the Russian regions and worst of all in the eastern national republics. The party in non-Russian regions frequently divided along ethnic lines. Usually a Russian faction, allied with a minority national faction, was pitted against a majority national faction. In this situation, *korenizatsiia* could be used to place political allies and dependents in positions of power: "Kazakhization is sometimes used in support of factional considerations."[85] Along with Crimea and Tatarstan, Kazakhstan was one of the republics most plagued by factionalism.[86] In 1925, the same year Kaganovich was sent to

---

[83] *2 plenum oblastnogo komiteta VKP/b/ Tatarskoi respubliki II sozyva. Stenograficheskii otchet* (Kazan, 1926): 16–17.

[84] *RTsKhIDNI* 62/2/220 (24–27.01.27): 35.

[85] *5-aia vsekazakskaia konferentsiia*, 17.

[86] On Tatarstan, see *RTsKhIDNI* 17/112/535 (06.05.24): 91/3; 17/112/700 (12.10.25): 113/1; *7-aia oblastnaia partiinaia konferentsiia Tatrespubliki. Stenograficheskii otchet* (Kazan, 1923);

Ukraine, Stalin removed the Kazakh national communist Khodzhanov and sent the old Bolshevik Filipp Goloshchekin to Kazakhstan. Like Kaganovich, Goloshchekin's job was to manage *korenizatsiia* so that it would not be a source of political discord.

Goloshchekin immediately set out to replace the discredited strategy of "mechanical *korenizatsiia*" with a new policy, which he introduced in May 1926 under the "slogan of functional *korenizatsiia*."[87] Following Kaganovich, Goloshchekin also informed the recipients that henceforth the party must consider the implementation of *korenizatsiia* their own business. Functional *korenizatsiia* involved four changes in policy. First, general quotas would be replaced with a list of specific jobs (a *nomenklatura*) to be fulfilled. These jobs would theoretically be those most necessary for supporting linguistic Kazakhization and to servicing the Kazakh masses. Second, the criteria for holding these jobs would not be ethnicity, whether one is Kazakh, but mastery of the Kazakh language. Third, *praktikanstvo* would be abolished and replaced with specialized short-term courses. Fourth, the Kazakh *korenizatsiia* commission would be abolished and supervision for *korenizatsiia*, again following Ukraine's example, would be transferred to Rabkrin.[88]

Goloshchekin made perfectly clear that the reason for the switch to functional *korenizatsiia* was Russian resentment. In his letter, he wrote: "The mechanical replacement of Europeans with Kazakhs . . . provokes a sharpening of interethnic conflict. Fired Russians . . . carry their understandable discontent to other employees, who are not guaranteed from a similar fate." Moreover, the employees' mood influences "the mood of the union masses, [who say] '*korenizatsiia* equals privileges for Kazakhs,' 'Kazakhstan is for the Kazakhs,' 'we need to move away from here.'"[89] Since ethnic conflict was both ubiquitous and severe in the factories of Kazakhstan and Central Asia, this latter point was a major concern. Functional *korenizatsiia* addressed Russian resentment in two ways. First, it limited the number of jobs where *korenizatsiia* applied, in particular the leadership positions held by influential Russian communists. Second, Russians in a *nomenklatura* position could keep their jobs as long as they learned the Kazakh language. Of course, Goloshchekin did not really expect more than a handful of Russians to learn Kazakh.[90] However, it was psychologically helpful to replace crude ethnic preferences with preferences based on a real skill: mastery of the indigenous language.

Stenograficheskii otchet IX oblastnoi konferentsii tatarsk. organizatsii RKP/b/ (Kazan, 1924); on Kazakhstan, see *5-aia vsekazakskaia konferentsiia*; RTsKhIDNI 17/85/77 (1926).

[87] *RTsKhIDNI* 17/69/61 (1926): 14–23. This was the first mention I found of the policy in the central archives.

[88] Ibid., 16–20.

[89] Ibid., 17.

[90] *RTsKhIDNI* 17/69/61 (1926): 138; 17/69/60 (1926): 24. In practice, the switch to functional *korenizatsiia* produced a brief surge in Russians' studying the native language, then a sudden collapse. *RTsKhIDNI* 17/69/61 (1926): 133–134; *GARF* 3316/20/431 (1927): 88.

Functional *korenizatsiia* also addressed the perceived failure up to then in preparing technical workers, since most of the nomenklatura jobs fell into that category. In Kazakhstan, the republican-level *nomenklatura* consisted of 1036 jobs, only 158 of which were occupied with Kazakh-speakers. In all of Kazakhstan, there were 13,000 *nomenklatura* positions, with 2300 held by Kazakhs.[91] The functional *korenizatsiia* plan called for a variety of courses, ranging from six months to two years, to train Kazakh-speakers (in practice, Kazakhs) to fill these 10,700 open *nomenklatura* positions. A TsIK investigation soon reported that there were "courses everywhere and in all places."[92] The functional system also had the advantage of recognizing, as Zelenskii put it, that "we do not have limitless resources."[93] Comprehensive *korenizatsiia* as practiced in Ukraine and Belorussia simply was not feasible anywhere in the east.

Goloshchekin's new policy met with initial resistance. He wrote a detailed letter to Stalin outlining five new policies he had adopted, one being functional *korenizatsiia*. He received a terse answer: "Comrade Goloshchekin! I think the policy outlined in this letter is in general the only correct policy. I. Stalin."[94] With approval from Stalin and later official endorsement by the Andreev commission, functional *korenizatsiia* spread rapidly to the other major eastern republics in the period from 1926 to 1927.[95] It is difficult to judge the success of functional *korenizatsiia* since the years from 1926 to 1928 were particularly difficult ones for republican governments. A massive reduction in the size of the government bureaucracies in the Soviet Union's autonomous republics and oblasts was undertaken in 1927.[96] In the summer of 1927, the number of individuals employed by the Soviet Union's twenty-three autonomous republics and oblasts was reduced by 26.5 percent, from 15,398 to 11,249. Kazakhstan lost 390 jobs (39.1 percent) and Tatarstan 782 (25.2 percent).[97] Theoretically, titular nationals were favored during these reductions. However, Tatarstan and Bashkiria reported reduced tempos of *korenizatsiia*.[98] Uzbekistan likewise saw the percentage of Uzbeks in the central government apparat drop from 18.0 percent to 16.8 percent and in the central economic apparat from 22.8 percent to 12.9 percent.[99]

Functional *korenizatsiia*, then, was more important as evidence of Soviet concern about Russian resentment than for its dramatic effect on the implementation of *korenizatsiia*. The success of *korenizatsiia* was much more closely linked to patterns in overall government hiring. As Table 17 nicely indicates, the

[91] *RTsKhIDNI* 17/85/206 (1927): 20; *6-ia vsekazakskaia konferentsiia*, 292–293.

[92] *GARF* 3316/20/431 (1927): 27, 89.

[93] *RTsKhIDNI* 62/2/220 (24–27.01.27): 10.

[94] *6-ia vsekazakskaia konferentsiia*, 90–95.

[95] *GARF* 1235/122/168 (1927): 57–60; 3316/19/852 (1926): 1–5; *RTsKhIDNI* 17/32/111 (1927): 25–26; 17/113/335 (07.10.27): 149/1; 62/1/220 (24–27.01.27): 2–49; *SU Tatarskoi respubliki*, no. 11 (1927): 153–159.

[96] On these reductions, see *GARF* (TsGA) 406/11/1005 (1927): 1–49.

[97] *XV s"ezd*, 413.

[98] *RTsKhIDNI* 17/69/58 (1927): 182; *GARF* 1235/122/168 (1927): 570b.

[99] *RTsKhIDNI* 62/2/1743 (1929): 44–45.

Table 17. Tatars in Central Tatarstan Government Apparat, 1921–1930

Year	Tatar (Percent)	Year	Tatar (Percent)
1921	7.8	1926	17.0
1922	8.9	1927	16.6
1923	9.7	1928	19.7
1924	14.0	1929	24.6
1925	16.8	1930	35.4

GARF 1235/122/40 (1925): 24; *RTsKhIDNI* 17/33/443 (1925): 290b.

number of Tatars in Tatarstan's government apparat grew steadily from 1921 to 1925 when the government apparat was expanding, leveled off from 1925 to 1927 when it was contracting, and surged again during the expansion of the socialist offensive.

The second major factor constraining *korenizatsiia* was the availability of trained cadres and professionals. The Bolsheviks preferred to recruit government employees from two sources: the proletariat and institutions of higher education. In the eastern republics in the early 1920s, there was virtually no native proletariat and an extremely small native presence in higher education. The Bolsheviks set out to correct this situation through aggressive Affirmative Action in industrial hiring and in higher education. In the following sections, I analyze these programs and their social impact, considering as well the enormous impact of the cultural revolution on Affirmative Action in the Soviet east.

Affirmative Action and Ethnic Conflict in the Industrial Workplace

The 1923 nationalities policy decrees placed great emphasis on the creation of a national proletariat in the Soviet east.[100] If there had been a gaping divide between the Russian proletariat and Ukrainian peasantry that led to "the cruel lesson of 1919" in Ukraine, an even more severe divide existed in Central Asia and Kazakhstan, where the Bolsheviks had relied almost exclusively on Russian settlers and railway workers.[101] The antinational, often overtly racist, policies of the first Bolshevik governments in Turkestan greatly exacerbated the Central Asian Basmachi rebellion.[102] As noted in Chapter 2, the center took decisive measures in 1921 with a radical land reform that transferred land from Russian settlers to the local peasantry. The national

[100] *Dvenadtsatyi s"ezd*, 693–695; *Tainy natsional'noi politiki*, 283.
[101] Alexander G. Park, *Bolshevism in Turkestan, 1917–1927* (New York, 1957), 3–58; Richard Pipes, *The Formation of the Soviet Union* (2nd ed., New York, 1980), 172–184.
[102] Baymirza Hayit, *"Basmatschi"* (Köln, 1992).

peasantry could be placated, but a national proletariat had to be created. As late as December 1926, there were still only 81 Tajik factory workers, 139 Kirgiz, 306 Turkmen, 2215 Kazakh, 7684 Uzbeks, and a grand total of 7 Yakut proletarians.[103] The 1921 and 1923 nationalities policy decrees promised to transfer factories from the central Russian regions to Central Asia but, as we have seen, under the constraints of NEP this program was quietly abandoned. Only with the first five-year plan would there be a substantial expansion of industry in the Soviet Union's eastern national regions. This meant that local authorities had to rely on aggressive use of Affirmative Action hiring in a tight labor market.

The use of Affirmative Action in the proletarian sphere was one of the most controversial aspects of the Soviet nationalities policy for both practical and ideological reasons. In Ukraine, Affirmative Action was not used for proletarian hiring due to Stalin's concern that it would provoke ethnic strife within Ukraine's politically valuable proletariat. Transcaucasian Bolsheviks, because of the horrendous ethnic violence of the revolutionary years, were extremely reluctant to use Affirmative Action in industry.[104] Ordzhonikidze went so far as to state that "among workers there can be no differences in nationality."[105] Many Bolsheviks agreed with Ordzhonikidze that *korenizatsiia* might be fine for bureaucrats (especially non-party ones), but the proletariat was a purely international group and so Affirmative Action in industry was inadmissible on ideological grounds alone. Most learned to hold their tongues, but not Mikhail Kalinin, who, to the distress of his colleagues, did not firmly grasp the new Soviet nationalities policy and frequently expressed his heterodox views publicly. At the first Uzbekistan party congress, Kalinin said that "the national question is purely a peasant question . . . the best way to eliminate nationality is a massive factory with thousands of workers . . . , which like a millstone grinds up all nationalities and forges a new nationality. This nationality is the universal proletariat."[106]

Despite these ideological and pragmatic concerns, Affirmative Action was practiced in industrial hiring throughout the Soviet east. Kazakhstan instituted a "system of preferences for Kazakh workers in all hiring and firing decisions."[107] In Central Asia, local nationalities were legally given "advantages in registration at labor markets, in hiring and in dismissals."[108] Such preferential treatment in hiring was known to and accepted by the all-union TsK and TsKK.[109] Nor was Affirmative Action confined to national republics. In 1928, the North Caucasus region initiated a five-year plan to recruit a thousand Mountaineers

---

[103] Calculated from *Natsional'naia politika v tsifrakh*, 126–128.

[104] *RTsKhIDNI* 17/17/12 (28–29.05.27): 227; 17/17/30 (06–14.03.29): 64–65.

[105] *III-i s"ezd kommunisticheskikh organizatsii Zakavkaz'ia. Stenograficheskii otchet* (Tiflis, 1924), 32.

[106] *RTsKhIDNI* 78/1/149 (1925): 109.

[107] *RTsKhIDNI* 17/69/61 (1926): 6.

[108] *RTsKhIDNI* 17/24/15 (09.09.28): 170/3.

[109] *GARF* 374/27s/1708 (1929): 35; *RTsKhIDNI* 17/113/725 (08.05.29): 725/1, 98.

a year into factories in Rostov and other major North Caucasus cities.[110] Such programs existed in other Russian regions as well, such as Moscow, which had a plan to recruit five thousand Gypsies into the city's factories.[111] Affirmative Action quotas emerged shortly after 1923 and continued openly through 1933.

As with the *korenizatsiia* of the government bureaucracy, Affirmative Action in industrial hiring also frequently involved the direct replacement of Russians with titular nationals. Kazakhstan noted the widespread "method of the mechanical introduction of Kazakhs into industry by firing other nationalities and replacing them with Kazakhs."[112] In Uzbekistan, the *korenizatsiia* commission sent seventy Uzbeks to a factory "with the recommendation to hire them, and if there weren't enough places, to lay off Europeans."[113] Buriat-Mongolia legally sanctioned such replacements.[114] The OGPU reported that Russian workers were enraged at the unions for permitting this and quoted a Russian worker: "If they fire me and hire a Buriat in my place, I'll kill that Buriat first of all, and then they can do with me as they please."[115] A TsK investigation found such direct replacements were common and that as a result, "Russian workers have become embittered against Soviet power and against the unions."[116] The Andreev commission condemned the replacement of Russians but did not call for abandoning the quota system since functional *korenizatsiia* made no sense for the hiring of unskilled industrial workers.[117]

Unsurprisingly, such crude Affirmative Action greatly exacerbated ethnic conflict in Kazakhstan and Central Asia. It was, of course, not the sole or even primary cause. The ethnic mixing of previously segregated populations typically brings an upsurge in ethnic conflict.[118] Moreover, as we have seen, in the early and mid-1920s violent rural ethnic conflict in Central Asia and Kazakhstan, as well as in regions of Buriat-Mongolia and Bashkiria, was ubiquitous and severe. As peasants entered the labor force, much of this ethnic conflict would naturally migrate to the cities. Through 1926, OGPU political reports on ethnic conflict highlighted rural ethnic conflict.[119] In 1927, rural ethnic conflict began to decline and the Central Asian OGPU reports began to emphasize "growing interethnic hostility based on the battle for work."[120] From 1927 onward, the factory (and labor market) became the predominant site for ethnic conflict in the Soviet Union.

[110] U., "Formiruetsia natsional'nyi proletariat," *Revoliutsiia i gorets*, nos. 11–12 (1929): 64–66.

[111] S. Abramov, *Natsional'naia rabota sovetov v gorodakh* (Moscow, 1935): 14.

[112] *RTsKhIDNI* 17/69/61 (1926): 6.

[113] *RTsKhIDNI* 17/85/206 (1929): 5.

[114] *RTsKhIDNI* 17/113/298 (03.06.27): 118/10.

[115] *RTsKhIDNI* 17/87s/201 (1927): 83.

[116] *RTsKhIDNI* 17/113/298 (03.06.27): 118/10, 102.

[117] *RTsKhIDNI* 17/113/336 (07.10.27): 149/1, 92.

[118] Horowitz, *Ethnic Groups in Conflict*, 95–140.

[119] *RTsKhIDNI* 17/87/196–200a (1925–1926); 62/2/535–536 (1926).

[120] *RTsKhIDNI* 62/2/882 (1927): 5.

The Tashkent labor market provides an excellent case study of the relationship between ethnic conflict and *korenizatsiia*. The deputy head of the Tashkent labor market, Valikhodzhaev, was an uncompromising and untactful *korenizatsiia* militant. For instance, in March 1927, in the presence of two hundred unemployed on the floor of the labor market, Valikhodzhaev objected to Russians being sent to a job site and screamed: "Send Uzbeks, the indigenous population, if you won't send Uzbeks, I'll complain to the obkom." On another day, a sign was hung on the door to the labor market: "Uzbek workers needed." On still another occasion, in February 1928, when the labor market had given a paper to a Russian woman for a position as a cleaning lady at the Commissariat of Trade, Valikhodzhaev took it and gave it to an Uzbek women and said: "I'm sending her as part of *korenizatsiia* and that's it."[121]

On several occasions, such behavior led to incidents, including ethnic brawls, on the floor of the labor market. For instance, in April 1927, a representative of the Tashkent oblast *korenizatsiia* commission arrived at the market and publicly announced that he needed "only members of the indigenous nationality" for a new job. The unemployed "Europeans" started to yell: "What are the Russians supposed to do, or do they not want to eat? Russians fought and won freedom for you devils, and now you say Uzbeks are the masters [*khoziaeva*] in Uzbekistan. There will come a time and we'll show you. We'll beat the hell out of all of you." The Uzbeks replied: "Just wait, it won't be long until we'll ask all you Europeans to go back to your homeland [*rodina*] and find work there." The GPU agent reported that the mood was tense and the outnumbered Uzbeks fled.[122] On another occasion, in February 1928, the unemployed Russians and Uzbeks did come to blows[123]:

> On the floor of the market a fight broke out between the Uzbeks and Russians due to national hostility. The Uzbeks declared they would soon drive the Russians out of Uzbekistan since they would soon have their own specialists and because the Russians always try to drive the Uzbeks out of their jobs. The Russians said that during the revolution the Uzbeks were *Basmachi* and now they are sneaking into power. Due to this [exchange] a fight broke out which was liquidated by the militia.

Fights broke out at the labor market on many other occasions as well.[124]

Valikhodzhaev's provocative behavior was partially explained by the bitter resistance he encountered in attempting to implement *korenizatsiia*. Russian enterprise directors frequently returned the Uzbeks he sent them. The director of a bottle factory returned nine Uzbek women "on the grounds that Uzbek women don't know how to wash bottles."[125] Moreover, the GPU took seri-

---

[121] *RTsKhIDNI* 62/2/881 (1927): 105; 62/2/1351 (1928): 29; 62/2/1349 (1928): 94.

[122] *RTsKhIDNI* 62/2/881 (1927): 125.

[123] *RTsKhIDNI* 62/2/1351 (1928): 191.

[124] *RTsKhIDNI* 62/2/881 (1927): 105.

[125] *RTsKhIDNI* 62/2/883 (1927): 21–22.

ously threats by unemployed Russians "to beat [Valikhodzhaev] mercilessly" for implementing *korenizatsiia*.[126] In mid-1927, the GPU was also concerned about threats of the unemployed to raise "the black flag" and attack the labor market.[127] This was not implausible. In 1928, in the town of Sergiopol in Kazakhstan, unemployed Russians and Russian workers from the Turksib railway construction site went on a rampage, beating Kazakhs (over fifty were injured) and sacking the town's GPU headquarters in order to free comrades who had been arrested during previous ethnic brawls. Although the rioters were brutally punished, such pressure from unemployed Russians seeking work in Kazakhstan was a major reason the Turksib construction administration failed to fill its Kazakh quota.[128] The same situation prevailed in Central Asia. A 1926 Uzbek report noted that "on the [Tashkent] labor market, unemployed Europeans arriving from the RSFSR gather and under their pressure, the labor market fails to hold to a correct political line on the nationalities policy."[129] Russian threats and actual acts of violence were often spontaneous outbursts in the face of what they perceived to be the gross injustice of *korenizatsiia*, but violence could also be a calculated form of resistance. At a mill in Kazakhstan, the GPU reported the following comment: "They will probably fire some of the Russian workers and replace them with Kazakhs. If this happens, we'll give the Kazakhs a good whipping and that way we'll put a fright into them and others."[130]

The ubiquitous politics surrounding *korenizatsiia* had the effect of turning every hiring and firing decision into a political event. At a butter factory in Turkmenistan, two Turkmen workers got in a fight and both were fired. The remaining Turkmen asserted this was an excuse to replace them with Russians.[131] After the dismissal of an Uzbek at a wine factory, Uzbek workers began a strike with the demand of "real Uzbekization."[132] Ethnic conflict, then, was not confined to the unemployed. Fights were common in the factories as well. Much of this conflict was also related to fear of losing jobs. In particular, attempts to apprentice Central Asians to Russians proved futile. As Zelenskii noted, the Russian view was that "I'm here today and tomorrow you'll drive me away, so the hell with you. You can spend as much time with me as you please and I won't teach you more than how to shovel coal."[133]

However, it would be a gross exaggeration to attribute ethnic conflict to Affirmative Action and employment concerns alone. In fact, ethnic conflict increased after 1929 when the first five-year plan had eliminated unemployment and created a labor shortage. Ethnic conflict usually involves not only competition over employment and other benefits, but also a symbolic battle over status

[126] *RTsKhIDNI* 62/2/882 (1927): 275.
[127] *RTsKhIDNI* 62/2/882 (1927): 275–2750b; 62/2/883 (1927): 9–24.
[128] Payne, "Turksib," 237, 256–258, 288–296.
[129] *RTsKhIDNI* 62/2/489 (1926): 7.
[130] *RTsKhIDNI* 17/87/196 (1925): 374.
[131] *RTsKhIDNI* 62/2/1809 (1929): 28.
[132] *GARF* 374/27s/1708 (1929): 36.
[133] *RTsKhIDNI* 62/1/220 (24–27.01.27): 47.

and priority in a given territory.[134] We have already noted this phenomenon in rural ethnic conflict in Central Asia and much of the Soviet east. Russians interpreted *korenizatsiia* as a deep and undeserved status insult. During ethnic incidents, Russians again and again appealed to their revolutionary service: "We fought, shed blood, and now they consider us guests. Are we not people, just like the Uzbeks?" When Russians saw a sign on the labor market asking for Uzbeks only, they lamented: "Where were they with these announcements when we shed blood and died like flies in the Central Asian deserts? If a war breaks out, we'll go to the front, but to fight against an administration like this." On another occasion, when Uzbeks received jobs over Russians, a Russian complained: "Russians fought to achieve the revolution, we died like flies and as a result, everything goes to the animals, who are now proud and declare: 'You fought the war. Thank you. Now we will work.'"[135] Two themes predominated in Russian complaints: first, that Russians had made enormous sacrifices on behalf of the revolution and been unjustly denied their deserved rewards; and second, that *korenizatsiia* made them outsiders, guests in what they had considered to be their homeland. Russians particularly resented the fact that *korenizatsiia* implied that Uzbekistan belonged to the Uzbeks, that "we conquered Turkestan and now the Uzbeks are the masters."[136]

Most Uzbeks appear to have understood *korenizatsiia* in the same fashion. They took the Soviet rhetoric of decolonization seriously and interpreted *korenizatsiia* as giving them an unqualified priority in all aspects of life in Uzbekistan, not the selected priority in certain spheres related to national culture that the Soviet leadership meant by *korenizatsiia*. During fights at the labor market, Uzbeks would tell Russians: "We are the masters of Uzbekistan and therefore they should give us jobs first."[137] Although the phrasing was hardly Soviet, in this case the policy implication was acceptable. In another instance, however, Uzbeks were being paid more for the same work at a factory. One Uzbek worker explained this simply: "Power belongs to us and therefore we receive more."[138] This sense that Uzbekistan belonged to them led Uzbeks to refer to Russians as "guests" and, during ethnic fights, to tell them "to get the hell out of Uzbekistan" and return to "your homeland [*rodina*]."[139] The tendency of the non-Russians to essentialize what the Soviets conceived of as an instrumental policy was an ongoing problem in the reception of *korenizatsiia*. Nor was this interpretation confined to non-Russians. Despite the fact that Russians remained dominant throughout the 1920s in both the government apparat and in the industrial workplace, Russians again and again expressed the fear that they were being "driven out of Central Asia."[140] This disproportionate

---

[134] See Horowitz, *Ethnic Groups in Conflict*.
[135] *RTsKhIDNI* 62/2/881 (1927): 141; 62/2/1351 (1928): 29; 62/2/1350 (1928): 103.
[136] *RTsKhIDNI* 62/2/1808 (1929): 109.
[137] *RTsKhIDNI* 62/2/1351 (1928): 156.
[138] *RTsKhIDNI* 62/2/882 (1927): 274ob.
[139] *RTsKhIDNI* 62/2/882 (1927): 274; 62/2/881 (1927): 125.
[140] *RTsKhIDNI* 62/2/1809 (1929): 73.

fear must be taken seriously, as it was not only expressed during public conflicts, but in intercepted letters as well: "I tried to get work at a factory but they are hiring only Uzbeks. Soon all Russians will probably have to leave here for Russia"; "The time will soon come when they politely ask all Russians to leave for the European part of Russia."[141]

This existential conflict was responsible for at least three characteristic aspects of ethnic relations in the industrial workplace in the Soviet east: pervasive ethnic segregation, the sudden and spontaneous nature of ethnic conflict, and a tendency for that conflict to take certain symbolic forms. Outside observers were almost always shocked by the pervasiveness of ethnic segregation. A report on working conditions at a Turkmen oil field noted that "the first thing that strikes the observer is that the workers are divided by nationality into three different barracks."[142] The same was true of Mountaineers in Rostov, where an appalled observer found that even within a mixed dormitory, workers were "distributed by room by 'national identity' or, to be more accurate, into 'national cells.' "[143] In another instance where only one barrack was available for Kazakhs and Russians, "a wooden barrier was erected in the middle to divide the two nationalities."[144] The Andreev commission found this division a common practice in the Soviet Union's eastern regions.[145] This segregation penetrated daily life. There were separate clubs and cafeterias. Zelenskii was particularly appalled by the custom of forming separate lines for water.[146]

This de facto practice of segregation bothered Soviet authorities, not only because it violated their internationalist principles, but also because it pointed to a disturbing quality of their own nationalities policy. Most Bolsheviks were outraged by the practice of segregation within the putatively internationalist proletariat.[147] And Soviet nationalities policy did indeed oppose extraterritorial nationality on these grounds and insisted that all nationalities in a given territory be served equally. However, it also insisted on the need to service all nationalities in their own languages. As we have seen, this led to the formation of village-sized national territories, a form of territorial segregation. In practice, it was not clear why this principle should not be applied to large factories as well. The Urals region, for instance, celebrated its formation of 337 national work brigades as an example of enlightened nationalities policy.[148] A hostile observer might call it segregation. After a serious ethnic riot, the Magnitogorsk authorities did not respond with a renewed push for integration, but rather with

---

[141] *RTsKhIDNI* 62/2/1808 (1928): 74; 62/2/1349 (1928): 106.

[142] *RTsKhIDNI* 62/2/2245 (1930): 189.

[143] I. Kar, "Kak zhivut, v chem nuzhdaiutsia i na chto zhaluiutsia rabochie-natsionaly v kraevoi promyshlennosti," *Revoliutsiia i gorets*, nos. 6–7 (1931): 86.

[144] *GARF* 1235/131/23 (1936): 52.

[145] *RTsKhIDNI* 17/113/336 (1927): 46.

[146] *RTsKhIDNI* 62/2/882 (1927): 274; 62/2/1349 (1928): 91; I. Zelenskii, "Protiv velikoderzhavnogo shovinizma i mestnogo natsionalizma," *Partrabotnik* (Tashkent), no. 3 (1930): 10. See also "Dve ocheredi uzbekskaia i russkaia," *Pravda vostoka*, no. 204 (27.07.31): 3.

[147] "Khronika," *Revoliutsiia i gorets*, nos. 6–7 (1930): 104.

[148] Ibragimov and S. Sady, *Uspekhi leninskoi natsional'noi politiki na Urale* (Sverdlovsk, 1932), 26.

an expanded system of national work brigades.[149] This was the path of least resistance. Attempts to integrate work brigades or dormitories frequently met violent resistance.[150] When a Central Asian *Biuro* inspector asked local authorities why they set up segregated barracks, they received a simple answer: "There are less brawls that way."[151]

The authorities, then, accepted a segregated workplace, despite their discomfort with it, both because it was convenient and because their nationalities policy gave it a certain superficial sanction. The Bolsheviks inherited a segregated society in Central Asia. They abolished legal segregation but preserved much of it in practice and even in thought. It is striking how Central Asian Bolsheviks, including Zelenskii himself, quickly adopted the prerevolutionary categories of "Europeans" and "Asians."[152] A 1929 TsKK investigator was astounded by the ubiquitous use of these terms, which he considered "incompatible with notions of brotherhood and the unity and equality of the laborers of all nations." This division was not purely racial, because the term *European* applied to "all newcomers," including the Turkic Azerbaijanis and Volga Tatars, and "Asian" signified the local population.[153] Tatars were in fact treated as Europeans, living in "European" barracks and standing in "European" lines.[154] It is striking that *korenizatsiia* had less impact on breaking down the "European" term (since *korenizatsiia* did treat nontitulars similarly) than it did in transforming the local undifferentiated "Asians" into Uzbeks, Tajiks, Turkmen, and Kirgiz.

The segregated workplace, combined with the status conflicts associated with *korenizatsiia*, created an exceedingly tense workplace environment where minor incidents could and did erupt into ethnic violence. The GPU noted that "national relations are so strained that the smallest everyday incident provokes misunderstandings and gives the Uzbeks cause to speak about European repression."[155] In typical fights, a conflict would break out between a Russian and a Central Asian and then their co-ethnics would join in to create an ethnic brawl.[156] Large fights tended to flare up in tense situations in which large numbers of ethnic groups congregated outside of work. The most common sites for such fights were the long lines at factory stores: "Lines are the breeding-ground of great power Russian chauvinism and local nationalism. In lines you can hear the Europeans call the nationals asses, morons and so forth and the nationals call the Russians dogs."[157]

[149] Azmat Nugaev, "Praktika natsional'noi politiki na Magnitogorske," *Revoliutsiia i natsional'nosti*, no. 8 (1931): 18.

[150] *RTsKhIDNI* 62/2/946 (1927): 3.

[151] *RTsKhIDNI* 62/2/2280 (1930): 9.

[152] For an example from a Zelenskii speech, and by no means the only example, see Zelenskii, "Protiv velikoderzhavnogo shovinizma," 10.

[153] *GARF* 374/27s/1707 (1929): 206.

[154] *RTsKhIDNI* 62/2/2245 (1930): 187; 62/2/2541 (1931): 51.

[155] *RTsKhIDNI* 62/2/1808 (1929): 20.

[156] *RTsKhIDNI* 62/2/881 (1927): 72.

[157] *RTsKhIDNI* 62/2/2245 (1930): 154.

One of the largest ethnic riots in Central Asia emerged out of exactly this type of situation. In April 1931, a group of 300 Uzbeks sacked the silk-weaving factory where they worked in Margelan (Samarkand oblast), "under the slogans of 'Russian oppression' and 'beat the Russians.'" During the fight, one worker was killed and two Russians and four Uzbeks severely wounded. The incident began with insults being traded between a Russian worker, Kulichnov, and an Uzbek, Karimov. A fight broke out and Kulichnov beat Karimov until the latter was unconscious. The militia escorted Kulichnov into their offices to protect him from a group of 250 to 300 Uzbeks who gathered outside the factory and cried out: "For a murdered Uzbek, beat the Russians. We should destroy the factory and the Russians. Then we'll go to the *Basmachi*. They'll support us and help us destroy the factory and drive out the Russians."[158] Finally, the Uzbeks sacked the militia office, while the militia fled with Kulichnov into the city of Margelan. Many smaller ethnic riots broke out in similar circumstances.[159]

Most conflict, of course, was not violent. More frequent were acts of symbolic violence. Given the conflict over who had the right to consider the Central Asian republics their own, symbolic issues took on a particular importance. Russians, for instance, were outraged that they were told to celebrate Christmas on January 2 in 1929. "They force us to celebrate Uzbek holidays, and our holidays they order celebrated not on the proper day"; "the Muslim Sarts are laughing at us, that the Russian fools celebrate their holidays on the wrong day."[160] Another fight broke out over whether Mohammed or Christ was superior.[161] By far the most frequently reported act of symbolic violence, however, was Russians rubbing pork fat on the lips of Muslims or forcing them to eat pork.[162] This was clearly intended to humiliate the Islamic peoples in the most profound way and thereby display Russian dominance on the factory floor. Russian dominance of the industrial workplace in the Soviet east was, in fact, never challenged. The Soviet response to this dominance and its manifestation in chronic ethnic conflict was conditioned by the dramatic changes that accompanied the launching of the socialist offensive in 1928.

Cultural Revolution and *Korenizatsiia* in the Soviet East

The socialist offensive had a dramatic impact on the implementation of the Soviet nationalities policy. We have already seen that the centralization and statism embodied in the new policy fatally undermined linguistic *korenizatsiia*

---

[158] *RTsKhIDNI* 62/2/2198 (1931): 1; 5.
[159] *RTsKHIDNI* 62/2/2541 (1931): 49–52.
[160] *RTsKHIDNI* 62/2/1808 (1929): 34.
[161] *RTsKHIDNI* 62/2/2278 (1930): 5.
[162] *GARF* 374/27s/1708 (1929): 35; *RTsKhIDNI* 62/2/943 (1927): 7–8; *7-aia vsekazakskaia partiinaia konferentsiia VKP/b/. Stenograficheskii otchet* (Alma-Ata, 1930): 253; Payne, "Turksib," 285; I. Gutte, "Bol'noi vopros," *Revoliutsiia i gorets*, nos. 11–12 (1930): 71; F. Makarov, "Ogon' po velikoderzhavnomu shovinizmu!" *Revoliutsiia i gorets*, no. 3 (1931): 43.

in Ukraine. The effect on *korenizatsiia* in the Soviet east was quite different because of the influence of the cultural revolution. For our purposes, cultural revolution can be divided into two processes. First, there was the destructive process associated with the intensification of class warfare, which involved the mobilization of militant "proletarian" Bolsheviks against various formerly tolerated "bourgeois elements" and institutions: academics and universities, priests and religion, fellow-traveling writers and their journals. This process was accompanied by a state-led terror campaign, initiated by the *Shakhty* trial in 1928, that signaled which population categories were now stigmatized and therefore vulnerable. In the national regions, the principal target of the cultural revolutionary terror was the *smenovekhovtsy*, the nationalist intellectuals who had accepted the Bolshevik offer to work on behalf of *korenizatsiia*. The nationalities trials (discussed in Chapter 5) also served to compromise *korenizatsiia* by signaling that its most avid supporters were in fact counterrevolutionaries. The destructive aspect of cultural revolution in the Soviet east was also distinctive, in that it involved a mass campaign against "feudal" practices that began already in 1927 with the campaign to stop the practice of female veiling.[163]

The second constructive aspect of cultural revolution involved a wave of utopian projects and experiments that aimed at the creation of a new socialist way of life (*byt*) to replace the bourgeois institutions then under attack.[164] This process also involved the unleashing of utopian energies temporarily constrained by the pragmatism of NEP. In the sphere of nationality, the initial assumption of most Bolsheviks was that the abolition of NEP and the attack on the nationalist *smenovekhovtsy* meant that the unloved compromise with national identity was at an end. The utopian project they favored was the creation of a purely internationalist Soviet non-national identity. This widespread interpretation was squelched by Stalin in a series of private comments in 1929 and then a decisive public declaration at the June 1930 party congress. There he provided an alternative utopian project: "The period of the construction of socialism is the period of the flowering of national culture, socialist in content and national in form . . . the development of national culture should unfold with new strength."[165] Stalin's intervention channeled the utopian strain of cultural revolution in the direction of the rapid acceleration of nation-building rather than the creation of a non-national Soviet identity.

Only in the Soviet East, as a result of its "cultural backwardness," could accelerated nation-building take on a sufficiently utopian character to satisfy cultural revolutionary utopianism. The creation of national territories, languages, and cultural institutions for the small peoples of the north, for instance, was celebrated in 1931 as "the creation of new nationalities out of tribes which had earlier

---

[163] Gregory J. Massell, *The Surrogate Proletariat* (Princeton, NJ, 1974). Douglas Northrop, "Uzbek Women and the Veil: Gender and Power in Stalinist Central Asia" (Ph.D. diss., Stanford University, 1999). Edgar, "The Creation of Soviet Turkmenistan", 145–201.

[164] Stephen Kotkin, *Magnetic Mountain* (Berkeley, 1995): 72–105.

[165] *XVI s"ezd VKP/b/. Stenograficheskii otchet* (Moscow, 1930): 55–56.

Implementing the Affirmative Action Empire

never dreamed of national existence . . . [and] their transition in just six years through all the stages of development, which for other peoples required thousands of years."[166] This was classic cultural revolutionary utopianism. It helps explain the differing fates of *korenizatsiia* in the Soviet east and west during the cultural revolution. If the pragmatism of NEP favored projects based on the rhetoric of indigenousness and was hostile to those based on cultural backwardness, the utopianism of the cultural revolution supported only those indigenization projects involved in the developmentalist project of overcoming cultural backwardness. I will now turn to an analysis of three cultural revolutionary campaigns that affected the development of *korenizatsiia* in the Soviet east: the campaign against great-power chauvinism, the establishment of Affirmative Action programs in higher education, and a major push to implement *korenizatsiia* in the eastern national territories.

The Campaign Against Great-Power Chauvinism

In the same June 1930 speech in which Stalin declared that cultural revolution meant the flourishing, not the liquidation, of national cultures, he likewise rebuked those activists who had questioned the established principle that great-power chauvinism was a greater danger than local nationalism.[167] Since this principle was a crucial pillar of *korenizatsiia*, Stalin's comments greatly relieved its advocates. The past few months had witnessed a series of show trials directed against the non-Russian *smenovekhovtsy* intellectuals on the charge of local nationalism with no comparable attack on any great-power chauvinists. As a result, many Bolsheviks believed the old principle had been overturned. However, Stalin did not state which great-power chauvinists should be attacked. Lacking central instructions, local authorities focused on their most pressing nationalities problem: ethnic tension, conflict, and prejudice among the proletariat. As the examples cited earlier indicated, and as subsequent Soviet studies confirmed, Russians were typically the aggressors in violent ethnic incidents.[168] Ethnic conflict continued to worsen during the socialist offensive.[169] As a result, a decision was made, reflected in a Central Asian press campaign immediately following Stalin's speech, to attack the mistreatment of non-Russians at the workplace under the slogan of fighting

---

[166] *2 sessiia VTsIK 15 sozyva. Stenograficheskii otchet* (Moscow, 1931): 16.

[167] *XVI s"ezd*, 54. Stalin called it "Great Russian chauvinism" but the press, official documents, and most other officials continued to use Lenin's preferred phrase, "Great Power chauvinism."

[168] See also "Na bor'bu s shovinizmom," *Sovetskaia iustitsiia*, no. 22 (1934): 8–9.

[169] For a list of published accounts of ethnic conflict in only three journals, see *Revoliutsiia i natsional'nosti*, no. 3 (1930): 9–10; no. 7 (1930): 102–103; nos. 8–9 (1930): 25–34; nos. 2–3 (1931): 76–81; 129–131; no. 8 (1931): 18–25; no. 9 (1931): 86–91; 151–156; no. 3 (1932): 19–22; no. 3 (1933): 92–96; no. 1 (1934): 80–86; *Prosveshchenie natsional'nostei*, nos. 4–5 (1930): 45–49; *Sovetskaia iustitsiia*, no. 4 (1929): 83–85; no. 2 (1931): 29–31; no. 15 (1931): 31; no. 19 (1931): 16–19; no. 3 (1932): 34–35; no. 11 (1932): 8–10; no. 19 (1932): 18–20; no. 9 (1933): 18; no. 5 (1934): 10–11; no. 16 (1934): 13; no. 22 (1934): 8–9.

great-power chauvinism.[170] Thus, the campaign against local nationalism that focused on the cultural intelligentsia would be balanced by a campaign against great-power chauvinism that focused on the Russian factory administration and Russian workers.

The campaign against Great Russian chauvinism did not focus on segregation, which would have been the logical target of an internationalist campaign, but rather on the fact that conditions were separate *and* unequal. National dormitories were almost always inferior to Russian ones.[171] At construction sites, Kazakhs and Uzbeks were often given no housing at all and slept "under the open sky."[172] At Karaganda, Kazakh housing was said to be worse than that given to the dekulakized peasants.[173] Eastern nationals were discriminated against in the distribution of food and consumer goods.[174] They were often paid less for the same work, and sometimes told this was due to their inability to speak Russian.[175] As noted above, they were constantly taunted with ethnic slurs, and Muslims were often forced to eat pork.

The authorities feared that this discrimination was sabotaging their attempts to create a national proletariat. Turnover among national workers in the Soviet east was much higher than among Russians. The authorities blamed high turnover for the relatively slow growth of the native proletariat as a percentage of the workforce, despite the favorable conditions brought about by industrial growth and aggressive Affirmative Action.[176] Just as unemployed Russians used violence to frustrate Affirmative Action in hiring, a 1931 Justice Commissariat circular accused chauvinists of intentionally using discrimination "to drive national minorities out of the work force."[177] Local authorities agreed. An

---

[170] See Zelenskii, "Protiv velikoderzhavnogo shovinizma," "Bor'ba s velikoderzhavnym shovinizmom nasha osnovnaia zadacha," *Pravda vostoka*, no. 179 (06.08.30): 2; "Ogon' protiv velikoderzhavnogo shovinizma i mestnogo natsionalizma!" no. 181 (08.08.30): 2; "Bezposhchadno vytravliat' velikoderzhavnyi shovinizm i mestnyi natsionalizm," no. 186 (14.08.30): 3.

[171] *RTsKhIDNI* 17/113/336 (07.10.27): 149/1, 46; 17/113/725 (08.05.29): 117/1.

[172] *RTsKhIDNI* 62/2/2278 (1930): 8; Payne, "Turksib", 277–278.

[173] *GARF* 1235/141/1565 (1933): 24–28.

[174] *RTsKhIDNI* 62/2/2245 (1930): 62; Payne, "Turksib", 278–279.

[175] *RTsKhIDNI* 62/2/2278 (1930): 5.

[176] Unfortunately statistics for the major eastern nationalities were not published and archival data are spotty. By January 1933, *korenizatsiia* of the factory proletariat in the RSFSR's ASSR and AO had achieved the following levels: Komi AO 62.9 percent Komi of a total proletariat of 1077; Karelia 16.3 percent/20078; Udmurtia 20.7 percent/5503; Mari AO 20.0 percent/5205 [for 1932]; Chuvashia 41.9 percent/7441; Bashkiria 24.3 percent/35546; Tatarstan 36.8 percent/52130; Mordovia 19.6 percent/4217; Volga German ASSR 64.9 percent/6711; Kalmykia 45.0 percent/324; Adygeia 9.5 percent/929; Ingushetia 8.2 percent/976; Kabardinia-Balkaria 16.2 percent/2366; Karachai AO 18.1 percent/451; North Ossetia 26.0 percent/4464; Chechnya 7.7 percent/19008; Cherkess AI 4.1 percent/447; Dagestan 23.2 percent/9263; Crimea 7.3 percent/40336; Kirgizia 27.2 percent/7505; Buriat-Mongolia 8.8 percent/7433; Kara-Kalpakia 81.6 percent/745. *Itogi razresheniia natsional'nogo voprosa v SSSR* (Moscow, 1936), 140–141.

[177] "Bor'ba organov iustitsii s velikoderzhavnym i mestnym shovinizmom," *Sovetskaia iustitsiia*, no. 3 (1932): 34–35.

Uzbek TsK report on the transport industry, a notoriously anti-*korenizatsiia* institution, noted that "the voluntary departure of Uzbek workers in the overwhelming majority of cases must be seen as not voluntary but the result of the failure to create satisfactory work conditions."[178] The North Caucasus *kraikom* blamed "outrageous facts of insults, rude treatment, persecution and even beatings of some nationals" for the fact that sixty-two of sixty-nine Mountaineers sent to work at one Rostov factory left within months.[179]

The campaign against great-power chauvinism soon evolved beyond propaganda alone to the use of show trials against great-power chauvinists. In November 1930, at the Magnitogorsk construction site, a brawl broke out between a Russian and a Tatar work brigade when the Russians attacked the Tatars, yelling "Beat the Tatars, beat the Tatar dogs!"[180] This one brawl led to four "large trials" of fifteen offenders and sixteen smaller trials in the first half of 1931. When Russians attacked twenty newly arrived Tatars at the Bereznikovskii factory in the Urals and beat up five of them, the Russian perpetrators were tried in public and sentenced to a severe term of five years of hard labor.[181] Show trials were not reserved only for such large episodes, but were also used periodically for individual fights that previously had resulted in the lesser charge of hooliganism. In May 1931, the GPU reported that during a fight over the distribution of sugar at the store of a Tashkent brick factory, a Russian beat an Uzbek senseless and concluded: "We petitioned the Justice Commissariat to conduct a show trial of Semenov at the factory."[182] In the North Caucasus, where mistreatment of Mountaineer workers in Rostov was rampant, the kraikom dissolved a factory's party committee and ordered "public show trials," not because of an actual fight, but as a result of general mistreatment of Mountaineers that had led to their leaving the factory.[183] In the first two months of 1932, the North Caucasus procurator processed sixty-two cases dealing with the crime of great-power chauvinism.[184]

This campaign was picked up by the RSFSR Commissariat of Justice, which in April 1931 issued a circular calling for greater attention to the battle with great-power and local chauvinism. The latter category seems to have been included purely to echo Stalin's formulation, since all of the cases subsequently reported dealt with great-power chauvinism. In December 1931, the commissariat issued another circular calling the campaign "extremely unsatisfactory" thus far and demanding a more aggressive fight with chauvinism, "in particu-

[178] *RTsKhIDNI* 62/2/2866 (1932): 7.

[179] "Postanovlenie sevkavkaraikoma VKP/b/," *Revoliutsiia i gorets*, no. 3 (1931): 10–12; see also "Khronika," no. 4 (1931): 64–65; "O vovlechenii natsionalov v promyshlennost' Groznefti," no. 5 (1931): 80–81; Voronkov, "Vnimanie podgotovke promyshlennykh natskadrov," no. 8 (1931): 9–12.

[180] Nugaev, "Praktika natsional'noi politiki," 18.

[181] P. Vagrov, "Kak vedetsia rabota po obsluzhivaniiu natsmen organami Urala," *Sovetskaia iustitsiia*, no. 11 (1932): 9–10.

[182] *RTsKhIDNI* 62/2/2541 (1931): 150.

[183] "Postanovlenie sevkavkraikoma," 10–12.

[184] *Materialy i resheniia 3 obshchegorodskogo natsmen-soveshchaniia* (Rostov-na-Donu, 1932): 24.

lar great power chauvinism."[185] In 1932, a study of five oblasts found eighty-seven trials on the charge of chauvinism. In each case the accusation was great-power chauvinism.[186] Overall, judging by the fragmentary statistics and reports published by the commissariat's journal, the campaign against great-power chauvinism peaked in 1931–1932, continued at a modest level through 1934, and then disappeared.

The campaign against great-power chauvinism was a unique episode in the implementation of *korenizatsiia*, as it was the only time that the judicial organs were mobilized in a systematic and propagandistic fashion against those who impeded the implementation of *korenizatsiia*. As we shall see, all other judicial campaigns targeted local nationalists who were too eager in support of *korenizatsiia*. Of course, the campaign against great-power chauvinism lacked the political message of the nationalities terror campaigns of 1928–1930, 1932–1933 and 1937–1938, since they involved only criminal charges against individuals, not political charges of counterrevolution against representatives of entire population categories. What were the results of the campaign? There are no data to answer that question, but it is certain that the impact could not have been the same as in the nationalities terror campaigns. Those had a major impact on *korenizatsiia* by signaling to party members and government officials that the charge of local nationalism could end up getting you arrested or executed, whereas the charge of great-power chauvinism might at worst get you demoted. Ordinary Russian workers, in particular those most likely to engage in ethnic brawls, were simply not looking for such signals. They wanted to avoid trouble with the state, and the campaign against great-power chauvinism was far less threatening than many others. So it is unlikely the campaign had more than local effects in the limited number of factories where show trials took place.

Affirmative Action in Higher Education

The Russian proletariat, then, remained numerically, politically, and sociologically dominant in the Soviet Union's eastern regions. However, despite the enormous problems Affirmative Action encountered, Soviet efforts did produce a native proletariat numbering in the hundreds of thousands. By January 1933, in nine eastern autonomous republics and twelve eastern autonomous oblasts of the RSFSR, there was a native industrial proletariat numbering 164,459 (14.9 percent).[187] In the eastern union republics, the industrial proletariat was larger in both absolute and relative terms—20.1 percent in Kazakhstan, 36.7 percent in Azerbaijan, 29.7 percent in Uzbekistan—though everywhere it remained a minority.[188] This new eastern proletariat represented a pool, albeit a shallow one, from which titular nationals could now be recruited into higher education

[185] "Bor'ba organov," 31–32.

[186] E. Petrova, "Mobilizirovat' vnimanie obshchestvennosti na bor'bu s shovinizmom," *Sovetskaia iustitsiia*, no. 9 (1933): 18.

[187] Calculated from *Itogi razresheniia*, 140–141.

[188] Zinger, *Natsional'nyi sostav proletariata*, 39, 46, 64.

to train them to take over technical positions in government and industry, following the pattern of Russian workers during the great *vydvizhenie* campaign of 1928 to 1931.[189] However, there were many demands being placed on this slender reed. Both non-Russian and central leaders were in a hurry to fulfill the cultural revolution's renewal of the 1923 promise to raise the cultural level of the backward nationalities to the level of the advanced Soviet nationalities. Therefore, the campaign to recruit eastern nationals into higher education took place simultaneously with the campaigns to create a national proletariat, to accelerate the implementation of *korenizatsiia*, and to create a system of universal primary education. All of these goals could not be accomplished, but the utopianism of the cultural revolution led to an adamant refusal to admit, or even seriously consider, this fact.

Affirmative Action programs for higher education existed before the cultural revolution. Indeed, as soon as VUZy were formed in the eastern republics, they established quotas for titulars and often other "culturally backward" nationalities.[190] This practice was authorized in 1924 by a TsK commission that stated: "In all rabfaks and institutes of higher education [VUZy] of the national republics and oblasts, a sufficient number of places [should] be reserved for the indigenous nationality."[191] A reservation or quota was referred to as a *bronia* (short for *bronirovanie*—reservation). The *bronia*, however, was usually better described as a target or an aspiration, since it was usually set so high that it could not possibly be fulfilled.[192] This was especially true during the cultural revolution when the all-union commissariats started to reserve 70 percent of the places in the VUZy they administered in national republics for titular nationals, while the Central Asian Biuro demanded that 75 percent of places in industrial-apprenticeship schools be reserved for local nationals.[193] Filling even half such quotas was utopian.

Perhaps the most striking thing about local Affirmative Action quotas in the period from 1924 to 1932 was their visibility. Not only did all VUZy have quotas, they publicly advertised them. During every admissions season, the Central Asian newspaper *Pravda Vostoka* printed dozens of advertisements from Central Asian universities, which openly stated their preferences and quotas for local nationalities: "70 percent titular nationals, 20 percent national minorities, 10 percent Europeans"; "for local indigenous nationalities, exceptions [to enrollment requirements] allowed"; "the majority of admissions must be local

[189] Sheila Fitzpatrick, *Education and Social Mobility in the Soviet Union, 1921–1934* (Cambridge, UK, 1979): 181–205.

[190] *GARF* 1235/120/101 (1925): 260b; *RTsKhIDNI* 17/26/60 (1926): 119; *Biulleten' TsIK . . . Chuvashskoi ASSR*, nos. 13–14 (1926): 2–7; *Biulleten' Narkomprosa Karel'skoi ASSR*, nos. 3–4 (1927): 17–28.

[191] *RTsKhIDNI* 17/84/485 (1924): 18.

[192] On systematic underfulfilment, see *RTsKhIDNI* 62/2/2245 (1930): 35; 62/2/2597 (1931): 2–3.

[193] *GARF* 3316/24/854 (1932): 36–37, 64, 71; 3316/24/768 (1934): 35. *RTsKhIDNI* 62/2/2597 (1931): 3.

nationals."[194] In some cases, the quotas were quite elaborate: "local nationalities not less than 85 percent (among them, *natsmen* not less than 10 percent), women 45 percent, workers not less than 40 percent, *batraki* 20 percent, *kolkhozniki* and *bedniaki* 30 percent, employees and peasants 10 percent. Members of Party and Komsomol, not less than 90 percent."[195] Obviously such quotas made titular nationals with the right class and gender profile exceedingly valuable to university admissions officials.

What is striking about these blunt advertisements of quotas was the seeming lack of concern shown for the feelings of Russians and other western nationalities. Unsurprisingly, Russians did resent such preferences. A GPU report recorded a typical remark from a Russian in Uzbekistan: "The Sarts and Kirgiz are studying in universities on our money and so there's no place for our Russian brother."[196] Ethnic conflict between Russians and eastern nationals was common in both central and republican universities, though such incidents were less frequent and much less violent than those in the industrial workplace.[197]

The more important site for Affirmative Action was the central VUZy of Moscow and Leningrad. The eastern republics had a skeletal structure of VUZy and technicums, most of which were pedagogical and agricultural. Only the central RSFSR VUZy could provide the education necessary to produce the technical cadres that the national republics needed to implement *korenizatsiia*. The RSFSR Education Commissariat did establish a special *bronia* for national minorities in the mid-1920s.[198] By 1928–1929, this *bronia* amounted to about one thousand places.[199] If it had been fulfilled, it would have made a substantial impact on the number of eastern nationals in higher education. However, the *bronia* was poorly designed. Although motivated by the problem of cultural backwardness, it targeted all "national minorities," with the result that Belorussia and Ukraine were also given a quota.[200] More importantly, the *bronia* was distributed to republics, not to individuals. As a result, the eastern republics, lacking qualified titular nationals, sent primarily Russians and Jews.[201] In January 1927, Zelenskii complained that the Central Asian republics

---

[194] *Pravda vostoka*, no. 232 (07.10.32): 4; no. 171 (24.06.31): 4.

[195] *Pravda vostoka*, no. 12 (03.01.31): 4.

[196] *RTsKhIDNI* 62/2/1808 (1929): 35.

[197] *RTsKhIDNI* 17/87/200 (1926): 1290b; 17/69/60 (1926): 16–18; K. Oshaev, "Za bol'shevistskie tempy podgotovki kadrov dlia gorskikh oblastei," *Revoliutsiia i gorets*, no. 3 (1931): 17–20; L. P., "Shkola eshche ne podniala oruzhiia protiv shovinizma i natsionalizma," *Pravda vostoka*, no. 281 (04.12.30): 3.

[198] It is not clear when exactly the *bronia* for national minorities began. The Sovnatsmen and nationalities department archive contains papers for the 1925–1926 admissions and after. *GARF* 1235/120/13 (1925–1926): 199–204; *GARF (TsGA)* 296/1/257 (1926): 1–40; 296/1/98 (1925): 18–22. Dagestani representatives to the Orgburo mentioned a *bronia* for communist VUZy in the center in 1924–1925. *RTsKhIDNI* 17/112/608 (03.11.24): 46ob.

[199] Dimanshtein, "O prakticheskom provedenii natsional'noi politiki v oblasti narodnogo prosveshcheniia v SSSR," *Narodnoe prosveshchenie*, no. 5 (1929): 46.

[200] At least this was the case in 1925–1926. *GARF (TsGA)* 296/1/257 (1926): 31, 38.

[201] *RTsKhIDNI* 17/69/58 (1927): 247; 17/113/270 (04.03.27): 95/2, 76–80.

fulfilled 90 percent of their *bronia* with Europeans.[202] As a result, the first central *bronia* did little to further the interests of the "culturally backward" eastern nationalities.

Table 18 gives a sense of the representation of "culturally backward" eastern nationalities at all levels of "professional education" (that is, education outside the grade 1–9 system) in the late 1920s.

The absolute number of eastern nationalities in higher education was quite respectable considering their literacy rates, but the general downward trend from 1926–1927 through 1929–1930 in all schools save the rabfak, which in national regions tended to function as a substitute for the almost complete absence of middle schools (grades 5 to 9). Moreover, these statistics represented enrollments, not graduations, and thus did not reflect the much higher drop-out rates of the eastern nationalities. By November 1, 1928, the number of eastern nationalities enrolled in VUZy had declined from 6.9 percent to 4.4 percent, in *Profshkoly* from 3.5 percent to 2.3 percent, and in technicums from 8.1 percent to 6.3 percent.[203] Graduation rates were still lower. Finally, as Table 19 shows, the eastern nationalities were disproportionately located in less prestigious specialties. The eastern nationalities, then, were heavily concentrated in pedagogical schools and comparatively weakly represented in the more prestigious industrial-technical, medical, and social-economic schools. All of these statistical indicators led nationalities specialists to conclude that the *bronia* had thus far failed to address the backwardness of the eastern nationalities.

The onset of cultural revolution led to a renewed effort to attract eastern nationalities into higher education. After all, higher education was at the center of the cultural revolution. The Shakhty affair in 1928 was staged to signal the need to replace the old disloyal intelligentsia with a new proletarian intelligentsia. To produce these new Red specialists, TsK ordered that 65 percent of all admissions to technical VUZy in the fall of 1928 be workers or children of workers.[204] Initially, this *vydvizhenie* (promotion) campaign affected primarily ethnic Russians and Russified western nationalities, since they represented the majority of the proletariat and in particular those with the minimal skills to enter the overwhelmingly Russian-language technical VUZy. The *vydvizhenie* campaign lasted from 1928 to 1931, when the center intervened to rehabilitate the old specialists and to scale back the mass promotion of workers.

Cultural revolution in the field of non-Russian education began later, just as the campaign against great-power chauvinism lagged behind the terror campaigns against the old Russian and national intelligentsias. The old national

---

[202] *RTsKhIDNI* 62/1/220 (24–27.01.27): 31.

[203] Calculated from a table reproduced in *GARF (TsGA)* 296/1/492 (1929): 10–11; 296/1/460 (1930): 87; Dimanshtein, "O prakticheskom provedenii," 45; A. Estrin, "K voprosu planirovaniia podgotovki natsional'nykh kadrov spetsialistov," *Revoliutsiia i natsional'nosti*, no. 2 (1930): 51. Rabfak enrollment declined only from 14.5 percent to 14.1 percent.

[204] Fitzpatrick, *Education and Social Mobility*, 184.

Table 18. Professional Education in the Russian Soviet Federated Socialist Republic by Nationality, 1925–1926 to 1929–1930 (Percent of Students)

Year	Profshkoly			Technicums		
	Russian	Cultured	Backward	Russian	Cultured	Backward
1925–1926	88.0	6.6	5.4	77.9	10.3	11.8
1926–1927	86.5	8.8	4.7	76.2	9.9	13.9
1927–1928	n/a	n/a	n/a	n/a	n/a	n/a
1928–1929	n/a	n/a	3.5	83.3	8.6	8.1
1929–1930	n/a	n/a	3.5	n/a	n/a	8.0
Percent of RSFSR Population	73.4	10.4	16.2	73.4	10.4	16.2

Year	Rabfaks			VUZy		
	Russian	Cultured	Backward	Russian	Cultured	Backward
1925–1926	80.4	9.4	10.2	74.7	21.1	4.6
1926–1927	75.4	11.5	13.1	75.4	16.0	8.6
1927–1928	75.0	11.0	14.0	75.6	19.1	5.3
1928–1929	74.0	11.5	14.5	74.7	18.4	6.9
1929–1930	n/a	n/a	n/a	n/a	n/a	6.0
Percent of RSFSR Population	73.4	10.4	16.2	73.4	10.4	16.2

GARF 1235/122/5 (1929): 87–88; 1235/141/562 (1930): 16; *GARF (TsGA)* 406/11/1285 (1930): 1710b; A. Rakhimbaev, "Novyi etap," *Prosveshchenie natsional'nostei,* no. 1 (1929): 54.

Table 19. RSFSR Professional Education by Nationality and Specialization, 1928–1929 (Percent of Students)

Type of School	Cultured	Backward
Industrial-technical	31.7	18.7
Agricultural	13.7	15.8
Pedagogical	14.4	45.5
Medical	14.3	0.0
Social-economic	14.9	10.5
Artistic	11.0	9.5
Total	100.0	100.0

Dimanshtein, "O prakticheskom provedenii," 45.

minorities *bronia* continued in 1928–1929 and 1929–1930, but no special effort was made to expand it.[205] Also, as with the chauvinism campaign, it was an intervention by Stalin that changed the situation. In an unpublished speech to a Ukrainian writers' delegation in February 1929, Stalin specifically cited the need for universal primary school education in native languages: "In what language can we achieve [universal education]? In Russian. No, only in

[205] Dimanshtein, "O prakticheskom provedenii," 46.

the native language. If we want to raise the broad masses to a higher level of culture . . . we must develop the native language of every nationality maximally." This was followed by his call for "the flowering of national culture" at the Sixteenth Party Congress in June 1930, which resulted in a party resolution "to assist in all ways the development of national culture and native languages."[206]

In late 1929, the RSFSR Education Commissariat, whose original five-year plan had disregarded national minority education entirely, met to cobble together a "national minority education five-year plan."[207] As a result of this lag, the period of cultural revolution in non-Russian education extended from 1930 to 1934, rather than from 1928 to 1931. The eastern republics had severely limited cultural resources and a plethora of pressing educational tasks. Among these were the liquidation of adult illiteracy, the achievement of universal primary education, the introduction of native-language instruction, the expansion of elementary school education (grades 5 to 9), and the training of technical cadres in central RSFSR universities. Faced with these difficult choices, the commissariat characteristically refused to choose: "The cultural five-year plan for national minority education should be constructed so that by the end of the first five-year plan, these culturally-backward nationalities will be raised to the median level of the oblasts and regions where they reside."[208] The previous plan calling for universal primary education by 1937 was scrapped in favor of an absurdly optimistic goal of 1931–1932.[209] Although many eastern republics had literacy rates under 10 percent (see Table 13), universal adult literacy for 16- to 40-year-olds was also to be achieved in two years. Native-language instruction was to be introduced not only in all primary schools, but even up to the level of VUZy. Elementary education was to be maximally expanded. Finally, a new and more ambitious *bronia* was to be established for "culturally backward" nationalities to study technical subjects in central RSFSR VUZy.[210] This comprehensive plan was a typical species of cultural revolutionary utopianism. It could not possibly be fulfilled. However, the very energetic and sincere attempts made to fulfill it had certain important consequences.

First, it dramatically increased the number and percentage of eastern nationals who studied pedagogy and became teachers. The number of students in the primary schools of the RSFSR's autonomous republics almost doubled from 1,085,097 in 1929–1930 to 1,861,038 in 1931–1932.[211] This required an enormous

---

[206] *XVI s"ezd*, 10, 55. RTsKhIDNI 17/113/860 (16.06.30): 203/2, 74.

[207] V. N. Panfilov, *Kul'turnaia revoliutsiia i piatiletka natsmenprosveshcheniia* (Moscow-Leningrad, 1930): 3–13.

[208] Panfilov, *Kul'turnaia revoliutsiia*, 14.

[209] *SU RSFSR*, no. 131 (1929): 851; no. 39 (1930): 479. "Reshitel'naia skhvatka: voprosy vseobucha v natsional'nykh oblastiakh severo-kavkazkogo kraia," *Prosveshchenie natsional'nostei*, no. 1 (1931): 45–48.

[210] Panfilov, *Kul'turnaia revoliutsiia*, 14, 49, 55; *Revoliutsiia i natsional'nosti*, nos. 4–5 (1930): 138. *GARF (TsGA)* 296/1/485 (1931): 32–34; 296/1/499 (1932): 112–1120b; 296/1/452 (1931): 86–94.

[211] *Itogi razresheniia*, 192–193.

increase in teachers. Since primary schools were simultaneously being made almost entirely native language, these teachers had to be non-Russians. To this end, the number of national pedagogical technicums in the RSFSR increased from 85 in 1928–1929 to 199 in 1932–1933. By the latter date, they were training a total of 48,000 students. In addition, non-Russians represented a whopping 30 percent of all students at general Russian pedagogical technicums. The number of national pedagogical VUZy grew from three to twenty-four in the same period and the number of students from 2242 to 9667. There were also 37 national pedagogical rabfaks in 1932–1933 with 10,300 students. Despite this mass of pedagogical students, in 1931–1932 these schools only produced 15 to 20 percent of the teachers required to fulfill the universal education plans and were expected to produce no more than 25 percent in 1932–1933. To fulfill this need, 10,140 nationals were rushed through short-term pedagogical courses in 1931–1932 and another 11,500 in 1932–1933.[212]

As a result of these efforts, the percentage of eastern nationals studying in pedagogical schools increased from an already high 45 percent (vs. 14.4 percent for western nationalities) in 1928–1929 to 63.8 percent in 1930–1931.[213] This had important short- and long-term consequences. First, it made it difficult, indeed impossible, to fulfill the generous *bronia* for eastern nationals in the prestigious technical and industrial central VUZy during the cultural revolution. Thus, at the time that a new proletarian technical intelligentsia was being created, eastern nationalities were being funneled into teachers' schools. In addition, this was also the period when a massive increase in the number of VUZy and technicums took place. TsK ordered that in national regions priority be given to the establishment of pedagogical schools.[214] Thus, the academic infrastructure in eastern national regions was biased toward pedagogy. All of this reinforced the long-term trend toward a bifurcated intelligentsia in the eastern national regions with a Russian technical intelligentsia and a national humanitarian intelligentsia.

The rush to establish universal primary school education in native languages had several other consequences. Since capable eastern nationals had many other more desirable options than teaching, those who enrolled in pedagogical schools represented, in the words of one Narkompros official, "inadequate human material." Many were illiterate in Russian and barely literate in their native language. As a result, instruction in Russian was miserable, which was a further impediment to eastern nationals in seeking entrance to central technical VUZy.[215] In addition, the exclusive focus on enrolling all eight-year-olds in the first grade often overshadowed the task of keeping them in school. As late as 1933, 64 percent of local nationals in Central Asia attended first grade, 26 percent second grade, 7 percent third grade, and only 2 percent fourth grade.[216] The focus on primary school also led to a relative neglect of

[212] *GARF (TsGA)* 296/1/529 (1933): 32, 920b–93, 950b–96, 98.

[213] A. R. Rakhimbaev, "Natsional'no-kul'turnoe stroitel'stvo na sovremennom etape," *Revoliutsiia i natsional'nosti*, nos. 8–9 (1930): 98.

[214] *RTsKhIDNI* 17/113/860 (16.06.30): 82.

[215] *GARF (TsGA)* 296/1/529 (1933): 930b, 118.

[216] *RTsKhIDNI* 62/1/1039 (29.08.33): 62–63.

elementary school (grades 5 to 9), which barely existed in many eastern regions by 1934.

In addition to this focus on primary school education, there was a renewed effort to attract eastern nationals into higher education. A new *bronia* was established for the 1930–1931 academic year that differed from the old one in specifically targeting "culturally backward nationalities."[217] This was part of the general shift during the cultural revolution toward a developmentalist ideology favoring the conquest of cultural backwardness rather than territorial nation-building in the stronger western republics such as Ukraine. The first year was largely a failure, but for the 1931–1932 academic year, an ambitious *bronia* of 7958 places was proposed in the following central VUZy, technicums, and rabfaks shown in Table 20. Only 18.7 percent of places were reserved for pedagogical schools, while 37.6 percent were reserved for technical VUZy (24.3 percent for the prestigious VSNKh VUZy). Narkompros reported a 50 percent fulfillment rate for the *bronia* in 1931–1932, which greatly disappointed them, but still it represented a massive growth in eastern representation in higher education.[218] As late as 1929–1930, there were only a few hundred easterners in central VUZy.

Narkompros continued to complain that national republics were sending "cultured" nationalities to fulfill their quotas. Some sent Russians. The Transcaucasus sent Armenians and Georgians, both of whom were overrepresented in higher education.[219] This spurred Narkompros to produce in 1932 an authoritative list (Table 21) of nationalities who were officially labeled "culturally backward" and so "eligible for preferential assistance, and enjoying appropriate awards and privileges."[220] At this point, Narkompros also singled out 5 official characteristics of culturally backward nationalities[221]:

1. an extremely low level of literacy—both the entire population and especially the active adult group
2. an insignificant percentage of children in school overall, and especially in native-language schools
3. the absence of a written script with a single developed literary language
4. the presence of everyday social vestiges—the oppression of women, religious fanaticism, nomadism, racial hostility, clan vengence and so forth
5. a complete lack or enormous dearth of national cadres in all aspects of soviet construction

This list followed conventional usage, except that it included Greeks and Bulgarians as culturally backward, and made the interesting distinction that

---

[217] *GARF (TsGA)* 406/11/1285 (1930): 161ob–162. *RTsKhIDNI* 17/113/820 (16.06.30): 203/2, 82–86. *Revoliutsiia i natsional'nosti*, no. 7 (1930): 93; A. Takho-Godi, "Podgotovka vuzovskikh kadrov natsmen," *Revoliutsiia i natsional'nosti*, no. 6 (1930): 85.

[218] *GARF (TsGA)* 296/1/463 (1932): 113.

[219] *GARF* 3316/24/854 (1932): 8–80b.

[220] *GARF (TsGA)* 296/1/476 (1932): 138.

[221] Ibid., 128.

Table 20. Bronia for Culturally Backward Nationalities, 1930–1931

Institution Receiving	Number of Students	Region Sending	Number of Students
Industrial	3029	RSFSR ASSRs	3104
Agricultural	1449	RSFSR AOs	3258
Trade	754	RSFSR krai/oblast	724
Medical	917	Union republics	872
Law	404	Total	7958
Pedagogical	1505		
Total	8058		

GARF 3316/24/854 (1932): 7–8; *GARF* (TsGA) 296/1/463 (1932): 115-116. In both sources, the first column sums to 8058, but 7958 is given as the correct figure for the *bronia*.

Table 21. Official List of "Culturally Backward" Nationalities

1. Abkhazy	26. Kazakhs	51. Mordvinians	76. Udegei
2. Adyghei	27. Kara-Kalpaks	52. Mari	77. Uzbeks
3. Ajary	28. Kara-Nogaitsy	53. Moldavians	78. Uigurs
4. Assyrians	29. Chinese	54. Manegry	79. Udmurts
5. Avars	30. Koreans	55. Nentsy	80. Ul'chi
6. Aleuty	31. Koriaki	56. Nagaibaki	81. Khakass
7. Baksan	32. Kirgiz	57. Nogaitsy	82. Roma
8. Balkars	33. Kumyks	58. Ostiaki	83. Chukchi
9. Bessermiane	34. Krymchaki	59. Oirots	84. Chechens
10. Bolgarians	35. Kumandintsy	60. Orochi	85. Cherkess
11. Buriats	36. Kabardinians	61. Orocheny	86. Chuvash
12. Bashkirs	37. Karachai	62. Ossetians	87. Chud
13. Volugy	38. Kaitaki	63. Persians	88. Chuvantsy
14. Vody	39. Kurds	64. Rutul'tsy	89. Shapsugi
15. Vepsy	40. Kurd-ezid'	65. Soioty	90. Shortsy
16. Giliaky	41. Komi-Zyriane	66. Tungusy	91. Eskimoes
17. Goldy	42. Komi-Permiaki	67. Teptyars	92. Iukagiry
18. Greeks	43. Karelians	68. Teleuty	93. Yakuts
19. Darginy	44. Karagassy	69. Tajiks	94. Tavgi
20. Dolgany	45. Kety	70. Tats	95. Negidal'tsy
21. Dungans	46. Lopary	71. Turkmen	96. Iuraki
22. Ingush	47. Lamuty	72. Taranchi	97. Samagiry
23. Izhortsy	48. Laki	73. Tabassarany	
24. Kalmyks	49. Lezgins	74. Azerbaijani	
25. Damchadaly	50. Mongolians	75. Tatars (outside ASSR)	

Tatars were only culturally backward outside the Tatar ASSR, a curious tribute to Tatarstan's zealous pursuit of *korenizatsiia*.

The 1932–1933 academic year marked the high point of the national *bronia*. A total of 13,616 places were reserved (7500 in VUZy, 2138 in technicums, 3978 in rabfaks).[222] The number of eastern nationalities sent came close to fulfilling

[222] *GARF* (TsGA) 296/1/463 (1932): 20–22; *GARF* 3316/24/854 (1933): 63. By territory, RSFSR and ZSFSR ASSRs received 4970 places, RSFSR AOs received 3802, RSFSR *krai* and oblasts 3550, and union republics 1294.

the *bronia* in VUZy (95.4 percent), technicums (59.0 percent), and rabfaks (77.8 percent).[223] These results were somewhat misleading, since central institutions often turned back unqualified students or eliminated their stipends and dormitory rights, a practice denounced by TsIK in March 1933.[224] This contributed to their very high drop-out rate. For the 1933–1934 academic year the responsibility for the *bronia* was transferred from the Education Commissariat to the Committee on Higher Technical Education (KTVO), which, as a representative of the all-union economic commissariats, was indifferent to national minority education.[225] Moreover, with the demise of the cultural revolution, central institutions were reluctant to accept poorly qualified national minorities. As a result, KTVO proposed a reduced *bronia* of 5678 places in central VUZy alone, but only 1026 were actually enrolled, an abysmal rate of 18 percent.[226] The next year the *bronia* was eliminated as a failure: "mechanical [and] not reflecting the cadre needs of the national republics and oblasts."[227]

This was undoubtedly an overly harsh judgment. Still, it is worth reflecting on why it proved so difficult to fulfill the central *bronia*. Central authorities blamed three actors: the central VUZy and the commissariats that administered them, the eastern students, and the eastern republics. The all-union commissariats were an easy target because their hostility to *korenizatsiia* was well known. They were accused of arbitrarily rejecting eastern nationals, denying them stipends or room and board, and generally failing to consider the national *bronia* "of sufficient political importance."[228] Although the commissariats certainly were unenthusiastic about the *bronia*, they were often faced with a *bronia* candidate sent to a prestigious Moscow technical VUZ, who was completely illiterate in Russian, the school's language of instruction. TsIK repeatedly called on the national republics to improve their teaching of Russian.[229] In fact, the experience of the *bronia* was at the root of the 1938 campaign to improve the teaching of Russian in the national republics. When KTVO was attacked for the abysmal failure of the 1933–1934 *bronia*, they responded: "the evil is not that the doors to higher education are in any way closed to culturally-backward nationalities, but that the national republics and oblasts are doing too poor a job of preparing cadres for entrance to VUZy and VTUZy."[230] TsIK was forced

---

[223] *GARF (TsGA)* 296/1/463 (1932): 14–15, 20. These figures represent total enrollment, some of which represent national minorities who showed up at central schools on their own initiative and were granted *bronia* places. Those officially sent as part of the *bronia* amounted to 49.2 percent for VUZy, 53.1 percent for rabfaks, and 31.9 percent for technicums.

[224] *GARF (TsGA)* 1/296/463 (1933): 35–40. *GARF* 3316/24/854 (1933): 117–119.

[225] *GARF* 3316/24/854 (1933): 137.

[226] *GARF* 3316/24/768 (1934): 14.

[227] Ibid., 16.

[228] *GARF* 3316/24/854 (1932): 1; *GARF* 1235/128/1 (1934): 19; *GARF (TsGA)* 296/1/441 (1932): 30; 296/1/463 (1933): 1–2; 296/1/475 (1931): 19.

[229] *GARF* 3316/24/854 (1933–1934): 117, 136, 144.

[230] *GARF* 3316/24/768 (1934): 14.

to accept this explanation. The problem was that the republics were simply not sending enough candidates.

For many central nationalities specialists, this considerably deepened the mystery of the *bronia* failure. They expected sinister deeds from the heartless all-union commissariats, sympathized with the eastern republics when they complained that the center refused to provide them with the necessary funds to implement *korenizatsiia*, and now found that when they had crafted an ambitious program to train in centrally funded VUZy an almost unlimited number of technical cadres, those same eastern republics consistently failed to send sufficient candidates to fill the reserved places. This seemed to reflect a lack of zeal for *korenizatsiia*. However, as Z. Ostrovskii, one of VTsIK's most perceptive nationalities specialists, explained, the reason for this failure was *exactly* that zeal for swift *korenizatsiia*: "We should understand that an [eastern national] literate in Russian, with the qualifications to enter a VUZ, will not be allowed to go study. Such comrades sit in leadership positions and are not sent to study."[231] Goloshchekin gave the same explanation from the student's perspective: "Why study, receiving a miserly stipend, when the demand for minimally literate Kazakhs is so great that one can receive a leadership position and a good salary."[232] When republics set up preparatory courses for entrance to VUZy, which consisted primarily of studying Russian, these courses instead prepared the student for immediate entry into the government apparat.[233] It was the desire to achieve as high a level of *korenizatsiia* as possible in the short term that led the republics to forego the opportunity to achieve a deeper long-term *korenizatsiia* of their technical cadres.

Although, as Ostrovskii pointed out, the republican leadership often refused to allow literate nationals to study, officials such as Goloshchekin also blamed students for their selfishness. Already in 1927, the Andreev commission worried that educational preferences would "spoil the nationals."[234] In the North Caucasus, Mountaineers who exploited the heavy demand for them in North Caucasus VUZy by constantly transferring from one school to another were called "fliers" (*letuny*). One official demanded "a boycott of these fliers," who exploited "the need for every even slightly literate Mountaineers" to leave schools for "positions paying two or three times more than their stipends."[235] Razumov complained that a system had evolved whereby Tatars were automatically given stipends 10 to 15 percent higher than Russians.[236] Again, this strategic manipulation of ethnic capital irritated Bolshevik officials.

The competition for relatively high-paying government jobs alone was not sufficient to explain the republics' reluctance to exploit the *bronia* fully. About

[231] *GARF* 3316/24/854 (1933): 62.

[232] *6-ia vsekazakskaia konferentsiia*, 66.

[233] On these courses, see *GARF* 3316/24/768 (1934): 76.

[234] *RTsKhIDNI* 17/113/58 (1927): 249.

[235] K. Oshaev, "Za bol'shevistskie tempy podgotovki kadrov dlia gorskikh oblastei," *Revoliutsiia i gorets*, no. 3 (1931): 18–20.

[236] *Ob"edinennyi plenum OK i OKK VKP/b/. Stenograficheskii otchet* (Kazan, 1933): 49.

half of the eastern nationals who enrolled in central VUZy in the early 1930s did not arrive through the official *bronia*, but simply showed up on their own volition (*samotekom*).[237] Some of these might have been refused a place in the *bronia* and decided to circumvent local authorities, but the majority undoubtedly could have been recruited. Ostrovskii again proffered an explanation: "Those finishing VUZy are not returned [to their home republics]. This places the localities in such a position that they fulfill their quota completely superficially, just to rid themselves of the task. They will not send a valuable individual."[238] From the very beginning of the *bronia* in the mid-1920s through the late 1930s, the republics consistently complained about the failure to return graduates to their home republics.[239] A Cherkess official declared that "if we have any [Cherkess] engineers and technical workers, then all of them, as a rule, graduated in Moscow and remained there."[240] The center several times issued decrees requiring all eastern nationals to be returned home after their graduation.[241] However, many students who reached the promised land of Moscow and Leningrad were reluctant to budge eastward. Strategic marriages to facilitate continued residence in the two capitals were not uncommon.[242]

To sum up the educational experience of the "culturally backward" eastern republics during the cultural revolution, the utopian refusal to choose educational priorities led to severe competition for qualified individuals. The crash program to achieve universal native-language primary education in only two years siphoned off an enormous number of titular nationals into pedagogic schools and then into the classroom. This reinforced the emerging split between a native humanities and Russian technical elite in the eastern republics, which would continue until the end of the Soviet Union. The focus on primary and pedagogic education at home left the republics reliant on Moscow for the training of technical cadres. The center provided a generous Affirmative Action program, but the lack of qualified eastern nationals, hostility from the central economic commissariats, and, above all, the reluctance of the eastern republics to risk losing an educated titular national all combined to undermine this program. The ultimate goal of both the campaign against great-power chauvinism and the *bronia* for higher education was to advance *korenizatsiia* in the eastern republics. I will now conclude this chapter with a discussion of the fate of *korenizatsiia* during the cultural revolution.

---

[237] For statistics, see *GARF (TsGA)* 296/1/463 (1932): 14–15, 20. For the overall phenomenon, *GARF* 3316/24/854 (1932): 80b, 66.

[238] *GARF* 3316/24/854 (1933): 62.

[239] *RTsKhIDNI* 17/112/668 (05.06.25): 83/1; *GARF* 1235/141/1587 (1934): 2; *GARF* 3316/13/27 (1936): 32; *GARF (TsGA)* 406/11/1285 (1930): 22.

[240] *GARF* 3316/13/27 (1936): 189.

[241] *RTsKhIDNI* 17/112/668 (05.06.25): 83/1; *GARF* 1235/141/1587 (1934): 1; *GARF* 3316/24/854 (1933): 117.

[242] *GARF* 3316/29/536 (1936): 156.

Utopian *Korenizatsiia*, 1928 to 1932

The developmentalist utopianism of the cultural revolution not only favored the eastern republics in general, but also the smaller and least developed in particular. In January 1931, a Dagestani delegate to the Soviet of Nationalities gloated at this shift in attention to "small national regions" and away from Ukraine and Belorussia, the formerly dominant "whales."[243] As we have seen, the period of NEP had marked a retreat in the Soviet east from ambitious plans for comprehensive *korenizatsiia* to the more modest project of limited functional *korenizatsiia*. With the onset of cultural revolution, the former optimism returned. In March 1929, Yakutia, whose central apparat was then only 13 percent Yakut, abruptly announced a goal of 50 percent Yakut representation in only nine months. In late 1929, the Komi government called for complete linguistic Komizatsiia within a few months.[244] Unlike during NEP, when VTsIK restrained its national regions, it now encouraged their ambitions. From June 1929 to November 1931, VTsIK criticized the inadequate implementation of *korenizatsiia* in sixteen different national regions of the RSFSR.[245]

I will focus on the North Caucasus autonomous oblasts, since these were considered among the very most "backward" of all the RSFSR's national regions. Despite this fact, in October 1928, VTsIK ordered these regions to complete comprehensive *linguistic korenizatsiia*, at all levels of government, by January 1, 1932.[246] Since Ukraine itself had achieved only a 65 percent rate of linguistic Ukrainization after three years of intense efforts, the prospects for North Caucasus success were not auspicious. Still, the project was pursued with vigor. Tens of thousands of Mountaineers (of a total population of just over a million) were put through short-term courses—the all-purpose solution to all difficulties during the cultural revolution—to train them for positions as modest as kolkhoz accountant. Virtually nothing was accomplished in the field of linguistic *korenizatsiia*.[247] In mid-1931, a North Caucasus decree protested "the outrageous fact that the completion dates for *korenizatsiia* have been put back four or more times."[248] They would be rolled back a few more times until the project was quietly abandoned in late 1933.

[243] *3 sessiia TsIK SSSR 5 sozyva. Stenograficheskii otchet* (Moscow, 1931): 5.
[244] "Iz reshenii obkoma VKP/b/. Ob iakutizatsii (ot 06.03.29)," *Po zavetam Il'icha*, no. 3 (1929): 37–39; "Postanovlenie biuro OK o komizatsii," *Komi mu—Zyrianskii krai*, no. 21 (1929): 41.
[245] B. Rodievich, "Korenizatsiia apparata v avtonomiiakh i raionakh natsmenshinstv RSFSR," *Revoliutsiia i natsional'nosti*, no. 12 (1931): 12–21. *GARF* 1235/123/68 (1928–1935): 1–366.
[246] *GARF* 1235/140/1051 (1928): 34. P. Beliachkov, "Ocherednye zadachi sovetskogo stroitel'stva v natsional'nykh oblastiakh kraia," *Revoliutsiia i gorets*, no. 2 (1929): 14.
[247] Again, with the exception of Ossetia, which did shift most of its rural apparat to Ossetian. V. Sabinin, "Voprosy korenizatsii apparata postavit' v tsentre vnimaniia," *Revoliutsiia i gorets*, no. 5 (1931): 66; A. Tliuniaev, "Korenizatsiia apparata v natsoblastiakh—odna iz osnovnykh zadach sotsialisticheskogo stroitel'stva," *Revoliutsiia i gorets*, nos. 8–9 (1932): 43–46; *GARF* 1235/123/68 (1931): 3–5.
[248] "Slomit' opportunisticheskoe soprotivlenie korenizatsii, provesti ee v srok," *Revoliutsiia i gorets*, no. 9 (1931): 68.

The North Caucasus example illustrates how the pragmatic strategy of functional *korenizatsiia* was quickly abandoned during the cultural revolution. Only Tatarstan continued its meticulous and successful efforts to gradually increase the number of Tatars in skilled positions.[249] In the North Caucasus, the old mechanical *korenizatsiia* ran rampant. Quotas were set and Russians replaced with no evident concern about their reactions. The Cherkess autonomous oblast even set a quota of 100 percent Cherkess in the oblast's leadership positions.[250] In early 1930, the North Caucasus government ordered the percentage of Chechens in leadership positions in their oblast raised from 27 percent to 50 percent in the course of four months.[251] To fulfill this measure, Russians would of course have to be replaced. Surprisingly, VTsIK was no less cautious. In a 1931 decree, they demanded that the percentage of titular nationals in the government apparat be raised from their current levels (20 to 30 percent) to 70 percent in less than six months.[252]

Or course none of these quotas were met, but that does not mean they were only propagandistic. Aggressive Affirmative Action did lead to a rapid growth of Mountaineers in leadership positions. In the Karachai autonomous oblast, Karachai increased from 34.4 percent in leadership positions in 1929 to 61.4 percent in 1931, but the number of Karachai in the overall government apparat inched forward from 21.5 percent to 24.6 percent.[253] Such modest but real progress was typical for the period from 1929 to 1932, with a sharp drop-off in 1933 as cultural revolutionary enthusiasm waned. By mid-1933, as Table 22 shows, despite the massive government efforts to promote titular nationals, the number of Mountaineers in government positions had actually declined since late 1928.

Table 23 shows that in some RSFSR national regions, modest progress was made in the *korenizatsiia* of the government apparat during the cultural revolution, whereas others witnessed an overall decline.[254] Overall, Bolshevik leaders found "cultural backwardness" much more intractable than either the ideology of the cultural revolution or NEP had predicted.

The situation in the union republics of Central Asia was similar, as a discussion of the Uzbek experience will demonstrate. From December 1923 to August 1928, Uzbekistan had passed no less than twelve *korenizatsiia* decrees and still seen the percentage of Uzbeks in the central government apparat drop from

---

[249] On Tatarstan's continued use of functional *korenizatsiia*, see *SU Tatarskoi respubliki*, no. 16 (1929): 236–248; no. 22 (1930): 435–436; no. 3 (1932): 35–38.

[250] A. Tliuniaev, "Plan korenizatsii apparata Cherkesii," *Revoliutsiia i gorets*, nos. 7–8 (1929): 21.

[251] "Khronika," *Revoliutsiia i gorets*, no. 3 (1930): 98.

[252] Tliuniaev, "Plan Korenizatsiia apparata," 47.

[253] N. Baronov, "Korenizatsiia—uzkoe mesto v Karachae," *Revoliutsiia i gorets*, nos. 10–11 (1931): 86–89.

[254] I removed the Bashkir ASSR, which increased from 6.8 percent to 25.6 percent from 1930 to 1933 while Bashkirs represented only 23.7 percent of the republics' total population, because Tatars were often counted together with Bashkirs in *korenizatsiia* statistics, and I suspect this explains the otherwise remarkable leap in *korenizatsiia* recorded there.

Table 22. Korenizatsiia in North Caucasus Autonomous Oblasts (AOs), 1929–1933 (Titular Nationals as Percent of Total Government Apparat)

Region	1929	1932	1933
Kabardino-Balkar AO	21.8	30.0	16.2
Karachai AO	21.5	24.6	20.4
North Ossetian AO	70.1	60.4	43.4
Cherkess AO	15.7	27.0	16.6
Ingush AO	n/a	51.9	n/a
Chechen AO	n/a	20.3	11.1

Dzhangir Nagiev, "Zadachi korenizatsii sovetskogo apparata v nats. obl. Sev.-Kav. kraia," Revoliutsiia i gorets, nos. 1–2 (1929): 34; Tliuniaev, "Korenizatsiia apparata," 43; D. Ts., "Po-bolshevistski, borot'sia Za Korenizatsiia" Revoliutsiia i gorets no. 9 (1933): 10–11, 12.

Table 23. Korenizatsiia of RSFSR ASSR and Autonomous Oblasts (AOs), 1930–1933 (Titular Nationals as Percent of Total Government Apparat)

Region	1930	1933	As Percent of Total Population
Karelian ASSR	17.9	16.7	37.4
Chuvash ASSR	46.6	54.5	74.6
Tatar ASSR	30.7	38.5	44.9
Mari AO	28.0	35.4	54.1
Mordvinian AO	18.2	17.6	29.3
Crimean ASSR	10.6	14.8	25.7
Dagestan ASSR	23.2	15.0	62.5

Adapted from Simon, Nationalism and Policy, 39. I removed the Bashkir ASSR, which increased from 6.8 percent to 25.6 percent from 1930 to 1933 while Bashkirs represented only 23.7 percent of the republics' total population, because Tatars were often counted together with Bashkirs in korenizatsiia statistics, and I suspect this explains the otherwise remarkable leap in korenizatsiia recorded there.

19.0 percent in April 1925 to 12.1 percent in April 1928.[255] Therefore, with the onset of cultural revolution, the Uzbek government was also ready to throw aside functional korenizatsiia and adopt strategy of comprehensive Uzbekization. A December 1928 decree called for all paperwork in all state institutions in Uzbekistan, from the village soviet to the republican level, to be conducted in Uzbek. The decree followed a slightly more gradual approach than in Ukraine. Institutions were divided into three categories. The first category (soft-line central institutions such as TsIK and Narkompros) had to switch to Uzbek by January 1, 1930; the second category (hard-line central institutions such as the Commissariat of Finance and VSNKh) by January 1, 1931; and the third

[255] GARF 374/27s/1707 (1929): 112–119.

category (economic trusts and large city institutions), by January 1, 1932, when Uzbekization would be complete. After October 1, 1929, it was forbidden to hire anyone who did not speak Uzbek.[256] All Europeans were required to study Uzbek with the threat of dismissal if they failed to do so.[257] The Central Asian Biuro even authorized a raise of up to 10 percent for those who learned the republican language.[258]

The attempt to force Europeans to study Uzbek was initially taken quite seriously. A Rabkrin investigation reported that "Europeans were studying [Uzbek] very energetically."[259] More tellingly, letters intercepted by the GPU in January 1929 warned acquaintances in the RSFSR not to come to Tashkent as "one needs to know the Uzbek language, which is now mandatory in all institutions."[260] An Uzbek TsK report said that initially 60 percent of Europeans enrolled in Uzbek-language courses but the percentage then dropped rapidly.[261] Uzbekistan lacked the enforcement bureaucracy that Ukraine put in place, so Europeans quickly learned they could avoid the courses with impunity. As a result, the December 1928 decree had virtually no impact on the number of Europeans with a knowledge of Uzbek.[262] Since Uzbeks remained a minority in their own government apparat throughout this period, this fact alone effectively doomed linguistic Uzbekization.

With one instructive exception, no Uzbek central organs did more than occasionally include Uzbek translations with the Russian directives they sent out. The exception was the paradigmatically soft-line Education Commissariat, which in August 1931 did indeed shift its working language entirely to Uzbek.[263] Their experience was instructive. Their internal work continued at previous tempos, but their correspondence with other institutions either went unanswered or was returned with a request for a Russian translation. They joked that this was one great benefit: "The legislative organs, particularly Sovnarkom, began to accept all our proposals just as we had prepared them (that is, in the Uzbek language)."[264] This experiment continued for over a year, but in 1933 they drifted back to work in Russian. This happened to countless village and district soviet institutions across Uzbekistan (and elsewhere), which switched to the native language but received all communication in Russian, and so gradu-

[256] Ibid., 114. *GARF* 3316/24/595 (1931): 45; *RTsKhIDNI* 62/2/1743 (1929): 14–15.

[257] A. B., "Sabotiruiut korenizatsiiu," *Pravda vostoka*, no. 186 (14.08.30): 3; Prepodavatel', "Korenizatsii apparata ugrozhaet sryv," *Pravda vostoka*, no. 286 (10.12.30): 3.

[258] *RTsKhIDNI* 62/2/1262 (1928): 4.

[259] *GARF* 374/27s/1707 (1929): 114.

[260] *RTsKhIDNI* 62/2/1808 (1929): 73.

[261] *RTsKhIDNI* 62/2/2272 (1930): 27.

[262] Ibid., 3. A. B., "Sabotiruiut korenizatsiiu," 3; "Rech' tov. Kakhiani na 5-m kurultae KP/b/Uz," *Pravda vostoka*, no. 138 (18.06.30): 2; RTsKhIDNI 62/2/2866 (1932): 19; 62/2/2280 (1930): 7.

[263] "Vtoroi etap bor'by za korenizatsiiu apparata narkomprosa UzSSR," *Pravda vostoka*, no. 281 (12.10.31): 3.

[264] "Vtoroi etap bor'by," 3.

ally switched to Russian.[265] Since the cultural revolution marked an enormous increase in the center's influence in rural regions, this ironically led to a decline in the level of linguistic *korenizatsiia*.[266] As in Ukraine, increased centralization undercut linguistic *korenizatsiia*.

The prospect for promotion of Uzbeks into government was more promising, since the socialist offensive led to a sudden spurt in the size of the government apparat. This meant Uzbeks could be promoted without displacing Russians. However, the increased class vigilance of the cultural revolution worked against *korenizatsiia*. The terror campaigns against the *smenovekhovtsy* national intelligentsia led eastern governments to remove these "former people" (*byvshikh*) from government jobs.[267] A central Rabkrin investigation claimed this process had gone too far: "Under the line of our class policy, nationals are being fired. This is a hidden persecution of nationals, an incorrect line."[268] GPU reports noted a pervasive atmosphere of fear among Uzbek *byvshikh*: "It is impossible to live this way anymore, when your every move is followed by one hundred suspicious eyes. God forbid that someone write a bad denunciation on me or if I quarrel with someone. They'll surely arrest me as I'm the son of a well-known imam."[269] The removal of members of the old national intelligentsias from government positions was particularly damaging for *korenizatsiia* as they tended to be the best educated and most qualified of the eastern national cadres.

In Russia, the purge of the old intelligentsia was accompanied by the mass *vydvizhenie* (promotion) campaign to train and promote workers to replace those purged. However, as we have seen, there was neither a sizable eastern proletariat nor sufficient literate titular nationals to fill the university places provided for by the *bronia*. Therefore, in the east, *vydvizhenie* took on a different meaning. It referred instead to the direct promotion of workers and peasants from blue-collar or agricultural labor into white-collar managerial positions. This campaign again lagged behind the central *vydvizhenie* initiative. It began in earnest only with a December 1931 Central Asian *Biuro* decree that was accompanied by a list of sixty-one local nationals to be promoted immediately into leadership positions in various economic organs.[270] For instance, Sherif Nurmatov, a locomotive driver with twelve years of work experience and five

---

[265] "Rech' tov. Kakhiani," 2.

[266] There were no reliable statistics kept on linguistic *korenizatsiia* in the countryside with the exception of Tatarstan, where the situation did worsen despite government efforts to the contrary. A. Osharov, "Iz opyta korenizatsii v Tatarskoi ASSR," *Sovetskoe gosudarstvo i pravo*, no. 4 (1930): 139. Based on numerous anecdotal reports, it seems certain that a similar decline took place elsewhere.

[267] *RTsKhIDNI* 17/113/756 (22.07.29): 138/1, 116; *RTsKhIDNI* 17/113/847 (06.05.30): 847/1, 280b.

[268] *GARF* 374/27s/1483 (1929): 121.

[269] *RTsKhIDNI* 62/2/1809 (1929): 28.

[270] "O vydvizhenii," *Revolivtsiia i natsional'nosti*, no. 3 (1931): 2.

years of party membership, was made assistant director of the Central Asian railway and head of its cadres department. The decree instructed all lower party organs, at the republican, regional, and district level, to do likewise. Kirgizia responded with a promotion of 125 local nationals to central jobs and 240 to district-level positions.[271] This alone improved their rate of *korenizatsiia* from 9.8 percent in January 1931 to 17.0 percent in June 1931. They planned to promote over one thousand local nationals in the course of 1931 and felt that through "decisive and bold promotion [*vydvizhenie*]" they could solve the problem of *korenizatsiia* within a few years.

The experience of the new *vydvizhentsy* was rarely a happy one. Mistreatment of *vydvizhentsy*, after ethnic conflict in the factory, was the favorite theme of newspaper articles denouncing great-power chauvinism. At best, they were treated as "an unavoidable evil," ignored and left, in the words of an official report, "to stew in their own juices."[272] European hostility cannot be attributed to racial prejudice alone. Many *vydvizhentsy* were not qualified and the Central Asian Biuro required economic enterprises "to organize special courses, study groups and individual training" for *vydvizhentsy* with time off from work for these activities.[273] Naturally having a major leadership position occupied by someone in need of basic training was undesirable. Many *vydvizhentsy*, therefore, were systematically mocked, denied apartments and generally given "disgusting living and work conditions." Such conditions drove one *vydvizhenets*, who had worked in the Agricultural Commissariat for a year and a half, to declare "he would return home to his kolkhoz at the first opportunity, where there are better living conditions." A committee studying the extremely high turnover rate of *vydvizhentsy* concluded that "they were given instructions and materials exclusively in Russian, which guaranteed they would commit errors, and therefore, fearing the loss of their Party cards, they fled work at the first opportunity."[274] This mirrored the high national drop-out rates in higher education and the high turnover among the native proletariat. In all three cases, the attempt to force a short-term solution on a long-term problem produced unsatisfactory results.

The overall development of *korenizatsiia* in Central Asia echoed the North Caucasus experience. Through 1932, there was solid growth in the rates of *korenizatsiia*: from 9 percent in January 1930 to 18.8 percent in March 1932 in Turkmenistan; from 6.4 percent in November 1930 to 20.8 percent in December 1932 in Kirgizia.[275] As in the North Caucasus, the growth occurred mostly in leadership positions. The overall rate of *korenizatsiia* in Uzbekistan grew, after

---

[271] A. Konstantinov, "Vydvizhenie, podgotovka natskadrov i zadachi korenizatsii v Kir. ASSR," *Pravda vostoka*, no. 260 (21.09.31): 3.

[272] Galkina i Filonov, "Zdes' gnezdiatsia shovinisty," *Pravda vostoka*, no. 230 (05.10.30): 2; RTsKhIDNI 62/2/2390 (1930): 62.

[273] "O vydvizhenii," 2.

[274] RTsKhIDNI 62/2/3133 (1933): 21–25.

[275] RTsKhIDNI 62/2/3313 (1933): 1; Konstantinov, "Vydvizhenie, podgotovka natskadrov," 3; RTsKhIDNI 62/1/1038 (25.08.33): 125.

six years of stagnation, from 16.9 percent in 1931 to 19 percent in 1932 and 22.5 percent in 1933. The comparable rates for leadership positions were 47.5 percent, 49.4 percent, and 77.0 percent, while for specialists they were 5.5 percent, 8.5 percent and 7.7 percent.[276] With the relaxation of effort that accompanied the end of the cultural revolution, again following the North Caucasus pattern, there was then a sudden drop in late 1932 and early 1933: in Turkmenistan from 18.9 percent to 13.8 percent, in Tajikistan from 16.3 percent to 15.1 percent, and in Kirgizia from 20.7 percent to 13 percent.[277] As in the entire Soviet east, the massive efforts expended during the cultural revolution to complete *korenizatsiia* had led to surprisingly meager progress. By 1933 it was clear that if *korenizatsiia* was to be accomplished, it would be a long process.

Conclusion: *Korenizatsiia* in East and West

The evolution of *korenizatsiia* in the numerous and diverse regions of the Soviet east, through the changing environments of NEP and cultural revolution, was an extremely complex process. Nevertheless, this complicated story supports several important generalizations. First, concerning the unity of Soviet policy, it raises the question of whether there was one or two Soviet nationality policies. The initial answer given in 1923 was unambiguous. There was a single policy of *korenizatsiia* that involved the promotion of national territories, elites, languages, and cultures for all Soviet nationalities regardless of their size, their level of development, or the strength of their nationalist movement. After the 1923 decrees had been issued, both western and eastern republics attempted to implement comprehensive linguistic *korenizatsiia* and Affirmative Action. It was only in the process of implementation that the policy bifurcated. In the western republics, the creation of an indigenous elite was relatively uncomplicated, so the major focus became the formidable task of linguistic *korenizatsiia*. In the eastern republics, the achievement of linguistic *korenizatsiia* proved utterly impossible, so all energies were devoted to Affirmative Action programs to create an indigenous elite. It is important here to recognize that these decisions were made at the local level, based on the judgments of the republican leaderships, and were only subsequently ratified by the center. They were not imposed from above. In both east and west, local conditions were decisive.

This of course does not mean that the categories of east and west only emerged as a result of the implementation of *korenizatsiia*. If the center proposed a single policy in 1923, it nevertheless offered two justifications for that policy: a primary principle of indigenousness and a secondary principle of cultural backwardness. The latter principle preserved the prerevolutionary dichotomy between east and west, although, in the characteristic manner of the

---

[276] *RTsKhIDNI* 62/2/3163 (1933): 203.
[277] *RTsKhIDNI* 62/2/3133 (1933): 8; 62/2/3163 (1933): 163.

Affirmative Action Empire, it reversed its political implications by granting preferences to the culturally backward. If the Soviets inherited rather than created the east/west dichotomy, it is fair to say that they increased its systematization. For instance, the general problems of implementing *korenizatsiia* in the east were given a single solution, the policy of functional *korenizatsiia*, that central authorities applied throughout the Soviet east, as if the region were a single, unified whole. Likewise, the problems in recruitment for higher education led to a shift from an affirmative action *bronia* based on indigenousness (for all national minorities) to one based on "cultural backwardness" for only eastern nationalities, and then ultimately to a complete systematization of the category of "eastern" by a definition of exactly which ninety-seven nationalities were culturally backward. Thus, a developmentalist continuum that ran rather seamlessly from the small peoples of the north to the Latvians and Estonians was divided into a stark dichotomy between east and west, advanced and backward.

The changing background of Soviet politics, in particular the abrupt transition from NEP to cultural revolution, intersected with the dual principles of indigenousness and cultural backwardness in a way that led to further differences in the course of *korenizatsiia* in east and west. Due to financial pragmatism and less aggressive centralization, NEP favored the principle of indigenousness, and so the years 1925 to 1928 represented the zenith of *korenizatsiia* in Ukraine and Belorussia. The centralization of the socialist offensive as well as the class warfare aspect of cultural revolution undermined linguistic *korenizatsiia* in Ukraine, Belorussia, and even Georgia. On the other hand, both centralization and the constructive utopianism of the cultural revolution favored the developmentalist project of overcoming cultural backwardness, so that the zenith of *korenizatsiia* in the east was the period from 1928 to 1932.

Here an important distinction can be made between the effect of the cultural revolution on relations between center and periphery and those between Russians and non-Russians. The socialist offensive and cultural revolution represented an intensification of the strategy of the Affirmative Action Empire, an intensification of both the project of building a centralized economy and polity, and an intensification of the policy of downplaying and stigmatizing Russian national culture and identity while promoting non-Russian identity. This again favored east over west. Linguistic *korenizatsiia* in Ukraine was undermined by a conflict between the Ukrainian republic and central institutions. The east welcomed centralization as it brought with it both greater financial assistance and support in the conflict between Russians and non-Russians, which it received in the form of the campaign against Great Russian chauvinism.

This divergent course of *korenizatsiia* during the cultural revolution can also be understood in terms of the hard-line and soft-line distinction. The socialist offensive and cultural revolution marked a decisive turn toward the implementation of the core Bolshevik projects of rapid industrialization, collectivization, complete political hegemony of the party, and the persecution of the bourgeoisie and other "former peoples." These policies undermined the attempt to establish Ukrainization as a hard-line policy. Why didn't this also happen in the Soviet east? To a degree it did. All-union central authorities did obstruct the *bronia* in Moscow and *vydvizhenie* in Central Asia, as well as any attempt to achieve linguistic *korenizatsiia*. The important difference was that in the Soviet east *korenizatsiia* could be furthered successfully as a soft-line policy. As noted earlier, hard-line and soft-line policies typically coexisted, with hard-line policies having a categorical priority and soft-line policies being implemented to the extent they did not contradict the core hard-line policies. In Ukraine, intensified centralization produced such a contradiction. However, in the Soviet east, the developmentalist project of overcoming cultural backwardness through Affirmative Action complemented perfectly the highly centralized but paternalist and anticolonial statism of the socialist offensive and cultural revolution. A contradiction would emerge only when the centralized state became re-identified with the core Russian people.

In addition to these generalizations about *korenizatsiia* in the east and west, a second important point that needs to be made concerns the social structure that had emerged in the Soviet east by 1933 and would remain, to a considerable degree, characteristic of the eastern national regions through to the collapse of the Soviet Union in 1991. This is what I referred to as "the hole in the middle," the absent national technical and clerical white-collar workers who would have made possible linguistic *korenizatsiia*, as well as complete indigenous control over the eastern republics. This result was largely conditioned by objective factors, in particular the limited number of well-educated titular nationals. Only through meticulous and well-conceived efforts, such as those made by Tatarstan, could the hole in middle be gradually filled. Instead, the widespread utopian refusal to choose priorities exacerbated the problem. The attempt to create a universal native-language primary school system virtually overnight diverted a huge percentage of educated titular nationals into pedagogy and elementary school teaching. The more talented titulars were promoted immediately into positions of leadership. This made it impossible to fulfill the generous *bronia* provided for "culturally backward" nationals in the most prestigious industrial and technical VUZy of Moscow and Leningrad. In this way, the eastern nationalities missed the great wave of *vydvizhenie* that created the new Soviet technical intelligentsia. The creation of a divided intelligentsia in the eastern republics—a national creative and Russian technical intelligentsia—dates back to this missed opportunity.

This outcome leads to a third and final general observation about the policy of *korenizatsiia*. It was, to a striking degree, a policy devoted exclusively to the problem of creating national elites at the republican level and below. It was largely silent about the promotion of non-Russian elites into *central* institutions. This is important since theories of nationalism have again and again emphasized the crucial importance of blocked upward mobility of peripheral elites in spawning nationalist movements.[278] Indeed, David Laitin's recent analysis of the Russian-speaking communities of Estonia, Latvia, Ukraine, and Kazakhstan uses exactly this variable to create a typology of three patterns of peripheral incorporation in the Soviet Union: a "most-favored lords" model in which the titular nationals can and do easily move into influential all-union positions (Ukraine); an "integralist" model in which the titular nationals dominate their own republic but either cannot or do not want to move into all-union positions (Latvia, Estonia); and a "colonial" model in which titular nationals share influence in their republics with Russians and have virtually no prospect of moving into important all-union positions (Kazakhstan).[279]

This typology is useful as it helps clarify both the goals and blind spots of *korenizatsiia*. The blind spot was non-Russian representation in the center. The goal was, at the local level, to move each republic from the colonial to the integralist model. By 1932, this goal had been largely achieved in the western republics. At the very least, there was a critical mass of non-Russians in the party and soviet bureaucracy to form a network of ethnicized patron–client ties that would gradually produce titular national control of these republics.[280] The transition failed to develop a critical mass in the Soviet east, due to the necessity of relying on Russians for the crucial white-collar positions. Even when ethnicized patron–client networks did gain a dominant position in the Brezhnev period, they still had to rely overwhelmingly on Russian specialists.[281]

This still leaves the issue of the incorporation of non-Russians into the central elite. Why was this not a more salient part of *korenizatsiia*? Were non-Russians excluded from the central elite? Of course they were not. The Affirmative Action Empire assumed a non-national central state elite, modeled on the historical experience of the Bolshevik Party, which always included a large representation of the Russian empire's western nationalities but which nevertheless conceived of itself as a non-national, or supranational, rather than multinational party. Throughout the 1920s and 1930s, Georgians, Armenians, Ukrainians, and other western nationalities rose into dominant positions in the all-union party and government, although beginning in the mid-1930s diaspora nationalities (Poles, Latvians, eventually Jews) began to be removed as potentially disloyal. Eastern nationalities, however, remained confined to the soft-line organs in charge of nationalities policy such as the Soviet of Nationalities (from 1927 to 1935, headed by a Turkmen and an Uzbek) and the Nationalities Department (run by a series of Kazakhs). Did this represent an intentional obstacle to eastern mobility reflecting a conscious or subconscious racism? Perhaps, but the more likely

---

[278] Benedict Anderson, *Imagined Communities* (London, 1991): 47–65. Ernest Gellner, *Nations and Nationalism* (Ithaca, N.Y., 1983): 52–87.

[279] David Laitin, *Identity in Formation* (Ithaca, N.Y., 1998).

[280] The classic work on ethnicized patron–client ties in the Stalinist period is Charles Fairbanks Jr., "Clientelism and the Roots of Post-Soviet Disorder," in Ronald Grigor Suny, ed., *Transcaucasia, Nationalism, and Social Change* (Ann Arbor, Mich., 1996): 341–376.

[281] For a good case study, see Nancy Lubin, *Labor and Nationality in Soviet Central Asia* (Princeton, N.J., 1984).

explanation was the same one that explained the failure of the all-union *bronia*. Any sufficiently talented and reliable eastern nationals were in a major leadership position in their own republic and could not be spared for central assignments. The easterners who were sent to Moscow were those who had lost out in factional struggles and were being exiled to a distant and insignificant assignment. As with so much of *korenizatsiia* in the East, it was a supply rather than a demand problem.

5

The Latinization Campaign and the Symbolic Politics of National Identity

The latinization campaign was about language, but it was more about what language symbolized. And language—not the public use of language, but its vocabulary, grammar, and script—symbolized national culture. National culture was the most ambiguous of the four central elements of *korenizatsiia*. The formation of national territories, support for the increased use of national languages, and the creation of national elites, the subject of Chapters 2 to 4, were clear, if often challenging, goals. But what exactly was national culture?

Stalin, of course, famously defined Soviet national cultures as being "national in form, socialist in content." But this just begged the question as to what "national in form" meant, and Stalin purposefully chose not to clarify this concept. The very existence of national culture was controversial. The left oppositionist, Vaganian, spoke for many party members when he asserted that national culture was an inherently bourgeois and nationalist concept and that the Bolsheviks should do no more than build international or socialist culture in national languages. Although he would never have admitted it, this is close to what Stalin had in mind. When he referred to tasks in building national culture, Stalin's first example was typically native-language schools.[1] In lists of accomplishments in "national-cultural construction," authors would add native-language literature, theater, and opera (which was considered especially cultured). Since the content of the schools and literary works was to be socialist, this all amounted to little more than Vaganian's socialist culture in national languages.

---

[1] I. Stalin, *Marksizm i natsional'no-kolonial'nyi vopros* (Moscow, 1934): 157–158.

Did Soviet national culture include any of the features now typically associated with national cultures, such as distinctive patterns of belief and social practices? It did not. In theory, Stalin included a distinctive *byt* (customs, way of life) in his 1913 definition of a nation and reiterated this in his canonical 1925 remarks on national culture. In practice, however, nationalities specialists never established what aspects of national *byt* should be preserved and promoted. All of the most significant national beliefs and practices—religion, gender relations, social stratification, economic organization—were either to be abolished or homogenized into what Stalin called both "socialist content" and "universal human culture" (*obshchechelovecheskaia kul'tura*).[2] Of course, Stalin did maintain, against Vaganian, that national culture existed in the present, and its vestiges would continue to exist for a long period of time. This was one of the justifications of having local nationals run their own republics. However, this did not mean that such vestiges should be preserved or encouraged. Quite the contrary.

This still leaves the positive content of national culture unspecified. As I argued in Chapter 1, the translation that best captures Stalin's *natsional'naia kul'tura* is not "national culture" but "national identity," or what the American sociologist Herbert Gans called "symbolic ethnicity."[3] Promoting "national culture" meant aggressively promoting national identity, while undermining distinctive national beliefs and social practices. Both Lenin's and Stalin's justifications of the Soviet nationalities policy were highly psychological. Lenin emphasized the necessity of overcoming the formerly oppressed nationalities' "distrust" of Russians, Stalin the need to make national governments feel "close and comprehensible to the [non-Russian] laboring masses."[4] By encouraging the growth of national identity and resolutely opposing assimilation, the Soviet government showed an ostentatious and unthreatening respect for the national identity of all non-Russians. This was a central aspect of the Affirmative Action Empire's strategy of preventing the growth of nationalist sentiment.

Such demonstrative respect was especially necessary because Soviet policy would involve an attack launched from the center (and so likely to be perceived as "Russian") on traditional national beliefs and practices, above all, religion. If "mistrust" was overcome, and the non-Russians felt "close" to their own government, these attacks would be understood as being non-national, based on the universal class ideology of socialism. They would therefore not be resisted so strongly (or rather resisted only by class enemies), and the homogenous socialist "universal human culture" would emerge, adorned with symbolic markers of national identity. The symbolic markers of identity favored by Soviet authorities were strikingly similar to those dear to independent nationalists worldwide: national folklore, dress, food, revolutionary heroes, progressive

[2] Ibid., 158.
[3] Herbert Gans, "Symbolic ethnicity: The future of ethnic groups and cultures in America," *Ethnic and Racial Studies* 2, no. 1 (1979): 9–17.
[4] Stalin, *Marksizm*, 157.

historical events, and classic literary works. As we shall see in Chapter 10, national poets became particularly important in the 1930s. A more ambiguous and therefore interesting symbolic marker was the national alphabet.

Although it would hardly seem to be a central concern of nationalities policy in a complex state like the Soviet Union, alphabet reform emerged in the 1920s and 1930s as a major practical project in language construction and an even more important symbolic battleground in the politics of national identity. The prominence of alphabet politics not only surprises the outside observer, but it also caused a contemporary publicist to puzzle over "the unclear political significance of questions of the development of alphabets, and the incomprehensible penetration of fierce class conflict into this narrow, specialized area, seemingly of interest only to professors, the problem of alphabets."[5] Alphabet politics assumed such significance because the written script proved an extraordinarily multivalent symbol, capable of communicating a variety of different messages about the national constitution of the Soviet Union as a whole, as well as about the cultural and political orientation of its component nations and groups of nations. Among the national orientations that could be signaled by, or inferred from, one's preference in alphabets were pan-Turkism, internationalism, Russophobia, allegiance to western Europe, allegiance to the eastern colonial world, treasonous irredentism, loyalist irredentism, and Russian nationalism. Among the political orientations were the cultural revolutionary, greatpower chauvinist, religious reactionary, and local nationalist.

This chapter is devoted to a case study in the symbolic politics of national identity. This might not seem a topic worthy of its own chapter. However, symbolic politics were a crucial component of Soviet politics under Stalin. Because the Bolshevik Party subscribed to a hegemonic and comprehensive ideology, instructions concerning the many aspects of daily administration that conflicted with that ideology could not be communicated directly. Therefore, the state itself often communicated through a process of symbolic politics called *signaling*. In Chapters 3 and 6, I discuss the role of terror campaigns in signaling to local officials which central policies were to be considered hard-line core Bolshevik policies and so to be implemented at all costs, and which were secondary soft-line policies that should be implemented only if they did not conflict with the core policies. Terror was, of course, only the most extreme form of central signaling. Most such signals were sent through the press. The center's decision to communicate with its officials and its population in this manner created a form of symbolic politics that could in turn be appropriated by different elites both within and without the government in an attempt to send their own preferred messages. Central symbols could be subtly slanted or new symbols could be advanced. The Bolshevik leadership was well aware of this process of symbolic politics and therefore monitored its publications carefully to control the signals being emitted.

---

[5] D. Orlinskii, "Natsional-demokratizm v voprosakh iazyka i pis'mennosti," *Bol'shevik*, no. 6 (1934): 81.

The Latinization Campaign

The latinization campaign was a paradigmatic example of this latter type of entrepreneurial symbolic politics initiated from below, in this case by eastern regional elites, and only gradually embraced by central authorities. Latinization involved either changing the alphabet of a language from a script such as Arabic or Cyrillic to the Latin script or creating a new written language using the Latin script for previously exclusively oral languages.[6] The success of the latinization movement was made possible by the inter- section of an urgent requirement created by the new Soviet nationalities policy and the symbolic agenda of a particular eastern elite. The urgent require- ment was clear. The Soviet nationalities policy demanded that all education and government work be conducted in native languages. Since the written languages of the majority of the Soviet Union's small nationalities were in a very rudimentary state, this created a sudden need for rapid linguistic reform.

This alone would not raise the issue of changing alphabets. It was the combination of radical linguistic reform with the decolonizing ideology sweeping the non-Russian peoples, an ideology endorsed (within limits) by the Bolsheviks' nationalities policy. The Cyrillic alphabet was strongly associ- ated with Orthodox missionary activity and Russian colonialism. Most of the Russian empire's newly converted Christian peoples, primarily the Finnic peoples of the middle Volga and far north, had a Cyrillic-based written lan- guage provided for them by Orthodox missionaries. The famous Orthodox missionary and educational reformer Nikolai Ilminskii extended this practice to Islamic peoples. In the linguistic chaos following the revolution, before any central policy could be established, some spontaneous latinization occurred. The Yakut in 1920 and the Ossetines in 1923 abandoned their Cyrillic scripts for the Latin.[7] Similar movements arose among the Christian nationalities of the Volga (the Mari, Mordvinians, Chuvash, Udmurt), but they instead opted to reform their existing Cyrillic alphabets.[8] The Komi also considered adopting the Latin script, but instead created their own distinctive Cyrillic script. The Kalmyks, who used the ancient Mongolian script, adopted Cyrillic. Their elites argued that since they lived among Russians and had to learn Russian, this choice made sense.[9] Other small peoples in a similar

---

[6] On latinizatsiia, see Michael Smith, *Language and Power in the Creation of the USSR* (New York, 1998): 121–142; M. I. Isaev, *Iazykovoe stroitel'stvo v SSSR* (Moscow, 1979); Michael Kirkwood, ed. *Language Planning in the Soviet Union* (New York, 1990). Adrienne Edgar, "The Creation of Soviet Turkmenistan, 1924–1938" (Ph.D. diss., University of California-Berkeley, 1999): 332–390.

[7] *Pervyi vsesoiuznyi tiurkologicheskii s"ezd. Stenograficheskii otchet* (Baku, 1926): 289 ff.; P. Tedeev, "Novyi alfavit v Osetii," *Kul'tura i pis'mennost' vostoka* 1 (1928): 101–106.

[8] A. Gren, "K voprosu o primenenii latinskogo alfavita k iazykam Komi i Udmurt," *Komi mu— Zyrianskii krai*, no. 3 (1924): 50–59; "O chuvashskom pravopisanii," *Biulleten' TsIK avtonomnoi chuvashskoi SSR*, no. 21–22 (1926): 6–18.

[9] *Pervyi tiurkologicheskii s"ezd*, 294.

situation (the Oirots, Khakassy, Shortsy, Gypsies, Assyrians) also adopted Cyrillic.[10]

The choice of alphabet was most controversial among the Islamic peoples, and it was from the Islamic regions that latinization emerged as a movement. The Arabic script was strongly identified with Islam, which made it attractive to conservative elites and suspect to reforming elites. Reformers also argued that the Arabic script had insuperable technical deficiencies. Its letters were difficult to distinguish and had different meanings according to their place in the word. Most important, the Arabic script lacked vowels, a serious handicap given many Turkic languages' use of vowel harmony. The Cyrillic alphabet was symbolically anathema, especially among the Turkic peoples, since it was associated with Tsarist missionary endeavors and with the putative apostasy of the Turkic Chuvash and Kryashen Tatars (baptized Volga Tatars), both of whose languages used the Cyrillic script. Initially, a compromise emerged in the Turkic regions in favor of a reformed Arabic alphabet. The most comprehensive reforms were attempted in Tatarstan and Kazakhstan.[11] Those Islamic peoples who lacked a written language, however, leaned toward the more neutral Latin script. The Islamic mountain peoples of the North Caucasus all adopted vernacular Latin alphabets between 1923 and 1927.[12]

This was the environment in which an Azerbaijani elite, consisting of former non-Bolshevik leftists who had joined the party and assumed prominent leadership positions in the new Soviet Azerbaijani government, initiated a campaign for latinization of the Turkic peoples' Arabic scripts. The leader of this campaign was Samed Agamali-Ogly, an experienced Azerbaijani revolutionary who was a veteran of the 1905 revolution and former member of the socialist Hummet party. In 1920, he joined the new Bolshevik government as its Commissar of Agriculture, and from 1922 to 1929 served as head of the Azerbaijani TsIK. Agamali-Ogly made latinization his personal crusade.[13] In 1922, he convinced the Azerbaijani government to support the formation of a committee for the new Turkic alphabet (*Komitet NTA*) and the establishment of a latinized Azerbaijani-language newspaper, *Jeni Jol* (*The New Road*). As the name *new Turkic alphabet* suggests, Agamali-Ogly's ambitions extended far beyond Azerbaijan. Success in Azerbaijan came quickly. In October 1923, the Latin script was given equal status with Arabic and in 1924 was made the sole official script throughout Azerbaijan.[14]

[10] N. Iakovlev, "Nekotorye itogi latinizatsii i unifikatsii alfavitov v SSSR," *Revoliutsiia i pis'mennost'*, nos. 4–5 (1932): 25–46. The attempt to shift Assyrian to Cyrillic failed.

[11] For a defense of these reform efforts, see *Pervyi tiurkologicheskii s"ezd*, 163 ff., 243 ff., 287 ff., 306 ff.

[12] U. Aliev, "Latinizatsiia pis'mennosti, bor'ba za novyi alfavit i nashi uspekhi," *Revoliutsiia i gorets*, no. 1 (1928): 29–39.

[13] U. Aliev, "Pobeda latinizatsii—luchshaia pamiat' o tov. Agamali-Ogly," *Kul'tura i pis'mennost' vostoka*, nos. 7–8 (1931): 17–30; also published in *Revoliutsiia i natsional'nosti*, no. 7 (1930): 17–28.

[14] Aliev, "Pobeda latinizatsii," 24.

Agamali-Ogly then set out to propagandize latinization among the Soviet Union's other Turkic peoples. First, however, he made a canny pilgrimage to the sick Lenin's bedside, where, Agamali-Ogly later claimed, he received the dying leader's benediction for his movement: "Latinization is the great revolution in the east." This would serve as the ubiquitous proof text for latinization.[15] Armed with a quotation from Lenin, Agamali-Ogly toured the Turkic republics in 1924 and 1925 agitating for latinization, wrote and commissioned a series of brochures, and formed alliances in both the Turkic republics and in Moscow. His efforts bore fruit in February–March 1926 when the first Turkological congress was held in Baku with representatives from all the Soviet Union's Turkic peoples. The congress endorsed Azerbaijan's latinization program. The next year Agamali-Ogly got official sanction from the Soviet central government to become the chairman of an all-union committee of the new Turkic alphabet (*VTsK NTA*), which was given leadership over the latinization movement throughout the Soviet Union.[16] By mid-1928, all of the Turkic republics had legislatively accepted NTA and begun its practical implementation.[17] This was a brilliant example of the prospects for entrepreneurial symbolic politics in the early Soviet Union.

It had not been easy. The central Soviet government's initial response to the latinization movement was lukewarm. Until 1926, the central party organs did not address latinization.[18] However, on February 18, 1926, a week before the opening of the first Turkological congress, the Politburo passed the following resolution[19]:

> On the Turkological Congress in Baku.
> 1. Communists at the congress will take the line, that the congress will confine itself to deliberating the possibility of shifting to the Latin script, not taking any categorical decision on an immediate shift to this script.
> 2. The congress will not leave behind any functioning, elected organ. . . .

These instructions contradicted the Azerbaijanis' intention to use the congress to endorse their own latinization movement and to initiate a program of all-union latinization.

[15] Until January 1928, the slogan was only "Latinization is a revolution in the east." Then Agamali-Ogly "remembered" that Lenin had actually responded to his description of latinization thus: "He said 'yes, it is a great revolution in the east!' ('*Da, eto velikaia revoliutsiia na Vostoke!*'). But alas, from the definition of that great man I left out the word 'great,' and so it remained: 'It is a revolution in the east.' After five years I remembered how profoundly correct comrade Lenin had been, and hurried to correct the definition of that great man." *Stenograficheskii otchet 2 plenuma VTsK NTA* (Baku, 1929): 2–3.
[16] Aliev, "Pobeda latinizatsiia."
[17] I. Nazirov, "Provedenie novogo tiurkskogo alfavita v SSSR i blizhaishie perspektivy," *Kul'tura i pis'mennost' vostoka*, no. 1 (1928): 11–33.
[18] A possible exception may have been the attempts made in 1924–1925 by N. F. Iakovlev, one of the most important latinists, to establish a "*Komitet iazykovykh kul'tur vostochnykh narodnostei.*" The Soviet of Nationalities turned down these requests. GARF 3316/17/695 (1924); GARF 3316/16a/167 (1924): 10b, 20b; GARF 3316/16a/211 (1924): 3.
[19] RTsKhIDNI 17/3/547 (18.02.26): 11/25.

This decision confirmed an Orgburo resolution made three days earlier on the basis of a memorandum by A. K. Abolin, deputy head of the Central Committee's Agitprop Department. Abolin had taken a cautious stance. He noted that any script change from Arabic would be viewed with hostility by religious Moslems, but that the Latin script would be "less odious" then the Russian. He concluded that while "all motives for and against Latin are weighty enough, one must conclude a shift to Latin is expedient; the whole question is how." He felt the most important thing was "not to give cause to accuse the central authorities of forcibly imposing a new script on the eastern peoples. The resolutions of the Turkological Congress will be viewed by the Moslem masses as a decree from the highest authority." He therefore suggested not forcing the latinization movement, and especially not leaving a central latinization organ, which would inevitably include "a large number of non-party Orientalists and professors."[20] Thus, the party was granting the latinization movement only highly conditional support. Its principal concern at this point, in keeping with the ideology of NEP, was not to antagonize Moslem public opinion unnecessarily.

Remarkably, the Azerbaijanis chose to flout the Politburo's authority. The congress passed a resolution, with only the Tatar delegation opposing, which praised the Azerbaijanis' latinization program and recommended it as a model to the other Turkic republics.[21] Still more audaciously, a meeting was held the day after the congress ended, which voted to consider the Azerbaijani *Komitet NTA* the guiding center for the spread of NTA throughout the entire Soviet Union, and to make Agamali-Ogly its chairman. They also passed fourteen other resolutions, all designed, in contradiction of Abolin's wishes, "to force" the issue of latinization.[22] This unilateral action, however, soon encountered obstacles. First, the Azerbaijani party, which was controlled by another faction and was unimpressed by Agamali-Ogly's attempt to establish in his words "Azerbaijani hegemony," demanded central government approval. The all-union Sovnarkom then refused to finance a purely Azerbaijani body.[23]

So the issue of latinization was taken to the central government for a second time. It won the approval of TsIK, whose party fraction on July 30, 1926 voted that "due to the important political significance of shifting all the Turkic peoples' alphabets from Arabic to Latin, to recognize the Komitet NTA as all-union and take it into the supervision of TsIK SSSR."[24] TsIK authorized Kulbesherov, who was then chairman of the Soviet of Nationalities and had sponsored this measure, to present it to the Orgburo. Kulbesherov was a Turkmen and an active supporter of NTA.[25] It is likely that his support and

---

[20] *RTsKhIDNI* 17/113/169 (15.02.26): 9/6, 185–187.

[21] *Pervyi tiurkologicheskii s"ezd*, 401.

[22] *GARF* 3316/65/10 (1926): 4.

[23] *RTsKhIDNI* 17/17/1 (1926): 152–159; *GARF* 3316/65/10 (1926): 17.

[24] *RTsKhIDNI* 17/113/219 (13.08.26): 49/7, 76.

[25] B. Kul'besherov, "Itogi 2-go plenuma vsesoiuznogo tsentral'nogo komiteta novogo tiurkskogo alfavita i ocherednye zadachi dela vvedeniia etogo alfavita," *Kul'tura i pis'mennost' vostoka* no. 2 (1928): 6–21.

that of the sizable eastern nationalities contingent in TsIK's presidium were important.

The Orgburo considered TsIK's petition on August 13, 1926. Abolin voted to reject it, as did Semen Dimanshtein, who would later become a prominent NTA supporter. The Orgburo, however, did not reject the petition, but rather called for further study.[26] Further study, as it so often did, dragged on for six months, until Agamali-Ogly again took matters into his own hands. At the February 1927 TsIK session, he gathered the Turkic delegations and they elected an all-union Komitet NTA.[27] For some reason, this second unilateral action provoked immediate Orgburo action and capitulation. On February 28, 1927, the Orgburo confirmed the All-Union Komitet NTA (VTsK NTA) and voted to grant it funding.[28] TsIK officially formulated this decision on May 11, and shortly thereafter, Agamali-Ogly's committee got 500,000 rubles funding.[29] This gave Agamali-Ogly the official state support and funds to ram through latinization.

Why did the central government give in? In the 1920s, it regularly did submit to local intransigence on issues that were not of principal significance. Moreover, Agamali-Ogly had organized his support well and stood firm. Therefore, a compromise line was adopted. VTsK NTA would not become a formal government body (it was under the supervision [v vvedenii] of TsIK, not part of TsIK [pri TsIK]). This would allow the government to deflect potential Moslem hostility away from the government and onto an "independent" organization, as it attempted to do with the League of Militant Godless in religious policy. As Dimanshtein put it at VTsK NTA's first plenum: "We are an organization created by the eastern peoples themselves, which the central power supports, but it does nothing to force [the latinization issue]; they are neutral in the fight between arabists and latinists."[30] While obviously not formally true, this statement nicely summarized the latinization compromise. VTsK NTA would use implied government support to force the issue of latinization; the government would use stated government neutrality to hold VTsK NTA responsible for any problems that might emerge. As noted above, by mid-1928 NTA had been formally adopted by all the Soviet Union's Turkic republics.

How can we explain this remarkably swift triumph, especially given the initially uncertain linguistic situation that prevailed after the revolution and the fact that the center endorsed the program only with great hesitation? What made the movement so attractive to the Turkic elites that forced its adoption? There seem to be two answers: cultural revolution and pan-Turkism. In Chapter 4, we examined cultural revolution from the central Bolshevik point of view and noted its two major aspects: a destructive class warfare movement directed at class enemies, their institutions, and their traditions; and a constructive

---

[26] RTsKhIDNI 17/113/219 (13.08.26): 49/7, 71–72.
[27] Stenograficheskii otchet 1 plenuma, 7.
[28] RTsKhIDNI 17/113/268 (28.02.27): 94/11.
[29] GARF 3316/20/13 (1927): 5.
[30] Stenograficheskii otchet 1 plenuma, 105.

utopian movement to build a new socialist way of life. We also noted that in the Soviet east, this utopian movement took a developmentalist form, with the goal being to overcome with great rapidity the "cultural backwardness" of the Eastern peoples. For this reason, cultural revolution furthered the implementation of *korenizatsiia* in the Soviet east.

The latinization campaign allows us to examine cultural revolution from the perspective of those eastern national elites who sympathized with and supported the Bolshevik leadership in the period directly following the revolution. For them, cultural revolution was a compelling idea and an even more attractive rhetorical stance. Throughout NEP, when cultural revolution was being downplayed by central authorities, it was absolutely central to the rhetoric of latinization. It was a rare speech, article, or resolution on latinization that did not include a paean to cultural revolution.[31] As we have seen, the dying Lenin's putative words to Agamali-Ogly, that "latinization is the great revolution in the east," became the endlessly repeated rallying cry of the movement. The linguist N. F. Iakovlev invoked this spirit in his account of the first latinized Chechen primer: "When the first teacher arrived in the mountains with a primer in Chechen, printed in the Latin script, they literally shot at him in the field, and during the shooting 'wounded' and executed that primer."[32] Similarly, Agamali-Ogly loved to relate the anecdote, "that in Dagestan, if an Islamic mountaineer finds a crumpled piece of newspaper written in the Arabic script, he will immediately pick it up, carefully preserve it, and carry it home. Why? Because in the letters themselves is a drop of divinity."[33] Latinization was designed to free the superstitious Moslem from this slavish worship of an archaic script that left him dependent on the Arabic-literate clergy.

The rhetoric of latinization, then, presented the campaign as in service of the destructive role of cultural revolution: the assault on Islam and "feudal" ways of thinking. It is not surprising that the largely symbolic campaign of latinization assumed such a large presence during the early years of NEP and in fact became the first eastern cultural revolutionary project to earn central sanction. For these were the same years when the coercive cultural revolutionary campaign against Islam and the veiling of women had stalled. In the mid-1920s, Islam was in a much stronger position than Orthodoxy. There had been no time for a campaign against Islam analogous to the one carried out against Orthodoxy from 1918 to 1922. Islamic schools, courts, and charitable organizations were all still functioning in the mid-1920s and were often more influential than the competing Soviet organizations.[34] Likewise female veiling remained the

---

[31] Umar Aliev, "Kul'turnaia revoliutsia i latinizatsiia," *Kul'tura i pis'mennost' vostoka*, no. 2 (1928): 22–30; S. A. Agamali-Ogly, "Kul'turnaia revoliutsiia i novyi alfavit," no. 3 (1929): 3–9; and others.

[32] *Pervyi tiurkologicheskii s"ezd*, 219.

[33] *Stenograficheskii otchet 2 plenuma*, 19.

[34] Shoshana Keller, "The Struggle Against Islam in Uzbekistan, 1921–1941" (Ph.D. diss., Indiana University, 1995).

largely unchallenged norm in many regions of Central Asia and the Caucasus.[35] In this environment, latinization allowed eastern reformers to undertake at least a symbolic assault on Islam.

Much nearer to the hearts of the eastern reformers, however, was the constructive project of cultural revolution: the crusade to overcome cultural backwardness. The Arabic script was held solely responsible for Turkic backwardness, for it had cut off the Turkic peoples from the advanced cultures of the west.[36] In the words of one representative to the Turkological congress, the Arabic script "prevent[ed] the adaptation of the Turkic-Tatar masses to culture and civilization, until now the property only of European peoples."[37] There were few sins not attributed to the Arabic script. Agamali-Ogly even somewhat strangely speculated that the Arabic script "greatly blunted the analytic capacities [of children], their ability to operate with abstract categories."[38] It is no surprise, then, that he believed that learning the new Turkic alphabet was the equivalent of "crossing the Rubicon": one "undergoes an internal revolution."[39]

This spiritual notion of internal conversion is rather distant from characteristic militant Bolshevik rhetoric. Indeed, latinization was an adaptation of the prerevolutionary modernizing Islamic reform movement, with its central concern of explaining and overcoming eastern backwardness, to a context of Bolshevik hegemony.[40] An early latinization skeptic, Stalin's deputy at the Commissariat of Nationalities, G. I. Broido, picked up on this quality and denounced latinization's non-Bolshevik style: "the extremely foul and in particular *intelligent*-far-fetched, utopian and SR-ish [*intelligentski-nadumannyi utopicheskii i eserovskii*] approach to matters."[41] As a nationalities specialist, Broido was familiar with this phenomenon. As we have seen, in order to fulfill *korenizatsiia*, the Bolsheviks had to recruit, in Stalin's words, all national cadres "up to and including Octobrists."[42] This policy of recruiting non-Russian nationalists, known as non-Russian *smenovekhovstvo*, was made possible by an intersection of the interests of the non-Russian *smenovekhovtsy* and Bolshevik nationalities policy. The intersection was cultural revolution, in particular the developmentalist project of overcoming cultural backwardness. Despite this intersection, it is not surprising that the eastern elites would bring their own concerns and their own psychological attitudes to this project. And latinization represented an indigenously sponsored project of cultural revolution.

[35] See Gregory Massel, *The Surrogate Proletariat* (Princeton, N.J., 1974).

[36] For instance, B. Kul'besherov, "Itogi 2-go plenuma vsesoiuznogo tsentral'nogo komiteta novogo tiurkskogo alfavita i ocherednye zadachi dela vvedeniia etogo alfavita," *Kul'tura i pis'mennost' vostoka*, no. 2 (1928): 7; B. Choban-Zade, "Itogi unifikatsii alfavitov tiurko-tatarskikh narodov," no. 3 (1929): 18–19.

[37] *Pervyi tiurkologicheskii s"ezd*, 11.

[38] Agamali-Ogly, "Rubikon pereiden," *Kul'tura i pis'mennost' vostoka*, no. 2 (1928): 5.

[39] *Stenograficheskii otchet 2 plenuma*, 20; also Agamali-Ogly, "Rubikon pereiden."

[40] Adeeb Khalid, *The Politics of Muslim Cultural Reform* (Berkeley, Calif., 1998).

[41] G. I. Broido, "Moim opponentam," *Zhizn' natsional'nostei*, no. 1 (1924): 163.

[42] *Tainy natsional'noi politiki*, 102.

This continuity across the revolutionary divide manifested itself most clearly in the latinization movement's extraordinary concern, indeed obsession, with the history of latinization. VTsK NTA's theoretical journal was filled with articles on latinization's prerevolutionary antecedents, beginning with the Columbus of latinization, the Azerbaijani dramatist Mirza Fatali Akhundov, who presented a latinization project to the Turkish sultan in 1857.[43] As critics would later point out, these histories presented a timeless succession of above-class heroes and villains: the latinists, some of whom were even princes, and the arabists.[44] The message seemed to be that the October revolution created a more favorable environment for latinization, but otherwise the movement remained the same.

Latinization as a symbolic expression of cultural revolution in the east was something central authorities could and eventually did support. The second component of the initial latinization campaign, pan-Turkism, was considerably riskier. The Bolsheviks were extremely suspicious of both pan-Islamic and pan-Turkic movements and generally inclined to exaggerate their strength and to punish expressions of them with great severity. The arrest and programmatic denunciation of Mir-Said Sultan-Galiev, who was accused of pan-Turkic nationalism and an excessive respect for Islam, was the most prominent instance of the danger of this accusation.[45] The genius of latinization was to advance pan-Turkic sentiments through a purely cultural and symbolic movement that officially served the orthodox Bolshevik goal of overcoming "eastern cultural-backwardness." Latinization was formally oriented toward the entire Soviet and non-Soviet east (hence its journal, *Culture and Written Languages of the East*). However, 95 percent of its energies were directed at Turkic peoples. And its goal was a new *Turkic* alphabet. In fact, the other nationalities who initially embraced NTA, the North Caucasian mountain peoples and a few small ethnicities of Central Asia and the Transcaucasus, were all seen as belonging to the Turkic sphere of cultural influence. The notion of such a cultural sphere was, of course, itself a rather pan-Turkic idea. The idea of this cultural sphere was well illustrated by the Dagestani government's 1923 decision, later reversed, to make Azerbaijani Turkic its government language.[46] The latinization movement's major foreign focus was Turkey, home of an analogous modernizing anti-Islamic movement, Kemalism. The Turkish republic's adoption of the Latin script in 1928 was a major triumph for the pan-Turkic component of the latinization campaign.

[43] *Kul'tura i pis'mennost' vostoka*, no. 2 (1928): 58–61; 146–148; no. 3: 10–17; 91–102; no. 4: 7–16; 69–73; 127–157.

[44] L. Rovinskii, "Ob odnoi natsional-demokraticheskoi kontseptsii," *Pravda*, no. 47 (17.02.34): 3; D. Orlinskii, "Natsional-demokratizm."

[45] A. A. Bennigsen and S. E. Wimbush, *Muslim National Communism in the Soviet Union* (Chicago, 1979); Mirsaid Sultan-Galiev, *Stat'i, Vystupleniia, Dokumenty* (Kazan, 1992).

[46] A. Takho-Godi, "Problema iazykov Dagestana," *Revoliutsiia i natsional'nosti*, no. 2 (1930): 68–75.

Nowhere was this pan-Turkism more vividly on display than at the 1926 Turkological Congress in Baku. Its very occurrence, with invited guests from Turkey and Hungary (the latter being considered a member of the larger Altaic language group), was striking. It is difficult to imagine an analogous pan-Finnic congress in Karelia, much less a pan-Slavic one in Minsk. The congress' speeches were filled with Turkic pride and calls for Turkic unity. An Uzbek objected to being confused with the Iranian Tajiks: "In their features, there is absolutely nothing Turkic." An Oirot spoke movingly of how he had only recently discovered "that I am a Turk." He protested another delegate's claim they were only turkicized Mongols: "I protest against such a definition, because I want to be a member of that *nation*, which is represented at this congress [my emphasis]." He then asked that "the Turkological congress uncover the history of the Oirots."[47]

Linguistic unity was a major concern. The official speaker on terminology, the Azerbaijani linguist Choban-Zade, argued so forcefully for cleansing the Turkic languages of Arabic and Persian terms and for creating new terms only using Turko-Altaic roots that one speaker accused him of favoring "a united Turkic national language." A more moderate delegate apologized for advocating only "a federation of Turkic languages."[48] Indeed, the tendency to borrow Turkish words in Azerbaijani was sufficiently strong that the party's first secretary warned of an Ottomanization of the Azerbaijani language.[49]

In addition to pan-Turkism and cultural revolution, the third notable feature of the latinization movement was its sanctioning of hostility toward Russian culture. There were comprehensible ideological (hostility to Islam) and practical reasons (major technical deficiencies) for rejecting the Arabic script. It was much less clear why Latin should be favored over Cyrillic. Before the Latin script was declared uniquely progressive for ideological reasons, most linguists found Latin and Cyrillic quite comparable on technical grounds.[50] Given that Russian was being taught (or was supposed to be taught) in all non-Russian schools and that it had already established itself as the Soviet Union's *lingua franca*, a strong pragmatic argument could be made for adopting the Cyrillic script.[51] As we noted earlier, the Kalmyks and several other small peoples living in Russian regions chose Cyrillic for exactly that reason. This and all other arguments, however, were overridden by one consideration: the presumed "distrust" of the non-Russians toward Russian culture and, therefore, by association, their distrust of the "Russian script" (as Cyrillic was always called in the 1920s and 1930s). The Russian script was felt to be fatally compromised by its connection to the

---

[47] *Pervyi tiurkologicheskii s"ezd*, 85–86.

[48] Ibid., 212, 165.

[49] *RTsKhIDNI* 17/17/12 (1927): 164.

[50] L. Zhirkov, "K reforme alfavitov vostochnykh narodnostei," *Novyi vostok* 10–11 (1926): 223–235; N. Iakovlev, "Problemy natsional'noi pis'mennosti vostochnykh narodov SSSR," 236–242.

[51] On this development, see V. N. Durdenevskii, *Ravnopravie iazykov v sovetskom stroe* (Moscow, 1927).

colonial, missionary russification policies of the Tsarist regime.[52] This attitude was sanctioned by the principle of the greater danger, that great-power chauvinism was a greater danger than local nationalism. One of the principal rhetorical advantages of the latinization movement was its initial ability to label any support of the Cyrillic script as great-power chauvinism.

The preceding analysis explains both the appeal and the significance of the latinization movement. The rhetoric of cultural revolution both appealed to eastern elites and provided an orthodox Bolshevik language in which they could symbolically advance an attitude, cultural pan-Turkism, that would otherwise be quite dangerous. It likewise provided a symbolic way in which to advance the eastern elite's reformist position against Islam during the relatively tranquil period of NEP. With the center's turn toward cultural revolution in 1928, the symbolic politics of latinization would move in a direction not anticipated by its founders. This was also not unusual in symbolic politics.

Latinization as Derussification

Since latinization had been presented from the beginning as a cultural revolutionary campaign, designed to help overcome eastern backwardness, it is not surprising that the onset of the all-union cultural revolution greatly speeded up the progress of latinization, just as it had furthered the implementation of *korenizatsiia* in the Soviet east. Prior to 1928, the central government had required VTsK NTA to take a cautious approach to latinization. As a result, although latinization had been formally adopted throughout the Soviet Turkic world, most of the relevant decrees passed in 1927 and 1928 had called for a five-year phase-in period.[53] In VTsK NTA's first oral report to the Soviet of Nationalities in April 1928, Agamali-Ogly was careful to emphasize strongly this gradualism, as did the Soviet of Nationalities in its resolution on his report.[54] As a result of this cautious approach, although by mid-1928 the Turkic republics had formally committed to latinization, the Arabic script was still dominant in most republics.

The latinization movement had strived from the beginning to get unambiguous central government support for its policies, so that they could be imposed by force. With the onset of the cultural revolution, they were granted that support. In October 1928, VTsIK and the RSFSR Sovnarkom issued a decree making NTA obligatory in all Turko-Tatar regions of the RSFSR.[55] Two months later, the third plenum of VTsK NTA reduced the phase-in period for latiniza-

---

[52] Zhirkov, "K reforme alfavitov," 227; Iakovlev, "Problemy natsional'noi pis'mennosti," 242.

[53] Kul'besherov, "Vtoroi plenum," 17; 28; Agamali-Ogly, "K delu i k delu!" *Kul'tura i pis'mennost' vostoka*, no. 1 (1928): 6.

[54] *GARF* 3316/20/218 (1928): 18–44; "V sovete natsional'nostei," *Sovetskoe stroitel'stvo*, no. 4 (1928): 122–124.

[55] *SU RSFSR* (10.15.28): 130/846.

tion to only two years, that is, by the end of 1930. Agamali-Ogly suggested most could do it even quicker.[56] Finally, in August 1929, the all-union TsIK and Sovnarkom decreed the Latin script obligatory from that point forward for all Turko-Tatar languages in the Soviet Union. The decree forbade the Arabic script in print, schools, government organs, and so forth; it even forbade the importing of an Arabic typography.[57] The Arabic script did not, of course, disappear the next day, but after this decree it began to disappear rapidly. With its primary mission accomplished, there was now talk of disbanding VTsK NTA.[58]

However, the latinization movement did not end, but rather expanded suddenly and rapidly to embrace almost all the languages of the Soviet Union. It did so by shifting its symbolic focus from pan-Turkism to internationalism, and by greatly accentuating its Russophobia. Thus far I have presented the latinization movement as largely monolithic. Of course, it was not. The most important division in the movement was between the politicians and the professors, many of whom (though not all) were Russians. The politicians, mostly leaders in the Turkic republics, were primarily concerned with driving the Arabic script out of their republics and with advancing a symbolic program of Turkic unity. The professors had a different crusade: unification. Unification, as endorsed at VTsK NTA's first plenum in 1927, meant that each letter of the new Turkic alphabet should represent the same sound in each of the languages adopting it.[59] In principle, the Turkic politicians supported this pan-Turkic goal. In practice, however, they defended their own Latin alphabets from change. Azerbaijan in particular, led by Agamali-Ogly, resisted unification.[60] The professors, mostly specialists on eastern languages, were after bigger game: not a pan-Turkic alphabet, but an international one. As an early proponent dreamed, "[NTA] will become the nucleus of alphabet unity, first in the entire east, and then, perhaps, in the entire world."[61] This was utopianism on a cultural revolutionary scale.

Indeed, it was internationalism that saved latinization from its pan-Turkic roots. The terror campaigns of the cultural revolution in the national republics were directed at the *smenovekhovtsy* national intelligentsia, many of whom were active in the latinization campaign in the Soviet east. The charge brought against the defendants was invariably nationalism and, in republics such as Tatarstan, Crimea, and Uzbekistan, pan-Turkism. Some of those purged were latinists, although no one was yet purged *as* a latinist. However, they were clearly threatened. An August 1930 Soviet of Nationalities resolution noted as one of the drawbacks of VTsK NTA's work[62]:

[56] Agamali-Ogly, "Itogi 3-go plenuma VTsK NTA," *Kul'tura i pis'mennost' vostoka*, no. 4 (1929): 3.
[57] *SZ SSSR* (07.08.29): 52/477; *Revoliutsiia i natsional'nosti*, nos. 8–9 (1930): 108–112.
[58] *Stenograficheskii otchet 4 plenuma VTsK NTA* (Moscow, 1931): 30.
[59] "Prilozhenie," *Kul'tura i pis'mennost' vostoka*, no. 1 (1928): 113–139.
[60] Agamali-Ogly, "K delu," 8.
[61] K. V. Iushmanov, "Opyty vsemirnogo alfavita," *Kul'tura i pis'mennost' vostoka*, no. 4 (1929): 70.
[62] "Khronika," *Revoliutsiia i pis'mennost'*, nos. 7–8 (1931): 225.

Certain elements of a pan-Turkic tendency have still not entirely been overcome, despite the correct line taken by VTsK on this line, in opposition to that tendency.

This was the first public rebuke VTsK NTA received for pan-Turkic tendencies. It helped confirm an orientation away from the movement's pan-Turkic origins, toward a new international mission, a shift reflected in the organization's new name. It was reduced to the All-Union Committee for the New Alphabet (VTsK NA).

The main obstacle to NA's world mission, within the Soviet Union at least, was the Russian alphabet. There had been some talk after the Revolution of latinizing the Russian alphabet, but nothing came of it.[63] In 1929, with a second wave of utopian internationalism rising, the subject was again broached. Lunacharskii wrote several articles in support of latinizing Russian.[64] Like Agamali-Ogly, he claimed he had Lenin's endorsement. Most important, Lunacharskii helped put the educational bureaucracy behind the idea. On October 19, 1929, *Uchitelskaia gazeta* (Teachers' Newspaper) published a discussion article on the latinization of the Russian alphabet.[65] A month later, *Izvestiia* announced plans to reform the Russian orthography. Three committees had been formed within the Scientific Department of the Education Commissariat: on orthography, spelling, and the latinization of the Russian alphabet.[66] At the same time, another committee was formed within the Council on Defense and Labor (STO) to deal with the publishing consequences of the proposed reforms. At least one of its members also publicly advocated latinization.[67] The Communist Academy, an early supporter of latinization, hosted an exhibition devoted to the new alphabet, which showed how under the russificatory Tsarist regime the Russian alphabet had expanded outward, and how under the new progressive Soviet regime its domain was continually contracting.[68] This flurry of activity suggested that the latinization of Russian was being seriously considered.

Its most ardent supporter was undoubtedly N. F. Iakovlev, a specialist on Caucasian languages and an active latinist. Iakovlev was involved in latinization from the beginning. He helped design the North Caucasians' Latin alphabets, gave the keynote address on latinization at the Turkological Congress, and propagandized tirelessly for the movement. He was chosen to organize and

[63] A. Samoilovich, "Novyi turetskii alfavit," *Novyi vostok*, no. 5 (1924): 390.

[64] A. Lunacharskii, "Latinizatsiia russkoi pis'mennosti," *Krasnaia gazeta*, nos. 5–6 (06–07.01.29); "Latinizatsiia russkoi pis'mennosti," *Kul'tura i pis'mennost' vostoka*, no. 6 (1930): 20–26.

[65] *Kul'turnaia zhizn' v SSSR, 1928–1941: Khronika* (Moscow, 1976): 146; some responses are preserved in *GARF* 2307/15/4 (1930).

[66] "Reforma orfografii," *Izvestiia*, no. 273 (23.11.29): 3.

[67] "Za internatsional'nyi apparat," *Komi mu—Zyrianskii krai*, no. 22 (1929): 35–38, which reprints an article by Prof. M. Shchelkulov.

[68] *Pravda*, no. 272 (22.11.29): 5; Levin, "Novaia pis'mennost' narodov SSSR," *Prosveshchenie natsional'nostei*, no. 3 (1930): 55–59; "Khronika," *Revoliutsiia i gorets*, no. 4 (1928): 88.

chair the Scientific Department's latinization subcommittee, which held five meetings in November and December of 1929. At the second meeting, Iakovlev presented a series of theses on the latinization of Russian that contained a startling indictment of the Russian alphabet.

No document conveys the anti-Russian character latinization had assumed by 1929 better than Iakovlev's theses[69]:

2. The Russian civic alphabet in its history is the alphabet of autocratic oppression, missionary propaganda, Great Russian national chauvinism; this in particular shows itself in its russificatory role in relation to the national minorities of the former Russian Empire. . . . At the same time this alphabet is the weapon of propaganda of Russian imperialism abroad (slavophilism and its role in the battle for the straits). . . .

3. [Even after the 1917 reform, the Russian alphabet] continues to remain the alphabet of national-bourgeois Great Russian ideology. This especially clearly shows itself in the endeavor of nationalities which use the Russian alphabet to shift to Latin (Ossetines, Abkhazians, the Komi movement and others), as an alphabet ideologically more neutral and international. . . .

5. . . . In replacement of our inherited national-bourgeois alphabet should come an alphabet of socialist society. We are speaking not simply of the creation of a new national-bourgeois cacophony of a Latin alphabet, as we have in modern western Europe, but of one international latinized alphabet of socialism. . . .

7. The Russian alphabet is at the current time not only an ideologically alien to socialist construction script, but it also serves as the chief obstacle to latinization, both of other national alphabets (Hebrew, Armenian, Georgian), and of other Cyrillic scripts (Belorussian, Ukrainian, the eastern Finns and others). . . .

It is difficult to imagine a more comprehensive rejection. It should also be noted that Iakovlev's arguments logically ought to apply equally to the Russian language and to Russian culture as a whole. If October had not purified the Russian script, how could it have purified the language and culture that script carried?

Iakovlev was a skilled, if excessive, practitioner of the new cultural revolutionary rhetoric. His arguments here against the Russian alphabet would be repeated, in a more moderate form, during the latinists' new assault on the Cyrillic script in other non-Russian republics. If the Russian script could be linked to Russia's colonizing, missionary past, then any defense of it would be great-power chauvinism, a deviation canonized by Stalin as the greatest danger in the nationalities policy. Nor could the latinists be accused of local chauvinism. That charge was reserved for those who wanted to retain obsolete national alphabets.[70] Only the latinists were true internationalists. It was this sense of

[69] *GARF* 2307/14/81 (1929): 27–28; see also Iakovlev's article, "Za latinizatsiiu russkogo alfavita," *Kul'tura i pis'mennost' vostoka*, no. 6 (1930): 27–43.

[70] For a classic statement of this position, see Latinist, "Alfavitnoe stroitel'stvo v SSSR," *Natsional'naia kniga*, no. 7 (1931): 3–7.

ideological invulnerability that for a few years gave the latinization movement its cocksure iconoclastic confidence.

Nevertheless, the assault on the Russian alphabet failed. The movement was ended with a laconic Politburo resolution of January 25 1930[71]:

> On latinization
>   Order *glavnauka* to cease its work on the question of latinizing the Russian alphabet.

The origins of this decision remain obscure. After the reversal of latinization, critics claimed Lunacharskii and Iakovlev were acting as loose cannons. However, the substantial publicity surrounding the potential shift belies this notion. Also, at least one document from TsK's Kultprop Department mentioned the forthcoming latinization of Russian. It does seem, however, that VTsK NA did not wholeheartedly support Iakovlev's actions. On only one occasion did its journal publish articles on the latinization of Russian.[72] Moreover, at VTsK NA's fourth plenum in May 1930, Iakovlev was criticized for not informing VTsK NA about his work at the Scientific Subdepartment.[73] In any case, the important fact was that the Politburo decision was not publicized and neither latinization of the Russian language nor any of its supporters was denounced. As a result of this lack of publicity, nationalities journals continued to report on the coming latinization of Russian.[74] The assault on the Russian alphabet therefore continued, but through a flanking maneuver rather than direct assault.

By May 1930, thirty-six languages had adopted NA.[75] In addition to the Turkic and North Caucasian peoples, three Mongolian nationalities shifted in 1929–1930. These included the Kalmyk, who gave up their Russian script for latin; the Buriat-Mongols; and the Mongols of the Soviet client state of Mongolia. They held their own miniature pan-Mongol summit in Moscow to unify their alphabets.[76] Seven Iranian languages adopted NA, including the Mountain Jews of Dagestan and the Central Asian Bukharan Jews, who both abandoned the Hebrew script.[77] In good cultural revolutionary rhetoric, this was referred to as "the Port Arthur of Hebraism."[78] Numerous Soviet Jewish organizations passed resolutions on the latinization of Yiddish, and this step was

---

[71] *RTsKhIDNI* 17/3/774 (25.01.30): 115/26.

[72] Lunacharskii, "Latinizatsiia," and Iakovlev, "Za latinizatsiiu," in *Kul'tura i pis'mennost' vostoka*, no. 6 (1930).

[73] *Stenograficheskii otchet 4 plenuma*, 78–82; 116–117.

[74] "Za internatsional'nyi alfavit," 35; "Khronika," *Revoliutsiia i gorets* (1930): 88; Levin, "Novaia pis'mennost'," 56.

[75] *Stenograficheskii otchet 4 plenuma*, 13.

[76] "Khronika," *Kul'tura i pis'mennost' vostoka*, no. 9 (1931): 66–67.

[77] F. N. Nechaev, "Novyi persidskii alfavit," no. 10 (1932): 41–42.

[78] L. Shaulov and R. Razilov, "Gorskie evrei i latinskii alfavit," *Revoliutsiia i gorets*, no. 5 (1929): 61.

considered only a matter of time.[79] The Assyrians also rejected Cyrillic in favor of Latin. A committee was even formed in Baku (though not Yerevan!) to latinize the ancient Armenian script, although nothing came of this move.[80] The only script where one finds absolutely no evidence of any intention to latinize was, unsurprisingly, Georgian.

From 1930 to 1932, VTsK NA focused its latinization efforts on three further goals: the latinization of Chinese and Korean, the formation of latin alphabets for the small peoples of the north, and, most importantly, the latinization of the Cyrillic alphabets of the eastern Finns and the Chuvash. The latinization of Chinese and Korean were significant for two reasons. First, it represented an attempt to force the issue of latinization for peoples where the overwhelming majority lived abroad, and also where there were considerable hopes for a communist revolution. Objections that this policy would make Soviet Chinese and Korean culture (there were several hundred thousand Koreans and Chinese in the Soviet far east) inaccessible to their compatriots abroad were brushed aside with characteristic bravado: "Not the twenty million strong population of Korea, but the 170 thousand strong Korean population of the Soviet Union should become the advance-guard of the cultural revolution of the Korean people."[81]

Second, these alphabets were hieroglyphic and therefore it was much more complicated to replace them with a phonetic latin alphabet. Indeed, there was no single Chinese oral language, but rather a series of mutually incomprehensible dialects. Opponents of latinization argued that only the hieroglyphic alphabet united China. Latinists replied that this argument contradicted Soviet nationalities policy, which always preferred the dialect over artificial "state languages."[82] Indeed it did. Chechen and Ingush were extremely close linguistically, but two separate literary languages were created with the additional consequence that two separate autonomous oblasts emerged. Similarly, attempts to merge the mountain and meadow dialects of Mari into one literary language failed, again leading to successful demands of the mountain Mari to form their own autonomous region. This principle was called "national-linguistic *raionirovanie*."[83] It was eventually decided to form five separate Latin alphabets for five major Chinese dialects.[84]

[79] A. Zaretskii, "K probleme latinizatsii evreiskogo pis'ma," *Revoliutsiia i pis'mennost'*, nos. 1–2 (1932): 15–32.

[80] *Stenograficheskii otchet 4 plenuma*, 36.

[81] I. Bulatnikov, "O latinizatsii koreiskoi pis'mennosti," *Prosveshchenie natsional'nost i*, no. 6 (1930): 107.

[82] E. Siao, "Revoliutsiia v kitaiskoi pis'mennosti," *Natsional'naia kniga*, no. 7 (1931): 11; M. Laikhter, "O latinizatsii kitaiskoi pis'mennosti," *Kul'tura i pis'mennost' vostoka*, no. 9 (1931): 25.

[83] A. M. Sukhotin, "K probleme natsional'no-lingvisticheskogo raionirovaniia v iuzhnoi Sibiri," *Kul'tura i pis'mennost' vostoka*, nos. 7–8 (1931): 93–108.

[84] "Pervaia vsesoiuznaia konferentsiia po latinizatsii kitaiskoi pis'mennosti," *Revoliutsiia i pis'mennost'*, nos. 1–2 (1932): 130. The five dialects, in Russian transcription, were severnoi/shandunskii, guandunskoi, futszianskoi, tsziansu/chzhetsziana, khunaii/tsziansi.

Any Chinese who were worried about the consequences of this move for the territorial integrity of a future communist China were reassured that "even in the boundaries of bourgeois democratic revolutions, the free development of national languages and cultures and the right of nations to full self-determination, including formation of their own state, is the condition which contributes to the integrity of multinational democratic states."[85] In practice, only a Latin alphabet for the northern Shandunskii dialect was approved and put into use for the Soviet Chinese.[86] Plans for a Latin Korean alphabet were approved but apparently not actualized.

The small peoples of the north represented a completely different test case. Throughout the 1920s, they were considered to be too small, too geographically dispersed, and above all too backward to be granted the status of full-fledged nationalities.[87] With the advent of cultural revolution, such doubts were cast aside: "In a socialist country there are no and can be no unequal peoples, no matter what their level of development."[88] The small peoples of the north would be given their own literary languages, their own native-language schools, and their own autonomous national oblasts. The alphabet question here was controversial. In many northern regions, Russians formed the majority. The small peoples had a very high rate of bilingualism. At best, native-language schools would go through fourth grade and then switch to Russian. All logic, therefore, indicated a choice of Cyrillic. Even Iakovlev, as late as 1928, had argued that in ethnically heterogeneous territories where a high rate of bilingualism prevailed, one should choose the script of the "culturally influencing nationality."[89] However, proponents of latinization again raised the issue of the Cyrillic script's "associations with the russificatory policies of Tsarist Russia," and so VTsK NA approved in early 1931 twelve Latin-based literary languages for the small peoples of the north.[90]

The climactic latinization campaign was the attempt to shift the eastern Finnic and Chuvash languages from Cyrillic to Latin. In 1929, there were eleven Soviet languages using the Cyrillic script.[91] Russian, Ukrainian, and Belorussian were off-limits after the Politburo decree. Bulgarian, Romany (gypsy), and Moldavian (which was shifted in 1932) represented insignificant populations. That left the eastern Finns (Komi, Udmurt, Mordvinians, Mari) and the Christianized Turkic Chuvash. These five nationalities had all received written languages from Russian missionaries in the nineteenth century. However, by 1930 they already had in their native languages a substantial literature, growing literacy rates, education to the high school level, and, at least for the Komi, much of their

[85] Laikhter, "O latinizatsii," 26.

[86] "Khronika," Kul'tura i pis'mennost' vostoka, no. 9 (1931): 80.

[87] Yuri Slezkine, Arctic Mirrors (Ithaca, N.Y., 1994): 131–217.

[88] I. P. Al'kor, "Pis'mennost' narodov severa," Kul'tura i pis'mennost' vostoka, no. 10 (1931): 18.

[89] Iakovlev, "Razvitie natsional'noi pis'mennosti," 228.

[90] Al'kor, "Pis'mennost' narodov severa," 25–27.

[91] A. Suhkotin, "K voprosam alfavitnoi," Prosveshchenie natsional'nostei, nos. 4–5 (1930): 97.

government bureaucracy. Moreover, while these peoples fit one Soviet defini-tion of being eastern, since they were categorized as "backward," the fact that they were Finns gave them a western face as well. This risked the danger of pan-Finnic accusations, not unlikely given that already in 1924 a Komi latinist had called for "a united Finno-Ugric bloc on questions of general cultural-historic character, a bloc which can only be created by the adoption of the latin script by all Finno-Ugric peoples."[92]

The movement for latinization revived in the Komi press in 1928. The Sci-entific Department, which was then pushing to latinize Russian, responded by arranging a Komi linguistic conference in July 1929. The conference resolved to shift to Latin in tandem with the Russians and other Finns.[93] In early 1930, the Komi obkom approved the shift to the Latin script and the oblast execu-tive committee formed a latinization committee.[94] Latinization arose simulta-neously in Udmurtia, where it was debated from 1928 to 1930 in the party and press, with neither side winning a decisive victory. As a result, the Komi and Udmurt governments appealed together to the central authorities. A com-mittee was formed within VTsK NA, which unsurprisingly recommended in January 1931 a shift to Latin. The Soviet of Nationalities endorsed this decision in April, and the Udmurt government confirmed it in June. By early 1932, a united Udmurt-Komi alphabet had been worked out.[95] The other Finnic nationalities moved more slowly. By December 1931, the Middle Volga krai had formed a commission on latinizing Mordvinian and Chuvash.[96] In 1932, VTsK NA approved Latin alphabets for the two main Mordvinian languages and was working on Chuvash and Mari variants.[97] In addition, three small Finnic peoples who lacked literary languages—the Veps, Izhor, and Tver Karelians—were given literary languages using the Latin alphabet in 1932.[98]

In principle, then, by 1932 all of the Finnic languages were on the verge of being latinized. In practice, only the Komis made the actual shift. Latinization ground to a halt in Udmurtia. A number of influential party figures opposed the shift.[99] Presumably, they realized Russian was and would remain the dom-inant language in their oblast. Without openly opposing latinization, they nev-ertheless made two damaging charges. First, they successfully tarred a number of local latinists as pan-Finns.[100] This broke the latinists' charmed invulnerabil-

[92] Gren, "K voprosu," 53.

[93] I. Razmanov, "Rezul'taty rabot Komi lingvisticheskoi konferentsii Glavnauki," *Komi mu—Zyrianskii krai*, nos. 16–17 (1929): 38–45.

[94] Nechaev, "Unifikatsiia Komi i Udmurtskogo," 15–16.

[95] Ibid., 18–21; B. Grande, "Latinizatsiia pis'ma v Udmurtskoi A. O. missionerskie alfavity," *Revoliutsiia i pis'mennost'*, no. 1 (1933): 59–62.

[96] "Latinizatsiia mordovskogo i chuvashskogo alfavitov," *Pravda*, no. 331 (02.12.31): 4.

[97] "Khronika," *Revoliutsiia i pis'mennost'*, nos. 1–2 (1932): 156–158; 165–166.

[98] N. Iakovlev, "Nekotorye itogi latinizatsii i unifikatsii alfavitov v SSSR," *Revoliutsiia i pis'mennost'*, nos. 4–5 (1932): 34.

[99] Grande, "Latinizatsiia pis'ma v Udmurtskoi A. O.," 59.

[100] T. Ivanov, "Ob unifikatsii udmurtskogo (votskogo) alfavita," *Kul'tura i pis'mennost' vostoka*, nos. 7–8 (1931): 169–170; Nechaev, "Unifikatsiia komi i udmurtskogo," 17.

ity to the charge of local chauvinism. This charge was furthered by an internal squabble within the language reform movement. A number of supporters of N. I. Marr, who had his own scheme for a universal alphabet also based largely on a Latin script, attacked VTsK NA as promoting only "family unification," that is unifying only families of languages: Turkic, Mongolian, Japhetic (a Caucasus group theorized by Marr), and now Finnic.[101] This nasty dispute, complete with a public disputation, weakened the latinization movement by undermining its internationalist profile.[102]

The second and more dangerous charge was that the latinists were anti-Russian. The anti-latinists argued: "What does it matter who created our alphabet? So what if it was at some point created by missionaries? At the present time it represents a weapon in the hands of the proletariat and serves the goal of Soviet construction."[103] This argument was deployed alongside the revived assertions that the Russian language was "the language of Lenin, the language of the October Revolution."[104] This was a commonplace rhetorical trope of the 1920s; its revival in 1931–1932 heralded the end of cultural revolution and a drastic change in the fortunes of latinization.

The high water mark for latinization came in 1932. N. F. Iakovlev presented the statistics on the total number of languages that had been latinized by year to the end of 1932 (Table 24). As late as November 1932, the Soviet of Nationalities gave VTsK NA a largely positive resolution on their biannual report.[105] However, by February 1933, at the first plenum of VTsK NA's scientific council, an entirely new ideological atmosphere had emerged, in which the question was not which languages remained to be latinized, but whether latinization would be reversed.

The lead address at the plenum, given by Semen Dimanshtein, not only attacked pan-Turkism—"a great many delegates had a harmful, purely nationalist, pan-Turkic orientation"—but also sounded a new note on the attitude toward the Russian language: "Has the Russian language remained for the non-Russian peoples the same after the revolution as it was before it? No, it has not. First, in that language the non-Russians acquire voluntarily much of great value . . . the original works of Lenin and Stalin and all the principal documents of the revolution appeared in Russian . . . besides that, the Russian language now has a different class content."[106] Such an attitude toward the Russian language and Russian culture presaged a fundamental revision of the Affirmative Action Empire.

[101] B. Grande, "K voprosu o novom komi-udmurtskom alfavite," *Prosveshchenie natsional'nostei*, nos. 2–3 (1932): 67.

[102] "Tribuna," *Revoliutsiia i pis'mennost'*, nos. 1–2 (1932): 87–95.

[103] Grande, "Latinizatsiia pis'ma," 60.

[104] B. Grande, "Na fronte terminologicheskogo stroitel'stva," *Prosveshchenie natsional'nostei*, nos. 8–9 (1932): 88.

[105] *Revoliutsiia i pis'mennost'*, no. 1 (1933): 140–141.

[106] S. M. Dimanshtein, "Printsipy sozdaniia natsional'noi terminologii," *Pis'mennost' i revoliutsiia*, no. 1 (1933): 31, 33–34.

Table 24. Number of Languages Shifted to Latin Script

Year	Latinized Languages
1922	2
1923	6
1925–1926	10
1926–1927	16
1928	28
1929	35
1930	39
1931	52
1932	66

[At the end of 1932, seven more languages were in the process of being latinized.]

Revoliutsiia i pis'mennost', no. 1 (1933): 140–141.

As noted in Chapter 4, the cultural revolution represented an intensification of the principles of the Affirmative Action Empire. This case study of latinization further demonstrates that point. A fundamental principle of the Affirmative Action Empire was that Russian culture and Russian national interests should be de-emphasized so as not to threaten the mistrustful non-Russians and provoke defensive nationalism. The endeavor to latinize the Russian alphabet on the grounds of its inherently missionary-colonizing character, and the production of maps showing the outward march of the Cyrillic alphabet under the Tsars and its retreat under the Soviets, marked a high point in the hostile attitude of the Soviet state to traditional Russian culture. The Affirmative Action Empire was also premised on the non-national nature of the Soviet Union as a whole, the refusal to create a Soviet nationality. This internationalism was also reflected in the latinization campaign during the cultural revolution, with the attempt not only to form a universal alphabet for the Soviet Union but to export it to the Chinese, Koreans, and eventually the entire world. Finally, the Affirmative Action Empire was based on a principle of ethnic proliferation, in which all ethnic groups, no matter how small, should not be forced to assimilate and should be granted national forms. The multiplication of national languages during the cultural revolution exemplified this policy.

The remarks of Dimanshtein in February 1933 marked not only the end of latinization but also a major change in the Soviet nationalities policy. The origins of this sea change in ideological atmosphere were not tied to latinization itself, but rather were the consequence of the political crisis of Ukrainization in December 1932. This event will be discussed in Chapter 7. However, the roots of this new attitude to Russian national identity can be seen by turning briefly to a consideration of language politics and language terror in Ukraine and Belorussia.

Language and Terror in the Soviet West

Latinization was almost entirely confined to the Soviet east. However, just as there was one episode where the latinization of the Russian language was proposed, there were likewise two occasions when the latinization of Belorussian and Ukrainian emerged as issues. The symbolic connotations of latinization in the Soviet west were entirely different. The cultural revolutionary element was entirely absent. Ukrainians and Belorussians were not considered "culturally backward" and their latinization was not discussed in context with the utopian scheme to develop a single universal alphabet. The national issue at stake, moreover, was not a broad cultural movement like pan-Turkism, but cross-border national ties between Soviet Belorussia and Ukraine and the Belorussian and Ukrainian communities of Poland. Cross-border nationalism was not necessarily anti-Soviet. As we have seen, the Piedmont Principle called for using cross-border ethnic ties to undermine neighboring states, above all Poland. There was loyalist irredentism and treasonous irredentism. This section will discuss how the language reform projects in Belorussia and Ukraine were construed as treasonous irredentism. Again, the pattern in the Soviet west differed from the east. In the east, an orientation on western culture and Russophobia were sanctioned during the cultural revolution. In the west, they were treason.

In 1926 and 1927, respectively, Belorussia and Ukraine hosted international conferences to discuss reforming their languages.[107] These were the western equivalents to the 1926 Turkological congress, save that the western congresses involved only a single nationality, not a supranational group. The Belorussian conference took place in November 1926 and included Belorussian guests from various European countries. The conference lay the groundwork for an orthography reform and gave the Soviets a chance to propagandize their nationalities policy, but it also provoked a scandal. Immediately after its conclusion, the Biuro of the Belorussian Central Committee met to rebuke the conference organizers: the conference hall had been decorated exclusively in national colors; no Soviet flag was hung; Lenin's portrait had been removed from the hall; the Belorussian nationalist Alekhnovich was greeted much too warmly; in his keynote address, the Education Commissar, Balitskii, had ignored the Communist Party's role in building Belorussian national culture. Letters of explanation and apology were sent to Stalin and the all-union TsK.[108]

In particular, the Belorussian Party Biuro was furious that a group of delegates, including prominent communists, proposed adopting the Latin script. A major Belorussian national communist leader, Adamovich, had raised the issue. A candidate member of the Belorussian central committee, Zhilunovich, gave

---

[107] George Y. Shevelov, *The Ukrainian Language in the first Half of the Twentieth Century* (Cambridge, Mass., 1989): 131–140.

[108] *GARF* 374/27s/1693 (1929): 57; *RTsKhIDNI* 17/33/468 (1927): 14–17; 36–42.

a speech advocating the move, excerpts of which were printed in the local press.[109] When the conference's official organizer, Biuro member Ignatovskii, received this proposal, he authorized it, adding only the qualification that the shift must take place in tandem with the other peoples of the Soviet Union.[110] Although the petition was subsequently rejected, an impression was created that Belorussia had voted to adopt the Latin script, and several foreign Belorussian papers reported this as a fact.[111] In response to this scandal, the Belorussian Party Biuro passed the following resolution: "The raising of this question objectively reflects a tendency on part of our intelligentsia toward an orientation on 'independence' and an orientation on the west."[112] Thus, it was deemed to be a nationalist deviation even to discuss in Minsk a policy that eight months earlier in a similar international conference in Baku had been adopted almost unanimously and heralded as uniquely progressive.

The all-Ukrainian conference on spelling reform held in Kharkov in May–June 1927 did not produce similar controversy. Like its Belorussian counterpart, it did not produce final agreement on an orthography reform, but it did lay the groundwork for a subsequent reform approved in September 1928.[113] The issue of latinization was raised by the writer and literary politician, Serhii Pylypenko, but without any apparent widespread support.[114] Of more long-term significance, the conference's organizer, Mykola Skrypnyk, proposed introducing two Latin letters, s and z, to represent the sounds dz and dzh. This reform was not accepted.[115] The 1928 reform did introduce the Galician "Г" to represent the hard g. In general, the spelling reform represented a compromise of east and west Ukrainian practices and therefore had the effect of slightly differentiating literary Ukrainian from Russian.[116]

These two conferences seemed to have had no more impact other than a slightly unpleasant, but short-lived, scandal in Minsk. This all changed with the onset of cultural revolution. In 1929–1930, language politics became enmeshed with the noisy political purges that took place in Belorussia and Ukraine. In the Union for the Liberation of Ukraine (SVU) show trial in Ukraine and the Union for the Liberation of Belorussia (SVB) political purge in Belorussia, both of which targeted the *smenovekhovtsy* intelligentsia, linguists were prominent among the accused. Indeed, the GPU placed Belorussian linguists literally at the center of the putative SVB conspiracy. The counterrevolutionary organization was said to have been established within the Scientific Terminological

[109] *RTsKhIDNI* 17/85/365 (1929): 69–70.
[110] *RTsKhIDNI* 17/33/468 (1927): 170.
[111] *RTsKhIDNI* 17/85/365 (1929): 70.
[112] *RTsKhIDNI* 17/33/468 (1927): 156–157.
[113] Shevelov, *The Ukrainian Language*, 132.
[114] A. Khvylia, "Vykorinyty, znyshchyty natsionalistychne korinnia na movnomu fronti," *Bil'shovyk Ukrainy*, nos. 7–8 (1933): 49; James Mace, *Communism and the Dilemmas of National Liberation* (Cambridge, Mass., 1983): 134.
[115] Khvylia, "Vykorinyty," 49.
[116] Shevelov, *The Ukrainian Language*, 132–134.

Commission of the Education Commissariat. They were said to have organized the 1926 language conference. They favored an orientation on Poland and therefore aimed at "the flooding of the Belorussian language with Polish words, the introduction of the Latin script, and so on." Their major base was the Belorussian Academy of Sciences, and "the chief problem that the national democrats occupied themselves with was the working out of Belorussian terminology. To the national democrats this was not only important scientifically, but above all politically. They needed to produce not only ordinary terminology, but terminology which would fence off Belorussian culture from all-union culture."[117] The role of language sabotage, as it was called, grew even larger in the articles written after the purge announcement.[118] This would become a pattern in future national purges. The role of language in the rhetoric of the purge played a greater role than in the politics leading to the purge itself. Language and terror were linked.

A similar pattern emerged in the 1929–1930 Ukrainian SVU show trial. As in Belorussia, the major controversies leading up to the purge trial had been literary politics and control of the Ukrainian Academy of Science.[119] However, also as in Belorussia, language politics played an important role in the show trial itself, but because of terminological sabotage rather than latinization. In his report on the trial, Skrypnyk noted that "a large number of old linguists are now sitting on the bench of the accused at the trial of SVU, for it has become known that in the area of terminology, they engaged in wrecking."[120] A number of articles after the trial reiterated this charge.[121]

Thus by 1930, what would become a persistent connection between language and terror had established itself in the western republics. It would appear to have arisen first in the Soviet west as issues of cultural hegemony were more sensitive there. Ukrainian and Belorussian culture were very close to both Russian and Polish culture. Therefore, any perceived rejection of Russian culture was apprehended as a move toward Polish culture, and given the hostility between the Soviet Union and Poland, the charge quickly became ideological. In the east, hostility to Russian culture was seen as hostility to Tsarist colonialism. In the west, however, it was seen as hostility to central control and an unhealthy orientation on the neighboring west. In a slightly different fashion, this echoed the pattern noted in Chapters 3 and 4, where an anti-Russian campaign was sanctioned in the east and anti-central impulses were suppressed in Ukraine. As we shall see, the charge of treasonous irredentism would recur with

[117] GARF 374/27s/1968 (1930): 2, 4, 26, 66.
[118] A. Sian'kevich, "Barats'ba z ukhilami u natsyianal'nim pitan'ni i natsarabotse," *Bol'shevik Belarusi*, no. 5 (1930): 12–15; A. V. "Politychnaia sutnas'ts' Belaruskaga natsyianal-demokratyzmu," nos. 10–12 (1930): 40–53.
[119] George S. N. Luckyj, *Literary Politics in the Soviet Ukraine, 1917–1934* (New York, 1956); I. I. Shapoval, *Ukraina 20–50-kh rokiv* (Kiev, 1993): 64–81.
[120] M. Skrypnyk, "Kontr-revoliutsiine shkidnytstvo na kul'turnomu fronti," *Chervonyi Shliakh*, no. 4 (1930): 142.
[121] Shevelov, *The Ukrainian Language*, 154–155.

the political crisis of Ukrainization in December 1932 and in the 1933 Ukrainian and Belorussian terror campaigns, during which language once again played a prominent role in the indictments leveled against Ukrainian and Belorussian nationalists. The origins of these events and their impact on the policy of *korenizatsiia* are the subject of the next two chapters.

PART TWO

THE POLITICAL CRISIS OF THE AFFIRMATIVE ACTION EMPIRE

6

The Politics of National
Communism, 1923 to 1930

Having analyzed the implementation of the Affirmative Action Empire in Part One, I now turn to a consideration of the political crisis of *korenizatsiia*. This chapter traces the emergence of a hard-line critique of *korenizatsiia* during NEP and its subsequent intensification with the launching of Stalin's socialist offensive. Chapter 7 will show how conflict between Ukraine and the RSFSR eventually led to the triumph of this new hard line during the grain requisitions crisis in December 1932, when the Politburo issued two anti-Ukrainization decrees. These decrees would usher in a fundamental revision of the Affirmative Action Empire.

In April 1925, Kaganovich had arrived in Ukraine and attempted to establish a consensus that Ukrainization was a core hard-line Bolshevik policy. As we have seen, he had considerable success before hard-line Ukrainization was ultimately undermined by the increased centralization accompanying the socialist offensive. This failure of hard-line Ukrainization should not be exaggerated. Ukrainization was not repudiated. It was not even criticized. Its implementation was simply undermined, because it was now firmly categorized as a secondary, soft-line policy. Before the December 1932 anti-Ukrainization decrees could emerge, much more was required: not just a belief that the implementation of *korenizatsiia* was a secondary concern, or that *korenizatsiia* sometimes impeded the accomplishment of core Bolshevik projects, but rather a conviction that *korenizatsiia* itself was in fundamental opposition to core Bolshevik principles.

This belief emerged as the political struggle surrounding *korenizatsiia* in the national republics gradually convinced a growing number of influential Bolsheviks that *korenizatsiia* was exacerbating rather than preventing the growth of nationalism. A number of factors converged to foster this belief: first, the persistence of national identity politics; second, growing concern over the influence of the national *smenovekhovtsy*; third, growing concern that cross-border ties were being used to the detriment of the Soviet Union rather than to its advantage; fourth, the persistence of the Russian question; and fifth, the increasing centralization that accompanied the socialist offensive.

The Shumskyi Affair

We already touched briefly on the Shumskyi affair in Chapter 3. It flared up suddenly in early 1926 during Ukrainian Politburo deliberation on how best to proceed with Ukrainization after the highly successful, but still incomplete, forced Ukrainization campaign of 1925. At a March 19 Politburo meeting, Kaganovich had put forward the slogan that the party should not "forcibly Ukrainize the proletariat." This was orthodox party policy, but Shumskyi apparently felt it sent a dangerous signal of weakness. As a result, on March 31, at a second Politburo meeting devoted to the Ukrainization of the central TsK newspaper *Kommunist*, Shumskyi launched into a bitter attack on Kaganovich and the rest of the Ukrainian Politburo over the slow pace of Ukrainization.[1] He accused Kaganovich of having said the party would not Ukrainize the proletariat, omitting the key word "forcibly." The other Politburo members denied Kaganovich had said this. In a rage, Shumskyi lashed out at the entire Politburo with superb invective[2]:

> In the Party the Russian Communist dominates and conducts himself with suspicion and hostility—to speak mildly—towards the Ukrainian Communist. He dominates and by relying on the contemptible self-seeking type of Little Russian [*prezrennyi skurnicheskii tip malorossa*], who in all historical epochs has been equally unprincipled and hypocritical, slavishly two-faced, and traitorously sycophantic. He now prides himself in his false internationalism, boasts his indifferent attitude to things Ukrainian and is ready to spit on them (perhaps even sometimes in Ukrainian), if that gives him the chance to serve and get a position.

Kaganovich naturally rebuked Shumskyi, and the latter in turn declared he could no longer work in Ukraine.[3]

There are two important background facts to this episode. First, Shumskyi was a member of the Ukrainian Socialist Revolutionary Party from 1909 to 1918, and in 1918 he helped found the new Ukrainian Communist Party, *borot'bisty* (named after its journal *Borot'ba*, "The Struggle"), which was formed from the

---

[1] *RTsKhIDNI* 17/26/3 (02.04.26): 17/3.

[2] Quoted in E. Hirchak, "Shums'kyzm i rozkol u KPZU," *Bil'shovyk Ukrainy*, no. 5 (1928): 39–40. There was a stenogram for this session, but it apparently has not survived.

[3] *TsDAHOU* 1/6/102 (12.05.26): 129. RTsKhIDNI 558/11/738 (1926): 14–16.

left wing of the Ukrainian Socialist Revolutionary Party and entered into a close alliance with the Ukrainian Bolsheviks.[4] In March 1920, under Bolshevik pressure, the *borot'bisty* liquidated their party and its most influential members entered the Ukrainian Communist Party (KP/b/U). Lenin personally specified that Shumskyi should be made a member of the Ukrainian TsK. Shumskyi was typical of the large number of national communists, who were recruited by the Bolsheviks from nationalist leftist parties. Agamali-Ogly, a member of the leftist Azerbaijani Hummet Party, was another. These individuals often served as nationalities policy specialists. Shumskyi himself was first a liaison to the Communist Party of Western Ukraine (KPZU) in Poland and then Ukraine's Commissar of Education. He gave the important keynote address at the April 1925 plenum that led to the adoption of hard-line Ukrainization.

Second, Shumskyi's attack has to be seen in the context of the rampant factionalism within the Communist Party in all the national republics. The Ukrainian national communist faction had just successfully rid themselves of Emmanuel Kviring and Dmitrii Lebed in a manner that produced a Politburo rebuke.[5] Shumskyi clearly hoped the same could be done with Kaganovich. Already in October 1925, during an audience Stalin held with a KPZU delegation in Moscow, Shumskyi suggested that Kaganovich should be replaced with an ethnic Ukrainian. Stalin reportedly agreed this would be desirable in principle, but argued that politically it was too soon to do so.[6] This certainly did nothing to slow Shumskyi's factional struggle with Kaganovich.

Shumskyi's conflict with Kaganovich, then, would have been of little political significance had he not again appealed to Stalin, in a meeting on April 20, to remove Kaganovich. He suggested Kaganovich be replaced by Chubar, and that Chubar's position as head of Sovnarkom might be filled by either Zatonskyi, Skrypnyk, or Hryhorii Hrynko. All were ethnic Ukrainians, and Hrynko was a fellow former *borot'bist*, who would become better known in the 1930s as the all-union Commissar of Finance, Grigorii Grinko.[7] Stalin initially counseled patience.

In the meantime, however, Kaganovich had written Stalin a savvy letter summarizing his conflict with Shumskyi.[8] He initially downplayed the affair, asserting that although Shumskyi claimed the conflict was over Ukrainization, it really had "no basis in substantive policy whatsoever" and instead reflected

---

[4] All biographical detail taken from "Spravka o byvshem chlene TsK i Orgbiuro TsK KP/b/U Shumskom Aleksandre Iakovleviche," *TsDAHOU* (Uncatalogued Document): 1–9. On the *borot'bisty*, see Iwan Majstrenko, *Borot'bism: A Chapter in the History of Ukrainian Communism* (New York, 1954).

[5] *RTsKhIDNI* 17/3/497 (16.04.26): 57/32. The decree read: "1. Do not oppose the removal of Comrade Kviring from Ukraine. 2. Tell TsK KP/b/U that they should have consulted with TsK RKP before they took the decision to remove Kviring from Ukraine. . . ."

[6] "Spravka," 6–7. Also, Shapoval, *Ukraina*, 21–22. Janusz Radziejowski, *The Communist Party of Western Ukraine, 1919–1929* (Edmonton, 1983): 118, 126n.

[7] *TsDAHOU* 1/6/102 (12.05.26): 129–130, 176, 191; *RTsKhIDNI* 17/33/552 (1926): 107.

[8] *RTsKhIDNI* 558/11/738 (1926): 12–14. The letter is not dated so it is unclear if it was written before or after Stalin's April 20 meeting with Shmuskyi.

Shumskyi's anger that he had not been elected to the Ukrainian Politburo. With some justice, Kaganovich claimed he could more plausibly be accused of pushing Ukrainization too much rather than too little. After this innocent beginning, Kaganovich cleverly inserted two damaging claims. First, he asserted that Shumskyi had "called a meeting of former *borot'bisty*, in which he mobilized his forces" against Kaganovich. To Stalin this would not at all signify a nonpolitical personal conflict but rather a serious attempt at political opposition by a Ukrainian nationalist non-Bolshevik movement. Second, Kaganovich attached six pages of inflammatory excerpts from the recent pamphlets of the flamboyant Ukrainian national communist writer, Mykola Khvylovyi, in which Khvylovyi argued aggressively for orienting Ukrainian culture toward western Europe rather than Moscow.[9] Kaganovich noted that Shumskyi defended Khvylovyi and suggested that their recent activity was evidence of a "growth in petit-bourgeois chauvinism." Kaganovich then ended his letter by wondering "what significance you, Comrade Stalin, will give to [Khvylovyi's] writings" and by requesting that Stalin "write a brief letter with his thoughts about this incident."

Stalin took Kaganovich's bait. On April 26, he escalated the affair with a letter addressed to Kaganovich and the Ukrainian TsK. Stalin noted that Shumskyi "had several correct ideas": that Ukrainian culture was growing, that the party must master it or lose influence to hostile forces, and therefore that "the spirit of irony and skepticism towards Ukrainian culture" reigning in the party must be overcome. However, Stalin also noted "at least two serious errors"[10]:

> First, [Shumskyi] mixes up the Ukrainization of our Party and Soviet apparat with the Ukrainization of the proletariat. We can and should, while observing the proper tempo, Ukrainize our party, state and other apparats. But we must not Ukrainize the proletariat from above. We must not force Russian workers *en masse* to give up the Russian language and culture and declare their culture and language to be Ukrainian. This contradicts the principle of the free development of nationalities. This would not be national freedom, but a novel form of national oppression. There is no doubt that the make-up of the Ukrainian proletariat will change as Ukrainian industry develops, as Ukrainian workers enter industry from the surrounding villages. There is no doubt that the proletariat will Ukrainize, just as in Latvia and Hungary, where it was once German, it became Latvian and Hungarian. But this process is a slow and spontaneous one. Replacing this natural process with a forced Ukrainization of the proletariat from above would be a utopian and harmful policy, capable of provoking anti-Ukrainian chauvinism in the non-Ukrainian parts of the proletariat in Ukraine.

---

[9] Ibid., 17–22.
[10] Stalin, "Iz pis'ma tov. Kaganovichu i drugim chlenam TsK KP/b/U," (1926) in *Marksizm*, 172–173.

In both these positive and negative assessments, Stalin endorsed the existing line on Ukrainization.

Stalin was particularly outraged by the excerpts of Mykola Khvylovyi's pamphlets that Kaganovich had sent him, and he criticized Shumskyi for defending Khvylovyi.[11] Khvylovyi was one of the most popular and admired of a talented group of young Ukrainian Bolshevik authors. In April 1925, Khvylovyi published a provocative, scornful attack on the Ukrainian literary organization *Pluh* ("The Plough"), whose goal was to create a mass organization of peasant authors, a kind of rural *Proletcult*. This article initiated the Ukrainian literary discussion of 1925 to 1928.[12] Khvylovyi sketched an "explanation of two psychological categories: Europe and *Prosvita*."[13] *Prosvita* was a pre-revolutionary organization devoted to the spiritual and material improvement of the Ukrainian peasantry. For Khvylovyi, however, *Prosvita* was synonymous with traditional Ukrainian backwardness, provincialism, and cultural servility: "the saccharine, populist premises which retard national development . . . a servile psychology . . . a psychological category of a repressive type . . . our 'Khokhlandia.'" Adopting a leftist stance akin to the all-union "On Guardists," Khvylovyi denounced *Pluh* as the bearer of a kulak ideology, "a red *prosvita*." However, in conscious contrast to the On Guardists, he advocated an elitist literary strategy: an orientation on an eternal "psychological Europe," for "the classic type of the civic person was developed by the West."[14] Khvylovyi's article was a manifesto for a modernist, urban, westernized high Ukrainian culture to replace a despised traditional, rural Ukrainian folk culture.

As the literary discussion continued, Khvylovyi grew bolder and specified the object of traditional Ukrainian servility[15]:

> Since our literature can at last follow its own path of development, we are faced with the following question: by which of the world's literatures should we set our course? *On no account by the Russian.* This is definite and unconditional. Our political union must not be confused with literature. Ukrainian poetry must flee as quickly as possible from Russian literature and its styles. . . . The point is that Russian literature has weighed down upon us for centuries as master of the situation, as one that has conditioned our psyche to play the slavish imitator. . . .

[11] Stalin's copy of the excerpts is covered with violent underlining in the text and margins. RTsKhIDNI 558/11/738 (1926): 17–22.

[12] On the literary discussion, see Myroslav Shkandrij, *Modernists, Marxists and the Nation* (Edmonton, 1992); George S. N. Luckyj, *Literary Politics in the Soviet Ukraine, 1917–1934* (rev. ed., Durham, N.C., 1990).

[13] Mykola Khvylovyi, *The Cultural Renaissance in Ukraine*, ed. Myroslav Shkandrij (Edmonton, 1986): 41.

[14] Ibid., 125; 124; 185; 97; 52; 116–121. "*Khokhol*" is a perjorative name for Ukrainians that connotes backwardness and provinciality.

[15] Ibid., 222.

As a committed leftist, Khvylovyi insisted that only a fully Ukrainized proletariat could overcome Russian cultural hegemony: "the point is the immediate
derussification of the proletariat . . . we demand that the authorities take a
serious attitude to the Ukrainization of the proletariat."[16] Finally, in the fateful
month of April 1926, Khvylovyi lashed out more generally at traditional "Russian
messianism" in a pamphlet entitled "Ukraine or Little Russia": "Today the
center of all-Union philistinism is Moscow, in which the proletarian factories,
the Komintern and the All-Union Communist Party figure as an oasis on the
world scale."[17]

Khvylovyi's intentional provocation succeeded in raising Stalin's ire[18]:

> Second . . . Shumskyi does not see that given the weakness of native Commu-
> nist cadres in Ukraine, the [Ukrainian cultural] movement, led completely by
> the non-Communist intelligentsia, may in places take on the character of a battle
> for the alienation of Ukrainian culture and Ukrainian society from all-union
> culture and society, the character of a battle against Russian culture and its
> highest achievement—against Leninism . . . [I have in mind] the demands of
> Khvylovyi for "the immediate derussification of the proletariat" in Ukraine, his
> belief that "from Russian literature, from its style, Ukrainian poetry should flee
> as quickly as possible," his declaration that "the idea of the proletariat is known
> to us without Moscow's art." . . . At a time when the West European proletariat
> is full of sympathy towards "Moscow" as a citadel of the international pro-
> letarian movement and Leninism . . . Khvylovyi has nothing to say in favor of
> "Moscow" except to call on Ukrainian actors to flee from "Moscow" "as quickly
> as possible." . . . Comrade Shumskyi does not understand that one can master
> the new movement in Ukraine for Ukrainian culture only by fighting extremes,
> such as Khvylovyi, within the Communist ranks. . . .

Both of Stalin's criticisms, then, focused on the sensitive Russian question: fear
of Russian proletarian resentment toward Ukrainians and Ukrainian culture, and
fear of Ukrainian intellectuals' growing resentment of Russian culture.

The version of Stalin's letter first published in 1934, and quoted from extensively in 1926, contained only criticism of Shumskyi. However, the unpublished
version also mildly censured Kaganovich: "It is possible that Kaganovich has
some defects in the sense of being overly administrative. It is possible that
organizational pressure [*nazhim*] is truly practiced by Comrade Kaganovich."[19]
The unpublished version also ended with some support for Shumskyi and
strong support for Ukrainization[20]:

> One conclusion: we must not persecute former *borot'bisty* because of their past.
> We must forget that at one time they sinned—we have no one without sins. We

[16] Ibid., 215, 212.
[17] Ibid., 228–229.
[18] Stalin, *Marksizm*, 173.
[19] *RTsKhIDNI* 81/3/135 (1926): 4.
[20] Ibid., 4–5.

must recruit them to Party work both at the local and central levels, unconditionally and without fail. We must include Comrade Shumskyi in leading Party work. We must intensively forge new cadres out of Ukrainians. We must pay special attention to schools, to the Ukrainian youth in schools, recruiting the most capable people. We must seriously work to master the new movement in Ukraine, while battling with the extremes of such comrades like Comrade Khvylovyi.

Stalin's letter backed Kaganovich, but not unconditionally.

A Ukrainian Politburo meeting was convened to discuss future plans for Ukrainization and the emerging Shumskyi affair. Shumskyi remained characteristically defiant. He reiterated his criticisms of Kaganovich and Ukrainization and, despite Stalin's intervention, defended Khvylovyi as "a talented writer" and "a major figure of our Party." Finally, he defended his *borot'bist* activities from 1917 to 1920 in a statement that particularly outraged the Politburo: "I have a [revolutionary] tradition from October on and in all that time I have not retreated from it one iota."[21] Hrynko, who had been distancing himself from Shumskyi, also infuriated his audience by declaring Kaganovich "a temporary figure . . . [who was not] deeply and organically tied to Ukraine," a reference to Kaganovich's Jewish roots and his revolutionary activity outside Ukraine.[22]

Kaganovich, on the other hand, was much more deferential to his audience. He presented a firm but modest persona, emphasized collective leadership, and stressed Ukraine's stature[23]:

> To what degree I am suitable—I find it difficult to say. I should declare that it is impossible to work in such a massive organization as Ukraine without errors. . . . Just try and find such a hero—Kaganovich or no Kaganovich—let him try to work in such a highly qualified institution as the [Ukrainian] Politburo, let him try to dominate with such major political figures as Vlas Iakovlevich [Chubar] and Comrade Petrovskii. In the Politburo, we have no hierarchy. Of course there could be concrete errors. Are we mortals? Mortals. Could it happen that I say to Grigorii Ivanovich [Petrovskii] something indelicate? It could. As to political abilities and leadership, I agree that in Ukraine you cannot simply be an organizer. Here politics is needed. This is no simple *gubkom*, or oblast, like the Urals.

He regretted the conflict with Shumskyi and insisted he could work with him. Kaganovich's performance was successful. The entire Politburo unanimously praised Kaganovich in a letter to Stalin and called Shumskyi's charge that Kaganovich was a despot "absolutely without foundation, it produces in us a

[21] *TsDAHOU* 1/6/102: 4–5, 119, 121–125, 176–177, 191.
[22] Ibid., 184.
[23] Ibid., 198–200.

feeling of indignation."[24] This unanimous support from his colleagues allowed Kaganovich to dictate terms to Shumskyi. After almost a year of struggle during which Shumskyi was required to confess his errors repeatedly, which he did with great reluctance and little conviction, he was finally exiled to Saratov. He later moved to Leningrad, where he was arrested in 1933 as the head of an imaginary counterrevolutionary Ukrainian nationalist group.[25]

Despite Stalin's intervention, the Shumskyi affair would have been of limited political significance had it not intersected with Soviet foreign policy ambitions in Poland. The Soviet leadership had authorized the formation of an independent Communist Party of Western Ukraine (KPZU) to exploit the national discontent of Poland's Ukrainian population. This strategy was compromised severely at a February–March 1927 Ukrainian TsK plenum, convened to put a formal end to the Shumskyi affair, when the KPZU's official representative, Karlo Maksymovych, defiantly defended Shumskyi. Maksymovych stated his unequivocal support for the KP/b/U line on the nationalities question, but he went on to express incredulity at the severity of Shumskyi's denunciation over a seemingly minor difference of opinion. He noted Shumskyi's past services to the KPZU and said the plenum's decision would not be well received in Western Ukraine. The Ukrainian TsK immediately drafted a letter to the KPZU demanding a condemnation of Maksymovych's position. This letter and a subsequent KP/b/U resolution denouncing Maksymovych's comments were summarily rejected. For the next eight months, the Komintern attempted to avoid a total defection of the KPZU leadership, but ultimately failed.[26] In January 1928, the majority of the KPZU leadership passed a resolution condemning "the bureaucratic deformation of the process of Ukrainization . . . the denial of the need to Ukrainize the urban proletariat . . . the driving away of the best Ukrainian forces on the pretext of national deviation (Shumskyi, Hrynko)."[27] The Komintern was then forced to dissolve the entire Central Committee of the KPZU and form an entirely new party leadership, an unprecedented embarrassment for the Komintern. An enraged and embarrassed Ukrainian party leadership responded by declaring Shumsky-

---

[24] *RTsKhIDNI* 17/85/4 (1926): 1–7. Kaganovich added a postscript testifying to the Politburo's "collective friendly work" and in particular his close relationship with Grigorii Ivanovich and Vlas Iakovlevich.

[25] For Shumskyi's confessions, see *Budivnytstvo radians'koi Ukrainy*, vol. 1 (Kharkov, 1928). *RTsKhIDNI* 17/85/4 (1926): 9–13; 17/33/552 (1926): 107–111; 85/27/91 (1926): 3–14. *TsDAHOU* 17/20/2247 (13.12.26): 95–114. On his transfer to Saratov, *RTsKhIDNI* 17/113/306 (01.07.27): 126/38; and for his later fate, Shapoval, *Liudyna i systema*, 134–151. Hrynko was sent off to Moscow, where he flourished and later rose to become all-union Commissar of Finance.

[26] Janusz Radziejowski, *The Communist Party of Western Ukraine, 1919–1929* (Edmonton, 1983): 108–169; *Budivnytstvo; Natsional'ne pytannia na Ukraini ta rozlam v KPZU: zbirnyk statei i dokumentiv* (Kharkov, 1928); M. Skrypnyk, *Dzherela ta prychyny rozlamu v KPZU* (Kharkov, 1928). *TsDAHOU* 1/16/6 (18.03.27): 1–9; 1/16/3 (1927): 193, 196, 318, 327, 338; *RTsKhIDNI* 17/162/6 (22.12.27): 1/11; (05.01.28): 4/31, 11–12; (09.02.28): 9/24.

[27] Radziejowski, *The Communist Party*, 154–155.

ism, and its ideological twin Khylovyism, "the theoretical formulation of Ukrainian fascism."[28]

The Shumskyi affair, then, escalated dramatically over the course of two years from typical factional struggle in the non-Russian republics to an international scandal and the condemnation of a fascist deviation within the Ukrainian Communist Party. As we have seen, this extended political battle had surprisingly little short-term impact on the implementation of Ukrainization. However, it had an important long-term impact, because it marked the crystallization of a new anti-*korenizatsiia* hard line stance. This new hard line emerged from a convergence of four overlapping issues: concerns with the policy of supporting national culture, the role of *smenovekhovstvo*, the Piedmont Principle, and, above all, the status of Russians and Russian culture. Since these concerns were not confined to Ukraine but contributed a growing concern over the impact of *korenizatsiia* throughout the Soviet Union, I will pause to analyze each of these four issues and their combined impact.

As we saw in the discussion of latinization in Chapter 5, the Soviet policy of supporting national cultures was filled with ambiguity. Indeed, from the center's perspective, it would ideally involve only the support of national identity through a set of symbolic identity markers. National identity would be, in Stalin's formula, empty of national "content." However, Soviet policy also called for creating national elites. Indeed, one justification for recruiting these elites was that distinct national cultures did exist in the present, and one needed leaders who understood them. This necessitated recruiting all moderately revolutionary titular nationals into important leadership positions in the non-Russian republics. They in turn naturally brought their own concerns about national culture and identity into the Communist Party. Agamali-Ogly and his Azerbaijani cohort from the Hummet Party, for instance, brought their concern for a spiritual renewal of the backward east. Such language made the Bolsheviks nervous. Shumskyi and his fellow *borot'bist* party members likewise brought with them a characteristic Ukrainian obsession with Ukrainian national identity. As a result, in mid-1926, the Ukrainian party found itself in the enormously embarrassing position of discussing at Politburo sessions and party plenums the pressing issue: who exactly was a true Ukrainian?

Shumskyi's attack on the "contemptible self-seeking Little Russian" both enraged and befuddled Ukrainian party members. It was a dominant theme at the June 1926 plenum. When Zatonskyi started to read statistics on how many Ukrainians there were in the party, one wit yelled out: "And how many Little Russians?" People were convinced they had been insulted but were uncertain as to what the insult meant. A Russian from the Donbass seemed to think it referred to Russians: "[According to Shumskyi] all communists

[28] *RTsKhIDNI* 17/26/15 (12–16.03.28): 3; 558/11/738, 28–80.

are Russian 'Little Russians,' harmful elements who surround the TsK, and many comrades are saying, 'we'll have to flee [to Russia].' And why? You work and work, and suddenly you get labeled a Little Russian." An ethnic Ukrainian speaker sarcastically said that "someone just asked me what my nationality is and, who knows, am I Ukrainian or Little Russian?"[29] Kaganovich recognized this anger and zeroed in on this issue for a nasty attack on Shumskyi[30]:

> We have previously divided the party into Russians, Ukrainians, Jews and now they say: "Little Russians." What political sense is there in such a term? How should we understand it? Really, Comrades, is this not moral and political terror against this or that Ukrainian? Does it not mean a planned attempt to terrorize Ukrainian youth and those who might not agree with these incorrect opinions. They are named "Little Russians" with a few other added epithets.

Most party members associated Shumskyi's un-Bolshevik terms of abuse to his *borot'bist* past. The ex-*borot'bisty* were universally known in the party as *byvshie* (formers), the same term used for privileged members of the prerevolutionary ruling class. There was considerable resentment of the *byvshie*. For instance, the Ukrainian leadership had to pressure the rank-and-file to elect Hrynko and Shumskyi to the Ukrainian TsK.[31] The *byvshie* were valued, however, as Ukrainian cultural specialists. An early Ukrainian party history even argued that the Ukrainian Communist Party had "twin roots": Bolsheviks rooted in urban Russian culture and *borot'bisty* rooted in rural Ukrainian culture. This model had already been denounced by late 1925.[32] However, the idea that the *byvshie* were uniquely qualified to implement nationalities policy remained. Zatonskyi, who as an old Bolshevik and ethnic Ukrainian strongly resented this claim, noted that "on one hand, the *byvshie* demand the reservation of certain positions for themselves on the grounds that only they can implement the nationalities policy properly; on the other hand [they complain] that they are called *byvshie*."[33] Most Ukrainian communists assumed (probably correctly) that Shumskyi identified *byvshie* as the true Ukrainians and other ethnic Ukrainian Bolsheviks as Little Russians.

If even ethnic Ukrainian Bolsheviks were too estranged from Ukrainian culture to be able to implement the Soviet nationalities policy properly, then clearly Russians and Jews were even more incapable. Hrynko's reference to Kaganovich as a "temporary figure," not "organically connected" with Ukraine, made this *byvshii* opinion crystal clear to the party's Russian and Jewish majority. This pointed to an important contradiction. Comprehensive Ukrainization

---

[29] *RTsKhIDNI* 17/26/1 (1926): 79; 93; 96.

[30] Ibid., 145.

[31] *RTsKhIDNI* 17/85/4 (1926): 6.

[32] M. Ravich-Cherkasskii, *Istoriia kommunisticheskoi partii Ukrainy* (Kharkov, 1923): 9; *RTsKhIDNI* 17/16/1396 (19.11.25): 98/9.

[33] *TsDAHOU* 1/6/102 (12.05.26): 161.

aimed at establishing the hegemony of Ukrainian culture, or rather Ukrainian identity, since the culture would be drained of its national "content" and so available to all territorial Ukrainians. Yet, Soviet Affirmative Action privileged ethnic Ukrainians. Moreover, for the implementation of nationalities policy, it privileged "organic" Ukrainians because they knew Ukrainian culture, although the Ukrainian culture they knew was itself to be drained of its national "content." Many influential Ukrainians, including Chubar, were uncomfortable with this emphasis on "pure-blood" (*chistokrovnyi*) Ukrainians.[34] The June 1926 plenum defended Kaganovich by denouncing the view that "all Party members, in particular non-Ukrainians, lack an organic tie to Ukraine if they worked in Ukraine before and after the revolution, but conducted their Communist work outside Ukraine for a certain period after October."[35] Many would have liked to go further and abandon any priority for ethnic Ukrainians.

Here Stalin stood firmly in the way. In his letter to Kaganovich, Stalin stated that "Shumskyi is correct that the Party leadership in Ukraine should become Ukrainian." Since the list of eminent Ukrainians he provided did not include Kaganovich, he clearly meant ethnic Ukrainians.[36] Moreover, on the exact same day he wrote to Kaganovich, Stalin also attended an Orgburo session, which he rarely did, devoted to the work of the Bashkir obkom. Stalin made only one proposal: "Couldn't we, say, find a Bashkir to serve as second party secretary—wouldn't that be a good thing?"[37] Surprisingly, the Bashkir party leader, Razumov, disagreed and made reference to the republic's large Tatar and Russian populations. Stalin, now somewhat irritated, insisted on his proposal[38]:

> I ask you: who in Bashkiria is chairman of Sovnarkom? A Bashkir. Who is chairman of TsIK? A Bashkir or a Tatar? A Bashkir. Why not a Tatar? Why on the soviet side [*po sovetskoi linii*], which interacts with the whole population, which interacts with the party, why on the Soviet side do you accept a Bashkir as chairman of Sovnarkom, chairman of TsIK. . . . The Bashkir language differs from the Tatar less than the language of industrial cadres [*khoziastvennikov*] from professionals [*professionalistov*] [Laughter]. I propose we decide this question. We can promote a Bashkir, the Tatars won't be insulted. The chairman of Sovnarkom and TsIK are Bashkirs, but the Tatars aren't upset, they got used to it. You need a helper with ties to the Bashkir and Tatar Party mass who can help you work. Why don't you want this?

Stalin's jocular reference to the similarities of the Bashkir and Tatar languages only reinforced the point that Stalin wanted a Bashkir exclusively because he would be an ethnic Bashkir. So Stalin made his position quite clear. On April

---

[34] *TsDAHOU* 1/6/102 (12.05.26): 89.
[35] *RTsKhIDNI* 17/33/552 (1926): 7.
[36] *RTsKhIDNI* 17/85/4 (1926): 5.
[37] *RTsKhIDNI* 17/113/190 (26.04.26): 56.
[38] Ibid., 62.

26, 1926, he twice advocated ethnic Affirmative Action for the highest positions in the party leadership of the national republics.

I have pointed out several times that *korenizatsiia* was a deeply psychological strategy. Stalin clearly believed, and contemporary theories of nationalism would generally support him, that it was crucial to have titular nationals occupy most, but not all, of the high positions in their national territories. Modern nations, however, typically desire not only to be ruled by co-ethnics, but that those rulers also share and love their culture. Indeed, Shumskyi declared that "if the commanding staff of the party does not roll up its sleeves with love for this task [Ukrainization], then without love nothing will be accomplished."[39] This struck many party members as yet another instance of Shumskyi's fundamental non-Bolshevism. Kaganovich disagreed and rebuked his colleagues[40]:

> All interpretations, all hints that Ukrainization is just some kind of concession [*ustupka*] to someone, that we are conducting Ukrainization due to some terrible necessity, under the pressure of hostile forces, all this is absolutely incorrect. . . . [This helps our enemies who say that] the Bolsheviks are insincere, the Bolsheviks lie when they speak about Ukrainization, it's a Bolshevik maneuver, the Bolsheviks are doing it just to trick you, the Bolsheviks conduct Ukrainization not desiring it, not believing in it, not loving it and so on. . . .

Korenizatsiia was in fact an instrumental strategy, but to be effective it had to be presented as an essential goal. *Korenizatsiia* aimed at reducing national culture to national identity, and yet it needed passionate believers in those national cultures to implement it. These tensions pointed to a potentially larger contradiction: Might not *korenizatsiia* be transformed from an instrumental strategy into an essential goal? Might it not strengthen the exclusivist love of national cultures? And the key question: Did *korenizatsiia* defuse nationalism or did it perhaps exacerbate it? Many party members would answer yes, but as of April 26, 1926, Stalin was not one of them.

A second closely related concern about *korenizatsiia* had to do with the impact of Ukrainian *smenovekhovstvo* (*zminovikhivtsvo*). As noted earlier, the term *smenovekhovstvo* came from the Russian nationalist émigré *smena vekh* (Change of Landmarks) movement, which argued that Russian nationalists should cease their struggle with Bolshevism, and in fact cooperate with it, since Bolshevism was now serving Russian national interests.[41] Stated in this way, one can immediately see that, given the Soviet nationalities policy, non-Russian *smenovekhovstvo* would be a vastly larger phenomenon, as it in fact was. Dozens of prominent Ukrainian nationalists, attracted by the Bolshevik project of Ukrainization, returned from abroad.[42] The most

---

[39] *TsDAHOU* 1/6/102 (12.05.26): 129.
[40] *RTsKhIDNI* 17/26/1 (1926): 139.
[41] Hardeman, *Coming to Terms.*
[42] Shapoval, *Liudyna i systema*, 108–128; Ruslan Pyrih, *Zhyttia Mykhaila Hrushevs'koho: ostannie desiatylittia, 1924–1934* (Kiev, 1993).

dramatic return occurred on March 7, 1924, when Mykhailo Hrushevskyi, the dean of Ukrainian historians and president of the Ukrainian government, the Central Rada, during its conflict with the Bolsheviks in 1917–1918, returned to Kiev to assume the chairmanship of the Ukrainian Academy of Science's historical section. In 1926, with Bolshevik permission, a festive jubilee was held to commemorate his sixtieth birthday.[43] Moreover, the all-union Politburo accepted a Ukrainian proposal, also in the crucial month of April 1926, to have Hrushevskyi elected head of the Ukrainian Academy of Sciences, although in the end this did not occur.[44] One can hardly imagine Pavel Miliukov being granted such honors. Ukrainian *smenovekhovstvo* was allowed such scope for three reasons: It provided much needed Ukrainian cultural specialists; it helped convince Ukrainian intellectuals that the Bolsheviks were serious about Ukrainization; and, as we shall see, it served Bolshevik foreign policy goals.

There were clear similarities between the *smenovekhovtsy* and the *byvshie*. Both were attracted to the Bolsheviks by their nationalities policy and both were attractive to the Bolsheviks due to their value as national cultural specialists. However, they were never confused. *Smenovekhovtsy* were bourgeois and antirevolutionary. They were sought out as tactical allies. They were not expected, or even encouraged, to convert to Bolshevism. They tended to serve in cultural and academic institutions or in the bureaucratic apparat, although in the Soviet east they could rise to positions of authority within the government, but usually not in the party. The *byvshie*—whom I will call national communists because they combined a sincere belief in both nationalism and communism as well as in their compatibility—were recognized by the Bolsheviks as fellow revolutionaries. They were allowed to convert and could occupy very high leadership positions. Khodzhanov became Kazakhstan's first party secretary. Said-Galiev, Faizulla Khodjaev, and Panas Liubchenko served as heads of Sovnarkom in Tatarstan, Uzbekistan, and Ukraine. There was also a third small category of native nationalities specialists. These were titular national old Bolsheviks who developed a passionate commitment to the implementation of the Soviet nationalities policy. Mykola Skrypnyk in Ukraine was the prime example, but there were dozens of others. I also call these individuals national communists, since they shared the belief in the compatibility of nationalism and communism. The interaction of national communism and *smenovekhovstvo* would prove crucial.

Zminovikhivstvo, then, was encouraged to serve Ukrainization, but it also made the Bolsheviks very nervous. As Kaganovich once commented: "In Kharkov and Kiev we have a whole series of governments. For instance, Golubovich walks about and works perfectly freely. These are people who not only have passed through the school of political battle but also served in a series of governments. Take Hrushevskyi, who has legalized himself as a

[43] Pyrih, *Zhyttia Mykhaila Hrushevs'koho*, 55–72.
[44] *RTsKhIDNI* 17/3/556 (15.04.26): 20/4. Pyrih, *Zhyttia Mykhaila Hrushevs'koho*, 36–89.

smenovekhovets."[45] On his arrival in Ukraine, Kaganovich met with Hrushevskyi and other *zminovikhivtsy* and, alarmed at their self-confidence, formed a secret Politburo commission on the Ukrainian intelligentsia and ordered the GPU to increase its surveillance efforts.[46]

The GPU's reports were not comforting. For instance, a September 1926 internal GPU circular "On Ukrainian Separatism" painted a dark picture of the *zminovikhivstvo* intelligentsia[47]:

> Their hopes to overthrow Soviet power failed. The nationalists were forced to accept Soviet power as an unavoidable fact. Therefore, a new battle tactic was forged. The new weapon of "cultural work" is to be used against Soviet power. . . . [To increase nationalism], all possibilities are used. Ukrainization is exploited to place supporters of the national idea in all important parts of the state organism. They created the Ukrainian autocephalous church, which is a powerful bulwark of nationalism and a superb agitational weapon. The Ukrainian Academy of Science gathered around itself a compact mass of important figures of the former Ukrainian People's Republic. In general, representatives of Ukrainian nationalism work without rest to embed nationalist feelings in the masses. . . .

Nor did they neglect members of the party:

> Chauvinist circles devote enormous attention to the poet Khvylovyi, despite the fact he is a member of the KP/b/U. The chauvinist foreign press sometimes prints his works from our journals and tries to influence him in a nationalist direction. Internal chauvinist circles are also interested in young authors, including Communists. An authoritative representative of the Kharkov right-wing said the following: "We can support Khvylovyi. We should exert our influence on Ukrainian Communists and conduct our work so that they do not depart from us, but that we together with them fight for Ukrainization, for Ukraine."

This last quotation raised a crucial issue: If Ukrainization could be exploited by the Bolsheviks to change the landmarks of Ukrainian nationalists toward Soviet Ukraine, might it not also be exploited by *zminovikhivtsy* to change the landmarks of Ukrainian communists, such as Khvylovyi and Shumskyi (and even Skrypnyk?), to Ukrainian nationalism? Might national communists become *smenovekhovtsy*?

---

[45] *TsDAHOU* 1/6/102 (12.05.26): 44. Golubovich was chairman of the first independent Ukrainian government's cabinet in January 1918.

[46] *TsDAHOU* 1/16/1 (26.06.25): 178.

[47] Iurii Shapoval et al, eds., *ChK-HPU-NKVD v Ukraini* (Kiev, 1997): 256–257; 263–264. For a similar GPU report, see Volodymyr Prystaiko and Iurri Shapoval eds., *Mykhailo Hrushevskyi: Sprava "UNTs" i ostanni poky (1931–1934)* (Kiev, 1999): 139–157.

The GPU was the most consistent propagator of the new anti-*korenizatsiia* hard line. In the aftermath of the Shumskyi affair their arguments appeared more convincing. In his analysis of the Shumskyi affair, Kaganovich accepted the traditional arguments that Ukrainization served to disarm Ukrainian nationalism and instead blamed the rise in Ukrainian chauvinism on the NEP environment, which Stalin had predicted would lead to a growth in both Russian and non-Russian chauvinism. However, Kaganovich also included an argument that contradicted these premises, that the *zminovikhivtsy* "came over to our side calculating that they could re-orient us." Rather than disarming them, Ukrainization actually "made them grow bolder rapidly"[48]:

> We witness the growth of two parallel processes: the process of our growth, the growth of Soviet culture and society; and the process of the growth of hostile forces, which attempt to master this process. Our Ukrainization naturally gives birth to these hostile forces. One must see this, one must grasp it. Whoever is scared by this does not understand that we should have foreseen it. We know that it is unavoidably tied to the conflict we have now.

In Kaganovich's new model, Ukrainization had two effects. On the positive side, it helped the party govern the Ukrainian masses. On the negative side, it strengthened *zminovikhivstvo*, both without and within the party. Ukrainization was, then, no longer an unambiguously positive policy, but rather a dangerous one with high pay-offs but considerable costs as well. The anti-*korenizatsiia* hard line now had a foothold.

This concern over the defection of national communists intersected in a potent way with foreign policy concerns tied to the Piedmont Principle. Soviet policy attempted to exploit cross-border ethnic ties to undermine neighboring states. Prior to 1923, this policy focused on the east. In June 1923, however, after the majority Ukrainian region of eastern Galicia was formally granted to Poland, Stalin declared that Ukraine now had the same significance for the west that Turkestan had for the east.[49] In December 1924, the Komintern passed a resolution calling for the eventual transfer of all majority Ukrainian territory from Poland, Czechoslovakia, and Romania to Ukraine. Separate communist parties were formed for Poland's Ukrainians (KPZU) and Belorussians (KPZB). One of the goals of Ukrainization was to make the Ukrainian SSR "a center of attraction for the mass of discontented Ukrainians [in Poland]."[50]

Ukraine's role in undermining Polish rule in West Ukraine gave it an unusual latitude in foreign affairs. For instance, the Ukrainian wire service, RATAU, was the only republican wire service granted a role in the presentation of foreign news. The Ukrainian Politburo had a standing commission on foreign affairs. Ukraine successfully claimed a role in the granting of Soviet citizenship to

[48] *TsDAHOU* 1/6/102 (12.05.26): 45–46.
[49] *Tainy natsional'noi politiki*, 261.
[50] *RTsKhIDNI* 17/69/58 (1927): 166.

Ukrainian émigrés. Most important, Ukraine was allowed to impinge on Komintern authority through its right to supervise the KPZU, which had a formal representative, Karlo Maksymovych, as a candidate member of the Ukrainian TsK.[51] Ukraine's major nationalities specialists—Shumskyi, Zatonskyi, and Skrypnyk—were all regularly involved in foreign Ukrainian affairs and did not shrink from attacking the communist parties of Czechoslovakia and Poland for neglecting Ukrainian issues. No other republic could come near to rivaling Ukraine's privileged foreign policy status.

The defection of the entire KPZU leadership in defense of Shumskyi was a crushing blow to Ukraine's foreign policy aspirations as well as a major embarrassment to the Komintern. Still, this development might not have unduly alarmed Soviet leaders had it not occurred at the height of the 1927 war scare. Marshal Pilsudski's *coup d'etat* in Poland in May 1926 was, after some initial confusion, soon interpreted as the first step in an imminent attack by world imperialism on the Soviet Union.[52] Pilsudski's well-publicized domestic policy initiatives to improve relations with Poland's Ukrainian and Belorussian populations further alarmed the Soviet leadership as they were seen as an attempt "to secure his rear in case of a conflict with the USSR, and he is definitely conducting a policy aimed at such a conflict."[53]

The defection of the KPZU was naturally assimilated to this war scare scenario. Those west Ukrainian social classes who had previously, due to the policy of Ukrainization, adopted a positive attitude toward Soviet Ukraine (cross-border *smenovekhovtsy*) were said to have now "changed their position" and formed a united Ukrainian nationalist front in tactical alliance with Pilsudski. This greatly aided the attempt by "international and especially English imperialism . . . and today's Polish fascism . . . to turn West Ukraine into a bridgehead (*platsdarm*) for an attack on Soviet Ukraine."[54] This analysis used the favored Soviet category of *smenovekhovstvo*: "the shift [in orientation] of the west Ukrainian bourgeoisie . . . is a decisive break with the tendency towards a Soviet orientation and the forms of solving the national and especially the Ukrainian question undertaken by Soviet power."[55] In March 1928, Kaganovich and Skrypnyk insisted on an identical explanation for the "treason" of the KPZU leadership. They had not simply been masked scoundrels. They had sincerely adopted Bolshevism. Faced with new class pressures and Pilsudski's

---

[51] *RTsKhIDNI* 17/60/847 (1923): 38–39; 17/60/888 (1923): 1–6; 17/113/592 (30.01.28): 89–107; 17/3/683 (19.04.28): 23/16; 17/162/6 (22.12.27): 1/11; (05.01.28): 4/31, 11–12; TsDAHOU 1/16/1 (12.11.23): 5; (20.06.24): 51; (04.09.24): 90; (07.08.24): 99; (08.09.24): 108–111; (03.04.25): 160; (09.07.26): 6; 1/16/1 (20.02.24): 23; (04.07.25): 194.

[52] *RTsKhIDNI* 17/162/3 (20.05.26): 27/1; (22.05.26): 28/79; (24.05.26): 28/35; (27.05.26): 28/1; (29.05.26): 29/84. Jon Jacobson, *When the Soviet Union Entered World Politics* (Berkeley, Calif., 1994): 206–232.

[53] *TsDAHOU* 1/16/3 (07.01.27): 133–134. Radziejowski, *The Communist Party*, 94–96. RTsKhIDNI 17/33/468 (1926): 380b–39.

[54] Ibid., 124.

[55] Ibid., 127.

Ukrainian initiative, however, they defected to their original nationalist orientation.[56]

This failure of cross-border *smenovekhovstvo* implied not only a potential failure of the Piedmont Principle, but its potential reversal. Zatonskyi noted with alarm that "due to the clever policy of Pilsudski," West Ukraine was being turned into a "Piedmont to attract discontented elements within [Soviet] Ukraine."[57] In other words, the Piedmont Principle was now being turned against the Soviet Union. Kaganovich made this concern crystal clear in his speech at the March 1928 plenum[58]:

> In today's complicated international circumstances, imperialism is trying to exploit the Ukrainian national question in its battle against us, in as much as the Ukrainian national question is now taking on international significance, and the Polish bourgeoisie in the person of Pilsudski is preparing for an attack on the Soviet Union and Soviet Ukraine.

That Ukrainization might lead some national communists to defect to a Ukrainian nationalist position was an important but not fatal defect. The fact that it might lead to the defection of a neighboring foreign communist party in an atmosphere of imminent war was a much more serious defect.

The final key element in this interpretation of the Shumskyi affair was the highly sensitive Russian question. The Russian question arose in three separate venues in March–April 1926. In the Ukrainian politburo, Shumskyi opposed Kaganovich's refusal to forcibly Ukrainize the Russian proletariat, which led Stalin to rebuke him for supporting the forced derussification of the proletariat. In the Ukrainian press, Khvylovyi called for an orientation of Ukrainian culture away from hidebound Russia and toward the civilized west, which also led to a rebuke by Stalin. Finally, as discussed in Chapter 2, Iurii Larin, with Enukidze's backing, raised the "Russian question" openly at the April 1926 TsIK session with his charge that Ukraine was repressing its Russian minority. Larin was consciously breaking a nationalities policy taboo. The Soviet nationalities policy was premised on the absence of a Russian question. Ukraine viewed Larin's criticisms as a dangerous provocation, as almost a call to a pogrom: "In Ukraine they're oppressing our people [*Na Ukraine nashikh dushit'*]."[59] Stalin was opposed both to a public airing of the Russian question and even more to any policies that provoked Russian discontent.

For our purposes, the important aspect of the Russian question was its intersection with the war scare and defection of the KPZU. In this context, Khvylovyi's call for an orientation on the civilized west and away from Russia

---

[56] *Budivnytstvo*, 231–239; Skrypnyk, *Dzherela*, 78–107.

[57] *RTsKhIDNI* 17/69/58 (1927): 167.

[58] *Budivnytstvo*, 235.

[59] A. Khvylia, "Pro natsionalistychni zbochennia Lebedia, Vahaniana, Zinov'eva i Laryna," in *Budivnytstvo; Natsional'ne pytannia na Ukrainy*, 33.

appeared like a dangerous call for Ukrainian separatism. A Ukrainian plenum echoed Khvylovyi's language in calling the KPZU and Pilsudki's goal a war "for European culture [and] for the union of Ukraine with European culture."[60] Semen Dimanshtein, head of the party's Nationalities Subdepartment and an avid defender of the Soviet nationalities policy, nevertheless expressed considerable concern at a 1927 meeting of the Orgburo *korenizatsiia* commission[61]:

> My first question is whether in Ukraine a strong alienation from Russia is making itself felt in connection with Ukrainization. Without a doubt this is the case. If now in Ukraine the Russian language has an equal status with Ukrainian, if the village now by and large knows it, we are now moving towards a situation where in the next ten to fifteen years an overwhelming majority of Ukrainians will not know Russian.

He noted that old Bolshevik workers in the Donbass currently formed a "link" (*smychka*) with the RSFSR but that "this connecting link will increasingly disappear." He also raised the danger of foreign intervention: "If it were not for the danger of the separation of Ukraine, of the isolation of Ukraine [then a western orientation would be fine], but for now this is not the case, and we should slow down, if necessary by artificial means, this rapid pace of Ukrainization."[62] In Chapter 5, we likewise noted criticism of the Belorussian and Ukrainian language reform endeavors for their orientation on the "west."

To sum up, an anti-*korenizatsiia* hard line gradually emerged during the long Shumskyi affair. It consisted of a growing belief that *korenizatsiia* was exacerbating rather than defusing nationalism. *Korenizatsiia* abetted national communists in introducing non-Bolshevik nationalist concerns into the party and society, such as Shumskyi's concern with who was a true Ukrainian. They were aided by the Ukrainian *smenovekhovstvy*, whose ideas were leading important Ukrainian communists, such as Shumskyi and Khvylovyi, to defect to Ukrainian nationalism. Moreover, the initial foreign policy advantages of Ukrainization in attracting West Ukrainian support for Soviet Ukraine proved illusory, since making nationality the central aspect of cross-border ethnic influence allowed West Ukrainian nationalists to exert an increasing influence on Soviet Ukraine. Finally, this reverse *smenovekhovstvo* had taken on an anti-Russian dimension, which was increasing the strength of Ukrainian separatism.

Nationality and the Left Opposition

I now turn briefly to the politics of *korenizatsiia* in the Soviet east. Once again there were substantial differences between east and west. The anti-*korenizatsiia* hard line could only have emerged in the Soviet west, since only

[60] Skrypnyk, *Dzherela*, 127–128.
[61] *RTsKhIDNI* 17/69/58 (1927): 144.
[62] Ibid., 145–147.

there was the foreign threat overwhelming. Likewise, only in the west was national communism a strong enough movement to plausibly dominate republican politics. On the other hand, there were fundamental similarities. In both east and west, factionalism ran rampant. In both regions, the role of *smenovekhovstvo* was important and controversial. A distinctive aspect of eastern politics was the tendency of titular nationals to divide into two competing party factions labeled "left" and "right." This was potentially significant in terms of Stalin's battle with the all-union left opposition throughout NEP.

The left–right national split emerged in virtually every republic of the Soviet east, but most strongly in the two Tatar republics of Crimea and Tatarstan.[63] This was because these republics had the strongest prerevolutionary intelligentsia, both nationalist and leftist, and the intelligentsia's fierce rivalries were imported into the Bolshevik Party. I will focus on Tatarstan. The unchallenged leader of the Tatar right, until his first arrest in May 1923, was Mirsaid Sultan-Galiev.[64] Other prominent members were K. G. Mukhtarov, Mansurov, A. M. Enbaev, and Sabirov. The leaders of the Tatar right came from the left wing of the prerevolutionary nationalist movement and were attracted to Bolshevism almost exclusively due to the nationalities question: "They nursed the hope they could reconcile nationalism with Communism."[65] In other words, they were national *smenovekhovtsy*. In Ukraine, *zminovikhovtsy* were almost entirely excluded from important government positions and confined to the academy. In the Soviet east, where the dearth of national cadres was especially severe, *smenovekhovtsy* could and did rise as high as head of the republican Sovnarkom. As *smenovekhovtsy*, the Tatar right was naturally zealously committed to *korenizatsiia*. The Tatar right controlled the government of Tatarstan, but not the party, from August 1921 to February 1924.[66]

The leadership of the Tatar left, on the other hand, consisted mostly of former Socialist Revolutionaries. They were joined by militant young Tatar Bolsheviks with no prerevolutionary political loyalties. In 1920 and 1921, their leader was a moderate leftist, Sagibgirai Said-Galiev, who was chairman of the Tatar Sovnarkom. More radical leftists, such as G. K. Shamigulov, Sagidullin, and S. Atnagulov, denied the legitimacy of national culture entirely and called for the liquidation of Tatarstan and other national republics. They proudly called themselves "internationalists" and "Bukharinites," consciously modeling themselves after the pre-1923 Bukharin who, along with Piatakov, had denied the existence of an above-class national culture.[67] They bitterly attacked the Tatar right as cryptonationalists, who had "made a fetish out of the nationalities

---

[63] In the typology of Chapter 2, the Tatar variant was particularly susceptible to factionalism, the Kazakh variant slightly less so, and the Uzbek variant still less so.

[64] Alexandre A. Bennigsen and S. Enders Wimbush, *Muslim National Communism in the Soviet Union* (Chicago, 1979); Mirsaid Sultan-Galiev, *Stat'i. Vystupleniia. Dokumenty* (Kazan, 1992).

[65] L. Rubinshtein, *V bor'be za leninskuiu natsional'nuiu politiku* (Kazan, 1930): 4.

[66] *RTsKhIDNI* 17/112/525 (21.03.24): 81/8; 17/112/535 (06.05.24): 91/3; 17/84/742 (1924–25): 5–10.

[67] Sultan-Galiev, *Stat'i*, 329, 364–370, 433; *Tainy natsional'noi politiki*, 26–31, 35–36, 49. *RTsKhIDNI* 17/112/535 (06.05.24): 31–32.

question in Tatarstan" due to their "distrust of the Russian proletariat."[68] The left controlled the Tatarstan government from June 1920 to June 1921 and again from February 1924 to October 1925.

"Left" and "right," then, simply signaled one's attitude towards *korenizatsiia*. This was not the case in Ukraine. Khvylovyi consciously styled himself as an ultra-leftist with a provocative admiration for Trotsky; Shumskyi despised Trotsky and, when categorized, was considered on the right.[69] Similarly, the anti-Ukrainization forces during the civil war consisted of Piatakov's leftist internationalist faction in Kiev and Kviring's rightist pro-RSFSR faction in Katerynoslav. There would seem to be two explanations for this pattern. First, although the nationalities question was a huge issue in Ukraine, it was still not so dominant *for titular nationals* that the entire party would split on the issue. Second, the greater social distance between Russians and titular nationals in the Soviet east meant that the left titular national faction could not merge with the anti-*korenizatsiia* Russian forces, but instead existed independently and in an uneasy alliance with them.

The first five years of Tatarstan's existence witnessed an open and continuous battle between two united and disciplined national factions: the Tatar "left" and "right." In 1923, this local conflict emerged briefly onto the all-union stage. Sultan-Galiev, aware that Lenin had invited Trotsky to attack Stalin on the nationalities question at the April 1923 Party Congress, approached Trotsky to form an alliance against Stalin.[70] Trotsky was not interested, but this warned Stalin that the deep fissures in the Soviet Union's eastern republics could quite easily be manipulated by a future all-union opposition. In April 1923, the center intercepted two conspiratorial letters written by Sultan-Galiev, which revealed he had Basmachi ties and indicated his willingness to exploit them to further his faction's agenda. With this evidence in hand, Stalin engineered Sultan-Galiev's arrest in May 1923 and his formal denunciation at the June 1923 TsK conference on nationalities policy. Given the nature of Soviet symbolic politics, the left interpreted this as a signal that their time had come and attacked the right bitterly at this conference.[71] Shamigulov crowed, undiplomatically, that the left "had declared in 1918–1919 that if TsK would orient themselves on those nationalists with a bourgeois background [i.e., the Tatar right], it would commit an error and [the right] would eventually take action against Soviet power."[72]

---

[68] *7-ia oblastnaia partiinaia konferentsiia Tatrespubliki. Stenograficheskii otchet* (Kazan, 1923): 168; "Stenograficheskii otchet soveshchaniia chlenov Tatobkoma i OKK sovmestno s otvetstvennymi rabotnikami po natsional'nomu voprosu" (1923) in *Tatarstan*, no. 2 (1991): 50.

[69] Khvylovyi, *The Cultural Renaissance*, 43, 59, 66, 130. Hirchak, *Khvyl'ovyzm*, 87. N. Lovyts'kyi, "Shcho take Shums'kyzm," *Bil'shovyk Ukrainy*, no. 6 (1928): 64.

[70] Bulat Sultanbekov, "Vvedenie," *Stat'i*, 14.

[71] Sultan-Galiev, *Stat'i*, 327–331; *Tainy natsional'noi politiki*, 29–37, 280–281; "Stenograficheskii otchet soveshchaniia chlenov Tatobkoma," *Tatarstan*, no. 2 (1991): 49–52; no. 3 (1991): 47–52; no. 6 (1991): 38–45.

[72] *Tainy natsional'noi politiki*, 35.

Stalin, however, had no interest in driving the right, which was the larger of the two factions and the one with greater popular support, into the arms of Trotsky or any other future opposition faction. Stalin pointedly reminded the June 1923 gathering that he had been Sultan-Galiev's patron and that he had also defended the Bashkir leader, Akmet-Zaki Validov, who later defected to the Basmachi. He defended the practice of aggressively recruiting eastern *smenovekhovtsy*: "*Intelligenty*, thinking people, even literate people, are so few in the eastern republics that you can count them with your fingers—how then can we not treasure them?" Stalin attacked the right for failing to become "a reliable bulwark against the nationalist trend . . . which is growing and strengthening due to NEP." However, Stalin attacked the left still more fiercely: "They do not know how to, and do not want to maneuver in attracting [loyal national] elements . . . if they think that one can transplant Russian models into distinct national conditions without considering local customs and circumstances, if they think that they can battle nationalism by throwing overboard all things national . . . then of the two dangers, the left danger may end up being the greater danger."[73] These remarks again demonstrate Stalin's serious commitment to *korenizatsiia* and his conscious decision to promote it through *smenovekhovstvo*.

In fact, between 1923 and 1926, Stalin repeatedly intervened personally in support of *korenizatsiia* and in opposition to the frequent local harassment of the *smenovekhovtsy*. A few months before the nationalities conference, Stalin had instructed the new party leadership of Kirgizia: "It is impossible to govern the Kirgiz republic without Kirgiz. You need to teach and transform the human material that you have. There are no better people to be found. Therefore you must not declare war on the existing Kirgiz elite."[74] In August 1924, Stalin wrote the Belorussian party leadership the following terse note objecting to the removal of Belorussian *smenovekhovtsy*: "I've discovered that Zhelukov and Balitskii and several other ethnic Belorussian assistant commissars have been purged from the party. Considering this step a fatal error, I strongly request that you take measures to prevent this error. Confirm receipt of this."[75] In January 1925, Stalin defended the head of the Tatar TsIK, the national communist Veli Ibragimov, from harassment by the head of the Crimean obkom secretary, Shvarts, by sending an open letter to the Crimean obkom instructing Shvarts to work with Ibragimov and, in general, "adopt more flexible and more expedient tactics in the nationalities question."[76] Finally, in April 1926, two months before the outbreak of the Shumskyi Affair, Stalin wrote the head of the Central Asian Biuro, Zelenskii, with yet another ringing defense of the policy of employing the *smenovekhovstvo* intelligentsia in pursuit of *korenizatsiia*[77]:

[73] Ibid., 81; 83; 84–85.
[74] *RTsKhIDNI* 558/11/31 (13.03.23): 23. Kirgiz here refers to Kazakhs.
[75] *RTsKhIDNI* 558/11/32 (27.08.24): 102.
[76] *RTsKhIDNI* 558/11/33 (26.01.25): 24.
[77] *RTsKhIDNI* 558/11/34 (23.04.26): 56.

In cultural work, you should be guided by the principle that even the most minimally loyal Uzbek *intelligenty* should be recruited into government work instead of being driven away. One must not view the Uzbek noncommunist intelligentsia as a single reactionary mass and threaten them with widespread arrests, as some comrades do, instead of appealing to them and attracting the best of them. Therefore I request that in this matter by the decrees of the nationalities conference that were passed several years ago and that remain to this day obligatory.

The newly available archival evidence contradicts any assertion that Stalin's support for *korenizatsiia* in the NEP years was either soft or cynical. On the contrary, the policy was identified with him personally and he backed it vigorously on numerous occasions.

From 1923 to 1928, TsK also consistently and persistently attempted to minimize the chronic national divisions within the Communist Party organizations of the Soviet east by categorically denying that these divisions had any ideological content. This new policy line was articulated in a June 1924 Orgburo decree, which instructed "the Tatar obkom and especially first party secretary, Morozov, not to divide officials into 'left' and 'right.'"[78] This principle was applied to other eastern republics as well and likewise guided Kaganovich's handling of the Shumskyi affair. Despite this effort to will the left/right conflict away, the Orgburo had to intervene dozens of times in the affairs of the national republics to resolve divisions whose primary causes were disagreements between titular nationals over the implementation of *korenizatsiia*.[79]

National factionalism was chronic because its cause was structural. As a rule, Stalin placed titular nationals at the head of each republic's Soviet organs—that is, head of Sovnarkom, TsIK, and the independent republican commissariats—and a nontitular, though by no means always a Russian, in the position of first party secretary.[80] Stalin did this, as he explained to Shumskyi privately and at the June 1923 gathering publicly, because he realized most titular nationals were, if not outright *smenovekhovtsy*, then communists too passionately committed to *korenizatsiia* to be relied on to resist "the nationalist trend."[81] This task was assigned to the first party secretary, which placed him in an exceedingly difficult position, since he was responsible for seeing that *korenizatsiia* was implemented, but also that it was not implemented too fast. This inevitably led to conflict with the titular national "right," which was usually entrenched in the Soviet organs (even when leftists controlled the leadership positions),

[78] *RTsKhIDNI* 17/112/566 (04.06.24): 1/5.

[79] *RTsKhIDNI* 17/112/568 (09.06.24): 3/2; 17/113/171 (22.02.26): 13–15; 17/113/268 (28.02.27): 94/2; 17/113/725 (08.05.29): 117/1; 17/113/756 (22.07.29): 138/1; 17/113/656 (10.09.28): 63/2; 17/112/691 (31.08.25): 105/1. Stalin also frequently intervened in this manner. See *RTsKhIDNI* 558/11/33 (15.10.25): 106; (18.10.25): 115; 558/11/1103 (08.12.24): 153–4.

[80] The exception to this pattern was again Georgia and Armenia, where titular nationals ran the party and government throughout Stalin's rule.

[81] *Tainy natsional'noi politiki*, 83.

was well-disciplined, and could mobilize extensive personal connections against the outsider first secretary. They could also appeal to their special status as "formerly oppressed nationalities" and to their expertise in solving the nationalities policy.

Given these formidable enemies, the first secretary naturally sought allies among the minority national left faction, both to secure protection against the charge of great-power chauvinism and as a valued source of local information. For example, in March 1924, without TsK permission, Tatarstan's first party secretary, Morozov, allied with the Tatar left to remove Tatarstan's rightist government. They even knowingly (and successfully) ignored a Politburo resolution ordering them not to remove the rightist Mukhtarov as head of Sovnarkom.[82] The position of a non-Russian first secretary in a national republic in the 1920s, then, was an exceedingly difficult one. Stalin greatly esteemed administrators, like Kaganovich, who could successfully implement *korenizatsiia* and control the local national communists.

Most could not. From the formation of Tatarstan in May 1920 to October 1925, the Tatarstan assignment defeated six different first party secretaries. In October 1925, the Orgburo convened to censure and remove the latest failure, Morozov, and to instruct the new first secretary once again to ensure cooperative work between the "left" and "right" (ignoring its own ban on these terms) and to implement *korenizatsiia* at the proper pace. One person in attendance, I. M. Vareikis, who had experience working in Central Asia, objected that this goal was simply unrealizable[83]:

> As to the problem of group conflict [*gruppirovka*], it is absurd to issue a demand that group conflict be extinguished in Tatarstan. One must not understand the conditions of work in a national republic to say that TsK can send a circular "On the Elimination of Group Conflict." There will be group conflict. Each one of us who has spent his time working in any national republic knows very well the strength of these group conflicts. Each of us set for ourselves the task of extinguishing this group conflict and in reality failed, because to extinguish these group conflicts completely and totally is impossible.

Unfortunately for Vareikis, another person who rarely attended Orgburo sessions, Stalin, was present this time and objected[84]:

> Comrade Vareikis is not correct if he thinks that we cannot issue a resolution on overcoming group conflict. Why not? We can. It is unacceptable that there are two camps who conduct open battles. Cooperation among oblast organizations has not been achieved—that's a fact. Comrade Morozov was exploited in

---

[82] *Stenograficheskii otchet IX oblastnoi konferentsii Tatarsk. organizatsii RKP/b/* (Kazan, 1924): 10–18; *RTsKhIDNI* 17/112/525 (21.03.24): 81/8; 17/112/535 (06.05.24): 91/3; 17/112/566 (04.06.24): 1/5.

[83] *RTsKhIDNI* 17/112/703 (19.10.25): 115/1, 77.

[84] Ibid., 84.

all ways by the current obkom majority to inflame passions and wipe out the
minority. Did we really give such a directive? No, TsK never gave such a directive. TsK said that it was time to overcome group conflict and nationalism. . . .
Comrade Morozov did not take all measures so that these disagreements and
group conflicts did not escalate into a battle between the two camps.

Stalin backed up his words with the decision to send an important figure to
run Tatarstan, the head of TsK's influential Cadres Department, M. M.
Khataevich.[85]

On his arrival in Tatarstan, Khataevich quickly decided that reconciliation was
impossible. He believed, as had Morozov, that to restore order he had to discipline those infected with Tatar nationalism. In order not to appear anti-Tatar,
he simultaneously had the party take a more active role in the implementation
of *korenizatsiia*, modeling himself on Kaganovich in Ukraine and Goloshchekin
in Kazakhstan. At the same time, he interpreted any breach of strict party discipline by Tatar communists as evidence of national group conflict. As a result,
he had soon quarreled not only with the Tatar right but with much of the left
as well, whom he now creatively labeled "the ultra-left" faction. The "ultra-
left," he claimed, used internationalist rhetoric to oppose Moscow's centralism,
"not noticing that in this way they sometimes slid into true nationalism."[86]
Within months of his arrival, Tatar communist delegations were traveling to
Moscow to lobby for Khataevich's removal.[87] Even the ethnic Russians worried
that Khataevich was excessively "rude" and that "apparently TsK will have to
interfere in Tatar affairs still one more time."[88] At the December 1926 Tatar
party conference, Stanislav Kosior, then a TsK secretary, attended and publicly
rebuked Khataevich for ignoring TsK instructions on the left–right division:
"Comrade Khataevich has tried to give some ideological content to the terms
left and right, but he has failed."[89]

Khataevich interpreted the aggressive Tatar campaign to have him removed
as evidence that Tatar nationalism had gone on the offensive. At a party gathering in June 1926, he attempted to revise a standard plank of the Soviet nationalities policy: "Although in the USSR as a whole, great power chauvinism is the
greater danger, within the Tatar republic both deviations are equally dangerous. The situation here is not the same as it was before the twelfth congress.
The national bourgeoisie is growing rapidly."[90] In December, he asserted that
local chauvinism often carried "an offensive character" and Russian chauvinism
"a defensive character."[91] Many Tatar communists reacted to this proposed revision with panic and spread rumors that the liquidation of the Tatar republic

---

[85] *RTsKhIDNI* 17/3/524 (22.10.25): 84/29.
[86] *RTsKhIDNI* 17/69/60 (1926): 33.
[87] *2 plenum*, 18.
[88] *RTsKhIDNI* 17/31/180 (1926): 1–5.
[89] *Stenograficheskii otchet zasedanii XII oblastnoi partiinoi konferentsii* (Kazan, 1927): 135.
[90] *RTsKhIDNI* 17/85/206 (1927): 59.
[91] Ibid., 59.

was being planned. Moscow apparently also grew concerned, which explains why a major figure like Kosior was dispatched to the 1926 Tatar party conference, where he publicly criticized this policy innovation.[92] Khataevich may well have misinterpreted the Shumskyi affair as a signal to attack national communists in other republics. In reality, the center neither provoked nor desired the Shumskyi affair. Despite strong Tatar resistance and Moscow's ambivalence, Khataevich survived for more than two tumultuous years. Finally, a "strike of the commissars" (*zabastovka narkomov*) broke out. A delegation of ten commissars and other major Tatar officials, including two obkom *Biuro* members, traveled to Moscow where they were received by Kosior, then TsK secretary, who listened to their petition to have Khataevich removed. At this point, Khataevich agreed to accept reassignment quietly and in early 1928, after almost appointing Nikolai Ezhov as first party secretary, TsK transferred M. O. Razumov from Bashkiria to Tatarstan.[93] The Tatar example demonstrates how difficult it was to run a national republic in the 1920s.[94] Khataevich was, after all, a talented Soviet politician and Stalin continued to give him sensitive assignments. Only when the socialist offensive allowed a massive increase in coercion and terror were national first party secretaries gradually able to turn their republics into personalistic fiefdoms.[95]

The Tatar example illustrates how deep the divisions in the eastern national republics were and how easy it would have been for the opposition to exploit them. Until the summer of 1927, however, none of the successive opposition movements even addressed the nationalities question.[96] There were three main reasons for this omission. First, as the Stalin group pointedly emphasized during the nationalities controversies in 1923, they were the nationalities specialists, and the future opposition leaders had virtually no personal experience in nationalities policy. Thus, when Trotsky finally did consult with a Kazakh communist in March 1927, his notes on the conversation revealed an ignorance of the politically salient issues in national regions and a confusion as to how they related to the opposition's principal concerns.[97]

Second, the left opposition was ignorant about nationalities policy because it was fundamentally uninterested. It reflected the average Russian party member's sense that nationalities policy was not a major issue. For instance, Kazakhstan's

---

[92] *Stenograficheskii otchet zasedanii XII oblastnoi*, 99–100; 137.

[93] Bulat Sultanbekov, "Nikolai Ezhov: palach i zhertva," *Tatarstan*, no. 1 (1992): 32.

[94] Tatarstan was admittedly a particularly difficult republic. However, for analogous factionalism in Crimea, Dagestan, Uzbekistan, Kazakhstan, Azerbaijan, and the Mari and Udmurt oblasts, see RTsKhIDNI 17/113/171 (22.02.26): 11/1, 103; 17/113/171 (22.02.26): 171/1; 17/113/314 (25.07.27): 133/1; 17/113/644 (01.08.28): 53/1; 17/112/568 (09.06.24): 3/2; 17/113/268 (28.02.27): 94/2; 17/113/725 (08.05.29): 117/1; 17/113/756 (22.07.29): 138/1; 17/113/656 (10.09.28): 63/2; 17/112/691 (31.08.25): 105/1.

[95] Charles H. Fairbanks Jr., "Clientelism and the Roots of Post-Soviet Disorder," in Suny, Ronald Grigor, ed., *Transcaucasia, Nationalism and Social Change* (Ann Arbor, Mich., 1996): 341–376.

[96] *Arkhiv Trotskogo. Kommunisticheskaia oppozitsiia v SSSR, 1923–1927*, vols. 1–4 (Moscow, 1990).

[97] "Natsional'nye momenty politiki v Kazakhstane," *Arkhiv Trotskogo*, vol. 2, 197–199.

first party secretary, Fillip Goloshchekin, reported in 1927 that "when I mentioned [the nationalities] question at our *krai* conference, one opposition supporter yelled out that we have more important questions [to discuss]."[98] Third, many oppositionists were not only uninterested, but actively hostile to Lenin's nationalities policy. This was a continuation of Piatakov's principled internationalism. Vaganian's 1927 book, *On National Culture*, followed Piatakov in arguing that the party should promote a single international culture, not separate national cultures. His book was not an official opposition document, but since its arguments reflected well-known opposition opinions and since Vaganian signed the opposition's "Platform of 83" in May 1927, his book became widely viewed as an opposition manifesto on national culture.[99] As we have seen, had the opposition decisively advocated Vaganian's strong internationalist position, there would have been a receptive audience in the national regions among both Russians and the national left faction. In fact, the Tatar leftist S. Atnagulov even initiated a polemic in support of Vaganian's views on national culture in Tatarstan in mid-1927.[100]

However, the opposition could never formulate a coherent stance on the nationalities question. At a June 24, 1927 TsKK meeting, Zinoviev accused Stalin of "colonialism" and of failing to implement Lenin's nationalities policy adequately. However, he likewise maintained that "in Ukraine, they are conducting a 'Ukrainization' that clearly contradicts our nationalities policy. It's awful! They are supporting the *Petliurovshchina* and not fighting true chauvinism."[101] A letter Stalin wrote in September 1927 revealed his scorn for Zinoviev's efforts and his confidence in his own mastery of the national question: "I am waiting with impatience for the opposition to risk even a hiccup about the theoretical side of the national question in an open polemic during the [15th] Party Congress. I am afraid they won't risk it, since after Zinoviev's unsuccessful speech at the TsK/TsKK plenum, the opposition preferred to be completely silent about national culture in their recent 'platform.'"[102]

Stalin was mistaken. The opposition did include a substantial section on nationalities policy in its final platform submitted to TsK in September 1927. This section abandoned Vaganian's and Piatakov's principled internationalism and instead, with the exception of a reiterated critique of Ukrainian chauvinism, attempted to outbid Stalin with a program of what might be called "*super-korenizatsiia*." For instance, the opposition's program advocated the following policies[103]:

[98] *XV s"ezd VKP/b/. Stenograficheskii otchet* (Moscow-Leningrad, 1928): 174.

[99] V. Vaganian, *O natsional'noi kul'ture* (Moscow-Leningrad, 1927); idem., *Ne soglasen ni s odnim iz moikh opponentov* (Moscow, 1927); "Zaiavlenie '83'," *Arkhiv Trotskogo*, vol. 3, 60–72.

[100] *Stenograficheskii otchet zasedanii XIII oblastnoi*, 98–99; Bulat Sultanbekov, "Poslednii boi Galimdzhana Ibragimova," *Tatarstan*, nos. 7–8 (1995): 46–58.

[101] Quoted in A. Khvylia, "Pro natsionalistychni zbochennia Lebedia," 17.

[102] Stalin, "Tovarishchu M. I. Ul'ianovoi. Otvet tovarishchu L. Mikhel'sonu," *Sochineniia*, vol. 10, 151–152.

[103] "Proekt platformy bol'shevikov-lenintsev (oppozitsii) k 15 s"ezdu VKP/b/," *Arkhiv Trotskogo*, vol. 4, 142–146.

Faster industrialization in national regions

A revision of resettlement policies in favor of non-Russian interests

A conscientious *korenizatsiia* of the soviet, party, cooperative, and union apparats

A fight with Great Russian chauvinism, especially in central commissariats and the central government apparat

Making the Soviet of Nationalities into an organ capable of defending national interests

Devoting more attention to forming a national proletariat and having union work carried out in national languages

Calling a fifth TsK conference on nationalities policy, with real representation of titular nationals "from below"

This program was clearly aimed at winning support among the right faction in the non-Russian regions. However, it was much too late. The Ukrainians were delighted to be singled out for criticism and gleefully lambasted Zinoviev as a great-power chauvinist.[104] In the east, where party divisions over nationalities policy were particularly deep, the opposition's platform had almost no resonance. In republics such as Tatarstan, Crimea, and Kazakhstan, where the left–right division was most prominent, neither side took an active interest in the opposition. The left had been spurned, and the right remembered the anti-*korenizatsiia* stances of oppositionists such as Piatakov, Vaganian, Preobrazhenskii, Krestinskii, and others. They assumed the opposition was hostile to national self-expression and, probably correctly, viewed their platform as hypocritical.[105] The opposition's only significant national support came in Georgia, where many members of the former Georgian leadership, who bore a grudge again Stalin and Ordzhonikidze dating back to the Georgian affair of 1922–1923, joined the opposition.[106]

Nationalities policy, then, played no role in determining the ultimate fate of the left opposition. However, the opposition's belated decision to address the nationalities question did play an important role in directing further central attention to the local left–right national schisms and linking them to all-union high politics. Despite the opposition's hypernationalizing platform, popular party opinion continued to associate the left with the internationalist stance of Piatakov and Vaganian. Given these associations, when in 1928 Stalin launched his revolution from above, declared the right deviation to be the greatest danger, and initiated the abolition of NEP, there was a widespread assumption in the party that this would mean the triumph of the true leftist position in nationalities policy as well. Neither Stalin nor his close associates

---

[104] *Desiatyi z'izd*, 125; Khvylia, "Pro natsionalistychni zbochennia," 13–41; *XV s"ezd*, 647–649. *TsDAHOU* 1/20/2315 (1926): 17–170b.

[105] *Oppozitsiia i natsional'nyi vopros* (n.p., 1927), 11; *XV s"ezd*, 150–152, 174–175, 1160.

[106] The Opposition promised to abolish the hated Transcaucasus federation. *V s"ezd KP/b/ Gruzii. Stenograficheskii otchet* (Tiflis, 1927), biul. 2: 46–53; 3: 26; 8: 17; *Piatyi s"ezd kommunisticheskikh organizatsii zakavkaz'ia*, 22–23; 285–286; *XV s"ezd*, 225–226; *XV konferentsiia VKP/b/. Stenograficheskii otchet* (Moscow-Leningrad, 1927): 84. *Arkhiv Trotskogo*, vol. 4, 142.

shared the Vaganian/Piatakov internationalist position on the nationalities question. They would, however, grow increasingly sympathetic to the anti-*korenizatsiia* hard-line stance that crystallized during the Shumskyi affair and that maintained that *korenizatsiia* was in fact often exacerbating rather than defusing nationalism.

The Socialist Offensive and Cultural Revolution

The launching of the socialist offensive in 1928 marked a pivotal moment in the evolution of the national constitution of the Soviet Union. I have been using "socialist offensive" as shorthand for the period from 1928 to 1932 and for the extraordinarily rapid restructuring of Soviet society that was undertaken at that time: rapid industrialization, the abolition of private trade, the collectivization of agriculture, dekulakization, and greatly intensified and centralized dictatorship.[107] I have been using "cultural revolution" to refer to two specific aspects of the larger socialist offensive: a destructive process of "class warfare," involving both state terror and the mobilization of militant Bolshevik proletarians, which was directed against formerly tolerated "bourgeois elements" and institutions; and a constructive process that involved a wave of utopian projects and experiments to create a new socialist way of life.[108] Cultural revolution can be profitably thought of as a strategy and a mood. The strategy was to mobilize Bolshevik militants to destroy stigmatized population categories. The mood was militant and utopian, and both the militancy and utopianism influenced the overall conduct of the socialist offensive. In Chapters 4 and 5, I discussed the constructive aspect of cultural revolution in the Soviet east. In this section, I focus on the impact of the destructive aspect, in particular the state-led terror campaign. However, the main focus will be on the overall impact of the socialist offensive on both the implementation of *korenizatsiia* as well as the larger evolution of the Affirmative Action Empire.

The official Stalinist history of the Bolshevik Party, the *Short Course*, famously described the socialist offensive as follows: "The distinguishing feature of this revolution is that it was accomplished from above, on the initiative of the state."[109] It is useful to consider the socialist offensive as a "Revolution from Above."[110] Barrington Moore and his students have contrasted the different causes and outcomes of popular social revolutions from below (France, Russia, China) and elite-led revolutions from above (Germany, Japan,

---

[107] As, for instance, in R. W. Davies, *The Socialist Offensive. The Collectivisation of Soviet Agriculture, 1929–1930* (Cambridge, Mass., 1980).

[108] Sheila Fitzpatrick, ed., *Cultural Revolution in Russia, 1928–1931* (Bloomington, Ind., 1978).

[109] *History of the Communist Party of the Soviet Union/Bolsheviks/Short Course* (Moscow, 1945): 305.

[110] For a different approach, see Robert C. Tucker, "Stalinism as Revolution from Above," in *Political Culture and Leadership in Soviet Russia* (New York, 1987): 72–107. Robert C. Tucker, *Stalin in Power* (New York, 1990).

Turkey).[111] Although this distinction is necessary, it is also important to note the similarities between Stalin's revolution from above and similar paradigmatic instances of revolution from above, such as Japan's Meiji Restoration and Ataturk's creation of a transformed Turkish Republic.[112] Each took place in a country that felt itself to be socially and economically backward and in need of rapid modernization to catch up to the more advanced Western nations. In each case, the need for rapid modernization was driven by the perception of a military threat to the state's independence or even existence. Modernization involved a state-led fundamental transformation of the country's social structure, with the principal goal being forced industrialization.[113] Finally, in each case the revolution's ideology was statist and its effect was a centralization of political, military, and economic power.

Of course, there were also fundamental differences. The ideology of a canonical revolution from above is typically not only statist but nationalist, with the national ideal usually defined as a past essence to be retrieved through the social and cultural purification of a decadent present. This nationalism manifests itself in a statist paternalist populism, which asserts the unity and subordination of the nation's population. Their duty is to make sacrifices for the nation's good, which is generally equated with the strength of the central state. In turn, the state is to care for the population. The state does not seek to mobilize the masses on behalf of social change, but rather to neutralize them. In addition, the revolutionary state gradually disarms and co-opts the former ruling class rather than destroying it suddenly and violently.[114]

None of these were true of Stalin's socialist offensive. Stalin aimed at the rapid and violent annihilation of class enemies, to which end he solicited mass popular participation. More important, Stalin sought to mobilize the population primarily through an ideology of class warfare rather than nationalism. This was the strategy of cultural revolution. On the other hand, the examples just given of the canonical revolution from above—state paternalism, popular demobilization, an emphasis on popular unity and submission—describe very well the *outcome* of the socialist offensive. Stalin's revolution from above, then, differed from canonical revolutions from above more in its tactics, the strategy of cultural revolution, than in its ultimate direction. Cultural revolution intensified the Affirmative Action Empire while at the same time, as we shall see, Stalin's revolution from above undermined certain of its premises. However, before drawing conclusions about the overall impact of the socialist offensive, I begin with a discussion of the initial popular cultural revolutionary

---

[111] Barrington Moore Jr., *Social Origins of Dictatorship and Democracy* (Boston, Mass., 1966). Theda Skocpol, *States and Social Revolutions* (Cambridge, UK, 1979). Ellen Kay Trimberger, *Revolution from Above* (New Brunswick, N.J., 1978).

[112] In addition to Trimberger, see Stephen M. Walt, *Revolution and War* (Ithaca, N.Y., 1996), 299–310; Bernard Lewis, *The Emergence of Modern Turkey* (Oxford, 1968).

[113] On the perception of backwardness and the commitment to forced growth in socialist states, see Janos Kornai, *The Socialist System* (Princeton, N.J., 1992): 160–163.

[114] Trimberger, *Revolution from Above*, 13–39, 105–146.

mood and its hostility to *korenizatsiia* and indeed the category of nationality itself.

The Popular Attack on Nationality

Nothing is more revealing of the popular party attitude toward *korenizatsiia* than the initial response to the launching of the socialist offensive and the public denunciation of the right deviation in 1928. The following interpretation of the socialist offensive quickly took shape, particularly in Ukraine: under NEP, the left deviation had been the greatest danger and manifested itself in the great-power chauvinism of Piatakov, Zinoviev, and Vaganian; under the socialist offensive, the right deviation was now the greatest danger; therefore, local nationalism, which was the manifestation of the right deviation in the national republics, had likewise become a greater danger than great-power chauvinism, which was now identified as a left deviation.[115] Since the thesis that great-power chauvinism was the greater danger was a pillar of the Soviet nationalities policy, this meant the authorities had finally abandoned their NEP-era concessions to local nationalism, just as they were abandoning their concessions to the peasantry and bourgeois intelligentsia. Sensing a chance to get his former ideas rehabilitated, Dmitrii Lebed managed to get an article published in *Bol'shevik*, the party's main theoretical journal, which argued that Ukrainian nationalism had now become a greater danger than Russian chauvinism.[116]

This argument had become influential enough for Stanislav Kosior, now Ukraine's first party secretary, to feel the need to rebut it at a Kiev party conference in December 1928[117]:

A few words about how the right deviation manifests itself in the national question here in Ukraine. Certain comrades, especially among you here in Kiev, maintain the view that Ukrainian chauvinism is the right deviation and Great Power [chauvinism] is the "left." Therefore in Ukraine the right deviation manifests itself predominately in the form of Ukrainian chauvinism. Let us decode this viewpoint: since we are to direct our fire first of all at the right deviation, this means we should direct our fire first of all at Ukrainian chauvinism. Is this view correct? Of course, it isn't. Both chauvinisms—Ukrainian and Great Power—have a right character, both push the Party towards hostile elements, both contradict the correct line. Neither of them is "superior," with both we must fight relentlessly. Those who say the fight with Russian Great Power chauvinism can be relaxed are deeply in error. This is not at all the case.

---

[115] *TsDAHOU* 1/20/2921 (16.05.29): 1–62. Mykoly Skrypnyk, "Natsional'ni peretynky. Teoretychna i politychna borot'ba na tereni natsional'noho pytannia v USRR u suchasnyi moment rekonstruktyvnoi doby," *Statti i promovy*, vol. 2, part 2, 274–329; E. F. Hirchak, *Natsional'ne pytannia ta pravyi ukhyl* (Kharkov, 1930); A. Senchenko, "Natsional'ne pytannia v period rozhornutoho sotsialistiychnoho nastupu na vs'omu fronti," *Bil'shovyk Ukrainy*, no. 17 (1929): 47–61.

[116] D. Lebed, "Vnimanie ideologicheskomu frontu," *Bol'shevik*, no. 7 (1928): 79–87.

[117] Hirchak, *Natsional'ne pytannia*, 3.

This became the standard response of the Ukrainian leadership. It was endorsed by Stalin in February 1929 during a meeting with a Ukrainian writers' delegation.[118] Stalin's speech was not published, but since it was addressed to non-party members, his words were clearly intended to become widely known in Ukrainian intellectual circles, as they did, by word of mouth.

Despite these authoritative interventions, the argument that Ukrainian nationalism was now the greatest danger continued to be made publicly, further evidence for the strength of this sentiment. A Ukrainian historian published an article in a Moscow journal, a favored strategy for evading Ukrainian censors, arguing that Great Russian chauvinism was no longer an important problem in Ukraine.[119] Two episodes particularly disturbed the leadership because they both occurred at party meetings organized to correct this interpretive error. In January 1929, at a special Kiev *okruzhkom* meeting devoted to nationalities policy, only a few weeks after Kosior's remarks, several speakers again hinted that Ukrainian nationalism should be considered the greatest danger.[120] Four months later, during a discussion of "the right deviation and the nationalities question" at the Ukrainian Institute of Marxism-Leninism, several graduate students did likewise.[121] This latter episode particularly embarrassed the leadership since the institute existed to defend party orthodoxy and had its own nationalities department chaired by Skrypnyk himself. Moreover, it was also disturbing that young party activists seemed most attracted to an anti-Ukrainization stance.[122]

The Ukrainian leadership responded energetically to this challenge. Its major nationalities specialists and leading politicians all published articles or delivered speeches on the impact of the socialist offensive on nationalities policy.[123] A December 1929 Kharkov *okruzhkom* decree, later confirmed by the Ukrainian TsK, rebuffed the Institute of Marxism-Leninism for allowing a "majority and minority" faction to form on nationalities policy.[124] The decree declared that great-power and Ukrainian chauvinism were linked to neither the left nor the right, but could mask themselves in the phraseology of either deviation. Both

---

[118] *RTsKhIDNI* 558/1/4490 (12.02.29): 1–12.

[119] Published in *Na literaturnomu postu*, no. 3 (1929) and cited in Skrypnyk, "Natsional'ni peretynky," 284.

[120] Senchenko, "Natsional'ne pytannia," 60–61; M. Skrypnyk, *Do rekonstruktsiinykh problem* (Kharkov, 1929): 29.

[121] *TsDAHOU* 1/20/2921 (1929); Skrypnyk, "Natsional'ni peretynky," 285–329.

[122] On this concern, see "Doklad tov. L. M. Kahanovycha na VII vseukrains'komu z'izdi LKSM," *Visti*, no. 103 (04.05.28): 2. M. Skrypnyk, *Neprymyrennym shliakhom* (Kharkov, 1929): 82–85.

[123] Skrypnyk, *Neprymyrennym shliakhom*; idem., *Do rekonstruktsiinykh problem*; idem., "Natsional'ni peretynky"; V. Zatonskyi, "Na frontakh natsional'noi kul'tury abo 'De toi pravyi, a de livyi bik," *Visti*, no. 259 (07.11.29): 2–3; N. Popov, "Natsional'naia politika partii v period sotsial-isticheskoi rekonstruktsii," *Pravda*, no. 252 (31.10.29): 2–3; Khvylia's speech in *Druha konferentsiia KP/b/ Ukrainy. Stenohrafichnyi zvit* (Kharkov, 1929), 109–110; Hirchak, *Natsional'ne pytannia*; Kosior's speech in *XI z'izd KP/b/ Ukrainy. Stenohrafichnyi zvit* (Kharkov, 1930): 274–289; P. Postyshev, *U borot'by za lenins'ku natsional'nu polityku* (Kharkov, 1934), 53–77.

[124] Hirchak, *Natsional'ne pytannia*: 145–151.

would increase during the socialist offensive and so both must be combatted. However, only a public intervention by Stalin in June 1930 would finally silence the anti-*korenizatsiia* militants.

The movement to revise the Soviet nationalities policy in Ukraine was distinctive in that the battle lines were consciously drawn between Ukrainian and Russian chauvinism. Elsewhere, the movement to declare local nationalism the greater danger contrasted it to internationalism, which represented the positive utopian goal of the cultural revolution. This internationalism was opposed to all national cultures, but above all to Russian culture. We have already seen this utopian internationalism in the latinization campaign. Other manifestations were the movement in support of Esperanto and the ascendancy of Marr's ideas about the plasticity of ethnicity.[125] It likewise found expression in the national press. In December 1928, the Transcaucasus *kraikom* newspaper, *Zaria Vostoka*, published an article openly asserting this position: "For the 'left,' the nation and national cultural are things of the past. For the right, nation and national culture remain and are the nearest truth . . . therefore, the right deviation, not the 'Piatakovshchina' or 'Vaganianshchina,' is now the central danger in national relations. Not an underestimation, but an overestimation of the national question, falling sick with nationalist ideology and forgetting about internationalism."[126]

This same interpretation flared up in Moscow in the summer of 1929 when Semen Dimanshtein addressed the Communist Academy in Moscow on the controversial problem of the socialist offensive and nationalities policy.[127] This was a big event because the topic was controversial and Dimanshtein was one of the Soviet Union's leading nationalities specialists. His opinions were typically painfully orthodox, but on this occasion he attempted to anticipate a policy shift. Dimanshtein set up a contrast between all-union, international, urban, proletarian culture and rural national cultures, and heterodoxly argued that there was a contradiction between them[128]:

> We now observe certain contradictions in the development of national culture. With regard to the question of the fusion of cultures, this contradiction lies in the fact that, on one side, we are undertaking great efforts in international education in order to draw together nationalities, strengthen their brotherhood, but at the same time we are also conducting great nationalities work and, against one's will, this divides one nation from another, isolates the culture of one nation from another. . . .

Dimanshtein's critics quickly pointed out that orthodox party policy asserted that the two policies complemented one another. Dimanshtein was,

---

[125] Michael Smith, *Language and Power in the Creation of the USSR, 1917–1953* (Berlin, 1998): 81–102.

[126] Ionov, *Zaria vostoka* (14.12.28), cited in Hirchak, *Natsional'ne pytannia*, 48.

[127] S. M. Dimanshtein, "Problema natsional'noi kul'tury i kul'turnogo stroitel'stva v natsional'nykh respublikakh," *Vestnik kommunisticheskoi akademii*, no. 31 (1929): 113–143.

[128] Dimanshtein, "Problema natsional'noi kul'tury," 121.

of course, perfectly aware of this fact. He was anticipating a change in this policy line.

In the most significant passage of his lecture, Dimanshtein argued that the social and economic changes that had begun during NEP and were now greatly accelerating (such as electrification, railway and industrial construction, the formation of a native proletariat, the liberation of women, and land reform) made the old nationalities policy redundant: "We cannot justify the practice of the right deviation in nationalities policy. We cannot carry over to the present period that which was correct for another period. Of course, this doesn't mean that all national differences will disappear, but their importance will decline markedly."[129] In other words, as his critics angrily pointed out, he argued that under current conditions, the further implementation of the 1923 nationalities policy decrees would represent a right deviation.[130] Dimanshtein guessed wrong. There was no policy shift and he was attacked in the party's major theoretical journals and in Ukraine on the grounds that he had, like Vaganian, taken a great-power chauvinist position under the false cover of internationalism.[131]

The increasing economic centralization that accompanied the socialist offensive also led the economic organs to assert their longstanding "internationalist" agenda: administrative territories based on socialist economic criteria and not on nationality. Gosplan had in fact already pushed this agenda in 1921, when economic *raionirovanie* was first being planned, but had been rebuffed. Beginning in 1928, however, smaller autonomous oblasts and republics were forced, often against their will, to become part of the larger administrative *kraia*.[132]

This did not threaten the actual existence of the national republics. With the onset of the socialist offensive, however, the idea that national territories themselves were outdated was revived. In 1929, Stalin reported that he often received letters hinting that national republics should be abolished.[133] In late 1929, an open debate on this issue flared up in TsIK's house journal, *Sovetskoe stroitel'stvo*. A journalist, Totskii, argued that national-territorial units were appropriate for the first phase of socialism, but the new second phase just beginning would be "characterized by the formation of state territories based chiefly on economic concerns." National territories, "in particular those of the culturally backward republics, do not at all serve their economic, social and cultural

[129] Ibid., 124.

[130] Hirchak, *Natsional'ne pytannia*, 62–66.

[131] K. Tabolov, "Protiv velikorusskogo shovinizma v voprosakh natsional'noi kul'tury," *Bol'shevik*, no. 13 (1930): 88; "Za pravil'nuiu natsional'nuiu politiku partii," *Kommunisticheskaia revoliutsiia*, no. 4 (1931): 71–74. Hirchak, *Natsional'ne pytannia*, 61–87; I. Hekhtman, "Do problemy natsional'noi kul'tury (Z pryvodu dopovidi t. S. Dimanshteina v Komakademii))," *Bil'shovyk Ukrainy*, nos. 21–22 (1929): 98–114; Senchenko, "Natsional'ne pytannia"; "Krytyka i bibliografiia," *Bil'shovyk Ukrainy*, no. 1 (1931): 81–84. Skrypnyk also attacked Dimanshtein at a session of the Soviet of Nationalities. *3 sessiia TsIK SSSR 5 sozyva* (Moscow, 1931), biul. 11: 25.

[132] M. Eremeev, "Raionirovanie RSFSR i avtonomnye respubliki," *Sovetskoe stroitel'stvo*, no. 10 (1928): 14–27.

[133] RTsKhIDNI 558/1/4490 (12.05.29): 2.

development."[134] It was not surprisingly that Totskii was immediately attacked for perverting the party line. It was very surprising, however, that the editors responded by opening the issue to further debate. They then published a rebuttal by Totskii and a further attack by his antagonist, Angarov, before closing the debate equivocally.[135] This suggested the editorial staff was still waiting for an authoritative pronouncement on this issue. Warnings were simultaneously published elsewhere about various plans to liquidate national-territorial units.[136]

Collectivization gave a further impetus to this abolitionist tendency. Already in January 1930, reports appeared complaining of the tendency of local officials "to liquidate national village soviets" during collectivization, and there were also reports of the widespread belief that complete collectivization meant the liquidation of "the linguistic and other particularities of national minorities, which made necessary the formation of national-administrative territories."[137] Another article likewise reported the widespread notion that collective farms should be international in composition.[138] The presidium of the Soviet of Nationalities considered this tendency alarming enough to plan how best to combat it.[139]

This prolonged uncertainty was due to the center's delay in producing an authoritative statement on the relationship between the socialist offensive and nationalities policy. In fact, after the two major discussions of nationalities policy in 1923, while the party devoted considerable energy to the implementation of nationalities policy, there was virtually no high-level discussion of possible policy alternatives. In 1926, TsK did form two committees to discuss emerging national problems in a fundamental manner. Despite great fanfare, Kalinin's Politburo commission on the RSFSR failed entirely to propose any fundamental reforms.[140] Likewise, Andreev's Orgburo commission on *korenizatsiia* produced no more than a simple reaffirmation of the 1923 decrees.[141] By 1928–1929, there was a widespread desire among the non-Russian leadership for a fifth TsK nationalities conference (the June 1923 conference was the fourth), enough that the left opposition included a demand for it in their last program.[142] In 1928, TsK instructed TsKK, which previously had not played a role in nationalities policy, to undertake a comprehensive investigation of

[134] N. Totskii, *Sovetskoe stroitel'stvo*, no. 12 (1929): 85.

[135] A. Angarov, "Burzhuaznaia teoriia raionirovaniia," *Sovetskoe stroitel'stvo*, no. 1 (1930): 59–64; N. Totskii, "Otvet A. Angarovu," *Sovetskoe stroitel'stvo*, no. 2 (1930): 70–74; A. Angarov, "Eshche raz o burzhuaznoi teorii raionirovaniia N. Totskogo," 75–79.

[136] I. Gebrart, "Perestroit' rabotu sovetov v nemetskikh raionakh," *Revoliutsiia i natsional'nosti*, no. 1 (1930): 45; P. Somoilovich, "Organizatsionnoe ukreplenie natsional'noi raboty v RSFSR," 85.

[137] Somoilovich, "Organizatsionnoe ukreplenie," 85.

[138] A. Osharov, "Korenizatsiia v sovetskom stroitel'stve," *Revoliutsiia i natsional'nosti*, nos. 4–5 (1930): 115.

[139] "V sovete natsional'nostei," *Revoliutsiia i natsional'nosti*, nos. 8–9 (1930): 143–148.

[140] See Chapter 10.

[141] For the materials and final report of the Andreev commission, see *RTsKhIDNI* 17/69/58 (1926–1927); 17/85/206 1926–1927); 17/114/336 (07.10.27): 6–148.

[142] *Arkhiv Trotskogo*, vol. 4, 145.

korenizatsiia in preparation for a special TsK conference.[143] TsKK did in fact investigate dozens of national republics in 1929.[144] In the case of Belorussia, their investigation had enormous political consequences. However, this was an exception. Otherwise, the investigation did not even produce a formulaic resolution, much less a TsK conference. The uncertainty continued up to the eve of the sixteenth Party Congress in June 1930. As a result, the discussion on nationalities policy in *Pravda* prior to the congress was, for the Soviet press in 1930, strikingly interesting.[145] It was at this congress that Stalin intervened decisively in the debate on the relationship between the socialist offensive and nationalities policy.

Stalin's Intervention

Long after his acknowledged expertise expanded far beyond being "master of the nationalities policy," Stalin continued to follow developments in the nationalities policy sphere carefully. He was thus fully aware that the policy of *korenizatsiia* and support for national culture was not popular with the party rank-and-file. In an unpublished 1927 letter, Stalin answered complaints he had received about the incompatibility of national culture and socialism.[146] Likewise in early 1929, Stalin noted that he often received letters that "hint that the existence of national governments and national republics with national Sovnarkomy is not our real policy, but a tactic, if you will, a little short-term concession. I often get such letters."[147] He said he regretted he lacked the time to gather materials on this question and make a formal address.

Stalin realized, therefore, the necessity of addressing the relationship between the socialist offensive and the nationalities question. During a two-month vacation in the fall of 1928, Stalin worked intensively on a major article on nationalities policy. He asked for and received from his personal secretary, Tovstukha, dozens of works on the nationalities question, including everything Lenin had ever written on the question.[148] By February 1929, he had a draft article ready

---

[143] *GARF* 374/27s/1374 (18.01.28): 207. TsKK did undertake an investigation of *Ukrainizatsiia* in 1927. See *RTsKhIDNI* 89/3/86 (1927). *GARF* 374/27s/1382 (26.11.28): 312. *TsDAHOU* 1/7/120 (03.04.29): 105/1, 33; 65.

[144] *GARF* 374/27s/1691–1709 (1929).

[145] S. Dimanshtein, "Voprosy natsional'nostei na XVI parts"ezde," *Pravda*, no. 162 (14.06.30): 4; P. Angarov, "O formakh kolkhozov v zhivotnovodcheskikh natsional'nykh raionakh i o natsional'noi politike," (20.06.30): 4; A. Avtorkhanov, "Za vypolnenie direktiv partii po natsional'nomu voprosu," *Pravda*, no. 170 (22.06.30): 4; K. Tabolov, "O natsional'noi politike partii," *Pravda*, no. 174 (26.06.30): 4; L. Gotfrid, "O pravil'nykh i pravooportunisticheskikh predlozheniiakh tov. Avtorkhanova," *Pravda*, no. 178 (30.06.30): 3; "Klassovoe soderzhanie natsional'noi politiki," *Pravda*, no. 180 (02.07.30): 7; A. Avtorkhanov, "Pis'ma v redaktsiiu," *Pravda*, no. 182 (04.07.30): 6; K. Tabolov, "Natsional'nyi vopros na XVI s"ezde partii," *Pravda*, nos. 204–205 (27–28.07.30): 2.

[146] Stalin, "Tovarishchu M. I. Ul'ianovoi."

[147] *RTsKhIDNI* 558/1/4490 (12.02.29): 2.

[148] For the correspondence between Stalin and Tovstukha and an extensive list of the books Stalin received, see *RTsKhIDNI* 558/11/72 (1928): 58–59, 67–69.

to rebut the "widespread opinion" that the "period of the transition from capitalism to socialism . . . that this period is the period of the liquidation of nations, the period of the dying away of national cultures and national languages. I decisively dispute this widespread opinion that has nothing in common with Marxism."[149] Stalin first made these ideas public during a February 1929 meeting with a Ukrainian writers' delegation in Moscow. He began his address to the writers with a quick sketch of popular party sentiment on this topic[150]:

> They claim . . . that socialism is already causing the dying away of national culture and that a common, world language should be established in the transitional period from capitalism to socialism. In our Union, it would seem all this should lead to the digestion of national cultures into one single culture and one language, *obviously Russian*, as the most advanced. . . . They hint that the existence of national governments and national republics with national Sovnarkomy, that this is not our policy, but a tactic; if you will, understand it as a kind of little concession, very temporary. I often receive such letters. [my emphasis]

Stalin categorically rejected this position. Indeed, the parenthetical "obviously Russian" reiterated his and Lenin's long-term stance that in Soviet conditions anti-*korenizatsiia* internationalism was typically a superficial cover for Russian chauvinism.

In rebuttal of the prediction of assimilation, Stalin repeated his favorite argument that just as Latvian and Hungarian cities had once been German and had subsequently been nationalized, this would also happen in the Soviet Union: "This is a general law." He also reiterated the argument that nationhood was a stage all peoples had to pass through on their way to internationalism: "We are undertaking a policy of the maximum development of national culture in order that it exhaust itself completely so that a base will be created for the organization of international socialist culture, not only in content but in form as well." This would happen, Stalin cautioned, only after the triumph of socialism worldwide, not during or after its complete triumph within the Soviet Union alone. Stalin assured his audience that national culture would not disappear: "What perspectives are there [for national culture]? These perspectives, that the national cultures of even the very smallest peoples of the USSR will develop and that we will help them develop."[151]

Stalin's speech to the Ukrainian writers was clearly designed to reassure them that Ukrainian culture and Ukrainization were not under threat. However, Stalin's speech was not published. Only in June 1930, at the Sixteenth Party Congress, did Stalin supply a fully public and authoritative denunciation of the internationalist position. Once again Stalin began with a summary of his

[149] *RTsKhIDNI* 558/11/132 (22.02.29): 38. In a later version, this article was published as "Natsional'nyi vopros i leninizm" in Stalin's complete works.
[150] *RTsKhIDNI* 558/1/4490 (12.02.29): 1–2.
[151] Ibid., 16; 9; 8; 11.

opponents' viewpoint, although now he unambiguously labeled it as Great Russian chauvinism[152]:

> The essence of the Great Russian chauvinist deviation is the desire to do without the national differences of language, culture and way of life; the desire to prepare for the liquidation of national republics and oblasts; the desire to undermine the principle of national equality and to overthrow the Party's policy of the *natsionalizatsiia* of the apparat, the *natsionalizatsiia* of the press, schools and other state and social organizations.
>
> Supporters of this deviation reason that since with the triumph of socialism nations should merge into one, and their national languages should be transformed into a single common language, therefore the time has come to liquidate national differences and to reject the policy of support for the development of the national cultures of the formerly oppressed peoples.

This deviation, Stalin went on, "hides itself under the mask of internationalism and the name of Lenin and so is the most subtle and therefore the most dangerous form of Great Russian chauvinism."[153] At the same congress, Kaganovich identified Gosplan as one of the institutions most infected with this form of chauvinism, presumably a reference to their new economic *raionirovanie* plans. Kosior cited the central soviet apparat in general. And Skrypnyk once again lit into the national communists' favorite punching bag, Semen Dimanshtein.[154]

There could hardly be a more definitive rejection of the position advanced by the nationalities policy militants and sympathized with by a broad segment of popular party opinion. However, Stalin now went beyond the rejection of the militants' position and asserted a positive interpretation of the impact of the cultural revolution on national culture[155]:

> The deviationists are mistaken when they assume that the period of the construction of socialism in the USSR is the period of the collapse and liquidation of national culture. The opposite is true. In reality, the period of the dictatorship of the proletariat and the construction of socialism in the USSR is the period of the flowering of national culture, socialist in content and national in form. They obviously do not understand that the development of national culture should unfold with new strength with the introduction and establishment of mandatory universal elementary education.

As we saw in Part One, these remarks provided an unambiguous program for cultural revolution in the sphere of nationalities policy: an acceleration in the pace of *korenizatsiia* and the development of national culture, with a

---

[152] *XVI s"ezd VKP/b/. Stenograficheskii otchet* (Moscow, 1930): 54.

[153] Ibid., 54.

[154] Ibid., 77; 180; 243.

[155] Ibid., 55–56.

particularly strong emphasis on the developmentalist project of overcoming "cultural backwardness" among the Soviet Union's eastern nationalities. The Affirmative Action Empire would be strengthened, not abandoned. Acceleration provided an outlet for the utopian energies of the cultural revolution.

Only a week before Stalin delivered this speech, the Orgburo met to discuss the practical forms that the cultural revolution should take in national regions. In line with Stalin's comments, the Orgburo endorsed "a significant increase in the tempos of cultural construction."[156] At the party congress, Kaganovich had noted that "if we have some achievements in the more progressive republics, such as Ukraine, in a series of eastern republics, [korenizatsiia] is still in a very bad condition."[157] The Orgburo agreed and recommended the state's energies be directed toward "the more backward, eastern nationalities."[158] As we have seen, the cultural revolution did in fact mark a shift in attention from the Soviet west to the east. In practical terms, cultural revolution as acceleration involved the following policies:

Accelerated tempos for the achievement of universal primary school education (Chap. 4)

Aggressive Affirmative Action programs for "culturally backward" nationalities (the bronia) in central universities (Chap. 4)

Affirmative Action to create a native proletariat in the Soviet east (Chap. 4)

Renewed efforts at the korenizatsiia of government in the eastern national republics (Chap. 4)

The completion of the network of national Soviets (Chaps. 2 and 7)

The recognition of new Soviet nationalities—ethnic proliferation (Chap. 2, 5, and 11)

The creation of new written languages (Chap. 5)

The latinization of a large number of Soviet languages, including several that used the Cyrillic script (Chap. 5)

Increased efforts to promote and strengthen the Soviet Union's national cultures (Chap. 11)

With the exception of the attack on national smenovekhovstvo, which we will turn to shortly, the cultural revolution resulted in a practical strengthening of the Affirmative Action Empire.

Stalin's categorical rejection of internationalism in 1929–1930 was a pivotal moment in the evolution of the Soviet national constitution. It marked the last time under Stalin that the idea of creating a united Soviet nationality was seriously considered. It also marked the last time that the regime had sufficient energy and purpose to pursue such a radical strategy. Therefore, the Soviet

---

[156] RTsKhIDNI 17/113/860 (16.06.30): 79.

[157] XVI s"ezd, 77.

[158] RTsKhIDNI 17/113/860 (16.06.30): 203/2.

Union would remain a multiethnic state. Stalin had unambiguously defended his own policy of *korenizatsiia* (or as he always preferred to call it, *natsional-izatsiia*). He had, however, also called for a more intense struggle against local nationalism and great-power chauvinism (or Great Russian chauvinism as he preferred to call it). In Chapter 4, we saw how Stalin's comments led to an immediate campaign against great-power chauvinism in the industrial workplace in the Soviet east. This campaign was dwarfed in significance by the terror campaign against local nationalists launched already in 1928 and continued with little interruption through 1933. This striking and consistent asymmetry between terror against local nationalists and great-power chauvinists would continue throughout Stalin's rule and have enormous significance for the evolution of the Affirmative Action Empire.

The Cultural Revolutionary Show Trial in Ukraine

Terror and show trials were the Soviet government's favored techniques for promoting the cultural revolution. Indeed, the announcement of the discovery of the Shakhty conspiracy is often seen as marking the beginning of the cultural revolution.[159] Terror and show trials were no less important in the national republics. Show trials targeting the non-Russian intelligentsia took place in most of the republics with a prominent prerevolutionary intelligentsia: Ukraine, Belorussia, Tatarstan, Crimea, Uzbekistan.[160] Less publicized purges took place in other national regions.[161] The trial of the Union for the Liberation of Ukraine (*Spilka Vyzvolennia Ukrainy—SVU*), however, received much more attention than all the other national show trials and purges combined. It served as the nationalities Shakhty. It received massive publicity not only in Ukraine, but also in Moscow and in other national republics. From February to April 1930, *Pravda* devoted over thirty long articles to coverage of this trial.[162] The other national show trials received extensive coverage only in their home

---

[159] Fitzpatrick, *Cultural Revolution*, 12; Kuromiya, *Stalin's Industrial Revolution*, 14–17.

[160] On Ukraine and Belorussia, see below. On Tatarstan, see L. Rubinshtein, *V bor'be za lenin-skuiu natsional'nuiu politiku* (Kazan, 1930); G. Kasymov, *Pantiurkistskaia kontrrevoliutsiia i ee agentura—Sultangalievshchina* (Kazan, 1931); Mirsaid Sultan-Galiev, *Stat'i. Vystupleniia. Doku-menty* (Kazan, 1992): 458–517; On Crimea, see D. K. Bochagov, *Milli Firka. Natsional'naia kontrrevoliutsiia v Krymu* (Simferopol, 1930); also, *RTsKhIDNI* 17/113/644 (01.08.28): 53/1; 85/27/219 (1928); On Uzbekistan, see the massive coverage of the "Kasymovshchina" in *Pravda vostoka* from March to October 1930; also, *RTsKhIDNI* 78/7/162 (1930); 62/2/2338 (1930); 62/2/2455 (1930); 62/2/2126 (1930); 62/2/2125 (1930).

[161] Ksenofont Sakunov, "Stalinist Terror in the Mari Republic: The Attack on 'Finno-Ugrian Bourgeois Nationalism'" *Soviet and East European Review* 74 (1996): 658–682; F. Tarakanov, "Protiv meshaniny i otsebiatiny v voprosakh natsional'noi politiki partii," *Komi mu—Zyrianskii krai*, nos. 18–19 (1929): 42–46; A. Minskii, "Strannoe i neponiatnoe" *Po leninskomu puti*, nos. 3–4 (1930): 6–10; "Reshenie ob"edinennogo zasedaniia biuro OK i prezidiuma OKK ot 14 fevralia 1930 g," nos. 3–4 (1930): 12–13; F. Il'chukov, "O natsional'nom shovinizme sredi rukovodi-ashchego aktiva partorganizatsii," nos. 3–4 (1930): 15–21.

[162] *Pravda*, nos. 57–110 (27.02–21.04.30).

republics.[163] The SVU trial was thus yet another example of the leading role in nationalities policy assigned to Ukraine by the center.

The SVU Show Trial

The SVU show trial took place with great fanfare from March 9 to April 19, 1930 in the Kharkov Opera Theater.[164] The forty-five defendants were carefully hand-picked to represent the following overlapping categories: members of the All-Ukrainian Academy of Science (VUAN), leaders of the Ukrainian Auto-cephalous Orthodox church, members of former Ukrainian "national socialist" parties, and other prominent ethnic Ukrainian nonparty intellectuals. The target of the trial, then, was clear: Ukrainian *smenovekhovtstvo*. SVU's purported leader and organizer was Serhii Efremov, a prominent Ukrainian literary critic, a leading member of the Ukrainian Socialist Federalist Party during the civil war, and former vice-president of VUAN.[165] The VUAN connection was not an acci-dent. The SVU trial was the culmination of the party's gradual process of cur-tailing and then abolishing the autonomy of VUAN, which they correctly saw as the heart of Ukrainian *smenovekhovstvo*.[166] The forty-five defendants repre-sented only the tip of the SVU iceberg. Already by December 1, 1929, seven hundred people had been arrested across all of Ukraine in connection with SVU. The final total would be in the thousands. The GPU's overall investigation produced 254 volumes of materials.[167]

Because of recent publications, we know more about the preparation of the SVU affair than about most other Stalinist show trials. In May 1928, the Ukrainian GPU was ordered to increase repression against kulak elements in the countryside and hostile intelligentsia elements in the city.[168] At the same time, the GPU was ordered to "renew work on the Efremov case."[169] A year later, on May 18, 1929, the Kiev GPU arrested a student, M. V. Pavlushkov, who lived with Efremov. He was forced to confess that he was a member of a coun-terrevolutionary group called the "Union of Ukrainian Youth" (SUM) and that Efremov had "ideologically inspired and organized the group."[170] On June 7, Balitskii reported to the Ukrainian TsK about the existence of this group.[171] On June 27, Pavlushkov began to confess the existence of a superior organization,

[163] *Pravda* largely ignored the prominent *Kasimovshchina* in Uzbekistan and *Sultan-Galievshchina* in Tatarstan. "Kasimovshchina," *Pravda*, no. 82 (24.03.30): 6; K. Tabolov, "Sot-sialisticheskoe nastuplenie i aktivizatsiia burzhuaznykh natsionalistov," no. 256 (04.11.29): 2.
[164] *Sprava "Spilky Vyzvolennia Ukrainy,"* ed. Volodymyr Prystaiko and Iurii Shapoval (Kiev, 1995); *"Spilka Vyzvolennia Ukrainy." Stenohrafichnyi zvit sudovoho protsesu*, vol. 1 (Kharkov, 1931); *Ukrains'ka kontrrevoliutsiia sama pro svoiu robotu. Vypusk II–III* (Kharkov, 1930).
[165] Shapoval, *Liudyna i systema*, 82–96.
[166] *TsDAHOU* 1/16/6 (17.02.28): 146–168; 1/16/6 (21.09.28): 307. *Sprava*, 131. Shapoval, *Ukraina 20-50-kh rokiv*, 76.
[167] Shapoval, *Ukraina 20-50-kh rokiv*, 76.
[168] *RTsKhIDNI* 17/67/384 (1928): 99–101. *TsDAHOU* 1/16/6 (04.05.28): 49–53.
[169] *RTsKhIDNI* 17/67/384 (1928): 99–101; *TsDAHOU* 1/16/6 (04.05.28): 49–53; *Sprava*, 36.
[170] *Sprava*, 36.
[171] Ibid., 108–110.

SVU, which was headed by Efremov himself. This led to Efremov's arrest on July 21. Efremov initially denied the existence of SVU, but by September 10, he had been forced to confess its existence.[172]

On November 3, the Ukrainian politburo authorized a show trial in Kharkov with no more than forty defendants. By December 1, the Ukrainian GPU had worked out the an elaborate historical scenario about the growth of SVU and a series of pedagogical "lines" to be emphasized at the coming show trial: academic (i.e., VUAN); school, youth, church (autocephalous); literary-publishing; cooperative; and rural "lines."[173] They had also already worked out a "preliminary list of those arrested in Kiev, who are proposed as representatives at the trial 'SVU.'" The list included forty-one individuals plus nine "possible" additions representing seven of the trials' proposed "lines." Another list of "candidates for the trial 'SVU' from the periphery" was compiled with fourteen individuals from eight Ukrainian *okrugi* plus the Moldavian ASSR.[174] During the preparation for the trial, the Ukrainian TsK received regular instructions from the All-Union Politburo, including at least one telegram from Stalin, who, foreshadowing the Doctors' Plot, insisted on the inclusion of a "medical" line.[175] The Ukrainian TsK appointed Panas Liubchenko, a former *borot'bist*, as prosecutor. It was his job to explain the meaning of the SVU show trial to the public.

The Ukrainian GPU and Ukrainian TsK, with oversight by the all-union TsK (and presumably the OGPU), devoted considerable attention to the pedagogical function of the SVU show trial. I will now attempt to explicate the meaning that the Ukrainian and all-union party leadership intended the SVU trial to convey to various sectors of the Soviet population. Soviet show trials of the cultural revolution era had at least four main functions. They had, first of all, a positive mobilizing function. Shakhty, for instance, was designed to energize working-class support for the socialist offensive. Second, show trials had a scapegoating function. Shakhty deflected working-class anger away from Bolshevik institutions toward the bourgeois specialists. Third, they also had a negative intimidating function. Shakhty aimed to terrify the bourgeois specialists and so preempt any opposition to the socialist offensive. Finally, show trials served to mark the regime's policy priorities. Shakhty signaled that the regime was deadly serious about their agenda of rapid industrialization.

The positive mobilizing function was marginal in both the SVU show trial as well as the other national show trials of the cultural revolution. The group that could be mobilized by SVU consisted of the anti-*korenizatsiia* militants. However, at the same time it was publicizing the SVU trial, the Ukrainian leadership was struggling to demobilize these militants. The only major instance

---

[172] Ibid., 115–127, 366–370.
[173] Ibid., 131–208. The GPU also suggested three other potential lines: engineering-technical, agronomy, and medicine.
[174] Ibid., 213–217.
[175] *RTsKhIDNI* 17/162/8 (05.11.29): 106/14; (25.01.30): 115/1; (05.02.30): 116/27; *Sprava*, 236.

where cultural revolutionary militants were mobilized to implement nationalities policy came with the campaign to unveil women in Central Asia and other Islamic regions.[176] As a substitute for the mobilization of Bolshevik militants, the Ukrainian leadership somewhat half-heartedly argued that the SVU trial would mobilize young ethnic Ukrainian students to replace the old discredited bourgeois Ukrainian intelligentsia with a new purely proletarian Ukrainian intelligentsia committed to an even more rapid implementation of Ukrainization.[177] The difficulty with this strategy was that, as we have seen, the student body was not militantly in favor of Ukrainization, but rather lukewarm if not openly hostile.

The negative intimidating function of the Soviet show trial was, however, well developed in Ukraine. The SVU show trial was directed overwhelmingly at Ukrainian *smenovekhovstvo*. Indeed, the cultural revolution show trials in all national regions were used to decisively mark the end of the era of national *smenovekhovstvo*. The elaborate historical narrative concocted by the Ukrainian GPU for the SVU trial emphasized exactly this point. According to the GPU scenario, after the defeat of the Polish invasion in 1920, Efremov took over the leadership of a Ukrainian conspiratorial group, which collapsed in 1924 due to the "*smenovekhovstvo* mood" of the anti-Soviet Ukrainian intelligentsia.[178] As the GPU put it, "*smenovekhovstvo* is a counter-revolutionary bourgeois conception that emerged due to the necessity to fight against the dictatorship of the proletariat by using all legal means to exert anti-Soviet ideological influence on the broad masses."[179] With this new goal in mind, Efremov's group went to work in VUAN[180]:

> Exploiting the circumstance that Soviet power was extensively recruiting specialists and *intelligenty* to work in cultural and economic construction, the members maliciously took advantage of that trust that was put in them, as qualified specialists, and used the broad possibilities given to them by the will of the worker and peasant masses, not to the benefit but to the harm of those masses, organizing active sabotage in all areas where they worked (the Academy of Science, schools, cooperatives).

This passage perfectly represented the regime's conflicted attitude toward *smenovekhovstvo*. On the one hand, they sponsored the movement to dissolve anti-Soviet groups; on the other hand, this only gave the groups still greater opportunities to work legally against Soviet power.

[176] Gregory J. Massell, *The Surrogate Proletariat* (Princeton, N.J. 1974). Douglas Northrop, "Uzbek Women and the Veil: Gender and Power in Stalinist Central Asia" (Ph.D. diss., Stanford University, 1999).

[177] *XI z'izd*, 274; "Bankouty," *Visti VUTsIK*, no. 57 (09.03.30): 1; "Sprava 'Spilky Vyzvolennia Ukrainy'. Promova hromads'koho obvynuvacha tov. Liubchenka," *Visti VUTsIK*, no. 85 (13.04.30): 3.

[178] *SVU. Sten. zvit*, 14–15.

[179] Ibid., 17.

[180] Ibid., 15.

One SVU defendant testified that "the Academy of Science [formed an] island within Soviet power, which enjoyed a unique political extra-territoriality."[181] This quotation was repeated frequently in the SVU propaganda. Again, it served as a symbol of VUAN and of Ukrainian *smenovekhovstvo*: an ideologically foreign and inassimilable presence within the Soviet organism. The GPU narrative, with its fantastic conspiracies, served to give this psychological disposition a concrete counterrevolutionary form. In their scenario, by mid-1926 the VUAN intellectuals were not only distressed by their inability to reorient Soviet power, but they were also actively plotting with west Ukrainian nationalists to form SVU. They were not only opposed to and afraid of the socialist offensive, but they had formed a plot to provoke a popular uprising as a prelude to foreign intervention.[182] Presumably, the party leadership hoped the population would literally believe this story.[183] For the party leadership, it represented a psychological truth. With the advent of the socialist offensive, the *smenovekhovstvo* intelligentsia would surely act this way if given an opportunity and therefore they must be preemptively annihilated. To sum up, then, the SVU trial and its cousins in other national regions purposefully targeted the national *smenovekhovstvo* intelligentsia and likewise decisively marked the end of national *smenovekhovstvo*.

The Ukrainian Terror, then, was clearly directed at the old Ukrainian intelligentsia. It also had an implied audience in Europe, as a telegram sent by Stalin to the Ukrainian politburo on January 2, 1930 made clear[184]:

When do you propose to hold the trial on Efremov and the others? Here we think that at the trial you should not only elaborate on the defendants' plans for uprisings and terrorist acts, but also their medical trickery [*fokusy*] aimed at murdering responsible workers. We have no reason to hide from the workers the sins of our enemies. Moreover, let so-called "Europe" know that the repression against the counter-revolutionary segment of specialists, attempts to poison and murder Communist patients, have a complete "justification" and in fact [these repressions] pale before the criminal activity of these counter-revolutionary scoundrels. We ask you to confirm with Moscow the plan for conducting the trial.

Stalin's odd phrase, "so-called 'Europe,'" appears to be a mocking reference to Khvylovyi's idealized "Europe." In this sense, the SVU trial represented a crude message to Khvylovyi's supposed European friends—in particular the west Ukrainian nationalist parties and Marshall Pilsudski—that any attempts to influence Soviet Ukraine would be cruelly rebuffed. In this sense, the trial

---

[181] P. Liubchenko, *Z varshavs'kym dohovorom proty piatyrichky (do protsesu SVU)* (Kharkov, 1930): 12.

[182] *SVU. Sten. zvit,* 14–30.

[183] According to a GPU report, there was a mixed reaction. *TsDAHOU* 1/20/3192 (1930): 87–93.

[184] *Sprava,* 236.

again represented a concretization, in the imaginary form of a real conspiracy between the entire *zminovikhovstvo* intelligentsia and their West Ukrainian counterparts, along with the governments of Poland and Germany, of what the Soviet leadership feared was, under the proper circumstances, a potential possibility. The SVU trial, then, represented yet another step in the progressive abandonment of the Piedmont Principle, the growing suspicion of all foreign ties and the Soviet decision to adopt an aggressively defensive foreign policy stance.

This foreign policy aspect raises the question of whether the national communists, those ethnic Ukrainians who were most committed to Ukrainization, were also an implied target of the SVU trial. After all, the principal concern that emerged during the Shumskyi affair was that foreign Ukrainian nationalists would change the landmarks of Ukrainian communists to nationalism rather than being themselves recruited to Bolshevism. No communists were arrested in connection with SVU. However, in almost all the other national show trials, prominent communists were included.[185] The position of education commissar, often held by exnationalists, was a frequent target.[186] Therefore, it would be naive to assume that because they were not arrested in Ukraine, national communists were not a target for intimidation in the SVU trial. Certainly, Nikolai Popov, in a prominent *Pravda* article, made a direct connection between the supposed defection of the SVU *zminovikhovstvo* intelligentsia after Pilsudski's seizure of power and the simultaneous defection of Shumskyi and the KPZU leadership.[187]

Terror as a System of Signaling

This warning to the national communists raises the further question of the policy impact of the SVU trial in particular and the cultural revolutionary terror in national republics in general. We have noted one clear policy impact: the end of national *smenovekhovstvo*. What, however, was the impact of the SVU trial on Ukrainization? According to the official propaganda line associated with the show trial, it would speed up the implementation of Ukrainization by removing the counterrevolutionary old Ukrainian intelligentsia and making way for a new proletarian one. As we saw in Chapter 3, it is true that a new campaign of Ukrainization in proletarian regions was undertaken during the period between the announcement of the SVU conspiracy and the show trial. Anti-

---

[185] For example, in Tatarstan and Crimea most of the prominent members of the former right factions were arrested. Kasymov, *Pantiurkistskaia kontrrevoliutsiia*, 79; *RTsKhIDNI* 17/3/763 (18.10.29): 104/14.

[186] For instance, in Belorussia, the commissar of education, Balitskii, see below; and in Uzbekistan, the education commissar, Batu, see *RTsKhIDNI* 62/2/2199 (1930): 20–42.

[187] N. Popov, "Sudorogi ukrainskoi kontrrevoliutsii," *Pravda*, no. 69 (11.03.30): 2–3. See also Liubchenko's prosecutorial speech, "Promova hromad'skoho obvynuvacha t. Liubchenka," *Visti VUTsIK*, no. 84 (12.04.30): 5.

Ukrainization militants, however, could and did see SVU as a signal for an attack on Ukrainization. If national *smenovekhovstvo*, which had been endorsed by the 1923 nationalities policy decrees, had now been rejected, then why not other NEP-era nationalities policies?[188] The GPU's internal reports on SVU give some support to this view. They frequently cite the conspirators' exploitation of Ukrainization and Ukrainian studies (*Ukrainoznavstvo*) courses both to place their cadres in influential positions and to recruit new supporters.[189] However, this confidential material dropped out of the final published GPU narrative.

Moreover, in an extremely important passage at the 1930 Ukrainian party congress, Kosior singled out the anti-Ukrainization interpretation of SVU for criticism[190]:

> In connection with the SVU trial some conversations have appeared—in some cases in whispers and in others out loud—on the theme that as a result of party policy, the party itself has planted Ukrainian nationalism and now is being forced to harvest crops such as SVU. Conversations of this type have taken place in Kiev and elsewhere.
>
> If one wants a true evaluation of the SVU trial, then it is characteristic that it showed a brilliant victory of our party as a result of the correct implementation of our nationalities policy. In this trial we not only uncovered and politically liquidated a counter-revolutionary nationalist organization, not only dethroned the most significant centers of the old Ukrainian bourgeois nationalism, but isolated them, split them off from the remaining vacillating parts of the old Ukrainian intelligentsia. This was possible only as a result of our enormous successes in the implementation of our nationalities policy. This is our triumph, not a defeat. Those who attempt to present the SVU trial as a defeat for the party, in fact repeat the words of Zinoviev who, in June 1927 at a meeting of the TsKK Presidium . . . , announced: "In Ukraine they are conducting a 'Ukrainization' that clearly contradicts our nationalities policy . . . helps the *Petliurovshchina* and gives no rebuke to true chauvinism."

I have quoted Kosior at length, because the position he attacks—that Ukrainization was actually arming rather than disarming Ukrainian nationalism—was one that only those in open opposition could state publicly but that clearly had growing party support. For the time being, however, Kosior successfully enforced the existing party line, that great-power chauvinism remained the greater danger.

If great-power chauvinism was indeed the greatest danger, then why was terror being mobilized exclusively against Ukrainian nationalism? This question had long preoccupied Mykola Skrypnyk. Already in April 1923, he objected to Stalin's "double bookkeeping": "All the time we try to achieve balance in

---

[188] *XI z'izd*, 287–288.
[189] *Sprava*, 136, 141, 187–188, 196, 210.
[190] *XI z'izd*, 287–288.

the nationalities question. Everyone tries to find a middle line. Every criticism of great-power chauvinism has to be compensated with an opposing criticism of the chauvinism of the non–state-bearing peoples, and so we end up with double bookkeeping . . . in this way, we never end up fighting great-power chauvinism."[191] Two months later, when confronted with the case against Sultan-Galiev, Skrypnyk abandoned his call for terror biased against great-power chauvinists and merely pleaded for equality. Skrypnyk began with an anecdote about how in antiquity a new building was dedicated by pouring the blood of a sacrificial victim under the cornerstone. Skrypnyk portrayed the persecution of Sultan-Galiev, whose guilt he in fact doubted, as a blood sacrifice poured under the edifice of the new Soviet nationalities policy. However, he complained that there were also many Great Russian chauvinists in Ukraine who falsely persecuted ethnic Ukrainian communists: "It seems to me that the blood of one of these criminals ought also to be placed under the cornerstone of a correct party policy, along with the blood of the criminal type, Sultan-Galiev."[192] With this appalling metaphor, Skrypnyk candidly pointed to the connection between terror and policy implementation.

This asymmetrical use of terror continued throughout the Stalinist period. For the NEP period, a comparison between the fate of Lebed and Shumskyi is instructive. Lebed openly attacked the official party line on the eve of the Twelfth Party Congress. After losing that polemic, he continued to espouse his views in a published pamphlet. He was never forced to undergo a public self-criticism. Lebed continued to work in Ukraine as a TsK secretary for two more years until, in Zatonskyi's words, "Comrade Lebed went to work in a higher culture, that is here in Moscow, and we remained in Ukraine to implement another line."[193] In Moscow, he became deputy Commissar of Rabkrin and a member of TsK. In 1928, to the enormous annoyance of Skrypnyk, he published an attack on the Ukrainian party's nationalities policy in the prestigious all-union theoretical journal, *Bolshevik*.[194] Shumskyi, on the other hand, only complained privately about the pace of the implementation of Ukrainization. Yet, he was required on numerous occasions to engage in self-criticism, and when he failed to do so sufficiently abjectly, he was denounced as the ideologue of a fascist national deviation. He was exiled first to Saratov and then to minor posts in St. Petersburg, where he could not publish. In 1933, he was arrested and convicted as the leader of a counterrevolutionary Ukrainian nationalist organization.

This asymmetry of terror increased with the cultural revolution. For instance, in April 1929 the TsKK inspection team headed by Azatian accused the Ukrainians of fighting Russian chauvinism more than Ukrainian chauvinism.[195] The

[191] *Dvenadtsatyi s"ezd*, 572.
[192] *Tainy natsional'noi politiki TsK RKP*, 62.
[193] *RTsKhIDNI* 17/85/206 (1927): 66.
[194] D. Lebed, "Vnimanie ideologicheskomu frontu"; M. Skrypnyk, "List do tov. Lebedia," *Statti i promovy*, vol. 2, part 1, 302–324.
[195] *TsDAHOU* 1/20/2631 (1929): 1–23.

Ukrainians reacted with indignation and bewilderment. Ukraine's GPU representative presented a long list of Ukrainian nationalist organizations that the GPU had uncovered. Others noted Lebed's current unscathed position.[196] Skrypnyk was outraged[197]:

> Skrypnyk: I would like to ask in recent time who we have beaten as a Russian chauvinist. What campaigns have we conducted against great-power chauvinism. Who have we attacked?
> Khvylia: This is our shortcoming.
> Liubchenko: Malitskii.
> Skrypnyk: And what did we do [to Malitskii]? We gave him a reprimand [*vygovor*] when as a member of the [Ukrainian] Supreme Court, he demanded, and did so vehemently, that we speak with him only in Russian. After that, how can you say we fight more with Great Russian chauvinism? Did we conduct a campaign [against Malitskii]? No. We had a resolution. And against Shumskyi we conducted a massive battle. . . .

Malitskii was not only a member of the Ukrainian supreme court but also its president. In January 1928, he had complained bitterly when the book he wrote in Russian was published first in a Ukrainian translation. He was called before TsKK, given a strong reprimand, denounced once in *Komunist*, but allowed to keep his position.[198]

The SVU trial naturally alarmed Skrypnyk, but he deployed a creative strategy for defusing the trial's potential to undermine Ukrainization. Skrypnyk defined SVU as a necessary attack on the nationalism of Ukrainian bourgeois specialists in order to balance the previous attack on the Great Russian chauvinism of the Shakhty specialists, who "were tenacious Russian nationalists. You know the desperate and conscious resistance they offered to . . . Ukrainization and the creation of Ukrainian national culture."[199] In this scenario, both trials primarily targeted nationalism and so politically canceled each other out. However, Skrypnyk later lamented that his interpretation had failed[200]:

> One unfortunately must confess that this aspect of the Shakhty trial was not emphasized by our press as a separate subject and analyzed from the perspective of nationalities policy theory. And yet this fact is important, very significant. The written declarations, confessions and testimony of the Shakhty wreckers clearly

[196] *TsDAHOU* 1/20/120 (03.04.29): 50–54.
[197] Ibid., 68.
[195] *TsDAHOU* 1/20/2631 (1929): 1–23.
[196] *TsDAHOU* 1/20/120 (03.04.29): 50–54.
[197] Ibid., 68.
[198] *Budivntystvo*, 158–161; *Natsional'ne pytannia*, 49–54.
[199] M. Skrypnyk, "Kontr-revoliutsiine shkidnytstvo na kul'turnomu fronti," *Chervonyi shliakh*, no. 4 (1930): 139; see also M. Skrypnyk, "Spilka Vyzvolennia Ukrainy," *Bil'shovyk Ukrainy*, no. 8 (1930): 23.
[200] Skrypnyk, "Natsional'ni peretynky," 282–283.

show how hostile they were to the Party's nationalities policy in Ukraine. They
showed their Great Russian orientation. In their practical work, they offered
fanatical resistance to the Ukrainization of the economic organs, . . . rejecting
. . . all that even smelled of the Ukrainian language.

This quotation again showed that Skrypnyk was acutely aware of the policy
impact of terror. He was not only desperate that Shakhty be used to balance
SVU, but that it also be given a clear policy "line." The Shakhty saboteurs were
being punished for the passionate resistance shown to Ukrainization by the all-
union economic organs. In this he clearly failed. On March 20, 1930, in the
middle of the SVU trial, Skrypnyk pleaded in a letter to Kosior that some
balance be achieved within the SVU trial. He asked that a positive witness
be allowed to speak about VUAN's potential for positive work on behalf of
Ukrainian national culture.[201] He again failed. SVU established a pattern of
asymmetric terror in Ukraine and the other national republics, which continued with the Ukrainian National Center in 1931, the Ukrainian Military Organization in 1933, and a plethora of other affairs from 1933 to 1938. Trials of Great
Russian nationalists did take place frequently, but they typically took place in
the center, received less publicity, and, most significantly, lacked the connection
to nationalities policy that Skrypnyk attempted to attach to Shakhty.[202]

This asymmetric deployment of terror was crucial to the fate of Ukrainization. The regime had great difficulty in getting its decrees implemented. By the
time of the socialist offensive, "verifying implementation" (*proverka ispolnenii*)
was perhaps the leadership's most pressing concern.[203] One response was to use
terror to mark those hard-line policies where no opposition would be tolerated.
Soft-line policies were still consistently supported, but terror was not mobilized
to force their implementation. As we have seen, the key to Kaganovich's early
successes was his construction of a hard line on Ukrainization, which featured
the use of "pressure" (*nazhim*) in the form of dismissals for resisting Ukrainization. This hard line, however, was not backed up with terror. All-union institutions would rehire those fired, hire others who did not speak Ukrainian, and
even openly use Russian in their paperwork. They never received a signal,
in the form of a show trial, that this bureaucratic resistance would not be tolerated. On the contrary, they frequently received the contrary signal that
Ukrainian nationalists, those too committed to Ukrainization and Ukrainian
national culture, were the main danger. In this case, the hard-line language of
terror trumped the soft-line insistence that Great Russian chauvinism remained
the greater danger.

Why did this peculiar divergence between party line and practice of terror
emerge? There are at least four reasons that nationalities policy remained a

[201] *Sprava*, 250–251.

[202] On the post-SVU terror in Ukraine, see Shapoval, *Ukraina 20-50-kh rokiv*, 82–240; Rublov
and Cherchenko, *Stalinshchyna*, 104–183.

[203] O. V. Khlevniuk et al., eds., *Stalinskoe politbiuro v 30-e gody. Sbornik dokumentov* (Moscow,
1995): 82–86.

soft-line policy whereas national repression earned a hard-line response. First, as argued earlier, Bolshevik culture did not view the construction of an Affirmative Action Empire as a core Bolshevik task, whereas the fight against bourgeois nationalism was viewed as such. Pressure was considered appropriate for the former task, terror for the latter. Second, in practical terms, local nationalism usually expressed itself in written form, whereas Russian chauvinism expressed itself as bureaucratic infighting. Third, as shown in the Shumskyi affair, due to cross-border ethnic ties, local nationalism became associated with the threat of foreign influence and ideological defection, a threat serious enough to warrant terror.

Finally, the socialist offensive markedly increased the centralization of the Soviet state and therefore the reach of all-union enterprises and commissariats. Since central bodies worked in the Russian language, centralization exacerbated local linguistic conflicts. It also increased the perception of the center as Russian and the periphery as non-Russian. Accusing central officials of Russian chauvinism, then, could easily be interpreted as resisting legitimate centralization and an expression of localism (*mestnichestvo*). Here an exchange between Ukrainian representatives and Stalin in February 1929 is relevant. One Ukrainian complained that Ukraine had conscientiously fought with local nationalism according to the formula of the 1923 decrees[204]:

> But this formula is poorly understood in the governing organs, even in Moscow. If one speaks of a fight with great power chauvinism then now we need to uncover that chauvinism in some kind of concrete form. In Ukraine we had such a concrete form, Shumskyism, and we fought against it. But in practice, Moscow workers and RSFSR workers don't do this, although one could name many facts of chauvinism in relation to Ukraine. This question has great significance and should be publicized in a concrete form.

Clearly, the Ukrainian representative was asking for some sort of exemplary punishment. Stalin responded:

> You have produced some sort of declaration. I spoke about this several times with comrades Petrovskii, Chubar and Kaganovich, when he worked in Ukraine. They expressed unhappiness that the apparats of the central commissariats demonstrated a complete neglect of the economic and cultural needs of Ukraine. These comrades can confirm this. Every time I asked them: name at least one person whom we could cut down in the eyes of everyone . . . I asked them and not once did they try to name anyone. Every time they would gather to discuss it and not once did they name anyone. They'd go, get scared, retreat and the matter would come to an end. Not once did they name anyone.

As Stalin made clear, there was obviously something to be afraid of or the Ukrainians could have named hundreds of individuals. However, they clearly

---

[204] *RTsKhIDNI* 558/1/4490 (12.05.29): 35–36.

felt that a call for exemplary punishment, much less terror, against central officials for neglecting national interests would be neither successful nor welcome.
The SVU trial, then, exhibited a characteristic ambiguity between the targets
of terror and the content of nationalities policy. Official policy remained largely
unchanged throughout the cultural revolution, yet terror was deployed to
intimidate the executors of that policy, the national communists, and this
seemed to signal the advent of a policy reversal on *korenizatsiia*. In the other
national republics, a few prominent national communists were arrested and
publicly tried, but again policy remained fundamentally unchanged.

Terror and Policy Reversal in Belorussia

The cultural revolutionary terror in Belorussia represented a revealing exception to this rule. A significant number of the republic's highest-ranking ethnic
Belorussian communists were arrested. More important, those Belorussian
national communists were accused of having defected to nationalism in exactly
the scenario previously mapped out in the Shumskyi affair. As a result of the
terror in Belorussia, the remaining party leadership formally declared Belorussian nationalism the greatest danger and ceased implementing Belorussization.
This aborted policy reversal presaged the major turn in nationalities policy that
took place in December 1932. It represented the first, if brief, triumph of the
anti-*korenizatsiia* hard line.

The nationalities question in Belorussia bore striking similarities to that in
Ukraine, a fact frequently commented on by both ethnic Russian and Belorussian communists working in the republic.[205] The existence of both nations
had been denied under Tsarism. The Soviet-Polish border divided the two
nations. A separate Communist Party had been formed in Poland for both the
Ukrainian (KPZU) and Belorussian (KPZB) minorities. In both republics, the
rural population was predominantly native and the urban population Russian
and Jewish. Belorussia, however, had a much more weakly developed sense of
national self-consciousness. Many Belorussian peasants bitterly opposed the formation of a Belorussian republic. As late as 1929, peasants sincerely explained
to Zatonskyi's TsKK commission that they spoke only Russian, unaware that
they were explaining themselves in fluent Belorussian.[206] Despite this weak
national self-consciousness, the implementation of *korenizatsiia* was eased by
the fact Belorussia lacked a strong russified Communist Party and had a smaller
Jewish and a much smaller Russian population than Ukraine. Given these similarities, the Belorussian government modeled its program of Belorussization
after Ukrainization. They formed the same network of mandatory courses,

---

[205] For some examples of this parallel, see *RTsKhIDNI* 17/31/4 (1924): 4; A. Siankevich,
"Kliasavaia barats'ba u belaruskai litaratury," *Bol'shevik Belarusi*, nos. 8–9 (1930): 28.
[206] *GARF* 1235/121/2 (1926): 23; 3316/16a/175 (1926): 48–51; *RTsKhIDNI* 17/69/59 (1927): 17;
17/85/365 (1929): 98–99.

issued the same threat to fire delinquents, proclaimed the same "hard line," required Belorussian studies courses, encouraged the return of Belorussian *smenovekhovstvo* nationalists, and so forth.[207]

Given Belorussia's reputation today as the least nationalist and most thoroughly russified of the former Soviet republics, one must strongly emphasize the remarkable success of Belorussization in the 1920s. The Belorussian leadership was obsessed with the process of nation-building and devoted more attention to it than even Ukraine. In 1926, the TsK *biuro* discussed nationalities policy fifty-one times. For comparison, in 1926 the Georgian *biuro* discussed the issue six times.[208] Central officials with a working knowledge of Belorussian exploded upward from only 21.9 percent in 1925 to 80 percent by the end of 1927 and approximately 90 percent by 1929, a considerably higher percentage than in Ukraine at the same time. As in Ukraine, almost all paperwork was shifted from Russian to Belorussian, whereas oral work was carried out in Russian.[209]

The press became almost exclusively Belorussian. By 1929, there was only one exclusively Russian-language newspaper and no Russian-language journals.[210] The TsK's official newspaper, *Zviazda*, was switched from Russian to Belorussian in early 1927.[211] Similar success was achieved with primary-school education, which rose rapidly from being only 28.4 percent Belorussian language in 1924–1925 to a whopping 93.8 percent in 1929–1930.[212] As in Ukraine, higher education and unions were much more resistant, but even here the Belorussian language secured a strong foothold.[213] The most striking proof of the success of Belorussization was that, again as in Ukraine, russified Belorussians in large numbers were shifting their official identity from Russian to Belorussian.[214] Zatonskyi, who knew Ukrainian conditions well, thought Belorussia had not moved as far along as Ukraine, but it is clear from the materials his TsKK commission collected that Belorussia no longer lagged far behind Ukraine and was rapidly closing the remaining gap.[215]

Zatonskyi's TsKK commission arrived in Belorussia on May 9, 1929 as part of the massive 1929 TsKK investigation of the Soviet nationalities policy.

[207] *Prakticheskoe razreshenie natsional'nogo voprosa v Belorusskoi sotsialisticheskoi respublike,* vol. 1 (Minsk, 1927): 87–146; A. Budzin, ed. *Natsyianal'nae pytan'ne,* (Minsk, 1930): 252–330. Durdenevskii, *Ravnopravie iazykov v sovetskom stroe,* 162–174.

[208] *RTsKhIDNI* 17/32/100 (1927): 8; 17/18/2 (1926): 11/1; 18/10; 25/12; 25/16; 30/1; 39/2. None of these, by the way, discussed Georgian nation-building. All were devoted to national minorities.

[209] *GARF* 374/27s/1694 (1929): 290b; 79; *RTsKhIDNI* 17/85/365 (1929): 47–48; *XI z'ezd kamunistychnai partyi/b/ Belarusi. 22–29 listapada 1927 hodu. Stenahrafichnaia spravadzdachav* (Minsk, 1927): 403; *RTsKhIDNI* 17/85/365 (1929): 27–28; 47–48.

[210] *RTsKhIDNI* 17/85/365 (1929): 41–43. Three newspapers and six journals were in mixed languages.

[211] *Natsional'ne pytannia,* 283.

[212] *Prakticheskoe razreshenie,* 44; A. Khatskevich, "Azhits'tsiaulben'ne leninskai natsiianal'nai palityki u Belaruskai SSR," *Bol'shevik Belarusi,* nos. 10–12 (1930): 24.

[213] *Prakticheskoe razreshenie,* 19–26; 55–59; *GARF* 374/27s/1694 (1929): 6–8; 50–58.

[214] *GARF* 374/27s/1691 (1929): 40; *RTsKhIDNI* 17/33/414 (1929): 12; 17/85/365 (1929): 54.

[215] *RTsKhIDNI* 17/85/365 (1929): 27–63.

Zatonskyi spent fifty-two days in Belorussia, collected several thousand pages of material, and sent a devastatingly critical report to Ordzhonikidze along with an even more damaging letter to Stalin.[216] Zatonskyi's report was the only one of the 1929 TsKK investigations to provoke a political purge. This was at least partially due to Zatonskyi's considerable authority in nationalities policy— Ordzhonikidze had singled him out as indispensable for the success of the 1929 investigations—as well as his enormous personal self-confidence.[217]

Zatonskyi's TsKK report not only supported Belorussization, but also advocated that it be implemented more aggressively. Zatonskyi was more disturbed, however, by the sharply anti-Russian mood he encountered in Belorussia. He wrote to Stalin that "I have seen all kinds of things in Ukraine, but the degree of animosity towards Moscow that oozes out at every gathering of writers or academics here is greater by several degrees than the most frenzied nationalism of the *Petliurovshchina* in 1918. A large number of Communists are caught up in this chauvinist intoxication."[218] As a committed national communist, Zatonskyi was particularly insulted by the provincialism of this Belorussian nationalism: "In Belorussia the expression 'love of the fatherland' and even 'Mother Belarus' ['*Matsy Belarus'*] do not at all sound ironic as does '*Nen'ka Ukraina*' and '*Rus' Matushka*'"; "There is an orientation on the West here, but nevertheless there is a much stronger orientation on *lapti* [peasant sandals], on indigenous *lapti*."[219] Zatonskyi noted that nationalists in Ukraine, such as Khvylovyi, had complete scorn for such provincialism.

Zatonskyi cited a series of incidents in support of this accusation. In November 1928, *Savetskaia Belarus* published a letter from a number of prominent Belorussian writers attacking the Belorussian national theater for staging translated Russian plays. They unwisely singled out the revolutionary classic, *Bronepoezd* [The Armored Train], as an example. *Savetskaia Belarus* had earlier published a similar attack by Belorussian communists on the russified nature of the Belorussian cinema, and then a month later again published complaints about the hostile atmosphere for Belorussian writers at the Belorussian State University.[220] These articles led Zatonskyi to sneer "that it's about time we Sovietized 'Soviet Belorussia.'"[221] He concluded that "in all these articles an anti-Moscow stance shone through, a mockery of the all-union status of these [literary] works and a desire for a [Belorussian] 'Renaissance' of a petty-

[216] For the extremely interesting materials collected by Zatonskyi, see *GARF* 374/27s/1691–1698 (1929); for his report to Ordzhonikidze, see *RTsKhIDNI* 17/85/365 (1929); for the letter to Stalin, *GARF* 374/27s/1691 (1929): 2–10; for another letter to Ordzhonikidze, *RTsKhIDNI* 85/27/345 (29.06.29): 1–2; for the time spend in Belorussia, *RTsKhIDNI* 17/85/365 (1929): 64.

[217] On Ordzhonikidze's endorsement, see *GARF* 374/27s/1382 (26.11.28): 312.

[218] *GARF* 374/27s/1691 (1929): 2.

[219] *RTsKhIDNI* 17/85/365 (1929): 103; *GARF* 374/27s/1691 (1929): 43.

[220] *GARF* 374/27s/1691 (1929): 43; *RTsKhIDNI* 17/85/365 (1929): 75–77. For other accounts of these episodes, see A. Nekrashevicha, "Belaruski natsiianal-fashizm i natsiianal-demakratizm," *As'veta*, nos. 11–12 (1929): 30–31; "Natsiianal-demokrati za 'pratsai'," *As'veta*, no. 12 (1930): 18–32.

[221] *GARF* 374/27s/1691 (1929): 42.

bourgeois type."[222] Zatonskyi also noted that the Belorussian party's top nationalities specialist, Ignatovskii, a member of the TsK *Biuro*, had published a history
of Belorussia that was later recalled as nationalist.

Zatonskyi was of course familiar with such incidents from his work in Ukraine.
What alarmed him, therefore, were not the events themselves, but what he
saw as the irresponsibly "delicate" response to them by the Belorussian party
leadership.[223] Based again on his Ukrainian experience, Zatonskyi felt the
Belorussian party leadership was far too deferential to its *smenovekhovstvo* intelligentsia and had in fact fallen under their ideological influence. As in Ukraine,
a large number of prominent Belorussian nationalists, including the prime min-
ister of the civil war–era Belorussian republic, had returned to Belorussia as
smenovekhovtsy and been given positions in what became the Belorussian
Academy of Science. In his letter to Stalin, Zatonskyi painted a grim portrait
of the Belorussian party leadership's relationship with their *smenovekhovstvo*
intelligentsia[224]:

> During the most tense periods of our battle with Shumskyism, even Shumskyi's
> most frenzied supporters never spoke aloud such things as those that are pub-
> lished completely openly and with no rebuttal in Belorussia's newspapers and
> journals. No matter how much Shumskyi differed with the Party line, no one
> ever dared suspect that after a fight in the TsK *Biuro* he would go to Hrushevskyi
> and drink tea and consult on tactics for their joint battle. Yet in Belorussia
> all this is the normal course of affairs. If the highest Communist leaders now
> consult with their Belorussian Hrushevskyis less frequently, they still maintain
> intimate ties and do not fight back against an aggressive Belorussian national-
> ism. And a whole number of figures slightly lower in the hierarchy, but still
> members of the government and close to the TsK, are so intertwined with
> non-Party nationalists that you can't find a border between them.

Zatonskyi noted that TsK biuro secrets immediately became known to the
smenovekhovstvo intelligentsia.[225]

Zatonskyi gave numerous examples of an excessive respect for the *smenovekhovstvo* intelligentsia. He noted with disgust that they were officially praised
as "the pioneers of Belorussian culture" and that even the TsK newspaper
Zviazda competed to publish their articles.[226] As a veteran of the Shevchenko
wars, Zatonskyi accepted the need to claim prominent national literary figures.
He was appalled, however, that the Belorussian lyric poets Ianka Kupala and
Iakub Kolas, both of whom were anti-Bolshevik nationalists throughout the
civil war and even now rather hesitant *smenovekhovtsy*, had been officially
declared "People's Poets of Belorussia" by the Belorussian TsK itself. Kupala's

[222] *RTsKhIDNI* 17/85/365 (1929): 76.
[223] *GARF* 374/27s/1691 (1929): 44.
[224] *GARF* 374/27s/1691 (1929): 2.
[225] *RTsKhIDNI* 17/85/365 (1929): 86.
[226] *RTsKhIDNI* 17/85/365 (1929): 75; 84.

portrait, Zatonskyi noted acidly, was hung alongside Lenin's in every Belorussian school.[227] Zatonskyi provided a psychological explanation for this deference.
The Belorussian leaders were unsure of their status as true Belorussians and of
their ability to oversee the construction of Belorussian national culture, and so
sought validation from "the pioneers of Belorussian culture" that they really
were "one hundred percent Belorussian." At a meeting of the Belorussian TsK
biuro, Zatonskyi told them this to their faces[228]:

> You play around with the nationalists far too much. I understand that there
> was a time when emigrants returned from abroad and that it was necessary
> for our foreign policy to greet them and give them positions in institutions and
> so forth. We did this with Hrushevskyi. I received him in my office as Com-
> missar of Education, but I never drank tea with him. I never invited him to my
> home. I understand that there was a time when we had to use them for our
> goals. This was correct, but you cannot tiptoe around them forever. . . . It is
> characteristic that up to now there is still the desire that they acknowledge you
> as one hundred percent Belorussians. You wait on them, play with them, instead
> of gradually distancing yourselves from them and replacing them with new
> cadres.

In addition to chastising their psychological capitulation, Zatonskyi was also
informing them of their failure to recognize that the onset of the socialist offensive meant the abolition of *smenovekhovstvo*.

The Shumskyi affair caused the Ukrainian leadership to fear that the strategy
of using the *smenovekhovstvo* intelligentsia to influence West Ukrainian popular
sentiment might backfire. Instead of changing the West Ukrainian population's
landmarks to Bolshevism, Ukrainian Bolsheviks might be seduced into changing their landmarks to Ukrainian nationalism. In Belorussia, Zatonskyi believed
this Ukrainian nightmare had materialized. To a considerable extent, the
Belorussian party leadership itself had become *smenovekhovstvo*. In his letter
to Stalin, Zatonskyi identified a number of Belorussian communists who had
become nationalists: the Commissar of Agriculture, Dmitrii Prishchepov, who
conducted "an unambiguously right deviationist agricultural policy"; the
Commissar of Education, Anton Balitskii, a "typical nationalist"; and the former
head of the TsK Press Department, Aleksandr Adamovich, who supported the
"one hundred percent Belorussian" intelligentsia.[229]

Moreover, even ethnic non-Belorussians could became accultured to their
local surroundings. For instance, Zatonskyi described the Belorussian second
secretary, Vasilevich, as "a solid revolutionary" and party member since
1918, "but having arrived in Belorussia, to a significant degree he got sick
with the local illness."[230] By this, Zatonskyi meant that individuals such as

---

[227] *RTsKhIDNI* 17/85/365 (1929): 102.
[228] *GARF* 374/27s/1691 (1929): 49.
[229] *GARF* 374/27s/1691 (1929): 5–6.
[230] Ibid., 5.

Vasilevich either fell under the influence of the national communists (in his case, Adamovich) and their *smenovekhovstvo* allies, or at least showed no inclination to fight them decisively. Among the higher leadership, Zatonskyi exempted only the newly appointed first secretary, Ian Gamarnik, and the future head of Sovnarkom, N. M. Goloded. This belief led Zatonskyi to deliver an ominous warning to Stalin: "At a time when Poland is openly preparing for war, the position of Soviet power and the proletarian dictatorship in Belorussia is very weakly secured. An openly kulak land policy has greatly consolidated kulak strength, which is now clearly beginning to exploit the national moment as their ideological banner."[231]

Zatonskyi's TsKK report and cover letters to Stalin and Ordzhonikidze were an unambiguous call for a purge of the Belorussian political leadership. In this, Zatonskyi was successful. In late 1929, a new attack was begun on Belorussian nationalism. Arrests were made in the Belorussian Academy of Sciences. Prishchepov, Balitskii, and Adamovich were removed from their positions.[232] By September 1930, they had all been arrested by the OGPU, along with a fourth and less important party leader, Petr Iliuchenko. The OGPU transformed Zatonskyi's TsKK report into a narrative account of the emergence of a counterrevolutionary organization: the "Union for the Liberation of Belorussia" (*Saiuz vyzvalennia Belarusi*—SVB). The SVB narrative closely followed its Ukrainian prototype.[233] Like the Ukrainian SVU, SVB was composed of Belorussia's *smenovekhovstvo* intelligentsia, and the conspiracy was centered on the Belorussian Academy of Science. SVB was also portrayed as an alliance of Belorussian intellectuals living in Belorussia and Poland, who took orders from the Polish government. Like SVU, the goal of SVB was to prepare and, at the proper moment, unleash a popular uprising to pave the way for foreign intervention and the formation of a separate Belorussian state under Polish hegemony. The chronological developments of SVU and SVB were almost identical.[234] Efremov was even said to have made contact with the leaders of SVB to coordinate efforts as part of a planned "union of nationalities" (*spilka narodnostei*).[235]

[231] Ibid., 2.

[232] A. Nekrashevicha, "Belaruski natsiinal-fashizm i natsiianal-demakratizm," *As'veta*, nos. 11–12 (1929): 21–37; A. Sian'kevich, "Barats'ba z ukhilami u natsiianal'nim pitan'ni i natsarabotse," *Bol'shevik Belarusi*, no. 5 (1930): 12–15.

[233] For the internal OGPU narrative, see *GARF* 374/27s/1968 (1930): 58–69; for later published versions, see E. F. Hirchak, *Bilorus'kyi natsional-demokratyzm* (Kharkov, 1931); *Suprots' kontrrevoliutsiinaha belaruskaha natsiinal-demokratizmu* (Minsk, 1931); also, a whole series of articles in *Bol'shevik Belarusi* and *As'veta* for 1930–1931.

[234] For instance, both organizations were preceded by a smaller group formed in the civil war era. Both organizations emerged after Pilsudski's rise to power in 1926 and key national events in their home republics: the literary discussion and Shumskyi affair in Ukraine and the academic conference in Belorussia. The formation of both organizations was preceded by the return to their home republics of two important émigrés: Nikovskyi in Ukraine and Lastovskii in Belorussia. SVU was formed in mid-1926 and SVB in early 1927.

[235] *GARF* 374/27s/1968 (1930): 62; *SVU: Sten. zvit*, 35.

There was, however, one enormous difference between SVU and SVB. The latter included prominent Belorussian party leaders. The OGPU narrative asserted that the four accused party figures were not formally part of SVB, but rather met regularly with the conspirators and together they formed a united front.[236] It is striking to what degree the OGPU's invented narrative integrated Zatonskyi's concern over social contacts between party leaders and the Belorussian intelligentsia. According to the OGPU, the SVB leadership worked out its agricultural policy "under the 'noise' of social gatherings [*pod 'shumok' vecherom*]" with Prishchepov and likewise discussed educational policy "through the invitation [of Balitskii] to all sorts of social gatherings [*vecherinki*]." Balitskii and Prishchepov said they conducted these meetings "to discuss issues preliminarily." Again, picking up on Zatonskyi's concerns, the OGPU had these meetings take place at the offices of *Savetskaia Belarus* and the apartment of the "people's poet," Kupala.[237] This blunt message of the SVB affair was quickly absorbed by the remaining Belorussian leadership. Shortly after an account of SVB was first published in the press, the head of Belorussia's Agitprop Department, A. Sankevich, who was not implicated in the affair, wrote a self-critical letter to TsKK. He defended himself on all counts except for "the crudest political error of attending social gatherings and banquets" with the Belorussian intelligentsia.[238]

The OGPU narrative, then, merely translated into conspiratorial form Zatonskyi's concern that part of the Belorussian leadership had psychologically defected to the *smenovekhovstvo* intelligentsia and was implementing its political line. The OGPU had one SVB leader say that in 1926, "the leadership [of SVB] set itself the goal that all questions, before being decided by the government, should be preliminarily discussed by the Belorussian intelligentsia and then ratified by the government." Another conspirator described this "as an attempt to replace the dictatorship of the proletariat with a dictatorship of the Belorussian intelligentsia." Moreover, since SVB followed the orders of the Polish government, the OGPU had one SVB defendant boast that "the budget of the Belorussian SSR was confirmed not in Moscow, but in Warsaw."[239] This again transformed into a conspiratorial narrative, Zatonskyi's real worry that the anti-Russian mood of the Belorussian leadership could be exploited by Pilsudski's government. The OGPU, in fact, did accuse SVB of conspiring to seize neighboring RSFSR territory, and to derussify and polonize the Belorussian language. Their goal, according to the OGPU, was to isolate Belorussia from all Russian influences through "the creation of artificial barriers to the east."[240]

In Ukraine, the OGPU only hinted that Ukrainization might have helped produce the SVU conspiracy, and Kosior resolutely denounced the argument

---

[236] *GARF* 374/27s/1968 (1930): 13–14.
[237] Ibid., 15, 27, 21, 13, 17.
[238] *GARF* 374/27s/1959 (1930): 5.
[239] *GARF* 374/27s/1968 (1930): 20, 24.
[240] Ibid., 37.

that Ukrainization had strengthened, rather than disarmed, nationalism. In Belorussia, where the SVB affair implicated to some extent the entire Belorussian party leadership, the OGPU went further. As in the SVU trial, the SVB leaders confessed their aim was "to seize control of Belorussization." Since their co-conspirators included the Commissar of Education and the head of the TsK Press Department, however, it was more plausible to claim they had succeeded. Balitskii confessed to the OGPU that courses in Belorussian studies had been introduced on the advice of SVB and that "these courses, as a number of the arrested have testified, were a true school for the production of National Democratic propagandists and agitators." Adamovich was also denounced for his "aggressive Belorussization of the eastern regions [of Belorussia]; for instance, the Belorussization of Kalinin okrug at break-neck pace."[241] Since Belorussian studies courses and aggressive Belorussization were official party policy, their criticism here implied that Belorussization was in line for revision, if not abolition.

The shaken Belorussian party leadership took the hint. Zatonskyi's TsKK report and the subsequent OGPU purges led them to reverse a fundamental pillar of the Soviet nationalities policy. In late 1929, *Zviazda* published an article declaring that Belorussian nationalism was now the greatest danger in Belorussia. The major Belorussian journals immediately followed suit.[242] The argument was the same as the one made unsuccessfully by the Ukrainian revisionists in 1928–1929. The socialist offensive meant that the right deviation had become the greatest danger, and local nationalism was identified with the right.[243] In Belorussia, this argument was buttressed by the fact that Zatonskyi had already linked Prishchepov's kulak agricultural policy with his Belorussian nationalism. As in Ukraine, the foreign policy threat from Pilsudski, who had supposedly allied himself with Belorussian "national fascism," was also invoked: "Belorussian national fascism succeeded in recruiting the Communist [author] M. Zaretskii from a Soviet position. In connection with this activation of a battle against the Soviet Union . . . we must now direct our chief fire against Belorussian nationalism and national democracy . . . which is in fact conducting an assault on the USSR."[244]

As we have seen, the greatest danger principle was closely linked to *korenizatsiia*. Therefore, its reversal put the policy of Belorussization in doubt. No formal repudiation occurred, but, after years of insistent emphasis, the issue suddenly disappeared from the Belorussian press and from party resolutions. It turned out that the Belorussian leadership misinterpreted, understandably, the center's signals. In June 1930, Stalin declared great-power chauvinism was still

[241] Ibid., 9, 29–30, 38.

[242] The *Zviazda* article is summarized in Nekrashevicha, "Belaruski natsiianal-fashizm"; see also Kunitsa, "Natsiianal'nae budaunitstsva na Homel'shchine za aposhniia tri hadi," *Bol'shevik Belarusi*, nos. 1–2 (1930): 120–126.

[243] Kunitsa, "Natsiianal'nae budaunitstsva," 121.

[244] Nekrashevicha, "Belaruski natsiinal-fashizm," 36–37.

the greatest danger throughout the entire Soviet Union. The Belorussian press immediately shifted course and, as penance, launched an attack on poor Semen Dimanshtein.[245] Articles once again emphasized the threat of great-power chauvinism to Belorussization.[246] The Belorussian TsK formally reversed its policy at an October 1930 plenum.[247] The Belorussian leadership was officially rebuked for its error at a February 1931 Orgburo session. Kaganovich noted an "anti-Belorussian mood" in the Russified Gomel region and called for "militant work on the nationalities question."[248]

However, the reassertion of the Greatest Danger Principle rang even hollower in Belorussia than in Ukraine. In December 1930, after a year of high-profile work, the OGPU's uncovering of the SVB conspiracy was announced, which in turn unleashed another flood of articles attacking Belorussian nationalism.[249] Moreover, these articles did not condemn only the arrested "national democrats" from the Belorussian Academy of Sciences and the four party leaders. A whole series of "national opportunists," those who were not part of SVB but who had fallen under the conspirators' ideological influence, published self-critical articles in the press. These included Ignatovskii (a member of the TsK *Biuro*), Zhilunovich (a main party specialist on nationalities and literary affairs), and the two people's poets, Kupala and Kolas.[250] Earlier, the head of Sovnarkom, Cherviakov, was publicly denounced by TsKK for "national opportunism."[251]

The official party line, then, asserted great-power chauvinism was the greatest danger, but no one was being arrested for this crime. This deviation was criticized for no more than a slower implementation of Belorussization. Belorussian nationalism was officially the lesser danger, though it had led to a conspiratorial organization embracing the flower of the Belorussian intelligentsia and several major party figures, enjoyed the tacit support of other higher party figures, and was backed by a neighboring government intent on war. This asymmetry, even more pronounced than in Ukraine, between the formal

---

[245] Peradavaia, "Barats'ba na dva fronti u natsiianal'nim pitan'ni—barats'ba za diktaturu proletariiatu," *Bol'shevik Belarusi*, nos. 8–9 (1930): 3–6; A. Nekrashevich, "16 z'ezd UseKP/b/ ab natsiianal'nai polititsi," *As'veta*, nos. 9–10 (1930): 81–87.

[246] N. Krasina, "Ab vialikadziarzhaunim shoviniz'me," *Bol'shevik Belarusi*, nos. 8–9 (1930): 7–14.

[247] *Natsiianal'nae pitn'ne*, 304–314.

[248] *RTsKhIDNI* 17/114/212 (01.02.31): 36/1, 22–24; 75.

[249] A. V., "Politichnaia sutnas'ts' Belaruskaha natsiianal-demokratizmu," *Bol'shevik Belarusi*, nos. 10–12 (1930): 40–53; A. Al'shevski, "Belaruskaia ahentura interventav," *As'veta*, no. 12 (1930): 13–18; "Natsiianal-demokrati za 'pratsai," *As'veta*, no. 12 (1930): 18–32; *Suprots' kontrrevoliutsiinaha belaruskaha*; I. Skerskaia et al., "Belorusskii natsional-demokratizm na ideologicheskom fronte BSSR," *Pravda*, no. 357 (28.12.30): 3.

[250] Their letters were published in *Zviazda* in December 1930. For copies, see *As'veta*, no. 12 (1930): 32–41. For aftermath, see K. V. Gei, "KP/b/ Belorussii v bor'be za general'nuiu liniiu partii," *Pravda*, no. 6 (08.01.31): 3–4; "Natsional-opportunisty, fashistskie agenty Ignatovskii i Zhilunovich vybrosheny iz partii," *Pravda*, no. 23 (24.01.31): 5; K. Dunets, "Natsional-opportunistov gnat' iz partii," *Pravda*, no. 46 (16.02.31): 5.

[251] "Ab pozitsii tav. Charviakova na pitan'niakh barats'bi z pravim ukhilam i natsiianal-demokraizmam," *Bol'shevik Belarusi*, nos. 1–2 (1930): 172–173.

articulated policy direction and the policy direction implied by the use of terror was so great that the All-Union Politburo apparently decided a formal show trial would be overkill and instead confined the affair to a relatively brief, but intense, press campaign.[252]

The terror campaign of the cultural revolution, then, overwhelmingly targeted local nationalism, not great-power chauvinism. Although the campaigns were accompanied, in most republics though not in Belorussia, with official statements *and* actions in support of *korenizatsiia*, the use of terror nevertheless fundamentally undermined that policy. In the Soviet Union, one important function of terror was to mark policy priorities. The fact that the center withheld terror against great-power chauvinists, to the anguish of Mykola Skrypnyk, signaled rank-and-file party officials that this was a soft-line policy that could be passively resisted, not with impunity, but without lethal consequences. This asymmetric use of terror fatally undermined Kaganovich's hardline Ukrainization. The origins of the anti-*korenizatsiia* hard line lay in the Shumskyi affair and the growing suspicion that national communists, under the pressure of the *smenovekhovstvo* intelligentsia both within the Soviet Union and abroad, would defect to nationalism. The cultural revolution, despite its overt support for *korenizatsiia*, greatly solidified this anti-*korenizatsiia* hard line. It would triumph three years later with the Kuban affair and result in the 1933 Ukrainian nationalities terror.

Conclusion

By the end of 1930, then, the politics of *korenizatsiia* had resulted in an ambiguous situation. On the one hand, the constructive utopian aspect of cultural revolution, endorsed firmly by Stalin himself, was furthering the implementation of *korenizatsiia*. On the other hand, the destructive aspect was undermining it. Stalin's public statements remained generally positive, but he too was also not fully satisfied with the results produced by the Affirmative Action Empire. He too shared the growing concern that *korenizatsiia* was abetting the defection of national communists. Stalin's definition of local chauvinism at the Sixteenth Party Congress illustrated this concern[253]:

> The essence of the local chauvinist deviation consists of the desire to isolate oneself and withdraw into one's national shell, in the desire to minimize class contradictions within one's nation, in the desire to defend oneself from Great Russian chauvinism by distancing oneself from the general stream of socialist construction, in the desire not to see what brings together and unites the toiling masses of different nationalities within the USSR, and to see only that which can distance them from one another.

[252] *RTsKhIDNI* 17/162/9 (15.10.30): 12/21; (15.01.31): 23/3.
[253] *XVI s"ezd*, 56.

In order to address this perceived lack of unity, between 1929 and 1931 the Soviet leadership initiated a new campaign designed to foster "the brotherhood of the peoples." The visit of the Ukrainian writers' delegation to Moscow in February 1929, where Stalin defended *korenizatsiia*, was the first episode in this campaign. The campaign itself anticipated the new Soviet national constitution of the mid-1930s, which was known by the ubiquitous metaphor of "the Friendship of the Peoples."

One of the major features of the Friendship of the Peoples was the rehabilitation of traditional Russian culture and Russian nationalism as a force for Soviet unity. At first glance, the cultural revolution would seem to involve the exact opposite trend. In particular, the internationalism of the cultural revolution, as exemplified by government proposals to latinize the Russian alphabet, involved an attack on traditional Russian culture. However, at the same time, the extreme centralization and statism of the revolution from above pushed the Bolsheviks toward a greater reliance on the one nationality most closely identified with the Soviet state: the Russians. As we have seen, revolutions from above tend to evolve in an increasingly nationalist direction.

This tendency was nowhere so clearly exhibited as in Stalin's striking russification of the Bolshevik revolution from above in his remarks to a group of Soviet industrialists in February 1931[254]:

> To reduce tempos means to fall behind. And the backward are beaten. But we don't want to be beaten. No, we do not want that! The history of old Russia consisted, among other things, in continual beatings due to backwardness. The Mongol Khans beat Russia. The Turkish nobles beat Russia. The Swedish feudals beat Russia. The Polish-Lithuanian lords beat Russia. The Anglo-French capitalists beat Russia. The Japanese barons beat Russia. Everyone beat Russia, due to her backwardness. Due to military backwardness, cultural backwardness, state backwardness, industrial backwardness, agricultural backwardness. They beat Russia because it was profitable and done with impunity. . . . [If] you are weak that means you are wrong, hence one can beat and enslave you. If you are mighty, that means you are right, one must be careful of you. This is why we can lag behind no more. . . . We are 50–100 years behind the leading countries. We have to cover this distance in ten years. Either we do it, or they crush us.

Stalin's remarks were a classical statement of the agenda of a nationalist revolution from above. They were also an enormous distance from his June 1930 party congress remarks. In those remarks, overt internationalism was denounced as covert Russian nationalism. In these remarks, overt Russian nationalism was suddenly made state policy. Moreover, in his remarks Stalin went on to assert that overcoming Russia's historic backwardness was not only a duty before the

[254] I. Stalin, "O zadachakh khoziastvennikov," (1931) *Sochineniia*, vol. 13 (Moscow, 1953): 38–39.

Soviet working class, but "our duty before the world proletariat."[255] Thus, overt Russian nationalism became covert internationalism.

Where did this Russian nationalism come from? One can identify four possible sources. First, the centralization and statism of the socialist offensive led to a growing reliance on and trust of the Russians as the nationality most identified with the central state. Resistance toward central dictates, in particular Ukrainian resistance toward the use of the Russian language by all-union organs, could now be increasingly imagined as anti-Russian. A second source was foreign policy. As the Soviet Union increasingly abandoned the Piedmont Principle and adopted a defensive foreign policy stance, the cross-border ethnic ties of the non-Russians became increasingly suspect. The cultural revolutionary terror exemplified these suspicions. As the central Soviet nation, Russians were less marked by such foreign ties. Third, collectivization was resisted more fiercely and more violently in the Soviet Union's non-Russian regions.[256] This again made Russians seem a more reliable nationality. Fourth, Stalin was increasingly concerned about Russian resentment of the Affirmative Action Empire. In his unpublished remarks to the Ukrainian writers, he expressed concern about Russian resentment of *korenizatsiia* and Russian resentment over the transfer of Russian territory to non-Russian republics.[257] Since this resentment expressed itself *within* the Communist Party, it was cause for some concern. Popular party opinion favored internationalism. Having rejected that alternative, Stalin instead assuaged ethnic Russian feelings by an appeal to Russian nationalism. As the class warfare mobilization strategy of the revolution from above was gradually abandoned, state propagation of Russian nationalism increased.

Centralization, increased xenophobia, and collectivization were all aspects of the revolution from above. Russian resentment was an ongoing problem associated with the Affirmative Action Empire, although it did worsen during the socialist offensive. Therefore, while the socialist offensive brought an overt strengthening of the Affirmative Action Empire, it likewise covertly undermined its major premises. Russian nationalism, which gradually emerged into the regime's public discourse after 1933, was already present in Stalin's discourse in late 1930. In addition to his public speech to the industrialists in February 1931, Stalin wrote a striking private letter to Demian Bednyi in December 1930, in which he berated Bednyi for slandering the Russian people in a recent *feuilleton*[258]:

The revolutionary workers of all countries unanimously applaud the Soviet working class and, above all, the *Russian* working class [Stalin's emphasis], the advance-guard of the Soviet workers, its acknowledged leaders, having

[255] Ibid., 39–40.
[256] See Chapters 7 and 8.
[257] *RTsKhIDNI* 558/1/4490 (12.02.29): 16, 19–20.
[258] I. Stalin, "Tov. Demianu Bednomu" (12.12.30) *Sochineniia*, vol. 13 (Moscow, 1953): 24–25. For Bednyi's *feuilleton* and his letter defending himself, see *RTsKhIDNI* 558/1/2939 (1930).

conducted a more revolutionary and activist politics than any other proletariat of the world could dream of. The leaders of the revolutionary workers of all countries study eagerly the enormously instructive history of the Russian working class, knowing that in addition to reactionary Russia, there existed a revolutionary Russia, the Russia of Radishchevs and Chernyshevskiis, Zheliabovs and Ulianovs, Khalturinyis and Alekseevs. All of this instills in the hearts of the Russian workers (and cannot not instill) a feeling of revolutionary national pride, able to move mountains, able to create miracles.

This extraordinary passage foreshadowed the entire propaganda campaign of the 1930s. It is quite clear from this passage that Stalin aimed quite instrumentally to motivate Russian workers through an appeal to their national pride in order "to create miracles." It is therefore especially significant that Stalin first articulated this strategy in response to a "slander" of the Russian people[259]:

> And you? . . . you have proclaimed to the whole world that in the past Russia represented a vessel of iniquity and desolation . . . that "laziness" and the desire to "sit on the stove" are almost the national characteristics of the Russians overall, and that means the Russian workers as well, those who accomplished the October revolution, of course, did not stop being Russians. And you call this Bolshevik criticism. No, highly esteemed Comrade Demian, this is not Bolshevik criticism, but the *slander* of our people, the dethroning of the USSR, the dethroning of the proletariat of the USSR, the dethroning of the Russian proletariat. [Stalin's emphasis]

As in the mid-1930s, the appeal to Russian national "pride" was framed as a response to national "slander." The Russian pride propagated was designed to appeal to a resentful Russian audience, an audience that to a considerable extent did in fact exist. Finally, in the last sentences we see the identification of the Russian proletariat with both the Soviet proletariat and with Russian history. Russian history, culture, and tradition would become the new force uniting the Soviet peoples. The only major difference between Stalin's letter and the later propaganda campaigns of the mid-1930s was that the leading role in the Soviet Union was still being assigned to Russian workers, not the Russian people. Nation, however, would soon supplant class entirely.

[259] Ibid., 25.

7

The National Interpretation of the 1933 Famine

By 1931, a highly ambiguous political atmosphere surrounded the policy of *korenizatsiia*. On the one hand, an anti-*korenizatsiia* hard line had crystallized during the cultural revolution and caused a momentary policy shift in Belorussia. The terror campaign against the national *smenovekhovstvo* intelligentsia and against select national communists continued to send compromising signals about *korenizatsiia*. Growing centralization was undermining linguistic *korenizatsiia* in Ukraine and elsewhere. There was an increasing tendency to interpret anti-Russian sentiments and conflict between titular nationals and Russians as evidence of anti-center and pro-western feelings. Perhaps most important, foreign policy concerns about cross-border ethnic ties continued to intensify after the defection of the Communist Party of western Ukraine (KPZU). All of these factors combined to create a growing concern that *korenizatsiia* might be intensifying rather than disarming nationalism. On the other hand, the utopian strain in the cultural revolution had strengthened the developmentalist project of nation-building in the Soviet east. It had also intensified the stigmatization of traditional Russian culture. Finally, Stalin had publicly and decisively intervened in support of *korenizatsiia*, silenced its critics, and reversed the Belorussian policy change. Before Stalin would give his backing to the anti-*korenizatsiia* hard line, a further policy shock would be required. This shock was the grain-requisitions crisis of the fall of 1932, which culminated in the Kuban affair and the decisive December 1932 anti-Ukrainization Politburo decrees.

The Kuban affair had its origins in a prolonged territorial dispute between the Ukrainian SSR and the RSFSR. This dispute began over the delineation of the Ukrainian–RSFSR border and then persisted because of Ukraine's insistent demands that the RSFSR form Ukrainian national soviets. In fact, the creation of Ukrainian national soviets would be the completing act in the formation of the grandiose pyramid of national soviets (see Chap. 2), just as their abolition would initiate the pyramid's gradual dismantling. This decade-long territorial dispute would be increasingly interpreted by central authorities as important evidence in support of the anti-*korenizatsiia* hard line. It would be seen as an aggressive attempt by Ukrainian national communists to project Ukrainian influence into central RSFSR regions. Moreover, not only was this endeavor considered evidence of Ukrainian nationalism, it would also be connected to the growing concern over cross-border Ukrainian nationalist influence, the same cross-border influence that led to the defection of Shumskyi and Khvylovyi and that was now increasingly seen as an important threat to the unity of the Soviet Union itself.

The Piedmont Principle and Soviet Border Disputes

The connection between Soviet foreign policy goals and the formation of national territories within the Soviet Union, and particularly internal disputes over the borders of those territories, is not immediately apparent. However, it was surprisingly direct. In the 1920s, the Soviet leadership placed great hope in the Piedmont Principle: the belief that cross-border ethnic ties could be exploited to project Soviet influence into neighboring states. The Piedmont Principle was not the primary justification of either *korenizatsiia* or the formation of national territories—disarming and preventing the growth of nationalism within the Soviet Union was the main goal—but it was an important factor strengthening the leadership's commitment to *korenizatsiia* in all of its border regions. As we noted in Chapter 2, the Piedmont Principle was one of the reasons that national soviets emerged first in Ukraine. They served to embarrass Poland, which refused to provide such territories for their Ukrainian and Belorussian populations and whose treatment of these national minorities was under constant attack at the League of Nations.[1] Soviet newspapers regularly reviled Poland's mistreatment of their Ukrainians and Belorussians, and the Soviet Foreign Affairs Commissariat even made formal diplomatic protests.[2]

In one exceptional case, the Piedmont Principle was even the primary motivation for the formation of a national republic: the Moldavian ASSR. The Soviet Union never recognized Romania's annexation of the Tsarist province of Bessarabia. In 1924, they began to exert maximum pressure to provoke an uprising there. This pressure included the organization, training, financing, and even

---

[1] Laszlo Revesz, *Minderheitenschiksal in den Nachfolgestäten der Donaumonarchie* (Wien, 1990): 334–345.

[2] "Fakty hnoblennia natsmenshostei u Pol'shchi dovedeno," *Visti VUTsIK*, no. 129 (10.06.24): 1; "Ugnetenie natsional'nykh men'shinstv v Pol'she," no. 131 (10.06.24): 1.

operational direction of partisan groups in Bessarabia.[3] It also involved the formation of a Moldavian ASSR or, as Volodymyr Zatonskyi put it, "our own Moldavian Piedmont."[4] Despite its small size, the new territory was given the status of an autonomous republic "due to Moldavia's future political perspective": that is, the eventual annexation of Bessarabia.[5] For the same reason, despite the protests of Romanian communists, a Moldavian literary language was established and a separate Moldavian national identity cultivated.[6] Each detail of the republic's formation was crafted to produce the maximum political effect on Bessarabia.

The Moldavian ASSR remained a part of the Ukrainian SSR and so the Ukrainian leadership eagerly supported its formation. Both Ukraine and Belorussia, however, invoked the Piedmont Principle in order to claim territory from the RSFSR. This provoked an acrimonious struggle over the final borders between the three Slavic republics. Since the Belorussian leadership achieved their territorial goals, and thereby established a precedent for Ukrainian territorial claims, I begin with that episode. After the 1921 Treaty of Riga had ceded large swaths of majority Belorussian territory to Poland, the remaining Belorussian republic had a population of about 1.5 million, which its leaders lamented was "almost a caricature of an autonomous republic in its insignificant size."[7] Millions of Belorussians lived compactly in neighboring RSFSR regions, but these regions had been excluded from the original Belorussian republic formed in December 1918, because of both the weakness of Belorussian national consciousness and Soviet fears of Polish claims to Belorussian territory.[8]

By late 1923, the Soviet Union had reversed its foreign policy stance and adopted an aggressive posture toward Poland, which included attempts, similar to those undertaken in Bessarabia, to provoke uprisings among Poland's Belorussian and Ukrainian populations.[9] To further this use of the Piedmont Principle, the Politburo voted in November 1923 to expand Belorussia by transferring to it adjacent RSFSR territory inhabited by Belorussians.[10] This decision immediately triggered the familiar pattern of ethnic politics described in Chapter 2. The Russian leadership of the threatened Vitebsk and Gomel *gubernii* began an aggressive campaign among their population in opposition to this transfer. They were apparently very successful, since all sides in the dispute admitted that

---

[3] *RTsKhIDNI* 17/162/2 (26.03.25): 94–98.

[4] *GARF* 3316/64/933 (1930): 28. On the formation of Moldavia, see *TsDAHOU* 1/16/1 (1924–1925).

[5] *TsDAHOU* 1/16/1 (12.08.24): 95. The territory was in fact annexed in 1940 as part of the Nazi–Soviet division of eastern Europe and a Moldavian SSR formed.

[6] *TsDAHOU* 1/16/1 (19.09.24): 119–120. The original version of the language decree contained the phrase "attempt to make [the new Moldavian literary language] as close as possible to the language of the Moldavian population of Bessarabia."

[7] *GARF* 3316/16/206 (1923–1924): 2.

[8] Anatol Vialiki, "'. . . po prochtenii . . . eto pis'mo szhech'," *Belarus'ki histarychny chasopis*, no. 1 (1995): 35.

[9] *RTsKhIDNI* 17/162/1 (13.11.23): 45/13.

[10] Ibid., 8. This involved part of Smolensk *guberniia*, and most of Vitebsk and Gomel *gubernii*.

the relevant population, although overwhelmingly Belorussian, opposed the transfer.[11]

The Belorussian leadership's arguments for ignoring that sentiment anticipated those later mobilized by the Ukrainian leadership. First, they complained that the Russian authorities had artificially created this opposition[12]:

> As soon as the Politburo passed its resolution on expanding Belorussia, the Vitebsk gubkom passed a decree declaring that for Vitebsk, this question did not exist. They discussed it in the press; a calculated campaign was undertaken to demonstrate that the Belorussian question did not exist. They scared the population with the claim that immediately after the transfer to Belorussia, the Belorussian language would replace Russian everywhere. As a result, they got a [negative] response from the population.

Second, they admitted that Belorussian national consciousness was weak but argued that this was a tragic result of Tsarist russification and must be reversed. Finally, they played the foreign policy card: "The formation of an expanded Belorussia would attract the gaze of Belorussians abroad to their native Belorussia." The current situation, on the other hand, was a propaganda embarrassment: "the young are taught in school that there are three Belorussias: one occupied by Poland, the second Soviet . . . , and the third—joined for some incomprehensible reason to Russia."[13] This remark daringly analogized the Polish-Belorussian border, which official Soviet doctrine considered the result of Polish imperialist aggression, with the disputed Belorussian–RSFSR border.

The foreign policy argument prevailed. Avel Enukidze, chairman of the border dispute commission, made this clear[14]:

> One must speak frankly. This [transfer] is a blow to the local population and I understand the fear of the Belorussians. Their children understand Russian better than Belorussian, and from the cultural point of view, we sacrifice the interests of the people. . . . But in this case, we are guided by the political consideration that we must expand Belorussia and draw the attention of foreign countries to her. Based on this consideration, we are expanding the population of Belorussia, and thereby demonstrating the nationalities policy of Soviet power.

In March 1924, the border commission voted to transfer sixteen *uezdy* (approximately two million people) to Belorussia. This action illustrated both the influence of the Piedmont Principle in the Soviet Union's border republics and the rejection of the right to even voluntary assimilation.

[11] Ibid., 11–22, 34–46, 65. *XIII konferentsiia KP/b/ Belorussii. Stenograficheskii otchet* (Minsk, 1924): 45–46. Vialiki, "'. . . pro prochtenii'," 34–36.
[12] *GARF* 3316/16/206 (1924): 37–38.
[13] Ibid., 105.
[14] Ibid., 40.

Table 25. RSFSR Regions Bordering Belorussian SSR (Population by Nationality)

Region	Russian	Russian Percent of Total	Belorussian	Belorussian Percent of Total	Total
Pskov *guberniia*					
Velizhskii *uezd*	111,961	87.3	9,528	7.4	128,241
Nevel'skii *uezd*	125,156	83.4	16,746	11.2	150,030
Sebezhskii *uezd*	118,216	92.5	4,326	3.4	127,779
Smolensk *guberniia*					
Demidovskii *uezd*	162,949	98.7	141	0.1	165,024
Smolenskii *uezd*	498,279	92.3	10,246	1.9	539,871
Roslavl'skii *uezd*	351,316	95.8	3,171	0.9	366,630
Briansk *guberniia*					
Klintsovskii *uzed*	263,989	88.3	6,679	2.2	298,825
Novozybkovskii *uzed*	139,737	78.4	5,608	3.1	178,136
Eight *uezd* total	1,771,603	90.6	56,445	2.9	1,954,536

Calculated from *Vsesoiuznaia perepis' 1926 g.*, vol. I–II.

Table 26. Belorussian SSR Regions Bordering RSFSR (Population by Nationality)

Region	Belorussian	Belorussian Percent of Total	Russian	Russian Percent of Total	Total
Vitebskii *okrug*	454,402	77.9	53,508	9.2	583,391
Gomel'skii *okrug*	194,712	47.8	150,472	36.9	408,074
Kalininskii *okrug*	346,449	92.4	6,321	1.7	374,923
Orshanskii *okrug*	368,467	88.5	13,943	3.3	416,309
Four *okrug* total	1,364,030	76.5	224,344	12.6	1,782,697

Calculated from *Vsesoiuznaia perepis' 1926 g.*, vol. X.

In December 1926, another two *uezdy* were transferred from Gomel *guberniia* to Belorussia, which produced the final Belorussia–RSFSR border.[15] After this final land transfer, the border largely satisfied the Belorussian authorities and defused any possibility of a Belorussian question emerging within the RSFSR. Table 25 shows that very few Belorussians were left in bordering RSFSR *uezdy*. Likewise, Table 26 shows that with the exception of Gomel, Belorussians also formed an overwhelming majority along their side of the Belorussian–RSFSR border. Thus, the Belorussian–RSFSR border was drawn almost exactly along the ethnographic border between Belorussians and Russians, as reflected in the 1926 census results. In disputed areas, the border

[15] I. Lazovskii and I. Bibin, eds., *Sovetskaia politika za 10 let po natsional'nomu voprosu v RSFSR* (Moscow-Leningrad, 1928): 150, 171–172. For a fascinating account of the politburo debate on this issue, see Vialiki, "'. . . po prochtenii . . .'," 36–37.

favored the Belorussians slightly.[16] This outcome set a precedent for the drawing of the Ukrainian–RSFSR border.

Given the importance of the Piedmont Principle in the Belorussian–RSFSR border dispute, one would expect its prominence to have been even greater in determining the Ukrainian–RSFSR border. Poland's Ukrainian minority was larger than its Belorussian minority and more revolutionary.[17] Nevertheless, foreign policy concerns did not produce strong central support for an expanded Ukraine. Ukraine was already by far the largest economic and political unit within the Soviet Union. Indeed, central economic planners saw it as too large and had tried to divide Ukraine into two separate economic regions.[18] Moreover, Ukraine's eastern border with the RSFSR was ambiguous. The highly industrialized Donetsk region had developed an almost purely Russian urban culture, whereas the local Ukrainian-speaking peasantry lacked a strong national identity.[19] In January 1918, local Bolshevik leaders even made a bold attempt to separate from Ukraine by forming a short-lived Donets-Krivoi Rog republic.[20] In December 1919, the reestablished Ukrainian republic was given control of this region and part of the former Don Cossack territory.

Local Russian communists therefore felt Ukraine had already received preferential treatment. In 1924, the formation of a large and politically powerful North Caucasus region led instead to territorial claims on Ukraine's eastern border regions. The North Caucasus claimed the majority Russian region surrounding the industrial city Shakhty, as well as the majority Ukrainian region surrounding the port city of Taganrog. Following the now familiar pattern, the North Caucasus leadership successfully solicited support among the local population. The TsIK commission formed in April 1924 to adjudicate this dispute reported that it received "a whole series of petitions" from the local population supporting the North Caucasus position.[21]

The Ukrainian leadership reluctantly admitted that economic arguments and the local population's desires favored a territorial concession.[22] In a November 1924 decree, VUTsIK conceded the majority Russian Shakhty region and part, though not all, of Taganrog *okrug*. However, in the same decree they aggressively counterclaimed a much larger swath of RSFSR territory (with a population of 2,050,956 and a 69 percent Ukrainian majority) located along their northeastern border in the RSFSR *gubernii* of Briansk, Kursk, and Voronezh.[23] In these regions, Ukrainian propaganda efforts were more

---

[16] If one followed the ethnographic principle exactly, four majority Russian border districts of Gomel *guberniia*—Dobrushskii, Krasnobudskii, Nosovichskii, Svetilovichskii—would have been assigned to the RSFSR. These districts had a population of only 130,728.

[17] Janusz Radziejowski, *The Communist Party of Western Ukraine, 1919–1929* (Edmonton, 1983): 1–29.

[18] I. G. Aleksandrov, *Ekonomicheskoe raionirovanie Rossii* (Moscow, 1921).

[19] Hiroaki Kuromiya, *Freedom and Terror in the Donbas* (Cambridge UK, 1998).

[20] Mykola Skrypnyk, "Donbas i Ukraina," (1920) in *Statti i Promovy*, vol. 2, part 1 (Kharkov, 1929): 26–28.

[21] *GARF* 3316/17/718 (1925): 76.

[22] *TsDAHOU* 1/20/1984 (1924): 6–7.

[23] *GARF* 3316/17/718 (1925): 26; *TsDAHOU* 1/20/1984 (1924): 46–57.

successful. They attracted a large number of petitions and letters supporting a territorial transfer to Ukraine.[24] Local Russian authorities complained of illegitimate methods[25]:

> The policy of the Ukrainian authorities is to use various strategies to attract the [local] population such as granting higher salaries to village soviet workers, artificially raising the price of bread and collecting petitions to unite with Ukraine by individually canvassing each local household.

After nineteen months of haggling and lobbying, an October 1925 TsIK decree finally endorsed a compromise. The North Caucasus received the Shakhty region and three-quarters of Taganrog *okrug*. In exchange, Ukraine received about half the territory it had claimed from the RSFSR (with a population of 1,019,230 and a 58.1 percent Ukrainian majority).[26] This decision satisfied the North Caucasus but left Ukraine profoundly unhappy.

A comparison of the Belorussia–RSFSR and Ukraine–RSFSR borders at the time of the 1926 census helps explain Ukraine's dissatisfaction. As noted earlier, the Belorussia–RSFSR border was drawn almost exactly along the ethnographic boundary between Russians and Belorussians. Table 27 shows how much territory Ukraine would have received along its eastern border with the RSFSR using the same ethnographic principle. In total, therefore, Ukraine could legitimately claim RSFSR territory with a population of slightly over five million people. Not only in the size of its claim, but in having any claim at all on RSFSR territory, Ukraine was unique. In every other case throughout the entire Soviet Union, borders had been drawn to favor non-Russian territories at the expense of the Russian regions of the RSFSR.[27]

Ukraine's reply to the border compromise was encapsulated nicely in a striking *Visti VUTsIK* lead editorial signed by Ukraine's chief negotiator, VUTsIK secretary Butsenko. Butsenko rejected the finality of the border settlement, since "a million and a half Ukrainians live in areas directly bordering Ukraine but, despite this fact, are still included in the RSFSR." He argued that by ethnographic and economic considerations they should belong to Ukraine, and therefore "the state border between the Ukrainian SSR and RSFSR remains unregulated and the fate of the Ukrainian population of Voronezh and Kursk undecided."[28] Ukraine insisted, successfully, on the formation of yet another

---

[24] *GARF* 3316/17/718 (1925): 128. *TsDAHOU* 1/20/1984 (1925): 9–28.

[25] *GARF* 3316/17/720 (1928): 83.

[26] *TsDAHOU* 1/20/1984 (1925): 46–57. *GARF* 3316/17/719 (1925): 2–7. *SZ SSSR* (1926): 4/28.

[27] There is not a single exception to this rule. Tatarstan did sacrifice majority Tatar regions to Bashkiria, but not to any Russian region of the RSFSR. On the contrary, almost all autonomous republics and oblasts included majority Russian regions along their borders. For example, a strict enforcement of the ethnographic principle would have led the Oirot AO to lose 4 of 10 *raiony*; Buriat-Mongol ASSR, 4 of 11; Bashkir ASSR, 4 of 8; Tatar ASSR, 4 of 12; Dagestan ASSR, 2 of 16; Chuvash ASSR, 1 of 5; Volga German ASSR, 3 of 14; Mari AO, 4 of 9; Votskaia AO, 2 of 3. Kazakhstan would lose 9 *uezdy*.

[28] "Do vrehuliuvannia kordoniv USRR z RSFRR," *Visti VUTsIK*, no. 181 (11.08.25): 1.

Table 27. RSFSR Regions Bordering Ukrainian SSR (Population by Nationality)

Region	Ukrainian	Ukrainian Percent of Total	Russian	Russian Percent of Total	Total
Kursk *guberniia* (1 *uezd* + 7 *volosti*)	346,344	57.4	248,996	41.3	603,041
Voronezh *guberniia* (4 *uezdy* + 3 *volosti*)	970,028	65.9	499,595	33.9	1,472,229
North Caucasus *krai* (2 *okrugi* + 16 districts)	1,669,634	54.9	950,729	31.3	3,028,997
Total (5 *uezdy* + 10 *volosti* + 2 *okrug* + 16 districts)	2,986,004	58.4	1,669,320	33.2	5,104,267

Calculated from *Vsesoiuznaia perepis' 1926 g.*, vol. III (1929): 72–79; vol. V (1928): 252–266. In all cases, I include only majority Ukrainian territory that directly borders Ukraine.

commission, whose work continued through 1929.[29] The Ukrainian Politburo even sent a powerful delegation of Kaganovich, Chubar, and Petrovskii to argue their case at the all-union Politburo.[30] Only modest success was made. In 1926, Ukraine acquired three districts with a population of 178,508.[31]

Ukraine continued to hope the Politburo would intervene on its behalf. As late as 1929, Mykola Skrypnyk published an essay arguing the case for Ukraine's territorial expansion.[32] When Odessa's daily newspaper was Ukrainized in 1929, the new editor chose the name *The Black Sea Commune* (*Chornomors'ka komuna*) to emphasize the Ukrainian claim to the Black Sea region of Kuban.[33] In February 1929, during a meeting of Stalin with a Ukrainian writers' delegation, the Ukrainian nationalities specialist Andrii Khvylia raised the issue of Ukraine's borders. Stalin gave the following highly interesting response[34]:

We've discussed this question several times [in TsK], for we often change our borders, too often [laughter]—we change our borders too often. This produces a bad impression within the country and without.... Internally we must be especially careful, because such changes provoke enormous resistance from some Russians. One must consider this factor.... Every time we discuss this question, people start to growl that millions of Russians in Ukraine are being

[29] See *GARF* 3316/17/718 and 3316/17/720 for the records of these commissions.
[30] *RTsKhIDNI* 17/26/11 (02.08.27): 107/5.
[31] "Kharakter teritorii, shcho ii pryiednano do Ukrainy," *Visti VUTsIK*, no. 70 (23.09.26): 2.
[32] Mykola Skrypnyk, "Pro kordony USRR," *Statti i Promovy*, vol. 2 part I (Kharkov, 1929): 315–330.
[33] Ivan Maistrenko, *Istoriia moho pokolinnia* (Edmonton, 1985): 225.
[34] *RTsKhIDNI* 558/1/4490 (1929): 19–20. Khvylia is not identified by name in the stenogram, but his question is referred to in *TsDAHOU* 1/7/120 (03.04.29): 19–20, 26–27.

oppressed, that they can't use their native language, are being forcibly Ukrainized and so forth [laughter]. This is a purely practical question. We've discussed it twice and put it off both times—we change our borders very often. Belorussia now wants part of Smolensk *guberniia*. This provokes resistance from Russians. I think such a question should be decided carefully, not running too far ahead, so as not to produce a negative reaction from one or the other side of the population.

Stalin here acknowledged that the frequent border changes of the 1920s had exacerbated ethnic conflict. This realization explains why after 1928 the redrawing of internal borders largely ceased.

More important, Stalin showed his growing concern over Russian national sentiment. He was still able to joke about the passionate resistance to Ukrainization by Ukraine's Russian population, but not about the resistance of RSFSR Russians to the territorial expansion of Ukraine and Belorussia. Here he counseled great caution. This echoed several other contemporary episodes. As we have seen, in February 1930 the Politburo canceled plans to shift the Russian language to the Latin script. In December 1930, Stalin severely rebuked Demian Bednyi for insulting Russian national feelings[35]:

You've started to pronounce to the whole world that Russia in the past was a vessel of abomination and desolation . . . that "laziness" and the desire "to sit on the Russian stove" are almost the national traits of Russians in general, and that means Russian workers too, who having made the October Revolution, of course, do not cease to be Russians. . . .

Stalin's growing concern over Russian national feelings would eventually turn the RSFSR–Ukrainian border dispute into a decisive turning point in the Soviet nationalities policy.

However, Stalin also remained deeply concerned about Ukrainian national sentiment. His meeting with the Ukrainian writers had been organized to reassure the Soviet Ukrainian intelligentsia that the socialist offensive did not mean an abandonment of the Soviet nationalities policy. After his informal address, Stalin tellingly inquired of his audience, "How are things going in Galicia?" Stalin noted that prior to the revolution Galicia had been the political and cultural center of the Ukrainian movement and he wanted to know if "hegemony is [now] in your hands." Stalin was naturally assured that whereas Galicia had previously been considered "the Piedmont of Ukrainian culture," the opposite was now the case. When Stalin asked if Galicians could understand the Ukrainian spoken in Soviet Ukraine, one writer, picking up on Stalin's irredentist foreign policy goal, playfully replied: "You can unite Galicia to Ukraine—they understand us."[36]

---

[35] I. V. Stalin, *Sochineniia*, vol. 13 (Moscow, 1953): 25.
[36] *RTsKhIDNI* 558/1/4490 (1929): 22–23; 24; 21.

Stalin's meeting with the Ukrainian writers revealed two important facts about the Ukrainian–RSFSR border dispute: first, the increasing importance of Russian national sentiment; second, that despite the impact of the Shumskyi affair and the collapse of the KPZU, the Piedmont Principle remained an important factor in Stalin's foreign policy thinking. These conflicting claims led Stalin and the Politburo to temporize. They never definitively rejected Ukraine's claims, but they also did not authorize another territorial transfer after a final October 1928 TsIK resolution, which transferred a meager fourteen villages from the RSFSR to Ukraine.[37]

The Ukrainian Question in the RSFSR

Ukraine's second response to the unsatisfactory 1925 border resolution, also articulated in Butsenko's 1925 *Visti VUTsIK* lead editorial, was to defend the national rights of the RSFSR Ukrainians. Butsenko maintained that six and a half million RSFSR Ukrainians were being denied their national rights, and that Ukraine must interest itself in the "question of the RSFSR's Ukrainian population."[38] Butsenko's article was remarkable not only in publicly claiming RSFSR territory, but also in its open complaints about the RSFSR's mistreatment of its Ukrainian minority, which echoed in a more polite form the simultaneous shrill press campaign being undertaken to protect the Ukrainian minority in Poland. Mykola Skrypnyk, in fact, went so far as to make this analogy explicit. At an April 1925 Ukrainian TsK plenum, he praised a December 1924 Komintern resolution, which had called for the eventual transfer of all majority Ukrainian regions of Poland, Czechoslovakia, and Romania to Ukraine, and went on to advocate the extension of this principle to the majority Ukrainian regions in the RSFSR.[39] The Ukrainian SSR was adopting the role of Piedmont not only for Ukrainians living outside the Soviet Union, but also for those living in Russia.

The 1925 border compromise, then, led to the emergence of a Ukrainian question in the RSFSR. The Ukrainian question proved important for several reasons. First, the 1926 census registered 7,873,331 Ukrainians living in the RSFSR. Ukrainians were thus twice the size of the next largest minority (3.85 million Kazakhs) and represented 29.7 percent of all non-Russians living in the RSFSR. If one excludes autonomous republics and oblasts, Ukrainians made up 53.1 percent of all non-Russians living in the Russian regions of

[37] *GARF* 3316/17/120 (1928): 112.
[38] *Visti VUTsIK*, no. 181 (11.08.25): 1; see also an earlier article, "Stan ukrains'koi natsmenshosti v SRSR," *Visti VUTsIK*, no. 172 (30.07.25): 3. The 1926 census would reveal that there were actually 7.9 million Ukrainians in the RSFSR.
[39] Skrypnyk, "Zlikviduvaty liuksemburgiianstvo," (1925) *Statti i promovy*, 75–76; see also "Pro Kordony USRR," (1928) *Statti i promovy*, 315–330. In 1928, Skrypnyk even attempted to get Komintern backing for his position; see N. Skrypnik, *Natsional'nyi vopros v programme kominterna* (Kharkov, 1929): 35–37.

the RSFSR.[40] The status of these Ukrainians would largely determine whether the RSFSR (excluding its autonomous republics and oblasts) would become a multiethnic or an almost purely Russian national space. Second, the Ukrainian question also touched on the important issue of assimilation. In 1926, only 67 percent of RSFSR Ukrainians reported Ukrainian as their native language.[41] Most local officials viewed this process of assimilation as natural (in large part due to the popular belief that Ukrainians and Belorussians did not differ essentially from Russians), and argued it should not be artificially impeded. However, Soviet policy was consistently hostile to assimilation. The Ukrainian question therefore also represented a test case in the Soviet commitment to preventing even voluntary assimilation.

Third, the fate of the RSFSR Ukrainians became a major point of tension between Ukraine and its neighboring Russian territories and so intersected with Stalin's growing concern over Russian national resentment, in particular as it manifested itself within the local Russian party leadership. Fourth, in Kuban the Ukrainian question became intertwined with the Cossack question, and therefore with questions of land ownership, political reliability, and estate identity (*soslovie*). As we observed in Chapter 2, the presence of these factors made the resistance to the formation of national soviets in Kazakhstan, Kirgizia, and the North Caucasus autonomous oblasts particularly fierce and led to popular attempts to expel Russians from those territories. In Kuban, the Cossacks were ethnically Ukrainian and the peasantry a mixture of Russian and Ukrainian settlers. Nevertheless, this coincidence of conflict along *soslovie*, land ownership, and national and territorial lines once again proved particularly explosive.

Finally, the Ukrainian question exposed the awkward position of the RSFSR government. Whereas the Ukrainian and Belorussian governments aggressively pursued their republic's national interests, the RSFSR government functioned more as a second central government (Rykov and Kalinin were head of both the USSR and RSFSR Sovnarkom and TsIK, respectively) and therefore more often took a neutral stance in quarrels between Russian regions and their non-Russian neighbors. This was evident in the RSFSR's hesitant resistance to Ukrainian and Belorussian territorial claims, and especially in the RSFSR government's aggressive support of full national rights for its Ukrainian minority.

The RSFSR Commissariat of Education was particularly tenacious in its insistence on the formation of Ukrainian-language schools. Already in late 1924, it

[40] These numbers are calculated from the 1926 census results. *Vsesoiuznaia perepis' naseleniia 1926 goda. Tom IX. RSFSR* (Moscow, 1929): 65–95. In the RSFSR as a whole, the population was 100,623,474; 74,072,096 Russians; 7,873,331 Ukrainians; 26,551,378 non-Russians. In the twenty-three ASSRs and AOs of the RSFSR, the total population was 19,417,551; 5,404,981 Russians; 1,218,967 Ukrainians, 14,013,570 non-Russians. In the RSFSR minus ASSRs and AOs, the total population was 81,205,923; Russians, 68,667,115; Ukrainians 6,654,364; non-Russians 12,537,808.

[41] Ibid., 34–35. Of 7,837,331 RSFSR Ukrainians, 5,276,787 considered Ukrainian their native language. The numbers for Belorussians were 94,859 of 637,634 for 14.9 percent; Jews, 278,474 of 566,917 for 49.1 percent; Poles, 83,785 of 197,827 for 42.3 percent.

undertook an examination of the state of Ukrainian-language education in the RSFSR. This study found only 193 Ukrainian-language primary schools and a few secondary schools. Only 5 percent of Ukrainian children studied in Ukrainian schools.[42] Narkompros called a conference in April 1925 to discuss this glaring violation of Soviet principles. The uniquely dismal performance was attributed to popular doubts about the existence of a Ukrainian nationality: "Not one nationality in the Soviet Union has produced so many doubts as to its very existence as the Ukrainian nationality." Narkompros officials admitted that although the RSFSR Ukrainians "were coming to national consciousness after the dark Tsarist times . . . , they still had a disdainful attitude towards their own language [and] a negative attitude to the Ukrainization of their schools." The conference considered this a historical tragedy to be overcome, not an argument against Ukrainization, and ordered all primary and secondary education in Ukrainian areas to be shifted to Ukrainian.[43]

This decree was resisted by both local authorities and much of the RSFSR Ukrainian population. In Kursk *guberniia*, a Narkompros official sent to implement Ukrainization was told that "you are trying to build *Khokhliandiia* in Kursk *guberniia*."[44] This hostility was undoubtedly connected to fears of Ukrainian territorial pretensions. In Voronezh, a Ukrainian petition was returned with the comment: "Write in Russian, as we are not yet in Ukraine, but the RSFSR."[45] In Kursk, a bureaucrat asked some local Ukrainians if they wanted a Ukrainian school and "received an unexpected answer—in favor of joining Ukraine."[46] As a result of this resistance, by January 1, 1927 there were still only 590 Ukrainian-language schools servicing the RSFSR's 7.9 million Ukrainians. Narkompros, however, continued to press aggressively for more Ukrainian schools.[47] In particular, it rejected the argument that the local population should be given the right to decide the language of instruction in their schools. A 1926 programmatic Narkompros document on native-language education made this absolutely clear[48]:

> The fundamental principle for determining the language of instruction of a member of any nationality should be the native language of the child. . . . Determining the language of instruction by surveying the population, as is done in some places, must be rejected.

This formulation was repeated in an August 1927 Narkompros resolution on Ukrainization: "A survey of the population, as is often practiced when shifting schools to instruction in the native language, and sometimes even a plebiscite,

[42] *GARF (TsGA)* 296/1/97 (29–30.04.25): 3, 62.
[43] Ibid., 29, 62, 68, 83.
[44] *GARF* 1235/120/36 (1925–1926): 265–268.
[45] Z. Ostrovskii, *Problema Ukrainizatsii i Belorussizatsii v RSFSR* (Moscow, 1931): 60.
[46] *GARF (TsGA)* 296/1/323 (1926–1927): 66.
[47] *GARF (TsGA)* 296/1/444 (1928): 58; 296/1/97; 296/1/168; 296/1/172; also *GARF* 1235/120/36.
[48] *GARF (TsGA)* 296/1/169 (1926): 4–5.

must be rejected."[49] Once again, Soviet decolonization meant resistance to even voluntary assimilation.

Narkompros lacked the clout to force local authorities to implement its decrees, so it consistently called on central authorities to support its position.[50] Central party authorities intervened in the Ukrainian question only indirectly. In April 1925, a TsK plenum passed a resolution, based on a report by Syrtsov, on the Cossack question.[51] The resolution was motivated by OGPU reports of widespread Cossack dissatisfaction, of "mass counterrevolutionary work" among the Kuban Cossacks, and of the ongoing threat of a Cossack "Vendee."[52] Syrtsov noted that the non-Cossack population viewed Cossacks "as a single united counterrevolutionary mass." As a result, in Cossack regions, "divisions along *soslovie* lines" prevailed over class divisions, and an above-class alliance of wealthy and poor Cossacks had formed.[53] The plenum endorsed the accepted Soviet solution to this problem: Cossacks were granted national minority status, including their own national soviets. In Kuban, where the Cossacks spoke a Ukrainian dialect and the overwhelming majority declared themselves Ukrainians in the 1926 census, this meant Ukrainization.

Kuban would be the decisive testing-ground for Ukrainization in the RSFSR. The Kuban *okrug* had a Ukrainian population of 915,450 (61.5 percent), of which about 580,000 were Kuban Cossacks.[54] In 1917 and 1918, the Kuban Cossacks had formed a separatist local government (the *Kuban Rada*), and many Ukrainian-language schools and cultural institutions had been established. These were all abolished after the Bolshevik victory in the civil war, after which "the word 'Ukrainian' was understood as meaning counterrevolutionary."[55] However by 1924–1925, despite strong opposition from North Caucasus authorities, 150 Ukrainian schools had reemerged in Kuban.[56] The TsK Cossack resolution dramatically accelerated this process. The North Caucasus *kraikom* immediately relented and decreed the Ukrainization of schools throughout the North Caucasus.[57] Ukrainization was thus not confined to the 580,000 Kuban Cossacks, but extended to all three million North Caucasus Ukrainians. In Kuban itself, a June 1926 party conference resolution supported the Ukrainization of the entire Kuban *okrug* government.[58]

[49] "Po radnatsmenu," *Novym Shliakhom*, no. 1 (1927): 82.
[50] *GARF (TsGA)* 296/1/172 (1926): 15; 296/1/297 (1928): 100b; 296/1/97 (1925): 6.
[51] *RTsKhIDNI* 17/2/172 (25.04.25).
[52] *GARF* 1235/140/1149 (1928): 18. *RTsKhIDNI* 17/84/904 (1925): 82.
[53] *RTsKhIDNI* 17/2/172 (1925): 390–396.
[54] *Vsesoiuznaia perepis'* Tom V (1928): 252. *GARF* 1235/140/1149 (1928): 21. The 1926 census did not include Cossacks. The Kuban GPU reported 580,000 Ukrainian-speaking Kuban Cossacks and 170,000 Russian-speaking "line" Cossacks.
[55] *RTsKhIDNI* 17/112/670 (12.06.25): 103.
[56] "Kul'tosvitnia robota sered ukrains'koi natsmenshosti na Kubani," *Visti VUTsIK*, no. 196 (27.08.25): 3.
[57] *Visti VUTsIK*, no. 196 (29.08.25): 3. *RTsKhIDNI* 17/112/670 (12.06.25): 84/10. *GARF* 3316/64/576, "Materialy po ukrainizatsii na Severnom Kavkaze," (1928): 16.
[58] *GARF* 3316/64/576 (1928): 16.

However, these decrees were never realized due to fierce resistance from local Russian officials and from within the North Caucasus government itself. VTsIK sent a research team to investigate this resistance and found four local arguments against Ukrainization: (1) the Kuban "Ukrainians" spoke a distinct "Kuban" language; (2) they were already assimilated; (3) it would increase *soslovie* hostilities; (4) the Cossack leadership would interpret it as a concession and demand more autonomy.[59] The latter two arguments gave the Ukrainian question in Kuban its special force. One official bluntly told the VTsIK commission: "The question of Ukrainization is tied to the question of who will be in power—us [*inogorodnie*, i.e. non-Cossacks] or them [Cossacks]." Another official argued that the Cossacks "understand by Ukrainization, that they'll get their 'united, undivided' and kick out all the Communists." Another agreed that "if we carry through Ukrainization, then the GPU will have to be on special alert."[60] This concern found its expression in a secret North Caucasus circular in August 1926 that ordered an end to Ukrainization only a year after its official endorsement.[61]

During the VTsIK inspection, the head of the Kuban GPU, Mironov, wrote a perceptive letter explaining the failure of Ukrainization in 1925–1926.[62] He noted that after the civil war, large amounts of Cossack land had been seized and transferred to the non-Cossack population. This land reform was just taking place in 1925 at the same time that Ukrainization was being introduced. Mironov also emphasized that memories of Cossack political domination were very strong, and both sides were quite conscious of the "change in roles" that had occurred after the revolution. Mironov agreed that the majority of Cossacks still dreamed of reestablishing the Kuban *rada*, and that in 1925 mass Cossack counterrevolutionary actions still required constant repression[63]:

> [T]he entire party-soviet *aktiv* thought that [Ukrainization] meant giving power into the hands of Cossack counterrevolution, especially since it coincided with the land transfer and the vicious battle over land reform . . . the non-Cossack population, only just having received land, but not yet settled on it, met [Ukrainization] with panic and opposed it ferociously. . . .

Mironov's account bore a striking resemblance to the conflict in Kazakhstan. In each case, the combination of conflict along national, land ownership, status, and territorial lines proved exceptionally fierce.

In the North Caucasus, this conflict was complicated by the interference of Ukraine. As already noted, after the unsatisfactory 1925 border settlement, Ukraine pursued a two-pronged strategy: pressure for a revised border

[59] Ibid., 15.
[60] Ibid., 30; 58; 80. Ostrovskii, *Problema Ukrainizatsii*, 35.
[61] Ibid., 17–18; GARF 3316/22/56 (1929): 7–11; Ostrovskii, *Problema Ukrainizatsii*, 53–54.
[62] GARF 1235/140/1149 (1928): 16–22.
[63] Ibid., 18–19.

settlement and pressure to grant RSFSR Ukrainians full national minority status. In the latter campaign, Ukraine generally observed the proprieties of bureaucratic conflict and did not attack its rivals publicly. However, Iurii Larin's public attacks on Ukraine's national minorities policy in 1925–1926 led Ukrainian officials to counterattack. At the April 1926 TsIK session, in response to Larin's attack, Zatonskyi raised the issue of the treatment of Ukrainians in Kursk.[64] Khvylia likewise wrote an article on the RSFSR Ukrainians in the Ukrainian TsK newspaper *Komunist*.[65]

However, it was the secret reversal of Ukrainization in Kuban in 1926 that led Ukraine to launch a remarkable public press campaign against its RSFSR neighbors. Ukraine's government newspaper, *Visti VUTsIK*, published only a few articles on the RSFSR Ukrainians in 1925 and 1926, but in 1927 the paper inaugurated a regular column on "Ukrainians in the RSFSR."[66] These columns were striking for their polemical tone, attacking both North Caucasus officials and central Russian organs for failing to enforce the Soviet nationalities policy.[67] Most articles focused on the North Caucasus, but the 1927 press campaign expanded the scope of the Ukrainian question to cover the large Ukrainian populations in the Far East, Kazakhstan, and Siberia.[68] The most striking characteristic of these articles, however, was their passionate expression of ethnic solidarity[69]:

> We, citizens of the Ukrainian SSR, interest ourselves in how Ukrainians live beyond Ukraine. We are not indifferent to how Ukrainians in West Ukraine live, not indifferent to the living conditions of Ukrainians who emigrated to America. Likewise, we are interested in how those Ukrainians, who are scattered across the Soviet Union, live.

In this spirit, a twelve-article travelogue about the North Caucasus instructed Ukraine's readers about the historic Ukrainian presence there and about the interest of North Caucasus Ukrainians in their ethnic brothers in Ukraine.[70]

RSFSR Ukrainians did, in fact, appear to be increasingly aware of the Ukrainian SSR and increasingly disposed to view her as a cultural and political patron. Both Ukrainian state organs and Ukrainian newspapers reported receiving from RSFSR Ukrainians large numbers of complaints about mistreatment on national

---

[64] *2 sessiia TsIK SSSR 3 sozyva. Stenograficheskii otchet* (Moscow, 1926): 513.

[65] In *Komunist* (14.04.26). Noted in *TsDAHOU* 1/20/2522 (1927): 59; in addition, see "Ukraintsi v RSFRR," *Komunist*, no. 135 (16.06.26): 1.

[66] I counted four articles on the RSFSR Ukrainians in 1925 and six in 1926. In 1927 there were 34 columns on the RSFSR Ukrainians, most containing several articles.

[67] See, for example, "Ukraintsi v RSFRR," *Visti VUTsIK*, no. 37 (15.02.27): 3; no. 133 (18.06.27): 4; no. 233 (12.10.27): 5; no. 261 (15.11.27): 4.

[68] "Ukraintsi na Dalekomu Skhodi," *Visti VUTsIK*, no. 83 (13.04.26): 2; "Ukraintsi v Kazakstanu," nos. 194–198 (27.08–01.09.27); "Ukraintsi v Sybiru," no. 229 (07.10.27): 4.

[69] "Ukraintsi na Dalekomu Skhodi," *Visti VUTsIK*, no. 83 (13.04.26): 2.

[70] *Visti VUTsIK*, nos. 39–76 (27.04–13.06.27).

grounds and requests for Ukrainian cultural assistance.[71] Ukraine responded by sending books, journals, and even Ukrainian teachers.[72] Thus, Ukraine began to be perceived as and act as a Piedmont for RSFSR Ukrainians. This emerging relationship infuriated and threatened North Caucasus leaders[73]:

> I will not speak about the official polemic, which is being carried out on the pages of the Ukrainian press. Everyone knows about that. But we know of another, unofficial side. We have this on the basis of GPU information. This is a course directed towards an independent Ukraine.

This comment by the head of the North Caucasus government may have referred to a group arrested by the GPU in 1927 for organizing to help unite Kuban to Ukraine. Ironically, one member of this group confirmed North Caucasus suspicions by petitioning for clemency on the grounds that he had been inspired by Andrii Khvylia's 1926 newspaper article.[74] Or alternatively the comment might have referred to GPU informational reports, such as the following October 1928 report on the antisoviet movement in the countryside[75]:

> In the North Caucasus, one must not forget that in Kuban, besides estate antagonism, there also exists a national attraction of antisoviet elements to establishing ties with antisoviet elements in Ukraine; and the chauvinist slogans of the latter are also present in the Kuban anti-soviet movement. Therefore in investigating counterrevolutionary groups with a national character, one must probe to see if they are not tied to Ukrainian counterrevolutionaries.

It was exactly these putative nationalist ties between Kuban and Ukraine that would form the basis of the national interpretation of the famine that would emerge in December 1932.

With the spread of national soviets throughout the RSFSR in 1926 and 1927, VTsIK joined Narkompros RSFSR in its campaign for Ukrainian national institutions. In late 1927, a VTsIK instructor, Z. Ostrovskii, was sent to research Ukrainization in Voronezh and Kursk, where he found VTsIK's decrees on national soviets had been almost entirely ignored.[76] Ostrovskii issued a scathing

[71] *RTsKhIDNI* 17/112/670 (12.06.25): 96; *GARF* 1235/120/36 (1925): 220, 243; "Ukrains'ka knyzhka v Ukrains'kykh koloniiakh Soiuzu," *Visti VUTsIK*, no. 132 (13.06.25): 1; "Stan ukrains'koi natsmenshosti v SRSR," no. 172 (30.07.25): 3; "Neukrains'ki ukraintsi," no. 236 (15.10.27): 3.

[72] "Kul'tosvitnia robota sered ukrains'koi natsmenshosti na Kubani," *Visti VUTsIK*, no. 196 (29.08.25): 3; "Neukrains'ki ukraintsi," no. 236 (15.10.27): 3; Skrypnyk, "Zustrich" (1929) in *Statti i promovy*, 351–352.

[73] *GARF* 1235/140/1149 (1928): 12.

[74] *TsDAHOU* 1/20/2522 (1927): 58–60.

[75] A. Berelovich and V. Danilov eds., *Sovetskaia derevnia glazami VChK-OGPU-NKVD 1918–1939. Vol. 2. 1923–1929. Dokumenty i materialy* (Moscow, 2000): 817.

[76] Ostrovskii, *Problema Ukrainizatsii*, 46–47. Voronezh in 1927 had undertaken an experimental *Ukrainizatsiia* of three *volosti*. Kursk had passed a resolution for the Ukrainization of 35 village soviets but had done nothing. Skrypnyk, "Pro Kordony USRR," 321–327.

report. With Kazakhstan having capitulated and formed Russian national soviets in 1927, the RSFSR Ukrainians remained the major glaring flaw in the pyramid of national soviets. At VTsIK's 1928 national minorities conference, the Ukrainian question now predominated.[77] The combination of increased VTsIK attention and the onset of cultural revolution led to rapid progress. Voronezh and Kursk *gubernii* combined in 1929 to form the Central-Black Earth region, which immediately passed an ambitious plan calling for the Ukrainization of twenty-seven majority Ukrainian districts and 780 village soviets.[78]

The North Caucasus resisted central pressures more stubbornly. At first they refused even to send a representative to VTsIK's 1928 national minority conference and, when threatened by VTsIK, sent a representative who categorically denied the necessity of Ukrainization.[79] VTsIK responded with a coordinated campaign mobilizing four different central organs. In the spring of 1928 Narkompros sent a commission to Kuban that produced a resolution reiterating their call for Ukrainization.[80] In March 1928, the Soviet of Nationalities, on the initiative of Skrypnyk, authorized a major investigation of Ukrainians in the RSFSR, focusing on the North Caucasus.[81] Finally, in July and August 1928, Ostrovskii headed a combined VTsIK/TsKK investigation of nationalities policy in the North Caucasus.[82] These efforts finally induced the North Caucasus leadership to relent and, in December 1928, they approved a three-year plan for the Ukrainization of all thirty-seven of their majority Ukrainian districts.[83] The capitulation of the North Caucasus led to the rapid spread of Ukrainization to the Lower Volga, Kazakhstan, and the Far East.[84] The triumph of Ukrainization in the RSFSR marked the final victory of the system of national soviets, as well as a surprising victory for the central national minorities bureaucracy (the Soviet of Nationalities, VTsIK's Nationalities Department, Narkompros' Sovnatsmen) over strong local party resistance.

It was also a victory for Ukraine that led to a major strengthening of its role as a cultural and political Piedmont. RSFSR regions increasingly appealed to Ukraine for help in Ukrainization.[85] In February 1929, the Ukrainian Narkom-

---

[77] *Soveshchanie upolnomochennykh po rabote sredi natsional'nykh men'shinstv. Stenograficheskii otchet* (Moscow, 1928): 196–203; see also "Ukrainizatsiia trekh okrugov TsChO," *Pravda*, no. 248 (24.10.28): 4.

[78] Ostrovskii, *Problema Ukrainizatsii*, 70; N. Aristidov, "Obsluzhivanie natsmen'shinstv—na vysshuiu stupen'," *Rabota sovetov* [Voronezh], no. 12 (1932): 23–24.

[79] *Soveshchanie upolnomochennykh*, 83.

[80] *GARF* 3316/64/576 (1928): 13.

[81] *GARF* 3316/20/204 (1928): 3–5; 29–47; 60–61; 3316/22/56 (1929): 7–11.

[82] *GARF* 316/64/576 (1928); Ostrovskii, *Problema Ukrainizatsii*, 55–56.

[83] Ostrovskii, *Problema Ukrainizatsii*, 76; *GARF* 3316/22/56 (1929): 66–67.

[84] *O rabote sredi natsional'nykh men'shinstv v N.-V. krae* (Saratov, 1929): 7–9. T. Gorb, "Stanovyshche Ukrains'koi liudnosti Kazakstanu," *Bil'shovyk Ukrainy*, nos. 19–20 (1930): 60–66. *GARF* 1235/141/1356 (1931): 17. *II Sessiia VTsIK XV Sozyva. Stenograficheskii otchet* (Moscow, 1931): biul. 9: 1–9. Ostrovskii, *Problema Ukrainizatsii*, 70. *Smolensk Archive*, Reel 52, WKP 482 (1929): 1–8; WKP 483 (1929): 1–19.

[85] *RTsKhIDNI* 17/26/36 (21.04.30): 1/7; 17/26/48 (27.06.31): 62/1; *GARF (TsGA)* 296/1/475 (1931): 311.

pros passed a resolution outlining an impressive list of services they would provide: Ukrainian teachers, textbooks, literature, journals, pedagogical programs, art exhibits, musical and theatrical presentations, films, radio programs, help in setting up museums and in organizing literary societies, reserved places in Ukrainian universities, and much more. This decree began with a concise statement of the Piedmont Principle[86]:

> Narkompros, as an organ of the Ukrainian soviet state [*derzhavnist'*], which undertakes the leading role in the creation of general cultural values for the entire Ukrainian people [*narod*], is obligated to consciously place before itself the task of the practical servicing of the cultural interests and needs of the entire Ukrainian people, that is not only the population of the Ukrainian SSR, but also Ukrainians living in other soviet republics.

Ukrainian newspapers encouraged their readers not to be "indifferent" and to support help "for the distant settlements of Ukrainians . . . [in] fraternal republics."[87] Ukraine's most important export was teachers. The Far East, for instance, relied on Ukraine for 30 percent of its teachers.[88] These teachers often arrived spontaneously. In 1932, Narkompros officially sent only 85 teachers to the RSFSR, but over 5000 arrived on their own initiative.[89] This again demonstrated the spontaneous ties that were developing between Ukraine and the RSFSR Ukrainians.

Thanks to Ukraine's assistance and the RSFSR Ukrainians' relatively high cultural level, Ukrainization proceeded much more rapidly than similar programs for other RSFSR national minorities. By 1932, the Central-Black Earth region had almost completely Ukrainized its educational system, including the creation of dozens of universities.[90] The number of Ukrainians attending Ukrainian-language schools in the North Caucasus went from 12 percent in 1928–1929 to 80 percent in 1931–1932.[91] The Far East had no Ukrainian schools in 1929–1930, but two years later had 1076 primary and 219 secondary Ukrainian schools.[92] No other national minority had made such rapid progress. The creation of literary organizations, theaters, museums, institutes, and a large network of newspapers also took place unusually quickly.[93]

[86] "Postanova Kolehii NKO," *Biuleten' narodn'oho komisariatu osvity*, no. 11 (1929): 2.

[87] "Ukraintsi v soiuznykh respublikakh," *Visti VUTsIK*, no. 7 (09.01.30): 6; no. 31 (07.02.30): 3.

[88] *GARF (TsGA)* 296/1/544 (1932): 61.

[89] *TsDAVOU* 166/10/914 (1932): 69. The spontaneous outflow of teachers was undoubtedly a response to rural famine in Ukraine, which was already quite severe in 1931–1932 and then spread to the rest of the Soviet Union's other grain-growing regions in 1932–1933.

[90] *GARF (TsGA)* 296/1/475 (1932): 309–313.

[91] *GARF (TsGA)* 296/1/542 (1932): 87–101; TsDAVOU 166/9/784 (1931): 69–70.

[92] M. Golubovskii, *Leninskaia natsional'naia politika v deistvii* (Khabarovsk, 1932): 23.

[93] *GARF* 3316/22/56 (1932): 109–1090b; L. Saratovskii, "Boevye voprosy ukrainizatsii na Severnom Kavkaze," *Leninskii put'* (Rostov), no. 6 (1931): 34–39; O. Sosulia, "Kul'turno-natsional'noe stroitel'stvo v TsChO," *Rabota sovetov* (Voronezh), nos. 10–11 (1931): 40–42; I. Zamch, *Partorganizatsiia na bor'bu za ukrainizatsiiu* (Rostov-na-donu, 1932): 3–9.

Table 28. Number of National Soviets, 1931–1935

	Districts	Village Soviets
RSFSR Ukrainian	130 (approx.)	4000 (approx.)
RSFSR non-Ukrainian	161	3004
in ASSRs/AOs	54	660
outside ASSRs/AOs	107	2344
Ukrainian SSR	27	1085
Belorussian SSR	0	67
Transcaucasus SFSR	18	n/a
Central Asia	n/a	n/a

"Natsional'nye raiony i sel'skie sovety RSFSR" (Moscow, 1935), in *GARF* 1235/130/3 (1935). The Ukrainian figures are approximate. There were 37 national districts in the North Caucasus, 27 in Central-Black Earth, 29 in Kazakhstan, 9 in the Far East. I used census data to estimate another 28. The Central-Black Earth region had 780 village soviets. I used their ratio of Ukrainian districts-village soviets to approximate 4000 village soviets. A few regions there did not report village soviets and so that number is slightly understated. For comparison, in December 1933 VTsIK's *otdel natsional'nostei* reported 117 national districts and over 3000 village soviets, numbers that are comparable. N. N. Nurmakov, "III Vserossiiskoe soveshchanie rabotnikov sredi natsional'nykh men'shinstv," *Revoliutsiia i natsional'nosti*, no. 1 (1934): 81.

Ukrainization in the RSFSR had enormous significance for the entire Soviet national minorities system. Table 28 shows how the enormous size of the RSFSR Ukrainian population (7.9 million) meant that Ukrainian national soviets made up a significant part of the entire Soviet total.[94]

Ukrainian soviets represented a majority of national soviets in the Russian regions of the RSFSR. They were the principal reason that those regions were not almost purely Russian, since most of the other soviets represented the numerically small peoples of the north. In addition, Ukrainian soviets were important politically because they represented an ongoing point of tension between Ukraine and neighboring RSFSR regions.

The Kuban Affair

In late 1932, during that year's ferocious grain requisitions campaign, this tension finally exploded in the form of the Kuban affair. The Kuban affair linked

[94] The Ukrainian figures are approximate. There were 37 national districts in the North Caucasus, 27 in Central-Black Earth, 29 in Kazakhstan, 9 in the Far East. I used census data to estimate another 28. The Central-Black Earth region had 780 village soviets. I used their ratio of Ukrainian districts-village soviets to approximate 4000 village soviets. A few regions there did not report village soviets and so that number is slightly understated. For comparison, in December 1933 VTsIK's *otdel natsional'nostei* reported 117 national districts and over 3000 village soviets, numbers that are comparable. N. N. Nurmakov, "III Vserossiiskoe soveshchanie rabotnikov sredi natsional'nykh men'shinstv," *Revoliutsiia i natsional'nosti*, no. 1 (1934): 81.

the central authorities' growing concerns about *korenizatsiia* with their immediate famine emergency to produce a national interpretation of their grain
requisitions crisis. In December 1932, this led to two important anti-Ukrainization Politburo decrees that initiated a fundamental revision of the Soviet nationalities policy. Before we examine this important policy shift, it will be helpful to
summarize the forces that were already undermining *korenizatsiia* in the fall of
1932. First, the defection of the KPZU had not only cast doubts on the efficacy
of the Piedmont Principle, but had also caused concern that cross-border ethnic
ties might be used to undermine Soviet unity. The rise of extreme nationalism
in eastern Europe and, above all, in Germany exacerbated this concern and led
the Soviet Union to adopt a more defensive foreign policy stance. Second, the
persistence of factionalism along national lines in almost all the non-Russian
party organizations, exemplified in the most alarming form by the Shumskyi
affair, increased concerns that *korenizatsiia* might be exacerbating rather than
disarming nationalism, that instead of "changing the landmarks" of nationalists
to communism, it might be doing the exact opposite. National communism
might be transformed into nationalist communism.

Third, the terror campaigns of the cultural revolution had focused asymmetrically on "local nationalists," who supported *korenizatsiia* too eagerly,
rather than "great-power chauvinists," who resisted its implementation. Given
the use of terror as a system of signaling, this undermined the perception of
central support for *korenizatsiia*. Also, while the terror campaigns targeted the
national *smenovekhovstvo* intelligentsia, a number of national communists were
also arrested, which increased the growing sense that national communists were
potentially disloyal. Fourth, the growth in centralization that accompanied the
socialist offensive had undermined linguistic *korenizatsiia*. Perhaps more important, it had increased the tendency to interpret national communist assertiveness as fundamentally anti-center and therefore disloyal. Fifth, this emerging
belief that the Affirmative Action Empire was not providing sufficient Soviet
unity for the new environment created by the socialist offensive and an increasingly alarming foreign policy threat prompted a reconsideration of the Russian
question. The Affirmative Action Empire required a deemphasis of Russian
national self-expression in order to strengthen the unity of the multiethnic
Soviet state. By 1930, Stalin was expressing concern about the Russian national
resentment this strategy had produced. Symbolic hostility to traditional Russian
culture in Belorussia and Ukraine, though not in the Soviet east, was likewise
being interpreted as evidence of prowestern and therefore anti-Soviet sentiment.
The interpretation of local anti-Russian sentiment and the existence of Russian
resentment as evidence of anti-center and therefore anti-Soviet sentiment would
greatly compromise both the policy of *korenizatsiia* and the Affirmative Action
Empire itself.

Ukraine's campaign to annex neighboring RSFSR territory and to serve
as the cultural and political patrons of the RSFSR Ukrainians exacerbated most
of these five concerns. The campaign was justified by the Piedmont Principle
and therefore confirmed central concerns that cross-border ethnic ties could

be used not only to project communist influence into neighboring states, but also to project Ukrainian nationalist influence into the Soviet Union's key border republic and, even more alarming, into its core RSFSR regions. The Ukrainian campaign illustrated the strength of national communist sentiment as it pursued a long-standing project of the Ukrainian *smenovekhovstvo* intelligentsia: claiming southern Kursk, Voronezh, and Kuban for Ukraine. Finally, Ukraine's campaign increased local Russian resentment within the important party organizations of the North Caucasus and Central Black Earth regions. To the extent that Ukraine's aggressive behavior was interpreted as evidence of pro-western and anti-Russian sentiment, it would mark a fundamental threat to Soviet unity. For this interpretation to emerge, we have to add a sixth general factor: the impact of collectivization and the 1932 grain requisitions crisis.

Collectivization intensified central concerns about Ukrainian nationalism (as well as non-Russian nationalism in general) since it marked a return to civil war policies and so potentially to a revival of Ukrainian peasant nationalist resistance and a repetition of "the cruel lesson of 1919." However, such resistance would no longer come as a surprise. Soviet officials at the central and regional levels were strongly predisposed to distrust the peasantry of Ukraine and the Kuban Cossacks because of their strong support for the Petliura, Makhno, and white army movements during the civil war.[95] Already in March 1928, after the 1927–1928 forced grain requisition campaign, Kaganovich told a Ukrainian TsK plenum: "One must say that the grain requisition campaign has led to an increase in chauvinism . . . there are conversations that Moscow is taking our bread, sugar. And this chauvinism is not only coming from above [from intellectuals], but from below [from peasants]. The questions about [the colonial rule] of Moscow and the Soviet Union raised invidiously by Volubuev [a recently purged Ukrainian economist] are now being propagated vigorously by the kulaks."[96] OGPU reports consistently treated Ukraine and the Cossack regions of the North Caucasus as the most threatening regions for rural counterrevolution.[97] When a mass peasant uprising involving tens of thousands of Ukrainian and Polish peasants broke out in February–March 1930 along the Polish–Ukrainian border, Soviet authorities saw their worst fears being realized.[98] In March 1930, when resistance to collectivization peaked, 45.1 percent of the mass peasant revolts (2945 of 6528) took place in Ukraine (with 19.5 percent of the USSR's population). For the year 1930 as a whole, Ukraine provided 29.8 percent (4098 of 13,754) of all mass

[95] Andrea Graziosi, *Bol'sheviki i krest'iane na Ukraine, 1918–1919 gody* (Moscow, 1997).

[96] *RTsKhIDNI* 17/26/15 (12–16.03.28): 21.

[97] A. Berelovich and V. Danilov eds., *Sovetskaia derevnia.* Vol. 2, 814–17; 1016–1038. N. Ivnitskii et al. eds., *Tragediia sovetskoi derevni. Kollektivizatsiia i raskulachivanie. Dokumenty i materialy.* Vol. 2. *Noiabr' 1929–dekabr' 1930* (Moscow, 2000): 89–92; 94–98, 642.

[98] Andrea Graziosi, "Collectivisation, revoltes paysannes et politiques gouvernementales a travers les rapports du GPU d'Ukraine de fevrier-mars 1930," *Cahiers du monde russe et sovietique* 35 (1994): 437–632.

disturbances.[99] The Ukrainian GPU's 1930 reports on peasant resistance to collectivization and dekulakization, and particularly their accounts of this uprising, several times mentioned the presence of Ukrainian nationalist slogans and consistently noted when a resisting village had also been active during the civil war.[100]

Ukraine was not the only republic to witness mass uprisings against collectivization. Although resistance to collectivization was widespread across the entire Soviet Union, it was generally stronger and much more violent in the Soviet Union's non-Russian and Cossack regions.[101] In addition to the February 1930 Ukrainian uprising, the onset of collectivization sparked a mass emigration movement among the Soviet Union's western national minorities. Despite the fact that collectivization was pursued much less vigorously in the eastern national regions, violent resistance was much more common there. Of the 1197 rural Soviet officials and activists murdered in 1930, 438 (36.59 percent) died in the eastern republics of Central Asia, Kazakhstan, the Transcaucasus, the North Caucasus national regions, Bashkiria, and Tatarstan.[102] The Central Asian region of Fergana exploded in another February 1930 uprising, which involved 5200 participants and led to a revival of the Basmachi guerrilla resistance movement that was only suppressed with the intervention of the Red Army.[103] Red Army troops were also sent to Chechnya, Ingushetia, Karachai-Cherkesia, and Dagestan to put down armed bands typically numbering from 200 to 800, but in one case including a force of "1200 bayonets, 400 sabers and artillery.[104] In both Karachai-Cherkesia and Chechnya, the Red Army fought 10-day battles with the rebels, in the latter case suffering 8 dead, 18 wounded, and 278 taken prisoner.[105] An armed rebellion broke out in Chechnya as late as 1932.[106] In Kazakhstan, one armed group numbered two to three

[99] Lynne Viola, *Peasant Rebels Under Stalin. Collectivization and the Culture of Peasant Resistance* (Oxford, 1996): 138–139.

[100] Graziosi, "Collectivisation," 437–632; see also *TsDAHOU* 1/20/3184 (1930); 1/20/3195 (1927–1930); 1/20/2522 (1927–1931); 1/20/3185 (1930). Viola, *Peasant Rebels under Stalin*, 120–121. I strongly suspect the OGPU was in fact inclined to exaggerate the significance of Ukrainian nationalism in contributing to peasant revolt in Ukraine, but this exaggeration is in itself important.

[101] For statements to this effect, see Viola, *Peasant Rebels Under Stalin*, 164, and N. A. Ivnitskii, *Kollektivizatsiia i raskulachivanie* (Moscow, 1996): 92. See the extensive statistical tables provided in Viola, *Peasant Rebels Under Stalin*, 100–180. For numerous examples, see Ivnitskii et al., eds., *Tragediia sovetskoi derevni*. Vol. 2, 191–194, 235–241, 368, 405–409, 430–432, 704–706, 787–808.

[102] Viola, *Peasant Rebels Under Stalin*, 110. These regions account for 18.05 percent of the Soviet Union's population. The murder rate in these regions was 2.6 times higher than in the rest of the Soviet Union.

[103] *RTsKhIDNI* 62/2/2140 (1930): 88–91. Hayit, "*Basmatschi*," 362–375.

[104] Ivnitskii, *Kollektivizatsiia i raskulachivanie*, 156–157. *RTsKhIDNI* 17/162/8 (25.02.30): 118/17; *RGAE* 7486/1/131 (1930): 81–82. "Chechnia: vooruzhennaia bor'ba v 20–30 gody," *Voenno-istoricheskii arkhiv* 2 (1997): 118–175.

[105] Ivnitskii, *Kollektivizatsiia i raskulachivanie*, 157.

[106] "Chechnia: vooruzhennaia bor'ba v 20–30 gody," *Voenno-istoricheskii arkhiv* 8 (2000): 99–121.

thousand, with two others bands of about 500.[107] Red Army troops were likewise required in Azerbaijan where several thousand peasants formed armed insurrectionary bands.[108] Such violent, armed resistance occurred almost exclusively in the eastern national regions, although resistance was also extremely strong in the Cossack regions of the North Caucasus.

The Politburo responded to this severe resistance by convening an emergency TsK conference on collectivization in the east. This conference produced a secret February 20 decree, "On Collectivization and the Battle with the Kulaks in National Economically Backward Regions," which forbade applying methods used in advanced Russian regions to the national regions of Central Asia, Kazakhstan, Transcaucasus, the North Caucasus, and Buriat-Mongolia.[109] In implementing this decree, other eastern regions were also included.[110] In early March, Kalinin accused the head of Tatarstan's TsIK of "counter-revolution" for sponsoring mass dekulakization in a national republic.[111] The center, then, was forced to make a short-term concession on the pace of collectivization in eastern regions. In the long term, the strength of non-Russian resistance to collectivization was a further important factor in leading the Soviet leadership to view its Russian core as more politically reliable than its national periphery. This was also one of the preconditions of the Kuban affair.

By reviving civil war attitudes toward the Kuban Cossacks, as well as by provoking considerable resistance from them, collectivization stiffened North Caucasus resistance to Ukrainization. North Caucasus officials argued "that Ukrainization obstructed this campaign," and North Caucasus proponents of Ukrainization were frequently branded as "nationalists" who favored "the forced Ukrainization of the Russian population."[112] In late 1931, the scope of North Caucasus Ukrainization was abruptly reduced from thirty-seven to twenty districts.[113] The center, however, continued to support Ukrainization in both Ukraine and the North Caucasus. In October 1932, Ukraine's Narkompros met to discuss an ambitious plan for supplying the RSFSR with Ukrainian teachers.[114] More importantly, on October 28, *Pravda* published a long letter from I. S. Zamch, the most vocal North Caucasus proponent of Ukrainization, in which he vehemently denounced resistance to Ukrainization.

---

[107] Ivnitskii, *Kollektivizatsiia i raskulachivanie*, 158. *Golod v kazakhskoi stepi* (*Pis'ma trevogi i boli*) (Almaty, 1991): 142–143. M. Omarov, *Rasstreliannaia step'* (Almaty, 1994): 3–56.

[108] Ivnitskii, *Kollektivizatsiia i raskulachivanie*, 159. RTsKhIDNI 80/25s/1 (1929–1930); 80/25s/2 (1930).

[109] RTsKhIDNI 17/162/8 (20.02.30): 118/44.

[110] RTsKhIDNI 558/11/38 (06.04.30): 83. Ivnitskii et al., eds., *Tragediia sovetskoi derevni*, vol. 2, 260, 305.

[111] RTsKhIDNI 94/1/13 (10.03.30): 276–277.

[112] Suprenko, "V provedenii ukrainizatsii," 72. Nikolai Mikhaevich, "Nekotorye itogi sovetskoi ukrainizatsii na Severnom Kavkaze," *Revoliutsiia i gorets*, no. 1 (1932): 88; see also Goffert, "Na vyshuiu stupen'," no. 2 (1930): 17–18; Zamch, *Partorganizatsiia*, 12.

[113] GARF 3316/22/56 (1932): 109; Mikhaevich, "Nekotorye itogi," 90.

[114] TsDAVOU 166/10/914 (1932): 2–12.

The *Pravda* editors added a note stating they had several letters backing Zamch's accusations and demanded an explanation from North Caucasus officials.[115]

By November 1932, however, North Caucasus officials were preoccupied with a considerably more serious accusation: failure to meet their grain requisition quota. Since the onset of collectivization, central demands for grain delivery had grown increasingly onerous.[116] By the end of the 1931 campaign, Ukraine and the North Caucasus were already on the verge of catastrophic famine.[117] In the spring of 1932, the Politburo undertook several measures, such as the authorization of collective farm trade and the repeated granting (always "as an exception") of additional seed loans, which seemed to hint at a new, softer line.[118] However, the poor 1932 harvest was met with unreachably high grain requisition quotas. On June 21, Stalin and Molotov wrote the Ukrainian leadership that their quota must be fulfilled "at any price."[119] Kaganovich and Molotov were dispatched to the July 1932 Ukrainian party conference to enforce this line. On August 4, *Pravda* criticized the North Caucasus for failing to meet its grain quota.[120] Three days later, the famous August 7, 1932 law made the theft of state property, including grain, punishable by death.[121] Finally, on August 25, in response to a request by the North Caucasus for a quota reduction, the Politburo "decisively rejected all attempts to reduce the grain requisitions plan" and instead ordered an increase in the use of terror to extract grain.[122]

This summarizes briefly the formal bureaucratic record of the progress of the grain requisitions crisis in the summer of 1932. Thanks to a series of letters Stalin wrote to Kaganovich from June to September 1932, we now also have access to thoughts Stalin chose to share only with the inner circle of the Politburo.[123] On June 2, Stalin wrote an extremely caustic letter to Kaganovich and Molotov about the failings of the Ukrainian leadership[124]:

[115] I. S. Zamch, "Kak ne nado provodit' natsional'nuiu politiku partii (Pis'mo instruktora po ukrainizatsii)," *Pravda*, no. 299 (28.10.32): 3.

[116] D'Ann Penner, "Stalin and the *Ital'ianka* of 1932–1933 in the Don Region," *Cahiers du monde russe* 39 (1998): 27–68. E. N. Oskolkov, *Golod 1932/1933. Khlebozagotovki i golod 1932/1933 goda v Severno-Kavkazskom krae* (Rostov-na-donu, 1991): 9–19.

[117] On Ukraine, see *Holod 1932–1933 rokiv na Ukraini: ochyma istorykiv, movoiu dokumentiv* (Kiev, 1990): 121; on the North Caucasus, see Oskolokov, *Golod 1932/1933*, 9–20.

[118] On the seed loans, see *RTsKhIDNI* 17/162/12 (1932): 93/38, 93/41, 94/41, 94/55, 95/41, 95/13, 95/45, 97/29, 97/46, 98/23. R. W. Davies, *Crisis and Progress in the Soviet Economy, 1931–1933* (London, 1996): 201–228.

[119] *Holod 1932–1933 rokiv*, 186–187.

[120] "Pervye itogi khoda uborki na Severnom Kavkaze," *Pravda*, no. 214 (04.08.32): 1.

[121] For a splendid account of this law and its implementation, see Peter Solomon, *Soviet Criminal Justice under Stalin* (Cambridge, UK, 1996): 111–129.

[122] *RTsKhIDNI* 17/3/897 (25.08.32): 113/93; 17/162/13 (25.08.32): 113/54.

[123] *RTsKhIDNI* 81/3/99 (1932): 45–174. Stalin was on a working vacation in Sochi. Kaganovich was running the politburo in his absence. Some of Stalin's letters are addressed to Kaganovich alone, others to Kaganovich and various members of the Politburo's inner circle.

[124] Ibid., 45–47.

1. Pay serious attention to Ukraine. Chubar, through his rotten and oppor-
tunistic nature, and Kosior, through his rotten diplomacy (with TsK VKP) and
his criminally light-minded attitude to affairs, are completely ruining Ukraine.
These comrades are not up to leading today's Ukraine. If you go to the Ukrainian conference (and I insist you do), take all measures to turn around the mood
of the officials, to isolate the whiny and rotten diplomats (who won't look
you in the face!) and to achieve a truly Bolshevik decree. I am developing the
impression (perhaps even the conviction) that we will have to remove both
Chubar and Kosior from Ukraine. Perhaps I am wrong. But check out this
possibility at the conference. . . .

Thirteen days later, Stalin again vented his anger at the Ukrainians[125]:

. . . 4. I did not like the letters of Chubar and Petrovskii. The first engaged in
"self-criticism" in order to get yet again millions of kilograms of grain from
Moscow, the other plays the saint, portraying himself as a victim of "the directives of TsK VKP" in order to get a reduction in the grain requisition plan. . . .
Chubar is mistaken if he thinks that self-criticism is not for the mobilization of
our forces in Ukraine, but for getting "help" from outside. I think we've given
more to Ukraine than we should have. Giving more grain is pointless. The worst
thing in this affair is the silence of Kosior. What explains this silence? Does he
know about the letters of Chubar and Petrovskii?

As noted above, Molotov and Kaganovich did attend the Ukrainian party conference in early July and apparently achieved a sufficiently Bolshevik decree to
satisfy Stalin, since on July 25 Stalin authorized a plan reduction for Ukraine,
noting that his previous objections to a plan reduction had only been a
tactic to avoid "the complete demoralization of the already demoralized
Ukrainians."[126]

However, only a few weeks later, on August 11, Stalin lashed out at the
Ukrainian leadership with still greater fury[127]:

The *chief thing* now is Ukraine. Things in Ukraine are terrible. It's *terrible*
in the *party*. They say that in two Ukrainian oblasts (I believe Kiev and
Dnepropetrovsk) that around 50 *raikomy* have spoken out *against* the grain
requisitions plan, considering it *unrealistic*. In other *raikomy*, it appears the
situation is no better. What's this like? It's not a Party, but a parliament, a
caricature of a parliament. . . . It's *terrible* in the *soviet* organs. Chubar is not
a leader. It's *terrible* in the GPU. Redens is not up to leading the fight with
counterrevolution in such a large and unique republic as Ukraine.

[125] Ibid., 63. Copies of Chubar and Petrovskii's letters are found in *RTsKhIDNI* 82/2/139
(1932): 144–165.
[126] Ibid., 115–116.
[127] Ibid., 145–151.

If we don't make an effort now to improve the situation in Ukraine, we may lose Ukraine. Keep in mind that Pilsudski is not daydreaming, and his agents in Ukraine are many times stronger than Redens or Kosior think. Keep in mind that the Ukrainian Communist party (500 *thousand* members, ha-ha) includes not a few (yes, not a few!) rotten elements, conscious and non-conscious Petliurites, as well as direct agents of Pilsudski. As soon as things get worse, these elements will not be slow in opening a front within (and without) the Party against the Party. The worst thing is that the Ukrainians simply *do not* see this danger.

This cannot go on this way. We must:

a. Remove Kosior from Ukraine and replace him with you while *keeping you* as TsK VKP/b/ secretary.

b. *Immediately following* this, transfer Balitskii to Ukraine as head of the GPU . . . while *keeping him* as an assistant head of the OGPU, and make Redens Balitskii's assistant.

c. *A few months later*, replace Chubar with another comrade, perhaps Grinko or someone similar, and make Chubar Molotov's assistant in Moscow (Kosior can be one of the TsK VKP/b/secretaries).

Give yourself the task of quickly transforming Ukraine into a true *fortress* of the USSR, a truly model republic. We won't spare money on this task.

Without these and similar measures (ideological and political work in Ukraine, in the first place in her *border* districts and so forth), I repeat—we can lose Ukraine. . . . [all emphasis in the original]

These remarks were much more ominous than Stalin's attacks on Kosior, Chubar, and Petrovskii in June as incompetent and rotten, which were only particularly nasty versions of criticisms he was then making of the leadership of all grain-producing regions.[128] Stalin was now singling out Ukraine itself as a "unique" national republic whose party had been infiltrated by Ukrainian nationalists (Petliurites) who were in turn serving Pilsudski's ongoing project of exploiting Ukrainian nationalism to annex Ukraine. While Stalin's comments about losing Ukraine may have been somewhat hyperbolic, his future actions suggest that his concern was not being greatly exaggerated. Stalin quickly decided he could not afford to send Kaganovich to Ukraine.[129] Major personnel changes were made only in January 1933, after the Kuban affair and the December 1932 anti-Ukrainization Politburo decrees.

Stalin remained positively disposed to the North Caucasus leadership and their first party secretary, Boris Sheboldaev, throughout the summer of 1932 until Sheboldaev also erred by asking for a plan reduction. Stalin then lashed

[128] Ibid., 65–68.

[129] Ibid., 171–172. "One could only replace Kosior with Kaganovich. I can't see any other candidate. Mikoian is not suitable, not only for Ukraine—he's not suitable for the Supply Commissariat [his current job] (a clumsy and disorganized 'agitator'). But it is impossible to weaken the TsK secretariat by sending Kaganovich to Ukraine now (not expedient!). We'll have to wait for a while."

out at him in a letter to Kaganovich on August 23 and ordered that *Pravda* "curse out the North Caucasus *leadership* for their bad work on grain requisitions."[130] From this point onward, although escalating terror was used in all grain-producing regions, the primary targets were Ukraine and the North Caucasus. On October 22, the Politburo formed commissions headed by Molotov and Kaganovich to travel to Ukraine and the North Caucasus, respectively, to "increase the collection of grain."[131] When Sheboldaev came to Moscow to plead with Stalin for a quota reduction, the latter responded by adding authoritative representatives, in particular from the state's punitive organs, to the Kaganovich commission: A. I. Mikoian (Politburo), G. G. Iagoda (OGPU), M. F. Shkiriatov (TsKK), I. B. Gamarnik (Red Army).[132] This extraordinary commission met personally with Stalin for over an hour on October 29.[133] They arrived in the North Caucasus on November 1 and unleashed the wave of terror known as the Kuban affair.[134]

The primary target of this terror was the North Caucasus peasantry and especially the Kuban Cossacks. At a November 2 meeting with party leaders and activists in the North Caucasus capital of Rostov, Kaganovich explained to his listeners that the kulaks "no longer dare to oppose us openly. Instead the class enemy continues its battle against us in a masked form" through entering the collective farms to "sabotage" grain requisitions and "to transform the collective farm into a kind of peasants' union." The answer was increased repression: "to fight savagely [*zverski drat'sia*] and fulfill the plan."[135] Sheboldaev echoed Kaganovich's theme: "We must carry out a complete program of repression so that they dare not laugh at our helplessness."[136] In Kaganovich's presence, the North Caucasus *kraikom* passed a decree on grain requisitions in Kuban, which called for extraordinary economic and judicial sanctions in order to fulfill their grain requisitions quota.[137] The decree was telegraphed to Stalin in Moscow, who edited it and ordered it be published the next day in the Rostov paper, *Molot*.[138] The most "savage" measure involved placing three Kuban Cossack towns (*stanitsy*) on the black list (*"chernaia doska"*). As Kaganovich explained, being placed on the black list involved a complete economic blockade of these already starving towns, the arrest of "counterrevolutionaries" by the OGPU,

[130] Ibid., 161–162.

[131] *RTsKhIDNI* 17/3/904 (22.10.32): 120/39.

[132] Oskolkov, *Golod 1932/1933*, 27–29. The original commission included M. A. Chernov and T. A. Iurkin. The new commission also included A. V. Kosarev (Komsomol).

[133] "Posetiteli kremlevskogo kabineta I. V. Stalina," *Istoricheskii arkhiv*, no. 2 (1995): 154.

[134] On the Kuban affair, see Oskolkov, *Golod 1932/1933*, 30–79; Nobuo Shimotomai, "A Note on The Kuban Affair (1932–1933)," *Acta Slavica Iaponica*, no. 1 (1983): 39–56; Kaganovich's "diary" (actually, notes on his observations, conversations, and speeches as recorded by his personal secretary) for his two trips to the North Caucasus in November 1932 are available in *RTsKhIDNI* 81/3/214 (1932).

[135] *RTsKhIDNI* 81/3/214 (1932): 10; Oskolkov, *Golod 1932/1933*, 35.

[136] *RTsKhIDNI* 81/3/214 (1932): 8.

[137] Oskolkov, *Golod 1932/1933*, 38.

[138] Ivnitskii, *Kollektivizatsiia i raskulachivanie*, 50.

the performance of show trials, and a purge of the party and soviet organs.[139] If the towns failed to fulfill their grain quota, the entire population was threatened with deportation to the far north.[140] Ultimately, three entire Cossack towns and over sixty thousand individual Kuban Cossacks would be deported to the far north. In the month of November, over two hundred Cossacks were arrested as counterrevolutionaries. The OGPU arrested a total of sixteen thousand peasants in Kuban alone during the entire 1932 grain requisitions campaign, the majority of arrests occurring in November and December.[141]

The secondary target of the Kuban terror was lower-ranking rural communists. During his visit, Kaganovich again and again emphasized that Kuban's grain requisitions failure was not only the result of kulak sabotage, but also due to the actions of ignorant, weak-willed, and sometimes maliciously hostile local communists: "Our rural Communists have not honestly studied, not once even examined, not understood at all the new forms of class warfare. And the worst have become the leaders of the kulak sabotage of the sowing and grain requisition campaigns. . . . And a bad communist is worse than no communist at all, since their Party ticket sanctifies, gives a blessing to the kulak mood."[142] Shkiriatov was still blunter: "If a communist doesn't implement our decision, he is an enemy—not a communist."[143] Two measures were taken to terrorize local communists. First, a November 4 *kraikom* decree initiated a party purge in the North Caucasus, concentrated "first of all, in the regions of Kuban."[144] Kaganovich publicly informed the Kuban communists that the purged would not simply be removed from the party, as in previous purges, but "deported to the far northern regions as traitors of the working class, as politically dangerous."[145] In November and December 1932, 44.8 percent of communists reviewed by Shkiriatov's purge commission in Kuban were excluded from the party. Half of the party secretaries of town soviets and collective farm party cells in Kuban were purged.[146]

Communists were also now targeted for judicial repression. In total, five thousand communists were arrested in Kuban and fifteen thousand in the North Caucasus as a whole.[147] Moreover, communists were now being publicly executed. Prior to Kaganovich's arrival, the collective farm chairman N. V. Kotov had been given a ten-year sentence for doubling his *kolkhozniki's* grain advances. On November 4, a new trial was held, after which he and

---

[139] *RTsKhIDNI* 81/3/214 (1932): 1–4.
[140] *RTsKhIDNI* 17/21/3377 (02.11.32): 84. Significantly, this decree was forwarded only to the Ukrainian TsK. *TsDAHOU* 1/20/5244 (1932): 46–50.
[141] Oskolkov, *Golod 1932/1933*, 42–43, 50–51, 55, 66.
[142] *RTsKhIDNI* 81/3/214 (1932): 4, 11.
[143] Oskolkov, *Golod 1932/1933*, 34.
[144] *TsDAHOU* 1/20/5422 (1932): 49–50.
[145] *RTsKhIDNI* 81/3/214 (1932): 83.
[146] Oskolkov, *Golod 1932/1933*, 60–61.
[147] Ivnitskii, *Kollektivizatsiia i raskulachivanie*, 50.

two of his colleagues were summarily executed.[148] His case received enormous publicity in the North Caucasus and in Moscow. Kaganovich and Mikoian publicly endorsed his execution and threatened the same for any other communists who "turn soft, who approach the collective farm in a populist spirit [*po-narodnichestvo*]."[149] In the next few weeks following Kotov's execution, the North Caucasus kraikom newspaper, *Molot*, publicized the executions of dozens of other communists.[150]

The Kaganovich commission, then, insisted that the primary cause of the grain requisitions crisis was kulak sabotage, abetted by weak-willed and hostile rural communists. The solution was increased terror. However, a third, less-emphasized explanatory thread also surfaced during Kaganovich's visit: the pernicious influence of Ukrainian nationalists, in particular those arriving in the North Caucasus from Ukraine. Kaganovich included a brief reference to this problem in his speech to the North Caucasus party biuro on the night of his arrival: "Without a doubt, among those arriving from Ukraine were organized groups, carrying out [counterrevolutionary] work, especially in the Kuban, where the Ukrainian language is spoken."[151] Kaganovich emphasized the Cossack problem in explaining Kuban's poor performance, but he also called attention to the Kuban Cossacks (of Ukrainian identity), even using what he called "my mixed-up Ukrainian speech" during his visits to several Kuban towns.[152]

There had, in fact, been a massive outflow of Ukrainians into neighboring RSFSR regions in the spring of 1932, since at that point famine conditions were worse in Ukraine than in other grain-growing regions. In a June 18, 1932 letter to Kaganovich, Stalin had complained that "several tens of thousands of Ukrainian *kolkhozniki* have already fled across the entire European regions of the USSR and are demoralizing our collective farms with their complaints and whimpering," though he did not yet connect these refugees with counterrevolutionary activities.[153] This connection first emerged strongly during Kaganovich's second trip to the North Caucasus, after a brief sojourn in Moscow from November 12 to 16.[154] On November 23, he told the Rostov party activists: "In a series of Kuban collective farms we have uncovered Petliurite agents, who arrived in Kuban [from Ukraine] this spring. . . . Local cadres have not devoted enough attention to the destructive work [of these Ukrainians], despite the fact that we knew very well about the ties between the Kuban counter-revolutionaries and the Ukrainian Petliurites, as well as their probable ties with Polish espionage as well, since the Petliurites work together with the Poles closely."[155] The

[148] Oskolkov, *Golod 1932/1933*, 47–51.
[149] *RTsKhIDNI* 81/3/214 (1932): 10.
[150] Oskolkov, *Golod 1932/1933*, 50.
[151] *RTsKhIDNI* 81/3/214 (1932): 4.
[152] Ibid., 37.
[153] *RTsKhIDNI* 81/3/99 (18.06.32): 66.
[154] "Posetiteli kremlevskogo," *Istoricheskii Arkhiv*, no. 2 (1995): 154–157.
[155] *RTsKhIDNI* 81/3/214 (1932): 104.

Pilsudski-Petliurite infiltration of the Ukrainian Communist Party, discerned by Stalin in August, had now been extended to include Kuban as well.[156]

The National Interpretation of the Grain Requisitions Crisis

Kaganovich completed his second trip to the North Caucasus on November 25. At the same time, Molotov completed his commission's work in Ukraine and also returned to Moscow. Molotov's commission had presided over an intensification of the grain requisitions terror in Ukraine, only slightly less severe than in Kuban.[157] In the month of November and the first five days of December, under Molotov's supervision, the Ukrainian GPU arrested 1830 individuals from the leadership of various collective farms. In addition, 327 communists were also arrested.[158] By December 15, approximately 16,000 individuals had been arrested, including 435 party members and 2260 collective farm officials. Of these, 108 had been sentenced to be executed.[159] After the return of Kaganovich and Molotov, the Politburo convened on December 14 and issued a secret decree on grain collection in Ukraine and the North Caucasus.[160] This decree was the most important central intervention on nationalities policy since the 1923 decrees that first codified the Soviet nationalities policy. It marked the first time that the Soviet leadership officially declared that the 1923 policy of *korenizatsiia*, as implemented in Ukraine and the North Caucasus, had not disarmed nationalist resistance as was intended, but rather had intensified it.

The December 14, 1932 Politburo decree articulated the national interpretation of the 1932 grain requisitions crisis. Ukraine and the North Caucasus were singled out for their lack of vigilance, which had allowed "kulaks, former officers, Petliurites and supporters of the Kuban *rada* to penetrate the collective farm leadership." Likewise, their lack of vigilance empowered "the most evil enemies of the Party, working class and kolkhoz peasantry, the saboteurs of grain requisition with Party tickets in their pocket."[161] In both Ukraine and the North Caucasus, the Politburo blamed this lack of vigilance on Ukrainization[162]:

---

[156] For other references by Kaganovich and others to Ukrainian counterrevolutionary work in Kuban and other regions of the North Caucasus, see *RTsKhIDNI* 81/3/214 (1932): 71–75, 89–90, 133.

[157] See in particular the Ukrainian TsK resolutions of November 5 and 18 in *Holod 1932–1933 rokiv*, 247–248, 250–261; also *RTsKhIDNI* 17/162/14 (22.11.32): 123/71. Also, Ivnitskii, *Kollektivizatsiia i raskulachivanie*, 50–56.

[158] Ivnitskii, *Kollektivizatsiia i raskulachivanie*, 56.

[159] *RTsKhIDNI* 81/3/215 (1932): 3.

[160] *RTsKhIDNI* 17/3/910 (10.12.32): 125/6; 17/3/911 (14.12.32): 126/46. The December 14 decree is reprinted in *Holod 1932–1933 rokiv*, 291–294. The decree also included the Western Oblast, but the focus was on Ukraine and the North Caucasus.

[161] *Holod 1932–1933 rokiv*, 292.

[162] Ibid., 292.

TsK and Sovnarkom note that instead of a correct Bolshevik implementation of the nationalities policy, in many Ukrainian regions Ukrainization was carried out mechanically, without considering the specifics of each district, without a careful choice of Bolshevik Ukrainian cadres. This made it easy for bourgeois-nationalist elements, Petliurites and others to create a legal cover [*prikrytie*] for their counterrevolutionary cells and organizations.

The verdict on Ukrainization in the North Caucasus was much harsher[163]:

TsK and Sovnarkom instruct the North Caucasus *kraikom* that the light-headed [*legkomyslennaia*], non-Bolshevik "Ukrainization" of almost half the North Caucasus districts did not serve the cultural interests of the population, and with the total absence of surveillance by *krai* organs of the Ukrainization of schools and the press, gave a legal form to the enemies of Soviet power for the organization of opposition to Soviet power by kulaks, officers, re-emigrated Cossacks, members of the Kuban *rada* and so forth.

In short, the grain requisitions crisis was the product of resistance by traitors within the soviet and party apparat, and many of them received their positions due to the policy of Ukrainization. This represented the national interpretation of the grain requisitions crisis.

Three series of events converged to produce this interpretation. First, as outlined in Chapter 6, an anti-*korenizatsiia* hard-line stance that maintained *korenizatsiia* was exacerbating rather than disarming nationalism gradually emerged in response to the perceived defection of national communists such as Shumskyi to a position of nationalism, the perceived influence of cross-border ethnic ties in causing such defections, as well as the cultural revolution terror campaigns against the national *smenovekhovstvo* intelligentsia and the centralizing thrust of the socialist offensive. The December 14, 1932 politburo decree represented the first central endorsement of the anti-*korenizatsiia* hard-line position that, at least in this one case, *korenizatsiia* had exacerbated rather than contained the threat of nationalist counterrevolution. Second, as described in this chapter, Ukraine's effort to annex neighboring RSFSR regions and to serve as the patron of the RSFSR Ukrainians both exacerbated central concerns about Ukrainian national communism and created a perceived political link between the Soviet Union's two most important grain-growing regions: Ukraine and the North Caucasus. Third, collectivization both elicited more violent resistance in the Soviet Union's non-Russian border regions, further exacerbating central concerns about national separatism, and resulted in a major political crisis in the fall of 1932 that made the perceived separatist threat in Ukraine intolerable.

The national interpretation, then, was not a cause of the grain requisitions crisis and famine. Rather, it emerged as a consequence of it. Although Ukrainization had lost momentum by 1932, there were no signals in Ukraine

[163] Ibid., 292–293.

that the policy was being called into question in a fundamental way prior to December 14, 1932.[164] In fact, on the eve of that decree, the Ukrainian Commissariat of Education had just launched another campaign to verify the implementation of Ukrainization.[165] Likewise, as noted earlier, *Pravda* published an article in defense of Ukrainization in the North Caucasus only two days before Kaganovich's commission departed for Rostov. Most strikingly, in the available internal correspondence concerning grain requisitions in Ukraine, the national factor is mentioned only once prior to November 1932.[166] From his letter to Kaganovich, we know that by August 11, Stalin had already linked Ukrainian nationalist infiltration of the party with the grain requisitions crisis in Ukraine, but not yet with the crisis in Kuban and the North Caucasus. We have also seen that Kaganovich alluded briefly to counterrevolutionary sabotage by groups from Ukraine in a speech delivered on his arrival in Rostov on November 1. However, aside from that stray comment, Kaganovich overwhelmingly blamed the crisis on the kulaks, the Kuban Cossacks, and rural communists.

The available evidence suggests that the national interpretation emerged in full form and received central sanction after the initial missions of Molotov and Kaganovich to Ukraine and the North Caucasus in early November. Molotov and Kaganovich both returned to Moscow for extensive consultation with Stalin from November 12 to 16.[167] After these meetings, Molotov returned to Ukraine and Kaganovich traveled to both Ukraine and the North Caucasus. During these repeat visits, the Ukrainian question received much greater emphasis. On November 18, Molotov told the Kharkov party *aktiv* that, "you must fight with those remnants of bourgeois nationalism in the form of Petliurites and half-Petliurites; one must understand that not only is the internal enemy at work here, but also . . . the enemy from across the border."[168] The same day, two Ukrainian TsK decrees both referred to the need to fight the "*Petliurovshchina*" and "to liquidate kulak and Petliurite nests."[169] Likewise, as noted earlier, Kaganovich began to emphasize the role of Ukrainian counterrevolutionaries in Kuban. The Ukrainian factor provided a convenient explanation for why Ukraine and the North Caucasus (and, above all, Kuban) were the Soviet Union's two most delinquent grain-producing regions. Nor was this interpre-

---

[164] I found not a single article casting any doubt on the Ukrainization policy published in the two Ukrainian national newspapers, *Visti VUTsIK* and *Komunist*, for the year 1932.

[165] *Biuleten' NKO*, no. 59 (1932): 3–8.

[166] This is based on the large quantity of Ukrainian documents published in *Holod 1932–1933 rokiv* and *Kolektyvizatsiia i holod na Ukraini, 1929–1933. Zbirnyk dokumentiv i materialiv* (Kiev, 1993) and also on my examination of the Ukrainian and all-union *osobaia papka* Politburo decisions in *TsDAHOU* 1/16/20 and *RTsKhIDNI* 17/3/162. In an April 26, 1932 letter to Stalin, Kosior mentioned a recent "open counter-revolutionary action of a Petliurite character"; *Holod 1932–1933 rokiv*, 150.

[167] "Posetiteli kremlevskogo," 154–157.

[168] *RTsKhIDNI* 82/2/140 (18.11.32): 48.

[169] *Holod 1932–1933 rokiv*, 256, 260. See also Kaganovich's remarks about Petliurite infiltration on November 25. *RTsKhIDNI* 81/3/215 (1932): 18.

tation unpopular with local communists in the North Caucasus, who eagerly seconded Kaganovich's attacks on Ukrainian counterrevolutionaries.[170] As we have already seen, they greatly resented Ukrainian attempts to annex their territory and to promote RSFSR Ukrainization. Moreover, they were relieved that central terror was now being deflected somewhat on to national targets. Likewise, the 1933 nationalities terror in Ukraine focused on Ukrainian cultural and educational institutions, as well as on political émigrés from Galicia, and away from rank-and-file communists.

The Politburo's development of a national interpretation of their grain requisitions crisis in late 1932 helps explain both the pattern of terror and the role of the national factor during the 1932–1933 famine.[171] The 1932–1933 terror campaign consisted of both a grain requisitions terror, whose primary target was the peasantry, both Russian and non-Russian, and a nationalities terror, whose primary target was Ukraine and subsequently Belorussia. The grain requisitions terror was the final and decisive culmination of a campaign begun in 1927–1928 to extract the maximum possible amount of grain from a hostile peasantry. As such, its primary targets were the grain-producing regions of Ukraine, the North Caucasus, and the Lower Volga, though no grain-producing regions escaped the 1932–1933 grain requisitions terror entirely. Nationality was of minimal importance in this campaign. The famine was not an intentional act of genocide specifically targeting the Ukrainian nation. It is equally false, however, to assert that nationality played no role whatsoever in the famine.[172] The nationalities terror resulted from the gradual emergence of an anti-*korenizatsiia* hard-line critique combined with the immediate pressures of the grain requisitions crisis in Ukraine and Kuban, whose particularly intense resistance was attributed to Ukrainization. The December 14 Politburo decree formalized this national interpretation and authorized an additional nationalities terror against Ukraine and Kuban. A second Politburo decree, on December 15, formally abolished Ukrainization throughout the entire RSFSR.[173] A third Politburo decree, a day later, extended the nationalities terror to Belorussia as well.[174]

My analysis explains why the 1932–1933 grain requisitions terror embraced both Russian and Ukrainian territories and also why the terror was worse in

[170] *RTsKhIDNI* 81/3/215 (1932): 71–75.

[171] As is well known, the role of the national factor (especially the Ukrainian factor) in the 1932–1933 famine has been extremely controversial. For the argument that the famine was an intentional genocide, see Robert Conquest, *The Harvest of Sorrow. Soviet Collectivization and the Terror Famine* (New York, 1986); for the exact opposite argument, see Shtefan Merl', "Golod 1932–1933 godov—genotsid ukraintsev dlia osushchestvleniia Politiki rusifikatsii?" *Otechestvennaia istoriia*, no. 1 (1995): 49–61.

[172] Merl', "Golod 1932–1933 godov."

[173] *RTsKhIDNI* 17/3/911 (15.12.32): 126/50.

[174] *RTsKhIDNI* 17/3/911 (16.12.32): 126/1. Belorussian First Secretary Gikalo mentioned that they had received directives on nationalities policy from the Politburo at this December 1932 session. See *XVII s"ezd*, 72. A further Politburo decree on nationalities policy in Belorussia was issued in March 1933. *RTsKhIDNI* 17/3/917 (08.03.33): 132/26.

Kuban and Ukraine than in the Lower Volga. The Lower Volga was visited by an extraordinary Politburo commission headed by Postyshev in December 1932, which did unleash a wave of terror against both the peasantry and local communists, but the level of terror never reached that of Ukraine and Kuban.[175] By March 1933, as a result of the grain requisitions terror, there were 90,000 individuals in Ukraine's jails and concentration camps, 75,000 in those of the North Caucasus, and 29,000 in those of the Lower Volga.[176] These numbers understate the actual difference, since 30,000 individuals had been transferred out of the North Caucasus camps in January, and Ukraine's camp population had already been reduced in late November.[177]

Above all, my analysis explains why Ukraine and the Kuban were singled out in a January 22, 1933 TsK circular that called for the closing of the Ukrainian and North Caucasus borders to peasant out-migration[178]:

> TsK VKP/b/ and Sovnarkom have received information that in the Kuban and Ukraine a massive outflow of peasants "for bread" has begun into Belorussia and the Central-Black Earth, Volga, Western, and Moscow regions. TsK VKP/b/ and Sovnarkom do not doubt that the outflow of the peasants, like the outflow from Ukraine last year, was organized by the enemies of Soviet power, the SRs and the agents of Poland, with the goal of agitation "through the peasantry" in the northern regions of the USSR against the collective farms and against Soviet power as a whole. Last year the Party, Soviet, and Chekist organs of Ukraine were caught napping by this counterrevolutionary trick of the enemies of Soviet power. This year we cannot allow a repetition of last year's mistake.
>
> First. TsK VKP/b/ and Sovnarkom order the kraikom, krai executive committee, and OGPU of the North Caucasus not to allow a massive outflow of peasants from the North Caucasus into other regions or the entry into the North Caucasus from Ukraine.
>
> Second. TsK VKP/b/ and Sovnarkom order TsK KP/b/U, the Ukrainian Sovnarkom, as well as Balitskii and Redens not to allow a massive outflow of peasants from Ukraine into other regions or the entry into Ukraine of peasants from the North Caucasus.
>
> Third. TsK VKP/b/ and Sovnarkom order the OGPU of Belorussia and the Central-Black Earth, Middle Volga, Western and Moscow regions to

[175] On the Lower Volga, see Viktor Viktorovich Kondrashin, "Golod 1932–1933 godov v derevne Povolzh'ia" (kand. diss., Moscow, 1991): 93–192. The Politburo *osobaia papka* decisions for 1932–1933 authorize terror and deportations in Ukraine and North Caucasus numerous times, but not in the Lower Volga. *RTsKhIDNI* 17/162/13–14 (1932–1933).

[176] *RTsKhIDNI* 17/162/14 (08.03.33): 132/22. Although it is not usually considered as a major site of grain requisitions terror, this document also lists the Central-Black Earth region as having 43,500 individuals in jail or concentration camps.

[177] *RTsKhIDNI* 17/162/14 (01.02.33): 129/51; (24.11.32): 123/82. Ivnitskii provides a figure of 219,460 arrested through March 1933 but does not break down the figure by regions. Ivnitskii, *Kollektivizatsiia i raskulachivanie*, 61.

[178] *RTsKhIDNI* 558/11/45 (22.01.33): 106–107.

immediately arrest all "peasants" of Ukraine and the North Caucasus who have broken through into the north and, after separating out the counterrevolutionary elements, to return the rest to their places of residence.

Fourth. TsK VKP/b/ and Sovnarkom order the OGPU to give a similar order to the OGPU transport organs.

65Sh. Molotov, Stalin

This directive once again points to Stalin's concern over the political impact of Ukrainian out-migration. It is impossible to determine how many Ukrainian and North Caucasus peasant lives might have been lost due to this directive, but it clearly shows that Ukraine and Kuban were singled out for special treatment specifically because of the national interpretation of the famine.

My analysis also explains why the terror in Ukraine and Belorussia continued throughout 1933 and into 1934, long after the terror was over in Russian regions. In fact, as we shall see in Chapter 9, by late 1933 the nationalities terror extended all the way to the non–grain-producing regions of Central Asia. In brief, the grain requisitions terror triggered a nationalities terror that continued for over a year after the grain requisitions terror was halted (in May 1933). More important, it triggered a wide-ranging revision of the Soviet nationalities policy.

Conclusion: The Aftermath of the December 1932 Politburo Decrees

In retrospect, it is clear that the December 14, 1932 Politburo decree marked a decisive turning point in the evolution of the Soviet nationalities policy. At the time, however, this was not at all clear. The decree did not condemn Ukrainization wholesale, but rather its "mechanical" implementation and the failure to make "a careful choice of Bolshevik Ukrainian cadres." The suggested solution was not russification, but rather "serious attention to the proper implementation of Ukrainization" and "the careful choice and education of Bolshevik Ukrainian cadres."[179] Only time would tell what exactly the shift to "Bolshevik" Ukrainization would mean. It is true that the December 15 Politburo decree abolished Ukrainization throughout the entire RSFSR, and this was an unambiguous policy innovation. However, given the high levels of assimilation among the RSFSR Ukrainians, it could easily have been understood as a single exception that proved the rule (as it in fact was for four years). Moreover, the decree was issued in the midst of a major political crisis, which involved a large-scale year-long terror campaign. That campaign was officially brought to a halt on May 8, 1933.[180] At that point, the December 14 decree could easily have been

---

[179] *Holod 1932–1933 rokiv*, 293.
[180] Peter Solomon, *Soviet Criminal Justice under Stalin* (Cambridge, UK, 1996): 124–125.

allowed to lapse, especially since it was never published. This did not occur. Instead, the December 14 decree initiated a series of far-reaching changes in the Soviet nationalities policy: the onset of Soviet ethnic cleansing and the emergence of the category of the "enemy nation"; a fundamental revision, but not abolition, of *korenizatsiia*; a shift from ethnic proliferation to ethnic consolidation, accompanied by an administrative russification of the RSFSR; and, finally, the rehabilitation of the Russians and traditional Russian national culture as part of the process of establishing a revised Soviet national constitution, whose organizing metaphor would be the Friendship of the Peoples. The gradual and uneven emergence of the new Soviet national constitution will be the subject of Chapters 8 to 11.

PART THREE

REVISING THE AFFIRMATIVE ACTION EMPIRE

8

Ethnic Cleansing and
Enemy Nations

The emergence of the category of enemy nation and the practice of ethnic cleansing was one of the most momentous developments in the Soviet nationalities policy of the mid-1930s. Between 1935 and 1938, at least nine Soviet nationalities—Poles, Germans, Finns, Estonians, Latvians, Koreans, Chinese, Kurds, Iranians—were all subjected to ethnic cleansing (that is, the forcible relocation of an ethnically defined population away from a given territory).[1] In 1937–1938, these and many other diaspora nationalities were labeled enemy nations and specifically targeted for arrest and execution due solely to their ethnic identity. This practice would seem to stand in complete opposition to the principles of the Affirmative Action Empire. It is true that ethnic cleansing has been a regrettably common feature of the twentieth-century landscape and that the Soviet Union was an unusually violent state.[2] Ethnic cleansing, however, has typically been an extreme manifestation of the nationalist project of making state borders coincide with ethnic borders.[3] As we have seen, the Soviet Union was not a nation-state, nor was its leadership ever committed to

---

[1] On the term "ethnic cleansing," see Terry Martin, "The Origins of Soviet Ethnic Cleansing," *The Journal of Modern History* 70 (December 1998): 817–824; and Norman Naimark, *Fires of Hatred. Ethnic Cleansing in Twentieth Century Europe* (Cambridge, Mass., 2000): 1–16. On early Soviet deportations, Ian M. Matley, "The Dispersal of the Ingrian Finns," *Slavic Review* 38 (March 1979): 1–16; N. F. Bugai, *L. Beriia—I. Stalinu: "Soglasno vashemu ukazaniiu...."* (Moscow, 1995); Michael Gelb, "The Western Finnic Minorities and the Origins of the Stalinist Nationalities Deportations," *Nationalities Papers* 24 (June 1996): 237–268; and Gelb, "An Early Soviet Ethnic Deportation: The Far-Eastern Koreans," *The Russian Review* 54 (July 1995): 389–412.

[2] Martin, "The Origins of Soviet Ethnic Cleansing," 817–824. Naimark, *Fires of Hatred*.

[3] Ernest Gellner, *Nations and Nationalism* (Ithaca, N.Y., 1983).

turning it into a nation-state. No attempt was made to forge a new Soviet nationality, and even voluntary assimilation was strongly discouraged. The Soviet regime devoted considerable resources to the promotion of the national self-consciousness of its non-Russian populations. Moreover, as we shall see, this commitment continued throughout the 1930s. This would seem to have made the Soviet Union a highly unlikely site for the emergence of ethnic cleansing.

Indeed, the simultaneous pursuit of nation-building and nation-destroying in the 1930s is a paradox in need of explanation. Early studies of the Soviet nationalities policy tended to emphasize a shift from a moderate policy of national concessions in the 1920s to a repressive policy in the 1930s featuring ethnic deportations, national terror, and russification.[4] More recent studies have instead focused on the impressive continuity in the Soviet commitment to nation-building throughout the entire Stalinist period and beyond.[5] However, neither approach gives a satisfactory explanation of the most striking paradox of the last two decades of Stalin's rule: the simultaneous pursuit of nation-building and nation-destroying. My account of the origins of Soviet ethnic cleansing will attempt to address this paradox by showing how the same principles that informed Soviet nation-building in the 1920s, under certain conditions, could and did lead to ethnic cleansing and ethnic terror against a limited set of stigmatized nationalities, while leaving nation-building policies in place for the majority of nonstigmatized nationalities.

The Border Regions

Soviet policy in the 1920s was marked by a striking ethnophilia. Nevertheless, even then, one can trace certain preconditions for the emergence of Soviet ethnic cleansing. In Chapters 2 and 7, I analyzed three of these factors: popular ethnic cleansing, ethnically based agricultural resettlement, and the Piedmont Principle. Popular ethnic cleansing was the tendency of some national majorities to favor the expulsion of national minorities from the majority's national territory. Such extreme sentiments emerged when the ubiquitous conflicts among ethnic groups over the control of administrative territory also became intertwined with conflicts over the possession of agricultural land and with conflicts along former estate (*soslovie*) lines. Such serious ethnic conflict emerged in Kazakhstan, Kirgizia, and the North Caucasus Mountain regions, as well as in the Kuban. The popular belief that administrative and ethnic boundaries should coincide was reinforced by the regime's own practice of ethnically based

---

[4] For representative works, see Robert Conquest, *The Nation Killers* (London, 1977); Alexandre A. Bennigsen and Enders S. Wimbush, *Muslim National Communism in the Soviet Union* (Chicago, 1979).

[5] Ronald Grigor Suny, *The Revenge of the Past* (Stanford, Calif., 1993). Yuri Slezkine, "The USSR as Communal Apartment, or How a Socialist State Promoted Ethnic Particularism," *Slavic Review* 53 (1994): 414–452.

agricultural resettlement. Territorially dispersed nationalities, such as the Jews and Roma (Gypsies), were resettled into compact agricultural settlements in order to form national soviets, while free land within national soviets was reserved for the in-migration of the national majority. Finally, the Piedmont Principle extended this belief in the primacy of ethnic solidarity beyond the Soviet Union. The Piedmont Principle asserted that ethnic ties transcended political borders and therefore could be exploited by the Soviet Union to project Soviet influence abroad. The formation of the Moldavian ASSR and the territorial expansion of Belorussia were dictated by the Piedmont Principle. Already in the 1920s, then, Soviet nationalities policy had linked ethnicity to issues of administrative territory, land possession, foreign policy, and resettlement. In the 1920s, this recipe supported ethnophilia; in the 1930s, it would lead to ethnic cleansing.

To understand this dramatic shift from ethnic proliferation to ethnic cleansing, three further factors must be considered: Soviet xenophobia, the category of the border regions, and the politics surrounding immigration and emigration. Soviet xenophobia refers to the exaggerated Soviet fear of foreign influence and foreign contamination. It was not identical to traditional Russian xenophobia. Soviet xenophobia was ideological, not ethnic. It was spurred by an ideological hatred and suspicion of foreign capitalist governments, not the national hatred of non-Russians. Foreign intervention during the civil war did not create Soviet xenophobia. It merely confirmed a preexisting ideological inclination.

Soviet xenophobia was, however, given a national focus by ongoing low-intensity guerrilla warfare and sporadic partisan uprisings along the entire Soviet frontier. Whereas foreign military intervention had been brief and discrete, guerrilla warfare involved ongoing secretive border crossings and relied on an ambiguous combination of foreign and domestic support. Most famously, the Basmachi rebellion in Central Asia, which raged from 1920 to 1922 and was not fully extinguished until 1934, relied on clan and ethnic alliances linking northern Afghanistan and Soviet Central Asia.[6] Periodic uprisings flared up in other Soviet border regions: Chechnya and Dagestan (1920–1922), Karelia (1921–1922), Georgia (1924), Yakutia (1924–1925 and 1927–1928), Ajaristan (1927), and Kabardinia (1928). As noted in Chapter 6, collectivization sparked a series of major armed insurrections in the Soviet borderlands. Moreover, throughout the early 1920s, the OGPU reported ongoing political banditism in its border regions. GPU reports from the second half of 1922 note fourteen instances of long-term armed political "bands" with over one hundred members, all of which were operating in national regions along the Soviet border and surviving by frequently crossing into neighboring states.[7] Political banditism across the Soviet

[6] Baymirza Hayit, *"Basmatschi"* (Köln, 1992).

[7] Nine of the bands were operating along the Ukrainian–Polish border in Podolia and Volynia, three in Azerbaijan, and two in Georgia. This count is taken from the complete run of rural OGPU reports published in V. Danilov and A. Berelowitch, eds., *Sovetskaia derevnia glazami*

Polish–Ukrainian border remained a persistent problem and concern into the mid-1920s.[8] This problem deepened Soviet fears of surreptitious foreign penetration and focused Soviet xenophobia on the largely non-Russian border regions.

In July 1923, Soviet xenophobia was given an institutional embodiment by a government decree that delineated a special continuous administrative territory called "the border regions" (*pogranichnye raiony*).[9] All modern nations have clearly marked borders, some have had the concept of a border region, but no nation went as far as the Soviet Union in the ideological and administrative definition of distinct border regions.[10] The 1923 decree, which was drafted by the GPU, established a series of increasingly high-security border strips (*pogranichnye polosy*) running along the entire land and sea border of the Soviet Union at the depth of 4 meters, 500 meters, 7.5 kilometers, 16 kilometers, and 22 kilometers.[11] The entire 22-kilometer strip was placed under the special supervision of the GPU border guard, which was given an unlimited right of search and seizure.[12] Thus, a new legally defined territorial category had been established along the entire Soviet frontier: the border regions.

The 1923 decree focused exclusively on defensive security measures and so exemplified Soviet fear of foreign influence. As we saw in the previous chapter, however, the Soviet Union soon grew more confident and attempted to use its border regions to influence cross-border populations, particularly along the Soviet western border. To that end, on July 16, 1925, the Politburo passed a sweeping resolution establishing a variety of privileges for the western border regions: higher salaries for specialists, greater economic investment, a better supply of goods, permission to run budget deficits, and more cultural investment.[13] This decree was justified by "the unique position and significance of the border regions, both in a military-strategic and in a political sense."[14] Or as another decree put it: "Our border regions are that part

---

VChK-OGPU-NKVD. Dokumenty i materialy. Vol. 1. 1918–1922 (Moscow, 1998). This count is clearly incomplete as the many large armed Basmachi units in Central Asia are not included. Banditism was reported in some RSFSR regions, the largest band numbered 40 and operated in Stavropol. In the first half of 1922, the civil war–era "green" uprisings were still being suppressed across almost the entire Soviet Union.

[8] *RTsKhIDNI* 17/87/177 (1924); 17/87/178 (1923–1924). Exhaustive reports on cross-border banditism from 1923 to 1929 are now available in A. Berelovich and V. Danilov eds., *Sovetskaia derevnia glazami VChK-OGPU-NKVD 1918–1939. Vol. 2. 1923–1929. Dokumenty i materialy* (Moscow, 2000).

[9] *GARF* 3316/16a/22 (1923): 3–12. Based on a prior politbiuro resolution, *RTsKhIDNI* 17/3/339 (08.03.23): 53/6.

[10] On the concept of "borderlands" in prerevolutionary Russia, see Terry Martin, "The Empire's New Frontiers: New Russia's Path From Frontier to *Okraina*, 1774–1920," *Russian History* 19 (1992): 181–201. On the Imperial German concepts of the borderlands, see William Hagen, *Germans, Poles and Jews* (Chicago, 1980): 188–207.

[11] *GARF* 3316/16a/22 (1923): 3–4.

[12] Ibid., 3–7; *GARF* 3316/64/218 (1925): 51.

[13] *RTsKhIDNI* 17/16/1396 (28.08.25): 85/5. *GARF* 1235/120/11 (1925–1926): 1–21.

[14] *RTsKhIDNI* 17/3/511 (16.07.25): 71/34.

of our territory by which the toilers of neighboring nations concretely judge the RSFSR."[15]

Nationalities policy was naturally a crucial component of the border regime. The Piedmont Principle was based on the belief that cross-border ethnic ties could be mobilized to further Soviet influence in neighboring states, but it also implied the ability of foreign governments to exploit those ties against the Soviet Union. The Soviet leadership was most concerned about their Finnish, Polish, and German populations. A 1925 Rabkrin investigation of the western border regions reported that the Leningrad Finnish population was being exposed to a strong "Finnish influence, explained both by historic-cultural ties, and the efforts of Finland herself, who tries in all ways to widen her sphere of influence on the Finnish population of our border regions."[16] Similar concerns were registered about Ukraine's Polish and German populations[17]:

> Our information demonstrates the existence of national chauvinism in the Polish population, the enormous influence of priests, which creates a base for the influence of White Poles. The German, Polish and, to a degree, the Czech colonies are a foothold for spreading the influence of their governments, nests of spies in support of these governments. It is interesting to note that tied to the election of Hindenburg, in the German colonies a rumor is spreading about a 15-year German occupation of Ukraine.

Given these security concerns, one might have expected that the Soviet nationalities policy would have been implemented less vigorously in the border regions. The opposite was the case. The 1925 Politburo decree mandated an especially generous policy toward national minorities in the border regions of the Soviet Union. There should be more national schools, more national territories, an expanded native-language press, aggressive recruitment and promotion of national cadres, and strict punishment of all Russian chauvinism.[18] Far from attempting to further ethnic homogeneity, the Soviet government consciously aimed to emphasize and promote the ethnic diversity of their border regions.

A fundamental tension, then, lay at the heart of the Soviet nationalities policy in the border regions. Soviet xenophobia encouraged ethnic suspicions and a restriction on national self-expression, whereas the Piedmont Principle dictated an ostentatious promotion of national institutions. Throughout the 1920s, the latter tendency prevailed. It would take a series of domestic and foreign policy shocks, beginning with the Shumskyi affair and the defection of the KPZU, to provoke an abandonment of the ethnophilia of the 1920s and a turn toward the ethnic cleansing of the 1930s. In both the 1920s and 1930s, however, the adopted

---

[15] *GARF* 1235/120/11 (1925): 4.
[16] *GARF* 374/27s/594 (1925): 45.
[17] Ibid., 79.
[18] *RTsKhIDNI* 17/113/677 (12.11.28): 107–109.

policy was based on the exact same premise: the Bolsheviks' strong belief in the political salience of cross-border ethnic ties.

The Politics of Immigration

This tension between Soviet xenophobia and the Piedmont Principle was perhaps most dramatically exemplified in the Soviet attitude toward immigration. On the one hand, immigration was a victory for the Piedmont Principle, demonstrative evidence that the Soviet Union was attractive to cross-border populations. On the other hand, immigration was feared as an easy cover for foreign espionage. Still, despite this latter concern, illegal immigrants were usually not deported. In fact, they were granted the same national rights as indigenous Soviet nationalities. For instance, Afghan immigrants (Beluchi, Djemshid, Khazara) were given land in the border regions, their own national territories, and other national rights: "A positive Soviet mood among them will evoke sympathy and attract to us class-friendly elements from the foreign [Afghan] border regions."[19]

If the Soviet government nervously accepted new immigrants, it actively solicited the return of most non-Russian Soviet émigrés. Treaties with Finland and Poland both stipulated the right of émigrés to return to the Soviet Union. About 12,000 Finns and many more Poles took up this offer of amnesty.[20] Efforts were likewise made to entice Volga German émigrés to return.[21] In Central Asia, where the civil war and Basmachi uprising led to massive emigration, the government undertook aggressive measures to improve the economic conditions of its border regions and thereby to prevent further emigration and lure back émigrés: "It is politically extremely negative, that every year in the Afghan border regions, more and more forces openly hostile to us are gathering which, if political conditions worsen, will be used against us."[22]

However, the recruitment of immigrants also provoked considerable anxiety. As we have seen, the Soviet government made a major and highly successful effort to recruit Ukrainian and Belorussian nationalist émigrés (the *smenovekhovtsy*) to return to Soviet Ukraine and Belorussia. Upon their return, however, they were immediately placed under OGPU surveillance and treated as a serious internal threat. Likewise, illegal immigrants were frequently moved away from the border regions to thwart potential espionage.[23] This concern

[19] *RTsKhIDNI* 62/2/2205 (1930): 6, 33–34; *RTsKhIDNI* 62/1/829 (18.03.31); 62/1/467 (30.04.28); 62/1/882 (27.06.31); 62/3/465 (15.01.29): 18–23.
[20] Matley, "The Dispersal of the Ingrian Finns," 5. Mikolaj Iwanov, *Pierwszy narod ukarany* (Warsaw, 1991): 72.
[21] *RTsKhIDNI* 17/3/517 (27.08.25): 77/12.
[22] *RTsKhIDNI* 62/2/1261 (1928): 1. On the enormous efforts to recruit émigrés to return, see *RTsKhIDNI* 62/1/1106 (27.02.33): 92–102; 62/1/467 (30.04.28): 240–249; 62/1/829 (18.03.31): 49–61.
[23] *RTsKhIDNI* 62/1/467 (30.04.28): 248–249; 62/1829 (18.03.31): 51.

about immigrants was most evident in the Soviet Far East, where a massive influx of Koreans had created extremely tense ethnic relations. From 1917 to 1926, the Soviet Korean population tripled from 53,600 to 168,009. By 1926, Koreans represented over a quarter of the rural population of the Vladivostok *okrug* (145,511 of 572,031).[24] There was an enormous class and status difference between Koreans and Russians. In 1922, 84.3 percent of Korean households were landless and only 32.4 percent even possessed Soviet citizenship. In 1925, 68.8 percent of Koreans still cultivated exclusively rented land (vs. 7.8 percent of Russians). The average Korean household possessed less than one-third the land of local Russians (15.9 vs. 4.6 acres).[25] Conflict centered on land possession, since Soviet policy called for transferring land to those who cultivated it. This meant giving Russian land to immigrant Korean tenants. Russians responded by refusing to rent land and, according to the OGPU, by "demanding the resettlement of Koreans into a different region."[26]

Soviet policy, as dictated by the Piedmont Principle, however, demanded the exact opposite: the formation of an autonomous Korean national territory. Mass Korean immigration had eloquently demonstrated the attractiveness of the Soviet Union for the Koreans of Japanese-occupied Korea. The formation of an autonomous Korean territory would further attract Koreans and put pressure on the Japanese colonial regime. Such was the argument of the Komintern's Eastern Department when, in May 1924, it petitioned the Soviet government to form a Korean autonomous oblast.[27] This petition coincided exactly with the formation of the "Moldavian Piedmont" in the Soviet west, whose goal was to put political pressure on Romania. Table 29 shows that a Korean ASSR of almost the exact same size and ethnic preponderance could have been formed. The OGPU reported that Korean autonomy was extremely popular among Soviet Koreans, especially communists and Komsomol.[28] This proposal was seriously debated in TsIK and VTsIK but by 1925 had been decisively rejected.[29]

Two factors appear to explain the rejection of a Korean ASSR. Most importantly, the Soviet leadership felt politically and militarily weak in the Far East. They were, therefore, more concerned over potential Japanese influence on the Soviet Korean population than over projecting Soviet influence into Japanese-ruled Korea. A 1929 Rabkrin report bluntly stated that Japan viewed Korean immigration to the Soviet Union "as the natural expansion of the boundaries

---

[24] *GARF* 1235/140/141 (1925): 4; S. D. Anosov, *Koreitsy v ussuriiskom krae* (Khabarovsk-Vladivostok, 1928): 7–8; *Vsesoiuznaia perepis' naseleniia 1926 goda. Tom VII* (Moscow, 1928): 8, 126–127. When one includes the city of Vladivostok, Koreans represented 22.4 percent of the population.

[25] Ibid., 4.

[26] *RTsKhIDNI* 17/87/199 (1925): 96.

[27] *GARF* 1235/140/141 (1924): 20–34; for earlier efforts, see *Belaia kniga o deportatsii koreiskogo naseleniia Rossii v 30-40-kh godakh* (Moscow, 1992): 40, 46–47.

[28] *RTsKhIDNI* 17/87/199 (1925): 101; *GARF* 374/27s/1706 (1929): 34.

[29] *GARF* 1235/140/141 (1924–1925): 42–47.

Table 29. Moldavian ASSR and Proposed Korean Autonomous Territories

Actual Territory	Population of Titular Nationality	Total Population	Titular Nationality as Percent of Total
Moldavian ASSR	170,263	572,339	29.7
Proposed Territories			
Korean ASSR			
[Vladivostok *okrug*]	152,424	680,011	22.4
Korean AO			
[5 Border *raiony*]	85,299	157,438	54.2

Vsesoiuznaia perepis' 1926 goda, vol. VII, 126–127; vol. XI, 36.

of Korea, which at the proper moment could be claimed formally."[30] This fear led the Foreign Affairs Commissariat in January 1926 to demand emergency measures to stop Korean immigration.[31] In addition, the far eastern communist leadership gave expression to popular ethnic hostility. They supported the local Russian view of Koreans as potentially disloyal and economically detrimental illegal aliens, who should be resettled away from the sensitive border regions.[32]

As a result, a deeply contradictory policy line emerged. On the one hand, smaller Korean national territories were authorized: one Korean national region and 171 Korean village soviets.[33] Korean-language schools and newspapers were established. A far eastern national minorities bureaucracy was formed with a plenipotentiary on Korean affairs. Koreans were systematically promoted into the far eastern bureaucracy.[34] This policy line presented Koreans as a model Soviet national minority to be poignantly and publicly contrasted with the wretched Koreans living under Japanese colonial occupation.

On the other hand, at the exact same time this policy line was being implemented, the central government issued a December 6, 1926 secret decree confirming a plan to resettle most Koreans north of the 48.5th parallel (north of Khabarovsk). According to this decree, all Koreans who had not yet received land (slightly over half the population) would be resettled to the north.[35] Two large land funds were reserved for the Koreans. When this policy was justified publicly (which was rarely), it was portrayed as analogous to Jewish resettlement. Landless nationals were to be resettled compactly onto free government land, to provide them with land and to allow them to better

[30] *GARF* 374/27s/1706 (1929): 3.
[31] *GARF* 1235/140/141 (1926): 1410b.
[32] *GARF* 1235/140/141 (1925): 54–75; *Belaia kniga,* 46–49. Gelb, "An Early Soviet," 394–395.
[33] *GARF* 374/27s/1706 (1929): 25.
[34] *GARF* 1235/120/60 (1927): 71–78; *Belaia kniga,* 37–39; *GARF* 374/27s/1706 (1929): 28.
[35] *GARF* 1235/140/141 (1926): 144.

develop their national culture.[36] The comparison, however, was specious. Dispersed Jews were being voluntarily concentrated on excellent agricultural land. Koreans were already territorially concentrated on good agricultural land and were to be involuntarily dispersed and then immediately replaced with Slavic peasants from central regions.[37] It was this last measure that most infuriated Korean communists, since it clearly implied that the Soviet Koreans were disloyal.[38]

The Korean resettlement program would have been the first instance of Soviet ethnic cleansing had it in fact been implemented. However, through the end of 1928, virtually nothing had been done.[39] The opposition of Korean communists, passive resistance by Korean peasants, absence of central funding, lack of Russian settlers, and a deeply contradictory state policy caused the resettlement plan to go unfulfilled. The law nevertheless remained formally in effect and served to stigmatize the Soviet Koreans. In the Far East, then, a rough kind of balance between Soviet xenophobia and the Piedmont Principle prevailed. Before full-scale ethnic cleansing could emerge in either the Far East or the western border regions, two further policy shocks would have to occur.

Collectivization and Emigration

The first came in the form of collectivization and the emigration movement it triggered. The reintroduction of coercive grain requisitions in the winter of 1927–1928 immediately reversed the NEP-era immigration flow. Central Asia and the Transcaucasus reported a sudden growth in emigration and plans to emigrate.[40] The most dramatic and politically consequential emigration movement, however, took place in the fall of 1929. In September 1929, Soviet citizens of ethnic German descent began to converge on Moscow to demand exit visas to leave the Soviet Union permanently. Word of this development soon reached the German embassy, who sent out a representative, their agricultural attaché Otto Auhagen, to investigate. He was accompanied by two German and three American correspondents. They found that about 4500 Germans, mostly Mennonites, had congregated in the Moscow suburbs. The Germans told of horrible repression and reported they had sold or abandoned all their possessions and were resolved to emigrate to Canada.[41]

---

[36] GARF 1235/120/60 (1928): 17–20. Anosov, Koreitsy v ussuriiskom krae, 64.

[37] GARF 1235/140/141 (1926): 144.

[38] GARF 1235/140/141 (1928): 146–152.

[39] GARF 1235/141/1356 (1931): 3; GARF 3316/64a/1078 (1931): 5; GARF 374/27s/1706 (1929): 7–9.

[40] RTsKhIDNI 62/2/1261 (1928): 1–17; 42–43; 75–76; 157/5/83 (1927): 229–230.

[41] From 1923 to 1926, around 20,000 Mennonites had been permitted to emigrate to Canada. They now sought to resume this movement. Captured German Materials, Microfilm Reel 4763 (11.10.29): L192465–75; Harvey Dyck, Weimar Germany and Soviet Russia, 1926–1933 (New York, 1966): 162–174; Meir Buchsweiler, Volksdeutsche in der Ukraine am Vorabend und Beginn des Zweiten Weltkriegs—ein Fall doppelter Loyalität? (Gerlingen, 1984): 58–64.

The foreign correspondents immediately published sensational accounts of the repression these German peasants had suffered, which in turn triggered a storm of media coverage and provoked a significant political scandal in Germany. An organization named "Brothers in Need" was formed to raise money for the Soviet Germans, and President Hindenburg himself donated 200,000 Marks of his own money to it.[42] The German embassy, which had previously refused to intervene on behalf of ethnic German Soviet citizens so as not to offend their Soviet hosts, now interceded aggressively on their behalf.[43] Surprised by this unexpected development, the Soviet government behaved erratically, first allowing 5461 Germans to emigrate and then deporting the remaining 9730 to their original places of residence.[44] The episode ended up embarrassing the Soviet government at the height of the collectivization drive and significantly souring Soviet–German relations.

In theory, collectivization was not supposed to have had an ethnic dimension but, as the German emigration movement demonstrates, it quickly developed one. The anarchy and violence of collectivization, with its sudden reversal of the NEP order, enabled the expression of ethnic hostility. Where sentiments of popular ethnic cleansing existed, NEP "losers" took revenge. In Kazakhstan, local Russians revenged themselves on the suddenly vulnerable Kazakh nomads. Likewise, in Ukraine, popular opinion tended to view all Germans as kulaks. A TsK reported noted that "certain high officials have the incorrect opinion that all German villages are exclusively kulak."[45] Another communist put it more colorfully: All Germans were "kulak colonizers to the marrow of their bones."[46] The numerous internal reports attempting to explain the emigration movement unanimously agreed that these sentiments had led to an exceptionally harsh treatment of Germans during collectivization.[47] Such popular attitudes had likewise surfaced during the civil war and were linked to the Germans' privileged prerevolutionary status.

Similar treatment provoked smaller emigration movements in 1929–1930 among almost all of the Soviet Union's "western national minorities": Poles, Finns, Latvians, Greeks, Estonians, Lithuanians, Czechs, Swedes, Bulgarians.[48] These movements consisted largely of group and individual petitions to Soviet authorities and foreign consuls. There were also demonstrations and, most disturbing for the Soviets, illegal flights across the western border.[49] The most active were the Poles.[50] They were also subjected to the greatest degree of popular and local communist hostility during collectivization. The popular

[42] Dyck, *Weimar Germany*, 163, 171.

[43] CGM Reel 5213 (01.08.29): K480944–49; Reel 4763, L192270–475.

[44] *GARF* 3316/64/759 (1929–1930).

[45] *RTsKhIDNI* 17/113/786 (16.10.29): 44.

[46] *GARF* 1235/141/561 (1930): 59.

[47] *RTsKhIDNI* 17/113/786 (16.10.29): 42–46; 17/113/822 (06.02.30): 181/4, 1–250; *GARF* 1235/141/561 (1930); 3316/64/928 (1930); 3316/64/759–761 (1929–1930).

[48] *GARF* 3316/64/760 (1930); 3316/64/928 (1930); 3316/23/1356 (1930): 14–15.

[49] *GARF* 3316/23/1360 (1930): 6–60b; 3316/64/928 (1930): 12–16.

[50] *GARF* 1235/141/561 (1930): 135–137; 3316/23/1360 (1930): 6; 3316/23/1318 (1930): 12–15.

identification of Pole and kulak was summed up in the rhyme: "*raz Poliak—
znachit kulak*." Poles were bluntly told, "you are being dekulakized not because
you are a kulak, but because you are a Pole." This reflected a widespread sentiment of popular ethnic cleansing, reflected in this comment from a Russian
village: "If he's a Pole, he annoys us and should be driven out of the village,
as a foreign element."[51] Hundreds of Poles, including many communists,
succeeded in fleeing across the Polish–Soviet border. Other Poles engaged
in mass demonstrative marches to the border, in crowds of up to 2000, to
publicize their demand to be allowed to emigrate.[52]

These emigration movements dramatically confronted the Soviet leadership
with the failure of the Piedmont Principle. The Soviet Union's western national
minorities were meant to serve as attractive communist examples for their ethnic
brethren abroad. Instead, they themselves had been attracted by their respective "home" countries and had repudiated their Soviet fatherland in an exceedingly embarrassing fashion. Their actions had even led to official protests by the
German and Finnish foreign ministries.[53] In addition, as we have seen, the non-
Russian periphery in general offered more violent resistance to collectivization
than did the Russian core. Moreover, such resistance often focused on the
border regions. The Basmachi movement received cross-border assistance from
related clans in Central Asia. The worst peasant uprising of the collectivization
era broke out along the Polish–Ukrainian border in late February 1930. Both
the emigration movements and these mass uprisings deepened Soviet concerns
about the loyalty of their non-Russian periphery and about the security of their
border regions.

Given this outcome, one might have expected dramatic policy revisions.
However, the official response, both in secret and published resolutions, called
instead for an intensification of the existing nationalities policy.[54] The policy
had not failed, it was declared, but rather had never been properly implemented
and was seriously distorted during collectivization. This was not simply verbal
cover for a real change in policy. Throughout 1930, enormous effort was put
into increasing the number and quality of German national institutions.[55] The
same was true for Poles and other western national minorities.[56] Of course, there
was also an increase in repression against "notoriously malicious elements" but
the policy emphasis remained on promoting, rather than attacking, national
identity.

There were, however, two important exceptions. The mass processions of
Poles to the Polish border particularly alarmed Soviet authorities, since they

[51] *GARF* 3316/64/760 (1930): 79; 3316/64/1355 (1930): 19; 3316/64/928 (1930): 15.
[52] *GARF* 3316/64/760 (1930): 62–63; 3316/23/1360 (1930): 6; 3316/64/928 (1930): 12.
[53] CGM Reel 5213 (07.01.31): K481216, (09.02.30): K481276; (04.03.30): K480975–77.
[54] *RTsKhIDNI* 17/113/821 (06.02.30): 181/4; *GARF* 1235/141/561 (1930): 10–12, 23, 201;
3316/16a/443 (1930): 10–12.
[55] There are literally thousands of pages of documents devoted to this question. *GARF*
1235/141/561 (1930); 3316/64/928 (1930); 3316/64/968 (1929–1930); 3316/64/759–761.
[56] *GARF* 3316/16a/443 (1930): 1–2; *GARF* 3316/64/760 (1930): 8–10.

took place in late February 1930 during the mass uprising against collectivization in the Ukrainian border regions. Although this uprising involved mostly
Ukrainian peasants, Poles also participated.[57] OGPU and government reports
spoke of increased Polish espionage and Polish government encouragement for
the uprising.[58] The Soviet nightmare scenario was a mass Polish emigration
movement, akin to the German one, but directed toward the Polish border
rather than Moscow[59]:

> Recently we have registered facts that work is being undertaken in order
> to prepare a mass demonstrative departure of Poles from the USSR to
> Poland. . . . There is no doubt that this campaign has the goal of preparing
> popular opinion to justify an armed attack on the Soviet Union.

It was in this environment that the Soviet leadership authorized its first
explicitly ethnic deportation.

On March 5, 1930, the Politburo passed the following resolution[60]:

> Deport from the border *okrugi* of Belorussia . . . and right-bank Ukraine . . .
>
> a. the families of individuals condemned for banditism, espionage, active
>   counterrevolution and professional contraband.
> b. independent of whether they are regions of complete collectivization, kulak
>   households of all three categories—in the first line, those of Polish nation-
>   ality—in addition to the quota already fulfilled: from Belorussia 3000–3500
>   families and from Ukraine 10–15,000 families. . . .
>
> In Belorussia and Ukraine, as part of this total may be deported those Polish
> noble families [*shliakhetskie semeistva*], regardless of their material position,
> whose presence near the border is determined by the OGPU and local party
> officials as dangerous. . . .

The decree also called for the OGPU to increase its surveillance of the border
to stop "unauthorized border crossings." This was the first instance of ethnic
deportation.[61] A follow-up decree on March 11 made clear these deportations
were directed primarily against Poles (and not primarily nobles) and that foreign
intervention was a major concern[62]:

> From our data there is reason to believe that in the case of serious kulak-peasant
> uprisings in right-bank Ukraine and Belorussia—especially tied to the coming
> deportation of Polish–kulak counter-revolutionary and spying elements from the

---

[57] *TsDAHOU* 1/20/3184 (1930): 17–18.
[58] *TsDAHOU* 1/20/3184 (1930): 17; *GARF* 3316/23/1318 (1930): 3, 15.
[59] *GARF* 3316/64/928 (1930): 1.
[60] *RTsKhIDNI* 17/162/8 (05.03.30): 119/5.
[61] Unless one counts Cossacks as an ethnic group, in which case the civil war–era deportation
of Terek Cossacks was the first instance.
[62] *RTsKhIDNI* 17/162/8 (11.03.30): 120/72.

border regions—that the Polish government might decide to intervene. In order
to avoid this. . . .

5. Prepare the operation for the arrest and deportation of kulak Polish
counter-revolutionary elements with great care and carry out in a maximally
short period.

6. Carry out the operation of deporting kulak-Polish elements with maximum
organization and without fanfare [*bez shuma*]. . . .

Collectivization, dekulakization, the Polish emigration movement, and intense
Soviet concern over the security of their border regions, then, led to the first
case of Soviet ethnic cleansing.[63] Still, after this deportation, Soviet policy
toward the Poles did not undergo a dramatic change. Remarkably, in 1932 a
new Polish national district was even established along the Belorussian–Polish
border.[64]

In the Soviet far east, collectivization also provoked increased ethnic tension
and growing security concerns. Anti-Korean and anti-Chinese popular violence
increased dramatically from 1928 to 1932.[65] This atmosphere led to a mass outflow
of Chinese migrant labor.[66] Approximately 50,000 Koreans also fled back to
Korea.[67] The authorities did not oppose this emigration. In fact, they revived
plans to resettle much of the remaining Korean population away from the
Soviet–Korean border. On April 13, 1928, a decree was passed calling for "the
resettlement of Koreans from Vladivostok okrug and the more strategically
vulnerable points of *Primor'e* into Khabarovsk okrug." The land of the resettled
Koreans was to be immediately transferred to "settlers from overpopulated agrar-
ian regions of the Soviet Union."[68] The plan was to settle demobilized Red Army
soldiers into the far eastern border zones to form "Red Army collective farms."[69]
Disloyal Koreans were to be replaced with loyal Slavs.

An official five-year plan called for resettling 88,000 Koreans (over half the
Korean population) north of Khaborovsk.[70] All Koreans without Soviet citizenship were to be resettled, "except those having proved their complete loyalty

[63] There may have been a Finnish deportation as well. The March 5 Politburo decree called for
the OGPU to study the Leningrad border regions and propose measures. Groups in Finland
claimed there was an ethnically targeted deportation. See The Ingrian Committee, *The Ingrian
Finns* (Helsinki, 1935), 8. I found no decree to confirm this deportation (but I did not work in
St. Petersburg archives), and Gelb also doubts an ethnically targeted deportation took place. Gelb,
"Western Finnic Minorities," 238–242.

[64] *GARF* 3316/64/1284 (1932); Iwanow, *Pierwszy narod ukarany*, 128–138.

[65] See *GARF* 3316/64/1078 (1931): 1–4; 20–53; 76–77; *GARF* 374/27s/1076 (1929): 59–63;
A. Nugis, *Protiv velikoderzhavnogo shovinizma i mestnogo natsionalizma* (Khabarovsk, 1933),
26–28. *GARF* 3316/64/1078 (1931): 50b; Agi Zakir, "Zemel'naia politika v kolkhoznom dvizhenii
sredi koreitsev Dal'nevostochnogo kraia," *Revoliutsiia i natsional'nosti*, nos. 2–3 (1931): 76–81.

[66] *GARF* 374/27s/1706 (1929): 400b.

[67] Haruki Wada, "Koreans in the Soviet Far East, 1917–1937," in Daae-Sook Suh, ed., *Koreans
in the Soviet Union* (Honolulu, 1987): 40.

[68] *GARF* 3316/16a/384 (1928): 1–2.

[69] *GARF* 5446/15a/258 (1933): 41–42.

[70] *GARF* 374/27s/1706 (1929): 80b.

and devotion to Soviet power."[71] The suspected disloyalty of the majority of Soviet Koreans was thus assumed. Anyone refusing resettlement was now threatened with arrest. Leaders of Korean village soviets that harbored illegal aliens were likewise threatened, showing that even Korean Soviet officials were now suspect.[72] The deportation was scheduled to begin in 1930. Ten thousand Koreans were to be moved northward and 10,000 demobilized Red Army soldiers and their families to be settled in the far eastern border zones.[73] In reality, only 1342 Koreans were actually resettled in 1930, "including 431 resettled by force [*prinuditel'nym sposobom*]."[74] In 1931, the plan was officially abandoned. In the end, only 500 Korean families (about 2500 individuals) had been resettled.[75] It appears that the Foreign Affairs Commissariat concerns that Japan could use the deportation of Japanese subjects from the Soviet border regions as a *casus belli* led to the abandonment of Korean resettlement.[76]

In both the west and east, then, the Soviet government retreated from large-scale ethnic cleansing as the collectivization emergency subsided. The effects of this crisis, however, were felt in a greatly intensified regime in the border regions. By 1929, the term "border regions" had been expanded to include not only all districts (*raiony*) touching the Soviet border (called the primary border zone), but also all districts touching those border districts (the secondary border zone).[77] In Ukraine alone, this included a population of about two to three million.[78] In keeping with the new militant rhetoric, border districts were now often referred to as "front" (*frontovye*) districts in opposition to nonborder "rear" (*tylovye*) districts.[79] Each year likewise witnessed an increase in the size of the OGPU's border guard.[80] Deportations of "active counterrevolutionary and kulak elements" from the border regions intensified.[81]

A further innovation begun during collectivization was the formation of Red Army collective farms in the border regions. Ambitious plans were drawn up to settle tens of thousands of demobilized Red Army soldiers in the Far East's border regions, although only about 10,000 were actually settled there in 1930–1931, and about half of these immediately departed for home.[82] In response to this mass flight of demobilized Red Army soldiers, a March 16, 1932 TsK

[71] GARF 1235/141/359 (1929): 3.
[72] Ibid., 3–4.
[73] GARF 1235/141/1356 (1930): 18–19; 3316/64/1078 (1931): 83; RGAE 7486/42s/5 (1931): 113.
[74] GARF 1235/141/1356 (1930): 18–19.
[75] GARF 3316/64/1078 (1931): 83.
[76] GARF 5446/29/67 (1937): 18.
[77] GARF 393/1s/283 (1929): 1.
[78] TsDAHOU 1/16/8 (16.01.32): 167–173.
[79] RTsKhIDNI 62/1/829 (10.03.31): 33.
[80] RTsKhIDNI 17/162/8 (20.04.30): 124/80; 17/162/11 (01.12.31): 78/80; (27.02.32): 90/45; 17/162/12 (16.04.32): 96/21.
[81] TsDAHOU 1/16/8 (08.01.32): 136; 1/16/35 (21.03.31): 16; RTsKhIDNI 17/162/8 (20.04.30): 124/80; 17/162/14 (19.04.33): 136/94; "Spetspereselentsy-zhertvy 'sploshnoi kollektivizatsii'," Istoricheskii arkhiv, no. 4 (1994): 156.
[82] RGAE 7486/42s/8 (1932): 42–55; 7486/42s/5 (1931): 113; GARF 5446/15a/262 (1934): 20; 5446/15a/258 (1933): 41–42.

decree formed a Special Kolkhoz Corpus in the far eastern army, which consisted of 50,000 active recruits, who would serve their terms in Red Army collective farms in the far eastern border regions and then stay on as colonists after their demobilization.[83] Due to the famine crisis, however, only a fraction of this plan was realized and the enthusiasm for Red Army colonization waned. It would revive only with the next wave of ethnic cleansing swept through the far east in 1937.[84] Red Army collective farms emerged as part of the 1928 Korean deportation plan and would consistently accompany Soviet ethnic cleansing. If national territories in the border regions were the symbol of the Piedmont Principle, Red Army collective farms became the symbol of Soviet xenophobia.

The Ukrainian Crisis

Collectivization and the accompanying emigration movement focused Soviet xenophobia on the Soviet Union's diaspora nationalities—Germans, Poles, Koreans—whose flight was felt to have demonstrated greater loyalty to their foreign homelands than to the Soviet Union. Their actions naturally undermined the viability of the Piedmont Principle and exacerbated Soviet xenophobia. The diaspora nationalities, however, were of little importance to domestic Soviet nationalities policy and of less importance to Soviet foreign policy ambitions than were large border republics such as Ukraine and Belorussia, whose cross-border ethnic ties were key to the Soviet goal of undermining Polish rule in Poland's majority Ukrainian and Belorussian territories. More decisive here was the combined effect of the Shumskyi affair, Pilsudski's rise to power in Poland, the 1927 war scare, and the defection of the KPZU in not only undermining the Piedmont Principle, but also suggesting that "due to the clever policy of Pilsudski," Western Ukraine was being turned into a "Piedmont to attract discontented elements within [Soviet] Ukraine."[85] As cross-border ethnic ties were increasingly seen as an important conduit for the penetration of foreign capitalist influence, Soviet xenophobia became ethnicized.

The balance between the Piedmont Principle and Soviet xenophobia tipped decisively in favor of the latter with the national interpretation of the grain requisitions crisis in the fall of 1932. It was now official doctrine that cross-border ethnic ties had made a substantial contribution to a major domestic crisis. The December 14, 1932 politburo decree represented not only a turning point in the history of *korenizatsiia*, but also the triumph of an ethnicized Soviet xenophobia and an important milestone in the onset of Soviet ethnic cleansing. In addition to criticizing Ukrainization, the December 14 decree also ordered

[83] Ibid., 42–55; *GARF* 5446/15a/262 (1934): 20.

[84] *RTsKhIDNI* 558/11/65 (06.05.38): 115–119.

[85] *RTsKhIDNI* 17/69/58 (1927): 167.

the deportation of the entire population of the Kuban Cossack town of Poltava, "except those truly devoted to Soviet power and not involved in the sabotage of grain delivery."[86] This decree led to the deportation of all 9187 Cossack residents to the far north with only non-Cossacks being spared.[87] In the next month, all inhabitants of two more Kuban Cossack towns (Medvedovskaia and Urupskaia) and the majority of a third town (Umanskaia) were also deported.[88] The final total of deported Kuban Cossacks exceeded 60,000.[89] Following the emerging Soviet norm, the deported Cossacks were replaced with 14,090 demobilized Red Army soldiers.[90] The majority of these were Russians, but settlers were recruited from Belorussia and Ukraine as well. There is no evidence that the goal of Red Army settlement was russification.[91] The same was true of the resettlement, with ordinary peasant households, of the hardest-hit south Ukrainian famine regions.[92]

The deportation of the Kuban Cossacks marked an important transition from class-based to ethnic-based deportation. The launching of the dekulakization campaign in February 1930 began the great era of mass forced relocation that would continue until Stalin's death in 1953. Approximately 1.8 million individuals were deported as kulaks in 1930–1931, and another 340,000 in 1932–1933.[93] These exiles were given the status of "special settlers" and were used both as a source of forced labor for industrialization and to colonize remote regions in the far north, Siberia, and Kazakhstan.[94] The grounds for deporting a "kulak" were his class status or the possession of "kulak" political views as demonstrated by resisting collectivization. All "kulaks" were deported as individuals (or rather individual household heads). Entire villages were never deported or officially threatened with deportation.

The deportation of three large Kuban Cossack towns would appear to have been the first officially sanctioned mass deportation of an entire settlement since the deportation of the Terek Cossacks from the Mountaineer ASSR in 1920–1921. Throughout the Kuban affair, Sheboldaev and Kaganovich empha-

[86] Holod 1932–1933 rokiv, 293.

[87] RGVA 9/36s/613s (1933): 6; 46. Ivnitskii, 51.

[88] Oskolkov, 55.

[89] Oskolkov, 66. Oskolkov cites deportations from eight Kuban Cossack towns, totaling 63,500 individuals. The actual figure would certainly be considerably higher, perhaps approaching 100,000.

[90] RTsKhIDNI 17/162/15 (11.10.33): 147/112; RGAE 5675/1/39 (1933): 24–25, 88.

[91] RGAE fond 5675, opis' 1, dela 33, 39, 43, 52, 55; RGVA 9/36s/613s (1933); GARF 5446/16a/261 (1935). RTsKhIDNI 17/3/933 (22.01.33): 148/73.

[92] In late 1933 and early 1934, a total of 44,026 peasant households were transferred to Kharkov, Donetsk, Dnepropetrovsk, and Odessa oblasts. Of these, 21,557 were from the RSFSR, 16,983 from other Ukrainian regions, and 5486 from Belorussia. GARF 5446/16a/261 (1935): 1–4.

[93] V. N. Zemskov, "Spetsposelentsy (po dokumentatsii NKVD-MVD SSSR)," Sotsiologicheskie issledovaniia, no. 11 (1990): 4–6. The total for 1932–1933 would include the Kuban Cossacks, as well as those exiled from urban centers as part of the passportization campaign in 1933.

[94] On the history of the spetspereselentsy, see the splendid document collections compiled by V. P. Danilov and S. A. Krasilnikov, eds., Spetspereselentsy v zapadnoi Sibiri, 4 vols. (Novosibirsk, 1992–1996).

sized the principle of collective responsibility: "In current circumstances, everyone must answer for their neighbors."[95] Kaganovich also drew an explicit parallel to the previous Cossack deportations: "All the Kuban Cossacks must be reminded how in 1921 the Terek Cossacks were deported. It's the same situation now."[96] The Kuban Cossack deportation was not, strictly speaking, an act of *ethnic* cleansing. The Cossacks were a former privileged status (*soslovie*) group and their resistance to collectivization was understood as the response of the formerly privileged. In this sense, their deportation could be and was interpreted as a special instance of dekulakization.[97]

However, the Cossack deportations were much more similar to the coming wave of ethnic cleansing. First, entire villages were deported on the principle of collective responsibility and collective guilt. Second, the Kuban Cossacks were a peculiar *soslovie* group. They were not a "layer" of society like the nobility, but a complete regionally based society with its own traditions, dialect, and identity: in effect, an unrecognized Soviet ethnicity. Third, as in many future cases of ethnic cleansing, there was strong hostility between the Kuban Cossacks and the local Slavic peasantry due to the coincidence of conflict along status, territorial, land ownership, and ethnic lines. Fourth, the Kuban Cossacks were labeled Ukrainian nationalists by the December 14 decree and linked to Ukrainian nationalism in Soviet and Polish Ukraine. The Kuban Cossack deportation, then, marked a transition from the class-based deportations, which predominated prior to 1933, to the ethnic deportations that would predominate from 1933 until Stalin's death in 1953.

The national interpretation of the grain requisitions crisis also launched the 1933 Ukrainian terror, during which tens of thousands of putative Ukrainian nationalists were arrested for allegedly conspiring with the new Nazi leadership in Germany, as well as Pilsudski's Poland, to separate Ukraine from the Soviet Union. The pernicious role of cross-border ethnic influence was a major propaganda theme during the 1933 terror and the major target for arrest was the diaspora community of west Ukrainian émigrés, most of whom were communist refugees.[98] The attitude toward Ukraine's German and Polish populations in 1933 was ambiguous. Since the Ukrainian leadership was being accused of mistreating their national minorities, there was some effort to improve the national institutions (especially schools) of the Poles and Germans.[99] However, this tendency was dwarfed by the overwhelming fear of cross-border ethnic influence. For the first time, ethnic Germans and Poles (both Soviet citizens and noncitizens) were now specifically targeted for arrest.[100] The Ukrair.an

[95] *RGVA* 9/36s/613s (1933): 15.

[96] Oskolkov, 52.

[97] Ibid., 5–6.

[98] O. S. Rublov and A. I. Cherchenko, *Stalinshchyna i dolia zakhidnoukrains'koi intelihentsii. 20-50-ti roku XX st.* (Kiev, 1994).

[99] *TsDAHOU* 1/20/6213 (1933): 1–71.

[100] *RTsKhIDNI* 81/3/215 (1932–1933): 2–6. *GARF* 1235/128/3 (1933): 216–217. Iwanow, *Pierwszy narod ukarany*, 351–356.

GPU uncovered a putative covert Polish Military Organization (POV).[101] It was supposedly based in the Institute of Polish Culture in Kiev, where "a majority of the Institute's staff and students were arrested by the GPU." Other Polish institutes were also found to have been "in reality, dens of spies and counter-revolutionaries."[102] Similar purges took place in German academic institutions.[103] Ukraine's border regions regime was once again strengthened through the deportation of various categories of "unreliable elements," among which were now 1200 ethnic German households.[104] The Piedmont Principle had now been irrevocably abandoned. With the rise of fascist and authoritarian regimes throughout East-Central Europe, official Soviet propaganda, adopting a phrase from Stalin's August 11 letter to Kaganovich, now instead emphasized turning Ukraine, and indeed the entire Soviet Union, into a "fortress" against all foreign influence.[105]

Ethnic Cleansing

Large-scale ethnic cleansing began in the Soviet Union's western border regions in 1935. The targets were again diaspora nationalities, that is, national minorities (such as Poles, Germans, Finns) with cross-border ethnic ties to a foreign nation-state. As we have seen, the Soviet leadership already sanctioned "positive" ethnic resettlement in the 1920s. Also, the diaspora nationalities were subject to considerable popular ethnic hostility, which led to harsh treatment during collectivization and the resulting emigration movements that in turn raised concern about their loyalty. These concerns escalated in 1933–1934, when a campaign was launched in Germany to help their starving German "Brothers in Need" in the Soviet Union by sending tens of thousands of food packets and foreign currency remittances (called "Hitler help" by the Soviets).[106] This campaign provided further evidence that the diaspora nationalities could be used by foreign governments as weapons against the Soviet Union: "From the moment of Hitler's rise to power, there was a significant rise in activity in our German national soviets and among the German consuls in Ukraine . . . the Hitler government through its [pan-German] organizations organized in the fascist press a broad anti-Soviet campaign about famine in Ukraine, organized displays of photographs of starving [Ukrainians] and published provocational

[101] Piotr Mitzner, "Widmo POW," *Karta*, no. 11 (1993): 21–23. I. I. Shapoval, *Ukraina 20-50-kh rokiv: storinky nenapysanoi istorii* (Kiev, 1993): 131.

[102] *TsDAHOU* 1/7/328 (13.10.33): 48.

[103] *GARF* 1235/128/3 (1933): 216–217.

[104] *TsDAHOU* 1/20/6390 (1933): 2. Bugai, *Iosif Stalin—Lavrentiiu Berii*, 37.

[105] *RTsKhIDNI* 81/3/99 (1932): 150. P. Postyshev, "Radians'ka Ukraina—nepokhytnyi forpost velykoho SRSR," in *U borot'by za lenins'ku natsional'nu polityku* (Kiev, 1934): 5–32.

[106] *Ts DAHOU* 1/20/6426 (1933): 1–23. Buchsweiler, *Volkdeutsche in den Ukraine*, 64–71. CGM Reel 5213 (25.05.32): K481339–41 (06.06.32): K481348–50. *Nimtsi v Ukraini 20-30-ti rr. XX st.* (Kiev, 1994): 179–185.

declarations of the German population in Ukraine asking for help."[107] The Ukrainian GPU also reported that Poles were soliciting similar help from the Polish consul in Kiev.[108] As Hitler solidified power in Germany and destroyed the powerful German Communist Party with surprising ease, Soviet concerns escalated. They peaked with the ominous German–Polish nonaggression pact of January 1934.

In response to these events, the Soviet government undertook a reevaluation of its policy toward its Polish population and yet another, more thoroughgoing intensification of the western border regions' regime. The Polish investigation found "an incorrect policy and practice of introducing Polish schools into districts and villages with a majority Belorussian population and the compulsory instruction in Polish for Belorussian children."[109] The head of the Belorussian government, N. M. Goloded, gave this discovery a new sinister interpretation[110]:

> We forgot that with the formation of a Polish national district our task becomes considerably more difficult. The enemy also exploits this act of Soviet power. Do you really think that the defense and other organs of Poland did not take into consideration this act of Soviet power? They did and they acted—it can't be excluded that—in a closed plenum we can speak of this—that Polish organs may have specially worked on the Polonization of [our] schools . . . the possibility can't be excluded that special work was undertaken to Polonize the Belorussian population through these schools. The possibility can't be excluded that here we see an attempt by Polish fascism to build something for future contingencies. . . .

This statement represented a fundamental shift, for it sanctioned the view that Polish national institutions had fostered rather than disarmed nationalism, an interpretation that would justify both the abolition of national institutions and the onset of ethnic cleansing.[111]

In the fall of 1934, the Politburo formulated a new regime for its western border regions.[112] This regime created yet another border category, the "forbidden border zone" (*zapretnyi pogranichnyi zon*), into which no one could enter without special NKVD permission.[113] This zone was officially only 7.5 kilometers deep, but in Leningrad oblast it ran as deep as 90 kilometers

---

[107] Ibid., 13–14.

[108] *GARF* 3316/64/1537 (1934): 14.

[109] *RTsKhIDNI* 17/21/404 (03.08.34): 2, 18–21. Belorussian-speaking Catholics often considered themselves Poles and demanded Polish education for their children, a practice that was officially sanctioned prior to 1934. The same was true of Ukrainian-speaking Catholics. See, for instance, *TsDAHOU* 1/20/2019 (1925): 10.

[110] Ibid., 87–88.

[111] For a similar statement about covert Polish government activities aimed at the "forced Polonization" of Ukrainians in Soviet Ukraine, see *TsDAHOU* 1/20/6453 (1934): 1.

[112] *RTsKhIDNI* 77/1/425 (1934): 1.

[113] *TsDAHOU* 1/16/13 (26.08.36): 104–109; SZ (17.07.35): 45/377.

along the Latvian and Estonian borders.[114] A variety of security measures accompanied this decree. One of them was ethnic cleansing. Between February 20 and March 10, 1935, a total of 8329 families (about 41,650 individuals) were deported from the border regions of Kiev and Vinnitsa oblasts to eastern Ukraine. Although Germans and Poles made up only a few percent of the local population, they represented 57.3 percent of the deportees.[115] This limited initial action against "unreliable" elements was expanded in the course of 1935. In July 1935, Kiev officials wrote the Ukrainian Central Committee that "the number of households deported and resettled had not completely cleansed [*ochistit'*] the Markhlevskii [Polish] district of anti-Soviet elements." They asked for and received permission to deport 300 additional Polish households.[116] This was now a completely ethnic deportation. In October 1935, the Ukrainian TsK petitioned Moscow for permission to deport still another 1500 Polish households.[117] In response, NKVD chairman Genrikh Iagoda wrote Molotov that the spring deportations had "significantly cleansed [*ochistilo*] the border regions, especially Kiev oblast, from counterrevolutionary nationalist (Polish and German) and anti-Soviet elements . . . [but] in the border regions of Vinnitsa oblast there remain significant cadres of counterrevolutionary Polish nationalist elements."[118] The charge of counterrevolution and the language of ethnic cleansing had now fully emerged.

In January 1936, before this third deportation had even been completed, the order was given for a massive new deportation of 15,000 German and Polish households, now to Kazakhstan rather than eastern Ukraine.[119] In Kazakhstan, they were quickly reduced to the same status ("special settler") as the formerly deported kulaks, which meant they were placed under NKVD supervision and subject to forced labor and other deprivations.[120] These deportations, however, still remained partial. Not all Germans and Poles were labeled counterrevolutionary and deported. The deportations of 1935–1936 included approximately half the German and Polish population of the Ukrainian border regions.[121] No Poles or Germans from outside the border regions were deported.

---

[114] *Leningradskaia pravda*, no. 113 (23.05.35): 1; BFORC Reel 3 (03.06.35): vol. 19454, 171–174.

[115] Of the deported families, 2866 were Polish and 1903 were German. *GARF* 5446/16a/265 (1935): 14. *TsDAHOU* 1/16/11 (20.12.34): 316–317; 1/16/12 (23.01.35): 39.

[116] *TsDAHOU* 1/6/396 (17.08.35): 166–167; *TsDAHOU* 1/16/12 (05.09.35): 267–268.

[117] *TsDAHOU* 1/16/12 (16.10.35): 314.

[118] *GARF* 5446/16a/265 (1935): 14–15.

[119] *GARF* 5446/18a/209 (1936): 1; *TsDAHOU* 1/16/12 (25.11.35): 346; 1/16/13 (15.03.36): 25; *RTsKhIDNI* 17/42/186 (16.02.35): 6–10; 17/42/208 (31.03.36): 15.

[120] Initially, the deported were not formally deprived of their civil rights but were, like the kulaks, settled in NKVD work-settlements (*trudposelki*). Later they were formally reduced to the existing kulak status of *spetspereselentsy*. *GARF* 5446/18a/209 (1936): 30, 70–73. Nikolaj F. Bugaj, " 'Specjalna teczka Stalina': deportacje i reemigracja polakow," *Zeszyty Historyczie*, no. 107 (1993): 137–138.

[121] This is an approximation based on the 1926 census. By 1941, 70 to 80 percent of the Germans had been deported from the German Pulinskii *raion*. Buchsweiler, *Volkdeutsche in den Ukraine*, 157.

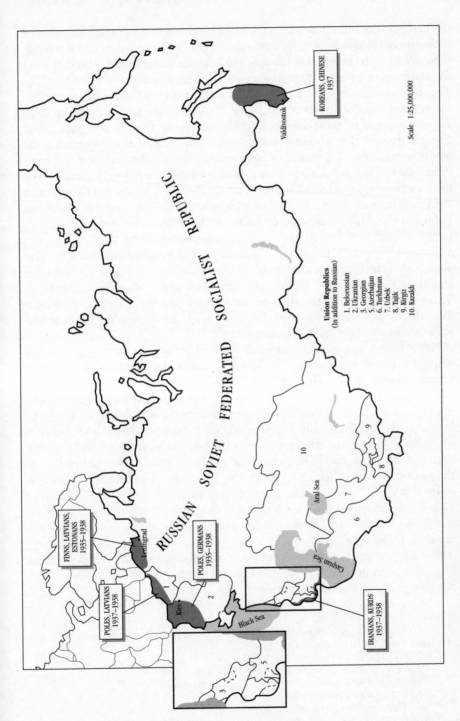

Map 3. Soviet Ethnic Cleansing, 1935–1938

The Germans and Poles who remained in Ukraine saw a gradual abolition of their national institutions.[122] By June 1935, 36 Polish village soviets and 367 Polish schools had been abolished in Ukraine and Belorussia. Both the deportations and the abolition of national institutions were marked, however, by an odd duality. The actions clearly indicated an intentional policy of national repression. However, unlike the former attacks on the "kulaks" or the Kuban Cossacks, there was no mention of these actions in the public press. On the contrary, public rhetoric insisted that nothing had changed. This duality even penetrated the Soviet bureaucracy. The Soviet of Nationalities, the paradigmatic soft-line institution supervising nationalities policy, fearing a tendency toward a total reversal of *korenizatsiia*, declared in June 1935 that the process of abolishing German and Polish institutions was over.[123] They were ignored. In July 1935, the Ukrainian Politburo abolished Ukraine's only Polish district, Markhlevskii, and the German border district of Pulinskii, both of which had been hard hit by the spring deportations.[124] Several major Polish and German cultural institutions were also abolished.[125] In October, 40 Polish village soviets and 117 Polish schools were abolished as "artificially created" (*isskustvenno sozdano, shtuchno utvoreno*).[126] This would become the patented phrase for justifying the abolition of national institutions. Belorussia followed Ukraine's lead. By September 1936, it had abolished nineteen of its forty Polish soviets.[127]

Nevertheless, the duality persisted. The majority of German and Polish national institutions continued to function. Public discourse about Poles and Germans remained largely unchanged. They were portrayed as loyal Soviet nationalities. A wide gap had opened between practice and discourse at all but the highest levels of the Soviet state. For instance, in responding to a censure by the Soviet of Nationalities, a Kiev official could only defend the abolition of Polish and German village soviets with this euphemistic reference to the 1935–1936 deportations: "The percentage of Polish and German population in the national soviets has changed in the direction of reduction [*v storonu umen'sheniia*]."[128] As a result, from 1934 to 1937 the Soviet of Nationalities consistently pressured local Ukrainian and Belorussian authorities to maintain Polish and German institutions. As late as 1937, the Soviet of Nationalities was accusing Ukraine of "distortions" in its policy toward Germans and Poles.[129] This duality, characteristic of Soviet nationalities policy in the aftermath of the December 1932 decrees, would only be resolved during the Great Terror with the emergence of the concept of enemy nations.

---

[122] Terry Martin, "An Affirmative Action Empire" (Ph.D. diss., University of Chicago): 757–759.
[123] *GARF* 3316/64/1537 (1935): 43.
[124] *RTsKhIDNI* 17/21/4676 (17.08.35): 46/30.
[125] *TsDAHOU* 1/16/12 (05.10.35): 303; (08.10.35): 309.
[126] *TsDAHOU* 1/16/12 (26.10.35): 325–330; (27.10.35): 333–339.
[127] *GARF* 3316/28/775 (1936): 232.
[128] *GARF* 1235/30/831 (1937): 151.
[129] *GARF* 3316/30/831 (1937); 3316/29/631 (1936); 3316/28/775 (1935–1937); 3316/27/766 (1934–1937); 3316/64/1869 (1937); 3316/64/1537 (1934–1936).

Ethnic cleansing in Leningrad oblast followed the Ukrainian pattern closely. A large deportation, authorized by the head of the NKVD, Genrikh Iagoda, on March 25, 1935, targeted the small Estonian and Latvian and larger Finnish populations of the Leningrad border regions.[130] According to Finnish sources, about 7000 to 9000 Finns were deported to Siberia and Central Asia.[131] As in Ukraine, this first deportation targeted independent peasants, *lishentsy*, and other stigmatized categories.[132] However, again following the Ukrainian pattern, in the spring of 1936, a second larger deportation of about 20,000 Finnish peasants to Siberia took place.[133] Still, not all Finns were deported. The removal of 30,000 Finns amounted to about 30 percent of the Leningrad Finnish population.[134] The deportations were accompanied, again as in Ukraine, by an abolition of many national institutions. The Soviet of Nationalities again vainly protested this development.[135]

The novel factor in Leningrad oblast was that the city of Leningrad itself lay within the border zone. The mass arrests and deportations of "unreliable elements" from Leningrad in late 1934, following the murder of Kirov, were actually part of the new border regime and had been planned prior to Kirov's murder. In a reply to an angry letter by Academic Pavlov protesting this repression, Molotov made clear this connection: "In Leningrad special measures are being taken against malicious anti-Soviet elements, which is tied to the special border position of this city."[136] Again, a major target of this wave of repression were the western national minorities: Finns, Latvians, Estonians, Germans, Poles.[137]

By 1936, then, the Soviet Union's western diaspora nationalities had been stigmatized as collectively disloyal and subjected to ethnic cleansing. In the far east, although Koreans had been threatened with deportation already in 1926, ethnic cleansing was delayed. There was a major wave of Korean arrests in 1935.[138] In July 1936, the far eastern *kraikom* first petitioned Sovnarkom for permission to implement the new border regime in the far east, in order to frustrate "the aggressive tactics of the local authorities in Manchuria and the Japanese, who exploit every border crossing from our side, either to recruit spies and saboteurs or to make various accusations against the Soviet

[130] *BFORC* Reel 3 (1935): vol. 19453, 259–264; vol. 19454, 171–174; Reel 5 (1936): vol. 20349, 169; Reel 6 (1936): vol. 20353, 14–17; *The Ingrian Finns* (Helsinki, 1935): 12–14. Gelb, "Western Finnic Minorities," 242–244; Bugai, *Iosif Stalin—Lavrentiiu Berii* (Moscow, 1992): 20. Iagoda had approved the deportation of 3547 families, not all of whom were Finns.

[131] *The Ingrian Finns*, 14.

[132] *BFORC* Reel 6 (1936): vol. 20353, 16.

[133] Matley, 9. *BFORC* Reel 16 (29.07.36): vol. 20353, 14–17. Gelb, "Western Finnic Minorities," 243.

[134] Matley, 8–10.

[135] *GARF* 3316/30/825 (1937).

[136] " 'Poshchadite zhe Rodinu i Nas'. Protesty akademika I. P. Pavlova protiv bol'shevistskikh nasilii," *Istochnik*, no. 1 (1995): 143. [Letter of Molotov to Pavlov, 15.03.35]

[137] *BFORC* Reel 5 (31.01.36): vol. 20349, 169–170.

[138] "Koreitsy," *Tak eto bylo*, vol. 1 (Moscow, 1993): 47–84. Gelb, "An Early Soviet," 397.

Union."[139] This appeal to Soviet xenophobia was opposed by Maxim Litvinov, who noted that the Portsmouth Treaty forbade "military measures on the Korean border."[140] At this point, the need to placate the Japanese outweighed concern over Japanese influence on the Korean population of the far eastern border regions. Only on July 28, 1937, after interventions by Nikolai Ezhov and Kliment Voroshilov, was the foreign ministry forced to accept the introduction of the new border regions' regime in the far east.[141]

On August 18, 1937, Stalin and Molotov sent a draft proposal for a Korean deportation to the far eastern leadership.[142] This proposal was similar to the 1935 deportations in Ukraine and Leningrad oblast in that the deportation was confined to twelve border districts, but distinct in that it targeted only Koreans and all Koreans were to be deported. Three days later, the official TsK and Sovnarkom deportation decree was expanded to include 23 districts, which increased the number of Koreans to be deported from 44,023 to 135,343.[143] Demobilized Red Army soldiers were also to be settled in formerly Korean collective farms.[144] The scope of the deportation continued to expand until finally, on September 22, 1937, the assistant head of the NKVD, V. V. Chernyshev, asked Ezhov for the right to deport every last Korean from the far eastern *krai*. His reasoning was highly revealing[145]:

> To leave these few thousand Koreans in the Far Eastern *krai*, when the majority have been deported will be dangerous, since the family ties of all Koreans are very strong. The territorial restrictions on those remaining in the Far East will undoubtedly affect their mood and these groups will become rich soil for the Japanese to work on.

In other words, we have injured some Koreans, therefore we can assume all Koreans are now our enemies. This psychology is extremely important not just for the spread of ethnic cleansing, but for the ratcheting up of all Soviet terror. Chernyshev's request was approved.[146] By October 29, Ezhov could report to Molotov that 171,781 Koreans had been deported to Kazakhstan and Uzbekistan and only about 700 scattered Koreans remained to be rounded up.[147] The first ethnic cleansing of an entire nationality, including communists, had been accomplished.

[139] *GARF* 5446/29/67 (1936): 42–43.
[140] Ibid., 18.
[141] Ibid., 18–25.
[142] *RGVA* 33879/2/181 (1938): 8–11.
[143] *Belaia kniga*, 64–67; *RGVA* 33879/2/181 (1937): 3–6.
[144] *GARF* 5446/29/113 (1938).
[145] *Belaia kniga*, 85–86, 88, 109–110.
[146] Ibid., 111.
[147] *GARF* 5446/29/48 (1937): 156. He noted that 700 dispersed Koreans remained to be rounded up. Approximately 11,000 Chinese were also deported with the Koreans, and 600 Poles, and several hundred Germans, Latvians, and Lithuanians were arrested. Nikolai F. Bugai, " 'Koreiskii vopros' na Dal'nem Vostoke i deportatsiia 1937 goda," *Problemy dal'nego vostoka*, no. 4 (1992): 158.

When the kolkhoznik Kim-Sen-Men was told that all Koreans were being deported to Central Asia, he responded that "in all likelihood, they will create for us a Korean Autonomous Oblast there."[148] Kim's comment was as revealing as Chernyshev's, for it illustrated the continuity between the 1920s' policy of ethnically based agricultural resettlement and the 1930s policy of ethnic cleansing. Surprisingly, Kim was not entirely mistaken. The deported Koreans were settled in separate Korean collective farms. Korean-language schools were formed.[149] Ezhov himself authorized the transfer of an entire Korean pedagogical school, a Korean publishing house, and a Korean newspaper to Central Asia.[150] Even in the midst of 100 percent ethnic cleansing, where every Korean had been declared a potential spy and traitor, the formulas of the Soviet nationalities policy could still not be entirely abandoned.

Enemy Nations

The Korean deportation took place at the onset of the mass operations of the Great Terror, which helps explain why that deportation spread so quickly to become a total deportation of all Koreans. The Great Terror witnessed the culmination of a gradual shift from exclusively class-based terror to terror that targeted (among others) entire nations. At this time, the duality that allowed for the simultaneous deportation of all Koreans and the formation of new national institutions in their place of exile was finally resolved. At the 1937 Ukrainian party congress, Oleksandr Shlikhter, an ideology specialist, spoke of the "wrecking of various nations" (*shkidnytstvo riznykh natsii*) in reference to the Germans and Poles of Ukraine.[151] Few others were so blunt in such a relatively public forum, but this sentiment underlay a new internal party discourse that justified collective terror against the Soviet Union's diaspora nationalities and ended the protests of soft-line institutions such as the Soviet of Nationalities.

The Great Terror saw an extension of ethnic cleansing to all the Soviet border regions and all of the Soviet Union's diaspora nationalities. On July 17, 1937, Sovnarkom issued a decree extending the new border regions' regime to territory bordering on Iran and Afghanistan. The new regime included ethnic cleansing: the deportation of over one thousand Kurdish families in late 1937 and two thousand Iranian families in 1938.[152] In September 1937, a separate TsK

---

[148] *Belaia kniga*, 133.
[149] GARF 5446/29/48 (1937): 156, 176.
[150] *Belaia kniga*, 100; GARF 5446/20a/509 (1937): 1–12.
[151] *Nimtsi v Ukraini*, 13.
[152] GARF 5446/20a/933 (1937): 7–8. GARF 5446/23a/50 (1938): 1–2; N. F. Bugai, "Kanun voiny: repressii v otnoshenii sovetskikh kurdov," in *Sovetskie kurdy: vremia peremen* (Moscow, 1993): 48; *Tak eto bylo*, vol. 1, "Kurdy," 95–125. GARF 5446/23a/29 (1938): 23. "Iranian" was actually not an ethnic term but embraced Persians, Azerbaijanis, and Kurds who originated in Iran (even if they were now Soviet citizens), again pointing to the key role of cross-border ethnic ties.

order called for the "cleansing" of the autonomous republic of Nakhichevan, which located along the Turkish border.[153] The next month, a further TsK order called for the deportation of "kulak and basmachi elements" from the border regions of Tajikistan, although this would not in fact be carried out until 1938.[154] By the end of 1938, the new regime had been extended along the entire Soviet border.[155] There were also further ethnic deportations from the western border regions. In November 1937, the Odessa obkom ordered the deportation of 5000 German households.[156] The decline in the German and Polish populations of Ukraine and Belorussia between the 1937 and 1939 censuses suggests there may have been other deportations as well.[157]

Most significantly, not only did ethnic cleansing spread outward to all the Soviet border regions, but terror against diaspora nationalities spread inward to embrace the entire Soviet Union.[158] This process began with the anti-German and anti-Polish campaigns during the 1933 Ukrainian terror. It took on all-union dimensions with the November 5, 1934 Politburo decree, "On the Battle with Counter-Revolutionary Fascist Elements in the German Colonies," which led to mass arrests and show trials not only in Ukraine, but also in central territories such as the Slavgorod German district in Siberia.[159] Likewise, the Leningrad repression following Kirov's murder also targeted (among others) diaspora nationalities. In 1936, the Party Control Commission (KPK) and the NKVD began a purge of all political émigrés in the Soviet Union, with Poles as the primary focus, a purge that quickly escalated into mass arrests.[160] With the onset

---

[153] *RTsKhIDNI* 558/11/56 (26.09.37): 99.

[154] *RTsKhIDNI* 558/11/56 (02.10.37): 117–118; 558/11/58 (17.12.38): 68.

[155] *GARF* 5446/29/96 (1938): 1–10; *GARF* 5446/29/67 (1938): 52.

[156] *TsDAHOU* 1/6/458 (19.11.37): 9/7, 63–70.

[157] Ukraine's Polish population declined by approximately 90,000 individuals and its German population by 40,000. In Belorussia, the Polish population declined from 119,881 in 1937 to 54,500 in 1939 (45.46 percent). Calculated (with adjustments for the inflated 1939 numbers) from *Vsesoiuznaia perepis' naseleniia 1937 g.*, 94, and *Vsesoiuznaia perepis' naseleniia 1939 goda*, 68. On the other hand, these population losses may reflect arrests and executions during the Great Terror, rather than deportations.

[158] The terror did not target those stateless diasporas whose co-ethnics did not live in concentrated communities adjacent to the Soviet Union, such as Jews, Assyrians, and Gypsies. Although they were treated with greater suspicion during the Great Terror, and some of their institutions were abolished, I have found no decrees specifically targeting them for repression. Nor have the statistics on the ethnic impact of the terror suggested they were targeted. According to Vaksberg, who had access to the former KGB archive in Moscow, the first specifically Jewish cases were initiated in 1939 after the Hitler–Stalin pact. Arkady Vaksberg, *Stalin Against the Jews* (New York, 1994): 80–102. See also Martin, "An Affirmative Action Empire," 782–785.

[159] *RTsKhIDNI* 558/11/51 (04.11.34): 71–72; 558/11/64 (20.07.34): 85. L. P. Belkovec, "Der Beginn des Massenterrors. Die Getreidequirierung von 1934 im westsibirischen Deutschen Rayon," *Forschungen zur Geschichte und Kultur der Russlanddeutschen*, no. 4 (1994): 121; Victor Chentsov, "Die deutsche Bevölkerung am Dnepr im Zeichen des stalinistischen Terrors," *idem*, no. 5 (1995): 11–13; *GARF* 3316/30/831 (1936): 7–8; 3316/29/631 (1935): 18–19; *Nimtsi v Ukraini*, 186–187.

[160] V. N. Khaustov, "Iz predystorii massovykh repressii protiv poliakov. Seredina 1930-kh gg.," in *Repressii protiv poliakov i pol'skikh grazhdan* (Moscow, 1997): 10–21; Nikita Pietrow, "Polska operacja NKWD," *Karta*, no. 11 (1993): 24–27.

of the Great Terror's "mass operations" in the summer of 1937, this elite terror against foreign communists merged with the mass ethnic cleansing of domestic diaspora nationalities to produce a mass terror campaign against the new category of enemy nations.[161] On August 9, 1937, the politburo confirmed NKVD decree 00485, "On the Liquidation of the Polish Sabotage-Espionage Group and the Organization POV."[162] Two days later, Ezhov formally issued this decree (accompanied by a massive historical account of POV's origins and activities as justification of the anti-Polish operations), which identified targets for arrest: all Polish political émigrés and refugees, as well as "the most active part of local anti-Soviet nationalist elements from the Polish national districts."[163] In October 1937, this category was extended to all Poles with "ties to [Polish] consuls" (*konsul'skie sviazi*), a category that could easily embrace any Soviet Pole.[164] By 1938, the NKVD was arresting Poles (and other diaspora nationalities) exclusively due to their national identity.[165]

The August 11, 1937 POV decree served as the model for a series of NKVD decrees targeting all of the Soviet Union's diaspora nationalities.[166] The NKVD referred to these decrees collectively as "the national operations" (to distinguish them from the other "mass operation" launched by NKVD decree 00447 on July 30, 1937, targeting "former kulaks, criminals, and other anti-Soviet elements").[167] A January 31, 1938 politburo decree extended until April 15, 1938 this "operation for the destruction of espionage and sabotage contingents made up of Poles, Latvians, Germans, Estonians, Finns, Greeks, Iranians, *Kharbintsy*, Chinese, and Romanians, both foreign subjects and Soviet citizens, according to the existing decrees of the NKVD." This decree also authorized a new operation "to destroy the Bulgarian and Macedonian cadres."[168] Koreans and

---

[161] There was also a July 25, 1937 NKVD decree, which targeted exclusively *foreign* Germans working in military plants or in transport. *Leningradskii martirolog, 1937–1938*, vol. 2 (St. Petersburg, 1996), 452–453.

[162] "Massovye repressii opravdany byt' ne mogut," *Istochnik*, no. 1 (1995): 125. The decree is reproduced in Pietrow, "Polska operacja NKWD," 27–29. POV was a real underground organization formed during World War I to support Pilsudski's legions. It ceased operations in Poland in 1918 and in Ukraine in 1921. Arrests by the NKVD for membership in POV began during the 1933 Ukrainian terror and continued through the Great Terror. Mitzner, "Widmo POW," 21–23.

[163] Both documents are reproduced in Iurii Shapoval, Volodymyr Prystaiko, and Vadym Zolotarov, eds., *ChK-HPU-NKVD v Ukraini: osoby, fakty, dokumenty* (Kiev, 1997): 347–377.

[164] N. V. Petrov and A. B. Roginskii, "'Polskaia operatsiia' NKVD 1937–1938 gg.," in *Repressii protiv poliakov*, 27. "*Konsul'skie sviazi*" were also a standard arrest category in the other national operations. See Chentsov, "Die deutsche Bevölkerung," 14.

[165] Petrov and Roginskii, "'Polskaia Operatsiia,'" 29–34; Pietrow, "Polska Operacja NKWD," 32; S. Bilokin, "Dokumenty z istorii NKVD URSR," *Nashe mynule*, no. 1 (1993): 40–41.

[166] Petrov and Roginskii, "'Polskaia Operatsiia,'" 28–29. N. Okhotin and A. Roginskii, "Iz istorii 'nemetskoi operatsii' NKVD 1937–1938 gg." In I. L. Shcherbakov ed., *Nakazannyi narod. Repressii protiv rossiiskikh nemtsev* (Moscow. 1999): 35–74. N. Okhotin and A. Roginskii, "'Latyshakskaia operatsiia' 1937–1938 godov. Arkhivnyi kommentarii," 30 *Oktabria* no. 4 (2000): 5.

[167] Petrov and Roginskii, "'Polskaia operatsiia,'" 30–31. For decree 00447, see "Limity terroru," *Karta*, no. 11 (1993): 8–15.

[168] *Tak eto bylo*, vol. 1, 253.

Afghans were also targeted by NKVD decrees.[169] The NKVD spoke of their "German operation" and "Latvian operation."[170] They arrested individuals "according to the Polish line" or "Finnish line" of the nationalities terror.[171] Most revealingly, internal NKVD documents refer to their operations as directed against "nationalities of foreign governments," a designation for the diaspora nationalities—the vast majority of whom were Soviet citizens and whose ancestors had resided for decades and sometimes centuries in the Soviet Union and Russian empire—that absolutized their cross-border ethnicities as the only salient aspect of their identity, sufficient proof of their disloyalty and sufficient justification for their arrest and execution.[172]

The national operations were not at all a minor part of the Great Terror. According to recently released statistics from the former KGB archive in Moscow, from July 1937 to November 1938, a total of 335,513 individuals were convicted in the national operations, while 767,397 were convicted in the operation carried out under decree 00447 (former kulaks, criminals, and other anti-Soviet elements).[173] We do not have an arrest total for this time period, but we do have a figure of 1,565,041 arrested on political charges between October 1, 1936 and November 1, 1938. Even using this extended time period, the national operations made up 21.4 percent and decree 00447 made up 49 percent of all arrests. When we examine total executions, the national operations assume a still larger role. Of the 681,692 executions in 1937–1938, the national operations made up 247,157 (36.3 percent) and decree 00447 made up 386,798 (54.1 percent). Of all those arrested on political and nonpolitical charges in 1937–1938, a total of 19 percent were executed; of those arrested on decree 00447, a total of 49.3 percent were executed; of those arrested in the national operations, 73.7 percent were executed. The execution rate on the Polish operation was slightly higher (79.4 percent) and the Greek, Finnish, and Estonian operations even higher, whereas the Afghan and Iranian execution rates were much lower.[174] To sum up, the national operations made up about a fifth of the total arrests and a third of the total executions during the Great Terror, and arrest in the national operations was much more likely to result in execution.[175]

---

[169] "Limity terroru," 8; Petrov and Roginskii, "'Polskaia operatsiia,'" 33. In July 1937, Stalin authorized the arrest of all Afghan citizens in Turkmenistan. *TsKhSD* 89/48/7 (25.07.37): 1.

[170] Rastsyslav Platonav and Mikola Stashkevich, "Dzve aperatsyi suprats' 'vorahav naroda'," *Belaruski histarychny chasopis*, no. 1 (1993): 78–79.

[171] Petrov and Roginskii, "'Polskaia operatsiia,'" 28.

[172] Petrov and Roginskii, "'Polskaia operatsiia,'" 34.

[173] Unless otherwise noted, all statistics in the following two paragraphs are taken from Petrov and Roginskii, "'Polskaia operatsiia,'" 32–33 and 37–38, and Pietrow, "Polskaia operacja, NKWD," 33, 39–40.

[174] This was the only information provided. The data follow the general pattern of greater severity in the west and the least severity in the south.

[175] For the national operations, no quotas were provided for executions and incarcerations as they were with decree 00447, although all executions in both operations had to be ratified by central authorities (albeit in the most rote fashion). This is one possible reason for the higher execution rates in the national operations.

Unfortunately, we do not know exactly how many members of the diaspora nationalities were arrested or executed, since not everyone arrested in the Polish operation was a Pole, nor were all arrested Poles included in the Polish operation. For instance, through September 1, 1938 in Belorussia, Poles made up only 43 percent of those arrested in the Polish operation, whereas Germans made up 76 percent of the German operation, and Latvians 74.6 percent of the Latvian operation.[176] Moreover, all three nationalities were included in all three operations. In Moscow oblast, through July 1, 1938, Poles made up 57 percent of the Polish operation, and for the entire Soviet Union from September to November 1938, Poles made up 54.8 percent of the Polish operation. Roginskii and Petrov report that 139,835 individuals were arrested in the Polish operation, while 118,000 to 123,000 Poles were arrested during the Great Terror in all the national operations and the decree 00447 operation combined. If this ratio of 84.4 percent to 88.0 percent holds for the other national operations, then diaspora nationalities still made up 25.7 percent to 26.8 percent of total arrests (and a still higher percentage of executions) during the mass operations of the Great Terror, although these same nationalities represented only 1.7 percent of the overall Soviet population.[177]

Mass ethnic cleansing and the national operations were unsurprisingly accompanied by decrees in December 1937 abolishing all national soviets and national

[176] "Dzve aperatsyi," 78–79.

[177] *Vsesoiuznaia perepis' naseleniia 1937 g.*, 83–84. The targeting of diaspora nationalities is also confirmed by evidence from Leningrad and Odessa *oblasti* as well as the Karelian ASSR. Using the biographical information of 11,547 individuals executed in Leningrad city and oblast from August to November 1937 as listed in *Leningradskii martirolog*, vols. 1–3 (the list is said to be almost comprehensive and so valid for statistical analysis—a small number of individual entries don't list nationality), I calculated the percentage of each nationality relative to the percentage that would be expected based on their total representation in the population of Leningrad city and oblast. Although the national operations (except the Polish one, which began August 20) were just beginning and most executions would have been part of the decree 00447 operations, the diaspora nationalities were still disproportionately affected: the number of Poles executed was 3094.2 percent of what would be expected based on their total representation in the population of Leningrad city and *oblast'*. In other words, due exclusively to their ethnicity, Poles were 30.94 times more likely to be executed than non-Poles. For other diaspora nationalities, the targeting was not yet so extreme: Finns 230.1 percent, Estonians 410.7 percent, Germans 372.3 percent, Latvians 159.1 percent. For Odessa *oblast'*, execution totals are available for the entire course of the mass operations and the comparable figures are: Poles 2236.3 percent, Germans 526.0 percent, Bulgarians 148.6 percent. In Karelia, arrest totals are available for the entire course of the mass operations (save the period from August 10 to September 20, 1938). Of those arrested, 85.97 percent were executed. The comparable figure for Finns was 1515.1 percent, that is, Finns were 15.15 percent more likely to be arrested. The execution figure would be slightly higher. For a comparison of these figures with non-diaspora nationalities, see Table 45. The published Gulag statistics for 1939 also show a substantial overrepresentation of diaspora nationalities and underrepresentation of indigenous nationalities. Statistics calculated from *Leningradskii martirolog, 1937–1938*, vols. 1–3 (1996–1998). N. N. Danilov, "Zaryty, no ne pokhoroneny," *Memorial-Aspekt*, no. 9 (1994): 5, as cited in Rittersporn, "'Vrednye elementy,'" 100. Takala, "Natsional'nye operatsii OGPU/NKVD," 194–195, 200. J. Arch Getty, Gabor T. Rittersporn, and Viktor N. Zemskov, "Victims of the Soviet Penal System in the Pre-war Years: A First Approach on the Basis of Archival Evidence," *American Historical Review* 98 (October 1993): 1028.

schools of the stigmatized diaspora nationalities.[178] These decrees allowed the party to articulate an internal nonpublic explanation for the nationalities terror. These national institutions were declared to have been "artificially created" (*iskusstvenno sozdano*), that is, they were not even historically justified. Moreover, Malenkov stated that it was often not even the party that had created them: "It has now been established that in numerous cases national districts were created by the initiative of enemies of the people in order to ease the development of counterrevolutionary espionage and wrecking."[179] Likewise, a delegate to the October 1937 TsK plenum stated: "The Poles, through their national fascist and Trotskyist agents filled the border regions with their people (*svoimi liud'mi*), such that their person (*svoi chelovek*) became head of the kolkhoz, head of the village soviet, and so forth."[180] Although expressed in the paranoid vocabulary of the Great Terror, these comments essentially express the following realization: we thought national soviets would disarm nationalism, but they have strengthened it; we thought they would ensure loyalty from our diaspora nationalities, but they have undermined it; we felt they would help project our influence abroad, but the exact opposite occurred.

The previously unappreciated scope of the mass terror against diaspora nationalities has important consequences for our understanding of the Great Terror. Approximately 800,000 individuals were arrested, deported, or executed in the ethnic cleansing and mass national operations from 1935 to 1938. This represents around a third of the total political victims in that time period.[181] That fact alone requires at least two revisions to our interpretations of the Great Terror. First, in terms of the origins of the Great Terror, in addition to elite political explanations that focus on Stalin and his circle, regional explanations that highlight tensions in center–periphery relations, ideological explanations that emphasize the continuation of class-based terror (the "former kulaks" in decree 00447), and social explanations that focus on leadership

---

[178] *RTsKhIDNI* 17/3/994 (11.12.37): 56/75, 56/76. 17/114/633 (01.12.37): 75/6, 75/7. There was one major exception. The Volga German ASSR and German schools within that republic were not abolished. The Soviet Union's stateless diasporas—Jews, Gypsies, Assyrians—fell into an intermediate category. There were no central decrees targeting them for terror, nor do we have evidence that they were disproportionate victims of the Great Terror. However, some of their national institutions began to be abolished in late 1937. Jewish and Gypsy national soviets were not mentioned by the December 1937 TsK decree, and the original decree abolishing diaspora nationalities' schools also did not mention Jewish, Gypsy, or Assyrian national schools. However, during the implementation of this decree by Narkompros RSFSR in early 1938, the national schools of Jews, Gypsies, and Assyrians began to be liquidated at the same time as the schools of the Soviet Union's other diaspora nations. Yiddish cultural institutions, in contrast to the institutions of other diaspora nations, only gradually declined during the late 1930s but were not totally abolished. And while Jews were not specifically targeted for repression by any central decree, anti-Semitism did markedly increase during the Great Terror, and any state effort to combat it largely disappeared.

[179] *RTsKhIDNI* 17/114/829 (01.12.37): 75/6, 122.

[180] *RTsKhIDNI* 17/2/627 (11–12.10.37): 55–56.

[181] This is a rough estimation. I do not have arrest figures for 1935–1936 or comprehensive deportation figures for 1937–1938.

panic over crime (the "criminals" in decree 00447), we must add the national or xenophobic explanation that I have outlined here.[182] In other words, the origins of Soviet ethnic cleansing are an important part of the origins of the Great Terror.

Second, in terms of the course of the Great Terror, it is striking that the terror itself exemplified, and to some degree completed, the larger transition from a primary focus on class-based terror to a preponderant emphasis on ethnic-based terror, which would then continue until Stalin's death. Roginskii and Petrov, based on extensive work in the central NKVD archives, conclude that from January–February 1938 (that is, six to seven months into the sixteen-month period of mass terror), the national operations eclipsed decree 00447 as the primary focus of NKVD activity. By the final months of the terror, they were virtually the exclusive focus.[183] Indeed, with only minor exaggeration, one might say that by November 1938 the Great Terror had evolved into an ethnic terror.

Conclusion

This chapter began with a paradox: How did a state with no ambition to turn itself into a nation-state—indeed with the exact opposite ambition—nevertheless become the site of large-scale ethnic cleansing? In fact, the Soviet turn toward ethnic cleansing in the 1930s was not even accompanied by a trend favoring assimilation, but rather by an increased emphasis on the distinct primordial essence of the Soviet Union's nationalities. Three factors converged to create this outcome. First, the Soviet leadership was already committed to ethnic resettlement in the 1920s to promote ethnic consolidation and the formation of national territories. Lenin and Woodrow Wilson were the two great propagandists for the right of nations to self-determination. While Lenin and Stalin opposed the creation of a Russian nation-state, they accepted the principle of the nation-state and sought to create the basic essentials of the nation-state— a national territory, elite, language, and culture—for each Soviet ethnic minority. They were, if you will, Affirmative Action nationalists.[184]

---

[182] On elite political explanations, see Robert Conquest, *The Great Terror: A Reassessment* (New York, 1990). On regional explanations, see J. Arch Getty, *Origins of the Great Purges: The Soviet Communist Party Reconsidered, 1933–1938* (Cambridge, UK, 1985). For a "class-based" explanation, see Sheila Fitzpatrick, *The Russian Revolution* (Oxford, 1994): 163–170. For the social explanation based on crime, see David Shearer, "Crime and Social Disorder in Stalin's Russia: A Reassessment of the Great Retreat and the Origins of Mass Repression," *Cahiers du monde russe* 39 (1998): 119–148. This is, of course, not meant to be a complete catalogue of factors leading to the terror.

[183] Petrov and Roginskii, " 'Polskaia operatsiia,' " 30.

[184] In this sense, there is a direct line connecting Soviet ethnic consolidation projects in the 1920s and Soviet participation in and sponsorship of the internationally sanctioned "liberal" ethnic cleansing that accompanied the conclusion of World War II: the Soviet Union's own population "exchanges" with Poland and Czechoslovakia and the expulsion of the German minority from eastern Europe. These actions were not undertaken in the pursuit of russification or the creation

Second, popular ethnic hostility played a role in the origins of Soviet ethnic cleansing. Due to the coincidence of status and ethnic divisions with conflicts over land and territory, some of the most important diaspora nationalities (Koreans, Germans, Finns, Poles) became the target of popular ethnic hostility. This hostility led to harsh treatment during collectivization, which helped provoke mass emigration movements. It led local communists to stigmatize these groups. Here there is again a link to the spread of Soviet ethnic cleansing beyond diaspora nationalities during World War II to embrace several North Caucasus nationalities (Chechens, Ingush, Balkars, Karachai). These nationalities had been involved in the most severe popular ethnic conflict during the 1920s and 1930s (as well, of course, as in the Tsarist period).[185]

Third, and most important, the Soviet belief in the political salience of ethnicity, which was reflected in their entire policy of supporting national institutions, led to their adoption of the Piedmont Principle: the attempt to exploit cross-border ethnic ties to project influence abroad. However, the exaggerated Soviet fear of foreign capitalist influence and contamination, what I have called Soviet xenophobia, also made such cross-border ties potentially suspect. Once it became clear to the Soviet leadership that cross-border ethnic ties could not be exploited to undermine neighboring countries, but instead had the exact opposite potential, their response was ethnic cleansing of the Soviet borderlands and, ultimately, ethnic terror throughout the Soviet Union. Again, ethnic cleansing of nationalities with suspect cross-border ethnic ties away from the Soviet borderlands continued throughout the late Stalinist period with the removal of the Crimean Tatars, Greeks, Armenians, Bulgarians, Meskhetian Turks, Kurds, Iranians, and Khemshils from the Black Sea and Transcaucasian border regions.[186]

Diaspora nationalities have often been seen as disloyal and so as an impediment to nation-building, and therefore have been subject to ethnic cleansing. However, the Soviet case is unusual since, as I have emphasized, Soviet xenophobia was an ideological rather than an ethnic concept. It became ethnicized only due to the Piedmont Principle's focus on cross-border ethnic ties, which, given the Soviet Union's geography, were exclusively non-Russian. In the late 1930s, alongside ethnic cleansing and ethnic primordialism, there was also a

---

of a Russian nation-state, but rather embodied Soviet sponsorship of the ethnic consolidation (through ethnic cleansing) of its future East European allies, particularly Poland and Czechoslovakia, as well as its own republics of Ukraine, Belorussia, and Lithuania. On these exchanges, see Martin, "The Origins of Soviet Ethnic Cleansing", 817–824. On the liberal ideology of national self-determination and ethnic cleansing, see David Laitin, *Ethnic Cleansing, Liberal Style*. MacArthur Foundation Program in Transnational Security. Working Paper Series, no. 4 (Cambridge, Mass., 1995).

[185] This is not to argue that all nationalities who were the subject of popular ethnic hostility were deported even in the North Caucasus, where Dagestan had been the site of much ethnic conflict (but there were no deportations) and Kalmykia was not (and the Kalmyks were deported). On these deportations, see Bugai, *L. Beriia—I. Stalinu*, 56–162.

[186] For evidence that these operations were considered "cleansing" of border regions, see Bugai, *L. Beriia—I. Stalinm*, 149–150, 163–185.

revival of a rather virulent state-sponsored Russian nationalist rhetoric, a revival that in fact peaked at the height of the Great Terror. However, this Russian nationalism is best understood as an effect rather than a cause of Soviet xenophobia. The growing fear of non-Russian nationalism and disloyalty due to the greater resistance to collectivization and the ethnicization of Soviet xenophobia through the reversal of the Piedmont Principle led the Soviet government to identify the state to a greater extent with its Russian core.

This did not prevent, however, under certain circumstances, even Russians from becoming an enemy nation. The January 1938 Politburo decree targeted the following diaspora nationalities for terror: Poles, Latvians, Germans, Estonians, Finns, Greeks, Iranians, Chinese, Rumanians, and *Kharbintsy*.[187] In this context, *Kharbintsy* sounds like some exotic Eurasian ethnicity. In fact, Kharbin was a town in northern China where the headquarters of the Chinese–Manchurian railway were located. Until the mid-1930s, the railway was owned and operated by the Soviet Union. *Kharbintsy*, who were primarily ethnic Russians, were the railway workers. After the sale of the railway to Japan, many returned to the Soviet Union. For the Soviet leadership, although they were ethnic Russians, their cross-border ethnic ties to the *Kharbintsy* remaining in China turned them into the functional equivalent of a diaspora nationality. And so, despite their Russianness, they too became an enemy nation targeted as part of the national operations during the Great Terror.[188] This seems convincing evidence that it was Soviet, not Russian, xenophobia that drove the practice of Soviet ethnic cleansing.

[187] *Tak eto bylo*, vol. 1, 253.

[188] In addition to the January 1938 Politburo resolution on the *Kharbintsy*, see the NKVD decree targeting the *Kharbintsy* (modeled after the Polish decree 00485), "Operativnyi prikaz NKVD SSSR No. 00593, 20.09.37," *Memorial-Aspekt*, no. 1 (3) (July 1993): 2.

9

The Revised Soviet Nationalities Policy, 1933–1939

For the Soviet Union's diaspora nationalities, the revisions made in the Soviet nationalities policy in the aftermath of the December 1932 Politburo decrees produced the unprecedented disaster of ethnic cleansing, mass arrests, and several hundred thousand executions. These nationalities, however, made up only 1.7 percent of the Soviet Union's total population (2.75 million), though during and after World War II the practice of ethnic cleansing was extended to numerous "indigenous" Soviet nationalities, and the Soviet Union's Jewish population gradually fell into the category of enemy nation as well.[1] Nevertheless, in the second half of the 1930s, none of the Soviet Union's indigenous non-Russian nationalities were categorized as enemy nations, and there is no compelling evidence that they were specifically targeted in any of the Soviet terror campaigns. However, the anti-Ukrainization decrees clearly put the future of *korenizatsiia*, both the promotion of non-Russian languages and non-Russian cadres, in considerable doubt. It was unclear to local elites if the decree's literal message that Ukrainization should be revised and pursued with renewed vigor was meant to be implemented, or if the terror campaign accompanying the decrees was a signal that *korenizatsiia* should be abandoned, or if the passing of the famine emergency and the end of dekulakization would lead to a restoration of the status quo ante. Moreover, since the decrees criticized only Ukrainization and Belorussization, it was equally unclear if their message was also intended for the eastern national republics or if, as was the case during the cultural revolution, there would be a divorce between policy trends in the Soviet east and west.

[1] Gennadi Kostyrchenko, *Out of the Red Shadows* (Amherst, N.Y., 1995).

The Skrypnyk Affair

These questions were answered not by the December 1932 decrees, but by the signals sent in the year-long terror and propaganda campaign in Ukraine known as the Skrypnyk affair. This was ironic, as Mykola Skrypnyk was an experienced and tough-minded Old Bolshevik who understood well the signaling function of Soviet terror campaigns, and he appealed vainly during the cultural revolution for a show trial of great-power chauvinists to balance the many trials of local nationalists. Instead, he himself became the object of the most significant nationalities terror campaign of the entire interwar period. Two questions are crucial for interpreting the signals sent by this, and indeed any other, Soviet terror campaign: First, what population categories were being targeted? Second, what criticism was being directed at the principal terror victims? During the 1933 Ukrainian terror, in addition to Germans and Poles, three main categories were targeted: national communists (as exemplified by Skrypnyk himself), Ukrainian cultural specialists (in particular, teachers and nationalities policy specialists), and the West Ukrainian émigré community. The multitudinous charges leveled against Skrypnyk can be divided into four general categories: creating a dangerous theoretical combination of nationalism and Bolshevism, grossly exaggerating the significance of the nationalities question, improperly invoking the Piedmont Principle, and attempting the forcible Ukrainization of Russian school children.

Mykola Skrypnyk was the Soviet Union's paradigmatic national communist. He was either the pioneer or one of the most avid proponents of numerous important Soviet nationalities policy initiatives: comprehensive Ukrainization, terror against great power chauvinists, the scientific study of the nationalities question, the Piedmont Principle, the pyramid of national soviets, territorial claims on the RSFSR, and Ukrainian linguistic reform. However, Skrypnyk was also an Old Bolshevik with party membership since 1899. He had been a member of the Military–Revolutionary Committee that planned the October Revolution. He was an influential member of the Ukrainian Politburo and the All-Union TsK. Therefore, both his national and communist credentials were impeccable. If Skrypnyk could be accused of defection to nationalism, no national communist was safe. This was, of course, exactly the message being sent in the Skrypnyk affair.

The Skrypnyk affair began with the December 14, 1932 Politburo decree and concluded with a November 1933 Ukrainization decree and an authoritative intervention by Stalin at the January 1934 party congress.[2] After Kaganovich's departure from Ukraine in 1928, Mykola Skrypnyk had assumed a dominant position as Ukraine's leading nationalities policy specialist. Publicly he was

---

[2] James Mace, *Communism and the Dilemmas of National Liberation* (Cambridge, Mass., 1983): 192–231, 264–301. Iurii Shapoval, *Ukraina 20-50-kh rokiv* (Kiev, 1993): 115–148; O. S. Rublov and I. Cherchenko, *Stalinshchyna i dolia zakhidnoukrains'koi intellihentsii* (Kiev, 1994): 104–130.

unassailable. However, Skrypnyk's vigorous pursuit of Ukrainization, advocacy of territorial expansion into the RSFSR, and support of cross-border cooperation with West Ukrainians all led to increasing attacks from both without and within Ukraine. He was denounced as a nationalist by a visiting TsKK delegation in 1929. Several times the Ukrainian Politburo had to reprimand Ukrainian party members for criticizing Skrypnyk.[3] The campaign against Ukrainian nationalism also began to claim his protégés. In 1931 and 1932, three of the six editors of his collected works were denounced as nationalists.[4] Moreover, Skrypnyk began to have conflicts with his Politburo colleagues.[5] In March 1932, the Ukrainian Politburo even asked him to provide a justification of his theoretical writings on the nationalities question, which he had just collected and ostentatiously republished in two large volumes.[6] However, the famine emergency deflected all attention to the countryside, and Skrypnyk made no reply to this request.

In January 1933, Stalin implemented a revised version of the personnel changes that he had first proposed to Kaganovich in August 1932. Pavel Postyshev, who had left Ukraine in 1930 and served as Stalin's right-hand man in the TsK Secretariat in 1931–1932, returned to Ukraine with the title of second party secretary, but in reality he functioned as Ukraine's first party secretary from January 1933 to January 1937. Vsevolod Balitskii, who was head of the Ukrainian GPU from 1923 to 1931, took over his old position. Nikolai Popov, a nationalities specialist who headed Ukraine's Agitprop Department from 1924 to 1927, also took up his old job as well, becoming a TsK secretary and editor of *Komunist*. Finally, M. M. Khataevich, another of Stalin's nationalities specialists, became a TsK secretary and head of the Dnepropetrovsk obkom.[7] Pressure on Skrypnyk began immediately. Already in January, Skrypnyk's mandatory nationalities policy course in all universities was abolished despite his protests.[8] Postyshev attacked Skrypnyk indirectly at a Ukrainian TsK plenum in early February.[9] Skrypnyk responded, in a speech to the Narkompros collegium on February 14, with a preemptive defense against the damaging charge of having

---

[3] *RTsKhIDNI* 17/26/32 (31.01.30): 103/11; 17/26/33 (27.07.30): 4/7.

[4] These were O. I. Badan, Andrii Richyts'kyi, and Matvei Iavorskyi. Skrypnyk, *Statti i Promovy*, vol. 2, part 2, 361. On Iavorskyi and Badan, see Rublov and Cherchenko, *Stalinshchyna*, 86–104.

[5] These conflicts are described in great detail in two letters from Panas Liubchenko to Stalin in early 1933. *RTsKhIDNI* 81/3/130 (1933): 76–84, 95–130.

[6] Ibid., 79–80. "Za rishuche provedennia lenins'koi natsional'noi polityky, za bil'shovyts'ku borot'bu proty natsionalistychnykh ukhyliv," *Visti VUTsIK*, no. 164 (23.07.33): 1–2; "Iz vystupu t. H. I. Petrovs'koho na zborakh partoseredku VUAMLIN'u 05.07.33 r.," *Visti VUTsIK*, no. 154 (11.07.33): 2.

[7] *RTsKhIDNI* 17/3/907 (25.11.32): 123/83; 17/26/68 (23.02.33): 104/4, 104/5, 104/14; Peredova, "Postanova TsK VKP/b/ z 24 sichnia 1933 r. ta zavdannia bil'shovykiv Ukrainy," *Bil'shovyk Ukrainy*, no. 3 (1933): 3–21. E. I. Veger also took over the Odessa obkom.

[8] *RTsKhIDNI* 17/26/74 (20.01.33): 133/16; (10–19.02.33): 134/3; 17/26/68 (20.02.33): 102/28; *Biuleten' NKO*, nos. 8–9 (1933): 3–4.

[9] *RTsKhIDNI* 17/26/66 (05–07.02.33): 58.

organized the forced Ukrainization of Russian children. He even attempted to publish his speech as a pamphlet.[10]

His efforts failed. On February 19, Skrypnyk's personal secretary, M. V. Ersteniuk, was arrested by the OGPU as a putative member of the counterrevolutionary Ukrainian Military Organization (UVO).[11] At this point, Skrypnyk traveled to Moscow for a 40-minute private audience with Stalin on February 23.[12] His appeal clearly failed. On February 28, Ersteniuk testified to the OGPU that Skrypnyk "with his nationalist activities encouraged me and other members of UVO in our counter-revolutionary activities."[13] From March to May 1933, a series of authoritative articles appeared in the Ukrainian press attacking positions associated with Skrypnyk—the Ukrainization of Russian children, the 1928 Ukrainian language reforms, his theoretical interpretations of the revolution in Ukraine—but without mentioning Skrypnyk by name.[14] Skrypnyk attempted for a last time to justify his past actions and writings with a 92-page treatise, entitled "Nationalities Policy at the Border of Two Five-Year Plans," but the Politburo once again rejected it as insufficient.[15]

On the eve of the June 8–11 Ukrainian TsK plenum, the Ukrainian Politburo finally authorized an open and devastating attack on Skrypnyk in *Bilshovyk Ukrainy*.[16] At the plenum itself, Skrypnyk confessed to errors on the linguistic and ideological fronts, as well as a too avid promotion of the Piedmont Principle.[17] However, Postyshev rejected his self-criticism[18]:

These [theoretical errors] are trivial in comparison to that wrecking that took place in the education organs that aimed at the confusion of our youth with an ideology hostile to the proletariat . . . these wreckers in Narkompros placed their people in our education system. . . . [As a result] Ukrainization often was put

[10] M. O. Skrypnyk, *Narysy pidsumkiv ukrainizatsii*. Skrypnyk delivered the speech on February 14, gave it to the publisher on February 16, and it appeared on February 23. However, the Politburo immediately ordered its confiscation. *RTsKhIDNI* 17/26/68 (03.03.33): 105/22; 17/26/69 (31.03.33): 108/8.

[11] Rublov and Cherchenko, *Stalinshchyna*, 116–117.

[12] "Posetitely kabineta I. V. Stalina," *Istoricheskii arkhiv*, no. 2 (1995): 168. Prior to Skrypnyk's February 23 meeting with Stalin, Kosior and Postyshev had met with Stalin (and Molotov and Iagoda) on February 15 for over three hours. On February 16 and 18, Kosior, Postyshev, and Chubar met with Stalin for about four hours on both occasions. Kaganovich and Molotov, along with OGPU representatives, were present.

[13] Rublov and Cherchenko, *Stalinshchyna*, 117.

[14] P. Liubchenko, "Pro 'natsional'-bil'shovyzm'," *Bil'shovyk Ukrainy*, no. 3 (1933): 84–91; V. P., "Likviduvaty zbochennia natsional'noi polityky po shkoli," *Komunist*, no. 82 (25.03.33): 3; A. Khvylia, "Za bil 'shovyts'ku pyl'nist' na fronti tvorennia ukrains'koi radians'koi kul'tury," no. 92 (04.04.33): 2–3; "Narada z pytan' natsional'noi polityky partii," no. 113 (29.04.33): 2; S. Shchupak, "Neprykhovanyi formalizm i natsionalizm," no. 119 (09.05.33): 3; A. Khvylia, "Znyshchyty natsionalistychne korinnia na movnomu fronti," no. 140 (03.06.33): 2. *SZ Ukrainy*, no. 18 (1933): 16–17.

[15] "Iz vystupu t. H. I. Petrovs'koho," 2.

[16] O. H. Shlikhter, "Za bil'shovyts'ku neprymyrennist' v teorii," *Bil'shovyk Ukrainy*, nos. 5–6 (1933): 69–86.

[17] *RTsKhIDNI* 17/26/66 (08–11.06.33): 82–84.

[18] Ibid., 85.

into the hands of Petliurite bastards [*svolochi*], and these enemies with Party cards in their pockets hid behind your broad back as a member of the Ukrainian Politburo, and you often defended them. You should have talked about that. That is the main issue.

Following the plenum, the Ukrainian press was filled with articles, some written by Politburo members, now directly attacking Skrypnyk.[19] On July 7, the Politburo declared "that Skrypnyk has not completed his obligation to give the TsK a short letter admitting his errors and decisively criticizing them for publication in the press."[20] This decision was taken in the absence of Skrypnyk, who had left the meeting earlier, gone to his office, and shot himself.[21] In the aftermath of his suicide, due to his status as an Old Bolshevik, Skrypnyk was not labeled an intentional counterrevolutionary, but rather a distinguished Bolshevik who regrettably "weakened his revolutionary vigilance and allowed wreckers with ties to counter-revolutionary organizations into important positions on our ideological front."[22] Stalin even resorted to theological language to describe "The Biblical Fall of Skrypnyk [*grekhopadenie Skrypnika*]."[23]

The press campaign against Skrypnyk's errors lasted through the fall of 1933.[24] Interestingly, the first error to be attacked publicly was a seemingly quite trivial one: Skrypnyk's use of the term "*natsional'-bil'shovyzm*" to describe members of the non-Bolshevik Ukrainian Communist Party (UKP), which was allowed to exist legally in Soviet Ukraine until 1925, as well as former members of the KPZU leadership.[25] Skrypnyk appears to have meant by this term a socialist

[19] F. Taran, "Proty idealizatsii, prykrashuvannia dribno-burzhuaznykh natsionalistychnykh partii," *Komunist*, no. 150 (15.06.33): 2; P. Liubchenko, "Pro 'derusyfikatsiiu' ta 'polurusiv," no. 161 (28.06.33): 2; "Neshchadno vykryvaty i vykoriniuvaty naslidky shkidnytstva ta natsional-oportunistychnykh perekruchen' na movnomu fronti," no. 162 (29.06.33): 3; O. H. Shlikhter, "Duzhche vohon' proty burzhuazno-natsionalistychnykh nedobytky," no. 164 (03.02.33): 2; Peredova, "Bil'shovytskyi vohon' proty perekruchen' natsional'noi polityky partii," no. 165 (04.06.33): 1; P. P. Liubchenko, "Pro deiaki pomylky na teoretychnomu fronti," no. 166 (04.07.33): 3.

[20] *RTsKhIDNI* 17/26/70 (17.06.33): 117/21; (26.06.33): 118/14; (05.07.33): 120/4; (07.07.33): 121/1.

[21] *RTsKhiDNI* 17/26/70 (07.07.33 evening): 122/1.

[22] "Promova tov. H. I. Petrovskoho," *Visti VUTsIK*, no. 152 (09.07.33): 2. See also "Pokhoron M. O. Skrypnyka," *Visti VUTsIK*, no. 152 (09.07.33): 2. "Pomer tov. M. O. Skrypnyk," *Komunist*, no. 169 (08.07.33): 4; "Vyshche revoliutsiinu pyl'nyst'," no. 170 (09.07.33): 2; "Mykola Oleksiievych Skrypnyk," *Bil'shovyk Ukrainy*, nos. 7–8 (1933): 103–105.

[23] *XVII s"ezd VKP/b/. Stenograficheskii otchet* (Moscow, 1934): 31.

[24] M. M. Popov, *Pro natsionalistychni ukhyly v lavakh ukrains'koi partorhanizatsii i pro zavdannia borot'by z nymy* (Kharkov, 1933). "Iz vystupu tov. H. I. Petrov'skoho na zborakh partoseredku VUAMLIN'u," no. 172 (11.07.33): 2. S. V. Kosior "Za rishuche provedennia lenins'koi natsional'noi polityky, za bil'shovyts'ku borot'bu proty natsionalistychnykh ukhyliv," no. 182 (23.07.33): 1–2; "Pro natsionalistychni ukhyly v lavakh Ukrainskoi partorhanizatsii ta zavdannia borot'by z nymy. Rezoliutsiia zboriv partaktyvu m. Tyraspolia z 15 lypnia 1933 r. na dopovid' sekretaria TsK KP/b/U tov. P. P. Liubchenka," no. 183 (24.07.33): 2.

[25] P. Liubchenko, "Pro 'natsional'-bil'shovyzm.'" According to Petrovskii, Liubchenko had already criticized Skrypnyk for using this term at the March 1932 politburo meeting. Petrovskii, "Iz vystupu t. H. I. Petrovs'koho." Zatonskyi already quarreled with Skrypnyk over this usage at the June 1927 Ukrainian TsK plenum. *RTsKhIDNI* 17/26/9 (03.08.06.27): 24–30.

version of *smenovekhovstvo*, Ukrainian socialists who became Bolsheviks through the nationalities question but who, in many cases, later defected back to their original nationalist position. However, his use of the term was now maliciously interpreted as an erroneous attempt to justify a blending of nationalism and Bolshevism. This ideology was said to have confused the Ukrainian youth and provided a path for the penetration of nationalist ideas into the Ukrainian Communist Party.[26] This in turn led to the infiltration of Petliurites into key positions and the resultant grain requisitions disaster. On this Postyshev was unequivocal: "Skrypnyk has most clearly demonstrated that any attempt to reconcile proletarian internationalism with nationalism inevitably leads that person into the bosom of nationalist counter-revolution."[27] Nothing could be clearer. National communism was now being presented as the ideology of nationalist defection. In this sense, the Skrypnyk affair marked an extension of the cultural revolutionary terror campaign against the *smenovekhovstvo* intelligentsia, who had failed to "change their landmarks" from nationalism to socialism, to national communists within the party, who were now accused of changing their landmarks from socialism to nationalism.

This new emphasis threatened the many influential former *borot'bisty* in the Ukrainian leadership, in particular the TsK secretary, Panas Liubchenko. In early January 1933, word reached Liubchenko that "at the December 14, 1932 session of the Politburo, [Stalin] gave an extremely severe evaluation of [his] role in implementing the nationalities policy in Ukraine."[28] In a panic, Liubchenko wrote Stalin two long letters detailing his many disagreements with Skrypnyk over the previous three years, including his denunciation of Skrypnyk's theory of "national Bolshevism" at a March 1932 Ukrainian Politburo meeting. He recounted how, on becoming a TsK secretary, he had removed the majority of *borot'bisty* and West Ukrainian émigrés from their positions in TsK and had failed to remove them from Narkompros only because of "the extraordinarily privileged position occupied by Skrypnyk, best characterized by the words, 'Everything was permitted for him.' "[29] Liubchenko survived and in 1934 was promoted to head of the Ukrainian Sovnarkom, but only because he had embraced the principle that all other *borot'bisty* were suspect as nationalists. This bloodless purge of the *borot'bisty* foreshadowed the mass operations of the Great Terror, when *borot'bisty* were one of the population categories targeted for arrest and execution, and when Liubchenko avoided that fate only by imitating Skrypnyk and preemptively committing suicide.[30]

The concern that nationalism was surreptitiously infiltrating the party under the cover of *korenizatsiia*, and that Skrypnyk's writings on "national Bolshevism" had abetted that process, was at the heart of the Kuban and Skrypnyk

[26] Liubchenko, "Pro 'natsional'-bil'shovyzm," 91; F. Taran, "Proty idealizatsii, prykrashuvannia dribno-burzhuaznykh natsionalistychnykh partii," *Komunist*, no. 152 (15.06.33): 2.

[27] *TsDAHOU* 1/1/420 (18–22.11.33): 125–126.

[28] From Liubchenko's letter to Stalin. *RTsKhIDNI* 81/3/130 (1933): 95.

[29] Ibid., 81, 95–98.

[30] *RTsKhIDNI* 17/3/990 (10.09.37): 990/751. Shapoval, *Ukraina 20-50-kh rokiv*, 223–240.

affairs. This concern led to the revival of Stalin's favorite civil war–era metaphor of the "national flag." Liubchenko, for instance, quoted a 1918 Stalin article: "The national flag is only attached to the cause to fool the masses, as a popular flag, useful for covering up the counter-revolutionary intentions of the national bourgeoisie."[31] Masking rhetoric pervaded the 1933 discourse: "the dominant tint of the class enemy, with which he masks himself, is above all the national flag, national clothes."[32] Using this metaphor, Skrypnyk was repeatedly accused of having "prettified [*prykrashuvaty*]" bourgeois Ukrainian parties and ideas.[33] Both Stalin and Lenin saw nationalism as a dangerous masking ideology that allowed hostile class interests to form a united national front. *Korenizatsiia* was designed to disarm this nationalist potential by granting the forms of nation-hood. Ten years later, however, Stalin considered that policy a failure in Ukraine[34]:

> I spoke about the vitality of the vestiges of capitalism. One should note that the vestiges of capitalism are much more vital in the realm of nationalities policy than in any other area. They are more vital because they have the possibility to mask themselves very effectively in a national costume. Many people think that the Biblical Fall of Skrypnyk was an isolated instance, an exception to the rule. This is not true.

This was an enormously important statement. It marked Stalin's growing con-viction that in many cases, nationalism could not be disarmed by *korenizatsiia*, but would remain a permanent, lurking danger necessitating periodic purges and terror campaigns.

In addition to his theoretical error concerning national Bolshevism, Skryp-nyk was also accused, in Kosior's words, "of greatly exaggerating, of fetishiz-ing the nationalities policy."[35] Citing Stalin, the Ukrainian leadership accused Skrypnyk of making "the nationalities policy something self-contained, [instead of] part of the general problem of the proletarian revolution."[36] His national-ities policy courses were much mocked. Liubchenko noted that Skrypnyk required that universities devote 110 hours to teaching nationalities policy and only 60 hours to Leninism: "the nationalities question was blown up to enor-mous proportions. In all [Skrypnyk's] speeches at the [nationalities policy] faculty [of the Institute of Marxism-Leninism], in all his articles on the nation-alities question, there is no class-based Marxism, no Marx, Engels, Lenin and Stalin, no citations to them."[37] The repeated attacks on Skrypnyk's exaggera-tion of the importance of the nationalities question marked the definitive death

---

[31] Liubchenko, "Pro deiaki pomylky," 3.
[32] *XVII s"ezd*, 199.
[33] "Mykola Oleksiievych Skrypnyk," 104.
[34] *XVII s"ezd*, 31.
[35] Kosior, "Za rishuche provedennia," 2.
[36] Liubchenko, "Pro deiaki pomylky," 3.
[37] *RTsKhIDNI* 81/3/130 (1933): 99–101. Liubchenko, "Pro deiaki pomylky," 3.

of hard-line Ukrainization, a mocking and incredulous dismissal of the notion, propagated by Kaganovich himself only eight years earlier, that the nationalities question could be a core Bolshevik concern. Skrypnyk's vocabulary—"the national cause," "national consciousness," "our national interests,"—was also described as more nationalist than Bolshevik.[38] As we saw in the Shumskyi affair, most Ukrainian party members were highly uncomfortable with the rhetoric of national identity that accompanied Ukrainization. That rhetoric was now discarded. After 1933, Ukrainization would continue to be implemented, though much less energetically, but it would no longer be incessantly discussed. This was not, in fact, a trivial difference. Russian party members resented being told on a daily basis that they were members of the former great-power nationality who must now make sacrifices on behalf of the formerly oppressed nations.

The propaganda campaign against mixing nationalism and Bolshevism, as well as exaggerating the importance of the nationalities question, was accompanied by a GPU terror campaign directed against Ukrainian cultural and nationalities policy specialists. In his letter to Stalin, Liubchenko noted that instructors teaching the nationalities question were "extremely suspect in the sense of the firmness of their Leninism." The majority of them were, in fact, fired or arrested in 1933.[39] By November 1933, 2000 employees had been removed from Narkompros as nationalists, over 300 scholars and editors arrested or fired, and another 200 individuals had been removed from eight central Soviet institutions as Ukrainian nationalists. The new Commissar of Education, Volodomyr Zatonskyi, reported to the November plenum that 16,000 new teachers had to be prepared by short-term courses as "the old teachers have amortized. Some of them died, some were fired and some were taken away by the GPU [laughter]."[40] When Zatonskyi reported that eleven of twenty-nine directors of pedagogical institutions had been fired, a TsK member joked: "eighteen still remain?"[41] This terror campaign reinforced the propaganda campaign's message that national communism was a dangerous phenomenon and that the nationalities question and building Ukrainian national culture were being downgraded to a secondary, soft-line status.

Skrypnyk was also criticized for his support of the Piedmont Principle. By the time of the November 1933 Ukrainian TsK plenum, with Hitler securely in power, the threat of foreign intervention to separate Ukraine from the USSR, a goal openly stated by Hitler's eastern specialist, Alfred Rosenberg, was now a dominant theme.[42] In a speech entitled, "Soviet Ukraine—The Unshakable

[38] Shlikhter, "Za bil'shovyts'ku neprymyrennist'," 82–83; O. Shlikhter, "Posylymo bil'shovyts'ku pyl'nist' na fronti borot'by za zdiisnennia lenins'koi natsional'noi polityky na Ukraini," *Bil'shovyk Ukrainy*, nos. 9–10 (1933): 63; Popov, *Pro natsionalistychni ukhyly*, 16.

[39] *RTsKhIDNI* 81/3/130 (1933): 79, 128.

[40] *TsDAHOU* 1/1/421 (18–22.11.33): 141; 144.

[41] Ibid., 145.

[42] *TsDAHOU* 1/1/420–21 (18–22.11.33); Kosior, *Itogi i blizhaishie zadachi*; Postyshev, *U borot'by za lenins'ku natsional'nu polityku*, 7–34.

Fortress of the Great USSR," Postyshev argued that Skrypnyk's errors could lead to "the separation of Ukraine from the Soviet Union, [which] would be the beginning of the end of the entire Soviet Union, the beginning of the end of proletarian and peasant power."[43] Before his suicide, Skrypnyk realized that his vociferous advocacy of the Piedmont Principle had become a major liability. During his last public defense at the June 1933 plenum, he stated that "in 1927, I said that Soviet Ukraine was the Piedmont of the entire Ukrainian people, all those living in Ukraine's ethnographic territory. [However], with the development of fascism in Poland and Germany, we have witnessed a change in the West Ukrainian people, who now use the slogan of a united Ukraine as the slogan of fascist union for battle against the Soviet Union." Skrypnyk likewise apologized for his advocacy of the 1928 reform of the Ukrainian script, which had made concessions to Galician usage and so "gave the opportunity for traitors and provocateurs arriving here [from West Ukraine] to do their vile and black deeds."[44]

In the 1920s, a large number of West Ukrainian intellectuals had emigrated to Soviet Ukraine to escape Polish persecution and to participate in Ukrainization. They now became the primary target of the 1933 Ukrainian terror. Galicians, as West Ukrainians were now called to emphasize their alien origins, began to be arrested in December 1932.[45] Since many of Skrypnyk's close allies were of Galician origin—Badan, Ersteniuk, Richytskyi—these arrests also compromised his position. In fact, the attack on Galicians was simultaneously an attack on a large number of the cadres who supervised the implementation of Ukrainization. In May 1933, the GPU forwarded a list of thirty-one arrested party members to the Ukrainian Politburo to be approved for inclusion in a show trial of Ukrainian nationalists. They were all "Galicians." [46] Unsurprisingly, the KPZU was now subjected to another devastating purge.[47] In 1938, it would be abolished. From 1933 onward, the Piedmont Principle only served to strengthen an ethnicized Soviet xenophobia and weaken the government's commitment to *korenizatsiia*.

The fear of Ukrainian separatism was accompanied by a new shrill rhetorical insistence on the unshakable unity of the Soviet Union. Here, Skrypnyk was blamed for his frequent protests against all-union organs during his tenure as Commissar of Justice in the 1920s.[48] Postyshev insisted that "Skrypnyk approached all-Union organs with hostility [*v shtyki*]. He saw the USSR as some

---

[43] *TsDAHOU* 1/1/420 (18–22.11.33): 119.

[44] *RTsKhIDNI* 17/26/66 (08–11.06.33): 83; 83–84.

[45] Rublov and Cherchenko, *Stalinshchyna*, 104–105. Galicians were also singled out as a terror category in an internal March 1933 draft of what would become the November 1933 Ukrainian TsK plenum resolution on Ukrainization. *RTsKhIDNI* 558/11/132 (1933): 108.

[46] *TsDAHOU* 1/16/10 (08.06.33): 90–93. The trial never occurred.

[47] V. Stasiak, "Ochystyty KPZU vid ahentiv natsionalizmu," *Bil'shovyk Ukrainy*, no. 3 (1934): 42–55.

[48] I. I. Zhygelev, "Skrypnyk proty SRSR, iak iedynoi soiuznoi derzhavy," *Chervonyi shliakh*, no. 1 (1934): 11–24.

kind of League of Nations, where people sit and chat periodically, but which has no influence on the life of each separate republic."[49] Of course, Chubar and Kaganovich had also frequently and vigorously protested all-union decisions during the 1920s. The attack on Skrypnyk's prior behavior merely served to signal that such localism would no longer be tolerated.

More important than this insistence on absolute political unity, which was always a part of the Affirmative Action Empire paradigm, was a new emphasis on the cultural unity of Russians and Ukrainians. Skrypnyk was accused of promoting "the weakening of economic, political and cultural ties between Ukraine and other Soviet republics . . . on the maximum alienation of the Ukrainian language from Russian through the replacement of Russian words with Polish, Czech and German."[50] This was part of a strategic rehabilitation of Russian culture and the Russian nationality, which after 1933 would no longer be downplayed according to the principles of the Affirmative Action Empire, but rather actively emphasized as the Soviet Union's unifying core. The rhetoric of the 1933 Ukrainian terror was filled with appeals to brotherhood: "the flowering of the Ukrainian SSR in the fraternal family of the USSR," "proletarian internationalism, strengthened by the brotherhood of the peoples."[51] Skrypnyk's promotion of a cultural competition between the RSFSR and Ukraine, as well as his efforts to support the annexation of neighboring RSFSR territory and to assist RSFSR Ukrainization, were now decisively condemned.[52] This newly emphasized rhetoric of the Brotherhood of the Peoples would be transformed in 1935 into "the Friendship of the Peoples," which would thereafter serve as the ubiquitous metaphor of the new Soviet national constitution.

Skrypnyk was accused not only of sowing discord between Ukraine and the RSFSR but also of threatening the status of Ukraine's Russians through forced Ukrainization. As we saw in Chapter 3, comprehensive Ukrainization had failed by 1932, and a bilingual public sphere had emerged in Ukraine. Skrypnyk's continued commitment to the comprehensive Ukrainization of primary education contradicted this development. His education policy was based on his theory that russified Ukrainians spoke a "mixed dialect" whose syntactical base was Ukrainian. Therefore, they should study in Ukrainian-language schools even if their parents declared their native language to be Russian. Skrypnyk was exceedingly fond of this theory and repeated it as late as the fall of 1932.[53] Immediately after Skrypnyk's removal, the new Education Commissar, Volodymyr Zatonskyi, denounced Skrypnyk's theory

---

[49] *TsDAHOU* 1/1/420 (18–22.11.33): 127.

[50] Kosior, *Itogi i blizhaishie zadachi*, 94.

[51] Peredova, "Marks i dyktatura proletariiatu," *Bil'shovyk Ukrainy*, nos. 5–6 (1933): 16; M. Popov, "Peremoha marksyzmu-leninizmu—peremoha partii Lenina," nos. 5–6 (1933): 28.

[52] *RTsKhIDNI* 81/3/130 (1933): 107–109.

[53] Shlikhter, "Posylymo bil'shovyts'ku pyl'nist'," 62. In fact, Skrypnyk did not even reject this theory in his February 1933 defense or in his June 1933 self-criticism. Skrypnyk, *Narysy pidsumkiv*; *RTsKhIDNI* 17/26/66 (08–11.06.33): 82–84.

as "forced Ukrainization" and "derussification."[54] One critic cleverly noted that Skrypnyk's theory bore a striking similarity to the old Tsarist theory that Ukrainian was at root a Russian dialect and therefore Ukrainians should speak Russian.[55]

Accompanying the criticism of Skrypnyk's theory was a strong sense that Russian honor had been slighted. Skrypnyk's reference to russified Ukrainians as "half-Russians" was taken as an ethnic slur.[56] An ethnographic survey was said to have described the speech of ethnically Russian Donbass miners "as if it were a thieves' [*blatnoi*] language."[57] Donbass students were said to be ashamed to speak Russian: "two students refused to repeat what they had said in Russian. Their motive—'I am ashamed [*Ia soromolis'*].' "[58] Zatonskyi, who in 1926 argued Russian culture was too strong to ever be threatened in Ukraine, now stated that Russian culture had been oppressed.[59] A sensational *Pravda* article quoted the letter of a ethnically Russian teacher from Belorussia, Stepuro, who was attacked for having written an appeal to his village soviet in Russian and was forbidden "to speak Russian with his own wife."[60] This letter prompted an immediate apology from the Belorussian leadership.[61] As we have seen, Russian resentment toward the Soviet nationalities policy was widespread throughout the 1920s and early 1930s. However, only in 1933 did it begin to receive a public forum and official backing.

Given this officially sponsored rhetoric of resentment, the actual revisions made to Ukraine's network of schools in 1933 were strikingly limited. Zatonskyi ordered a series of investigations to find out how many Russian-language students were studying in Ukrainian-language schools. According to these reports, approximately 40 to 60 percent of native Russian speakers attended a Russian-language school.[62] Remarkably, during the cultural revolution–era expansion of education, the number of Russian-language schools in Ukraine declined in absolute terms (from 1287 to 1004) as did the number of students attending them (285,500 to 211,000). In the major russified cities of Odessa, Nikolaev, and Kharkov, the figure was slightly lower (30 to 50 percent); in Kiev, just under 50 percent (8040 of 16,460). In the formerly heavily Russian city of Kherson, there was not a single Russian school. The most detailed study undertaken of thirteen industrial districts in the

---

[54] *TsDAVOU* 166/11/24 (1933): 6; "Ob obespechenii kul'turnykh potrebnostei," 16–17.
[55] Shlikhter, "Posylymo bil'shovyts'ku pylnist'," 65.
[56] P. Liubchenko, "Pro 'derusifikatsiiu' ta 'polurusiv'," *Komunist*, no. 161 (28.06.33): 2.
[57] *TsDAHOU* 1/6/308 (17.06.33): 73.
[58] *TSDAVOU* 539/11/1112 (1933): 64.
[59] V. P. Zatonskyi, "Z pytan' natsional'noi polityky na Ukraini," *Bil'shovyk Ukrainy*, nos. 9–10 (1933): 111.
[60] Referred to by Gikalo in his speech at *XVII s"ezd*, 72.
[61] *RTsKhIDNI* 81/3/224 (1937): 142. N. Gikalo and N. Goloded, "Ob oshibkakh partiinykh i sovetskikh organizatsii Belorussii v natsional'nom voprose," *Pravda*, no. 62 (04.03.33): 2.
[62] *TsDAVOU* 539/11/1112 (1933): 21–23, 62–65, 70–73, 92–93, 113–117; 539/11/1121 (1933): 50–56; Zatonskyi, "Z pytan' natsional'noi polityky na Ukraini," 111.

Donbass, the most russified region in all of Ukraine, found that even there only 62.7 percent (22,746 of 36,303) of native Russian speakers attended a Russian school.[63]

Zatonskyi made relatively modest corrections to the system for the 1933–1934 school year. The number of students in Russian-language schools increased from 6.9 percent in 1932–1933 to 8.7 percent in 1933–1934. This was still slightly below the ethnically Russian population of Ukraine (9.23 percent). The effect was greater in the large cities. The number of children in Russian-language schools in grade 1 increased from 20 percent to 39 percent in Kharkov, from 21 percent to 38 percent in Odessa, and from zero to 32 percent in Kherson.[64] In the Donbass, the percentage studying in Russian-language schools became equivalent to the percentage of Russian-language speakers in the region.[65] Efforts were also made to increase the number of Russian theaters. Amazingly, in 1933 there were only nine Russian-language theaters in all of Ukraine, whereas there were twelve Yiddish-language theaters. The capital, Kharkov, did not have a single Russian theater. In 1933, the Politburo ordered the creation of a Russian-language state theater in Kharkov and an increase in the number of Russian-language theaters across Ukraine. Newspapers were not a major focus. Ukrainian-language newspapers declined from 91.6 percent of those published in Ukraine in 1932 to 89.9 percent in 1933 and 88.2 percent in 1934, while Russian-language papers rose modestly from 4.7 percent to 6.3 percent to 8.3 percent.[66]

The following conclusions can be drawn from these reforms. First, 1933 did not mark a strong move toward russification in Ukraine. Rather, the modest reforms in education, the theater, and the press aimed at bringing those fields in line with the consensus that had emerged elsewhere by 1932: a bilingual public sphere with a strong Russian-language presence in Ukraine's major cities. Second, there was a particular focus on the Donbass. This meant that after ten years in which Ukraine's leadership attempted to project its cultural influence into the neighboring Central-Black Earth and North Caucasus regions of the RSFSR, now the reverse was taking place. The Ukrainization of those regions had been peremptorily ended and the Russian-language presence in the Donbass strengthened. This was clearly meant to solidify Ukraine's links to the RSFSR by strengthening the Russian character of Ukraine's border regions. Third, the educational reforms were carried out under the slogan of "the national self-determination of the population itself, that is their subjective wishes."[67] This marked a sea change in Soviet nationalities policy. Until 1933,

[63] V. P. Zatonskyi, "Shkoly Ukrainy rozpochynaiut' novyi navchal'nyi rik," *Visti VUTsIK*, no. 197 (01.09.33): 3; Zatonskyi, "Z pytan' natsional'noi polityky na Ukraini," 111; *TsDAVOU* 539/11/1112 (1933): 62; 539/11/1121 (1933): 51–54; *TsDAHOU* 1/1/421 (18–22.11.33): 142.

[64] *TsDAHOU* 1/1/421 (18–22.11.33): 142.

[65] *TsDAVOU* 539/11/1121 (1933): 55–56.

[66] *Presa Ukrains'koi RSR 1918–1973* (Kharkov, 1974), 176–177.

[67] *TsDAHOU* 1/20/6213 (1933): 8. "Ob obespechenii kul'turnykh potrebnostei," 17.

there had been no educational choice and assimilation was aggressively discouraged. After 1933, national minorities were increasingly granted the right to assimilation.

The Skrypnyk affair, then, sent the following signals. National communism was now seen as a dangerous threat to the unity of the Soviet Union. The nationalities question was definitively downgraded to a secondary, soft-line status. A policy of not discussing and theorizing the nationalities question excessively was inaugurated. The Piedmont Principle was abandoned and cross-border ethnic ties viewed as a threat rather than an opportunity. The cultural ties between Russia and Ukraine were emphasized as the glue linking together the Soviet Union into a Brotherhood, soon to be Friendship, of the Peoples. The status of Russians within Ukraine was strengthened, particularly in the regions bordering the RSFSR. Comprehensive Ukrainization was abolished but it was not replaced with a policy of russification.

The Greatest-Danger Principle

The November 1933 Ukrainian TsK plenum resolution that officially ended the Skrypnyk affair did not clearly articulate all these changes. It did, however, contain one major innovation: the declaration that "the greatest danger is now local Ukrainian nationalism, as it has allied itself with international intervention."[68] In 1923, the principle that great-power chauvinism was a greater danger than local nationalism was articulated as a core component of the Affirmative Action Empire. It justified downplaying traditional Russian culture and Russian national self-expression so as not to provoke reactive nationalism among the formerly oppressed nationalities. This principle was challenged several times, in Tatarstan, Ukraine, and Belorussia, but was always backed by central authorities, most decisively by Stalin in his authoritative comments at the Sixteenth Party Congress in 1930. The reversal of this principle in Ukraine, due to the threat of "international intervention," was therefore a particularly significant signal. It remained to be determined, however, what impact this change would have on policy in the rest of the Soviet Union.

The Skrypnyk affair received considerable publicity across the entire Soviet Union and was carefully followed by nationalities policy specialists. *Pravda* published the November 1933 Ukrainian TsK plenum's resolution and the speeches of Postyshev and Kosior, as well as a lead article on the issue.[69] These three documents were translated into dozens of Soviet languages, including Romany, Komi, and Mordvinian.[70] This was yet another example of the leading role

---

[68] Kosior, *Itogi i blizhaishie zadachi*, 96. For a series of earlier drafts of this resolution, see RTsKhIDNI 558/11/132 (1933): 104–119.

[69] "Itogi i blizhaishie zadachi provedeniia natsional'noi politiki na Ukraine," *Pravda*, no. 326 (27.11.33): 2; Peredovaia, "Leninskaia natsional'naia politika pobezhdaet," no. 327 (28.11.33): 1; for Kosior and Postyshev's speeches, see no. 331 (02.12.33): 4; no. 335 (06.12.33): 3.

[70] *Literatura natsional'nostei SSSR*, no. 3 (1934): 15; no. 7 (1934): 11; no. 8 (1934): 18.

Ukraine played in the formulation of the Soviet nationalities policy. Belorussia typically followed the Ukrainian pattern, and in 1933 a very similar nationalities terror campaign was unleashed in Belorussia. Belorussian leaders repeatedly stated that their nationalities policy failures were analogous to those of Ukraine.[71] A December 1933 Belorussian TsK plenum produced an identical resolution to the November 1933 Ukrainian one, including the exact same title and the same declaration that Belorussian nationalism was now the greatest danger in Belorussia.[72] Both the Ukrainian and Belorussian resolutions, however, also added that "Great Power Russian chauvinism remains, as before, the greatest danger in the Soviet Union as a whole."[73]

This declaration initiated a process of sorting out exactly where local nationalism had become the greatest danger. In Karelia, a December 1933 plenum also declared local nationalism the greatest danger, again due to the fact that "the remnants of bourgeois-kulak and nationalist elements of Karelia have united with the interventionist circles of Fascist Finland, with the goal of annexing Karelia and uniting her to Finland under the slogan of a 'Great Finland' extending all the way to the Urals."[74] Karelia's leadership had established Finnish as Karelia's state language and aggressively recruited Finnish settlers from Canada and the United States.[75] This practice was now condemned and the republic instructed to pursue a policy of Karelization.[76] As we have seen, the 1933 terror in Ukraine also led to arrests of Poles, Germans, and Finns, and initiated the process leading to the deportation of the Soviet Union's western national minorities, which began in late 1934. Finally in Crimea, despite the titular nationality's status as "culturally backward," local nationalism was also judged the greatest danger, again as a result of its putative alliance with interventionist forces in Turkey.[77]

The Crimean decision was particularly significant because it suggested that local nationalism could be declared the greatest danger in the Soviet Union's eastern "culturally backward" republics as well, in particular in the many Turkic republics such as Azerbaijan, Kazakhstan, and Uzbekistan. In Ukraine and Belorussia, korenizatsiia had already lost momentum from 1928 to 1932, and the 1933 decrees marked a continuation of this trend. In the Soviet east, however,

[71] RTsKhIDNI 17/21/401 (20–23.07.33): 38; P. Kirushyn, "Kontrrevoliutsyiny belaruski natsyianal-demakratyzm na sluzhbe interventsyi," Bol'shevik Belarusi, nos. 1–2 (1935): 115; XVII s"ezd, 72.

[72] Itogi i blizhaishie zadachi provedeniia leninskoi natsional'noi politiki v BSSR (Minsk, 1934).

[73] Kosior. Itogi i blizhaishie zadachi, 95–96; Itogi i blizhaishie zadachi . . . v BSSR, 9.

[74] P. Khiuppenen, "Mestnyi natsionalizm—glavnaia opasnost' v karel'shoi partorganizatsii, na dannom etape," Sovetskaia Kareliia, nos. 1–2 (1934): 16.

[75] Markku Kangaspuro, "Finskaia epokha Sovetskoi Karelii," in Timo Vihavainen and Irina Takala, eds., V sem'e edinoi (Petrozavodsk, 1998): 123–160. Michael Gelb, "'Karelian Fever': The Finnish Immigrant Community During Stalin's Purges," Europe-Asia Studies, vol. 45 (1993): 1091–1116.

[76] Khiuppenen, "Mestnyi natsionalizm," 19–22.

[77] K. P. Sizonov, "Znyshchyty do kintsia natsionalistychnu kontrabandu na fronti radians'koho budivnytstva i prava," Radians'ka Ukraina, no. 8 (1934): 33.

korenizatsiia did not begin to be implemented seriously until the cultural revolution, so a reversal would have marked a much more dramatic and unexpected change. In fact, in the first half of 1933, there was a renewed effort to speed up the implementation of *korenizatsiia* in Central Asia. In August 1933, a Central Asian Biuro plenum included a report on the implementation of *korenizatsiia* for the first time since 1927. The report excoriated great-power chauvinists for sabotaging the implementation of *korenizatsiia* across Central Asia.[78] A press campaign in support of *korenizatsiia* was launched in the wake of the plenum.[79] Within the RSFSR, a November 1932 VTsIK resolution calling for an accelerated implementation of *korenizatsiia* in the RSFSR's autonomous oblasts and republics likewise led to renewed efforts.[80] In Kazakhstan, the effect was even more dramatic. Goloshchekin was removed as first party secretary in 1933 and criticized by TsK not for local nationalism, but rather for great-power chauvinism.[81] In April 1933, the new Kazakh first secretary, an experienced Armenian nationalities specialist, L. I. Mirzoian, launched a vigorous revival of both linguistic and Affirmative Action *korenizatsiia*.[82] The All-Union Politburo supported Mirzoian and established a series of measures to train and promote Kazakh cadres.[83]

Although this renewed *korenizatsiia* campaign had been endorsed by TsK and VTsIK, the increasing publicity given to events in Ukraine after Skrypnyk's July 1933 suicide, culminating in the widespread distribution of the November 1933 Ukrainian nationalities policy resolution, sent powerful signals undermining that endorsement. Already on April 4, 1933, the head of the Central Asian Biuro, Bauman, sent Stalin the following telegram: "In order to deliver a sudden blow to the active counterrevolutionary elements in Central Asia, the Central Asian Biuro requests that the *polittroika* of the OGPU be granted the right to carry out the death sentence for crimes of sabotage, insurrection, banditism and theft." Stalin scrawled "in favor. I. St." on the telegram.[84] Although this telegram did not yet specify nationalists, the GPU soon began to arrest prominent national communists in all the Central Asian republics.[85] On September 24, 1933, the head of the Kirgiz Sovnarkom, Abdrakhmanov, was excluded from

---

[78] *RTsKhIDNI* 62/1/1038 (25–29.08.33): 110–166; 62/2/1039 (25–29.08.33): 1–168.

[79] K. Ablianov, "Za bol'shevistskie natsional'nye kadry," *Pravda vostoka*, no. 199 (28.08.33): 2; "Natsionalizatsiia sovetskogo apparata i voprosy kul'turnogo stroitel'stva v respublikakh Srednei Azii," no. 223 (26.09.33): 2–4.

[80] *Postanovleniia prezidiuma VTsIK ot 1.11.32 i prezidiuma Bashkirskogo TsIK ot 29.12.32 o korenizatsii apparata* (Ufa, 1933).

[81] *Shestoi plenum Kazakhskogo kraevogo komiteta VKP/b/. Stenograficheskii otchet* (Alma-Ata, 1936): 3–8.

[82] *O korenizatsii. Sbornik rukovodiashchikh materialov* (Alma-Ata, 1934): 21–25; "O korenizatsii," *Bol'shevik Kazakhstana*, no. 6 (1933): 1–7; Il'ias Kabulov, "Za reshitel'nuiu bor'bu na dva fronta v natsional'nom voprose v Kazakhstane," nos. 1–2 (1934): 9–14.

[83] *RTsKhIDNI* 17/3/933 (01.11.33): 148/44.

[84] *RTsKhIDNI* 558/11/64 (10.04.33): 21.

[85] In addition to the arrests in Kirgizia and Tajikistan, see the announcement about arrests in Turkmenistan and Uzbekistan in "Na VI s"ezde kompartii Turkmenii," *Pravda vostoka*, no. 13 (15.01.34): 2; *RTsKhIDNI* 17/27/54 (10–14.01.34): 124–129.

the party and handed over to the OGPU as a nationalist.[86] As in Ukraine, he was said to have sabotaged grain requisitions.

The most publicity was given to the arrest of Tajikistan's two leading national communists: Khajibaev, head of the Tajik Sovnarkom, and Maksum, head of the Tajik TsIK.[87] Their arrest was accompanied by a massive GPU terror campaign against Tajik national communists. By October 28, in the midst of this campaign, they had already arrested 693 individuals, including 14 members of the central republican apparat, 35 party and Soviet leaders, 141 officials at the district level, and another 145 at the village level.[88] In a republic the size of Tajikistan and with its limited reserve of literate Tajik communists, this was a massive campaign. The removal of Maksum and Khadjibaev was announced at the Tajik obkom plenum in December 1933 by the Central Asian first secretary, Bauman, who informed the delegates that Maksum and Khadjibaev had also sabotaged grain requisitions and were aggressively anti-Russian: "They constantly held conversations about the need to drive all Russians out of Tajikistan."[89] Bauman drew a direct parallel with the Ukrainian events[90]:

> You know that in the resolution on nationalities policy in Ukraine it is said that in the Soviet Union as a whole great power chauvinism is the greatest danger. However, in Ukraine at the current time it declares that the greatest danger is local Ukrainian nationalism.
>
> In Tajikistan, Khajibaev and Maksum, as heads of the government, conducted a bourgeois-nationalist line and objectively united with the kulak counter-revolution. Thus here in Tajikistan the battle with bourgeois nationalism must be increased. This is a crucial question. Bourgeois nationalists in Tajikistan are counting on the interventionist intentions of the imperialists. They are aiming at violating the unity of the laborers of the Soviet Union.

Bauman was all but saying that local nationalism should be judged the greatest danger in Central Asia. The first secretary of Uzbekistan, Ikramov, went further and stated that local nationalism was the greatest danger in Uzbekistan, since "Uzbek nationalist counter-revolutionaries have again and again allied themselves with foreign interventionists."[91]

At this point, Stalin intervened twice to moderate the movement for a reversal of the greatest danger principle in the Soviet east. His first intervention came

[86] "Rezoliutsiia ob"edinennogo zasedaniia biuro Kirgizskogo obkoma i prezidiuma OKK VKP/b/ . . . ," Pravda vostoka, no. 227 (30.09.33): 1; "O polozhenii v Kirgizskoi partorganizatsii. Stat'ia zam. Pred TsKK-NKRKI SSSR tov. N. Antipova," no. 228 (02.10.33): 1.

[87] RTsKhIDNI 558/11/63 (01.12.33): 65–67; 17/3/935 (05.12.33): 150/100; GARF 3316/7s/92 (1934): 10–42; RTsKhIDNI 121/2/362 (1933): 1–121; "Postanovlenie ob"edinennogo plenuma TsK i TsKK KP/b/Tadzhikistana ot dekabria 1933 goda," Pravda vostoka, no. 5 (05.01.33): 1.

[88] RTsKhIDNI 81/3/103 (1933): 74.

[89] K. I. Bauman, "Prevratit' Tadzhikistan v obraztsovuiu sovetskuiu sotsialisticheskuiu respubliku," Partrabotnik. Organ Sredazbiuro TsK VKP/b/, no. 1 (1934): 16.

[90] Ibid., 27.

[91] RTsKhIDNI 17/27/46 (11–15.02.34): 127.

in Kazakhstan. The November 1933 Ukrainian resolution had caused considerable concern for Mirzoian in Kazakhstan, since his arrival was linked to the ouster of Goloshchekin as a great-power chauvinist and he had placed his authority firmly behind the campaign to revive *korenizatsiia*. Mirzoian was justified in his concerns. Goloshchekin had noted the changed political environment produced by the Shrypnyk affair and, on August 4, 1933, had written Stalin and Kaganovich complaining that Mirzoian had gone too far in attacking him as a great power chauvinist and in promoting *korenizatsiia*. Mirzoian was instructed to tone down his propaganda campaign.[92] After the Ukrainian resolution, the Kazakh *kraikom* biuro gathered and passed a compromise resolution that "in Kazakhstan, the greatest danger remains Great Power chauvinism. At the same time, it is necessary to fight Kazakh nationalism more systematically and thoroughly." This decision not to adopt the new Ukrainian policy was justified by "the exceedingly weak *korenizatsiia* of the government apparat, the extreme backwardness of [Kazakh] national culture, the weak development of industry and national cadres, and the cultural backwardness of the Kazakh masses."[93] Mirzoian sent this decision to Stalin for comment along with a cover note explaining that "with the publication of the Ukrainian resolution and the speech of Kosior, the district and oblast *aktiv* are now demanding a discussion of the nationalities policy and the battle on two fronts," that is they were demanding a reversal of the greatest danger principle. Mirzoian requested Stalin's approval of the draft resolution.[94]

On the same day, Stalin sent back the following reply[95]:

> The fight with Great Russian chauvinism is carried out not only by local Party organizations but, above all, by TsK VKP/b/ as a whole. The current task for Kazakh Bolsheviks consists of concentrating their fire against Kazakh nationalism and the deviation towards it, while continuing the fight with Great Russian chauvinism. Otherwise one cannot build Leninist internationalism in Kazakhstan. One cannot say that in Kazakhstan international training is better than in Ukraine. Rather the opposite. If despite this, local nationalism is not at the current moment the greatest danger in Kazakhstan, this is explained by the fact that it is more difficult for Kazakh nationalism to connect with international interventionists than in Ukraine. However, this positive circumstance should not lead to a weakening of the battle against Kazakh nationalism or to compromise with it. On the contrary, the battle with local nationalism should be increased to create the conditions for the planting of Leninist internationalism among the laboring national masses of Kazakhstan. As material for orientation, we are sending the TsK resolution on Tajikistan.

[92] *RTsKhIDNI* 81/3/419 (04.08.33): 55–57.
[93] *VIII Kazakstanskaia kraevaia konferentsiia VKP/b/. Stenograficheskii otchet* (Alma-Ata, 1935): 221–222.
[94] *RTsKhIDNI* 558/11/48 (13.12.33): 640b.
[95] *RTsKhIDNI* 558/11/48 (13.12.33): 64. Stalin's telegram was published with no excisions in *VIII Kazakstanskaia kraevaia*, 222.

The Politburo resolution on Tajikistan referred to by Stalin was relatively mild. It condemned Maksud and Khajibaev's violation of Leninist internationalism but called into question neither *korenizatsiia* nor the greatest-danger principle.[96] Bauman did, in fact, send Stalin a further Tajik resolution that would reverse the greatest danger principle, but Stalin sent back a terse rejection of this move: "The TsK secretariat considers it inexpedient to issue this resolution, in particular we consider incorrect the formula about the greatest danger in national deviations that you have put forward. We propose that the resolution not be passed, and if it already has been, that it not be published.[97]

Stalin's intervention ended speculation that the greatest-danger principle would be reversed throughout the Soviet Union. It also established the principle that the nationalities living along the Soviet Union's western borders would be subject to the greatest scrutiny. In this sphere, then, the distinction between Soviet eastern and western nationalities did become a geographical rather than a developmental one. Not only in "backward" Kazakhstan, but also in "cultured" Georgia, Beria could resolutely and successfully state that "our situation is of course not like it was in Ukraine. The greatest danger here remains great power chauvinism."[98] In the Middle Volga autonomous republics, far from any border, the issue was not even raised.[99] Mirzoian's *korenizatsiia* campaign continued in Kazakhstan.

At the Seventeenth Party Congress in January 1934, Stalin publicly put an end to further debate about the greatest-danger principle[100]:

> People argue about which deviation represents the greatest danger, Great Russian chauvinism or local nationalism. In today's circumstances, this is a formal and therefore empty debate. It would be stupid to give a formula that would be valid for all times. Such formulas do not exist. The greatest danger is that deviation against which one ceases to battle and which therefore grows into a danger to the state. [extended applause]

Thus Stalin officially abandoned one of the pillars of the Affirmative Action Empire. This paved the way for the rehabilitation of Russian national culture. No longer were Russians or Russian culture held responsible for the sins of Tsarism. In practice, of course, terror had already been deployed asymmetrically against local nationalism rather than Russian chauvinism. Stalin's telegram

---

[96] *RTsKhIDNI* 17/3/935 (05.12.33): 150/100. For extensive background on this affair, see *RTsKhIDNI* 81/3/103–104 (1933–1934).

[97] *RTsKhIDNI* 558/11/48 (13.12.33): 64. Stalin's telegram was published with no excisions in *VIII Kazakstanskaia kraevaia*, 222.

[98] *IX s"ezd KP/b/Gruzii. Stenograficheskii otchet* (Tiflis, 1935): 72.

[99] See the 1934 party congress in the Mari autonomous oblast, *RTsKhIDNI* 17/21/2825 (1934): 69–74; and in the Bashkir congress (where concern was expressed only about "Tatar [Great] Power chauvinism towards Bashkirs and other local nationalities"), *RTsKhIDNI* 17/21/274 (13–17.01.34): 144; and for Tatarstan, M. Razumov, "Pobeda leninskoi natsional'noi politiki," *Bol'shevik*, no. 21 (1933): 28–41.

[100] *XVII s"ezd*, 32.

to Mirzoian, with its insistence that local communists concentrate their fire on local nationalism, indicated this pattern would continue, as it did. In January 1937, at the beginning of the next great wave of terror, the greatest-danger principle made its last appearance when Kazakhstan, the republic that had most insisted on the greatest danger of great-power chauvinism in 1933, formally declared that local nationalism was now the greatest danger in Kazakhstan.[101] This would remain the case for the rest of Stalin's rule. This meant recurrent terror campaigns against local nationalism but it did not, as we shall now see, mean the abolition of *korenizatsiia*.

Ukrainization after the Skrypnyk Affair

The December 14, 1932 Politburo decree condemned only the "mechanical" implementation of Ukrainization, not the policy itself, and it demanded not russification but the promotion of "Bolshevik Ukrainian cadres."[102] During the course of the Skrypnyk Affair, this phrase was transformed into a call for "Bolshevik *Ukrainizatsiia*" instead of "mechanical *Ukrainizatsiia*" or "*Petliurizatsiia*."[103] Postyshev provided a definition of mechanical Ukrainization at the June 1933 plenum: "Comrades, it is a fact that in the Party and Komsomol people were accepted only because of their national identity, only because they were Ukrainians . . . [the All-Union Politburo] directed our Party's attention to the need to abolish this mechanical implementation of Ukrainization."[104] At a Belorussian TsK plenum a month later, the first Party secretary, N. F. Gikalo, produced the same formula: "We must at last break with the non-Bolshevik attitude towards promoting cadres. We must conduct a furious battle against promoting cadres not by Bolshevik principles, but by the principle of whether one is Belorussian, Jewish, Russian, Ukrainian, etc."[105] Of course, no one had promoted cadres in this fashion more vigorously than Kaganovich, whose tenure as Ukrainian first party secretary was being fulsomely praised throughout 1933.[106] Therefore, it was easy for Ukrainian Bolsheviks to doubt the sincerity of Kosior's insistence in July 1933 and again in November 1933 that

---

[101] "Otchetnyi doklad tovarishcha L. I. Mirzoiana pervomu s"ezdu KP/b/Kazakhstana o rabote kraikoma KP/b/K," *Bol'shevik Kazakhstana*, nos. 6–7 (1937): 59.

[102] *Holod 1932–1933 rokiv na Ukraini* (Kiev, 1990): 292–293.

[103] For the introduction of these phrases, see M. Popov, "Peremoha marksyzmu-leninizmu," 28; Skrypnyk, *Narysy pidsumkiv*, 5. Draft versions of both the December 14, 1932 Politburo resolution and the November 1933 Ukrainian TsK plenum resolution have been preserved with Stalin's editorial revisions. In both case, Stalin repeatedly added the phrase "Bolshevik *Ukrainizatsiia*" to the document, so it seems clear that Stalin made the phrase central to both resolutions as part of his balancing act of preserving Ukrainization while severely punishing its putative nationalist version promoted by Skrypnyk. RTsKhIDNI 17/163/968 (14.12.32): 101–120; 558/11/132 (1933): 104–119.

[104] RTsKhIDNI 17/26/66 (08–11.06.33): 58.

[105] RTsKhIDNI 17/21/401 (20–23.07.33): 34.

[106] Andrii Khvylia, *Znyshchyty korinnia ukrains'koho natsionalizmu na movnomu fronti* (Kharkov, 1933): 3.

the Skrypnyk affair had made the promotion of reliable ethnic Ukrainian cadres a greater priority.[107]

In fact, the 1933 terror campaign, which annihilated the entire Narkompros apparat devoted to monitoring the implementation of Ukrainization, along with their influential patron, unsurprisingly led to a spontaneous wave of de-Ukrainization. Nikolai Popov noted that "in the provinces, there is a tendency to equate the excesses of Ukrainization with Ukrainization itself. Some comrades think that the liquidation of the excesses [of Ukrainization] means the liquidation of Ukrainization." He reported that everywhere factory newspapers were being shifted from Ukrainian to Russian. In Lugansk, the obkom newspaper had been changed over to Russian entirely while preserving only its Ukrainian title.[108] In Donetsk, the city government was emboldened to conduct all its paperwork in Russian, and mixed Ukrainian–Russian primary schools also began to teach entirely in Russian. The recently Ukrainized Odessa state university likewise switched back to Russian. The assistant director explained: "It's now time to start teaching people."[109] The Italian embassy reported that Russian was being increasingly used by the bureaucracy and that "a circular has been issued to all offices requiring that employees be asked if they have studied Ukrainian 'WILLINGLY'. . . or against their will."[110] The director of the Odessa fine arts technicum was the most honest: "Prior to the matter with Skrypnyk, all our courses were beginning to be taught in Ukrainian. But after the Skrypnyk Affair, everyone switched back to Russian fearing that otherwise they would be labeled a Ukrainian nationalist."[111]

This spontaneous wave of de-Ukrainization was sufficiently strong that it was felt necessary to renounce it already at the November 1933 plenum[112]:

> Great Power Russian chauvinists and Ukrainian nationalists attempt to interpret the Party's decisive battle with Petliurite elements as a revision of the nationalities policy. We must give the most merciless rebuttal to these slanderous and provocational attempts. . . . The Party will mercilessly expose all attempts to revise the decisions of the twelfth and sixteenth party congresses under the cover of leftist phrases about how the nationalities policy is no longer necessary, that national republics are not needed anymore.

Nevertheless, the November 1933 plenum did not call a halt to the terror campaign against "Ukrainian nationalists," a campaign that continued well into 1934 and that brought with it further spontaneous de-Ukrainization. After the plenum, public discussion of Ukrainization ceased, although there was renewed

---

[107] Kosior, "Za rishuche provedennia"; Kosior, *Itogi i blizhaishie zadachi*, 96–97. The same policy line was followed in Belorussia. *Itogi i blizhaishie zadachi . . . v BSSR*, 11–12.

[108] *TsDAHOU* 1/1/421 (18–22.11.33): 114; 114–115.

[109] *TsDAHOU* 1/20/6634 (1935): 28, 34; 100.

[110] James E. Mace and Leonid Heretz, eds., *Oral History Project of the Commission on the Ukraine Famine*, vol. 1 (Washington, D.C., 1990): 446–447.

[111] *TsDAHOU* 1/20/6634 (1935): 103.

[112] Kosior, *Itogi i blizhaishie zadachi*, 100–101.

attention to the celebration of acceptable Ukrainian national heroes, above all Taras Shevchenko.[113] This silence about Ukrainization after a year-long campaign against its abuses has understandably led to a widespread belief that Ukrainization was abandoned entirely after 1933.[114]

Although Ukrainization disappeared from public discourse from 1933 to 1937, archival documentation reveals that it remained an ongoing concern of the Ukrainian leadership throughout this period. Moreover, it is clear that Stalin himself set a limit to the revision of *korenizatsiia* in Ukraine and Belorussia. In mid-1934, he intervened directly in Belorussian affairs. Two events triggered this intervention. First, the head of the Belorussian Sovnarkom, Goloded, complained to Moscow that the Belorussian first party secretary, N. F. Gikalo, was interfering in matters reserved for the soviet bureaucracy.[115] Second, a TsK investigation reported the systematic Polonization of Belorussian children in the Polish national soviets of Belorussia. Goloded and Gikalo were called to Moscow to discuss these issues. At an August 1934 Belorussian TsK plenum, Gikalo reported Stalin's comments at the Moscow meeting[116]:

> In his comments and in a formal address, Stalin declared that there had been an underestimation of the importance of Soviet governmental work. In particular he said there had been an underestimation of the national moment in both party and soviet work. We cannot underestimate the difficulty of work in a national republic. Comrade Stalin pointed out that, for instance, we are not talking about some kind of Samara oblast here, where things aren't so complicated. To this one must add the border position of Belorussia. And Comrade Stalin bluntly indicated—and I most definitely committed this error in my work in Belorussia—that as a leader I made an error in my desire to forcibly control day-to-day matters, of underestimating the importance of soviet governmental work.

This is an exceedingly interesting passage. In December 1932, Stalin accused the Ukrainian party of failing to supervise the implementation of Ukrainization by the Soviet organs (Skrypnyk's Narkompros) and launched a wave of terror by the hard-line party and GPU against the soft-line soviet institutions.[117] Now, he was intervening to protect the soft-line soviet institutions, to whom he assigned the task of promoting *korenizatsiia*, from excessive control by the hard-line party bureaucracy. At the same time as he made this intervention in

[113] The silence of the press on Ukrainization is based on a reading of *Visti VUTsIK, Komunist, Bil'shovyk Ukrainy, Literaturna Hazeta,* and *Biuleten' NKO,* all of which dealt with Ukrainization continuously from 1925 to 1933. On Shevchenko, see N. Kahanovich, "Iak Ukrains'ki natsionalisty fal'syfikuvaly Tarasa Shevchenka," *Visti VUTsIK,* no. 7 (08.01.34): 2–3. E. Shabl'ovs'kyi, "Proty natsionalistychnoi fal'syfikatsii Shevchenka," *Literaturna hazeta,* no. 1 (03.01.34): 3.

[114] For example, Mace, *Communism and the Dilemmas,* 300–301. Shapoval, *Ukraina 20–50-kh rokiv,* 98–114.

[115] *RTsKhIDNI* 17/21/404 (03.08.34): 2–5; 86–93.

[116] Ibid., 23.

[117] On this, see Kosior, "Za rishuche provedennia."

Belorussian affairs, Stalin appointed the former *borot'bist* and nationalities specialist Panas Liubchenko to take over the Ukrainian Sovnarkom, thereby again revealing his preference for having a "true" Ukrainian in charge of the soft-line bureaucracy in Ukraine.[118]

Stalin's criticisms of the Belorussian leadership were formalized in a July 1934 TsK resolution.[119] At the August 1934 plenum, Gikalo condemned the fact that "at mass meetings, meetings of workers and demonstrations the Belorussian language is almost forgotten" and that Belorussian "had been driven out" of party meetings completely. Goloded called for a revival of *korenizatsiia*: "We must discuss this issue again at the TsK *Biuro* and work on the promotion of cadres from the native population, those knowing the language, customs and culture of the population living in Belorussia." The plenum also condemned the persecution of the Belorussian language in Polish regions and called for "a much greater protection of the interests of the Belorussian language."[120] It is not clear what impact Stalin's invention had on the implementation of Belorussization, though by 1935, Gikalo was at least bragging about the fact that 1624 of 1858 (87.4 percent) schools in Belorussia were Belorussian-language.[121]

Ukrainization also began to draw revived political attention in 1934. In March 1934, Kosior presented a proposal to the Ukrainian Politburo, calling for an investigation of the state of Ukrainization in government organs, and the forthcoming investigation was even to be publicly announced in the Ukrainian press.[122] By May 1934, TsK's Kultprop Department had produced a draft decree that read almost as if it had been written in the mid-1920s[123]:

TsK KP/b/U decrees:
1. Require all communists who know Ukrainian to use it in their work at meetings and in speeches.
2. All employees who either do not know Ukrainian or who know it insufficiently should continue the study of Ukrainian on their own efforts. Given the flowering of Ukrainian culture, there is no longer a need for the State Ukrainian Studies courses.
3. Reiterate that every employee of a state and cooperative institution is required to know Ukrainian . . . well enough to a/ understand exactly written and oral instructions, b/ carry out assignments, c/ write grammatically.
4. Require Commissar of Finance, Rekis, Commissar of Health, Kantorovich, Commissar of Light Industry, Tsutsulkivskyi, and head of the Cooperative Union, Kuzmenko, to immediately correct all defects in the implementation

---

[118] For evidence that Stalin personally intervened in support of Liubchenko, see *RTsKhIDNI* 558/11/64 (14.02.34): 60. Note also that in his August 11, 1932 letter to Kaganovich, Stalin had suggested the former *borot'bist* Hrynko for this position.

[119] *RTsKhIDNI* 17/21/404 (03.08.34): 2–5.

[120] Ibid., 20–21; 89; 2.

[121] N. Gikalo, "Bol'sheviki Belorussii v bor'be za sotsializm," *Bol'shevik*, no. 4 (1935): 22.

[122] *RTsKhIDNI* 17/21/4672 (14.03.34): 4/12.

[123] *TsDAHOU* 1/6/352 (03.05.34): 68–69.

of Ukrainization in their institutions. In the future, place the responsibility for the state of Ukrainization personally on the head of each institution. . . .

The Politburo created an authoritative commission (Kosior, Popov, Liubchenko) to revise this decree for publication. It was, however, never published.

Instead of this bold call for a revival of the linguistic Ukrainization of the 1920s, the Politburo instead initiated a dramatic return to the policy of promoting ethnic Ukrainians to leadership positions. On February 26, 1935, the Ukrainian Politburo ordered the TsK Cadres Department to[124]:

1. Draw up a list of 120 to 150 ethnic Ukrainians to promote to the position of *raikom* secretary and another 120 Ukrainians to promote to chairman of district executive committees.
2. Produce a list of ethnic Ukrainians who are now secretaries of a *raikom* or district executive committee to be promoted to work in the oblast or central party and soviet organs.
3. Draw up a list of agricultural students to be promoted into leadership positions in the district, oblast, and central party and soviet apparat.

In addition, all TsK departments were required to:

4. Find no less than 300 Ukrainians from among party committees and party activists for promotion to leading party and soviet work as well as work in the oblast, party, and soviet apparat.
5. Compose a list of all Ukrainians who work in the obkom, oblast executive committee, and central soviet apparat.

Finally, the Komsomol was ordered "to present proposals to TsK relating to the promotion of new Ukrainian cadres to leadership positions in the Komsomol." Such aggressive Affirmative Action had not been practiced in Ukraine since the height of Kaganovich's 1925 Ukrainization drive.

This surprising decree was followed up by an even more unprecedented June 3, 1935 TsK decree that required all Ukrainian commissariats to promote ethnic Ukrainians immediately into positions of leadership.[125] The resultant actions exceeded even the "mechanical Ukrainization" of the 1920s. A series of Orgburo decrees required ethnic Ukrainians to be promoted into high-ranking leadership posts. For instance, in the Commissariat of Health, ethnic Ukrainians were to be promoted to "the head of oblast health departments and city health departments, the director of health institutions, the directors of sub-departments and so forth."[126] In the Commissariat of (Justice), ethnic Ukrainians were to be installed in the positions of "assistant general procura-

[124] *RTsKhIDNI* 17/21/4675 (26.02.35): 33/1.
[125] Referred to in *RTsKhIDNI* 17/26/4701 (05.07.35): 40/3.
[126] *RTsKhIDNI* 17/26/4701 (05.07.35): 40/3.

tor, Commissariat of Justice procurator, members of the Supreme Soviet, oblast procurators and their assistants, heads and assistant heads of oblast courts."[127]

The Orgburo decrees made quite clear that ethnic Russians were being directly replaced with ethnic Ukrainians. In some cases, the Russians were reassigned to other work; in other cases, their fate was not specified.[128] Such crudely direct replacement of high-ranking ethnic Russians by ethnic Ukrainians purely on the basis of national identity did not take place even at the height of Kaganovich's Ukrainization. The 1935–1936 Orgburo decrees also revived the old practice of granting Ukrainians preferential access to open positions. The Commissar of Housing was instructed that "in all instances, when a leadership position becomes available, Ukrainians should be given preference." Law schools in Kiev and Kharkov were ordered to expand their faculty with the following instructions: "Staff these faculties primarily with Ukrainians, 75–85 percent." Orgburo decrees ordering the mass promotion of Ukrainians into leadership positions continued for over a year after the original February 1935 Politburo decree. In addition, the Politburo singled out Odessa, Dnepropetrovsk, and Donetsk oblasts as particularly delinquent and ordered them to immediately promote Ukrainians into leadership positions.[129]

Given the lack of public discussion and the loss of archival materials during World War II, it is difficult to determine the state of Ukrainization that prompted these decrees.[130] However, three extensive, though rather anecdotal, 1935 inspections of Ukrainization in Odessa, Dnepropetrovsk, and Donetsk have survived.[131] From these inspections, it is clear that all oral work was being conducted exclusively in Russian, while written work had largely been shifted to Russian in Odessa, Donetsk, and the city of Dnepropetrovsk, though the oblast authorities in Dnepropetrovsk were still using mostly Ukrainian.[132] The reports do not provide comprehensive statistics about the number of Ukrainians in leadership positions but do indicate that, although Ukrainians were a majority of the population in all three regions, they remained a minority in most leadership positions. In Dnepropetrovsk, for example, Ukrainians made up 25 percent of the oblast presidium and 42 percent of the city presidium, although they were 79.7 percent of the overall oblast population.[133] All of the reports found that no attention had been devoted to Ukrainization and that, as was the case prior to 1933 as well, "there was a negative attitude towards Ukrainization."[134]

---

[127] *RTsKhIDNI* 17/21/4701 (19.08.35): 43/33.

[128] *RTsKhIDNI* 17/21/4701 (19.08.35): 43/2.

[129] *RTsKhIDNI* 17/21/4702 (15.03.36): 65/13; 65/9 (28.06.36): 75/11; 17/21/4676 (10.09.35): 47/43.

[130] With the exception of the records of the highest party organs—the Secretariat, Orgburo, and Politburo—and a small number of records from the TsK departments, almost all relevant documentation in Kiev was destroyed by the Soviet authorities before the fall of Kiev to the Germans in 1941.

[131] *TsDAHOU* 1/20/6634 (1935): 1–124.

[132] Ibid., 1, 7–10, 27–28, 92–94.

[133] Ibid., 1–5. Neither Odessa nor Donetsk provided exact leadership figures.

[134] Ibid., 115.

One would have expected that this dramatic revival of Ukrainization, after the noisy Skrypnyk affair, would have required some public explanation. However, the Ukrainian press was silent and these promotions were ordered and presumably carried out conspiratorially. Besides this striking difference in publicity, the new Ukrainization differed from the old in two further ways. First, the focus was on Affirmative Action rather than on linguistic Ukrainization. Second, attention was devoted exclusively to the promotion of Ukrainians into leadership positions (from the district level up to the central commissariats). In the 1920s, the Ukrainization of the government apparat was the top priority. This was again due to the commitment to linguistic Ukrainization. To establish Ukrainian as the language of government, one needed Ukrainians in the positions where paperwork was being processed. With the subsiding of the 1933 nationalities terror, the goal seems to have been a reemphasis of the Ukrainian character of the republic's government. This required visible figures. Although Stalin eventually gave up on linguistic *korenizatsiia*, he never abandoned the reasonable belief that nationalist feelings would be assuaged if the republican leadership was predominantly composed of titular nationals.

It is difficult to judge the impact of the mid-1930s' Ukrainization campaign. From figures provided by Postyshev in January 1936 and Kosior in May 1937, it would seem that a sizable de-Ukrainization had occurred during the terror of 1933–1934, which was more than corrected for by the 1935–1936 campaign. Postyshev provided the following statistics on the number of ethnic Ukrainians in various jobs on January 1, 1934 and January 1, 1936: *raikom* and assistant *raikom* secretaries, 179 of 431; heads and assistant heads of oblast departments, 14 of 32; propagandists, 5000 of 9500; district newspaper editors, 213 of 319; directors of machine-tractor stations, 384 of 604; heads of district executive committees and city soviets, 250 of 332.[135]

According to Kosior, in 1936–1937, the number of Ukrainian students in universities ranged from a high of 74.4 percent in agricultural institutes to a low of 31 to 40 percent in industrial institutes. By comparison, in 1932–1933, 54.5 percent of students in Ukraine's institutes were ethnically Ukrainian.[136] In 1937, the state apparat was 52.7 percent Ukrainian, up slightly from 51.4 percent in 1930, while the party was 57 percent Ukrainian, up solidly from 52.9 percent in 1930.[137] The Komsomol expanded from 66.1 percent Ukrainian in 1928 to 74 percent in 1937.[138] These highly anecdotal statistics suggest that the representation of Ukrainians in higher education and government was slightly higher in 1937 than at the height of the Ukrainization campaign. Of course, given the massive influx of Ukrainians into the cities and the ongoing expansion of government and education, Ukrainian representation should have grown with no government efforts. This was why Affirmative Action was not a priority at the

[135] *RTsKhIDNI* 17/21/4668 (26–30.01.36): 126–127; 17/21/4665 (27.05–03.06.37): 44–47.
[136] *RTsKhIDNI* 17/21/4665 (27.05–03.06.37): 45.
[137] Ibid., 46–47; Khvylia, *Do rozv'iazannia*, 72–73. *TsDAHOU* 1/20/6197 (1935): 96.
[138] *RTsKhIDNI* 17/21/4665 (27.05–03.06.37): 47; *GARF* 374/27s/1709 (1929): 78.

Table 30. Newspaper Circulation in Ukraine, 1930–1939

Year	Ukrainian Language Circulation	As Percent of Total Circulation	Russian Language Circulation	As Percent of Total Circulation	Total Circulation
1930	349,290	76.7	85,080	18.7	455,406
1931	464,642	88.9	37,448	7.2	522,919
1932	950,295	91.7	48,948	4.7	1,037,164
1933	661,495	89.9	46,091	6.3	735,453
1934	480,611	88.2	45,480	8.3	545,104
1935	675,768	79.2	150,813	17.7	853,327
1936	756,193	83.7	113,108	12.5	903,708
1937	845,698	77.1	213,954	19.5	1,096,329
1938	817,480	68.5	351,075	29.4	1,193,948
1939	854,968	67.4	390,237	30.8	1,268,018

Calculated from *Presa Ukrains'koi RSR, 1918–1973*, 176–77.

height of Ukrainization. This natural growth of Ukrainian cadres was momentarily reversed by the 1933 terror and purges, but then corrected by the 1935–1936
Ukrainization campaign.

The use of Ukrainian in government, the dominant issue from 1925 to
1932, was a secondary concern in the mid-1930s.[139] As noted above, there was
a substantial linguistic de-Ukrainization after 1933, which led to a September
1935 Politburo decree berating the Donetsk, Dnepropetrovsk, and Odessa
obkoms.[140] In the press and primary education, the Ukrainian language
remained dominant. Table 30 shows that the percentage of newspapers published in Ukrainian peaked in 1932 and then began a decline that was briefly
reversed by the 1935–1936 Ukrainization campaign and then accelerated again
during the 1937–1938 terror.

These statistics undoubtedly overstate the dominance of Ukrainian since a
variety of sources suggest that newspapers with a Ukrainian title would sometimes publish in Russian.[141] In late 1935, Postyshev noted that none of Ukraine's
32 central newspapers and only one of its 23 oblast papers (*Stalino*) was Russian-
language. He also observed that there were currently 17,327 Ukrainian-language
schools and only 1394 Russian-language schools.[142] Book publication remained
relatively constant. In 1932, 71.7 percent of all books and 84.7 percent of tirage
was Ukrainian-language; in 1937, the same figures were 58.6 percent and 89.6
percent.[143] The Ukrainian language, then, remained dominant in the press and

[139] One orgburo decree did instruct the Commissariat of Health to keep its medical journals
in Ukrainian. *RTsKhIDNI* 17/21/4701 (05.07.35): 40/3.
[140] *RTsKhIDNI* 17/21/4676 (10.09.35): 47/43.
[141] *TsDAHOU* 1/20/6634 (1935): 32–33.
[142] P. Postyshev, "Radians'ka Ukraina na porozi 1936 roku," *Bil'shovyk Ukrainy*, nos. 11–12
(1935): 39–41.
[143] V. P. Zatonskyi, *Natsional'no-kul'turne budivnytstvo i borot'ba proty natsionalizmu* (Kiev,
1934): 13; *Kniga i knizhnoe delo v Ukrainskoi SSR* (Kiev, 1985): 399.

primary education, but its use declined significantly within the government apparat.

Surprisingly, the onset of the Great Terror inspired a short-lived movement to revive linguistic Ukrainization as well. On January 13, 1937, the All-Union Politburo issued a decree that criticized Pavel Postyshev for having allowed Trotskyists to infiltrate the Kiev obkom and TsK apparat.[144] Three days later, with Kaganovich present, Postyshev had to perform self-criticism and Kudriavtsev replaced him as Kiev obkom secretary.[145] Two months later, Postyshev also lost his position as second secretary and was removed from Ukraine. Following what would become a standard Great Terror scenario, Postyshev was immediately criticized for having created a cult of his own personality in Ukraine. There was special emphasis on his organization of "Postyshev corners in the schools, and how the students were instructed about 'the friend of children, Postyshev.' "[146]

Less typically, Postyshev was also blamed for inadequate Ukrainization. During his remarks at the Ukrainian politburo session where Postyshev was disgraced, Kaganovich spoke of "an underestimation of the nationalities question as it manifested itself in the choice of cadres. Organizational questions took precedence over political ones."[147] A February 1937 Ukrainian TsK plenum resolution repeated Kaganovich's criticism of "an underestimation of the nationalities policy in Ukraine, which is a most serious political error."[148] For once, it seemed as if terror would work to reinforce Ukrainization. Postyshev's replacement, Kudriavtsev, commented: "It is well known that Postyshev during the period of his work in Ukraine loved to remember the lessons of 1933," that is, the danger of Ukrainian nationalism, but "the nationalists [purged in 1933] were replaced with Trotskyists, Zinovievites and rightists, who engaged in wrecking."[149] Kudriavtsev's comments contained the assumption that the fall of Postyshev meant the repudiation of the policy with which he was most associated: the attack on Ukrainian nationalism in 1933. At the February–March All-Union TsK plenum, Postyshev was again attacked for having neglected nationalities policy.[150] Moreover, Stalin himself emphasized the importance of promoting local cadres, though he was referring not to nationalities policy, but rather the fight with "family circles" (semeistvennost'). His exemplary target was Mirzoian, who was chastised for bringing his clients with him from Azerbaijan rather than promoting local Kazakh cadres.[151]

The fall of Postyshev, Kaganovich's comments, the February 1937 plenum resolution, and Stalin's remarks at the February–March plenum, as well as the fact

[144] RTsKhIDNI 17/21/4682 (16.01.37): 77/1.
[145] RTsKhIDNI 17/21/4682 (16.01.37): 77/1; 81/3/220 (1937).
[146] RTsKhIDNI 17/21/4665 (27.05–03.06.37): 41.
[147] RTsKhIDNI 81/3/224 (1937): 56.
[148] Ibid., 91. RTsKhIDNI 17/21/4669 (31.01–03.02.37): 42.
[149] RTsKhIDNI 17/21/4665 (27.05–03.06.37): 47, 52.
[150] "Materialy fevral'sko-martovskogo plenuma TsK VKP/b/," Voprosy istorii, nos. 11–12 (1995): 10.
[151] Ibid., 12–13.

that by June 1937 the Great Terror was still targeting primarily putative "Trot-skyists" rather than "bourgeois nationalists," all led the Ukrainian leadership to believe that the center was signaling a revival of *korenizatsiia*. At the May–June 1937 Ukrainian party congress, Kosior announced the rehabilitation of even forced linguistic Ukrainization: "We in the Central Committee are now carry-ing out the policy of further Ukrainization through pressure [*natysk*] on those elements who work in our apparat and still have not learned Ukrainian. We will force [*prymushuvaty*] them to learn it. Everyone who works in Ukraine is required to know the language of the Ukrainian people."[152] His speech was filled with calls for a hard line on Ukrainization: "I think we need to exert more pressure to implement the Ukrainization of the apparat . . . this [policy] requires only attention and a firm hand [*tverda ruka*]."[153]

Postyshev's replacement, Kudriavtsev, went even further. He denounced the existence of a split between a Ukrainian cultural sphere and a Russian economic sphere, a split that had already emerged by 1932 and intensified after 1933[154]:

In the last years, in the speeches of a variety of comrades, and above all in the speeches of Postyshev, who set the tone, an identification of the Party's nation-alities policy and national-cultural construction has taken place.

If you look at the speeches of Postyshev on the nationalities question in these years, you see that . . . Postyshev considered the main content of the nationali-ties policy to be the construction of primary schools, the development of theater, literature, the ideological front, and so forth.

Is it not clear that this is an incorrect attitude towards the nationalities policy?

Is it not understood that national-cultural construction is part, but only part of the party's nationalities policy? . . . Is it not understood that the growth of industry, the development of agriculture, the rise of living standards, the growth of Ukrainian cadres, that all this is a result of our party's nationalities policy? . . .

Is it a coincidence that in Kiev we have a relatively significant layer of Ukrainian cadres in the cultural sector, but among economic cadres, the layer of Ukrainian cadres is completely negligible. . . .

Skrypnyk would have been proud of this speech. One would have to go back to 1930, or perhaps to 1927, to find a Ukrainian TsK plenum or party congress where the rhetoric was so hospitable to Ukrainization.

The Ukrainian leadership guessed wrong. In September 1937, mass arrests of putative "bourgeois-nationalists" began. Moreover, the actions of those arrested as bourgeois-nationalists in support of *korenizatsiia* were now described as wrecking. This marked a return to the usual Soviet linkage between terror and nationalities policy. Beginning in November 1937, a series of All-Union Politburo and Orgburo decrees raised the status of the RSFSR, the Russian

[152] *RTsKhIDNI* 17/21/4665 (27.05–03.06.37): 42.
[153] Ibid., 50.
[154] Ibid., 50.

language, and Russian culture. These decrees affected all republics equally. The only decree that singled out Ukraine was a December 1 Orgburo decree, "On Russian Newspapers in Ukraine"[155]:

> TsK VKP/b/ notes that one of the manifestations of wrecking by bourgeois nationalists in Ukraine is the lack of newspapers in Russian, above all in Kharkov, Dnepropetrovsk, Kiev, Nikolaev and other Ukrainian cities.
>
> TsK considers this attitude of TsK KP/b/U to the liquidation of Russian newspapers in republican and oblast centers of Ukraine incorrect and politically erroneous. In fact, it has eased the criminal work of bourgeois nationalists.

In a matter of only five months, the language of 1933 had returned with a vengeance.

In an accompanying memorandum, Mekhlis insisted that "in no other republic was the Russian-language press in such a shabby state as in Ukraine."[156] Also, reflecting the new political mood, he argued that "the Ukrainian population reads Russian-language newspapers with great interest."[157] The Orgburo decree ordered the formation of a republican Russian-language daily with as large a circulation as *Komunist*, as well as Russian dailies in Kharkov, Dnepropetrovsk, Odessa, and Nikolaev. *Sovetskaia Ukraina* began publication in January 1938.[158] The Russian-language press jumped rapidly from 12.5 percent of total Ukrainian circulation in 1936 to 29.4 percent in 1938. This marked the liquidation of the last remnant of comprehensive Ukrainization. In mid-1938, an observer might well have suspected that a decisive wave of russification had begun. However, with the end of the Great Terror and the annexation of West Ukraine in 1939, the situation again stabilized. Henceforth, Soviet Ukraine would be bilingual and bicultural.[159]

Silent *Korenizatsiia* in the Soviet East

The differing fate of the greatest-danger principle in 1933–1934 suggested that there would be a corresponding difference in the implementation of *korenizatsiia* in the Soviet east, as had been the case during the cultural revolution. In fact, similarities outweighed differences. As in Ukraine and Belorussia, discussion of *korenizatsiia* largely disappeared from the public sphere. *Korenizatsiia* was significantly downgraded in importance, but its implementation still remained a real internal concern for central and republican authorities. This

---

[155] *RTsKhIDNI* 17/114/633 (01.12.37): 75/8.
[156] *RTsKhIDNI* 17/114/829 (01.12.37): 135.
[157] Ibid., 135.
[158] *RTsKhIDNI* 17/21/4685 (04.12.37): 10/37. A Russian-language TsK daily also began publication in Belorussia in October 1937. Peredovaia, "'Sovetskaia Belorussiia'," *Sovetskaia Belorussia*, no. 1 (02.10.37): 1.
[159] Yaroslav Bilinsky, *The Second Soviet Republic* (New Brunswick, N.J., 1964).

practice of silent *korenizatsiia* would, in fact, characterize Soviet policy for the rest of the Stalin years. As in Ukraine, enforcement of *korenizatsiia* would be sporadic, with periods of neglect followed by campaign-like flurries of action. The growing emphasis on visible leaders was another similarity. Finally, the decline of linguistic *korenizatsiia* in Ukraine and Belorussia, a policy that was never a high priority in the eastern national regions, also contributed to the convergence between Soviet east and west. The major difference remained the chronic shortage of educated titular nationals in the Soviet east, which ensured that more attention would be devoted to higher education to train skilled workers for technical posts in government and industry. Therefore, I begin with an analysis of Affirmative Action in higher education, proceed to discuss *korenizatsiia* in the republican governmental bureaucracies, and conclude with a look at the problem of ethnic conflict.

Higher Education

From 1930 to 1934, elite all-union universities in Moscow and Leningrad were required to reserve a substantial number of their total admissions quota for culturally backward nationalities (the *bronia*). The abolition of the national minorities *bronia* in 1934 has led some commentators to assume that Affirmative Action for eastern nationalities in higher education also ended.[160] In fact, this was not the case. The April 1934 decree abolishing the *bronia* ran as follows[161]:

1. Given that the reservation [*bronirovanie*] of places in VTUZy, VUZy, technicums and rabfaks for those sent from the national republics and oblasts is being realized mechanically, without consideration of the cadre needs of the national republics and oblasts . . . it is not expedient to preserve the *bronia* for nationals in the system of schools run by the all-union commissariats.

2. Consider it necessary that a planned admission of nationals into the schools of the all-union commissariats be realized. In keeping with this, instruct Gosplan SSSR, in their planning for the preparation of cadres for the second five-year plan to single out particularly the need for cadres in the national republics and oblasts for each given specialty.

3. Require all All-Union Commissariats with VTUZy, VUZy, technicums and rabfaks to maintain control over the proper enrollment of nationals in them. . . .

VTsIK issued a comparable decree for RSFSR commissariats in December 1934, and so the *bronia* survived one academic year longer in the RSFSR.[162] The TsIK decree marked the end of cultural revolution in higher education. The language of this decree, with its reference to the "mechanical" implementation of ethnic Affirmative Action, followed the pattern established by the December 14, 1932

---

[160] Simon, *Nationalism and Policy Towards the Nationalities* (Boulder, Colo., 1991): 55. William Fierman, *Language Planning and National Development* (Berlin, 1991): 195.

[161] *GARF* 3316/24/768 (1934): 16.

[162] *GARF* 1235/130/1 (1935): 570b–58.

Ukrainization decree, which also called for a continuation of Affirmative Action in a revised form.

The actual changes made to the national *bronia* by the April 1934 TsIK decree were minimal. Under the old system, the republics proposed their own needs, which were usually accepted without emendation. Now Gosplan was to determine their needs in a planned and scientific manner that would focus on the glaring lack of technical cadres. Under the old system, the Commissariat of Education (and later TsIK's KTVO) supervised the fulfillment of the *bronia*, a task now left to the cadres sector of each commissariat. As before, the republics were responsible for recruiting candidates. In effect, quotas were still set and rates of fulfillment reported to TsIK.[163] A crucial difference, however, was the abolition of the term *bronia* itself and the annual public campaigns associated with it. Affirmative Action was no longer public and overt. Goals and timetables replaced quotas. *Pravda Vostoka* no longer published advertisements with admissions quotas. This practice of silent Affirmative Action was part of a larger strategy carried out from 1933 to 1938 to address the problem of Russian resentment.

There were two other changes as well, one symbolic and the other practical. The final point of the April 1934 TsIK decree read: "Communicate to all institutions about the incorrect usage of the term 'culturally backward' nationality in present times."[164] This was another marker of the end of the cultural revolution whose assigned task in the Soviet east had been to overcome cultural backwardness. This task was now officially accomplished. This change involved a "big fight" in the TsIK commission dealing with the abolition of the *bronia*, since the rhetoric of backwardness and the center's commitment to developmentalism in the Soviet east was a crucial component of the eastern nationalities' cultural capital. However, as with the abolition of the *bronia*, the change was mostly rhetorical. Affirmative Action continued for eastern nationalities, now more politely referred to as "formerly culturally backward nationalities."[165]

A second change also reflected the movement from the utopianism of the cultural revolution to the more pragmatic stance of the "great retreat" that followed it. From 1934 to 1937, more attention was focused on bridging the immense gap between primary school and higher education, in the words of one Turkmen official, "the preparation of cadres for [the preparation of] cadres."[166] Grades 5 to 10 barely existed in most eastern national republics. As late as 1935 in Tajikistan, only 130 Tajiks graduated from grade 7 and not one from grade 10, whereas the republican plan for 1935–1936 required 1402 Tajiks to enter its technicums.[167] In 1937 in Kirgizia, there were only thirty Kirgiz

---

[163] For reports every bit as detailed as those generated from 1930 to 1934, see GARF 3316/24/768 (1934–1935): 1–155; 3316/29/536 (1936–1937): 1–317.

[164] GARF 3316/24/768 (1934): 16.

[165] Ibid., 52.

[166] GARF 3316/29/536 (1937): 222–224; 3316/13/27 (1936): 27, 63, 76–77.

[167] GARF 3316/29/536 (1935): 12.

studying in grades 8 to 10 in the entire republic.[168] As a result, throughout the cultural revolution and into the 1930s, remedial courses and the rabfaks served as the primary links between primary school (grade 4 or often lower) and higher education.[169] The construction of a network of elementary schools had barely begun by 1938 when it was supplemented by a second campaign to improve the teaching of Russian as a second language. This was also aimed at improving access to higher education, since efforts at the linguistic *korenizatsiia* of more than pedagogical VUZy had also largely ceased with the end of cultural revolution.

As in Ukraine, the abolition of the *bronia* in 1934 was initially interpreted, despite the decree's wording, as a signal that Affirmative Action was being abolished. In 1934–1935, Gosplan failed to set targets for national minorities.[170] The commissariats argued that "since the *bronia* is abolished, no work need be done on the recruitment of nationals."[171] As a result, the 1934–1935 admissions rates for eastern nationalities in central VUZy declined. For example, the number of "formerly culturally backward nationalities" accepted by the Commissariat of Heavy Industry's VTUZy dropped dramatically from 1638 of 17,156 (8.72 percent) in 1933 to 1060 of 22,658 (4.47 percent) in 1934.[172] The Soviet of Nationalities, however, led energetically from 1935 to 1937 by the Belorussian nationalities specialist A. I. Khatskevich, made Affirmative Action in higher education one of its major priorities and intervened decisively to restore it.[173]

As a result of these efforts, by 1935–1936 Gosplan and the all-union commissariats were again setting quotas and reporting on their fulfillment.[174] For the 1935 admissions season, the Commissariat of Heavy Industry's VUZy accepted 1174 eastern nationals of a total 23,436 (4.77 percent), a slight improvement from the previous year. A 1936 TsIK decree unambiguously asserted preference for titular nationals: "Beginning in 1936, admissions to technicums should consist primarily of titular nationals."[175] At a special conference on the production of national cadres, Khatskevich called an agricultural VUZ in Turkmenistan where Turkmen made up only 30 of 450 students "a scandal" and "a crude violation of Party and government directives [that] specialists should be prepared primarily from indigenous nationalities."[176] At another special conference on preparing national cadres, Grigorii Petrovskii rebuked Gosplan and KTVO for insufficient promotion of nationalities and asserted: "If Comrade Stalin heard

---

[168] *GARF* 3316/30/872 (1937): 105.

[169] For an excellent account of the particular reliance of eastern nationalities on the rabfak system and its popularity with them, see A. S., "Rabfaki i gorskaia molodezh'," *Revoliutsiia i gorets*, nos. 6–7 (1930): 73–78.

[170] *GARF* 3316/29/536 (1935): 159.

[171] *GARF* 3316/24/768 (1935): 100.

[172] *GARF* 3316/27/768 (1935): 129–129ob.

[173] On Khatskevich's work, see *GARF* 3316/24/768 (1934–1935); 3316/3316/29/536 (1936–1937); 3316/13/27 (1936); 3316/13/24 (1935): 153–183; 3316/30/872–874 (1937).

[174] *GARF* 3316/24/768 (1935): 18–23; 29–62; 100–109; 115–135.

[175] *GARF* 3316/29/536 (1936): 205–206.

[176] *GARF* 3316/13/27 (1936): 86–87; 3316/29/536 (1935): 44.

Table 31. Indigenous Communist Party Membership in the Soviet
East (Titular Nationals as Percent of Total Party Membership)

Party Organization	1927	1932	1937
Kazakhstan	38	51	49
Uzbekistan	36	58	52
Tajikistan	49	53	45
Kirgizia	52	57	50
Tatarstan	32	42	42
Bashkiria	16	22	21
Chuvashia	58	62	61
Udmurtia	18	32	30
Mari	38	41	37

Simon, *Nationalism and Policy,* 32–33. The figure for Tajikistan is
1933, not 1932. The figure for Kazakhstan in 1932 is from Martha Olcott,
The Kazakhs (Stanford, Calif., 1987): 277.

about this, you know that it would be very bad [for you]."[177] The vehemence
of this intervention suggests that the all-union commissariats were not
fulfilling their quotas. It also demonstrates that the Soviet commitment to
Affirmative Action for eastern nationalities in both central and republican higher
education was being reaffirmed.[178] Silent Affirmative Action continued throughout the 1930s, albeit much less aggressively than during the cultural revolution,
and it would in fact persist through to the collapse of the Soviet Union
in 1991.[179]

The Government Bureaucracy

As in Ukraine, the end of the cultural revolution witnessed a spontaneous
decline in *korenizatsiia* levels in the Soviet east. After several years of impressive growth, the percentage of titular nationals in the central republican apparat
declined from 18.9 percent to 13.8 percent in Turkmenistan, from 16.3 percent
to 15.1 percent in Tajikistan, and from 20.7 percent to 13 percent in Kirgizia.[180]
This same pattern was evident elsewhere in the Soviet east. As Table 31
illustrates, native party membership also peaked in 1932 and then tapered off
slightly. This trend was briefly resisted in the second half of 1933 as the Central

[177] *GARF* 3316/13/27 (1936): 89.

[178] The Soviet of Nationalities' journal also devoted considerable attention to the need to
prepare skilled national cadres. S. Akopov, "Podgotovka natsional'nykh kadrov," *Revoliutsiia i
natsional'nosti,* no. 4 (1934): 54–60. B. R., "O natsional'nykh kadrakh spetsialistov," no. 10 (1935):
51–53. A. Telikhanov, "O natsional'nykh sovetskikh kadrakh," no. 12 (1935): 66–70. Ali Bogdanov,
"Podgotovka natsional'nykh kadrov," no. 4 (1936): 44–51. A. Bogdanov and I. Agishev,
"Podgotovka kadrov Uzbekistana," no. 7 (1936): 54–57.

[179] Victor Zaslavsky, *The Neo-Stalinist State* (Armonk, N.Y., 1994): 112–113. Robert Kaiser, *The
Geography of Nationalism in Russia and the USSR* (Princeton, N.J., 1994): 234. Nancy Lubin,
Labour and Nationality in Soviet Central Asia (Princeton, N.J., 1984): 154–158. Rasma Karklins,
Ethnic Relations in the USSR (Boston, Mass., 1986): 110.

[180] *RTsKhIDNI* 62/2/3133 (1933): 8; 62/2/3163 (1933): 163.

Table 32. *Korenizatsiia* in Udmurtia, 1932–1935 (Udmurts as Percent of Total Government Apparat)

Udmurt TsIK Apparat	1932	1933	1934	1935
Total employees	48.5	51.2	38.8	36.5
Leadership positions	62.1	65.2	53.5	68.7
Technical positions	45.8	33.3	19.4	15.0
District Department Heads				
Agricultural	84.7	69.2	66.7	36.0
Financial	47.3	62.2	44.4	35.4
Education	61.0	93.4	78.6	53.5
Planning	66.7	50.0	55.5	26.0

[Udmurts represented 59 percent of the total population in 1935.]

GARF 3316/28/822 (1935): 4–40b.

Asian Biuro and Kazakhstan launched new *korenizatsiia* campaigns, but by early 1934 these efforts had collapsed and, as in Ukraine, the issue of *korenizatsiia* disappeared from public discussion.[181]

With a few notable exceptions, central government officials also ignored *korenizatsiia* after 1933. The exceptions involved sporadic campaigns that identified particularly egregious failures to implement *korenizatsiia* and meted out exemplary punishment. As usual in such cases, punishment involved being shamed and rebuked in Moscow, not dismissed or arrested. The first such victim was the Udmurt ASSR leadership in 1935.[182] Table 32 shows that the percentage of Udmurts in the government apparat at the central and district level plummeted after 1933. It was the enormous decline in the number of Udmurt skilled technical workers (from 45.8 percent to 15.0 percent), at the same time that Udmurt representation in leadership positions was actually increasing (from 62.1 percent to 68.7 percent), that attracted central attention.

The problem of the national "hole in the middle"—strong *korenizatsiia* at the leadership and menial level but a minimal national presence at the skilled positions in between—had been recognized as the most troublesome *korenizatsiia* issue already in 1925 and led to the adoption of the method of functional *korenizatsiia*. This problem worsened after 1932. The reduced central commitment to *korenizatsiia* still involved a strong desire to keep titular nationals in visible leadership positions, which was not that difficult, but at the technical level administrative efficiency increasingly trumped ("mechanical") Affirmative Action in hiring decisions. This meant a greater reliance on ethnic Russians and therefore the dominance of the Russian language, which in turn

[181] It was discussed in a few small, specialized nationalities policy journals, in particular *Revoliutsiia i natsional'nosti*, under the rubric of "national cadres" and sometimes also as "*korenizatsiia*," as well as in *Vlast' sovetov*, *Sovetskoe stroitel'stvo* and *Revoliutsionnyi vostok*.
[182] *GARF* 3316/28/787 (1935): 114; 3316/28/822 (1935): 1–206; 3316/28/823 (1935): 1–21. I. Kravilnikov et al., "Voprosy korenizatsii v Udmurtii," *Revoliutsiia i natsional'nosti*, no. 8 (1935): 25–30.

made it still harder to promote non-Russians. In Udmurtia, an October 1928 Orgburo decree had demanded complete linguistic *korenizatsiia* in two years time, a typically utopian cultural revolutionary demand. It prompted a brief flurry of activity.[183] Within a year, 37 percent of village soviets and four of eighteen (22.2 percent) district soviets had adopted the Udmurt language, while the oblast Narkompros likewise began to use Udmurt. By 1933, this campaign had collapsed because, as an Udmurt district official explained, "in the last years we almost never received a directive from above in Udmurt and so we don't write [in Udmurt]."[184] This pattern repeated itself across the entire Soviet east.

The surprise was not this pattern but rather the sudden decisive intervention in 1935, after several years of silence, by the Soviet of Nationalities. The Soviet not only censured Udmurtia's current performance but, again following the Ukrainian pattern, demanded the implementation of the 1928 TsK resolution on Udmurtization, which had called for not only mass promotion of Udmurts, but also complete linguistic Udmurtization, including the mandatory study of Udmurt by local Russians.[185] All Udmurt officials would reasonably have assumed that the 1928 decree had long since expired. This intervention resulted in the usual flurry of short-term activity, which declined rapidly as the center's gaze shifted elsewhere.[186] In 1936, the gaze, in fact, shifted to the North Caucasus, where an identical campaign was launched by the Soviet of Nationalities against the North Caucasus authorities for neglecting *korenizatsiia* in their autonomous oblasts. Again, the demand was to implement several cultural revolution–era *korenizatsiia* decrees.[187] Finally, in 1936–1937, the Soviet of Nationalities launched a coordinated campaign to improve the training of national cadres by the all-Union universities and to promote those graduates to technical positions in the government and industrial bureaucracies of Bashkiria, Kirgizia, and Kazakhstan, all of whose *korenizatsiia* records were declared to be "catastrophic."[188] As in Ukraine, this campaign continued and indeed intensified in the period leading up to September 1937, the moment when the mass operations of the Great Terror began to target "bourgeois nationalists" and the resulting arrests decimated the leadership of the Soviet of

---

[183] *RTsKhIDNI* 17/113/669 (15.10.28): 73/1; *GARF* 3316/28/822 (1935): 60b.

[184] *GARF* 3316/28/822 (1935): 46.

[185] *GARF* 3316/28/787 (1935): 114.

[186] On actions taken, see *GARF* 3316/28/822 (1935): 1–206. "Korenizatsiia gosapparata v Udmurtskoi respublike," *Revoliutsiia i natsional'nosti*, no. 2 (1936): 34–37.

[187] *GARF* 3316/30/822 (1937): 1–9; 3316/28/787 (1935–1936): 115; 3316/13/25 (1936): 270b; 3316/13/27 (1936): 170–205; "O narushenii natsional'noi politiki v Severo-Kavkazskom krae," *Revoliutsiia i natsional'nosti*, no. 2 (1936): 73–74; no. 6 (1936): 39–43; "O khode vypolneniia postanovleniia prezidiuma TsIK SSSR ot 07.01.1936 g. po voprosu o narushenii natsional'noi politiki v Severo-Kavkazskom krae," no. 8 (1936): 75–76; T. Aiupov, "Korenizatsiia apparata v Checheno-Ingushetii," no. 2 (1936): 41–43. *O narushenii natsional'noi politiki v Severo-Kavkazskom krae* (Piatagorsk, 1936).

[188] *GARF* 3316/30/872–73 (1937). Ali Bogdanov, "Podgotovka natsional'nykh kadrov," *Revoliutsiia i natsional'nosti*, no. 4 (1936): 44–51. A. Bogdanov and I. Agishev, "Podgotovka kadrov Uzbekistana," no. 6 (1936): 54–57. Ibragimov Gali, "Po vuzam Kazakhstana," no. 5 (1937): 90–91.

Nationalities.[189] When the Soviet of Nationalities began functioning again in late 1938, its new leadership abandoned the *korenizatsiia* campaign. In fact, even at the height of the Great Terror, in an October 1937 telegram to Stalin from Tajikistan describing the purges he was carrying out there in the party and in the border regions, Andreev emphasized the need to transfer Tajik cadres from Uzbekistan to preserve *korenizatsiia* in the republic.[190] Stalin approved Andreev's proposals.[191]

Despite public silence, then, the policy of *korenizatsiia* did continue to receive active central support. This support, however, differed fundamentally from that received prior to 1933, since now only the soft-line Soviet of Nationalities was involved. In 1928, it was the Orgburo that issued a decree on Udmurtization, after an authoritative inspection by a TsK instructor and in the presence of the obkom first party secretary.[192] The Orgburo followed this pattern on dozens of occasions from 1923 to 1932. From 1933 to 1938, the Orgburo did not once intervene in support of *korenizatsiia*, nor did TsK instructors undertake any comparable investigations. Nothing remotely similar to the authoritative 1926–1927 Orgburo *korenizatsiia* commission, headed by A. A. Andreev, was established. Particularly in 1937–1938, however, the Orgburo and Politburo did carefully supervise and endorse the abolition of national institutions and a strengthening of the position of the Russian language and Russian culture. This division of labor reflected Stalin's intentions. The December 1932 decrees marked a decisive repudiation of hard-line *korenizatsiia* and an orientation of the party toward fighting "local nationalism." Stalin's 1934 Belorussian intervention in support of the soft-line Soviet organs, and in opposition to a complete neglect of *korenizatsiia*, made clear that soft-line *korenizatsiia* was not simply a rhetorical stance but a real, if secondary, policy concern.

Korenizatsiia in 1939

Given that *korenizatsiia* was implemented continuously from 1923 to 1939, albeit with great variations in intensity, one would like to be able to illustrate statistically the effects it had on the social structure of the non-Russian republics. This is difficult for two reasons. First, one simply cannot separate out the specific effects of *korenizatsiia* from the enormous changes produced by Stalin's socialist offensive: mass industrialization, urbanization, bureaucratization, migration. If we instead ask what were the effects of *korenizatsiia* in tandem with these larger social processes, there is still a major data problem. With a few exceptions, Soviet *korenizatsiia* statistics always tended to be anecdotal rather than systematic, and the quality of the anecdotal data worsened considerably with the onset of silent *korenizatsiia*. Fortunately, data from the 1939 census on

---

[189] The last archival document on the Bashkir-Kirgiz-Kazakh campaign is dated September 1 1937. *GARF* 3316/30/872 (1937): 101.

[190] *RTsKhIDNI* 558/11/56 (02.10.37): 117–18.

[191] *RTsKhIDNI* 558/11/56 (03.10.37): 116.

[192] *RTsKhIDNI* 17/113/669 (15.10.28): 73/1.

the social structure of the titular nationalities in the non-Russian republics (the RSFSR is perversely omitted) have recently been published.[193]

Due to the use of completely different census categories, fine-grained comparisons with the 1926 census are not possible. However, Table 33 provides a highly revealing comparison of the representation of titular nationals in all white-collar jobs in 1926 and 1939.[194]

These numbers eloquently demonstrate the enormous increase in titular national white-collar employment in the period from December 1926 to January 1939 (and the effect would have been still stronger if we had data from December 1922). Every non-Russian republic (except Armenia, where Armenians already dominated in 1926) experienced substantial growth in its white-collar *korenizatsiia* rates. The effect was much stronger in the Soviet east where autonomous republics witnessed an average 37.5 percent growth and union republics a 33.1 percent growth in white-collar *korenizatsiia*, whereas the comparable increase for the Soviet west was 11.5 percent. As a result there was a pronounced convergence between Soviet east and west. In 1939 Buriat-Mongolia, astonishingly, had a higher *korenizatsiia* rate than Ukraine, Belorussia, and the Volga German republic. The creation of a substantial indigenous white-collar class in the eastern national republics, in a mere fifteen years, was perhaps the single greatest success of the *korenizatsiia* policy.

The 1939 census data allow us to take a closer look at the composition of this new white-collar elite. Table 34 divides the titular national white-collar elite into the six official census categories. Two patterns emerge from these data. First, there is the familiar "hole in the middle." Remarkably, the *korenizatsiia* rates for leadership positions (a category that includes leaders of party, government, cooperative, and mass organizations from the village to republican level) in the eastern republics (90/82 percent) almost equal those in the Soviet west (91.8 percent). In fact, Ukraine and Belorussia's leadership *korenizatsiia* rates are lower than those for all but Kirgizia and Chechno-Ingushetia.[195] If we look at only the highest republican-level leadership positions (Table 35), the east lags slightly more (65.6/43.4 percent vs. 77.0 percent) but still not overwhelmingly (and Ukraine and Belorussia still perform poorly). On the other hand, the difference in *korenizatsiia* rates is enormous for technical positions. The rates in the Soviet west are more than twice as high as in the eastern ASSRs (86.6 percent vs. 41.4 percent) and three times the rate in eastern union republics (27.2 percent). The same pattern holds for medical and communications cadres. This leadership/technical split in the Soviet east was mirrored by a technical/

---

[193] *Vsesoiuznaia perepis' naseleniia 1939 goda. Osnovnye itogi* (Moscow, 1992): 148–227.

[194] Complete data were available only for the republics listed, all of which were autonomous or union republics in 1926. The *korenizatsiia* rate is calculated by dividing the second column by the first. For example, if Bashkiria in 1926 with a 23.5 percent Bashkir population had a 100 percent *korenizatsiia* rate, this would mean Bashkirs made up 23.5 percent of all white-collar employees. The summary average figures are obtained simply by dividing the *korenizatsiia* rates of all the republics, not by weighting them according to the population of the republics. The same is true of Tables 34 to 37.

[195] Also Moldavia (54.4 percent) and Kara-Kalpakia (72.4 percent).

| Republic | 1926 | | | 1939 | | | Change in Korenizatsiia Rate, 1926–1939 |
	Titular Nationals as Percent of Total Population	Titular Nationals as Percent of Total White-Collar Employees	Korenizatsiia Rate (Percent)	Titular Nationals as Percent of Total Population	Titular Nationals as Percent of Total White-Collar Employees	Korenizatsiia Rate (Percent)	
Bashkiria	23.5	6.8	28.9	21.2	14.9	70.3	+41.4
Buriat-Mongolia	43.8	7.6	17.4	21.3	19.1	89.7	+72.3
Dagestan	64.5	18.9	29.3	72.0	45.2	62.8	+33.5
Karelia	37.4	15.4	41.2	23.2	18.1	78.0	+36.8
Crimea	25.1	6.8	27.1	19.4	10.8	55.7	+28.6
Tatarstan	44.9	16.5	36.7	48.7	35.5	72.9	+36.2
Chuvashia	74.7	28.9	38.7	72.2	60.5	83.8	+45.1
Yakutia	81.6	48.0	58.8	56.5	36.9	65.3	+6.5
Eastern ASSR average			34.8			72.3	+37.5
Azerbaijan	62.1	25.9	41.7	58.4	37.7	64.6	+22.9
Kazakhstan	57.1	9.8	17.2	37.8	25.9	68.5	+51.3
Kirgizia	66.6	8.4	12.6	51.7	30.2	58.4	+45.8
Tajikistan	74.6	33.2	44.5	59.6	37.4	62.8	+18.3
Turkmenistan	71.9	8.0	11.1	59.2	29.3	49.5	+38.4
Uzbekistan	65.9	21.8	33.1	65.1	35.7	54.8	+21.7
Eastern SSR average			26.7			59.8	+33.1
Armenia	84.1	93.3	110.9	82.8	85.6	103.4	–7.5
Belorussia	80.6	49.0	60.8	82.9	73.5	88.7	+27.9
Georgia	67.1	65.6	97.8	61.4	65.1	106.0	+8.8
Ukraine	80.0	50.0	62.5	76.5	62.6	81.8	+19.3
Volga German	66.4	52.1	78.5	60.4	53.1	87.9	+12.4
Western average			82.1			93.6	+11.5

Calculated from *Natsional'naia politika VKP/b/ v tsifrakh* (Moscow, 1930): 44–51; and *Vsesoiuznaia perepis' naseleniia 1939 goda*, 148–227. Complete data were available only for the republics listed, all of which were autonomous or union republics in 1926. The *korenizatsiia* rate is calculated by dividing the second column by the first. For example, if Bashkiria in 1926 with a 23.5 percent Bashkir population had a 100 percent *korenizatsiia* rate, this would mean Bashkirs made up 23.5 percent of all white-collar employees. The summary average figures are obtained simply by dividing the *korenizatsiia* rates of all the republics, not by weighting them according to the population of the republics. The same is true of Tables 34 to 37.

Table 34. Social Structure of Non-Russian Republics, 1939 (Korenizatsiia rates in parentheses)

Republic	Titular Nationals as Percent of Total Employee Population	Titular Nationals as Percent of All Employees in Sector					
		Leadership	Technical	Medical	Cultural–Education	Artistic	Communication
Bashkiria	20.8	18.7 (90.0)	8.8 (42.3)	8.7 (41.8)	20.5 (98.6)	12.3 (59.1)	5.2 (25.0)
Buriat-Mongolia	23.2	22.8 (98.3)	7.6 (32.8)	8.1 (34.9)	30.3 (130.6)	21.7 (93.5)	8.6 (37.1)
Chechen-Ingushetia	63.4	46.6 (73.5)	7.4 (11.7)	10.5 (16.6)	53.0 (83.6)	24.7 (39.0)	12.9 (20.3)
Chuvashia	74.9	64.9 (86.7)	50.1 (66.9)	58.7 (78.4)	66.6 (88.9)	54.0 (72.1)	43.9 (58.6)
Crimea	16.7	15.2 (91.0)	6.1 (36.5)	10.5 (59.9)	16.3 (97.6)	15.1 (90.4)	7.3 (43.7)
Dagestan	71.0	59.4 (83.7)	21.1 (29.7)	24.2 (34.1)	66.7 (93.9)	39.5 (55.6)	16.8 (23.7)
Kabardino-Balkaria	52.6	45.3 (86.1)	10.0 (19.0)	15.7 (29.8)	39.2 (74.5)	32.8 (62.4)	23.9 (45.4)
Kalmykia	45.5	55.5 (123.1)	21.2 (46.6)	17.3 (38.0)	54.1 (118.9)	60.0 (131.9)	26.1 (57.4)
Karelia	20.9	24.1 (115.3)	11.2 (47.8)	17.3 (82.8)	25.7 (123.0)	6.9 (33.0)	15.7 (75.1)
Tatarstan	48.4	42.8 (88.4)	25.1 (51.9)	25.8 (53.3)	47.3 (97.7)	32.9 (68.0)	26.0 (53.7)
Yakutia	53.0	47.4 (89.4)	19.0 (35.8)	19.6 (37.0)	61.3 (115.7)	43.6 (82.3)	12.4 (23.4)
Eastern ASSR average		(90.0)	(41.4)	(47.5)	(96.9)	(69.8)	(45.9)
Azerbaijan	55.0	50.3 (91.5)	25.7 (46.7)	31.3 (68.4)	54.6 (99.3)	40.6 (73.8)	7.7 (14.0)
Kazakhstan	39.4	36.3 (92.1)	11.4 (28.9)	7.2 (18.3)	42.1 (106.9)	25.4 (64.7)	6.9 (17.5)
Kirgizia	52.1	38.2 (73.3)	9.6 (18.4)	5.1 (9.8)	51.8 (99.4)	34.0 (65.2)	4.8 (9.2)
Tajikistan	56.2	47.6 (84.7)	12.9 (23.0)	14.6 (26.0)	59.5 (105.9)	39.2 (69.8)	7.7 (13.7)
Turkmenistan	56.7	39.8 (70.2)	10.6 (18.9)	21.4 (37.7)	50.4 (88.9)	25.3 (44.6)	1.9 (3.4)
Uzbekistan	64.8	51.9 (80.1)	15.4 (27.2)	25.1 (38.9)	50.3 (78.0)	46.9 (72.7)	6.1 (9.5)
Eastern SSR average		(82.0)	(27.2)	(33.2)	(96.4)	(65.1)	(11.2)
Armenia	79.6	86.2 (108.3)	81.8 (102.8)	88.9 (111.7)	85.2 (107.0)	82.4 (103.5)	80.0 (100.5)
Belorussia	81.6	63.6 (77.9)	65.8 (80.6)	63.7 (78.1)	73.7 (90.3)	32.7 (40.1)	79.9 (97.9)
Georgia	59.7	67.1 (112.4)	62.3 (104.4)	69.0 (115.6)	71.4 (119.6)	44.3 (74.2)	55.4 (92.8)
Ukraine	76.9	59.6 (74.9)	60.4 (78.5)	58.4 (75.9)	71.3 (92.7)	46.8 (60.9)	69.7 (90.6)
Volga German	63.0	53.9 (85.6)	42.0 (66.7)	51.9 (82.4)	66.3 (105.2)	50.3 (79.8)	29.3 (46.5)
Western average		(91.8)	(86.6)	(92.7)	(103.0)	(71.7)	(85.7)

Calculated from *Vsesoiuznaia perepis' naseleniia 1939 goda*, 148–227. The average figures for eastern ASSRs include not only the eleven republics listed, but also the other eight republics for which data are available (Komi, Mari, Mordvinian, Udmurt, North Ossetian, Abkhaz, Kara-Kalpak, and Moldavian ASSRs; Nakhichevan and Ajaristan are not counted as they have the same titular nationality as their own republic).

Table 35. Korenizatsiia of Leadership Positions, 1939 (Korenizatsiia rates in parenthesis)

Republic	Titular Nationals as Percent of Total Employee Population	Leadership	Republican
Bashkiria	20.8	18.7 (90.0)	17.6 (84.6)
Buriat-Mongolia	23.2	22.8 (98.3)	31.1 (13.4)
Chechen-Ingushetia	63.4	46.6 (73.5)	23.4 (36.9)
Chuvashia	74.9	64.9 (86.7)	55.0 (73.4)
Crimea	16.7	15.2 (91.0)	13.1 (78.4)
Dagestan	71.0	59.4 (83.7)	29.6 (41.7)
Kabardino-Balkaria	52.6	45.3 (86.1)	34.4 (65.4)
Kalmykia	45.5	55.5 (123.1)	47.1 (103.5)
Karelia	20.9	24.1 (115.3)	9.6 (45.9)
Tatarstan	48.4	42.8 (88.4)	38.0 (78.5)
Yakutia	53.0	47.4 (89.4)	26.4 (49.8)
Average eastern ASSRs		(90.0)	(65.6)
Azerbaijan	55.0	50.3 (91.5)	33.1 (60.2)
Kazakhstan	39.4	36.3 (92.1)	25.8 (65.5)
Kirgizia	52.1	38.2 (73.3)	14.8 (28.4)
Tajikistan	56.2	47.6 (84.7)	24.7 (44.0)
Turkmenistan	56.7	39.8 (70.2)	15.9 (28.0)
Uzbekistan	64.8	51.9 (80.1)	22.3 (34.4)
Average eastern SSRs		(82.0)	(43.4)
Armenia	79.6	86.2 (108.3)	95.2 (119.6)
Belorussia	81.6	63.6 (77.9)	41.6 (51.0)
Georgia	59.7	67.1 (112.4)	62.6 (104.9)
Ukraine	76.9	59.6 (74.9)	42.1 (54.7)
Volga German	63.0	53.9 (85.6)	34.6 (54.9)
Average western		(91.8)	(77.0)

Calculated from *Vsesoiuznaia perepis' naseleniia 1939 goda*, 148–227.
The average figures for eastern ASSRs include not only the eleven republics listed, but also the other eight republics for which data are available (Komi, Mari, Mordvinian, Udmurt, North Ossetian, Abkhaz, Kara-Kalpak, and Moldavian ASSRs; Nakhichevan and Ajaristan are not counted as they have the same titular nationality as their own republic).

cultural split. *Korenizatsiia* rates for cultural-educational white-collar work are almost equally high in eastern (96.9/96.4 percent) and western republics (103 percent).

The technical/cultural split becomes even more pronounced when we break down the "technical," "medical," and "cultural-educational" census categories further. Table 36 reports *korenizatsiia* rates for six major technical and cultural jobs. For Bolsheviks, the engineer was a particularly esteemed "hard-line" profession. Tens of thousands of proletarians were trained to become "red engineers" during the mass proletarian Affirmative Action programs of the cultural revolution.[196] Many were later recruited into leading party positions, and

[196] Fitzpatrick, *Education and Social Mobility in the Soviet Union* (Cambridge, UK, 1979), 184–211.

Table 36. Titular National Representation in Select Occupations, 1939 (*Korenizatsiia* rates in parentheses)

Republic	Titular Nationals as Percent of Employee Population	Titular Nationals as Percent of all Employees					
		Engineers	*Tekhniki* (Technicians)	Doctors	Researchers/ Professors	Teachers	Authors/ Journalists
Bashkiria	20.8	3.2 (15.4)	5.3 (25.5)	4.3 (20.7)	10.8 (51.9)	20.2 (97.1)	31.8 (152.9)
Buriat-Mongolia	23.2	2.4 (10.3)	3.9 (16.8)	6.9 (29.7)	26.4 (113.8)	31.2 (134.5)	47.1 (203.0)
Chechen-Ingushetia	63.4	1.8 (2.8)	2.4 (3.8)	2.9 (4.6)	8.9 (14.0)	59.3 (93.5)	40.8 (64.4)
Chuvashia	74.9	28.0 (37.4)	37.7 (50.3)	38.5 (51.4)	53.4 (71.3)	68.5 (91.5)	82.0 (109.5)
Crimea	16.7	2.7 (16.2)	3.8 (22.8)	4.9 (29.3)	6.5 (38.9)	18.5 (110.8)	20.2 (121.0)
Dagestan	71.0	8.2 (11.5)	15.8 (22.3)	15.5 (21.8)	13.5 (19.0)	70.1 (98.7)	72.7 (102.4)
Kabardino-Balkaria	52.6	1.2 (2.3)	6.4 (12.2)	6.5 (12.4)	13.5 (25.7)	39.9 (75.9)	49.5 (94.1)
Kalmykia	45.5	17.0 (37.4)	8.9 (19.6)	16.3 (35.8)	7.7 (16.9)	56.9 (125.1)	72.7 (159.8)
Karelia	20.9	2.1 (10.0)	5.4 (25.8)	1.9 (9.1)	9.2 (44.0)	24.3 (116.3)	44.1 (211.0)
Tatarstan	48.4	14.5 (30.0)	15.5 (32.0)	16.5 (34.1)	17.2 (35.5)	48.5 (100.2)	56.3 (116.3)
Yakutia	53.0	2.6 (4.9)	8.2 (15.5)	7.4 (14.0)	19.6 (37.0)	65.6 (123.8)	62.3 (117.5)
Average eastern ASSRs		(16.2)	(25.1)	(25.5)	(43.9)	(100.6)	(131.5)
Azerbaijan	55.0	20.4 (37.1)	22.2 (40.4)	34.6 (62.9)	42.8 (77.8)	57.2 (104.0)	62.5 (113.6)
Kazakhstan	39.4	3.5 (11.7)	5.5 (18.3)	6.1 (20.3)	16.0 (53.3)	44.0 (146.7)	52.5 (175.0)
Kirgizia	52.1	0.9 (1.7)	4.9 (9.4)	3.9 (7.5)	13.0 (25.0)	56.5 (108.4)	53.2 (102.1)
Tajikistan	56.2	2.6 (4.9)	6.0 (11.4)	5.9 (11.2)	21.2 (40.3)	64.0 (121.7)	46.9 (89.2)
Turkmenistan	56.7	1.8 (3.2)	5.9 (10.4)	5.7 (10.1)	13.9 (33.5)	56.8 (100.2)	54.4 (95.9)
Uzbekistan	64.8	2.9 (4.5)	12.9 (20.0)	11.4 (17.6)	13.0 (20.1)	54.3 (83.8)	51.4 (79.3)
Average eastern SSRs		(10.3)	(18.3)	(21.6)	(41.7)	(110.8)	(109.2)
Armenia	79.6	80.9 (101.6)	85.5 (107.4)	91.3 (114.7)	90.2 (113.3)	84.2 (105.8)	81.9 (102.9)
Belorussia	81.6	32.8 (40.2)	55.2 (67.6)	33.3 (40.8)	40.8 (50.0)	78.8 (96.6)	54.1 (66.3)
Georgia	59.7	58.5 (98.0)	57.7 (96.6)	71.2 (119.3)	73.6 (123.3)	72.2 (120.9)	62.5 (104.7)
Ukraine	76.9	38.6 (48.5)	56.2 (73.1)	30.4 (39.5)	40.8 (53.1)	76.0 (98.8)	55.0 (69.1)
Volga German	63.0	10.8 (17.1)	16.1 (25.6)	29.2 (46.3)	49.3 (78.3)	68.3 (108.4)	59.5 (94.4)
Average western		(61.0)	(74.1)	(72.1)	(83.6)	(106.1)	(87.5)

Calculated from *Vsesoiuznaia perepis' naseleniia 1939 goda*, 148–227.

they eventually dominated the Brezhnev Politburo.[197] Despite an analogous Affirmative Action program for eastern nationalities, the *korenizatsiia* rates for engineers (and less-skilled technicians) remained abysmally low in 1939 (16.3/10.3 percent vs. 61.0 percent). Absolute numbers tell the story even more dramatically: 7 Bashkir engineers, 12 Buriats, 2 Kabardianians, 1 Balkar, 8 Chechens, 12 Turkmen, 102 Uzbeks, 1 Kara-Kalpak, 12 Tajiks, 108 Kazakhs, 5 Kirgiz (though 1084 Azerbaijanis and 300 Tatars) as opposed to 15,551 Ukrainians, 993 Belorussians, 4011 Georgians, and 896 Armenians. On the other hand, eastern titular nationals were on average overrepresented in the professions of teacher (100.6/110.8 percent) and author/journalist (131.5/109.2 percent). Perhaps most tellingly, their *korenizatsiia* rates were quite high for the positions of professor and scientific researcher (43.9/41.7 percent), despite the fact that these jobs required more higher education than the position of engineer or technician.

These data confirm the argument made in Chapter 4 that during the mass upward mobility of the cultural revolution, despite good-faith efforts by the center to train technical cadres (through the *bronia*), educated eastern nationals were diverted into visible leadership positions and into primary school education. Table 37 illustrates this process by presenting not *korenizatsiia* rates, but rather data on how the scarce resource of educated titular nationals were distributed by profession.[198] Leadership and cultural–educational cadres represented 61.4 percent of all white-collar employees in the eastern ASSRs and 75.1 percent in the eastern union republics, but just under half in the western republics (49.6 percent). The single job of primary and middle school teacher occupied about a third of the white-collar workforce in the eastern union republics and just under half in Tajikistan (45.2 percent) and Kirgizia (42.5 percent).

To sum up, by 1939 the policy of *korenizatsiia* in combination with the social transformation initiated by Stalin's socialist offensive had produced in the non-Russian republics, both eastern and western, a sizable indigenous white-collar class.[199] In leadership positions and the cultural sector, titular nationals had on average achieved proportionate representation (in some cases, overrepresentation). In the Soviet east, however, titular nationals were poorly represented in the technical, medical, and communication spheres, creating a "hole in the middle" (between leadership and menial positions) as well as a pronounced technical/cultural split. One might view this in purely developmentalist terms. Technical cadres simply take longer to develop and in one more generation the technical gap would be filled. The 1939 data and my analysis of Affirmative Action in Chapter 4, cast doubts on this scenario. Eastern titular nationals were already three to four times more likely to be a highly educated professor than

[197] Sheila Fitzpatrick, *The Cultural Front* (Ithaca, N.Y., 1992), 149–182.
[198] *Vsesoiuznaia perepis' naseleniia 1939 goda*, 148–227.
[199] For an analysis of *korenizatsiia* in the period from 1939 through to the death of Stalin, see Peter Blitstein, "Stalin's Nations: Soviet Nationality Policy between Planning and Primordialism, 1936–1953" (Ph.D. diss., University of California-Berkeley, 1999).

Table 37. Distribution of Titular Nationals by Employment Category, 1939

Republic	Total Titular National White-Collar Employees	Percent of Titular Nationals Employed As						
		Leadership	Technical	Medical	Cultural-Educational	Teachers	Engineers	Doctors
Bashkiria	16,570	29.2	9.9	3.7	38.0	27.7	0.2	0.1
Buriat-Mongolia	5,340	28.9	8.5	2.9	29.5	21.3	0.2	0.4
Chechen-Ingushetia	8,455	24.9	5.0	8.0	41.6	36.7	0.2	0.1
Chuvashia	21,831	26.2	12.6	7.0	30.2	23.7	0.1	0.2
Crimea	9,102	31.9	11.4	10.3	26.2	18.1	0.5	1.1
Dagestan	15,674	36.9	7.3	3.2	37.9	29.5	0.3	0.3
Kab.-Balkaria	4,498	39.3	6.0	4.1	35.7	25.8	0.1	0.3
Kalmykia	4,102	38.0	6.6	2.4	30.5	23.3	0.2	0.3
Karelia	6,606	29.4	14.3	7.8	22.8	12.1	0.2	0.1
Tatarstan	42,279	26.5	13.3	8.0	35.3	25.1	0.7	0.7
Yakutia	10,450	37.0	4.0	3.3	33.1	24.5	0.1	0.2
Average eastern ASSR		30.4	10.4	5.6	31.4	24.7	0.3	0.4
Azerbaijan	55,198	30.9	13.5	6.9	31.7	19.9	2.0	1.9
Kazakhstan	66,847	33.5	8.1	1.8	38.4	29.7	0.2	0.2
Kirgizia	16,951	32.0	5.0	1.0	49.1	42.5	0.3	0.1
Tajikistan	21,057	37.1	4.2	2.6	49.2	45.2	0.6	0.1
Turkmenistan	17,004	33.3	5.7	6.7	41.8	31.9	0.7	0.2
Uzbekistan	86,519	37.5	6.3	5.8	36.0	31.9	0.1	0.4
Average eastern SSR		34.1	7.1	4.1	41.0	33.5	0.7	0.5
Armenia	42,446	23.5	14.8	7.6	29.8	20.0	2.1	1.6
Belorussia	155,054	22.2	17.6	8.0	25.9	19.9	0.6	0.6
Georgia	110,983	22.9	17.7	8.9	27.1	19.9	3.6	2.6
Ukraine	953,419	19.5	21.3	8.3	23.8	17.3	1.6	0.8
Volga German	13,706	22.2	12.3	7.5	31.4	22.4	0.1	0.4
Average western		22.0	16.7	8.5	27.6	19.9	1.6	1.2

Calculated from *Vsesoiuznaia perepis' naseleniia 1939 goda*, 148–227. *Vsesoiuznaia perepis' naseleniia 1939 goda*, 148–227.

a much less educated engineer. *Korenizatsiia* created an insatiable demand for teachers, journalists, authors, artists, and folklore specialists, as well as for visible leaders in all fields. Titular nationals naturally gravitated to those spheres and established self-perpetuating patronage networks in those fields, whereas Russians came to dominate the technical sphere. As a result, both the "hole in the middle" and the technical/cultural split persisted in the eastern republics, particularly Central Asia, through to the end of the Soviet Union.[200]

Ethnic Conflict

Ethnic conflict was a substantial problem during the first fifteen years of Soviet rule. In the 1920s, rural ethnic conflict over control of agricultural land and the formation of national territories predominated. During the cultural revolution, this conflict migrated to urban sites, such as the universities and especially the industrial workplace, both of which were growing rapidly and mixing previously isolated ethnic communities. The Soviet government undertook numerous measures to eliminate this ethnic conflict. Chauvinism was always punished severely, and after 1933 the legal and propaganda campaign against great-power chauvinism was transformed into a more even-handed campaign in support of internationalism and friendship among the Soviet peoples. The practice of silent *korenizatsiia* and silent Affirmative Action aimed at preserving the positive aspects of those policies while also taking into consideration ethnic Russian feelings. National territorial boundaries were rarely revised in the 1930s and the policy of ethnic proliferation was abandoned. Finally, Soviet control of their peripheral national regions increased substantially after 1933, which allowed greater enforcement of antichauvinist laws. Did these efforts lead to a substantial reduction in ethnic conflict?

It is again difficult to answer this question definitively. Ethnic conflict was never widely discussed in the public press, and with the onset of silent *korenizatsiia*, this topic disappeared almost entirely.[201] Important archival documentation (above all, the NKVD informational reports) is also missing or inaccessible.[202] Conversely, the records of the Harvard Interview Project, which in 1950–1951 conducted in-depth interviews with several hundred Soviet citizens about their prewar life experiences, provide unique and valuable insights into

[200] Lubin, *Labour and Nationality*, 52–111. Kaiser, *The Geography of Nationalism*, 198–243. Simon, *Nationalism and Policy*, 265–78.

[201] For a few exceptions from the specialized nationalities policy literature, see S. Abramov, *Natsional'naia rabota sovetov v gorodakh* (Moscow, 1935): 10; A. Kochanov, "Obsluzhivanie rabochikh i trudiashchikhsia natsmen Moskovskoi oblasti," *Revoliutsiia i natsional'nosti*, no. 3 (1934): 87; A. Bogdanov, "Usilit' rabotu sredi natsmen," no. 2 (1935): 79; Anver Tazhurizin, "Obsluzhivanie natsional'nostei v Stalingradskom krae," no. 6 (1935): 68; A. Elbaev, "O rabote sredi natsmen Moskovskoi oblasti," no. 8 (1936): 18–19.

[202] Beginning in 1932, OGPU informational reports were returned to the OGPU and, as a rule, no longer kept in the working party archives. As a result, they are now located almost exclusively in the former KGB archives, where they are currently largely inaccessible. An exception is Leningrad oblast. On ethnicity in Leningrad, see Sarah Davies, *Popular Opinion in Stalin's Russia* (Cambridge, UK, 1997): 82–90.

popular perceptions of ethnic relations in the period immediately preceding World War II.[203] The interview sample is not ideal for our purposes, since it consists overwhelmingly of Ukrainians, Belorussians, and Russians from Smolensk and Leningrad regions, which were not areas of particularly high ethnic conflict. Moreover, the respondents' attitudes to the nationalities question were clearly influenced by their wartime experiences of Nazi racism (which they often contrasted with Soviet practices) as well as by the influence of émigré nationalist organizations who were active in the displaced persons camps where the interviews were conducted.[204] Nevertheless, keeping in mind these limitations, the interviews provide interesting insights into popular ethnic attitudes.

The interviewers did not ask the respondents directly about ethnic conflict. Instead, respondents were asked to list the "distinguishing characteristics" of Russians, Ukrainians, Jews, Georgians, Armenians, Kalmyks, and Tatars.[205] This request for ethnic stereotypes elicited a surprising response. About one-fifth of the respondents (49 of 250) initially denied that there were any ethnic differences whatsoever.[206] When pressed by the often astonished interviewer, it turned out that the respondents did not literally mean that there were no cultural differences between these nationalities. Rather, they had inferred (probably correctly) that the interviewer was really interested in two quite different questions. First, did the Soviet state treat their nationalities differently? In particular, did they engage in national persecution (as the Nazis did)? Hence, the following two responses to the question about "distinguishing characteristics": "Politically and in living standards, no. In national customs, yes"; "Yes. The Jews have the first place in the Soviet Union."[207] Second, the respondents often inferred an interest in the existence of widespread popular prejudice in the Soviet Union: "Yes of course there are [national differences]. But the nationalities are not enemies because of that"; "But that does not mean that there are necessarily antagonistic feelings between us."[208]

In fact, many respondents directly linked the absence of popular ethnic prejudice and conflict to official state policy. In response to the "distinguishing characteristics" question, a dozen respondents spontaneously asserted that there was no openly expressed national prejudice in the Soviet Union because the Soviet state punished such speech so severely:[209]

---

[203] The sample is described in Alex Inkeles and Raymond Bauer, *The Soviet Citizen* (Cambridge, Mass., 1959): 21–40.

[204] For comments contrasting Soviet and Nazi policies, see Harvard Interview Project. "A" Series. Respondent #4, p. 60. [Hereafter HIP A4, 60]; A26, 71; A108, 42. On the influence of nationalist organizations in the camps, see HIP A108, 43.

[205] Question P10e. "What are the distinguishing characteristics of the following nationalities: Ukrainians, Jews, Great Russians, Georgians, Armenians, Tatars?" In an earlier questionnaire, as question P2c, the question included Kalmyks.

[206] Statistics based on the P10e question (protocol A4). Due to interviewer error, not all respondents were asked the question (or their answers were not recorded).

[207] HIP A528, 34; A393, 40.

[208] HIP A385, 82; A349, 70.

[209] HIP A91, 55; A340, 47; A342, 69; A380, 29; A18, 62; A20, 33; A60, 24; B482, 16.

"No that is impossible. Everyone must love everyone in the Soviet Union.
. . . It was against the law to have national animosities."

"There is no chauvinism, you can get ten years for it."

"In the army, a soldier got seven years for calling a Jew 'Zhid.' "

"All are alike. You cannot tell somebody that he is a Ukrainian and brag that
you are a Russian or you would be arrested."

"It was strictly forbidden by law to offend the member of any nationality,
regardless of whether he was a Russian, Ukrainian, a White Russian, or anything
else."

"If you cussed out a member of the minority group, there was serious
trouble."

"If you call a Jew a 'zhid,' he can go to the police and you will get a prison
sentence."

"In the Soviet Union national animosity was forbidden and it was punished.
You could dislike a person of another nationality but you couldn't reveal that
dislike. The use of the one word 'zhid' would mean a 5–10 year sentence in a
concentration camp."

One primary school teacher even related a personal tale of how she had used
the Russian proverb, "An untimely guest is worse than a Tatar," in a public
place and almost lost her job after being denounced by a hostile colleague.[210]
When one considers that the interviewer neither asked about national prejudice
nor about state policy, these spontaneous responses are impressive testimony to
the success of the Soviet campaigns against great-power chauvinism and in favor
of internationalism and friendship among the Soviet peoples.

The majority of respondents agreed that the Soviet state treated its nationalities equally[211]:

"The equalization of the nationalities must be considered an achievement of the
Soviet system."

"All the nationalities are treated the same. There are no differences between
them."

"Legally and administratively, all the nationalities were treated alike."

A smaller sample of respondents was asked whether the 1936 constitution's
guarantee of equality for all nationalities was in fact observed. Despite their
assertions that the constitution was in general a complete fraud, the overwhelming majority answered in the affirmative: "correct"; "and this is true, it
was like that"; "in this case there is no conflict between the text of the constitution and reality"; "all nations have the same rights."[212] A small dissenting

---

[210] HIP A91, 6.

[211] HIP A131, 99; A145, 67; A1053, 49.

[212] Question P3c. "What is your opinion of the articles in the Soviet constitution dealing with
the equality of all USSR nationalities?" This question was asked of only the "A2/A3" sample, a
total of 61 respondents (and again, not all those interviewed were asked the question). HIP A13,
47; A23, 20; A25, 52; A46, 39.

group (thirteen in total) claimed that either Jews, Georgians, or Caucasians received preferential treatment, citing either Stalin's nationality or the putative disproportionate representation of Jews in leadership and white-collar positions.[213] Another nine respondents made reference to Soviet Affirmative Action policies, but there was no strong sense that these policies were a fundamental violation of national equality since they were referred to in a developmentalist framework as "help" for "the less cultured peoples."[214]

This assertion of national equality did not always indicate a positive evaluation of the Soviet nationalities policy. In fact, the most typical assertion was that all nationalities were equally oppressed:[215]

> "It's all the same. The Russians and the Ukrainians and the Belorussians, they all get the same raw deal."
> "I can't say [if there are 'distinguishing characteristics'], it is difficult to say. Everybody is the same. Everybody is equally impoverished."
> "Stalin's policy consists of making all nationalities slaves."
> "They have no real differences. Each one has suffered as much under Stalin as the other."

This response was particularly common in answer to the question about the 1936 constitution's guarantee of national equality:[216]

> "They are only equal in the sense that they are suffering equally under the Soviet regime."
> "Equal in their poverty, in their fear and in the treatment that they get in the concentration camp."
> "In the Soviet Union, there is no difference between different nationalities, because the unhappiness makes one people just like the next people."
> "Absolutely true, they are all the same in their lack of rights."
> "They are all equally under the thumb of the Communist Party."

This rhetoric is particularly helpful in understanding the evolution of ethnic conflict in the 1930s. Inkeles and Bauer, summarizing the results of the Harvard Interview Project, emphasized their respondents' tendency to use a we/they dichotomy to describe Soviet society, with "they" being an oppressive and alien party elite (what would later be widely known as the *nomenklatura*) and "we" being a largely undifferentiated and oppressed people (*narod*).[217] Sarah Davies found that the same we/they dichotomy was ubiquitous in the overheard conversations reported in the Leningrad NKVD and party informa-

---

[213] HIP A300, A1241, A41 asserted that Caucasians were privileged. HIP A60, A48, A1528, A493, A307 asserted that Jews were privileged. HIP A36, A10, A634, A520, A342 asserted that Georgians were privileged.

[214] HIP A20, A25, A29, A36, A58, A118, A188, A300, A454.

[215] HIP A107, 25; A379, 30; A516, 55; A633, 23.

[216] HIP A4, 26; A11, 40; A14, 75; A17, 75; A48, 49.

[217] Inkeles and Bauer, *The Soviet Citizen*, 321–337.

tional reports on popular mood.[218] Inkeles and Bauer argued that the ubiquitous we/they dichotomy explained their respondents' extremely low levels
of perceived class rivalry despite the overwhelming evidence that "objectively"
the Soviet Union in the 1930s was a class-based society.[219] It would appear that
the we/they dichotomy had the same effect on popular perceptions of ethnic
rivalry.

This was a somewhat ironic success for the Affirmative Action Empire
strategy, since one of its primary goals was to prevent non-Russians from interpreting unpopular Soviet policies (such as collectivization) as national oppression. At all costs, the center should not be perceived as Russian. In this, they
were successful. The Harvard interviewers asked a sample of their respondents
whether "the RSFSR and the Great Russian people can claim a leading role in
relation to the other nationalities in the Soviet Union" and whether the "equality of minorities [was] compatible with the outstanding role of the Russian
people."[220] These questions were responding to the Soviet propaganda campaign asserting a leading role for the Russians that was launched in the mid-
1930s and intensified during World War II. Again, almost half of the respondents
(16 of 36) denied the question's premise that the Russians *did* play a leading
role: "I can't see the eminent role of the Russian people. I just simply can't see
it."[221] Fifteen respondents denied that Russians should have a leading role,
without addressing whether they in fact enjoyed such a role. Only five respondents agreed that the Russians did and should have a leading role, and they all
stated that role in orthodox Soviet developmentalist terms as, in the words of
a Kalmyk respondent, offering "the help of the fraternal Russian people [to
regions where] the cultural level is low."[222] Not a single respondent asserted
that the Russians were dominant and oppressed other nationalities. Those who
denied a leading role for the Russians again invoked the we/they dichotomy:[223]

"The greatest role is played by the Kremlin."

"The chief differences in Russia are differences between party and non-party
people."

"I think that you have posed the question incorrectly, because the question
seems to imply that it is the Russian people who are playing the leading role.
You simply can't say that the Politburo is the Russian people. They are a group
torn off from the Russian people, who have no connection with them."

[218] Davies, *Popular Opinion in Stalin's Russia*, 124–146.

[219] Inkeles and Bauer, *The Soviet Citizen*, 299–320.

[220] Question P10b. "Do you think that the RSFSR and the Great Russian people can claim a
leading role in relation to the other nationalities in the Soviet Union?" Question P10d. "Is this
equality of minorities compatible with the outstanding role of the Russian people?." These two
questions were also asked only of the "A2/3" sample.

[221] HIP A1, 18.

[222] HIP A23, 19.

[223] HIP A8, 30; A104, 23; A20, 33; A11, 40; A104, 23. Voroshilov and Budennyi were both
Russian, but only Voroshilov was in the Politburo, and there were always other Russians in the
Politburo as well.

"Russians don't play a leading role. Take the Kremlin. Do you have many Russians in the Kremlin?"

"Some people believe that the Russians have a preferential status in Russia. But that is wrong. Look at the Politburo, where only Voroshilov and Budenny are Russians [sic!]."

Judging by this admittedly small and not fully representative sample, oppression was popularly perceived as Bolshevik or "party," not Russian.

The evidence marshaled here does not allow any definitive conclusions about the evolution of ethnic conflict in the second half of the 1930s. It does suggest, however, that in all likelihood ethnic conflict did decline after 1933 and probably substantially. If so, this decline could be attributed both to the influence of factors unrelated to nationalities policy and to several intentional state actions. The former would include collectivization, which stopped ethnic conflict over control of agricultural land by rendering the land worthless to the peasantry; the passage of time, which muted the initial shock of ethnic mixing during the cultural revolution; greater political control over the national periphery, which produced greater social order; and, finally, the enormous growth of state repression and the formation of a visibly privileged party elite, which led to the domination of the we/they axis of conflict in popular perception and a diminished consciousness of class and ethnic rivalry. The intentional state actions included propaganda in favor of internationalism and punitive action against both chauvinist words and deeds, actions that, judging from the Harvard materials, were perceived by the population to be both sincere and rigorous; ending the practice of frequent changes in the borders of national territories; and the shift from overt to silent *korenizatsiia*.

Conclusion

The evolution of *korenizatsiia* after 1933 reveals a scaling back and rationalization of the policy rather than its abolition. In 1934, after the previous year's nationalities terror had provoked a spontaneous retreat from *korenizatsiia*, Stalin intervened in Belorussia in support of the policy. Stalin remained, above all, committed to the policy of having titular elites occupy a substantial portion of the most visible leadership positions in the non-Russian republics. In this he was successful. In 1939, six years after the anti-Ukrainization decrees, titular nationals were increasingly occupying their proportionate share of leadership positions (Table 34). To achieve that goal, the Soviet state continued to practice Affirmative Action in higher education. When necessary, it was also willing to sanction, despite the outraged denunciations of "mechanical" *korenizatsiia* in 1933, the promotion of titular nationals based on their ethnicity alone. In Ukraine, the party even sanctioned the direct replacement of Russians with titular nationals. Indigenization did not end in 1933.

It did, however, change considerably. First of all, the association of *korenizatsiia* and national communism was severed as a result of the Skrypnyk affair. No longer would *korenizatsiia* be allowed to foster a general sense of the indigenous nationality's priority in their own republic. National assertiveness would be checked through terror. To avoid a reemergence of national communism, *korenizatsiia* was firmly categorized as a secondary, soft-line policy. In addition, due to increasing concern over Russian resentment, *korenizatsiia* and Affirmative Action were now implemented silently, without campaigns, advertisements, and denunciations of great-power chauvinists. Finally, although the commitment to linguistic *korenizatsiia* was never formally abandoned, it became an increasingly low priority and the Russian language assumed a dominant position in all the non-Russian republics except Georgia and Armenia.

The state's goal was to preserve the positive psychological impact of *korenizatsiia* in preventing the growth of non-Russian national resentment without the negative outcomes of unwanted national assertion and of Russian resentment. The Harvard Interview Project materials suggest that the new policy line had some success in muting ethnic rivalry. Conversely, the dearth of national technical cadres in the eastern regions ("the hole in the middle") persisted and would become a permanent feature of Soviet life. This necessitated the migration of Russians to occupy these technical positions. However, given the new status assigned to Russians after 1933 as the unifying glue of the multiethnic Soviet state, this was not necessarily an undesirable outcome. The next chapter looks at this dramatic reemergence of the Russians.

10

The Reemergence of the Russians

The most important process initiated by the December 1932 Politburo decrees was a thoroughgoing rehabilitation of Russian culture and the right of Russians to national self-expression. The status of the Russian nationality was raised dramatically in the period from 1933 to 1938, along with the status of the RSFSR. This development threatened the foundations of the Affirmative Action Empire, which demanded that Russian national self-expression be downplayed to avoid provoking defensive nationalism among the formerly oppressed non-Russians. The rehabilitation of Russian national self-expression did not, however, involve a shift from nation-building to russification. As we have just seen, *korenizatsiia* continued at a reduced pace throughout the 1930s and, as we shall see, the cultivation of non-Russian national identity actually intensified after 1933. Rather, the reemergence of the Russians involved three main processes: first, the formation of a Russian national space through the Russification of the RSFSR; second, the elevation of the status and unifying role of Russian culture within the entire USSR; third, the integration of the newly central Russians into the preexisting Soviet national constitution through the metaphor of the Friendship of the Peoples. This chapter discusses the first two processes; the third is the subject of the book's final chapter.

The Awkward Republic: The RSFSR

In July 1980, fifty-eight years after the formation of the Soviet Union, Viacheslav Molotov confessed to his scribe, Feliks Chuev, that the Communist Party had never adequately resolved the Russian question: the problem of what status the massive RSFSR and the Russian nation should have within the Soviet Union. To Chuev's complaint that only the Russian republic was denied its own Communist Party, Molotov responded that once under Stalin (1936–1937) and then again under Khrushchev (1958–1965), a special TsK Biuro on RSFSR affairs had been formed, but in neither case did it prove a success. "We didn't forget [to form an RSFSR Communist Party]," Molotov explained, "there was just no place for it."[1] There was, in fact, never a good place for the Russian nation. They were always the Soviet Union's awkward nationality, too large to ignore but likewise too formidable to give the same institutional status as the Soviet Union's other major nationalities.

Just over a decade after Molotov's conversation with Chuev, Boris Yeltsin would seize the Russian question and use it to destroy the Soviet Union. Many aspects of the collapse of the Soviet Union in 1991 undoubtedly were unimaginable to the state's founding fathers, but Yeltsin's use of the RSFSR against the USSR was most certainly not one of them. On the contrary, due to their realization of the unique threat the Russians posed to Soviet unity, both Lenin and Stalin insisted that the Russians be denied a full-fledged national republic as well as all of the other national privileges granted to the non-Russians. As noted in Chapter 1, Lenin and Stalin worked together closely from 1913 to mid-1922 in formulating the Soviet nationalities policy and can properly be considered the coauthors of the Affirmative Action Empire.

However, when it came time to specify a formal constitutional structure in mid-1922, Lenin and Stalin did differ, and it is not surprising that they quarreled over the crucial question of the status of the Russians and the RSFSR. On August 10, 1922, the Politburo formed a commission chaired by Stalin on the relations between the RSFSR and the then formally independent Soviet republics of Ukraine, Belorussia, Georgia, Armenia, Azerbaijan, Bukhara, Khiva, and the Far East.[2] Stalin immediately proposed that the independent republics should enter the RSFSR as autonomous republics. His plan called for three types of commissariats: united commissariats that would exist only at the RSFSR level (foreign affairs, military, etc.), divided commissariats where an RSFSR commissariat would supervise ASSR filials (supply, labor, etc.), and independent commissariats that would exist only at the ASSR level (justice, education, etc.). On September 24, the commission accepted Stalin's proposal.[3]

Lenin, however, immediately attacked Stalin's project for tactlessly compromising the status of the independent republics. He instead proposed constructing "a new floor" above the RSFSR that would be called the "Union of Soviet Republics of Europe and Asia." It would be a "federation of independent republics" into which the RSFSR and the independent Soviet republics would enter as equal members.[4] The existing autonomous republics would then

[1] Feliks Chuev, *Sto sorok besed s Molotovym* (Moscow, 1991): 208–209.
[2] "Iz istorii obrazovaniia SSSR," *Izvestiia TsK KPSS*, no. 9 (1989): 191.
[3] Ibid., 192–193; 200–205. Georgia dissented and Ukraine abstained.
[4] Lenin, *PSS*, vol. 45, 211–213.

have a lower status. Stalin initially resisted this proposal but, faced with Lenin's fierce resolve, quickly retreated and accepted Lenin's proposal.[5]

Lenin's conflict with Stalin over the constitutional form of the Soviet state has often been portrayed as Lenin's defense of national minorities from Stalin's great-power chauvinism.[6] This was certainly how Lenin framed it in his December 1922 article attacking Stalin, Ordzhonikidze, and Dzerzhinskii as great-power chauvinists.[7] However, this is enormously deceptive. With regard to the rights of the non-Russians, there was little difference between their rival constitutional proposals. Both plans had the identical three-tier commissariat structure. Lenin's proposal was slightly more favorable to the independent republics since it maintained the appearance of their equality with Russia (the RSFSR), raised them above the existing autonomous republics in status, and, most important, abolished the term "all-Russian" (*rossiiskii*) as a designation for the Soviet state. This term grated on non-Russian, especially Ukrainian, sensibilities.[8] Stalin's plan, however, was much more favorable to the existing autonomous republics, such as Tatarstan and Turkestan, who would be given the same status as Georgia and Ukraine.

The substantive disagreement between Lenin and Stalin was over the status of Russia and the Russians. Stalin readily agreed to give the independent republics a higher status than the existing autonomous republics, but he vigorously objected to the creation of a separate RSFSR TsIK and Sovnarkom[9]:

> I think that Comrade Lenin's corrections will lead unavoidably to the creation of a Russian TsIK with the eight autonomous republics currently part of the RSFSR excluded from it (Tatarstan, Turkestan, and so on). It will unavoidably lead to these republics being declared independent along with Ukraine and the other independent republics, to the creation of two chambers in Moscow (Russian and Federal), and in general to deep restructurings that are not called for by either internal or external necessities.

Stalin's concern here was not about raising the status of the eight autonomous republics to the level of Ukraine. His proposal already did that. He was worried exclusively about the creation of a separate, purely Russian TsIK that could become the vehicle for defending sectarian Russian interests and so create a situation of dual centers of power in Moscow: to be anachronistic, he was worried about Yeltsin versus Gorbachev. Stalin's proposal was actually more in keeping with the ideology of the Affirmative Action Empire. It recognized the Russians as the Soviet Union's state-bearing nationality and so denied them the

---

[5] "Iz istoriia obrazovaniia," no. 9 (1989): 205–215.

[6] This became the standard Soviet interpretation in the Khrushchev era. For a western example of this interpretation, see Moshe Lewin, *Lenin's Last Struggle* (New York, 1968): 43–63. For a convincing rebuttal of this interpretation, see Smith, *The Bolsheviks and the National Question* (London, 1999): 180–189.

[7] Lenin, "K voprosu o natsional'nostiakh ili ob 'avtonomizatsii'," *PSS*, vol. 45, 356–362.

[8] The same was true of the name All-Russian Communist Party, which was later changed to All-Union Communist Party. "Iz istoriia obrazovanii," no. 5 (1991): 175.

[9] "Iz istorii obrazovaniia," no. 9 (1989): 208.

independent national institutions granted to all non-Russians. Lenin's proposal, on the other hand, created a semi-Russian institution, the RSFSR, whose organs partially represented Russia and partially served as subordinate central institutions.

Stalin's concern that Lenin's proposal would lead to a Russian government in Moscow was fueled by the proposals of the Tatar national communist Mirsaid Sultan-Galiev. In October 1922, Sultan-Galiev and several of his Tatar colleagues proposed that the existing autonomous republics and oblasts be allowed to enter the Soviet Union directly, that is, to be removed from the RSFSR.[10] Sultan-Galiev called the current proposal an unfair division of Soviet nations into "step-sons and true sons."[11] Stalin angrily denounced Sultan-Galiev's proposal as "reactionary." He objected to it for exactly the same reason he opposed Lenin's proposals:

> Such a proposal demands dissolving our federation into pieces, together with the creation of a Russian TsIK—not an all-Russian [rossiiskii] but a Russian [russkii] TsIK and a Russian [russkii] Sovnarkom. [If the ASSRs leave the RSFSR], then how else will Russians enter into the Union. No other way. Either they remain outside the Union or they organize themselves. A Russian TsIK? A Russian Sovnarkom? Comrades, do we really need this? . . . I see no justification for such a proposal.

Stalin's remarks make it clear that his quarrel with Lenin was over the Russian question. Moreover, Stalin did not intend to exalt the Russians by maintaining the RSFSR instead of forming a new USSR, but rather to disarm them. His greatest fear was Sultan-Galiev's separate Russian republic, and he saw Lenin's RSFSR as a major step in that direction.

This was not just a passing concern on Stalin's part. He returned to it again in 1925 when Mikoian, in his capacity as head of the North Caucasus region, supported a proposal for uniting the south Ossetian AO (part of Georgia) and the north Ossetian AO (part of the RSFSR) as a united Ossetian ASSR within the Georgian republic.[12] Stalin initially backed the proposal since the division of the Ossetians into two bordering national territories was a violation of the Soviet nationalities policy.[13] However, Stalin quickly developed serious doubts about this policy during his 1925 vacation, when he traveled extensively throughout the north Caucasus and had the opportunity to think the issue through more carefully.[14] His written remarks on the possible implications of Ossetian reunification are instructive:[15]

> Now, living in the North Caucasus and looking closer at the real conditions here, I see that this policy, if taken to extremes, will unavoidably produce a number

[10] Natsional'nyi vopros na perekrestke mnenii (Moscow, 1992): 102–105.
[11] Mirsaid Sultan-Galiev, Stat'i. Vystupleniia. Dokumenty (Kazan, 1992): 229.
[12] RTsKhIDNI 558/11/765 (1925): 11.
[13] RTsKhIDNI 558/11/33 (23.05.25): 80.
[14] RTsKhIDNI 558/11/68 (1925).
[15] RTsKhIDNI 558/11/1105 (1925): 159–61.

of serious minuses, capable of worsening our political position in the Russian and non-Russian regions. Most distressing, these minuses have already emerged, at the very least, in the north Caucasus. First, as a consequence of transforming the Ossetines into a republic and their departure from the RSFSR, the Chechens will table the question of [leaving the RSFSR and] entering the Transcaucasus federation. Second, Dagestan is raising the question of leaving the RSFSR and entering the Transcaucasus federation. Without a doubt, they will be followed by the Ingush and others. Third, seeing all this, the Cossacks (for now the Terek and Kuban Cossacks, but then the Don Cossacks will join in) already talk of autonomy and the creation of a Cossack republic, declaring that they "are no worse than the Ossetines and Dagestani," that they "also have their own interests," that "why insult the Russians, denying them what is given to the non-Russians." These are the sprouts of Russian nationalism, and that is the most dangerous form of nationalism. I have not yet even mentioned that this policy cannot but incline the national republics of the northern and eastern parts of the RSFSR to leave the RSFSR and enter the USSR as union republics.

The collapse of the RSFSR—this is where we are going if we do not change our policy now. What should we do?

Either we agree that the North Caucasus autonomous republics will be transformed into republics and be transferred to the Transcaucasus federation—and then, first of all, we will have to create a similar federation out of the Tatar republic, the Bashkir republic, the Kirgiz republic, and others and so accept the collapse of the RSFSR; second of all, we will have to satisfy the growing "national" desires of the Cossacks. Or we reject the policy of transforming national oblasts into republics and firmly say that, above all, the Ossetines, Chechens, Dagestani, and others should remain within the RSFSR.

Once again, Stalin unambiguously highlighted the danger of the collapse of the RSFSR and the formation of an ethnically Russian republic with the accompanying growth of Russian nationalism, "the most dangerous form of nationalism" for the Soviet Union.

A few months later, at the December 1925 TsK plenum, Stalin was forced to address the Russian question yet again when a seemingly innocuous proposal to change the party's name from the "All-Russian (*rossiiskaia*) Communist Party /Bolsheviks/ (RKP/b/)" to the "All-Union (*vsesoiuznaia*) Communist Party /Bolsheviks/ (VKP/b/)" encountered fierce resistance.[16] Already in 1923, Khristian Rakovskii and Mykola Skrypnyk had argued that it was a violation of Soviet nationalities policy to use the term *rossiiskii* to refer to the unionwide Communist party, even if *rossiiskii* historically referred to the Russian state while *russkii* referred to the Russian ethnicity.[17] An attempt to rename the party at a 1924 TsK plenum had drawn controversy and therefore been postponed a year.[18]

---

[16] *RTsKhIDNI* 17/2/200 (15.12.25); 17/2/205 (15.12.25).
[17] *RTsKhIDNI* 17/2/200 (15.12.25): 16.
[18] *RTsKhIDNI* 558/11/1105 (15.12.25): 137.

Now a year later, a formal proposal introduced by Molotov and backed by Stalin drew criticism from some of Stalin's closest allies. Ordzhonikidze objected to the proposal with an argument familiar to Stalin: "We will fall into the position where alongside an all-union TsK, we will also have a Russian [*russkii*] Central Committee. Such a situation, in my opinion, will not help overcome nationalism, but will inflame it."[19] Voroshilov noted that similar objections had been raised when the issue had been discussed at the Politburo and seconded Ordzhonikidze: "Now that they want to rename the party after the name of the government, then logically one must organize a Russian [*russkaia*] Communist Party, . . . we will have to organize a Russian party so that the Russian comrades do not consider themselves insulted, and so that we do not inflame Russian nationalism."[20] Finally, Mikoian likewise warned of the possible danger to party unity that a Russian party would imply: "The danger of the formal contradiction [between the name of the party and the state] is much less than the danger of creating two party centers in Moscow, for alongside the general party TsK will be a TsK RKP [Russian Communist Party] that will unite two-thirds of our whole party. This circumstance will be a dangerous wedge, making a schism in the party much easier."[21]

These objections put Stalin in a difficult position. First, all three dissenters were close allies and all had extensive nationalities policy experience in Stalin's home region of the Caucasus. Second, their objections closely echoed Stalin's own concerns about the Russian question. Stalin's response was, therefore, interesting. He dismissed the concerns about Russians being insulted as "comical" and, presaging his 1930 letter to Demian Bednyi, called the Russians "the largest, the most cultured, the most industrial, the most active, and the most soviet of all nations in our country."[22] Most important, he drew his characteristic distinction between the RSFSR and a Russian republic: Ordzhonikidze, Voroshilov, and Mikoian "are talking about a Russian [*russkaia*] party, but we in fact do not have a Russian [*russkii*] republic. There is the all-Russian [*rossiiskaia*] Federated Republic. It is not Russian [*russkaia*]; it is all-Russian [*rossiiskaia*]."[23] For Stalin, this was the crucial distinction. In fact, he had ended his remarks on the Ossetine question with three proposals for strengthening the multiethnic nature of the RSFSR: "Adopt a course oriented on the strengthening of the RSFSR and the uniting around it the national oblasts and republics. Strengthen the budget of the RSFSR while taking into account the interests of the national oblasts and republics. Promote a national to the position of assistant head of the RSFSR Sovnarkom."[24]

[19] *RTsKhIDNI* 17/2/205 (15.12.25): 4.
[20] Ibid., 4.
[21] Ibid., 6.
[22] Ibid., 5. On Stalin's letter to Bednyi see Chapter 6.
[23] Ibid., 5.
[24] *RTsKhIDNI* 558/11/1105 (1925): 161.

Despite Stalin's efforts, the awkwardness of the RSFSR became increasingly apparent.[25] RSFSR organs always had a semicentral status. For instance, the RSFSR Narkompros supervised the all-union Affirmative Action program for central universities. This semicentral status made it difficult for RSFSR organs to defend Russian interests aggressively, a fact that was particularly evident during the Ukrainian–RSFSR border disputes of the 1920s. On the other hand, RSFSR organs were distinctly second-rate central institutions, always dominated by their all-union counterparts. Therefore, despite Stalin's claim that the idea of Russian resentment was comical, Russian regional leaders did feel that they lacked a republic and a republican party that would defend their interests as aggressively as the Ukrainian republic defended Ukraine's national interests. In June 1926, in response to this discontent, the Politburo formed a special commission with the grandiose title, "The Construction of the RSFSR, National Republics and Oblast Organs within the RSFSR."[26] The commission was charged with finding solutions, including constitutional ones, to the problematic relations of RSFSR institutions with both all-union authorities and with their own autonomous republics and oblasts.[27] Mikhail Kalinin was put in charge of the commission because, as head of the RSFSR TsIK, he was the Politburo member most identified with Russian national issues. The Kalinin commission worked laconically over the period of its nine-month existence and ultimately achieved nothing practical. However, its deliberations revealed issues and attitudes of fundamental importance.[28]

In particular, the Kalinin commission offered the first and only politically sanctioned opportunity for the expression of RSFSR resentment—resentment directed both at RSFSR domination by all-union organs and at the relatively privileged status of the other union republics. RSFSR officials were particularly envious of the audacity and success of Ukrainian protests against all-union decisions. Indeed, when a series of speakers complained of all-union dominance, Kalinin joked that "with all your talk of republican rights, if we had Ukrainians here, they'd be applauding you."[29] There were complaints that, unlike other republics, almost all RSFSR industry was under the control of all-union bureaucracies: "why does the RSFSR occupy the worst position in the Union?" Another member complained, "you can count on your fingers what belongs to the RSFSR." Stanislav Kosior, then a TsK secretary, declared that "the task [of the commission] is to give the RSFSR all those advantages that are enjoyed by

[25] *Natsional'nyi vopros na perekrestke mnenii*, 114.

[26] *RTsKhIDNI* 17/3/566 (07.06.26): 32/25.

[27] *GARF* 3316/64/188 (1926): 5–6.

[28] The materials of the Kalinin commission are scattered throughout the central state and party archives. *GARF* 1235/140/305 (1926–1927): 1–85; 1235/140/435 (1926–1927): 1–60; 3316/16a/211 (1926–1927): 1–3; 3316/16a/212 (1926–1927): 1–142; 3316/16a/272 (1926–1927): 1–24; 3316/64/188 (1926–1927): 1–230; 393/1s/196 (1926–1927): 1–96; RTsKhIDNI 17/33/485 (1926–1927): 1–77; 17/85/108 (1926–1927): 1–208; 78/7/61 (1926–1927): 1–97; 78/7/62 (1926–1927): 1–274; 78/7/83 (1926–1927): 1–18; 78/7/88 (1926): 1–67.

[29] *GARF* 1235/140/435 (1927): 1, 32, 37.

the other Union republics."[30] This amounted to TsK acknowledgment of the RSFSR's inferior status.

There were also complaints about the RSFSR's lack of certain institutions. VTsIK's secretary, Kiselev, even called for the formation of a Russian Communist Party with its own Central Committee, for which he was later criticized but not punished.[31] The habit of filling the same all-union and RSFSR positions with one person—Rykov and Kalinin were heads of the RSFSR and all-union Sovnarkom and TsIK, respectively—was condemned as belittling the importance of the RSFSR organs.[32] There were also complaints about central favoritism toward non-Russian regions, "that backward nationalities, for the most part, live off the central Russian peasantry."[33] The Kalinin commission, then, was a rare, perhaps unique, forum for the expression of grievances from "the great-power nationality."

However, it amounted to little more than venting anger. The Kalinin commission completed its work in March 1927 and forwarded its resolutions to the Politburo for consideration. Its demands were exceedingly modest and, as already mentioned, none of them were acted on. The Politburo delayed consideration of the Kalinin commission's report until February 1928, when it laconically transferred the commission's materials to the files of TsKK-Rabkrin with no further comment, an ignominious end to the commission's work.[34] The period of constitutional change and claims for sovereignty had passed. With the first five-year plan, RSFSR claims against the center became even less tenable.

The Internationalization of the RSFSR

In fact, as we have seen in earlier chapters, the status of Russian culture reached a nadir during the cultural revolution. The latinization campaign now embraced languages that used the Cyrillic or "Russian" alphabet, which was declared to be "in its history, the alphabet of autocratic oppression, missionary propaganda, Great Russian national chauvinism."[35] A renewed legal and propaganda campaign against great power chauvinism was launched. Moreover, after Stalin's declaration that the accelerated construction of socialism would witness a "flowering" of nations, the process of ethno-territorial proliferation also accelerated, which in turn led to a further internationalization of the RSFSR. By 1932, after the formation of Ukrainian and Belorussian national soviets, over the protests of local Russian officials, the RSFSR had a network of approximately

[30] RTsKhIDNI 78/7/62 (1927): 37–38, 51–52; 55–56; 78.
[31] GARF 1235/140/435 (1927): 10.
[32] GARF 3316/64/188 (1927): 198.
[33] GARF 3316/64/188 (1927): 21, 198.
[34] RTsKhIDNI 17/3/625 (24.03.27): 92/3; 17/3/626 (31.03.27): 93/1; 17/3/639 (16.06.27): III/17; 17/3/672 (09.02.28): 9/27.
[35] GARF 2307/14/81 (1929): 27–28.

290 national districts, 7000 national village soviets, and well over 10,000 national collective farms, in addition to its ten autonomous republics, twelve autonomous oblasts, and nine autonomous *okrugi*.

The flowering of nations during the cultural revolution even led to the discovery of new nations. The small Mari nation (200,000) splintered into "meadow" (*lugovoi*) and "mountain" (*gornyi*) Mari, with the latter, smaller group (50,000) being given its own national district within the Mari Autonomous Oblast.[36] In Georgia, the Mingrelians (250,000) demanded the same status and were likewise granted their own national press and schools, although not a national district.[37] Not only did the flowering of nations involve the recognition of new nations, it also meant the elevation of the tribe to the status of nationality.

In the early 1920s, the Soviet Union's numerous "small peoples of the north" (Nentsy, Chuchki, etc.) had been granted a special status and special institutions due to their extreme tribal "backwardness." They were organized in extraterritorial clan soviets, which represented only the native population and were supervised by a paternalistic committee of the north based in Moscow.[38] From the perspective of the cultural revolution, this system looked hopelessly antiquated and colonial. Passionate calls were made to grant the small peoples their "full national rights."[39] In December 1930, VTsIK passed a decree forming national soviets in the far north.[40] By 1931, the small peoples of the north had a network of nine national *okrugi*, 65 national districts, and 411 national village soviets.[41] Written languages were provided for populations numbering under one thousand. Despite these small numbers, Anatolii Skachko, a major patron of the small peoples, boasted that these national soviets were the site of "the creation of new nationalities out of tribes that had earlier never dreamed of national existence . . . [and] their transition in just six years through all the stages of development, which for other peoples required thousands of years."[42] Such rhetoric marked the height of the cultural revolution's developmentalist utopia and of the Soviet Union's commitment to ethnic proliferation.

---

[36] *GARF* 1235/141/1531 (1933): 42. By 1935, this district already had four newspapers publishing in the Mountain Mari language. *Letopis' periodicheskikh izdanii SSSR v 1935 g.* (Moscow, 1935), 780.

[37] *RTsKhIDNI* 17/18/34 (08.08.32): 21/18; 17/18/39 (02.09.33): 50/22; *Letopis' periodicheskikh izdanii*, 780–81.

[38] Yuri Slezkine, *Arctic Mirrors* (Ithaca, N.Y., 1994): 131–183.

[39] P. Smidovich, "Sovetizatsiia severa," *Sovetskii sever*, no. 1 (1930): 5.

[40] "Postanovlenie prezidiuma VTsIK 'Ob organizatsii natsional'nykh ob'edinenii v raionakh rasseleniia malykh narodov severa," *Sovetskii sever*, no. 1 (1931): 230–233; *GARF* 3316/23/1313 (1930–1931); Slezkine, *Arctic Mirrors*, 269–272.

[41] A. Skachko, "VIII plenum komiteta severa," *Sovetskii sever*, no. 5 (1931): 5; P. E. Terletskii, "Natsional'noe raionirovanie krainego severa," nos. 7–8 (1930): 13.

[42] *2 sessiia VTsIK 15 sozyva. Stenograficheskii otchet* (Moscow, 1931): 16.

The Russification of the RSFSR

It also marked the zenith of the internationalization of the RSFSR. The Kuban affair and the national interpretation of the grain requisitions crisis not only initiated a turn toward the pragmatism of silent *korenizatsiia* and the violent repression of the Soviet Union's diaspora nationalities, they also marked a rather dramatic shift from ethnic proliferation to ethnic consolidation. In fact, the key December 14, 1932 Politburo decree not only criticized Ukrainization and ordered the deportation of the Kuban Cossacks, it also ordered the abolition of Ukrainization and all Ukrainian national soviets in the North Caucasus[43]:

> Immediately shift paperwork in all soviet and cooperative organs of "Ukrainized" districts in the North Caucasus, as well as all newspapers and journals, from the Ukrainian language to the Russian language, as the latter is more understandable for Kuban residents. Also, prepare to shift teaching in the schools to Russian in the fall.

The next day a second Politburo decree extended the abolition of Ukrainization to the entire RSFSR[44]:

> TsK VKP/b/ and Sovnarkom SSSR decisively condemn the proposals of some Ukrainian comrades about the Ukrainization of a whole series of districts throughout the Soviet Union (for instance, in the Far East, Kazakhstan, Central Asia, the Central-Black Earth region). Such proposals can only benefit those bourgeois nationalist elements which, exiled from Ukraine as bad elements, will penetrate the newly Ukrainized districts and undertake destructive work there.

As we saw in Chapter 7, Ukrainian efforts on behalf of the RSFSR Ukrainians were now being portrayed as a form of Ukrainian imperialism toward the RSFSR.[45]

These two decrees abruptly initiated a reverse policy trend toward the Russification of the RSFSR. By this phrase, I mean the abolition of non-Russian national territories and other national institutions within the Russian regions of the RSFSR (*oblasti/kraia*) and the restriction of these institutions to the

---

[43] *Holod 1932–1933 rokiv na Ukraini* (Kiev, 1990): 293.

[44] *RTsKhIDNI* 17/3/911 (15.12.32): 126/50.

[45] O. Shlikhter, "Posylymo bil'shovyts'ku pyl'nist' na fronti borot'by za zdiisnennia lenins'koi natsyonal'noi polityky na Ukraini," *Bil'shovyk Ukrainy*, nos. 9–10 (1933): 77; M. Orlov, "Proty natsionalistychnykh nastanov u roboti URE," nos. 7–8 (1932): 67–68; P. P. Liubchenko, "Pro deiaki pomylky na teoretychnomu fronti," *Komunist*, no. 165 (04.07.33): 3. K. P. Sizonov, "Znyshchyty do kintsia natsionalistychnu kontrabandu na fronti radians'koho budivnytstva i prava," *Chervonyi Shliakh*, no. 8 (1934): 41–42.

RSFSR's autonomous republics and oblasts, which were not subjected to russification. RSFSR Ukrainians (7.9 million in the 1926 census) were more than twice the size of the RSFSR's next largest minority (3.85 million Kazakhs). They represented 29.7 percent of all RSFSR non-Russians and an absolute majority (53.1 percent) of all non-Russians in the Russian regions of the RSFSR.[46] Therefore, the abolition of all Ukrainian national institutions, as well as the institutions of the much less numerous RSFSR Belorussians (640,000), represented a major step toward the administrative Russification of the RSFSR.[47]

A comparison of the 1926 and 1937 censuses shows the remarkable impact of this administrative redefinition. In both censuses, respondents were allowed to choose their nationality. Table 38 shows an enormous decline in those describing themselves as Ukrainians and Belorussians in the RSFSR, a decline not observed in their home republics: As Table 39 shows, this decline was most precipitous in the regions bordering on Ukraine, especially in the North Caucasus and above all Kuban, where the terror against Ukrainians in 1932–1933 was most severe.

Only the Ukrainians and Belorussians saw their national territories abolished so abruptly. Elsewhere the Russification of the RSFSR took place more gradually. Nevertheless, already in December 1933, when VTsIK's Nationalities Department held its third national minorities conference, it was clear that the December 14–15, 1932 Politburo decrees had placed national soviets under threat.[48] The chairman of VTsIK's Nationalities Department, N. N. Nurmakov, praised the RSFSR's network of national soviets, but declared that the process of forming new soviets was over. In fact, he warned the process had already gone too far[49]:

> Some national minorities, fulfilling the task of bourgeois nationalist elements— whether consciously or not—demanded the formation of special districts for numerically insignificant groups of national minorities . . . the formation of such districts, without the necessary economic and financial conditions, does not at all further the rapid development of these national minorities. It creates purely Potemkin districts without any future perspective.

The policy of ethnic proliferation was now stigmatized as bourgeois nationalist.

---

[46] These numbers are calculated from the 1926 census results. *Vsesoiuznaia perepis' naseleniia 1926 goda. Tom IX. RSFSR* (Moscow, 1929): 65–95.
[47] There was no specific decree abolishing RSFSR Belorussian territories and institutions. The December 16, 1932 Politburo decree extending the nationalities terror from Ukraine to Belorussia appears to have been sufficient to imply analagous treatment of RSFSR Ukrainians and Belorussians.
[48] *GARF* 1235/128/2–3 (26–27.12.33).
[49] N. N. Nurmakov, "III vserossiiskoe soveshchanie rabotnikov sredi natsional'nykh men'shinstv," *Revoliutsiia i natsional'nosti*, no. 1 (1934): 81.

Table 38. Ukrainian and Belorussian Population by Republic, 1926–1937

| | 1926 Census | | 1937 Census | |
	Population	As Percent of Republic	Population	As Percent of Republic
RSFSR				
Ukrainians	7,873,331	7.8	3,087,022	3.0
Belorussians	637,634	0.6	349,214	0.3
Ukrainian SSR Ukrainians	23,218,860	80.1	22,212,525	78.2
Belorussian SSR Belorussians	4,017,301	80.6	4,361,804	83.9

Calculated from *Vsesoiuznaia perepis' 1926 goda, vol.* IX–XI; and *Vsesoiuznaia perepis' naseleniia 1937 g. Kratkie itogi* (Moscow, 1991): 85–86.

Table 39. Ukrainian Population in RSFSR by Region, 1926–1937

| | 1926 Census | | 1937 Census | |
	Population	As Percent of Region	Population	As Percent of Region
Region				
North Caucasus	3,106,852	37.15	212,857	2.84
Kuban/Krasnodar	915,450	61.48	51,588	2.82
Central-Black Earth	1,651,853	15.26	709,126	5.51
Kazakhstan	860,822	13.24	549,859	10.73
Far East	315,203	10.43	328,286	14.41

Calculated from *Vsesoiuznaia perepis' 1926 goda,* vol. IX–XI; and *Vsesoiuznaia perepis' naseleniia 1937 g. Kratkie itogi* (Moscow, 1991): 85–96. The high figure in the far east is largely explained by ongoing Ukrainian agricultural settlement to the region, which compensated for losses due to assimilation.

The new negative attitude toward ethnic proliferation was accompanied by a positive reevaluation of the role of Russian culture. Nurmakov asserted the need for a better knowledge of Russian and questioned the value of minority-language schooling: "We open national schools not in order to provide mandatory instruction in native languages, but in order to give an education to national minorities."[50] This statement completely contradicted existing policy and called into question all minority-language education. Nevertheless, the Education Commissariat's representative agreed that Russian must be given priority: "We must adapt to the language that has the higher culture."[51]

The striking contrast between this laconic comment and Skachko's hymn to the creation of new nations marks the distance between the height of the cultural revolution and the beginning of the great retreat: the language of utopia and ethnic proliferation versus the language of realism and ethnic

[50] *GARF* 1235/28/2 (1933): 204.
[51] Ibid., 147.

Table 40. National Soviets in RSFSR in 1935

Region	National Districts	As Percent of Total Districts	National Village Soviets	As Percent of Total Village Soviets
RSFSR	161	6.8	3004	7.0
Oblasts/*Krai*	107	6.2	2344	6.8
ASSR	50	9.5	615	7.5
AO	4	4.3	45	3.0

This gives an almost complete listing of all national districts and village soviets. When "mixed" soviets are listed, I have divided the number between the two nationalities. When districts are listed but not village soviets, I have calculated a village soviet figure proportionate to the number of districts.

consolidation. The Politburo decrees of December 1932 and the campaign against Ukrainian nationalism divided these two periods. The shock waves from these events were felt in all areas of nationalities policy, but, as noted in Chapter 9, their precise policy consequences were not immediately made clear. From 1933 to 1937, two possible outcomes remained in competition: the abolition of all national minority institutions and complete administrative russification, as with the RSFSR Ukrainians, or a modest correction leaving the existing national minorities system largely intact. The limited revision of *korenizatsiia* suggests the latter course was a real possibility.

It seemed, at first, as if the latter option might still triumph. As Table 40 shows, by 1935 the network of national soviets in the RSFSR, correcting for Ukrainian and Belorussian losses, remained about exactly the size it had been in 1932.[52] In 1935, the average national district had a majority national population and its own national-language school and newspaper, was staffed largely by titular nationals, and could count on favorable financial treatment from higher authorities. The districts did, however, conduct almost all their paperwork in Russian. Thus, the rural national minority system appeared to have stabilized.

Urban national minority institutions, however, fared much less well. Although there were some urban national soviets, this system could not be effectively transferred to cities. In compensation, an elaborate system of national urban institutions had been organized: national clubs, schools, work brigades, dormitories, red corners.[53] After 1933, this system went into rapid decline. In early 1933, Tatar demands for separate national Tatar workshops and cooperative stores in the Donbass were condemned as "building a Chinese wall between

[52] This gives an almost complete listing of all national *raiony* and village soviets. When "mixed" soviets are listed, I have divided the number between the two nationalities. When *raiony* are listed but not village soviets, I have calculated a village soviet figure proportionate to the number of *raiony*.

[53] S. Abramov, *Natsional'naia rabota sovetov v gorodakh* (Moscow, 1935); Ibragimov and S. Sady, *Uspekhi leninskoi natsional'noi politiki na Urale* (Sverdlovsk, 1932): 26–34; *Materialy i resheniia 3 obshchegorodskogo natsmen-soveshchaniia* (Rostov-na-donu, 1932).

Table 41. RSFSR National Minority Newspapers (Excluding ASSR/AO)

Year	Oblast/Krai	City	Total
1927	14	2	16
1928	15	2	17
1929	14	3	17
1930	16	4	20
1931	17	9	26
1932	26	12	38
1933	29	15	44
1934	25	12	37
1935	23	12	35
1936	19	7	26
1937	16	4	20
1938	12	3	15
1939	2	2	4
1940	0	0	0

Calculated from *Gazety SSSR 1917–1960. Bibliograficheskii spravochnik* (Moscow, 1970–1984). *Oblast/krai* level newspapers are those published by an *oblast* or *krai* level organization. City newspapers are published by a city or urban district organization or by a factory.

Russians and national minorities" and "foreign to a proletarian organization of labor."[54] These demands, though fully in line with the old system, were now labeled counterrevolutionary.

Industry and trade union officials had always shown the greatest hostility to the Soviet nationalities policy, in particular to Affirmative Action. Now they simply ceased to implement such policies in the Russian regions of the RSFSR. By 1934, model industrial Affirmative Action programs in the North Caucasus and Lower Volga were no longer functioning.[55] Affirmative Action in education was thereafter largely confined to the union and autonomous republics, and the silent Affirmative Action continued in the major Moscow and Leningrad universities. Urban national schools fared better, but their number also began a gradual decline after 1933.[56] In fact, the number of students enrolled in the RSFSR's national minority schools (excluding ASSRs) declined from over one million in 1932–1933 to 605,383 in 1935, and then to 417,316 in 1937–1938.[57] As Table 41 shows, urban national minority newspapers began a similar decline in 1933.[58] The decline of national minority institutions in Russian cities began the division of the RSFSR into a Russian space, where national minorities

---

[54] N. Safarov, "Protiv izvrashcheniia natspolitki," *Revoliutsiia i natsional'nosti*, no. 4 (1933): 75–76.

[55] Anver Tazhurizin, *Ocherki o khoziaistvennom i kul'turnom stroitel'stve v natsional'nykh raionakh Nizhnei Volgi* (Stalingrad, 1934): 40–41.

[56] GARF 3316/30/825 (1937): 92; 3316/30/831 (1937): 76.

[57] GARF (TsGA) 2306/70/935 (1935–1936): 37; RTsKhIDNI 17/114/633 (01.12.37): 75/7, 131–132.

[58] *Oblast/krai* level newspapers are those published by an *oblast* or *krai* level organization. City newspapers are published by a city or urban district organization or by a factory.

would not be granted a distinct status, and a non-Russian space: the RSFSR's autonomous republics and oblasts.

National institutions were increasingly concentrated in the RSFSR's autonomous republics and oblasts. In 1934, Moscow-based Tatar and Chuvash newspapers were moved to their respective republics.[59] Central national minorities institutions, such as Komnats (1934), which serviced national minority education, and Komsever (1935), which serviced the small peoples of the north, were abolished.[60] National minority journals also ceased publication.[61]

This overall trend, and in particular the new emphasis on Russian-language education, opened up the formerly taboo topic of assimilation. Prior to 1932, Soviet policy was unambiguously hostile to even voluntary assimilation. In 1929, Stalin had stated: "It is well known that assimilation is categorically excluded from the arsenal of Marxism-Leninism as an antinational, counter-revolutionary and fatal policy."[62] After 1933, a new attitude and a new rhetoric emerged. In 1934, the secretary of the Soviet of Nationalities, A. Tadzhiev, stated publicly that he was sending his own children, native Uzbek speakers, to Russian-language schools. He added the following remarkable comments[63]:

> Local misunderstandings develop because we observe an opposition to assimilation. One sometimes even observes this among Communists. In fact, we should not oppose assimilation. Our nationalities policy is absolutely clear and we can never permit forced assimilation. We won't allow that, but we should by all means welcome natural assimilation, we should welcome natural assimilation which takes place at its own pace. This is good as it leads to the formation of a single nation, a single language.

Two years earlier, on the authority of Stalin's speech to the 1930 party congress, these remarks would have been denounced as great-power chauvinism.

Nor was this an isolated instance. In 1936, Tadzhiev's successor as secretary of the Soviet of Nationalities, A. I. Khatskevich, made these similar comments[64]:

> Many incorrectly understand the *rights* of national minorities in their economic and cultural development. They say: "If you are a *natsmen*, then whether you want to or not, you must attend a national school . . . you must have your soviet's paperwork done in the national language." . . . [However,] more attention must be given to realizing *the right of free choice* to use any language

---

[59] *Gazety SSSR*, vol. I, 29.

[60] *GARF (TsGA)* 296/1/280–281.

[61] Komsever's *Sovetskii sever* ceased publication in 1935, the North Caucasus' *Revoliutsiia i gorets* in 1933, *Literatura natsional'nostei SSSR* in 1935, *Prosveshchenie natsional'nostei* in 1935. None were replaced by analagous publications.

[62] Stalin, "Natsional'nyi vopros i leninizm," *Sochineniia*, vol. II, 347.

[63] *GARF* 3316/27/766 (1934): 125–126.

[64] *GARF* 3316/13/27 (1936): 246–249.

according to the choice of the population itself and each citizen individually.
. . . Each *natsmen* should have the right to liquidate their illiteracy in their native
language, but if they want to liquidate it in Russian, *living somewhere in the kraia
and oblasts of the RSFSR*, then one must give them that *right* and possibility.
[emphasis mine]

Several things stand out here. First, Khatskevich singled out the Russian regions
of the RSFSR as the natural sites of assimilation. Second, like Tadzhiev, he
insisted on the "right" of assimilation, not forced assimilation. This became the
new standard position.[65] Third, Khatskevich invoked the desires of individual
non-Russians, not just the new goals of the state. This was not simply hypocrisy.
Many non-Russian parents did want to enhance their children's economic
prospects with a Russian-language education. The right of assimilation was not
only a new state policy but, for a significant segment of extraterritorial national
minorities, a long-standing popular demand.

The right of assimilation implied a rejection of ethnic proliferation in favor
of national consolidation. The 1934 union of Chechnya and Ingushetia into
a single Chechen-Ingush autonomous oblast, with the formation of a united
Chechen-Ingush literary language, was a forerunner of this change. The movement toward national consolidation was given a giant push forward by an off-
hand remark in Stalin's November 1936 address on the new constitution: "The
Soviet Union, as is well-known, consists of sixty nations, national groups, and
ethnicities."[66] Of course, this was not at all well known. The 1926 census list
had included about 200 peoples (*narodnosti*), and a revised list in 1927 recognized 172 peoples.[67] Moreover, in 1936 over one hundred separate nationalities
had their own national soviets.[68] Stalin's number barely embraced the fifty-one
Soviet nationalities with their own national okrug, oblast, or republic.[69]

Stalin's comment naturally affected the preparations for the 1937 census.
Already in early 1935, *Revoliutsiia i natsional'nosti* had published a discussion
article proposing a revised list of 121 Soviet nationalities for the new census.[70]
The final 1937 census list was reduced to 107 national categories (about a
dozen for foreign citizens).[71] The 1939 list was further reduced to 59 "major

---

[65] See also S. Dimanshtein, "Otnoshenie marksizma-leninizma k voprosu ob assimiliatsii
natsional'nostei," *Revoliutsiia i natsional'nosti*, no. 7 (1935): 57–63.

[66] I. V. Stalin, *Sochineniia*, vol. 1 [14] (Stanford, Calif., 1967), 146. Stalin uses the words "*60
natsii, natsional'nykh grupp i narodnostei.*"

[67] Francine Hirsch, "The Soviet Union as a Work in Progress: Ethnographers and the
Category *Nationality* in the 1926, 1937, and 1939 Censuses," *Slavic Review* 56 (1997): 263–264.

[68] B. Grande, "Materialy dlia utochneniia spiska narodov SSSR," *Revoliutsiia i natsional'nosti*,
no. 4 (1935): 78; *GARF* 3316/29/577 (1936): 1–132.

[69] *Administrativno-territorial'noe delenie soiuznykh respublik na 1 marta 1937 g.* (Moscow, 1937),
IV.

[70] Grande, "Materialy dlia utochneniia spiska narodov," 81–87.

[71] *Vsesoiuznaia perepis' naseleniia 1937 g.*, 83–84, 228–229. For an excellent and thorough discussion of the formation of the 1937 and 1939 lists, see Hirsch, "The Soviet Union as a Work in
Progress," 266–276.

Table 42. RSFSR Population by Nationality, 1926–1937

Year	Total Population	Non-Russian Population	As Percent of Total	Non-Russian Excluding Ukrainians and Belorussians	As Percent of Total
1926	100,623,474	26,551,378	26.39	18,040,413	17.93
1937	103,919,847	18,558,453	17.86	15,122,217	14.56
1939	109,397,463	19,089,187	17.45	15,271,344	13.96

Calculated from *Vsesoiuznaia perepis' 1926 g.*, vol. IX, 34–51, 65–79; *Vsesoiuznaia perepis' 1937 g.*, 85–96; *Vsesoiuznaia perepis' 1939 g.*, 59–79.

nationalities" (57 in the published version), finally bringing it into line with Stalin's 1936 comment.[72] The 1937 census was used to propagate the right to assimilation. The 1937 census was preceded by newspaper articles trumpeting the right to choose one's own nationality.[73] Given massive population movements and border changes, it is difficult to compare the 1926 and 1937 censuses. However, Table 42 does show evidence of considerable assimilation. These statistics, even corrected for the massive decline in Ukrainians and Belorussians, show a marked drop in non-Russians. The non-Russian population of the Russian regions of the RSFSR (*kraia*/oblasts) dropped from 12,841,825 (15.76 percent) in 1926 to an insignificant 4,116,241 (4.71 percent) in 1937.[74] By early 1937, then, considerable progress had been made toward the Russification of the RSFSR.

In late 1937, the administrative Russification of the RSFSR suddenly received a further impetus from above through a series of Politburo and Orgburo decrees. In December 1937, the Politburo issued a decree abolishing the schools and cultural institutions of the Soviet Union's diaspora nationalities (e.g., Germans, Poles, Finns, Estonians, Latvians).[75] In the course of this decree's implementation, it was expanded to include all "non-Russian schools in Russian regions," which meant the abolition of all 4598 national minority schools in the Russian regions of the RSFSR.[76] A further set of Orgburo decrees also abolished all pedagogical schools.[77] By mid-1938, then, only Russian schools were to be functioning in the Russian regions of the RSFSR.[78]

[72] Ibid., 275–276.
[73] Ibid., 268.
[74] Same sources as for Table 42.
[75] *RTsKhINDI* 17/3/994 (11.12.37): 56/75. This confirmed an Orgburo decree, 17/114/633 (01.12.37): 75/7.
[76] *RTsKhIDNI* 17/114/829 (01.12.37): 75/7, 129–132.
[77] *RTsKhIDNI* 17/114/640 (04.03.38): 82/11; 17/114/844 (04.03.38): 82/11, 171–174.
[78] Peter Blitstein, who is writing a dissertation on nationalities policy from 1934 to 1953, informs me that this decree was not systematically enforced and some non-Russian schools continued to exist in Russian regions.

Table 43. Rural District–Level National Minority Newspapers

Year	RSFSR Oblast/*Krai*	ASSR/AO	Union Republic
1930	7	7	6
1931	19	17	15
1932	32	25	23
1933	35	30	26
1934	34	35	31
1935	39	41	33
1936	39	41	33
1937	36	43	35
1938	27	41	41
1939	23	38	41
1940	22	39	41
1941	21	39	41

Calculated from *Gazety SSSR, 1917–1960.* The diaspora nationalities excluded are Finns, Estonians, Latvians, Poles, Germans, Bulgarians, Greeks, Czechs, Koreans, Chinese, Kurds, and Iranians, whose newspapers were all abolished by 1939.

In December 1937, the Politburo also issued a similar decree abolishing the national soviets of diaspora nationalities.[79] This decree was not formally extended to include other RSFSR national minorities. However, since the western national minorities had the strongest national soviets, their abolition fatally weakened the system. After 1938, national districts and village soviets ceased to be mentioned. Their fate can be inferred, however, from the evolution of the Soviet Union's network of district-level national minority newspapers (Table 43).[80] After 1937, national minority newspapers in the Russian regions of the RSFSR dropped off considerably (from 36 to 21), but in the Soviet Union's national territories (SSR, ASSR, AO), they actually increased slightly (from 78 to 80). In 1940, there were no national minority newspapers above the district level in the Russian regions of the RSFSR (see Table 43), but there were twenty such papers in the Soviet Union's national territories.[81] In other words, by 1940 the Soviet Union had been divided into a Russian space (the RSFSR's oblasts/*kraia*), where institutional russification had been almost entirely completed, and a non-Russian space, where national minority status continued to be recognized.

This process was complemented by the abolition of almost all remaining central nationalities institutions in 1937–1938. Komzet, which had organized the

[79] *RTsKhIDNI* 17/3/994 (11.12.37): 56/76. Based on a prior Orgburo decree 17/114/633 (01.12.37): 75/6.

[80] The diaspora nationalities excluded are Finns, Estonians, Latvians, Poles, Germans, Bulgarians, Greeks, Czechs, Koreans, Chinese, Kurds, and Iranians, whose newspapers were all abolished by 1939.

[81] Calculated from *Gazety SSSR, 1917–1960.* In 1940, there were three republic-level and one city-level national minority newspapers in the RSFSR's autonomous republics and oblasts, and nine republican or oblast and seven city papers in the Soviet Union's union republics.

agricultural resettlement of Jews, was abolished in 1938.[82] The reorganization of VTsIK into the RSFSR Supreme Soviet led to the abolition of VTsIK's Nationalities Department.[83] This was accompanied by the abolition of all Nationalities departments at the *krai*, oblast, and republic level. The special representatives of the autonomous republics and oblasts attached to VTsIK, who had served as valuable lobbyists, were also abolished.[84] The last Moscow-based national minority newspapers ceased publication in 1939.[85] Likewise, the few remaining central periodicals that dealt with nationalities issues were abolished.[86] The presidium of the Soviet of Nationalities, which had been very active from 1935 to 1937, ceased all noticeable work at the end of 1937.[87] It did, however, survive as the sole central political institution formally devoted to the nationalities question.

By 1938, then, a purposeful, comprehensive, and carefully targeted institutional Russification of the RSFSR had been set into motion. This process led to the division of the Soviet Union into a central Russian core and a non-Russian "national" periphery. This ethnogeography now seems a self-evident fact, hardly in need of explanation, but in reality it is a relatively recent historical construction. In the 1920s, due to state support for ethnic proliferation, nationality permeated the entire Soviet Union and, in particular, the RSFSR. There was no purely Russian space. The creation of that Russian space took place in the 1930s and was the result of a conscious strategy of national consolidation and institutional Russification.

This strategy, however, created a major contradiction at the heart of the emerging new Soviet nationalities policy. In the 1920s, the Soviet Union had created a coherent, if utopian, scheme to resolve the tension between their adopted system of territorial nationality and their commitment to preserving each individual's extraterritorial personal nationality: the pyramid of national soviets. The abolition of national districts and village soviets in 1937–1938 and the reduction in the number of national *okrugi* and oblasts at the time of the adoption of the 1936 constitution sliced out the middle layers of that pyramid (Table 44). The ethnic cleansing of World War II further weakened the center of the pyramid by abolishing several autonomous oblasts and republics. For a substantial minority of the Soviet population, this revived the tension between the individual's passport and territorial nationality. Extraterritorial national minorities lost state support for the maintenance of their ethnic identity. If they assimilated or, as the RSFSR Ukrainians and Belorussians, were required to

---

[82] On the abolition of Komzet and its foreign financial sponsor, Agrojoint, see *GARF* 5446/29/1–13 (1938).

[83] *GARF* 1235/141/1880 (1937): 1–13.

[84] *GARF* 1235/141/2153 (1938): 1–6; 1235/141/1880 (1937): 4–9.

[85] *Gazety SSSR, 1917–1960*, vol. 1, 11–66.

[86] *Revoliutsiia i pis'mennost* (1937), *Revoliutsiia i natsional'nosti* (1937), *Revoliutsionnyi vostok* (1937), *Sovetskoe stroitel'stvo* (1937), *Vlast' sovetov* (1938).

[87] For evidence of this abrupt rupture, see the records in *GARF fond* 3316 (especially *opisi* 30 and 65) and fond 7523 (especially *opis'* 65s).

Table 44. The Pyramid of National Soviets, 1932–1938

c. 1932		c. 1938	
National Territory	Number	National Territory	Number
1. Soviet Union	1	1. Soviet Union	1
2. Federal republic	2	2. Federal republic	1
3. Union republic	7	3. Union republic	11
4. Autonomous republic	15	4. Autonomous republic	16
5. Autonomous oblast	16	5. Autonomous oblast	8
6. Autonomous *okrug*	10	6. Autonomous *okrug*	10
7. National district	290		
8. National village soviet	7,000		
9. National *kolkhoz*	10,000		
10. Personal nationality	147,027,915	10. Personal Nationality	161,753,176

assimilate, there was no contradiction. As we shall see in the following chapter, however, the passport system and a growing primordialism erected new barriers to assimilation.

As this contradiction demonstrates, the Russification of the RSFSR had been an ad hoc response to a practical problem. It gradually evolved in the aftermath of the Kuban affair and the fundamental revision of the Soviet nationalities policy. One important factor driving the Russification of the RSFSR was the growing Soviet distrust of their national borderlands, driven by fear of cross-border ethnic ties and by their experience of national resistance to collectivization. This growing suspicion of the Soviet Union's "national periphery" led to a corresponding tendency to rely on the "Russian core." The Russification of the RSFSR was designed to solidify that Russian core.

Russian resentment toward the Soviet Affirmative Action Empire was another important, and more immediate, impetus for the Russification of the RSFSR. Such resentment was both ubiquitous and deeply felt. Russian peasants violently resisted the policy of giving non-Russians preferential access to agricultural land as well as the transfer of majority Russian territory to non-Russian republics. Russian workers violently resisted Affirmative Action in industry. Most important, Soviet Affirmative Action was unpopular among ethnically Russian Communist Party officials, who consistently opposed its implementation more vigorously than did noncommunists. The Russification of the RSFSR was a response to this Russian resentment. Affirmative Action was now largely confined to the Soviet Union's national periphery. To the extent that it continued in the central Russian regions, as it did to some extent in higher education, it was now implemented surreptitiously so as not to offend Russian sensibilities. The loud campaign of 1930–1934 against great-power chauvinism ceased. National minorities in the Russian regions of the RSFSR had to adapt to a hegemonic Russian environment. Russians, conversely, could now feel at home in their own national republic.

The Russification of the RSFSR, then, was part of a conscious effort in the 1930s to resolve the Soviet Union's persistently troubling Russian question: What role should Russians and Russian culture play in the constitution of the multinational Soviet state? Sultan-Galiev's proposal to establish a Russian republic had been rejected in 1923 because its size and power would be threatening to both the central Soviet state and the non-Russian republics. The Bolsheviks' solution to this problem was the Affirmative Action Empire. This strategy would promote a unified Soviet state in two ways. First, by downplaying Russian national culture and denying Russia its own ethnic republic, it would eliminate the likelihood that Russian national interests would dominate the state. Second, the establishment of the pyramid of national soviets ensured that nationality would permeate the entire Soviet Union so that each nationality would be ensured of national expression throughout the entire state. This would bind the Soviet Union together nationally. By 1933, however, the Soviet leadership felt this strategy had failed because of both the high levels of Russian resentment it had provoked and the feeling that it had abetted the emergence of a dangerous separatist national communism.

The Russification of the RSFSR addressed the problem of individual Russian national discontent in the RSFSR but not the problem of finding an institutional outlet for Russian national self-expression throughout the USSR. It was in fact a compromise solution that created a purely Russian space within the oblasts and *kraia* of the RSFSR, where individual Russians could feel at home nationally, but not a threatening Russian republic. The RSFSR did not evolve into the institutional representative of Russian national interests. The creation of a TsK Biuro on RSFSR affairs in September 1936, which served as compensation for the missing RSFSR Communist Party, could have furthered that goal.[88] However, the Biuro lacked influential members, met only seven times, discussed trivial issues with no Russian national content, and was disbanded in April 1937.[89] A similar attempt failed under Khrushchev. There were two possible ways to institutionalize the newly sanctioned Russian national self-expression, either through the RSFSR or at the all-union level. The rejection of the first option led to an adoption of the second one.

Script Russification and the Symbolic Politics of the Great Retreat

After December 1932, the centrality and the unifying function of the Russian nation and Russian national culture were gradually institutionalized at the all-union level. The rehabilitation and growing celebration of Russianness was an integral part of the process that Nicholas Timasheff called "the Great Retreat": the gradual abandoning of revolutionary and utopian social and cultural

---

[88] *RTsKhIDNI* 607/1/11 (1936): 2.
[89] *RTsKhIDNI* 607/1/11 (1936–1937): 1–166.

practices in favor of traditional, often prerevolutionary, values. Among the many examples cited by Timasheff were the abandonment of progressive education in favor of traditional teaching methods, the prohibition of abortion, increased obstacles to divorce, the condemnation of avant-garde art, and the promotion of realist literature, folk art, and the Russian classics, as well as a shift in emphasis from class-based internationalist propaganda to patriotic Russian nationalism.[90] Writing in 1946, Timasheff expected that the Great Retreat would continue and would, albeit fitfully, "direct the nation towards a situation which would have obtained if [the Bolsheviks'] utopia would not have interrupted the organic development [of the nation]."[91] That situation, Timasheff believed, would have been democracy and a market economy. In this, Timasheff proved both a poor prophet and, for all the brilliance of his *Zeitgeschichte*, an inadequate analyst of the 1930s. For in the political and economic spheres, the period after 1933 marked a consolidation, rather than a repudiation, of the most important goals of Stalin's socialist offensive: forced industrialization, collectivization, nationalization, abolition of the market, political dictatorship.[92] The "Great Retreat," then, is an unfortunate term. However, since its use is now standard, I will employ it to refer to the traditionalist turn in the social and cultural spheres after 1933, while rejecting Timasheff's teleology and his claims about the political and economic spheres.

The single most important aspect of the Great Retreat was the rehabilitation of the Russian nation. Its importance lay both in its far-reaching consequences—the rejection of the pre-1933 principle of Soviet unity (the Affirmative Action Empire) and the articulation of a new principle of unity (the Friendship of the Peoples)—but also due to its role in the larger process of the Great Retreat. In many ways, the rehabilitation of the Russians was a precondition for the Great Retreat, since it is difficult to imagine how a shift in the direction of traditional Russian social and cultural values could take place without it. In this sense, the gradual emergence of an ethnicized Soviet xenophobia that favored a reliance on the Russian core and a fierce resistance to all foreign influence was a major cause of the Great Retreat, though an equally important factor was the statist paternalism that emerged as a consequence of Stalin's revolution from above. This paternalism privileged the state as the motive force in initiating and guiding social change. It favored, therefore, an increasingly demobilized and ordered society, and it imagined that society as composed of a ruling elite and a largely undifferentiated people (*narod*), the state's version of the popular we/they dichotomy. This trend favored the traditionalist reforms of the Great Retreat, including the rehabilitation of the Russian nationality.

[90] Nicholas S. Timasheff, *The Great Retreat* (New York, 1946).

[91] Ibid., 19.

[92] The ongoing effects of these fundamental changes were vastly more consequential for the experience of everyday life and for the evolution of Soviet society than the effects of the "Great Retreat." For a brilliant analysis of the unintended consequences of similar political and economic changes in Maoist China, see Andrew Walder, *Communist Neo-Traditionalism* (Berkeley, Calif., 1986).

Thus, the Great Retreat and the rehabilitation of Russianness were mutually reinforcing.

Timasheff's metaphor does have one redeeming value. The word *retreat* accurately conveys the fact that the Great Retreat was gradual, uncertain, reactive, prone to occasional reversals, and not fully coherent. In nationalities policy, the Great Retreat began with a big bang: the Kuban affair, the December 1932 decrees, and the 1933 Ukrainian terror. These events dramatically signaled a change in nationalities policy but did not make clear whether a mild revision (as the literal text of the decrees stated) or a complete reversal (as the terror campaign suggested) was intended. Both options, as well as a return to the status quo ante, remained in play from 1933 to 1938. Such uncertainty was a prime characteristic of Great Retreat politics. With respect to ethnic cleansing and the Russification of the RSFSR, the policy of total reversal triumphed during the Great Terror. With respect to the broader policy spheres of *korenizatsiia* and Affirmative Action in higher education, the outcome was mild revision. The same uncertainty surrounded the rehabilitation of the Russian nationality.

In the period from 1919 to 1932, the symbolic politics of latinization allowed eastern national elites to express a limited pan-Turkism and Russophobia, as well as their own version of cultural revolution. From 1933 to 1940, the symbolic politics of alphabet russification and terminological reform likewise was used by other local elites and by central authorities to signal the new role of the Russian nationality and Russian culture in the Soviet Union as a whole. As we saw in Chapter 5, the latinization movement peaked in 1931–1932 with the latinization of several Cyrillic alphabets and proposals to latinize the Cyrillic scripts of the Eastern Finns and Chuvash. In November 1932, the Soviet of Nationalities heard VTsK NA's biannual report and gave them a largely positive resolution.[93] In 1933, VTsK NA intended to continue its efforts to latinize the alphabets of the Eastern Finns and Chuvash. By January 1933, however, these plans were already moribund. The first 1933 issue of VTsK NA's journal, published in anticipation of a February 1933 plenum of VTsK NA's scientific council, contained an unmistakable new tone, which quickly crystallized into a new message at the February plenum itself.[94]

The message was that latinization was over. The lead editorial on the plenum stated unequivocally: "Today we can say that the hard labor of latinization is finished. The next task is to solidify and further develop the successes we have achieved." This further work was to develop and regulate "terminology, orthography, the creation of literary languages, dictionaries, and grammars."[95] Terminology was the plenum's primary concern, and Semen Dimanshtein's address on that subject best illustrated the new ideological atmosphere. Dimanshtein

---

[93] *Revoliutsiia i pis'mennost'*, no. 1 (1933): 140–141.

[94] K. Alaverdov, "Na vysshuiu stupen'," *Revoliutsiia i pis'mennost'*, no. 1 (1933): 3–7.

[95] Peredovaia, "Vpered k dal'neishim pobedam na fronte iazykovoi kul'tury," *Pis'mennost' i revoliutsiia*, no. 1 (1933): 4.

attacked the twin symbolic pillars of latinization: pan-Turkism and Russophobia. The 1926 Turkological Congress had done much good, he said, "but a great
many delegates had a harmful, purely nationalist, pan-Turkic orientation." In
terminology, this showed itself in attempts at "the creation of a united great
Turkic or Turko-Tatar nation, a single Turkic language, the restoration of the
magnificence of the East."[96]

Dimanshtein's primary target, however, was Russophobia: "the attempt in all
ways, no matter what the cost, to avoid Russian terms, the argument that it is
better to use any other foreign words or phrases, but in no case Russian." This
linguistic "purism" was based on "the old attitude to the Russian language" as
the language of russification, an attitude no longer acceptable: "Has the Russian
language remained for the non-Russian peoples the same after the revolution
as it was before it? No, it has not. First, in that language the non-Russians
acquire voluntarily much of great value. . . . The original works of Lenin and
Stalin and all the principal documents of the revolution appeared in Russian.
. . . Besides that, the Russian language now has a different class content."[97]
Dimanshtein's message was unmistakable. Attacks on the Russian language were
now attacks on the revolution and therefore on the state itself.

The comment about Russian being the language of Lenin and Stalin was
not accidental. In the 1930s, this became a standard rhetorical trope. It led
to a growing obsession with the accuracy, indeed purity, of translations of
"Marxist-Leninist classics" into the non-Russian languages.[98] Dimanshtein
addressed this issue too. He noted a pernicious tendency to translate "international terms." These included not only such truly international Marxist terms
as *proletariat, klass, sotsialism,* but also purely Russian terms such as *sovet*
(council), *piatiletka* (five-year plan), *kulak* (wealthy peasant), and even "*generalnaia liniia partii.*" Finding native equivalents for such terms, which was
perfectly natural and quite easy, was now ideologically suspect: "From the
confusion of concepts, one gets a distortion of the class line, a distortion of
the general line of the party."[99]

Finally, Dimanshtein also attacked the principle of the supremacy of
the dialect and defended the principle of assimilation. It was wrong, he
said, to create a literary language for every ethnic group. Some should use the
literary language of a larger related nationality as the Mingrelians used
Georgian: "It makes no sense to engage in an endless dividing up of nations."
Others would adopt Russian. He correctly noted that many parents
were adamant on this score: "Don't impose our old language on us. Don't
force our children to become as helpless as we are."[100] This was an early

---

[96] S. M. Dimanshtein, "Printsipy sozdaniia natsional'noi terminologii," *Pis'mennost' i
revoliutsiia,* no. 1 (1933): 26–31.

[97] Ibid., 33–34.

[98] Michael Smith, *Language and Power in the Creation of the USSR, 1917–1953* (Berlin, 1998):
151–154.

[99] Dimanshtein, "Printsipy sozdaniia," 35–36.

[100] Ibid., 37; 38.

and decisive articulation of the emerging policy of ethnic consolidation and the right to assimilation.

Dimanshtein's speech and the plenum's resolutions were typical examples of central guidance on the nationalities policy in 1933. Like Nurmakov's December 1933 speech at the national minorities conference, the December 1932 and November 1933 Ukrainization decrees, and the abolition of the central *bronia*, Dimanshtein's speech and the plenum resolutions declared: (1) that the policy had contributed to counterrevolutionary actions and (2) that the policy should not be expanded but should continue as before with minor revisions. As in the other policy spheres, the formal reassurances were initially trumped by the intimidating charge of counterrevolution and the latinists understandably adopted a low profile. By mid-1933, VTsK NA had disappeared from public view. Without announcement or explanation, its journal ceased publication and its previously announced sixth plenum did not take place.[101]

If the latinists were intimidated, their enemies were emboldened. The first test of the new policy atmosphere took place in Tatarstan. In a public address in the summer of 1933, the Tatar obkom's first secretary, M. O. Razumov, proposed shifting the Tatar alphabet from the Latin to the Russian script. Two other obkom members defended the proposal in the press. It was discussed and approved with only one dissenting vote at a subsequent obkom plenum.[102] An obkom resolution formally authorized the shift on September 14, 1933. It likewise denounced the failure to introduce into Tatar international terminology "in its Russian form."[103] However, the shift did not occur. The latinists denounced the move through bureaucratic channels and the resolution was swiftly withdrawn.[104] In 1938, a Tatar politician remarked that Razumov and his allies had been "severely punished."[105] They had misread the signals.

Or had they? Razumov's punishment was hardly severe. He was made first secretary of the Eastern Siberia *kraikom* (in effect, a promotion) and continued his fight, now advocating a shift to Cyrillic for the small peoples of the north, some of whom lived in his new domain.[106] He even devoted the majority of his speech at the Seventeenth Party Congress in January 1934 to a blistering attack on latinization. He focused his attack on a short history of latinization published in 1932 by an obscure latinist, I. Khansuvarov, which included now archaic attacks on the "russificatory alphabet" and calls for an "international alphabet."[107] By keeping to the symbolic level and condemning Russophobia, Razumov hit the jackpot. His speech prompted denunciations of poor

---

[101] *GARF* 3316/28/766 (1935): 22–45; 3316/28/769 (1935): 198–206.
[102] *RTsKhIDNI* 17/21/4369 (1937): 50; 17/21/4370 (1937): 152–153.
[103] *RTsKhIDNI* 17/21/4390 (14.09.33): 170.
[104] *RTsKhIDNI* 17/114/571 (28.10.34): 222–223; GARF 3316/65/1525 (1934): 4.
[105] *RTsKHIDNI* 17/21/4353 (1938): 212.
[106] *GARF* 3316/65/1525 (1934): 4.
[107] *XVII s"ezd VKP/b/. Stenograficheskii otchet* (Moscow, 1934): 215.

Khansuvarov's brochure first in the party newspaper, *Pravda*, and then in its theoretical organ, *Bol'shevik*.[108]

The fate of Khansuvarov's brochure is instructive. Its attack on the missionary Russian alphabet was absolutely typical of the cultural revolution. The reviews of the book that appeared in late 1932 and early 1933 found it unexceptional.[109] A year later it was counterrevolutionary. *Pravda* was enraged by Khansuvarov's "war against the Russian language," which flowed from his "national-democratic conception of written scripts, which in principle differs in no way from the Ukrainian and Belorussian national-democratic conception in questions of language and literature."[110] This was the most damaging charge possible, because the Ukrainian and Belorussian linguists were a primary target of the 1933 nationalities terror. It was a call for the politics of language and terror to be applied in the east as well. VTsK NA's deputy chairman immediately wrote an apologetic letter to *Bol'shevik* disavowing Khansuvarov, and Dimanshtein published a denunciation of Khansuvarov in a highly self-critical article.[111] A purge atmosphere appeared to be developing.

However, a purge did not break out. Instead, an agonizingly slow review of latinization took place in the higher party and government organs. On August 7, 1933, the Orgburo ordered the Kultprop Department to undertake a comprehensive review of latinization and present its proposals within a month and a half.[112] The Kultprop review, delayed until May 1934, established a new official line on latinization. It reiterated that latinization had been a correct policy but that errors had been made in its implementation. The review proposed adopting the following principles: (1) do not latinize when the majority live abroad (e.g., Koreans, Persians); (2) do not create a separate written language if the group is bilingual or very small; and (3) in the future, do not latinize alphabets now using Cyrillic. These principles echoed the post-1932 changes in nationalities policy: (1) the triumph of Soviet xenophobia over the Piedmont Principle; (2) ethnic consolidation and the right to assimilation; and (3) the enhanced status of Russian culture. The review also criticized insufficient attention to terminological errors and wrecking. International terms such as *sovet*, *sovkhoz*, and *kolkhoz* were translated. In one case *partinyi* was translated as *pristrastnyi* (partial), *generalnaia liniia* as *shakhskaia doroga* (the Shah's road).[113] The review, which was finally published as a TsIK decree on August

---

[108] Rovinskii, "Ob odnoi natsional-demokraticheskoi kontseptsii"; Orlinskii, "Natsional-demokratism"; the work in question is I. Khansuvarov, *Latinizatsiia—orudie leninskoi natsional'noi politiki* (Moscow, 1932).

[109] "Kritika i bibliografiia," *Pis'mennost' i revoliutsiia*, no. 1 (1933): 211–213; V. S-nin, "Bibliografiia," *Revoliutsionnyi vostok*, no. 5 (1933): 157–159.

[110] Rovinskii, "Ob odnoi."

[111] S. Dimanshtein, "Bibliografiia," *Revoliutsiia i natsional'nosti*, no. 6 (1934): 96–103; on Korkmasov's apology, 102–103.

[112] *RTsKhIDNI* 17/114/357 (07.08.33): 151/22.

[113] *RTsKhIDNI* 17/114/571 (1934): 233–239. The review also criticized the unwieldy size of many alphabets and the proliferation of different latin characters.

17, 1935, was by no means a disaster for latinization.[114] Even if the enumerated errors were corrected, the vast majority of latinized alphabets would remain untouched.

This decree finally allowed the politics of latinization (and delatinization) to resume. VTsK NA's deputy chairman immediately published a programmatic article in the Soviet of Nationalities' journal.[115] VTsK NA's own journal began publishing, and their long-delayed sixth plenum finally took place. Local committees that had ceased to function were reconstituted.[116] On the other hand, local officials who had been intimidated by the Tatarstan affair now began to push to have their alphabets shifted to Cyrillic. Given the condemnation of latinizing the alphabets of small and isolated peoples, it is not surprising that the movement was led by the Kabardinians, with the backing of North Caucasian *krai* officials, and by the various regions (East Siberia, the far east, the northern *krai*) responsible for the small peoples of the north.

VTsK NA naturally resisted these attempts to roll back latinization. On numerous occasions, they were accused of obstructing, or failing to help, in shifting Latin alphabets to Cyrillic. N. F. Iakovlev, who helped develop the latinized North Caucasus languages, was accused of trying to stop the Kabardinian plans during two trips to the North Caucasus. He was also accused of helping to produce new Latin alphabets for several small Dagestani peoples.[117] Indeed, in 1935 two new Latin alphabets, the last ones as it turned out, were approved.[118] A. I. Khatskevich was exasperated by the latinists' impolitic resistance: "There is no government discipline in the apparat of VTsK NA. Technical workers of VTsK NA, while on government business, helped create new alphabets, despite the decisions of the Soviet of Nationalities (the 'work' of Professor Iakovlev). Such work distorts and undermines VTsK NA and doesn't help to solidify latinization."[119]

As his comments indicated, Khatskevich also wanted to save latinization.[120] In the policy spheres of western national minorities, Affirmative Action in higher education, *korenizatsiia* in the Soviet east, national minority soviets, and latinization, the soft-line soviet organs (TsIK and the Soviet of Nationalities, VTsIK and its Nationalities Department) consistently opposed the rollback of the pre-1933 nationalities policy. As late as February 1937, at VTsK NA's seventh plenum, Khatskevich publicly opposed sentiment to reverse latinization:

---

[114] For details on the further bureaucratic politicking that preceded this decree, see *GARF* 3316/65/1525 (1934): 1–20; 3316/65/1645 (1935): 2–5; 3316/13/23 (1935): 1110b. *RTsKhIDNI* 77/1/456 (1934): 2–5.

[115] D. Korkmasov, "Ot alfavita—k literaturnomu iazyku," *Revoliutsiia i natsional'nosti*, no. 9 (1936): 34–42.

[116] *Pis'mennost' i revoliutsiia*, no. 2 (1936). *GARF* 3316/28/769 (1935): 220–222; *RTsKhIDNI* 17/21/4399 (1936): 94/11.

[117] *RTsKhIDNI* 17/114/607 (19.05.36): 607/2, 36–37.

[118] N. Iakovlev, "O razvitii i ocherednykh problemakh latinizatsii afavitov," *Kul'tura i pis'mennost' vostoka*, no. 2 (1936): 33.

[119] *GARF* 3316/28/770 (1936): 76.

[120] *GARF* 17/13/27 (1936): 201; 256–258.

"We should deal with this seriously, and not jump from one alphabet to another
... we need to remember that every time we shift an alphabet, a certain
part of the population becomes illiterate."[121]

Defense of latinization, then, was concentrated in the central soviet organs.
The attack on latinization came from local party leaders, who appealed to central
party organs over the head of TsIK and the Soviet of Nationalities. The test
case for the reversal of latinization proved to be the Kabardinian alphabet. VTsK
NA was aware of the Kabardinians' desire to shift to Russian already in 1933 but
successfully stalled action on it for three years.[122] The Kabardinian party finally
responded in March 1936 by sending a delegation to Moscow, who ostentatiously snubbed VTsK NA by refusing to meet with them and instead appealed
directly to the party's Central Committee to approve a shift to Cyrillic. They
apparently received unofficial encouragement, as on April 7, 1936 the
Kabardinian-Balkar obkom voted to shift their alphabet to Russian. The Presidium of VTsK NA met on May 14 to discuss this development and divided
over the issue. Three days later, however, they approved the shift.[123] The reason
for this concession soon became clear. The All-Union Orgburo had discussed
the issue and backed the Kabardinian proposal. Among the materials supporting this decision was a blistering anti-latinization report from the head of TsK's
Scientific Department, K. Ia. Bauman.[124] The Soviet of Nationalities then
quickly endorsed the shift on June 5, 1936, making Kabardinian the first Soviet
language to be officially delatinized.[125]

This decisive intervention of TsK on behalf of the Kabardinians might have
been expected to start a stampede to Cyrillic. In fact, by mid-1937 only the
small peoples of the north (in February 1937) had been shifted to Cyrillic,
although the process had begun for the other North Caucasus peoples and for
the small Siberian ethnicities: the Oirot, Khakassy, and Shortsy. The reversal
of latinization, then, had been confined to the small ethnicities of the RSFSR,
those whose native languages had in fact already failed to establish themselves
as viable. As one Karachai delegate told the Soviet of Nationalities, "The
Karachai people are not only for the Russian alphabet, but for the Russian
language."[126] Thus, the explanation for shifting the Kabardianians was to make
the Russian language and Russian culture more accessible to them. This,
of course, had originally been the principal symbolic reason *not* to give them
the Russian alphabet.

From mid-1935 to mid-1937, then, there was continuous contestation over the
extent to which latinization, and the cultural politics it symbolized, would be

[121] "VII plenum VTsK NA," *Revoliutsiia i natsional'nosti*, no. 3 (1937): 65–66.
[122] *RTsKhIDNI* 17/114/571 (28.10.34): 15/8, 222. *GARF* 3316/28/769 (1935): 233; 3316/30/784
(1936): 1.
[123] *GARF* 3316/29/579 (1936): 1–10.
[124] *RTsKhIDNI* 17/114/607 (19.05.36): 51/2, 28–29; 38–45.
[125] *GARF* 3316/29/579 (1936): 13. The Komi-Zyrian actually shifted back to Cyrillic in 1935, but
did so on their own without any central authorization.
[126] *GARF* 3316/13/27 (1936): 193.

reversed, a process during which TsK gave maddeningly vague guidance. The symbolic politics of the Great Retreat seemed to be gradually moving toward a new cultural and political equilibrium, in which the Russian language and culture would be granted new prestige in the Soviet Union as a whole, and a still stronger assimilatory role among the "small and isolated" peoples of the RSFSR. However, a second process was simultaneously taking place during the Great Retreat, a subtext of terror.

Terror was linked primarily to accusations of terminological sabotage. Prior to 1933, these accusations had been made overwhelmingly in Ukraine and Belorussia, because of the particular security concerns over cross-border ethnic ties along the Soviet Union's western border with Poland.[127] The rhetoric accompanying the campaign to reverse latinization emphasized the positive attraction of the Russian language and culture, while the rhetoric of terminological sabotage emphasized the malicious and counterrevolutionary attempts of nationalists to undermine the unifying cultural ties between the Russian core and non-Russian periphery. The accusations of sabotage focused, above all, on the sabotage of translations of the Marxist-Leninist-Stalinist classics. From 1933 to 1937, this topic dominated the nationalities journals.[128] A whole industry was developed to train adequate translators and to supervise translation efforts. In 1937–1938, this growing subtext of linguistic sabotage would surface and lead to a complete reversal of latinization and a further enhancing of the unifying function of the Russian language and culture.

Language and the Great Terror

The two major historiographic constructs used to describe the Soviet Union in the 1930s, the Great Retreat and the Great Terror, carry on parallel existences and fail to intersect. The Great Retreat describes a fundamental shift in social and cultural policy across a broad range of issues. The Great Terror, in the existing historiography, has no policy content. It is a matter of power politics: in the traditional paradigm, Stalin establishing his personal dictatorship over all rivals and the party's totalitarian rule over an atomized society; or in the revisionist paradigm, the center lashing out at an inefficient and corrupt regional bureaucracy.[129] In neither case are the processes involved in the Great Retreat linked to the Great Terror.[130] In this respect, the Great Terror seems to differ from

---

[127] K. P. Sharaborin, "Zadachi kul'turnogo stroitel'stva i stroitel'stva iazyka," *Sovetskaia Iakutiia*, no. 1 (1936): 3–19; P. A. Oiunskii, "Iakutskii iazyk i puti ego razvitiia," no. 1 (1936): 20–34. See also *Revoliutsiia i gorets* for 1932; T. Zhurgenev, "Voprosy terminologii kazakskogo iazyka," *Bol'shevik Kazakstana*, no. 6 (1935): 44–51.

[128] See the journal *Revoliutsiia i natsional'nosti* for the years 1933–1937.

[129] Robert Conquest, *The Great Terror* (New York, 1990); Robert C. Tucker, *Stalin in Power* (New York, 1990): 366–584. J. Arch Getty, *Origins of the Great Purges* (Cambridge, 1985).

[130] An exception would be Stakhonovism as described in Lewis H. Siegelbaum, *Stakhanovism and the Politics of Productivity in the USSR, 1935–1941* (Cambridge, 1988). Stakhonovism, however, did not represent an enduring policy shift.

the previous terror waves of 1929–1930 and 1932–1933, which were accompanied by unambiguously radical shifts in policy.

In nationalities policy, however, the Great Retreat and the Great Terror quite clearly intersected, and the Great Terror had a strong policy impact. The nature of that impact was consistent across a variety of nationalities policy spheres. In each case, the Great Terror completed the policy change initiated by the December 1932 Politburo decrees and tentatively carried out during the first five years of the Great Retreat. During the Great Terror, diaspora nationalities were definitively categorized as enemy nations and subjected to mass deportation, arrest, and execution; decisive measures were taken to ensure a bicultural Ukraine and Belorussia; the Russification of the RSFSR was completed, as was the reversal of latinization. Moreover, the propaganda campaign celebrating the unifying role of the Russian nation and culture, as well as extravagantly praising the Russian language, literature, arts, and traditional heroes, escalated dramatically during the Great Terror. The Great Terror ended the gradualism of the Great Retreat and rapidly completed the changes initiated in December 1932.

However, the policy direction of the Great Terror was not immediately evident. In Ukraine, as we have seen, the fall of Postyshev in January 1937 was accompanied by a dramatic new campaign in support of Ukrainization that extended into the summer of 1937. A prominent accusation against Postyshev was neglect of Ukrainization. A similar interpretive error was made by Tatar elites concerning latinization. At the March 1937 Tatar obkom plenum, the former Razumov leadership was denounced and, in the catalogue of their many errors, a prominent place was given to the attempt to introduce the Cyrillic alphabet for the Tatar language.[131] Although the Ukrainian and Tatar leadership misjudged the policy implications of the terror, their guesses were not obtuse. Kaganovich had mentioned Postyshev's Ukrainization failings during the latter's removal in Kiev, and Stalin had stressed the necessity of using local cadres at the February–March TsK plenum. Moreover, in religious policy, the Great Terror did involve a temporary reversal of the Great Retreat tendency to mute the extreme antireligious mood and actions of the cultural revolution. In nationalities policy, however, the Great Terror would reinforce the Great Retreat.

The policy shift started to become evident in September 1937, a month after the launching of the mass operations of the Great Terror. Before that date, purged members of the Soviet elite were being categorized and denounced as Trotskyists. The major sin attributed to Postyshev, for instance, was allowing Trotskyists to infiltrate the Kiev obkom. In September 1937, however, *Pravda* and *Izvestiia* published a flood of articles on the discovery of bourgeois nationalist conspiracies in the non-Russian republics.[132] These articles, however, did

---

[131] *RTsKhIDNI* 17/21/4369 (1937): 50; 17/21/4370 (1937): 151–153, 172; 17/21/4372 (1937): 230–231.

[132] After an almost complete absence until September 1937, at least seven articles in *Izvestiia* and twenty-two articles in *Pravda* were devoted primarily to bourgeois nationalist conspiracies.

not yet connect the Great Retreat and the Great Terror. The putative bourgeois nationalists were not primarily anti-Russian, but rather enemies of their own people.[133] Their distinctive sin, beyond the same wanton malice characteristic of Trotskyists as well, was a failure to implement the Soviet nationalities policy, a failure to support their own native language, culture, and cadres.[134] Therefore, the terror was still policy-stabilizing. As a result, when the British foreign office eagerly inquired whether this new wave of terror meant there were indeed bourgeois nationalists in the republics, the ambassador had to disappoint his boss. A Trotskyist was what you called a purged Russian, he reported, and a purged non-Russian was a bourgeois nationalist.[135]

Was the British ambassador correct? Is it true that non-Russians were not intentionally targeted for disproportionate arrest and execution during the Great Terror? As a result of the frequent accusation of bourgeois nationalism and the much less common charge of Great Russian chauvinism, there has been a widespread sense that non-Russians were in general disproportionately and intentionally affected by the Great Terror.[136] As we have seen, the Soviet Union's diaspora nationalities were specifically targeted by unambiguous central decrees. Did such decrees exist for other non-Russian nationalities? They did not. The members of various non-Russian former political parties (e.g., *borot'bisty*, *Mussavisty*, *Dashnaki*) were targeted by decree, but this was also true of members of Russian parties (e.g., Mensheviks, Social Revolutionaries).[137]

Leaving aside specific decrees, were "indigenous" non-Russians nevertheless disproportionately affected by the Great Terror? We do not yet have sufficient evidence to answer this question definitively. The published GULag statistics suggest that they were not. In 1939, excluding the diaspora nationalities, only three of the ten other nationalities listed were overrepresented: Russians (108.5 percent), Belorussians (110.0 percent), Turkmen (154.3 percent).[138] The unusually high Turkmen figure was not the result of intentional targeting of Turkmen,

[133] "Vragi Tadzhikskogo naroda," *Pravda*, no. 250 (10.09.37): 2; "Dela vragov Armianskogo naroda," *Pravda*, no. 268 (28.09.37): 4.

[134] Of the twenty-nine *Pravda* and *Izvestiia* articles, there were only two exceptions, both from Dagestan, where bourgeois nationalists were accused of wrecking Russian-language instruction; "Gnilaia pozitsiia Dagestanskogo obkoma," *Pravda*, no. 265 (25.09.37): 2; "Burzhuaznye natsionalisty oruduiut v Dagestane," *Pravda*, no. 221 (21.09.37): 3.

[135] *BFORC* (1937): vol. 21101, 80–82.

[136] Robert Tucker, *Stalin in Power*, 486–491. Bohdan Nahaylo and Victor Swoboda, *Soviet Disunion* (New York, 1990), 73–80. Conversely, Robert Conquest, who wrote two books devoted to national persecution in the Soviet Union, argued that Russians and non-Russians were equal targets in the Great Terror. Conquest, *The Great Terror*, 223–227.

[137] *RTsKhIDNI* 17/3/751 (10.09.37): 52/751. O. V. Khlevniuk, *Politbiuro* (Moscow, 1996): 195–196. Gabor Rittersporn, " 'Vrednye elementy', 'opasnye men'shinstva' i bol'shevistskie trevogi: massovye operatsii 1937–38 gg. i etnicheskii vopros v SSSR," in Timo Vihavainen and Irina Takala, eds., *V sem'e edinoi* (Petrozavodsk, 1998): 102.

[138] The figure in parentheses is the percentage of the nationality in the GULAG divided by their percentage in the population as a whole. Calculated from data in "Table 4. Ethnic Groups in GULAG Camps, January 1, 1937–1940," in J. Arch Getty, Gabor Rittersporn, and Viktor

but rather because the Turkmen NKVD ran amok and dramatically overfulfilled its arrest quota, for which it was later investigated and rebuked.[139] The other seven nationalities were underrepresented: Ukrainians (83.8 percent), Tatars (75.0 percent), Uzbeks (65.5 percent), Jews (84.7 percent), Kazakhs (71.4 percent), Georgians (67.4 percent), Armenians (66.7 percent). Moreover, if we compare the GULag camp population on January 1, 1937 to that on January 1, 1939, we find (for the seven nationalities for which figures are available) that only the Russians (103.8 percent to 108.5 percent), Georgians (42.7 percent to 67.4 percent), and Armenians (50.8 percent to 66.7 percent) became more represented in the camp population as a result of the Great Terror (and the Georgians and Armenians were still significantly underrepresented in 1939). The Ukrainian, Belorussians, Jewish, and Uzbek populations all witnessed a proportionate decline during the Great Terror.[140] The GULag evidence would suggest that if any nondiaspora nationalities were disproportionately affected, it was the Russians.

Since execution rates greatly exceeded incarceration rates in the national operations of the Great Terror, however, execution statistics are more important for evaluating the targeting of nationalities. Unfortunately, comprehensive execution statistics have not yet been published by republic or by ethnicity. Table 45 provides statistics that have recently appeared on executions during the Great Terror in Leningrad, Odessa, and Karelia.[141]

These figures generally support the hypothesis that "indigenous" non-Russians did not suffer disproportionately during the Great Terror. Once one factors out the diaspora nationalities, Russians were slightly underrepresented in Leningrad *oblast'* (95.4 percent) and overrepresented in Odessa (162.6 percent), whereas the opposite was true of Ukrainians (200.0 percent and 75.0 percent). One might assume that titular nationals were underrepresented as more nontitulars are sent to the region to occupy risky, elite positions. However, Jews were only slightly overrepresented in Leningrad (112.2 percent) and substantially underrepresented in Odessa (66.3 percent). This result is quite

Zemskov, "Victims of the Soviet Penal System in the Pre-war Years: A First Approach on the Basis of Archival Evidence," *American Historical Review* 98 (October 1993): 1028. All GULag statistics are calculated from this table.

[139] On this episode, see Oleg Hlevnjuk, "Les mécanismes de la 'Grande Terreur' des années 1937–1938 au Turkménistan," *Cahiers du monde russe* 39 (1998): 197–208.

[140] Ukrainians (103.2 percent to 83.8 percent), Belorussians (158.8 percent to 110.0 percent), Jews (87.9 percent to 84.7 percent), Uzbeks (126.3 percent to 65.5 percent). I do not have an explanation for the dramatic drop in Uzbek representation. In fact, the Uzbeks were the only listed nationality to witness an absolute decline in their prison population during the Great Terror, from 29,141 in 1937 to 19,758 in 1939.

[141] Figures were not available for the Belorussian, Ukrainian, and Tatar rural populations in Leningrad *oblast'*, so estimates were made using the 1926 census data. The same data were used to estimate what percentage of the "others" category in the census figures for all three regions was composed of diaspora nationalities. Finally, for Odessa and Karelia, it was necessary to estimate what percentage of the "others" category were diaspora nationalities. In all cases, the numbers involved were very small so errors in estimation would make a trivial difference in the calculated percentages.

Table 45. Executions by Nationality during the Great Terror

	Leningrad oblast					Odessa oblast	
Nationality	Total Executions	Percent of Total Executions	Percent of Total Executions Divided by Percent of Total Population*	Percent of Total Executions Excluding Diaspora Nationalities	Percent of Total Executions Divided by Percent of Total Population Excluding Diaspora Nationalities*	Total Executions	Percent of Total Executions
Russians	6,719	58.19	66.1	88.23	95.4	920	14.44
Ukrainians	194	1.68	138.8	2.55	200.0	1,540	24.18
Belorussians	423	3.66	571.9	5.56	829.9	270	4.24
Jews	300	2.60	77.8	3.94	112.2	329	5.17
Tatars	9	.08	12.9	.12	18.2		
Karelians							
Moldavians						79	1.24
Finns	525	4.55	230.1				
Poles	2,465	21.35	3,094.2			997	15.65
Germans	202	1.75	372.3			1,876	29.46
Estonians	531	4.60	410.7				
Latvians	86	.74	159.1				
Bulgarians						142	2.23
Total	11,547					8,689	

Calculated from *Leningradskii martirolog, 1937–1938*, vols. 1–3 (1996–1998). N. N. Danilov, "Zaryty, no ne pokhoroneny," *Memorial-Aspekt*, no. 9 (1994): 5, as cited in Rittersporn, " 'Vrednye elementy'," 100. Takala, "Natsional'nye operatsii OGPU/NKVD v Karelii," 194–195, 200.

* This number illustrates whether a given nationality was over- or under-represented in the terror. For instance, if Russians represented half of population in the region and half of those executed, the number would be 100 percent. If they represented half the population and one-quarter of those executed, the number would be 50 percent. Figures were not available for the Belorussian, Ukrainian, and Tatar rural populations in Leningrad *oblast'*, so estimates were made using the 1926 census data. The same data were used to estimate what percentage of the "others" category in the census figures for all three regions was composed of diaspora nationalities. Finally, for Odessa and Karelia, it was necessary to estimate what percentage of the "others" category were diaspora nationalities. In all cases, the numbers involved were very small so errors in estimation would make a trivial difference in the calculated percentages.

surprising. Although Jews were not targeted as a diaspora nationality, since they lacked a foreign homeland, they had extensive cross-border ties and did have some national institutions abolished in 1937–1938. They were also overrepresented in elite white-collar jobs, and for that reason alone, it has logically been assumed that they suffered disproportionately.[142] Tatars and Moldavians were both underrepresented in Leningrad and Odessa, respectively. The Karelians, on the other hand, appear to have been sufficiently tied to Finland and the Finnish population to be three times more likely than Russians to be arrested in their own autonomous republic.[143]

[142] For example, Nora Levin, *The Jews in the Soviet Union Since 1917*, vol. 1 (New York, 1990): 323–329.

[143] For an impressive analysis of the national operations and their background in Karelia, see Irina Takala, "Natsional'nye operatsii." Karelia in Vihavainen and Takala, *V sem's edinoi. Nat-*

	Odessa oblast			Karelian ASSR			
Percent of Total Executions Divided by Percent of Total Population*	Percent of Total Executions Excluding Diaspora Nationalities	Percent of Total Executions Divided by Percent of Total Population Excluding Diaspora Nationalities*	Total Arrests	Percent of Total Arrests	Percent of Total Arrests Divided by Percent of Total Population*	Percent of Total Arrests Excluding Diaspora Nationalities	Percent of Total Arrests Divided by Percent of Total Population Excluding Diaspora Nationalities*
89.7	28.54	162.6	2,874	25.34	40.2	45.74	72.3
41.2	47.78	75.0					
1,059.8	8.38	2,043.2					
36.4	10.21	66.3					
			3,059	26.97	124.1	48.69	223.2
77.5	2.45	139.2					
			4,708	41.51	1,515.1		
2,236.3							
526.0							
148.6							
			11,341 (9,750 or 85.97 percent executed)				

By far the largest surprise in Table 45 is the Belorussian figures. Excluding diaspora nationalities, Belorussians were over eight times more likely to be arrested than non-Belorussians and over *twenty* times more likely in Odessa. In both Leningrad and Odessa, Belorussians were more overrepresented than any of the diaspora nationalities except Poles. This substantial Belorussian overrepresentation is probably due to the fact that many Belorussians (and a much smaller percentage of Ukrainians) were Catholics, who in the 1920s declared themselves to be Poles and sent their children to Polish schools. Therefore, they were arrested in large numbers during the Polish operation. For example, in Belorussia itself, Belorussians made up 47.3 percent of those arrested in the Polish operation (more than the Poles at 42.3 percent). They made up 14.2 percent of those arrested in the Polish operation from September to November 1938 in the USSR as a whole, more than any other non-Polish nationality (the vastly more numerous Ukrainians were next at 13.6 percent and the still more numerous Russians at 8.8 percent). Given the high Ukrainian figure, it would not be surprising, despite the Odessa figures, if Ukrainians were also slightly overrepresented in the Soviet Union as a whole. Because Belorussia and Ukraine were home to the largest diaspora nationality populations in the Soviet Union and were high-security border regions, the NKVD was likely to be generally more active in those republics (the same would be true of Leningrad, Karelia, and the far east).

sional'naia politika partii bol'shevikov i ee osushchestvlenie na Severo-Zapade Rossii v 1920–1950-e gody (Petrozavodsk, 1998).

In short, with the probable exception of Belorussians and the possible exception of Ukrainians, the evidence available suggests "indigenous" Soviet nationalities were not intentionally or unintentionally targeted.[144] For the purpose of signaling a policy change, however, it was not only important who was targeted. The crime attributed to the terror victim was equally as important, if not more so. If in September the putative bourgeois nationalists were accused of undermining the Soviet nationalities policy, by October their agenda had already been reversed. This sudden change was the result of a major intervention by the party's highest decision-making bodies. From October to December 1937, the Politburo, Orgburo, and a TsK plenum passed a series of resolutions that tightened the ideological supervision of the translation of Marxist-Leninist classics, made the Russian language a mandatory subject in all schools, liquidated national districts and village soviets, liquidated all non-Russian schools in the Russian regions of the RSFSR, and increased the number of Russian newspapers in Ukraine.[145] In each instance, the previous policy was not acknowledged as a past error to be corrected, but rather was blamed on the malicious intrigues of bourgeois nationalists: "Artificial [national districts] were created by enemies of the people with the intention of wrecking"; "Bourgeois nationalists liquidated Russian newspapers, even though there is a large Russian population in Ukraine"; "Enemies of the people, having wormed their way into Narkompros and its local organs, over a period of years wrecked the teaching of Russian language in non-Russian schools."[146] The majority of these resolutions aimed at enhancing the role of the Russian language and blamed counterrevolutionary nationalists for its insufficiently high status. Thus, language and terror were once again allied.

This internal rhetoric quickly made itself felt in public propaganda. Ukrainian nationalists were once again accused of attempts "to divorce Ukrainian culture from fraternal Russian culture and orient the Ukrainian people on the capitalist west, on fascist Germany."[147] Remarkably, the leader of the 1933 attack on Ukrainian linguists, Andrii Khvylia, was now labeled as a nationalist linguistic purist, whose language reform had actually served Ukrainian nationalist interests. As a result, yet another language commission was formed and another new Ukrainian language reform undertaken.[148] The greatest attention was devoted to the teaching of Russian. A series of newspaper articles was devoted to this theme. The lead editorial in Uchitel'skaia gazeta for August 7, 1938 provides a good example: "The great and mighty Russian language, the language of Lenin and Stalin, Pushkin and Gorky, Tolstoi and Belinskii, is profoundly dear to all citizens of the USSR, and is studied with love by children and adults . . . [which

[144] In the mountainous regions of Chechnya, the terror provoked an armed uprising that was put down with severe repression. TsKhSD 89/73/147 (1938): 1–8.
[145] RTsKhIDNI 17/2/628 (1937): 120–123; 17/114/631 (26.10.37): 73/2; 17/114/633 (01.12.37): 75/6–8; 17/114/635 (02.01.38): 77/2, 77/4; 17/3/994 (11.12.37): 56/75–76.
[146] RTsKhIDNI 17/114/633 (1937): 75/6, 75/8; 17/114/635 (1937): 26.
[147] "Kak 'ochishchali' Ukrainskii iazyk," Pravda (04.10.37): 4.
[148] RTsKhIDNI 17/21/4687 (20.05.38): 23/43.

shows] the exclusive interest of all nationalities to the study of the language of the great Russian people, first among equals in the fraternal family of the peoples of the USSR." The only blot on this idyll was that "Trotskyist-Bukharinites and bourgeois nationalist agents of fascism attempted to separate the fraternal peoples from the great culture of the Russian people, denied non-Russian students texts and teaching aids to study Russian."[149] This article exemplified the new linguistic and cultural paradigm. Russian culture was now to serve as the core of Soviet culture (though the two were not at all identical), and the Russian language was the principal path for non-Russians to participate in that culture. Anyone opposing this paradigm was a bourgeois nationalist.

This atmosphere naturally led to an acceleration of the delatinization campaign. VTsK NA was abolished in December 1937, ending its meager resistance.[150] By April 1939, thirty-five languages had been shifted to Cyrillic.[151] The principal concern in this process was to unify the new alphabets as closely with Russian as linguistically possible.[152] As Michael Smith nicely put it, the goal now was "the vertical unification of the non-Russian scripts under a Russian standard, not the horizontal unification between the scripts of the Turkic peoples."[153] Russophilia rather than pan-Turkism was the new norm. The final alphabets shifted to Cyrillic in 1940 were those of the union republics of Central Asia. This was done with little fanfare.[154] Latinization ended with a whimper.

Conclusion

The coincidence of language and terror is striking. And not only language and terror, but terror and the revision of nationalities policy, as well as terror and the increased emphasis on the centrality and unifying role of the Russians. We have seen the first two linkages emerge in the three major waves of terror that rolled across the Soviet Union in 1929–1930, 1932–1933, and 1937–1938. The third emerged in 1932–1933 and played a dominant role in the Great Terror, as it would during the post-war terror campaigns.[155] Why did these three linkages emerge?

If for the moment we accept the second two linkages, the first linkage between language and terror is not surprising. As we have seen, language politics served a highly important symbolic function in the politics of national identity. It allowed groups to give expression to an agenda or tendency in an

---

[149] "Dat' v srok uchebniki russkogo iazyka dlia nerusskikh shkol," *uchitel'skaia gazeta*, no. 106 (07.08.38): 1.

[150] *GARF* 3316/30/784 (1937): 48–49.

[151] "S latinizirovannogo na russkii alfavit," *Izvestiia*, no. 90 (17.04.39): 4.

[152] *GARF* 2306/75/2485 (1938): 18; see also further examples in *GARF* 2306/75/2497, 2499, 2484, 2486, 2489–91, 2494 (1937–1938).

[153] Smith, *Language and Power*, 158.

[154] *SZ SSSR* (11.05.40): 16/392; (06.07.40): 20/493; (22.10.40): 29/710; (11.11.40): 30/734.

[155] Kostyrchenko, *Out of the Red Shadows*.

oblique and more politically acceptable form. Latinization allowed the expression of a mild pan-Turkism and Russophobia. It is not surprising, then, that language fulfilled the same function in the Great Retreat and Great Terror. Language was the leading edge in the rehabilitation of Russian patriotism. It was easier to rehabilitate the Russian language than Russian history or Russian thought. The Bolsheviks emerged out of the culture of the radical Russian intelligentsia, which always took special pride in one aspect of the Russian past: its creative literature. Thus, the Great Retreat also involved a rehabilitation and celebration of Russian literary figures.

On September 3, 1938, in celebration of the fifty-fifth anniversary of Turgenev's death, *Uchitelskaia gazeta* published an article entitled, "The Great, Mighty Russian Language."[156] The article quoted Turgenev's linguistic nationalism with unreserved approval: "In my days of doubt, in days of painful reflection on the fate of my fatherland—you [*ty*] alone give me support, o great, mighty, just and free Russian language!" The author then exhorted his reader that, "a protective attitude to the great Russian language is a matter of honor for the Soviet people," and concluded: "Indeed, great and mighty is the language of Pushkin and Turgenev, Tolstoi and Gorky." Only as an afterthought did he add Lenin and Stalin to this pantheon. One can easily see how such linguistic patriotism would be attractive to both the old and new Soviet intelligentsia.

The linkage between terror and revisions in nationalities policy is less clear. Why did the asymmetric use of terror against "bourgeois nationalists" rather than "great-power chauvinists" that Skrypnyk so often lamented nevertheless recur again and again? Why did terror consistently undermine rather than strengthen the Soviet nationalities policy? There are two complementary approaches to these questions. The Soviet nationalities terror campaigns were directed against the perceived improper, and therefore dangerous, expression of national identity by non-Russian elites, first the *smenovekhovtsy* and then the national communists. There is a paradox here. The Affirmative Action Empire involved the systematic promotion of non-Russian national identity, not only through the formation of national territories and strengthening of national languages, but also through the promotion of such symbolic markers as national folklore, museums, dress, food, revolutionary heroes, progressive historical events, and classic literary works. Modifying Miroslav Hroch's typology again, we might call this "Phase A" nationalism: the promotion by an elite of a nonpolitical sense of national identity. The hope was that this would prevent "Phase B" nationalism: the emergence of a nationalist elite committed to a politicized national identity. However, already by the time of the Shumskyi affair, there was concern that, as Hroch would insist, Phase A nationalism was leading to Phase B nationalism. This led to prophylactic terror against the putatively emerging nationalist elite to remove the potentially dangerous and to intimidate others. However, Stalin remained committed to the strategy of promot-

---

[156] "Velikii, moguchii russkii iazyk," *Uchitel'skaia gazeta*, no. 119 (03.09.38): 2.

ing national identity. As a result, there tended to be periodic terror campaigns against bourgeois nationalism until the end of Stalin's rule.

This helps explain the asymmetric use of terror against bourgeois nationalists, but not the linkage of terror and revision of nationalities policy. Here the mutually reinforcing role of terror and Soviet xenophobia played a more important role. All Soviet terror campaigns were carried out in the idiom of Soviet xenophobia, the exaggerated fear of foreign capitalist influence and its potential supporters. Terror victims were invariably portrayed as spies linked to foreign anti-Soviet groups and their governmental patrons. As a result, Soviet terror campaigns tended to grow increasingly xenophobic as they proceeded. Given the ethnicization of Soviet xenophobia, this led to increasing suspicions of the non-Russian periphery and their cross-border ethnic ties (linked to their elites' potential "Phase B" nationalism). It also led to an increasing emphasis on the centrality and unifying role of the Russian nation, hence the third linkage between terror and the reemergence of the Russians. If we look at the period from 1928 to 1933 as an extended terror campaign, it began in an internationalist and Russophobic idiom and ended in a xenophobic and Russophilic mode. The Great Terror likewise initially seemed to promise a revival of *korenizatsiia* but turned increasingly xenophobic so that by the end of 1938, its primary targets were diaspora nationalities and its primary policy implication was the strengthening and celebrating of the centrality, primacy, and unifying function of the RSFSR and the Russian nation. In the next chapter, we will look at how the new status of the Russians was integrated into the preexisting nationalities policy to produce a new Soviet national constitution: the Friendship of the Peoples.

II

The Friendship of the Peoples

The major changes made to the Soviet nationalities policy after December 1932 necessitated the articulation of a new principle of unity for the multiethnic Soviet state. In December 1935, Stalin introduced the metaphor of the Friendship of the Peoples. The metaphor proved felicitous. It granted the Russians, Russian culture, and the RSFSR a primary role as the motive force that forged and sustained the friendship, but it did not imply either russification or the formation of a Russian-dominated Soviet nation. In fact, the large, compact, "indigenous" non-Russian nationalities that survived the process of ethnic consolidation in the mid-1930s saw their sovereignty and status as Soviet nations newly strengthened. Moreover, the gradual turn toward a primordial conception of nationality during the Great Retreat led to an intensified cultivation of the separate and historically deep national identities of the recognized Soviet nationalities, both Russians and non-Russians. As a result, the Friendship of the Peoples, as well as a xenophobic enmity of the peoples, was gradually projected backward in time. By 1938, the Friendship of the Peoples was the officially sanctioned metaphor of an imagined multinational community.

The Brotherhood of the Peoples

The roots of the Friendship of the Peoples as a metaphor to represent and further Soviet unity lay in an earlier and aborted Soviet campaign to promote a Brotherhood of the Peoples (*bratstvo narodov*). Brotherhood was the classic socialist metaphor for proletarian unity both within a given national culture and among the world proletariat. Throughout the 1920s, the Soviet government used the brotherhood metaphor in this manner.[1] However, it played a minor role in state efforts to promote Soviet unity. In fact, throughout the 1920s, it is striking how little attention was devoted to creating an image of the Soviet Union as a unified multiethnic state. Instead, discussions about national culture were confined to the non-Russian republics. There were vigorous debates, to cite a few examples, about the nature of the Ukrainian, Belorussian, Tatar, and Buriat-Mongolian national cultures, but not about the multiethnic dimension of Soviet culture.[2] This was intentional. The Affirmative Action Empire was premised on the belief that multiethnic Soviet unity would be furthered by granting the non-Russians maximal national self-expression within the constraints of a unitary Soviet state. Soviet unity would emerge spontaneously as a result of the disarming of non-Russian nationalism, which would in turn lead to a focus on class interests and so interethnic proletarian brotherhood. This was a highly indirect strategy for achieving Soviet unity.

The perceived need for a more direct and active promotion of Soviet unity emerged as a result of the Shumskyi affair in Ukraine. Mykola Khvylovyi's passionate advocacy of a western rather than a Muscovite (understood as Russian) orientation for Ukrainian culture provoked Stalin to insist firmly on a Muscovite (understood as proletarian) and not western (understood as Polish) orientation. It was not yet clear, however, what such an orientation on proletarian Moscow would imply. The initial phase of the cultural revolution led to a strong movement within the Bolshevik Party to repudiate the Affirmative Action Empire and form instead a united proletarian Soviet nation. Stalin decisively rejected this movement. Instead, an alternative strategy was proposed: a campaign to propagandize the Brotherhood of the Peoples, a campaign that required no repudiation of separate national identities but did involve more active efforts to foster multiethnic Soviet unity.

The brotherhood campaign was propagandistic and symbolic. It did not involve a repudiation of the Affirmative Action Empire. The principal device in this symbolic campaign was the visit of non-Russian delegations to Moscow— a city presented as the center of the proletarian revolution, not the capital of Russia—both to demonstrate and to further the Brotherhood of the Soviet Peoples. The first such visit to receive aggressive propagandistic treatment was the visit of a delegation of Ukrainian writers to Moscow in February 1929. Their visit would establish the paradigm for the entire 1930s' genre of fraternal visits. There were public meetings between Ukrainian and Russian authors, literary performances, exhibitions of Ukrainian art, plans to translate Ukrainian literary

---

[1] Joshua Sanborn, "Family, Fraternity, and Nation-building in Russia, 1905–1925," in Ronald Grigor Suny and Terry Martin, eds., *A State of Nations: Empire and Nation-Building in the Age of Lenin and Stalin* (Oxford, 2001).

[2] Myroslav Shkandrij, *Modernists, Marxists and the Nation* (Edmonton, 1992). Anthony Adamovich, *Opposition to Sovietization in Belorussian Literature* (New York, 1958). S. Ibragimov, *Voprosy natsional'noi kul'tury* (Ashkabad, 1928). *Materialy k pervomu kul'turno-natsional'nomu soveshchaniiu BMASSR* (Verkhneudinsk, 1926).

works into Russian, and meetings with the Moscow proletariat.[3] The Party's Agitprop Department sponsored a special "Party Conference on Fostering Closer Ties (*sblizhenie*) between Russian and Ukrainian Writers."[4] The goal of this visit, according to *Pravda*, was to overcome "the well-known isolation" of the literary intelligentsias of the two "fraternal peoples" and to promote an "alliance" (*smychka*) between them.[5] Mykola Skrypnyk defined the "historic and political significance" of this "brotherly visit" as "the final liquidation of the old misunderstandings and distrust," which he acknowledged had not yet been fully overcome.[6]

The climax of the Ukrainian visit, and this again served as a model for future fraternal visits, was a private audience with Stalin. The transcript of this meeting illustrates that, despite some provocative questions from the Ukrainian writers, Stalin made every effort to create a positive impression. Stalin took this occasion to present his first public address on the relationship of the socialist offensive to nationalities policy, during which he reassured the Ukrainian writers of his commitment to "the maximum development and protection of national culture." He playfully hinted at his ongoing interest in the annexation of Galicia. He even agreed to consider suppressing Bulgakov's *The Days of the Turbins*, which the Ukrainian writers denounced as egregious Russian *smenovekhovstvo*.[7] Like Skrypnyk, Stalin admitted that the historic distrust between Russians and non-Russians had not yet been fully overcome, but that such meetings would help achieve that goal. In a revised version of this speech, Stalin declared that once historic distrust had been overcome, the result would be a "friendship between the peoples" of the USSR.[8] Thus, Stalin had already made the connection in his mind between such fraternal visits and the future slogan of the Friendship of the Peoples.

This "Ukrainian week" was followed over the course of the next two years by a series of similar literary events in Moscow: a Tatar visit in September 1929 and a much-publicized "Belorussian week" in January 1931.[9] This visit was directly inspired by Volodymyr Zatonskyi's alarmist 1929 Rabkrin report on the growth of Belorussian nationalism. Zatonskyi had noted the positive impression made on the Ukrainian literary community by their Moscow visit and

[3] "Ukrainskie pisateli v Moskve," *Pravda*, no. 33 (09.02.29): 2; "Ukrainskaia nedelia nachalas'," no. 34 (10.02.29): 3; "Ukrainskaia nedelia," no. 35 (12.02.29): 3; "Smychka ukrainskikh pisatelei s moskovskimi rabochimi," no. 36 (13.02.29): 2; "Ukrainskie pisateli v Moskve," no. 37 (14.02.29): 3.

[4] "Partiinoe soveshchanie o sblizhenii russkikh i ukrainskikh pisatelei," *Pravda*, no. 33 (09.02.29): 2.

[5] "Ukrainskie pisateli," 2.

[6] M. Skrypnyk, "Ukrains'kyi tyzhden u Moskvi," in *Statti i promovy*, vol. 2, part 1, 353. See also his article, 349–352.

[7] *RTsKhIDNI* 558/1/4490 (12.02.29): 8, 22–28, 32.

[8] Stalin, "Natsional'nyi vopros i leninizm," *Sochineniia*, vol. 11, 338.

[9] "Pisateliam krasnogo Tatarstana—nash privet!" *Literaturnaia gazeta*, no. 22 (16.09.29): 1. On the Belorussian visit, see the numerous articles in *Literaturnaia gazeta*, no. 61 (1930), nos. 1–3 (1931); *Pravda*, nos. 4–7 (1931).

strongly recommended a similar event for Belorussia.[10] In addition to these single-nationality events, the summer of 1930 witnessed an all-union theatrical olympiad in Moscow, which featured fifteen different national theaters, ten national musical ensembles, and nine national film organizations.[11] The period from 1929 to 1931 also witnessed the first large wave of translations of non-Russian Soviet literature into Russian.[12] *Literaturnaia gazeta* began, for the first time, to publicize the literary achievements of the Soviet Union's smaller nationalities.[13] The Soviet Union's hegemonic writers' organization, VOAPP, which had been notorious for ignoring national literature, suddenly devoted a session of its May 1931 plenum to national culture.[14]

These literary campaigns shared common rhetorical tropes and were clearly part of a unified campaign to address the perceived national disunity of the NEP period. The most common theme was the need to overcome "national isolation" and "put an end to disunity."[15] These events were said to strengthen "the links between the fraternal union republics," promote "fraternal solidarity," and further the "consolidation of the national ranks of the Soviet proletariat." Most interestingly, they helped build an "alliance (*smychka*) between the Soviet peoples."[16] This was a new usage of the word *smychka*. In the 1920s, this term had been reserved, in nationalities policy discussions, for the alliance between the primarily native peasantry and primarily Russian proletariat within each national republic. This made it part of the larger peasant—proletariat *smychka*. Now *smychka* was being detached from its class referent and applied instead to an above-class alliance between entire nations. This was an important innovation that would eventually form the core of the doctrine of the Friendship of the Peoples in the late 1930s.

However, as both Stalin and Skrypnyk emphasized during the Ukrainian visit, the *smychka* had not yet been attained. Distrust between Russians and non-Russians had not yet been overcome. This distinguished the literary meetings of the cultural revolution era from their successors during the Great Retreat. The former were presented more as battles to attain unity than celebrations of an achieved unity. They took place against a background of

[10] *GARF* 374/27s/1691 (1929): 9.

[11] "Privet uchastnikam vsesoiuznoi olimpiady iskusstv narodov SSSR," *Literaturnaia gazeta*, no. 24 (16.06.30): 4. A miniature North Caucasian theatrical olympiad likewise took place in Rostov in late 1931. I. T., "Natsional'nomu iskussvu bol'shevistskoe razvitie (K itogam kraevoi olimpiady gorskikh iskusstv)," *Revoliutsiia i gorets*, no. 1 (1932): 81–86.

[12] "Pisateliam krasnogo Tatarstana," 1; "Nedelia belorusskogo iskusstva i literatury," *Literaturnaia gazeta*, no. 19 (12.05.30): 1; "Na fronte natsional'noi knigi," no. 24 (05.05.31): 3.

[13] "Za boevuiu mordovskuiu literaturu!" *Literaturnaia gazeta*, no. 40 (25.07.31): 2; "Nogaitsy smeiutsia," no. 44 (15.08.31); "Itogi tvorcheskogo goda v chuvashskoi literature," no. 44 (15.08.31): 4.

[14] "Smotr natsional'nykh otriadov proletarskoi literatury," *Literaturnaia gazeta*, no. 29 (30.05.31): 1. See also articles in *RAPP*, nos. 3–6 (1931).

[15] Peredovaia, "Sblizhenie natsional'nykh otriadov sovetskoi literatury," *Literaturnaia gazeta*, no. 8 (10.06.29): 1; Peredovaia, "Usilim vzaimodeistvie kul'tur narodov SSSR," no. 24 (16.06.30): 1; "Za literaturnuiu olimpiadu," no. 36 (20.08.30): 1.

[16] Peredovaia, "Zveno bratskoi sviazi," *Literaturnaia gazeta*, no. 3 (14.01.31): 1.

constant arrests and show trials of literary figures in the non-Russian republics.[17]
A December 1930 lead article in *Literaturnaia gazeta* noted that "it is no
accident that in almost all cases, the members of counterrevolutionary organizations are writers."[18] Only weeks before his anticipated arrival as the star
member of the Belorussian writers' delegation, the "profoundly national poet"
Ianka Kupala was arrested as a counterrevolutionary.[19] The literary visits, therefore, were presented as a form of class warfare that would "strike a devastating
blow at both petty-bourgeois chauvinists and reactionary Great Power attitudes."[20] As part of this class war theme, the national writers always visited
prominent Moscow factories to emphasize their proletarian credentials.[21] The
Belorussian writers' delegation was even accompanied by a group of Belorussian factory workers.

An uninhibited celebration of traditional national culture also still lay in the
future. The literary visits of the cultural revolution were marked by a strong
suspicion of völkisch tendencies. In particular, what we would now call orientalism was frequently denounced: "Great power chauvinists interpret national
culture as primarily exotica."[22] On the eve of the theatrical olympiad, another
polemicist likewise accused the Russian intelligentsia of viewing national art
purely "as exotica, as art with only an ethnographic interest and not an aes-
thetic or socio-cultural one."[23] National artists were also accused of catering
to this great-power prejudice, of engaging in "a hypertrophic fetishization of
national forms."[24] At a session of the May 1931 VOAPP plenum devoted to
national culture, Averbakh said that 90 percent of the time national folklore
was being used with no understanding of its class nature, which led to "an uncritical relationship to the national culture of the past."[25]

Finally, the status of Russian culture still remained uncertain. The brotherhood campaign brought new visibility to Russian culture since national culture was now being discussed in an all-union context. The metaphor of the
Brotherhood of the Peoples implied an equal status for Russian culture (the
"elder brother" had not yet appeared) and this would have involved a challenge

---

[17] For the constant stream of such reports, see *Literaturnaia gazeta*, no. 29 (04.11.29); no. 12
(24.03.30): 1; no. 21 (26.05.30): 2; no. 21 (26.05.30): 4; no. 33 (05.08.30): 2; no. 38 (30.08.30): 2;
no. 43 (24.09.30): 3; no. 54 (20.11.20): 4; no. 56 (29.11.30): 4; no. 57 (04.12.30); no. 59 (14.12.30):
1; no. 60 (19.12.30): 1; no. 2 (09.01.31): 2.

[18] Peredovaia, "Protiv natsional-demokratizma!" *Literaturnaia gazeta* (14.12.30): 1.

[19] "Ianka Kupala," *Literaturnaia gazeta*, no. 21 (26.05.30): 1.

[20] "Privet uchastnikam," 4.

[21] "Smychka ukrainskikh pisatelei," 2; "Pisateliam krasnogo Tatarstana," 1; "Za vsesoiuznuiu
literaturnuiu olimpiadu," *Literaturnaia gazeta*, no. 35 (15.08.30): 1; "Dnevnik 'nedeli'," no. 1
(04.01.31): 1.

[22] V. Kovalenko, "Proletarskaia literatura SSSR v bor'be za leninskoe natsional'no-kul'turnoe
stroitel'stvo," *RAPP*, nos. 1–2 (1932): 49.

[23] Peredovaia, "Usilim vzaimodeistvie kul'tur narodov SSSR," *Literaturnaia gazeta*, no. 24
(16.06.30): 1.

[24] E. Gal'perina, "Formy proiavleniia velikoderzhavnogo shovinizma v literaturovedenii i
kritike," *RAPP*, nos. 5–6 (1931): 47.

[25] L. Averbakh, "Stroitel'stvo sotsializma i natsional'naia kul'tura," *RAPP*, no. 3 (1931): 5.

to the Affirmative Action Empire. In line with this tendency, Russian literary figures were rebuked not only for their great-power condescension to and exoticization of non-Russian national culture, but also for "defining Great Russian culture as 'above-national' [*sverkh-natsional'naia*]. Under the concept national culture, they understand only the cultures of the formerly oppressed peoples. . . . [This is] a manifestation of great power swinishness."[26] The origins of such swinishness were clear enough. The Affirmative Action Empire did deny Russians ordinary national status and so did transform the Russians into a kind of "above-national" nationality, whose culture was either downplayed or identified with Soviet culture as a whole. However, despite this incipient movement toward establishing Russian culture as an ordinary Soviet national culture, Russians still continued to be labeled the former great-power nationality. Stalin still insisted that non-Russian distrust had not yet been overcome. Great-power chauvinism remained the greater danger. Therefore, Russians continued to occupy an awkward place in the emerging Soviet brotherhood. The cultural revolution, then, witnessed more the articulation of a problem, the need for a more active principle of Soviet unity, than a solution to that problem.

The Friendship of the Peoples

On December 4, 1935, the Kremlin hosted a gathering in honor of forty-three Tajik and thirty-three Turkmen "progressive" *kolkhozniki* who had distinguished themselves during the last cotton harvest. The most important members of the Politburo were all present: Stalin, Molotov, Kaganovich, Voroshilov, Ordzhonikidze, Mikoian, Chubar, Andreev, Rudzutak.[27] For two days, *Pravda* devoted most of its pages to this meeting.[28] This gathering was not original. Similar meetings had already been held in honor of Russian collective farmers and industrial Stakhanovites. The Central Asian gathering represented a national version of this new Soviet ritual. Following the established ceremonial procedure, the Soviet leadership listened to speeches from the participants about their accomplishments. Stalin periodically would interrupt with polite questions and earnest promises of aid.[29] One participant, Epa Geldyeva, presented Stalin with a hand-woven carpet featuring Lenin's portrait as a present from Turkmen women in thanks to Stalin for "the happy life given to us."[30] A ten-year-old pioneer girl, Mamlakat Nakhangova, likewise gave Stalin a copy of his own book, *Questions of Leninism*, in a Tajik translation. According to *Pravda*'s correspondent, "Stalin is touched . . . with rapid steps he approaches

[26] A. Selibanovskii, "O velikoderzhavnosti," *Literaturnaia gazeta*, no. 61 (24.12.30): 1.
[27] "Na soveshchanii v Kremle," *Pravda*, no. 334 (05.12.35): 1.
[28] See *Pravda*, no. 334 (05.12.35): 1–2; no. 335 (06.12.35): 1–3.
[29] "Soveshchanie peredovykh kolkhoznikov i kolkhoznits Tadzhikistana i Turkmenistana s rukovoditeliami partii i pravitel'stva," *Pravda*, no. 334 (05.12.35): 2.
[30] "Velikaia druzhba," *Pravda*, no. 334 (05.12.35): 1.

the pioneer girl, Mamlakat, and gives the happy girl a gold watch and then, in a fatherly fashion, he embraces and kisses her."[31]

As with its Russian counterparts, this meeting was designed to emphasize Stalin's paternal concern for the common people and their corresponding child-like gratitude and love for him.[32] Such statist paternalism was typical of the Great Retreat era. What was novel about the national version of these events was the extreme emphasis now being placed on national distinctiveness. The numerous photographs accompanying the Kremlin reception all showed the participants dressed in traditional native costumes.[33] The ceremony even involved the participants presenting each Politburo member with a national Turkmen or Tajik outfit.[34] Moreover, most of the published photographs of the event featured Central Asian women who, although not fully veiled, all wore scarves that modestly covered their hair and necks. This was true even of the gathering's star performer, the ten-year-old Mamlakut.[35] *Pravda*'s official accounts strongly emphasized the use of Turkmen and Tajik by all the national participants.[36] Molotov even opened his speech with a greeting of "Comrades!" in Turkmen and Tajik.[37]

Model "progressive" national *kolkhozniki*, then, did not abandon their national identity, but rather zealously preserved it and used it to express their Soviet loyalty. Stalin elaborated on this theme in his brief speech. Again following the pattern of previous Russian gatherings, after first announcing that each collective farm represented at the event would receive a truck and each participant would be given a watch and a gramophone with records, Stalin complimented the participants on their success with the cotton harvest.[38] He then continued:

> But comrades, there is one thing more valuable than cotton—that is the friendship of the peoples of our country. Today's gathering, your speeches, your deeds witness that the friendship between the peoples of our great country is strengthening. This is very important and noteworthy.

Stalin contrasted this current friendship with the Tsarist period, when the government attempted "to make one people—the Russian people—the ruling people and all others peoples—subordinate, repressed. This was a savage, wolflike policy." After eighteen years of Soviet rule, Stalin noted, the deleterious consequences of Tsarist policy had been overcome[39]:

---

[31] Ibid., 1.

[32] To cite *Pravda*, "with such love and devotion, so warmly and sincerely the *kolkhozniki* and *kolkhoznitsy* of Tajikistan and Turkmenistan greeted comrade Stalin."

[33] *Pravda*, no. 334 (05.12.35): 1–2, 6; no. 335 (06.12.35): 1–2, 4.

[34] "Na soveshchanii v Kremle," 1.

[35] *Pravda*, no. 334 (05.12.35): 1–2, 6; no. 335 (06.12.35): 1–2, 4.

[36] "Velikoe bratstvo svobodnykh narodov," *Pravda*, no. 335 (06.12.35): 1.

[37] "Rech' tov. Molotova," *Pravda*, no. 335 (06.12.35): 3.

[38] "Rech' tov. Stalina," *Pravda*, no. 335 (06.12.35): 3.

[39] Ibid., 3.

Today's meeting is a striking proof of the fact that the former distrust between the peoples of the USSR has already come to an end. That distrust has been replaced with a complete mutual trust. The friendship between the peoples of the USSR is growing and strengthening. That, comrades, is the most valuable of all that the Bolshevik nationalities policy has produced.

And the friendship between the peoples of the USSR is a great and serious victory. For while this friendship exists, the peoples of our country will be free and unconquerable. While this friendship lives and blossoms, we are afraid of no one, neither internal nor external enemies. You can have no doubt about this, comrades. [Wild applause, all present stand and yell: "Stalin, Hurrah!"]

Stalin's brief remarks initiated an important reimagination of the Soviet Union's national constitution.[40]

The next four months witnessed a series of highly publicized national "meetings" and "receptions" at the Kremlin that clearly formed part of a con-scious campaign to promote the newly announced Friendship of the Peoples. On December 19, "progressive" *kolkhozniki* from three other Central Asian republics—Uzbekistan, Kazakhstan, and Kara-Kalpakia—gathered in the Kremlin for a similar meeting.[41] Eleven days later, an all-class delegation from Armenia was publicly received in the Kremlin by the Politburo.[42] The Armenian meeting served as a model for Kremlin receptions of delegations from Azerbaijan (January 21), Buriat-Mongolia (January 27), and Georgia (March 19).[43] As with the Tajik-Turkmen event, the leading members of the Politburo, including Stalin, always attended these receptions. *Pravda* gave these events front-page coverage and liberally included symbolic photographs depicting the friendship.[44] The Buriat-Mongolian reception provided one of the most famous photographs of the Stalin cult, that of Stalin paternally holding in his arms a young Buriat-Mongol six-year-old, Geleia Markizovaia, who was smiling broadly while presenting Stalin with a bouquet of flowers.[45]

After the Georgian reception in March 1936, the campaign to promote the friendship of the Peoples returned to its literary roots. The favored symbolic demonstration of the friendship became periodic "weeks of national art" (*dekady natsional'nogo iskusstva*) held in Moscow. These festivals involved the

---

[40] Lowell Tillett, *The Great Friendship* (Chapel Hill, N.C., 1969).

[41] "Soveshchanie peredovykh kolkhoznikov i kolkhoznits Uzbekistana, Kazakstana i Kara-Kalpkii s rukovoditeliami partii i pravitel'stva," *Pravda*, no. 350 (21.12.35): 1.

[42] "Priem delegatsii trudiashchikhsia sovetskoi Armenii v Kremle," *Pravda*, no. 350 (31.12.35): 1.

[43] "Priem delegatsii sovetskogo Azerbaidzhana rukovoditeliami partii i pravitel'stva v Kremle," *Pravda*, no. 23 (24.01.36): 1; "Priem delegatov trudiashchikhsia Buriat-Mongol'skoi ASSR rukovoditeliami partii i pravitel'stva v Kremle," no. 29 (30.01.36): 1; "Priem delegatsii sovetskoi Gruzii rukovoditeliami partii i pravitel'stva v Kremle," no. 80 (21.03.36): 1. The formulaic titles demonstrate that these meetings were seen as part of a single larger campaign.

[44] For a few examples of such photographs, see *Pravda*, no. 350 (21.12.35): 1, 5; 352 (23.12.35): 1; no. 360 (31.12.35): 1; no. 1 (02.01.36): 2; no. 23 (24.01.36): 1; no. 27 (29.01.36): 3; no. 29 (30.01.36): 1; no. 80 (21.03.36): 1.

[45] *Pravda*, no. 29 (30.01.36): 1.

arrival in Moscow of a sizable delegation of artists from a given republic, who would organize artistic exhibitions and literary evenings and present a series of theatrical performances. The latter were always considered the highlight of the *dekady*. The favored theatrical form was the musical opera with a generous dollop of folk music and dancing. In 1936 and 1937, there were four major national *dekady*: Ukrainian (March 1936), Kazakh (May 1936), Georgian (January 1937), and Uzbek (May 1937).[46] The *dekady* received even more extensive press coverage than the preceding Kremlin receptions. Each *dekada* culminated with Politburo attendance at a theatrical performance. A Kremlin reception for the national artists would follow, at which awards would be lavishly distributed to the national artists.[47]

All of these events were suffused with the new rhetorical trope of the Friendship of the Peoples. This could hardly have been accidental. Prior to Stalin's use of this phrase at the Tajik-Turkmen meeting, it was almost entirely absent from Soviet rhetoric. The standard metaphor was the Brotherhood of the Peoples. Stalin also used the brotherhood metaphor more frequently prior to 1935, though he had occasionally employed the friendship motif. On one occasion, in an April 1917 editorial, Stalin even used the exact formulation he would later canonize, when he insisted that only granting the right of separation could "strengthen trust and the friendship of the peoples [*usilit' doverie i druzhbu narodov*]."[48] On a second occasion, in the revised version of his February 1929 speech to the Ukrainian writers, a speech in which he first seriously dealt with the problem of establishing a new principle of unity for the Soviet state, Stalin again spoke of the goal of "friendship among the peoples [*druzhba mezhdu narodami*]."[49] Already in 1929, Stalin associated the friendship metaphor with a future revision of the Soviet national constitution.

It is not surprising, then, that when Stalin turned to the task of providing a new formulation of the Soviet national constitution to assimilate the fundamental changes made to the Soviet nationalities policy after December 1932, he returned to the Friendship of the Peoples. Within months of the December 1935 Central Asian meeting, this metaphor had become ubiquitous. The next-day *Pravda*'s account of the Tajik-Turkmen meeting was entitled "The Great Friendship."[50] When the second meeting of Central Asian *kolkhozniki* assembled two weeks later, Molotov instructed his audience that "the friendship of the peoples of the Soviet Union [is] our great strength in the battle for a better life."[51] When Molotov published a collection of his speeches at the Kremlin

[46] "Dekada Ukrainskogo iskusstva v Moskve," *Literaturnaia gazeta*, no. 18 (27.03.36): 4; "Privet masteram literatury i iskusstva vozrozhdennogo Kazakhstana!" no. 28 (15.05.36): 2; "K dekade gruzinskogo iskusstva," no. 1 (05.01.37): 3; "Dekada Uzbekskogo iskusstva," no. 29 (30.05.37): 3;

[47] For example, see "Zakonchilis' spektakli Kazakhskogo muzykal'nogo teatra v Moskve," *Literaturnaia gazeta*, no. 30 (24.05.36): 1.

[48] Stalin, "Kontrrevoliutsiia i narody Rossii," (1917) in *Sochineniia*, vol. 3, 208.

[49] Stalin, "Natsional'nyi vopros i leninizm," 339.

[50] "Velikaia druzhba," 1.

[51] V. M. Molotov, *Velikaia druzhba narodov SSSR* (Moscow, 1936): 19.

gatherings of December 1935 to March 1936, he naturally gave it the title: "The Great Friendship of the Peoples of the USSR." Given this unprecedented promotion of a new metaphor for describing the multiethnic Soviet state by the Bolsheviks' highest leaders, a careful examination of its significance seems in order.

Already in August 1917, Stalin had linked the development of mutual "trust" (*doverie*) with the emergence of a "friendship of the peoples." Eighteen years later, he declared that this process was over: "The former distrust between the peoples of the USSR has already come to an end" and a Friendship of the Peoples had emerged.[52] In his speech on the adoption of the new Soviet constitution in November 1936, Stalin reiterated his belief that the former "feeling of mutual distrust has disappeared, a feeling of mutual friendship has developed among [the Soviet peoples], and thus real fraternal cooperation among the peoples has been established."[53] These two statements were exceedingly important. The historically justifiable non-Russian distrust (*nedoverie*) of Russians was a pillar of the Affirmative Action Empire. It dictated the principle that great-power chauvinism was the greatest danger and justified the corresponding downplaying of Russian national self-expression and stigmatizing of traditional Russian culture. By 1934, however, Stalin had declared the greatest-danger principle an irrelevancy and the rehabilitation of traditional Russian culture had already begun. Stalin's statements provided an ideological justification for both these processes. One aspect of the Friendship of the Peoples, then, was the rehabilitation of Russian national culture.

For that purpose, however, the existing brotherhood metaphor would have served equally well. Why, then, the abrupt switch to friendship? Oddly, although brotherhood literally denotes an intimate family tie, in communist rhetoric it was strongly associated with class militancy. It did not connote domestic affection, but rather public solidarity. As such, brotherhood was the ideal metaphor for the militant 1929–1931 campaign, whose stated goal was the direction of international proletarian solidarity against each nation's internal class enemies and against great-power chauvinists. With the end of cultural revolution and the onset of the Great Retreat, this class militancy disappeared from the 1935–1938 friendship campaign. Both factory visits and denunciations of nationalist and great-power deviations disappeared from the agenda of these visits. Instead of hatred for internal class enemies, the new emphasis was on the nationalities' "feeling of love" for one another and, of course, for Comrade Stalin.[54] The emotions being highlighted were now intimate and personal. Instead of factory visits, delegates now received watches and gramophones. The friendship metaphor better conveyed this new affective tie.

The Friendship of the Peoples did allow for one form of militancy, that directed against foreign enemies. In a frequently cited portion of his Decem-

[52] "Rech' tov. Stalina," 3.
[53] Joseph Stalin, *Marxism and the National Question* (New York, 1942): 218.
[54] A. Tatarishvili, "Poeziia druzhby narodov," *Pravda*, no. 244 (04.09.36): 3.

ber 1935 remarks, Stalin asserted that "while this friendship exists, the peoples of our country will be free and unconquerable. While this friendship lives and blossoms, we are afraid of no one, neither internal nor external enemies."[55] The internal enemies referred to here were no longer defined as class enemies, but "enemies of the [Soviet] people," a category that included the enemy nations who had been excommunicated from the Soviet family of peoples and subjected to ethnic cleansing. The adjectives most frequently attached to the Friendship of the Peoples emphasized defense against foreign aggression: "mighty," "unbreakable," "unconquerable."[56]

Stalinist Primordialism

The friendship campaign of 1935–1938 differed from the brotherhood campaign of 1929–1931 not only in the substitution of national amity for class hatred, but also in a changed attitude to the concept of nationality itself. The Affirmative Action Empire was premised on the belief that nations were fundamentally modern constructs, a product of capitalism and industrialization. Stalin had stated this belief clearly in his 1913 pamphlet, *Marxism and the Nationalities Question*[57]:

> What is a Nation?
>
> A nation is, above all, a definite community of people. This community is not racial, nor is it tribal. The modern Italian nation was formed from Romans, Teutons, Etruscans, Greeks, Arabs, and so forth. The French nation was formed from Gauls, Romans, Bretons, Teutons, and so on. The same can be said of the English, Germans and others, who consolidated into nations out of different races and tribes.
>
> Thus, a nation is not racial or tribal, but *a historically constituted community of people.* [my italics]

This was an unexceptional, orthodox statement of contemporary Marxist thought. In opposition to the widespread belief in the historic depth of national identity, Marxists asserted that nations were fundamentally modern constructs. In Stalin's words: "A nation is not merely a historical category, but a historical category belonging to a definite epoch, the epoch of rising capitalism."[58] During the Great Retreat, however, there was a dramatic

---

[55] "Rech' tov. Stalina," 3.

[56] Peredovaia, "Nerushimaia druzhba," *Pravda*, no. 80 (21.03.36): 1; M. Bazhan, "Druzhba narodov," no. 193 (15.07.36): 2; E. Evdokimov, "Nepobedimyi soiuz narodov," no. 308 (07.11.36): 6; Peredovaia, "Sviataia liubov' k rodine," no. 341 (12.12.36): 1.

[57] I. Stalin, "Marksizm i nasional'nyi vopros," (1913) in *Marksizm i natsional'no-kolonial'nyi vopros* (Moscow, 1934): 4.

[58] Stalin, *Marksizm*, 10.

turn away from the former Soviet view of nations as fundamentally modern constructs and toward an emphasis on the deep primordial roots of modern nations.[59]

This was evident in the changed attitude toward the national exotic. In the brotherhood campaign, the exoticization of national culture—the excessive and uncritical use of the folkloric—was one of the chief sins attributed to both nationalists and especially great-power chauvinists. In the friendship campaign, this concern disappeared entirely and the folkloric and exotic were celebrated uncritically. National dance and song were at the center of the 1936 Ukrainian *dekada*.[60] Even their operas included national dances and songs.[61] *Pravda* celebrated "the uniquely distinctive [*svoeobraznyi*] art of the Ukrainian folk."[62] At the Kazakh *dekada*, the star performers were the *Akyny*, traditional Kazakh musical improvisers who were asked to perform at the Kremlin reception for the Kazakh artists.[63] Similarly, the Kremlin reception for Georgian artists at the end of their *dekada* featured a performance by a Georgian "ethnographic choir."[64] Photographs of the *dekady*, like the Tajik-Turkmen Kremlin reception, invariably focused on national costumes.[65] A highly clichéd essentializing rhetoric of national character even began to appear. During the Georgian *dekada*, Georgia was invariably referred to as "sunny, socialist Georgia" and their fine weather was said to explain their "joyful" national art.[66]

In addition to this new affirmation of the exotic, there was a simultaneous classicizing trend. During the brotherhood campaign, new works about the revolution had been favored. This emphasis reversed with the friendship campaign, which instead favored, where they existed, prerevolutionary "classics." This dovetailed with the folkloric theme, since in both cases the intent was to stress the depth and historicity of national culture, as opposed to the previous empha-

[59] I use the word "primordial" here to refer to a belief in both the antiquity of modern nations and the fundamental continuity in a nation's essence across time. This is also sometimes called "essentialism." The primordialist/modernist dispute in nationalities studies is already an old and increasingly unproductive one. For a summary with bibliography, see the introduction to John Hutchinson and Anthony B. Smith, eds., *Ethnicity* (Oxford, 1996): 3–16.

[60] O. Litovskii, "Dekada Ukrainskogo iskusstva v Moskve," *Literaturnaia gazeta*, no. 18 (27.03.36): 4; "Fol'klor narodov SSSR," no. 20 (05.04.36): 4; Andrei Khvylia, "Ukrainskoe narodnoe tvorchestvo," *Pravda*, no. 35 (05.02.36): 4.

[61] "Ukrainskaia opera v Moskve," *Pravda*, no. 82 (23.03.36): 4.

[62] V. Kemenov, "Narodnoe iskusstvo Ukrainy," *Pravda*, no. 212 (03.08.36): 4.

[63] "Akyny Kazakhstana," *Literaturnaia gazeta*, no. 27 (10.05.36): 4; "Zakonchilis' spektakli," 1.

[64] "Priem v Kremle uchastnikov dekady gruzinskogo iskusstva," *Literaturnaia gazeta*, no. 3 (15.01.37): 1.

[65] See, for example, the photographs in *Literaturnaia gazeta* during the Kazakh *dekada* in nos. 27–28 (10–15.05.36).

[66] Tamara Vakhvakhishvili, "Gruzinskaia narodnaia pliaska," *Literaturnaia gazeta*, no. 1 (05.01.37): 3; Peredovaia, "Prazdnik sotsialisticheskoi kul'tury," no. 2 (10.01.37): 1; "Solnechnyi prazdnik iskusstva," no. 3 (15.01.37): 5.

sis on the novelty of Soviet national cultures. The popularization of the non-Russian classics was a major theme of the first all-union congress of Soviet Writers in August 1934: "Those peoples who prior to the revolution created cultural treasures, especially in artistic literature, only now have the possibility to acquaint other [Soviet] nationalities and the whole world with them."[67]

In particular, it was considered important that each nation have its own "people's poet" (*narodnyi poet*). Novelists were apparently too superficially modern, since almost all candidates were lyric or epic poets. The Shevchenko cult in Ukraine flourished.[68] Between 1933 and 1938, the Ukrainian Politburo discussed Shevchenko at least eleven times: celebrations of his birth and death, construction of a monument, publication of his works, newly discovered documents about Shevchenko.[69] *Pravda* devoted considerable attention to the erection of a Shevchenko monument in Kharkov.[70] The same was true of the even more elaborate cult of the medieval Georgian poet, Shota Rustaveli.[71] When adequate prerevolutionary poets did not exist, a contemporary poet had to be elevated. The most striking case was the populist nationalist, Ianka Kupala, who was made Belorussia's people's poet in the 1920s, then arrested as a nationalist in 1930, but quickly released and bestowed with an all-union cult in the 1930s.[72] The partiality for traditional folkloric poets was also evident in the all-union status given to the Dagestani and Kazakh people's poets, Suleiman Stalskii and Dzhambul, both traditional bards.[73] This same preference was evident in the choice of Russia's national poet, with the classic Pushkin being elevated over more revolutionary candidates such as Mayakovsky or Bednyi.

Perhaps the most striking new departure, however, was the sheer amount of attention devoted to national culture. Prior to 1933, national culture had been a much lower priority than linguistic *korenizatsiia*, Affirmative Action, or the formation of national soviets. As the attention devoted to those topics

---

[67] N. Davagian, "Sotsialisticheskii realizm i natsional'naia literatura," *Literaturnaia gazeta*, no. 127 (22.09.34): 2.

[68] N. Kahanovich, "Iak Ukrains'ki natsionalisty fal'syfikuvaly Tarasa Shevchenka," *Visti VUTsIK*, no. 7 (08.01.34): 2–3. Also at the same time, E. Shabl'ovs'kyi, "Proty natsionalistych-noi fal'syfikatsii Shevchenka," *Literaturna hazeta*, no. 1 (03.01.34): 3.

[69] *RTsKhIDNI* 17/26/70 (17.06.33): 117/15; 17/21/4672 (14.03.34): 4/54; 17/21/4675 (08.04.35): 37/1; (02.06.35): 41/16; 17/21/4676 (23.06.35): 42/41; (26.07.35): 44/26; 17/21/4678 (28.02.36): 55/43; 17/21/4679 (27.05.36): 60/39; 17/21/4682 (14.04.37): 86/11; 17/21/4685 (20.05.38): 23/7; 17/21/4690 (19.12.38): 5/169; 5/197.

[70] A. Khvylia, "Khudozhniki Ukrainy," *Pravda*, no. 74 (16.03.35): 4; "Segodnia v Khar'kove otkrytie pamiatnika Shevchenko," no. 82 (24.03.35): 3; Leonid Sobolev, "Otkrytie pamiatnika Tarasu Shevchenko," no. 83 (25.03.35): 6.

[71] The cult of Rustavelli began to take on all-union status in the mid-1930s and peaked with the all-union celebration of the 750th anniversary of Rustaveli's poem, *Vitiaz' v tigrovoi shkure*, in December 1937. Peredovaia, "Prazdnik sotsialisticheskoi kul'tury," *Uchitel'skaia gazeta*, no. 38 (27.12.37): 1.

[72] Kupala was rehabilitated remarkably quickly. Already in September 1932, his fiftieth birthday was celebrated at the all-union level. "50-letie narodnogo poeta Belorussii Ianki Kupaly," *Literaturnaia gazeta*, no. 41 (11.09.32): 4.

[73] A. Levshin, "Suleiman Stal'skii," *Uchitel'skaia gazeta*, no. 158 (22.11.38): 4; K. Altaiskii, "Dzhambul," *Literaturnaia gazeta*, no. 31 (30.05.36): 1.

plummeted, figures as prominent as national TsK secretaries began to devote entire speeches to the problem of national culture. After his fall in 1937, Posty-shev was accused, with some justification, of having reduced the nationalities question exclusively to the problem of national culture. At a 1937 Tatar TsK plenum, a delegate complained not of the neglect of the Tatar language or underrepresentation of Tatars in technical positions, but of the fact that "to the misery of the national pride of the Tatar toilers . . . it is no secret that when our Tatar theater went to the Moscow festival, it shamed itself by performing a work of vulgar plagiarism."[74] On the other hand, Kazakhstan's first party secretary, Mirzoian, boasted of their *dekada*'s success in Moscow and the fact that "Kazakh legends, songs and folklore have become known to the entire country."[75]

One of the most prominent features of the new fevered promotion of national culture was the proliferation of scientific research institutes of national culture. By 1936, there were over forty of these institutes in the Soviet Union's national republics.[76] Most of them had been formed after 1934.[77] An all-union Scientific Research Institute of National Culture was also established in 1934 in Moscow.[78] Its mission was not only "to study the unique characteristics of the national cul-tures of the different peoples of the USSR," but also "to give aid to the devel-opment of the national cultures of the USSR."[79] In other words, a massive state-sponsored academic apparatus was being established for the sole purpose of celebrating and promoting ethnic diversity. In service of the same goal, the publication of Russian translations of the folklore and literature of the peoples of the Soviet Union accelerated dramatically.[80] A Museum of the Peoples of the USSR was established.[81] The newly formed all-union Committee on Artistic Affairs devoted a considerable amount of its attention to the promotion of national culture.[82] In short, after 1933, an enormous amount of money and effort was invested in the celebration and promotion of the existence of ethnically distinct, folkloric, primordial national cultures. Moreover, this project was intimately linked to the simultaneous campaign to promote the Friendship of the Peoples.

The intensified promotion of folkloric national cultures might seem rather trivial and superficial in comparison with the now deemphasized *korenizatsiia* campaign of 1923 to 1933. Völkisch ethnicity, it might seem, was a poor substi-tute for nation- and state-building. However, in late 1936, Soviet propaganda suddenly began once more to emphasize the "stateness" (*gosudarstvennost'*) and

---

[74] *RTsKhIDNI* 17/21/4379 (10–11.03.37): 184–185.

[75] L. Mirzoian, "Kazakhstan—soiuznaia respublika," *Bol'shevik*, no. 4 (1937): 25.

[76] *GARF* 3316/29/601 (1936): 15–16.

[77] *GARF* 3316/29/605 (1936–1937): 1–54.

[78] *GARF* 3316/13/20 (1934): 320b.

[79] *GARF* 3316/29/601 (1936): 3, 6–7.

[80] "Knigi pisatelei narodov SSSR," *Literaturnaia gazeta*, no. 123 (14.09.34): 4; "Perevody s iazykov narodov SSSR," no. 72 (31.12.35): 1; "Tvorchestvo narodov SSSR," no. 15 (10.03.36): 6.

[81] *GARF* 3316/28/787 (1936): 19.

[82] *GARF* 3316/30/792 (1937): 1–3.

Map 4. Federal Structure of the USSR, 1939

"sovereignty" (*suverenitet*) of the union republics.[83] This was part of the propaganda campaign tied to the adoption of the new Soviet constitution in late
1936. The 1936 constitution created, in *Pravda*'s words, "five new Soviet
republics" and another five new autonomous republics.[84] By generous acts such
as these, it was argued, the Soviet state had not only facilitated the achievement
of stateness, but in many cases the consolidation of nationhood as well: "Many
nations in reality have consolidated only under Soviet power"; "the help of the
dictatorship of the working class insured that the consolidation of nations took
place immeasurably faster than could be conceived of in capitalist conditions";
"the consolidation of the Kazakh people into a nation represents one of the
remarkable victories of socialism in the USSR."[85] This emphasis on the recent
achievement of stateness and nationhood did not contradict the simultaneous
emphasis on the historic depth of völkisch ethnicity. Rather, the Soviet Union
had inherited ethnicities and had transformed them into nation-states. In doing
so, it had fulfilled its role as the vanguard of nations, which in turn had helped
create the Friendship of the Peoples.

In early 1937, the chairman of Kazakhstan's Sovnarkom wrote an article on
this popular theme, entitled "On the National Consolidation of the Kazakh
People," in which he stated that "the Kazakh people had evolved from backward and feudal tribes into a socialist nation and a socialist national state [*v
sotsialisticheskuiu natsiiu i v sotsialisticheskoe natsional'noe gosudarstvo*]."[86] The
terms "socialist nation" and "socialist national state," which entered Soviet
discourse during the propaganda campaign surrounding the 1936 constitution,
were a significant addition to the friendship paradigm. Their origins lay in
Stalin's unpublished March 1929 article, "The Nationalities Question and
Leninism." In this article, Stalin introduced the idea that in addition to bourgeois nations, "there are in existence other nations. These are the new Soviet
nations, which have been developing and taking shape on the base of the old
bourgeois nations since the overturning of capitalism in Russia."[87] The working
class and its internationalist party, Stalin went on, "bind together these new
nations and guide them." This was again the familiar idea of Bolshevism as the
vanguard of the nations. These new nations, Stalin continued, "may be qualified as socialist nations." Their achievement, he predicted, would lead "to the

[83] For examples, see L. Mirzoian, "Kazakhstan—soiuznaia respublika," *Bol'shevik*, no. 4 (1937):
26; I. Trainin, "Suverenitet soiuznykh respublik," *Pravda*, no. 348 (19.12.36): 2.

[84] Peredovaia, "Piat' novykh soiuznykh respublik," *Pravda*, no. 348 (17.12.36): 1. The five new
republics were Kazakhstan, Kirgizia, Georgia, Armenia, and Azerbaidzhan. The first two were
raised from autonomous to union republic status. The latter three had the intermediary
Transcaucasus Federal Republic abolished. Five autonomous oblasts—Kabardino-Balkaria, Komi,
Mari, North Ossetia, and Chechno-Ingushetia—were made autonomous republics.

[85] S. Dimanshtein, "Leninsko-stalinskaia natsional'naia politika i proekt novoi konstitutsii
SSSR," *Bol'shevik*, no. 13 (1936): 68; I. Trainin, "Bratstvo narodov v sotsialisticheskom gosu-
darstve," *Bol'shevik*, no. 8 (1938): 34; I. Isakov, "O natsional'noi konsolidatsii Kazakhskogo
naroda," *Bol'shevik Kazakhstana*, no. 5 (1937): 70.

[86] Isakov, "O natsional'noi konsolidatsii," 70.

[87] Stalin, "Natsional'nyi vopros i leninizm," 338–339.

establishment of a friendship between the peoples." Socialist nations, moreover, "were much more unified and much more viable [*zhiznesposobnye*] than any bourgeois nation." They were more united because they were "free from the unresolvable class contradictions that eat away at bourgeois nations." They were more viable because they "were much more popular [*obshchenarodnyi*] than any bourgeois nation."[88]

Stalin made the obvious point that it was only bourgeois nations that were liquidated with the end of capitalism, or rather not liquidated but transformed into socialist nations. He did not state that socialist nations were now permanent features of the socialist era. He still insisted they would disappear in the distant future after the worldwide triumph of socialism. However, he had come close to asserting the permanence of socialist nations. After World War II, Stalin's speech would be published and permanent socialist nations based on primordial ethnic roots would become a canonical plank of the Soviet nationalities policy.[89] However, it is quite clear that Stalin's socialist nations were already in place by 1936: nations with no class antagonisms, based on völkisch popular foundations, having consolidated and achieved stateness thanks to the actions of the Soviet state, and bound together by the Friendship of the Peoples.

There was a major contradiction in this new paradigm. On the one hand, as noted in Chapter 10, the Great Retreat marked a new emphasis on Soviet citizens' right to assimilation, the right to choose their own ethnic identity. On the other hand, primordial völkisch ethnicity and semipermanent Soviet social- ist nationhood were being promoted at the same time. The first trend implied that ethnicity was conditional and changeable, the latter that it was primordial and permanent. To some degree, this contradiction cannot be explained away. The Soviet nationalities policy of the mid-1930s was both more practical and less coherent than the utopian but logically coherent policy of the 1920s. The right to assimilate addressed two practical problems: first, the need to consoli- date the number of nationalities and national territories to a manageable size; second, the need to provide a national home for the ethnic Russians through the Russification of the RSFSR. The vast majority of Soviet nationalities were neither expected nor encouraged to assimilate. On the contrary, their nation- hood was to be further consolidated and the deep historic roots of their ethnicity emphasized and celebrated. Primordialism was the major trend in the Soviet nationalities policy during the 1930s and the one that triumphed decisively in the period of late Stalinism after World War II.

It is this trend toward primordialism that requires an explanation. The Affirmative Action Empire was based on a belief that ethnicity was a historically contingent phenomenon. It was not an irreducible part of human nature. In fact, it was easily manipulated. Nationalism was an attempt to manipulate ethnic

[88] Ibid., 339–341.
[89] Described splendidly in Slezkine, "The USSR as a Communal Apartment," 448–452; and Slezkine, *Arctic Mirrors*, 303–335.

feeling. It was a masking ideology that led legitimate class interests to be expressed in the illegitimate form of an above-class national movement. The Soviet nationalities policy was a strategy designed to disarm nationalism by granting the forms of nationhood. It was a *strategy*. It was not premised on a belief in primordial ethnicity. Indeed, it represented a pedagogical effort to move the Soviet population from the popular understanding of nations as primordial and immutable to the Bolsheviks' own sociological understanding of nations as historical and contingent. Again, the Communist Party as the vanguard of Soviet nations as well. Yet, by the 1930s the Soviet state was itself propagating a doctrine of primordial ethnicity and the permanence of Soviet nations. Why did this change occur?

It was partially the unintentional result of the extreme statism inherent in Bolshevik national vanguardism. The Affirmative Action Empire required a constant practice of ethnic labeling and so inadvertently indoctrinated its population in the belief that ethnicity was an inherent, fundamental, and crucially important characteristic of all individuals. To implement Affirmative Action programs, monitor their success, form national soviets, assign children to native-language schools, and administer dozens of other nationalities programs, the Soviet state constantly asked its citizens for their nationality. It also asked their employers, their party cell chairmen, trade union representatives, and so forth. All personnel forms had a line marked "nationality." Moreover, Affirmative Action turned nationality into a valuable form of social capital. The nationality line in a job application form was not a neutral piece of information but a crucial advantage or disadvantage. The message broadcast by the state was crystal clear: nationality is one of the most important attributes of any individual. This reinforced a popular belief in primordial ethnicity. It became second nature to label people nationally. When internal passports were introduced in 1932, there was no debate about whether to record nationality on them.[90] It was included without reflection, just as it was on all personnel forms, as a necessary and crucial datum about any Soviet citizen. Yet, the nationality line on Soviet passports became one of the single most important factors in reinforcing the belief, and the social fact, that national identity was primordial and inherited.

The shift to primordial ethnicity was also closely connected to the larger social and cultural processes driving the Great Retreat. After 1933, there was a shift in emphasis from class to people (*narod*). We have seen this in the transition from class-based to ethnically based deportation, from the persecution of class enemies to enemies of the people, and in the turn from an emphasis on class militancy to a society imagined as consisting of a powerful, paternalistic state and a largely undifferentiated, demobilized people. The 1936 constitution, which ended the practice of formal legal discrimination against class aliens (the *lishentsy*), symbolically marked this transition from class to people. One com-

---

[90] I was unable to find any discussion of nationality in the documentation surrounding passportization in 1932–1933, nor did Nathalie Moins, "Passeportisation, statistique des migrations et controle de l'identite sociale," *Cahiers du monde russe* 38 (1997): 587–600.

mentator noted: "The constitution should remind us that the popular [*narod-nost'*] is the highest criterium of all cultural work."[91] The enormous attention devoted to folklore (both non-Russian and Russian) and popular artistic expression in the mid-1930s was also part of the new cult of *narodnost'*.[92] The shift from class to people and the popular helps explain both the increase in attention given to national culture, as the literal embodiment of *narodnost'*, and the shift toward a more primordial, völkisch understanding of those national cultures.

The cult of the popular surrounding the 1936 constitution was not only associated with the introduction of the term "socialist nation" into Soviet discourse, but also increased use of the expression "Soviet people" (*sovetskii narod*).[93] This term might seem to indicate an attempt to construct a Soviet nationality. It did not. The phrase "*sovetskii narod*," or its close counterpart "*sovetskii patriotizm*," was most frequently used in discussions of the need to resist potential foreign aggression.[94] The *sovetskii narod* was always presented as "our multinational *sovetskii narod*." A *Pravda* article on Soviet patriotism spoke of "our great Soviet Union—common home to the toilers *of all nationalities* [author's emphasis]." Likewise, a lead editorial praised "the Ukrainian people [as] burning with Soviet patriotism, like all the peoples of the Soviet Union."[95] Stalin himself always emphasized the multiethnicity of the Soviet people. In his 1934 comments on a new textbook on the history of the Soviet Union, Stalin made the text's insufficient emphasis on the history of the non-Russian peoples of the Soviet Union one of his major criticisms.[96] The Soviet equivalent of the core nationality of a modern nation-state—of German, French, or Japanese—was not the *sovetskii narod* but the Friendship of the Peoples.

In addition to the effects of Soviet Affirmative Action and the new cult of the popular, both of which derived from extreme Stalinist statism, a third contributing factor in the turn toward primordialism was the emergence of an ethnicized Soviet xenophobia and the category of enemy nation, a category that could be understood only in primordial terms. On the one hand, the emergence of the category of enemy nation marked the triumph of primordialist thinking. On the other hand, since the concept of enemy nations was not compatible with a belief in modern constructed nations, it also represented a final factor fueling the Soviet turn toward primordial nationality. This latter effect was responsible for the official institutionalization of inherited passport nationality. As noted above, when passports were introduced in 1932, there was

[91] D. Mirskii, "O velikoi khartii narodov. Konstitutsiia pobedy," *Literaturnaia gazeta*, no. 41 (20.07.36): 2.

[92] *Sovetskii Fol'klor* tom. 1–7 (1934–1941).

[93] For example, V. Bystrianskii, "Sovetskii narod," *Pravda*, no. 95 (24.04.36): 2.

[94] V. Bystrianskii, "O sovetskom patriotizme," *Pravda*, no. 113 (18.05.36): 2.

[95] I. Trainin, "Suverenitet soiuznykh respublik," *Pravda*, no. 348 (19.12.36): 2.; Bystrianskii, "O sovetskom patriotizme," 2; Peredovaia, "Literatura Ukrainskogo naroda," *Pravda*, no. 193 (15.07.36): 1.

[96] I. Stalin, A. Zhdanov, and S. Kirov, "Zamechaniia po povodu konspekta uchebnika po 'Istoriia SSSR,'" *Partiinoe stroitel'stvo*, no. 3 (1936): 44–46.

no special concern about nationality, and individuals were allowed to choose their own nationality when acquiring a passport. At the height of the mass operations against diaspora nationalities, however, an April 2, 1938, NKVD decree declared that henceforth nationality should be determined by the nationality of the parents and not the free choice of the individual. As examples of nations to be watched particularly carefully, the NKVD cited "Germans, Poles and others" who were trying to present themselves as "Russians, Belorussians and others."[97] Obviously the concern was over members of enemy nations trying to change their national identity to avoid arrest and execution. Here is clear proof that the emergence of the category of enemy nation directly influenced the emergence of the single most important long-term prop of Soviet maintaining primordial ethnicity: inherited passport nationality.

Soviet primordialism, then, can be explained by a number of convergent factors. The pervasive Soviet practice of labeling individuals by national identity to administer Affirmative Action programs helped turn nationality into an ascribed hereditary status. Passportization reflected and exacerbated this trend. In addition, Stalin's statist revolution from above produced a paternalistic cult of the popular, which in turn encouraged a celebration of primordial, *völkisch* national culture. Finally, the emergence of the category of enemy nations both exemplified and further reinforced the tendency to think of nations primordially rather than instrumentally. The Soviet turn toward primordial nationality, then, was not intentional. It was the result of unforeseen consequences of the original Soviet nationalities policy combined with the affinity of primordial ethnicity with broader Soviet social processes such as the statist cult of the popular.

The First among Equals

Primordial ethnicity was one of the pillars of the Friendship of the Peoples. The other was Russian centrality.[98] When Stalin introduced the friendship in December 1935, he declared that non-Russian "mistrust" had been overcome. This implied the rehabilitation of Russian culture, a process that began already in 1933. By January 1937, Russian culture had its own official pantheon of classic literary, artistic, and scholarly heroes[99]:

> The Russian people in its historic development forged the remarkable culture of Lomonosov and Pushkin, Belinskii and Chernyshevskyi, Dobroliubov and Nekrasov, Tolstoi and Gorkii. Our country has the right to be proud of such names, and also of the names of the great Russian scholars, Mechnikov

[97] Roginskii and Petrov, 36.
[98] On the rise and reception of Russocentric propaganda, see David Brandenberger, "The 'Short Course' to Modernity" (Ph.D. diss., Harvard University, 1999).
[99] Peredovaia, "Privet izbrannikam velikogo naroda!" *Literaturnaia gazeta*, no. 3 (15.01.37): 1.

and Mendeleev, Sechenov and Pavlov, the great Russian musicians, Musorgskii and Borodin, Bakirev and Rimskii-Korsakov, great artists such as Repin and others.

Of course, such cultural figures had never been repudiated by the Soviet state, even at the height of the cultural revolution. What was new in the mid-1930s was the strong emphasis on their Russianness. For instance, a *Pravda* article on the "great Russian painter V. I. Surikov" began with the axiom: "History teaches that an artist's creations are only great and eternal when they are deeply popular [*narodnyi*] and national."[100] By July 1937, such titles as "On National Form in Soviet Russian Theater" were commonplace.[101] Russian culture now had been given the same deep historic past and the same emphasis on "the popular and the national" as the other peoples of the Soviet Union.

However, at the same time that the position of Russian culture was being normalized, a second process had begun that resulted in Russian culture being again assigned an unequal status, this time a privileged one. This new status was announced in a February 1, 1936 lead editorial in *Pravda*, entitled "The RSFSR," which contained an unambiguous declaration of Russian priority[102]:

> All the peoples [of the USSR], participants in the great socialist construction, can take pride in the results of their work. All of them from the smallest to the largest are equal Soviet patriots. But the first among equals is the Russian people, the Russian workers, the Russian toilers, whose role in the entire Great Proletarian Revolution, from the first victory to today's brilliant period of its development, has been exclusively great.

After this editorial, "first among equals" became a standard Soviet epithet for the Russian people.[103] Russian culture and the Russian people were now also regularly referred to as "great." Russian culture was "the most progressive culture" and a model for the other Soviet peoples.[104] Russian cultural priority was linked to an affinity with socialism and the dominant role of the Russian proletariat in the October Revolution.

As we have seen, Stalin himself shared this view of the Russian people. At the

[100] Igor Grabar, "Velikii russkii zhivopisets V. I. Surikov," *Pravda*, no. 357 (28.12.36): 4. For similar *Pravda* articles emphasizing the Russianness of various canonized Russian cultural figures, see Peredovaia, "Velikii russkii kritik," no. 162 (14.06.36): 1 on Belinskii; V. Kemenov, "Ilia Repin," no. 188 (10.07.36): 4; Peredovaia, "Genial'nyi syn velikogo russkogo naroda," no. 317 (18.11.36): 1 on Lomonosov. The year 1936 was the key year for the canonization of prerevolutionary Russian cultural figures.

[101] "O natsional'noi forme v sovetskom Russkom teatre," *Teatr*, no. 4 (1937): 15–22.

[102] Peredovaia, "RSFSR," *Pravda*, no. 31 (01.02.36): 1.

[103] "Privet izbrannikam," 1; G. M. Malenkov, "Torzhestvo leninsko-stalinskoi natsional'noi politiki," *Pravda*, no. 157 (09.06.38): 3.

[104] Peredovaia, "Edinaia sem'ia narodov," *Pravda*, no. 29 (30.01.36): 1; Peredovaia, "Znat' istoriiu narodov SSSR," *Pravda*, no. 231 (22.08.37): 1; B. Volin, "Velikii Russkii narod," *Bol'shevik*, no. 9 (1938): 26.

[105] RTsKhIDNI 558/11/205 (15.12.25): 5.

December 1925 TsK plenum, he called the Russians "the most industrial, the most active, and the most Soviet of all nations in our country."[105] In his December 1930 letter to Demian Bednyi, Stalin called the Russian working class "the advance-guard of the Soviet workers, its acknowledged leaders, having conducted a more revolutionary and activist politics than any other proletariat of the world could dream of."[106] Similarly, in a May 1933 speech in the Kremlin, Stalin again complimented the Russians as "the major nationality of the world; they first raised the flag of the soviets in opposition to the rest of the world. The Russian nation—it is the most talented nation in the world."[107] Significantly, all these remarks were either private or addressed to limited elite audiences and none of them were published at the time, since they contradicted the spirit of the Affirmative Action Empire. With his Friendship of the Peoples speech in December 1935, Stalin first combined the idea of Russian priority and Soviet unity. On the 21st anniversary of the October Revolution in 1938, he explicitly endorsed the "first among equals" trope: "The old Russia has now been transformed into the USSR, where all peoples are equal. The country is mighty and strong in its army, industry, and collectivized agriculture. Among the equal nations of the state and country of the USSR, the most soviet and most revolutionary is the Russian nation."[108]

By 1938, this Russian cultural priority had also increasingly grown primordial roots. Russian superiority was no longer confined to the era of socialism but extended back a millennium in time. By 1938, the Soviet government was propagating an extraordinarily crude essentialist Russian nationalism. A striking example of this propaganda was an article, "The Great Russian People," which appeared in the May 1938 issue of the party's main theoretical journal[109]:

> The history of the Great Russian people is the history of its heroic battle for independence and freedom against innumerable enemies, conquerors and interventionists, including against "German elements." . . . In this difficult battle full of dangers, the Great Russian people multiplied and developed its remarkable qualities as the People-Fighter and People-Freedom Lover [narod-borets, narod-svobodoliubets]. . . .

The author went on to recount the defeat of thirteenth-century "German elements," the Teutonic Knights, by Alexander Nevsky and concluded his description with a hymn to the primordial essence of Russianness[110]:

> The people is immortal. The military abilities of the Slavic warriors [druzhina] and the courage, endurance, inventiveness and resoluteness of the Russian fighters—all these qualities have been cultivated in the Russian people.

[106] I. Stalin, "Tov. Demianu Bednomu," (12.12.30) Sochineniia, vol. 13 (Moscow, 1953): 24–25.
[107] RTsKhIDNI 558/11/1117 (1933): 10.
[108] RTsKhIDNI 558/11/1122 (07.11.38): 158–159.
[109] Volin, "Velikii Russkii narod," 28.
[110] Ibid., 29.

This article, published at the height of the national operations of the Great Terror, conveys a sense of the Russian nationalism that was promoted in the party's main theoretical journal already three years before Hitler's invasion.

The most common theme of this new propaganda was "the right of the Russian people to be proud," the "justifiable pride" of the Russians.[111] This was clearly a response to the Affirmative Action Empire's previous sanctions against Russian national self-expression. An August 1937 *Pravda* article, with the characteristic title "On the National Pride of Russian Artists," directly repudiated this previous norm[112]:

> The combination of the words "Russian Soviet painting" seems unusual. We often speak about Georgian, Armenian and other Soviet artists, but we for some reason avoid the word "Russian," replacing it with epithets like "Muscovite," "our," "contemporary" or still more careful—"artists of the RSFSR." What is the reason for this national "shame"?

The author then answered his own question. It was due to intimidation: "Under the cover of the 'battle' against great power chauvinism, ['internationalist' critics] noisily declared all Russian culture and art landowner-bourgeoisie, reactionary-nationalist."[113] Similarly, in an article entitled "MKhAT— National Russian Theater," another author complained that "up until recent times, directors and critics have 'been ashamed' to speak of the national character of plays and in general about the national form of Russian art."[114] The shrillness of this propaganda campaign was aimed at Russians who resented the fact that they had been bullied into being ashamed of their national traditions and culture.

A second ubiquitous theme of the Russian nationalist propaganda was the immense "brotherly help" the Russian people had provided for the non-Russians, and in turn the gratitude and love that was owed to them.[115] Under the Affirmative Action Empire, Russians were required to sacrifice their national interests quietly and selflessly to help defuse the justifiable historic distrust of the non-Russians. Russian communist officials were always struck and disturbed by the failure of non-Russians to respond with the proper degree of gratitude. Instead, in the officials' opinion, non-Russians selfishly manipulated their ethnic

---

[111] Volin, "Velikii Russkii narod," 26; V. Kirpotin, "Russkaia kul'tura," *Bol'shevik*, no. 12 (1938): 61; "Gordost' Russkogo iskusstva," *Teatr*, no. 3 (1937): 19–21; Peredovaia, "Velikii Russkii poet," *Pravda*, no. 346 (17.12.35): 1; V. Bystrianskii, "Kriticheskie zamechaniia ob uchebnikakh po istorii SSSR," no. 31 (01.02.36): 2; "Velikii Russkii kritik," 1; L. Timofeev, "Osnovatel' russkoi literatury," no. 317 (18.11.36): 4.

[112] V. Kemenov, "O natsional'noi gordosti Russkikh khudozhnikov," *Pravda*, no. 222 (13.08.37): 4.

[113] Ibid., 4.

[114] V. Ivanov, "MKhAT—natsional'nyi Russkii teatr," *Teatr*, no. 4 (1937): 23.

[115] "Privet izbrannikam," 1; Volin, "Velikii Russkii narod," 27; "RSFSR," 1; Peredovaia, "Ot nevezhestva i otstalosti—k rastsvetu kul'tury," *Pravda*, no. 6 (06.01.36): 1; G. Torzhanov, "Dekada Kazakhskogo iskusstva," *Pravda*, no. 116 (28.04.36): 4; "Torzhestvo leninsko-stalinskoi," 1.

identities strategically to maximize their Affirmative Action benefits at the expense of the selfless Russians. The Great Retreat brought a role reversal. Non-Russians were required to express repeatedly and ritualistically their gratitude to the Russians for their "brotherly help" and their admiration and love for the great Russian culture.[116] *Korenizatsiia* and Affirmative Action were now implemented surreptitiously.

Finally, a third major theme was the ubiquitous "slander" (*kleveta*) that the Russian people and Russian culture had to endure. Some of this slander came from abroad, particularly from fascist Germany and Poland: "Hatred of the Russian people includes, of course, hatred to everything Soviet, to the USSR as a whole, but in their slander our enemies direct their fire [*ogon' napravliaetsia*] first of all at the Russian people, because they know very well its immense will, energy and endurance."[117] Of course, from 1923 to 1933 official Soviet policy was "to direct fire first of all" at great-power chauvinism because of the unique danger of Russian nationalism. Having renounced this policy, the Soviet leadership now increasingly labeled it fascist. Those who had followed that policy in the 1920s could now be attacked for their previous remarks. Bukharin was said to have, "to the advantage of the fascists, slandered the Russian people, calling them 'a nation of Oblomovs.'"[118] In short, then, with the resentful and boastful style of Russian nationalist propaganda, the regime was responding to what it perceived was Russian resentment of the Affirmative Action Empire.

The central, unifying role of the Russians was now added to the metaphor of the Friendship of the Peoples: "In the center of the mighty family of peoples of the USSR stands the great Russian people, passionately loved by all the peoples of the USSR, the first among equals."[119] The Russians bound together the Soviet Union in three ways. First, "the heroic, self-sacrificing Russian working class helped the peoples settling Russia throw off the yoke of national oppression forever."[120] Due to this selfless help, "the friendship and love of all the peoples of the USSR to the first among equals, the most progressive among the progressive—the Russian people—grew and solidified."[121] Second, "the culture of the Russian people, having become available to all the peoples of the Soviet country, provided a mighty and fruitful influence on the cultural development of the fraternal peoples of the USSR."[122] Third, the Russian language served both as a language of mutual communication and the language of the world socialist classics. Just as Russian culture was initially praised for its accomplishments in the Soviet era and then that praise was generalized to all of Russian

[116] *RTsKhIDNI* 17/21/4351 (10–19.07.38): 112; Uieir Gadzhibekov, "Dekada Azerbaidˀ nanskogo iskusstva v Moskve," *Sovety Azerbaidzhana*, nos. 3–4 (1938): 24; Peredova, "Braˀ ers'kyi pryvit velykomu Rosiis'komu narodovi!" *Visti VUTsIK*, no. 15 (15.01.37): 1.

[117] "RSFSR," 1.

[118] Trainin, "Bratstvo narodov," 39; Kirpotin, "Russkaia kul'tura," 61. "Edinaia sem'ia narodov," 1.

[119] "Privet izbrannikam," 1.

[120] "Torzhestvo leninsko-stalinskoi," 1.

[121] Volin, "Velikii Russkii narod," 27.

[122] "Privet izbrannikam," 1.

history, the Friendship of the Peoples, initially said to have formed during the Soviet period, likewise grew primordial roots[123]:

> The cultures of the peoples of the USSR are historically linked with the culture of the Russian people. They have felt and continue to feel, to an enormous degree, the beneficent influence of the progressive Russian culture.

Thus, an abstract concept, the Friendship of the Peoples, was given the primordial roots associated with essentialist nationalism. In this way, it could serve as an effective substitute for the unifying nationalism of a traditional nation-state.

The integration of the leading role of the Russian people into the Friendship of the Peoples did not dramatically alter the symbolic rituals associated with the friendship. The national *dekady* in Moscow continued. The major change was that Russian national holidays, anniversaries, and celebrations became part of the friendship symbolic. In particular, the largest single celebration of the friendship was the massive Pushkin jubilee of February 1937. Planning for this celebration began already in December 1935. It was then announced that Pushkin was not only "the great Russian poet," but a poet for "the toilers of all nationalities."[124] Pushkin's verses boasting that he would one day be read by "the proud grandson of the Slavs, the Finns, the now wild Tungus, and the friend of the steppe, the Kalmyk" were widely quoted.[125] In preparation for the jubilee, Pushkin was translated into fifty-eight of the Soviet Union's languages.[126] All the nationalities scrambled to find connections between Pushkin and their own national poets.[127] Although the jubilees of Shevchenko and Rustaveli were celebrated on an all-union basis, only the Russian poet Pushkin was declared the national poet of all the Soviet Union's peoples.

An aphorism frequently repeated during the 1937 Pushkin jubilee was that "for the very reason that Pushkin was so deeply national, he became an international poet."[128] This comment reflected an interesting continuity in the status of the Russians in the Soviet Union. Under the Affirmative Action Empire, Russians were identified with the state and asked to sacrifice their national interests and submerge their national identity, all to serve the goal of preserving the mul-

---

[123] Volin, "Velikii Russkii narod," 34.

[124] Peredovaia, "Velikii Russkii poet," *Pravda*, no. 346 (17.12.35): 1.

[125] Ibid., 1; N. Dmitriev, "Pushkin na iazykakh narodov SSSR," *Literaturnaia gazeta*, no. 33 (10.06.36): 5.

[126] E. Sikar, "Pushkin na iazykakh narodov SSSR," *Revoliutsiia i natsional'nosti*, no. 2 (1937): 71.

[127] E. Sharki, "Aleksandr Sergeevich Pushkin i narodnyi Tatarskii poet Abulla Tukaev," *Revoliutsiia i natsional'nosti*, no. 1 (1937): 40–45; Prof. A. M. Ladyzhenskii, "A. S. Pushkin i natsional'nosti," no. 2 (1937): 65–67; A. Arustamov, "Vliianie Pushkina na tvorchestvo Tumaniana," no. 2 (1937): 67–70; P. Ageev, "Pushkin i Shevchenko," no. 4 (1937): 67–71; A. Tagirov, "Pochemu Bashkiram dorog Pushkin," no. 4 (1937): 71–73.

[128] Volin, "Velikii Russkii narod," 32.

tiethnic state. By 1937, Russian national identity was no longer submerged—it was being crudely celebrated at every turn—but it was still identified closely with the state. The Russian regions of the RSFSR may have been made into a comfortable home for the Russian population, but the Soviet Union was their motherland. Since the Soviet state was socialist and international, Russian national identity was increasingly identified as socialist and international: "The Russian people are full of national pride because their motherland [has become] the most international . . . that the world has ever known."[129] Russian national identity was therefore still submerged in the Soviet whole. The following quotation illustrates tellingly the confused nature of Russian identity: "The Soviet patriotism of the Russian people—this is love to the socialist motherland [*rodina*], the fatherland [*otechestvo*] of the toilers of the whole world."[130] On the one hand, Russian national identity was extravagantly aggrandized, while on the other hand it was also diluted and confused with its close Soviet counterpart.

The most important practical policy associated with the new status of Russian culture was the March 13, 1938 TsK decree making the study of the Russian language mandatory in all non-Russian schools.[131] Legally this decree was unnecessary. The study of Russian was already mandatory in all non-Russian schools.[132] In practice, however, according to Narkompros statistics, only 190 of 984 primary schools in Dagestan offered any instruction in Russian. The comparable figures were 508 of 1351 for Chechno-Ingushetia, 321 of 728 for Turkmenistan, 189 of 667 for Kirgizia, 39 of 225 for grades 5 to 7 in Kazakhstan, and only 7 of 75 for grades 7 to 9. Conditions in Tajikistan and Uzbekistan were said to be no better.[133] The significance of the March 1938 decree, then, was not the legal obligation to teach Russian as a second language, but the central signal that this was now a major state priority, as well as the considerable financial resources directed toward the training of Russian teachers.[134] The ideology behind this decree was dictated by the friendship paradigm: "the immense significance of the Russian language as a mighty weapon of culture and as a means of communication between the fraternal peoples of the USSR."[135]

The problem of Russian language study in non-Russian schools was first publicly discussed at an all-union TsK plenum in November 1937.[136] Stalin

---

[129] Ibid., 27.

[130] Ibid., 26.

[131] *RTsKhIDNI* 17/3/997 (13.03.38): 59/166. For an excellent study of the adoption and consequences of this law, see Peter Blitstein, "Stalin's Nations: Soviet Nationality Policy between Planning and Primordialism, 1936–1953" (Ph.D. diss., University of California-Berkeley, 1999): 101–37.

[132] *RTsKhIDNI* 17/114/833 (02.01.38): 26–29.

[133] *RTsKhIDNI* 17/114/833 (02.01.38): 77/2, 27; 17/114/840 (16.02.38): 81/13, 76.

[134] For these plans, see *RTsKhIDNI* 17/114/833 (02.01.38): 26–31; 17/114/840 (16.02.38): 76–87; 77/1/857 (1938): 1–9, 36–42.

[135] *RTsKhIDNI* 17/114/833 (02.01.38): 25.

[136] *RTsKhIDNI* 17/2/628 (11–12.10.37): 120–123.

himself gave the official address on this question. As in his December 1935 speech, he linked the nationalities question directly to the defense of the Soviet Union[137]:

> This question was raised because we stand before a major enrollment of soldiers into the Red Army. We have a law that conscription applies to every citizen of the USSR when they reach a certain age, regardless of nationality. . . . But we encountered the problem that those conscripted into the army, for example, in Uzbekistan, Kazakhstan, Armenia, Georgia and Azerbaijan did not speak Russian. With such a situation, one is forced to leave them in their local regions and then our divisions and brigades are transformed into territorial ones. This is not an army. We don't look at our army that way. We think that every division should not be a local army, but an army of the entire Union, part of the army of the entire Union. . . . Otherwise, we will have no army.

Stalin was strongly understating his discontent with the existing territorial national divisions. In fact, a month earlier, he had received a telegram from Andreev, who was then in Central Asia supervising the purge of the local party leadership, reporting that the Uzbek and Tajik national divisions stationed in the border regions had been linked to the purged leaders of those republics: "[T]here will be attempts in the future as well to conduct hostile work among them from Afghanistan, Iran, and Turkey. It would be best to move these divisions into the European parts of the Soviet Union." On the telegram, Stalin scrawled: "Comrade Voroshilov: Andreev is signaling that it would be best to put Russian units in Tashkent and Stalinabad and, after first purging them, transfer [the national divisions] to other less distant places."[138] A March 7, 1938 TsK decree would eliminate the existing system of territorial national military units entirely.[139]

Stalin's speech made it clear that the two decrees were linked[140]:

> But we have only one language in which all citizens of the USSR can make themselves understood more or less—this is the Russian language. It would be a good thing if every citizen conscripted into the army could make themselves understood in Russian, so that if, say, an Uzbek division is shifted to Samara, they can make themselves understood to the local population. Here is where the absolute need was born, given universal conscription . . . that all Red Army soldiers master some one language, in which they can communicate in all regions of the Union. This language is Russian. We study German, French and English, but let me assure you, that in our everyday practice, French, German and English are less useful than Russian. [laughter. Voices: "Correct."]

---

[137] Ibid., 120–121.

[138] *RTsKhIDNI* 558/11/65 (03.10.37): 87.

[139] Simon, 153.

[140] Ibid., 121–122. The linkage is also made clear by a February 21 TsK telegram stating that the two issues would be discussed *jointly* at a March 7 conference in Moscow. *RTsKhIDNI* 558/11/58 (21.02.38): 5.

It was quite characteristic of Stalin to present this issue as one of practical convenience and downplay any suggestion of cultural russification. The measure was passed without discussion.[141]

Stalin addressed this issue once more at a March 8, 1938 session of Zhdanov's Politburo commission, which had been formed to draft the TsK decree on Russian language instruction.[142] Stalin's speech at this session is currently not available to researchers, but Zhdanov summarized Stalin's three main arguments in favor of the legislation[143]:

> First, in a multinational state such as the USSR, the knowledge of Russian should be a powerful means for creating ties and communication between the peoples of the USSR, furthering their continued economic and cultural growth. Second, [it will] help the further perfecting of the technical and scientific knowledge of national cadres. Third, it is a necessary condition for the successful performance of military service in the Red Army by all citizens.

These arguments followed from the new friendship paradigm. The Russian language was a unifying link language for the Soviet peoples and it also furthered the acquisition of higher culture by national cadres. Zhdanov also reported that Stalin emphasized "that there should be absolutely no repression or reduction of the use of the native language, that teachers should be warned that the Russian language is not to be used for instruction, but only as a subject of study."[144] Stalin's comments here might seem cynical, but in fact largely were not. With few exceptions, throughout Stalin's rule, native-language education remained mandatory in non-Russian schools and Russian remained only a subject of study. The March 1938 decree did not begin cultural russification. Its goal was only bilingualism or, at the very most, biculturalism. The friendship paradigm continued to insist on the cultivation of the non-Russians' distinct national identities.

The Russian language was not the only aspect of Russian culture to penetrate the non-Russian republics in the 1930s. It was joined there by an increasing number of Russian individuals. Kazakhstan's desperate resistance to Russian immigration had been broken in 1928. Karelia had successfully resisted Russian immigration and promoted Karelian and Finnish immigration through 1935, when the republican leadership was finally removed and a planned program of russificatory immigration set in motion. As a result of the center's refusal to allow national governments to regulate immigration, the large-scale construction of new factories in national regions, and the massive population movements during the chaos of the first five-year plan, the number of Russians living outside the RSFSR increased dramatically (Table 46).[145] As

---

[141] Ibid., 123.
[142] *RTsKhIDNI* 77/1/857 (08.03.38): 1–9.
[143] Ibid., 36–37.
[144] Ibid., 1.
[145] Adapted from V. Kabuzan, *Russkie v mire* (St. Petersburg, 1996), 279.

Table 46. Russians Living Outside the RSFSR, 1926–1939

| | 1926 | | 1939 | |
Republic	Russian Population	As Percent of Republic Population	Russian Population	As Percent of Republic Population
Ukraine	2,707,000	7.3	4,886,000	11.8
Belorussia	485,000	5.9	536,000	6.0
Uzbekistan	244,000	4.5	744,000	11.7
Tajikistan	6,000	0.7	135,000	9.1
Turkmenistan	75,000	7.7	233,000	18.6
Kazakhstan	1,280,000	20.6	2,447,000	40.2
Kirgizia	116,000	11.7	303,000	20.8
Georgia	96,000	3.6	309,000	8.7
Azerbaijan	220,000	9.5	528,000	16.5
Armenia	21,000	2.3	51,000	4.0
Total	5,250,000	8.0	10,121,000	13.5

Adapted from V. Kabuzan, *Russkie v mire* (St. Petersburg, 1996), 279.

the table shows, the number of Russians living outside the RSFSR almost doubled in the thirteen years between 1926 and 1939. Growth was most dramatic in the five Central Asian republics, where the Russian population more than doubled (from 1,721,000 to 3,862,000) in absolute terms and rose dramatically from 11.2 percent to 23.2 percent of the total Central Asian population.

From 1926 onward, Russian national soviets had been formed and Russians had been treated as national minorities. After 1933, the term *national minority* was increasingly not used to describe Russians living outside the RSFSR. After 1937, this usage disappeared altogether along with Russian national soviets. This did not represent a diminution in status. On the contrary, the status of national minority was considered insufficiently dignified for the Soviet Union's "first among equals." Measures were taken, such as the formation of republican Russian-language newspapers in Ukraine and Belorussia, to ensure that Russians need no longer feel like national minorities anywhere in the Soviet Union. In the 1920s, the fact that national soviets permeated the entire Soviet Union, in particular the RSFSR, helped bind the Soviet Union together nationally. With their gradual abolition in the 1930s, the Russians living outside the RSFSR, whose national identity was now systematically supported by the state, played the same unifying role as the non-Russians had under the old system.

Conclusion

By 1938, the Soviet Union had a new national constitution. I have chosen to call that constitution by the name given to it by Stalin: the Friendship of the Peoples. The Friendship of the Peoples involved the following elements. Those

Soviet nations not considered too small, and so subject to assimilation or ethnic consolidation, or too disloyal, and so subject to deportation and annihilation, were to be recognized as socialist nations with primordial ethnic roots. They were for all practical purposes recognized as a permanent, eternal part of the socialist Soviet Union. Their national cultures would continue to be patronized by the Soviet state. Affirmative Action and nation-building would continue, though not in such a way as to insult or demean Russians. They were under no threat of forcible assimilation, though individual members were free to assimilate if they so chose. All non-Russians, however, were required not only to learn the Russian language but also to familiarize themselves with the Russian culture. Indeed, the Russian culture should in some important way become part of their national cultures. Pushkin should be their national poet.

The Russians now played the leading role in the Soviet Union. They would never again be required to feel ashamed of their national past and its traditions. On the contrary, it was their duty to take pride in it. Russian culture was given even deeper primordial roots than the national cultures of other Soviet nations. The Russian people, language, and culture served to unify the Soviet Union. Their priority should be openly acknowledge and furthered. Russians should be able to feel at home nationally in the Russian regions of the RSFSR. Affirmative action and the promotion of non-Russian cultures should be confined to the Soviet Union's national regions (except for Moscow, which remained more a socialist than Russian city). Under no circumstances, however, should the RSFSR be turned into a purely Russian republic that could serve as a force for pursuing particularistic Russian national interests. Instead, Russians should be encouraged to identify their national interests with Soviet interests.

The Soviet Union was not a nation-state. No attempt was ever made to create either a Soviet nationality or to turn the Soviet Union into a Russian nation-state. The Soviet people were primarily a figure of speech, used most frequently as shorthand for the passionate patriotism and willingness of all the national distinct Soviet peoples to defend the Soviet Union from foreign aggression. The role played by the dominant nationality of traditional nation-state would be played in the Soviet Union by the Friendship of the Peoples. The Friendship of the Peoples was the Soviet Union's imagined community.

Glossary

agitprop: Central Committee department in charge of propaganda.

AO: Autonomous oblast; national territory ranked below ASSR.

ASSR: Autonomous republic; national territory included within a union republic.

Basmachi: Anti-Soviet guerilla movement in Central Asia.

borot'bisty: members or former members of the left wing of the Ukrainian Socialist Revolutionary Party.

bronia: A quota for admission to higher education.

commissariat: Equivalent of Soviet ministry.

gortsy: Member of one of the small nationalities of the North Caucasus mountain range.

Gosplan: State planning committee; responsible for central economic planning.

GPU: *See* OGPU.

guberniia: Large administrative territory; abolished in 1920s.

gubkom: Communist Party organ in charge of a *guberniia*.

kanton: *See uezd.*

Kharbintsy: Former workers on the Soviet-run Manchurian railway who returned to the USSR after the railway was ceded to the Japanese.

kholkol: Pejorative term for Ukrainian.

kolkhoz: Collective farmer.

kolkhoznik: Member of collective farm.

Komintern: The Communist International; oversaw world communist movement.

Komnats: The nationalities committee of the education commissariat.

Komsomol: Communist Youth League as well as member of Communist Youth League.

KP/b/U: Communist Party of Ukraine.

KPK: Commission on Party Control. Replaces TsKK in 1934.

KPZB: Communist Party of Western Belorussia.

KPZU: Communist Party of Western Ukraine.

krai: A large multiethnic province.

kraikom: Communist Party organ in charge of a *krai*.

korenizatsiia: The policy of supporting the use of the non-Russian languages and the creation of non-Russian elites in the non-Russian territories.

KTVO: Committee for Higher Technical Education.

kulak: Well-to-do peasant.

kultprop: Central Committee department in charge of culture and propaganda.

likuknep: Committee for the Liquidation of Ukrainian Illiteracy; formed within Ukrainian education commissariat to supervise mandatory adult study of Ukrainian.

Narkompros: The commissariat (or ministry) of education.

NEP: New Economic Policy, 1921–1928.

NKVD: Name of Soviet political police from 1934 to 1941.

obkom: Communist Party organ in charge of an oblast.

oblast: A large province.

OGPU: Name of Soviet political police from 1922 to 1934; local branches called GPU.

okrug: Administrative territory between *raion* and oblast.

orgburo: Organizational Bureau of the Central Committee; along with sekretariat, supervises work of Communist Party.

orgraspred otdel: Department of the central committee in charge of supervising regional party organizations.

rabfak: Special schools formed to provide basic education for adult workers.

raikom: Communist Party organ in charge of a *raion*.

raion: "District"; small administrative territory; replaces *volost'* and *uezd*.

rabkrin: Worker-Peasant Inspection; formed a united bureaucracy with TsKK until 1934.

raionirovanie: Regionalization; the formation of new administrative territories.

RSFSR: Russian Union of Federated Socialist Republics.

smenovekhovets: Russian or non-Russian nationalist who supports Soviet power because of a conviction that Soviet power is at least temporarily serving national ends.

smenovekhovtstvo: The movement associated with individual *smenovekhovtsy*.

smychka: Link; refers to link between workers and peasants during NEP.

soslovie: pre-revolutinary term for estate or status groups.

soviet: Governmental body in charge of any administrative territory.

Sovnarkom: Council of People's Commisariats; highest-ranking non-party body.

SSR: Union republic; largest national territories that together form Soviet Union.

technicum: Trade or professional school.

TsIK: Central Executive Committee; the Soviet legislature.

TsK: Central Committee of the Communist Party.

TsKK: Central Control Commission; body in charge of party discipline through 1934.

uezd: Administrative territory larger than *volost'* and smaller than *guberniia*; abolished in 1920s.

VKP/b/: All-union Communist Party.

volost': Small administrative territory; abolished and replaced by *raiony*.

VSNKh: Supreme Council of the People's Economy; highest economic organ.

VTsIK: All-Russian Central Executive Committee; the RSFSR legislature.

VTsK NTA (NA): All-Union Central Committee of the New (Turkic) Alphabet.

VTUZy: Higher technical educational institutes.

VUTsIK: all-Ukrainian Central Executive Committee; the Ukrainian parliament.

VUZy: Higher educational institutes.

vydvizhenie: Soviet term for the promotion of workers to white-collar jobs.

vydvizhentsy: Workers who have been promoted specially to white-collar jobs.

zminovikhivstvo: Ukrainian term for *smenovekhovstvo*.

ZSFSR: Transcaucasian Union of Federated Socialist Republics; includes Georgia, Armenia, and Azerbaijan; abolished in 1936.

Bibliography

I. ARCHIVAL SOURCES

i. *Rossiiskii Tsentr Khraneniia i Izucheniia Dokumentov Noveishei Istorii (RTsKhIDNI)*. Moscow.

Fond 5. *Lenin, Vladimir Ilich*
Fond 17. *Tsentral'nyi Komitet KPSS*
  Opis' 2. *Plenumy TsK*
  Opis' 3. *Politicheskoe biuro TsK*
  Opisi 17–21, 23–30. *Sektor informatsii otdela rukovodiashchikh partiinykh organov*
  Opisi 31–32, 87. *Informatsionnyi otdel TsK*
  Opisi 33, 84–86. *Sekretnyi otdel i biuro sekretariata TsK*
  Opis' 42. *Sektor partiinoi informatsii otdela partiinykh organov*
  Opis' 60. *Otdel agitatsii i propagandy TsK*
  Opisi 67–69, 74. *Organizatsionno-raspredelitel'nyi otdel*
  Opisi 112–114. *Organizationnoe biuro i sekretariat TsK*
Fond 62. *Sredneaziatskoe biuro TsK VKP/b/ (Sredazbiuro)*
Fond 77. *Zhdanov, Andrei Aleksandrovich*
Fond 78. *Kalinin, Mikhail Ivanovich*
Fond 80. *Kirov, Sergei Mironovich*
Fond 81. *Kaganovich, Lazar Moiseevich*
Fond 82. *Molotov, Viacheslav Mikhailovich*
Fond 85. *Ordzhonikidze, Grigorii Konstantinovich*
Fond 89. *Iaroslavskii, Emelian Mikhailovich*
Fond 94. *Fraktsiia RKP/b/, VKP/b/ vo vserossiiskom tsentral'nom ispolnitel'nom komitete (VTsIK), na s"ezdakh sovetov, v prezidiume TsIK SSSR*
Fond 121. *Upolnomochennyi TsKK VKP/b/—NK RKI v Srednei Azii*

Fond 157. *Tskhakaia, Mikhail Grigorevich*
Fond 445. *Tsentral'noe biuro evreiskikh kommunisticheskikh sektsii pri TsK VKP/b/*
Fond 558. *Stalin, Iosif Vissarionovich*
Fond 607. *Biuro po delam RSFSR pri TsK VKP/b/*
Fond 613. *Tsentral'naia kotrol'naia komissiia VKP/b/ (TsKK)*

ii. *Gosudarstvennyi Arkhiv Rossiiskoi Federatsii (GARF).* Moscow.

Fond 374. *Tsentral'naia kontrol'naia komissiia VKP/b/—Narodnyi komissariat raboche-krest'ianskoi inspektsii SSSR (TsKK-NKRKI SSSR)*
Fond 393. *Narodnyi komissariat vnutrennikh del RSFSR* (NKVD RSFSR)
Fond 1235. *Vserossiiskii tsentral'nyi ispolnitel'nyi komitet RSFSR* (VTsIK RSFSR)
Fond 3316. *Tsentral'nyi ispolnitel'nyi komitet SSSR* (TsIK SSSR)
Fond 3972. *Likvidatsionnaia komissiia narodnogo komissariata natsional'nostei*
Fond 5446. *Upravleniie delami Sovnarkoma SSR*
Fond 7523. *Verkhovnyi sovet SSSR*
Fond 7543. *Vsesoiuznyi tsentral'nyi komitet novogo alfavita* (VTsK NA)

iii. *Gosudarstvennyi Arkhiv Rossiiskoi Federatsii* [former TsGA RSFSR] (GARF-TsGA RSFSR). Moscow.

Fond 296. *Komitet po prosveshcheniiu natsional'nykh men'shinstv pri Narkompros RSFSR* (Komnats RSFSR)
Fond 406. *Narodnyi komissariat raboche-krest'ianskoi inspektsii RSFSR* (NKRKI RSFSR)
Fond 2306. *Narodnyi komissariat po prosveshcheniiu RSFSR* (Narkompros RSFSR)
Fond 2307. *Glavnauka Narkomprosa RSFSR*

iv. *Rossiiskii gosudarstvennyi arkhiv ekonomiki* (RGAE). Moscow.

Fond 5675. *Uchrezhdeniia po rukovodstvu pereseleniem v SSSR*
Fond 7486. *Narodnyi komissariat zemledelii SSSR* (NKZ SSSR)

v. *Rossiiskii gosudarstvennyi voennyi arkhiv* (RGVA). Moscow.

Fond 9. *Politicheskoe upravlenie RKKA*
Fond 33879. *Upravlenie dal'nevostochnogo krasnoznamennogo fronta*

vi. *Tsentr khraneniia sovremennoi dokumentatsii (TsKhSD)*

Fond 89. The Communist Party on Trial

vii. *Tsentral'nyi derzhavnyi arkhiv hromads'kykh ob'ednan' Ukrainy (TsDAHOU)*

Fond 1. *Tsentral'nyi komitet KP/b/U*
    Opis' 1. *Plenumy TsK KP/b/U*
    Opis' 6. *Politbiuro TsK KP/b/U*
    Opis' 7. *Orgbiuro TsK KP/b/U*
    Opis' 16. *TsK KP/b/U (osobaia papka)*
    Opis' 20. *Otdely TsK KP/b/U*

viii. *Tsentral'nyi derzhavnyi arkhiv vykonnykh orhaniv Ukrainy (TsDAVOU)*

Fond 166. *Narodnii komissariiat osvity URSR* (Narkomos URSR)

Fond 539. *Narodnyi komissariat raboche-krest'ianskoi inspektsii USSR* (NKRKI USSR)
Fond 2605. *Vseukrains'ka rada profesional'nykh spilok URSR* (VURPS URSR)

ix. *Harvard Interview Project* (HIP)

"A" Series. General Interviews.
"B" Series. Special Topics Interviews

x. *British Foreign Office: Russia Correspondence* (BFORC)

xi. *Captured German Materials* (CGM)

II. NEWSPAPERS

Bil'shovyk (Kiev)
Izvestiia TsIK i VTsIK (Moscow)
Komunist (Kharkov-Kiev)
Leningradskaia pravda (Leningrad)
Literaturnaia gazeta (Moscow)
Literaturna hazeta (Kharkov-Kiev)
Molot (Rostov-na-donu)
Pravda (Moscow)
Pravda vostoka (Tashkent)
Sovetskaia Belorussiia (Minsk)
Uchitel'skaia gazeta (Moscow)
Visti VUTsIK (Kharkov-Kiev)

III. JOURNALS

Arkhivy Ukrainy
As'veta
Bil'shovyk Ukrainy
Biuleten' narodn'oho komisariatu osvity Ukrainskoi RSR
Biulleten' narkomprosa Karel'skoi ASSR
Biulleten' narodnogo komissariata po prosveshcheniiu RSFSR
Biulleten' tsentral'nogo ispolnitel'nogo komiteta sovetov rab., krest. i krasnoarm. deputatov avtonomnoi Chuvashskoi sovetskoi respubliki
Bol'shevik
Bol'shevik Belarusi
Bol'shevik Kazakstana
Chervonyi shliakh
Istochnik
Istoricheskii arkhiv
Izvestiia TsK KPSS
Izvestiia TsK VKP/b/
Karta
Komi-mu—Zyrianskii krai
Kommunisticheskaia revoliutsiia
Kommunisticheskii vostok

Kommunisticheskoe prosveshchenie
Kul'tura i pis'mennost' vostoka
Leninskii put' (Rostov-na-donu)
Literatura natsional'nostei SSSR
Narodnoe prosveshchenie
Natsional'naia kniga
Novym shliakhom
Novyi vostok
Partiinoe stroitel'stvo
Partrabotnik (Tashkent)
Pis'mennost' i revoliutsiia
Planovoe khoziaistvo
Po leninskomu puti
Po zavetam Il'icha
Prapor marksyzmu
Prosveshchenie natsional'nostei
Put' Lenina (Ufa)
Radians'ka Ukraina
Revoliutsiia i gorets
Revoliutsiia i natsional'nosti
Revoliutsiia i pis'mennost'
Revoliutsionnyi vostok
Sobranie zakonov i rasporiazhenii SSSR
Sobranie uzakonenii i rasporiazhenii raboche-krest'ianskogo pravitel'stva Tatarskoi respubliki
Sobranie uzakonenii i rasporiazhenii raboche-krest'ianskogo pravitel'stva Ukrainskoi Sotsialisticheskoi Sovetskoi Respubliki
Sovetskaia Iakutiia
Sovetskaia iustitsiia
Sovetskaia Kareliia
Sovetskii fol'klor
Sovetskii sever
Sovetskoe gosudarstvo i pravo
Sovetskoe stroitel'stvo
Sovetskoe stroitel'stvo. Ezhemesiachnyi politiko-ekonomicheskii zhurnal gosplana BSSR
Sovety Azerbaidzhana
Teatr
Vestnik kommunisticheskoi akademii
Vlast' sovetov
Zhizn' natsional'nostei

IV. STENOGRAPHIC REPORTS

A. All-Union and RSFSR

i. TsK Congresses and Conferences

Vos'moi s"ezd RKP/b/. 18–23 marta 1919 g. Protokoly (Moscow, 1933).
Desiatyi s"ezd RKP/b/. Mart 1921 g. Protokoly (Moscow, 1933).

Dvenadtsatyi s"ezd RKP/b/. 17–25 aprelia 1923 goda. Stenograficheskii otchet (Moscow, 1968).

Trinadtsatyi s"ezd RKP/b/. Mai 1924 goda. Stenograficheskii otchet (Moscow, 1963).

XV konferentsiia vsesoiuznoi kommunisticheskoi partii/b/. 26 oktiabria—3 noiabria 1926 g. Stenograficheskii otchet (Moscow, 1927).

XV s"ezd vsesoiuznoi kommunisticheskoi partii—/b/. Stenograficheskii otchet (Moscow-Leningrad, 1928).

XVI s"ezd vsesoiuznoi kommunisticheskoi partii VKP/b/. Stenograficheskii otchet (Moscow, 1930).

XVII s"ezd vsesoiuznoi kommunisticheskoi partii/b/. 26 ianvaria—10 fevralia 1934 g. Stenograficheskii otchet (Moscow, 1934).

ii. Congresses of Soviets and Sessions of TsIK

III s"ezd sovetov Soiuza Sovetskikh Sotsialisticheskikh Respublik. Stenograficheskii otchet (Moscow, 1925).

Pervaia sessiia tsentral'nogo ispolnitel'nogo komiteta Soiuza Sovetskikh Sotsialisticheskikh Respublik vtorogo sozyva. Stenograficheskii otchet (Moscow, 1924).

Vtoraia sessiia tsentral'nogo ispolnitel'nogo komiteta Soiuza Sovetskikh Sotsialisticheskikh Respublik vtorogo sozyva. Stenograficheskii otchet (Moscow, 1924).

Tret'ia sessiia tsentral'nogo ispolnitel'nogo komiteta Soiuza Sovetskikh Sotsialisticheskikh Respublik vtorogo sozyva. Stenograficheskii otchet (Moscow, 1925).

Vtoraia sessiia tsentral'nogo ispolnitel'nogo komiteta Soiuza Sovetskikh Sotsialisticheskikh Respublik tret'ego sozyva. Stenograficheskii otchet (Moscow, 1926).

Tret'ia sessiia tsentral'nogo ispolnitel'nogo komiteta Soiuza Sovetskikh Sotsialisticheskikh Respublik piatogo sozyva. Stenograficheskii otchet (Moscow, 1931).

iv. VTsK NTA

Pervyi vsesoiuznyi tiurkologicheskii s"ezd. 26 fevralia—5 marta 1926 g. Stenograficheskii otchet (Baku, 1926).

Stenograficheskii otchet pervogo plenuma vsesoiuznogo tsentral'nogo komiteta novogo tiurksokogo alfavita, zasedavshego v Baku ot 3-ego do 7-go iunia 1927 goda (Moscow, 1927).

Stenograficheskii otchet vtorogo plenuma vsesoiuznogo komiteta novogo tiurkskogo alfavita, zasedavshego v g. Tashkente ot 7-go po 12-e ianvaria 1928 goda (Baku, 1929).

Stenograficheskii otchet chetvertogo plenuma vsesoiuznogo komiteta novogo tiurkskogo alfavita (Moscow, 1931).

Iazyk i pis'mennost' narodov SSSR. Stenograficheskii otchet 1-go vsesoiuznogo plenuma NS VTsKNA (Moscow, 1933).

iv. Other

Pervyi vsesoiuznyi s"ezd 'Ozet' v Moskve. 15–20 noiabria 1926 g. Stenograficheskii otchet (Moscow, 1927).

Soveshchanie upolnomochennykh po rabote sredi natsional'nykh men'shinstv pri TsIKakh avtonomnykh respublik, oblastnykh kraevykh i gubernskikh ispolnitel'nykh komitetakh, 1928 g. Stenograficheskii otchet (Moscow, 1928).

Tainy natsional'noi politiki TsK RKP. Chetvertoe soveshchanie TsK RKP s otvetstvennymi rabotnikami natsional'nykh respublik i oblastei v g. Moskve. 9–12 iiunia 1923 g. Stenograficheskii otchet (Moscow, 1992).

Vtoraia sessiia VTsIK piatnadtsatogo sozyva. Stenograficheskii otchet (Moscow, 1931).

B. Belorussia

XIII konferentsiia kommunisticheskoi partii/bolsh./ Belorussii. Stenograficheskii otchet (Minsk, 1924).

X-yi s"ezd kommunisticheskoi partii (bol'shevikov) Belorussii. 3–10 ianvaria 1927 goda. Stenograficheskii otchet (Minsk, 1927).

XI z"ezd kamunistychnai partyi/b/ Belarusi. 22–29 listapada 1927 godu. Stenahrafichnaia spravazdacha (Minsk, 1928).

C. Georgia

IV s"ezd kommunisticheskoi partii (bol'shevikov) Gruzii. 30.11—5.12 1925. Stenograficheskii otchet (Tbilisi, 1925).

V s"ezd kommunisticheskoi partii/b/ Gruzii. Stenograficheskii otchet (Tbilisi, 1927).

VI s"ezd kompartii/b/ Gruzii. 1–10 iulia 1929 g. Stenograficheskii otchet (Tbilisi, 1929).

Vtoroi ob"edinennyi plenum TsK i TsKK KP/b/ Gruzii. Iun' 1932 g. Stenograficheskii otchet (Tbilisi, 1932).

IX s"ezd kommunisticheskoi partii/b/ Gruzii. 10 ianvaria 1934 g. Stenograficheskii otchet (Tbilisi, 1935).

D. Kazakhstan

5-aia vsekazakskaia konferentsiia Rossiiskoi kommunisticheskoi partii (bol'shevikov). Stenograficheskii otchet i rezoliutsii. 1–7 dekabria 1925 g. (Kzyl-Orda, 1925).

6-aia vsekazakskaia konferentsiia VKP/b/. 15–23 noiabria. Stenograficheskii otchet (Kzyl-Orda, 1927).

7 vsekazakskaia partiinaia konferentsiia VKP/b/. Stenograficheskii otchet (Alma-Ata, 1930).

Shestoi plenum Kazakhskogo kraevogo komiteta VKP/b/. 10–16 iulia 1933 goda. Stenograficheskii otchet (Alma-Ata, 1936).

VIII Kazakhstanskaia kraevaia konferentsiia VKP/b/. 8–16 ianvaria 1934 g. Stenograficheskii otchet (Alma-Ata, 1935).

E. Tatarstan

7-ia oblastnaia partiinaia konferentsiia Tatrespubliki. 22–26 marta 1923 g. Stenograficheskii otchet (Kazan, 1923).

Stenograficheskii otchet IX oblastnoi konferentsii tatarsk. organizatsii RKP/b/ (Kazan, 1924).

Stenograficheskii otchet zasedanii XI oblastnoi partiinoi konferentsii (Kazan, 1925).

2 plenum oblastnogo komiteta VKP/b/ Tatarskoi respubliki odinnadtsatogo sozyva. Stenograficheskii otchet (Kazan, 1926).

4 plenum Tatarskogo oblastnogo komiteta VKP/b/. 15–19 sentiabria 1927 goda. Stenogramma otcheta biuro OK VKP/b/ (Kazan, 1927).

Stenograficheskii otchet zasedanii XII oblastnoi partiinoi konferentsii (Kazan, 1927).

Stenograficheskii otchet zasedanii XIII oblastnoi partiinoi konferentsii. 23–29 noiabria 1927 g. (Kazan, 1927).

Ob"edinennyi plenum OK i OKK VKP/b/. 19–23 fevralia 1933 g. Stenograficheskii otchet (Kazan, 1933).

F. Transcaucasus

III-i s"ezd kommunisticheskikh organizatsii zakavkaz'ia. 13–15 maia 1924 goda. Stenograficheskii otchet (Tbilisi, 1924).
Piatyi s"ezd kommunisticheskikh organizatsii Zakavkaz'ia. Stenogramma (Tbilisi, 1928).
VI s"ezd kommunisticheskikh organizatsii Zakavkaz'ia. Stenograficheskii otchet (Tbilisi, 1930).

G. Ukraine

Biulleten' VIII-i vseukrainskoi konferentsii kommunisticheskoi partii (bol'shevikov) Ukrainy. Stenogramma. 12–17 maia 1924 g. (Kharkov, 1924).
Deviatyi s"ezd kommunisticheskoi partii bol'shevikov. Stenograficheskii otchet (Kharkov, 1926).
Persha vseukrains'ka konferentsiia KP/b/U. 17–21 zhovtnia 1926 roku. Stenohrafichnyi zvit (Kharkov, 1926).
Desiatyi z'izd komunistychnoi partii (bil'shovykiv) Ukrainy. 20–29 listopada 1927 r. Stenohrafichnyi zvit (Kharkov, 1928).
Druha konferentsiia komunistychnoi partii (bil'shovykiv) Ukrainy. 9–14 kvitnia 1929 roku. Stenohrafichnyi zvit (Kharkov, 1929).
XI z'izd komunistychnoi partii (bil'shovykiv) Ukrainy. 5–15 chervnia 1930 roku. Stenohrafichnyi zvit (Kharkov, 1930).
Tret'ia konferentsiia komunistychnoi partii (bil'shovykiv) Ukrainy. 6–9 lypnia 1932 roku. Stenohrafichnyi zvit (Kharkov, 1932).
Pervoe vseukrainskoe soveshchanie po rabote sredi natsional'nykh men'shinstv. 8–11 ianvaria 1927 goda. Stenograficheskii otchet, rezoliutsiia, postanovleniia i materialy (Kharkov, 1927).
"Spilka Vyzvolennia Ukrainy": Stenohrafichnyi zvit sudovoho protsesu. Tom 1 (Kharkov, 1931).

V. PRIMARY SOURCES. BOOKS AND ARTICLES

Abramov, S. *Natsional'naia rabota sovetov v gorodakh* (Moscow, 1935).
Administrativno-territorial'noe delenie Soiuza SSR na 1 marta 1937 goda (Moscow, 1937).
Akademicheskoe delo, 1929–1931 gg. Vypusk 1. Delo po obvineniiu akademika S. F. Platonova (St. Petersburg, 1993).
Aleksandrov, I. G. *Ekonomicheskoe raionirovanie Rossii* (Moscow, 1921).
Anosov, S. D. *Koreitsy v ussuriiskom krae* (Khabarovsk-Vladivostok, 1928).
Arkhiv Trotskogo. Kommunisticheskaia oppozitsiia v SSSR, 1923–1927, 4 vols. (Moscow, 1990).
Ashnin, F. D., and Alpatov, V. M. *"Delo slavistov" 30-e gody* (Moscow, 1994).
Belaia kniga o deportatsii koreiskogo naseleniia Rossii v 30-40-kh godakh. Kniga pervaia (Moscow, 1992).
Berelovich, A., and Danilov, V., eds. *Sovetskaia derevnia glazami VChK-OGPU-NKVD 1918–1939. Vol. 2. 1923–1929. Dokumenty i materialy* (Moscow, 2000).

Bochagov, D. K. *Milli Firka. natsional'naia kontrrevoliutsiia v Krymu* (Simferopol, 1930).

Bottomore, Tim, and Goode, Patrick, eds. *Austro-Marxism* (Oxford, 1978).

Budivnytstvo radians'koi Ukrainy. Zbirnyk vypusk 1. Za lenins'ku natsional'nu polityku (Kharkov, 1928).

Budzin, A., ed. *Natsyianal'nae pytan'ne* (Minsk, 1932).

Bugai, N. F. *Iosif Stalin–Lavrentiiu Berii. "Ikh nado deportirovat'...." Dokumenty, fakty, kommentarii* (Moscow, 1993).

Butsenko, A. *Sovetskoe stroitel'stvo i natsmen'shinstva na Ukraine* (Kharkov, 1926).

Carynnyk, Marco et al., eds. *The Foreign Office and the Famine. British Documents on Ukraine and the Great Famine of 1932–1933* (Kingston, Ont., 1988).

"Chechnia: vooruzhennaia bor'ba v 20–30 gody," *Voenno-istoricheskii arkhiv* 2 (1997): 118–175.

"Chechnia: vooruzhennaia bor'ba v 20–30 gody," *Voenno-istoricheskii arkhiv* 8 (2000): 99–121.

Chuev, F. *Sto sorok besed s Molotovym. Iz dvenvika F. Chueva* (Moscow, 1991).

Danilov, V., and Berelowitch, A., eds. *Sovetskaia derevnia glazami VChK-OGPU-NKVD. Dokumenty i materialy. Tom 1. 1918–1922* (Moscow, 1998).

Danilov, V. P., and Krasilnikov, A., eds. *Spetspereselentsy v Zapadnoi Sibiri*, 4 vols. (Novosibirsk, 1992–1996).

Durdenevskii, V. N. *Ravnopravie iazykov v sovetskom stroe* (Moscow, 1927).

Gazety SSSR, 1917–1960. Bibliograficheskii spravochnik, 5 vols. (Moscow, 1970–1984).

Girchak, E. F. *Na dva fronta v bor'be s natsionalizmom* (Moscow-Leningrad, 1931).

Golde, I. *Evrei zemledel'tsy v Krymu* (Moscow, 1932).

Golod v kazakhskoi stepi. Pis'ma trevogi i boli (Almaty, 1991).

Golubovskii, M. *Leninskaia natsional'naia politika v deistvii* (Khabarovsk, 1932).

Graziosi, Andrea. "Collectivisation, Revoltes Paysannes et Politiques Gouvernementales a travers les rapports du GPU d'Ukraine de fevrier-mars 1930." *Cahiers du monde russe*, vol. 35 (July–Sept. 1994): 437–632.

Hirchak, E. F. *Bilorus'kyi natsional-demokratyzm* (Kharkov, 1931).

Hirchak, E. F. *Khvyl'ovyzm (Sproba politychnoi kharakterystyky)* (Kharkov, 1930).

Hirchak, E. F. *Natsional'ne pytannia ta pravyi ukhyl* (Kharkov, 1930).

Hirchak, E. *Zavdannia natsional'no-kul'turnoho budivnytstva. Do trymisiachnyka Ukrains'koi kul'tury* (Kharkov, 1929).

Holod 1932–1933 rokiv na Ukraini. Ochyma istorykiv, movoiu dokumentiv (Kiev, 1990).

Ianson, P. M. *Ot ugneteniia i bespraviia—k schastlivoi zhizni* (Leningrad, 1936).

Ibragimov and Sady, S. *Uspekhi leninskoi natsional'noi politiki na Urale* (Sverdlovsk, 1932).

Ibragimov, S. *Voprosy natsional'noi kul'tury* (Ashkhabad, 1928).

The Ingrian Finns (Helsinki, 1935).

Itogi i blizhaishie zadachi provedeniia leninskoi natsional'noi politiki v BSSR. Postanovlenie ob"edinennogo plenuma TsK i TsKK KP/b/B (Minsk, 1934).

Itogi raboty sredi natsional'nykh men'shinstv na Ukraine (Kharkov, 1927).

Itogi razresheniia natsional'nogo voprosa v SSSR (Moscow, 1936).

Ivnitskii, N. et al., eds. *Tragediia sovetskoi derevni. Kollektivizatsiia i raskulachivanie. Dokumenty i materialy. Vol. 2. Noiabr' 1929–dekabr' 1930* (Moscow, 2000).

Kaganovich, Lazar. *Pamiatnye zapiski* (Moscow, 1996).

Kalinin, M. I. *Evrei-zemledel'tsy v soiuze narodov SSSR* (Moscow, 1927).

Kantor, I. *Natsional'noe stroitel'stvo sredi evreev v SSSR* (Moscow, 1934).

Kasymov, G. *Pantiurkistskaia kontrrevoliutsiia i ee agentura—Sultangalievshchina* (Kazan, 1931).

Kazan'—tsentr Volzhsko-Kamskoi oblasti (Kazan, 1923).

Khansuvarov, I. *Latinizatsiia—orudie leninskoi natsional'noi politiki* (Moscow, 1932).

Khlevniuk, O. V. et al., eds. *Stalinskoe politbiuro v 30-e gody. Sbornik dokumentov* (Moscow, 1995).

Khvylia, Andrii. *Do rozv'iazannia natsional'noho pytannia na Ukraini* (Kharkov, 1930).

Khvylia, A. *Natsional'nyi vopros na Ukraine* (Kharkov, 1926).

Khvylia, Andrii. *Vid ukhylu—u prirvu (pro "val'dshnepy" Khvyl'ovoho)* (Kharkov, 1928).

Khvylia, Andrii. *Znyshchyty korinnia Ukrains'koho natsionalizmu na movnomu fronti* (Kharkov, 1933).

Khvylovyi, Mykola. *The Cultural Renaissance in Ukraine. Polemical Pamphlets, 1925–1926*, ed. Myroslav Shkandrij (Edmonton, 1986).

Kniga i knizhnoe delo v Ukrainskoi SSR. Sbornik dokumentov i materialov, 1917–1941 (Kiev, 1985).

Kolektyvizatsiia i holod na Ukraini, 1929–1933. Zbirnyk dokumentiv i materialiv (Kiev, 1993).

Kosior, S. *Itogi i blizhaishie zadachi provedeniia natsional'noi politiki na Ukraine* (Moscow, 1933).

Larin, Iurii. *Evrei i antisemitizm* (Moscow, 1929).

Lazovskii, I., and Bibin, I., eds. *Sovetskaia politika za 10 let po natsional'nomu voprosu v RSFSR* (Moscow, 1928).

Lebed, Dmitrii. *Sovetskaia Ukraina i natsional'nyi vopros za piat' let* (Kharkov, 1924).

Lenin, V. I. *Polnoe sobranie sochinenii*, 55 vols. (Moscow, 1976–1978).

Leningradskii martirolog, 1937–1938, 3 vols. (St. Petersburg, 1996–1998).

Letopis' periodicheskikh izdanii SSSR v 1935 g. (na 1 iulia) (Moscow, 1935).

Lih, Lars, ed. *Stalin's Letters to Molotov, 1925–1936* (New Haven, Conn., 1995).

Liubchenko, P. *Z Varshavs'kym Dohovorom proty p'iatyrichky. Do protsesu SVU* (Kharkov, 1930).

Lutskyi, Iurii, ed. *Vaplitians'kyi zbirnyk* (Oakville, Ont., 1977).

Maistrenko, Ivan. *Istoriia moho pokolinnia. Spohady uchasnyka revoliutsiinykh podii v Ukraini* (Edmonton, 1985).

Materialy i resheniia 3 obshchegorodskogo natsmen-soveshchaniia. 7–8 iulia 1932 goda (Rostov-na-donu, 1932).

Materialy k pervomu kul'turno-natsional'nomu soveshchaniiu BMASSR (Verkhneudinsk, 1926).

Molotov, V. M. *Velikaia druzhba narodov SSSR* (Moscow, 1936).

Natsional'naia politika VKP/b/ v tsifrakh (Moscow, 1930).

Natsional'ne pytannia na Ukraini ta rozlam v KPZU. Zbirnyk stattei i dokumentiv (Kharkov, 1928).

Natsional'nye men'shinstva leningradskoi oblasti (Leningrad, 1929).

Natsional'nyi sostav vybornykh organov vlasti RSFSR (Moscow, 1928).

Natsional'nyi vopros na perekrestke mnenii. 20-e gody. Dokumenty i materialy (Moscow, 1992).

Nimtsi v Ukraini 20–30-ti rr. XX st. Zbirnyk dokumentiv derzhavnykh arkhiviv Ukrainy (Kiev, 1994).

Nugis, A. *Protiv velikoderzhavnogo shovinizma i mestnogo natsionalizma* (Khabarovsk, 1933).

O korenizatsii. Sbornik rukovodiashchikh materialov (Alma-Ata, 1934).

O narushenii natsional'noi politiki v Severno-Kavkazskom krae (Piatigorsk, 1936).

O rabote sredi natsional'nykh men'shinstv v N.-V. krae (Saratov, 1929).

Oppozitsiia i natsional'nyi vopros. Iz stenogrammy 6-go ob"edinennogo plenuma TsK i TsKK KP/b/T po dokladu tov. Tera ob itogakh avgustovskogo plenuma TsK i TsKK VKP/b/. Materialy k 3-mu s"ezdu KP/b/T (n.p., 1927).

Ostrovskii, Z. *Problema Ukrainizatsii i Belorussizatsii v RSFSR* (Moscow, 1931).

Ot s"ezda k s"ezdu. Aprel' 1927–mai 1929 g. (Moscow, 1929).

Panfilov, V. N. *Kul'turnaia revoliutsiia i piatiletka natsmenprosveshcheniia* (Moscow, 1930).

Pipes, Richard, ed., *The Unknown Lenin. From the Secret Archives* (New Haven, Conn., 1996).

Platonau, Rastsislau, and Stashkevich, Mikola. "Dzve aperatsyi suprats' 'Vorahau naroda'." *Belaruski histarychny chasopis*, no. 1 (1993): 73–80.

Popov, M. M. *Pro natsionalistychni ukhyly v lavakh Ukrains'koi partorhanizatsii i pro zavdannia borot'by z nymy. Dopovid' na zborakh kharkivs'koho partaktyvu 9 lypnia 1933 roku* (Kharkov, 1933).

Postanovlenie 2-go respublikanskogo soveshchaniia natsmen Kir. ASSR (Frunze, 1932).

Postanovleniia prezidiuma VTsIK ot 1 noiabria 1932 goda i presidiuma Bashkirskogo TsIKa ot 29 dekabria 1932 goda o korenizatsii apparata (Ufa, 1933).

Postyshev, P. *U borot'bu za lenins'ku natsional'nu polityku* (Kharkov, 1934).

Prakticheskoe razreshenie natsional'nogo voprosa v Belorusskoi Sotsialisticheskoi Respublike. Chast' 1. Belorussizatsiia (Minsk, 1927).

Prakticheskoe razreshenie natsional'nogo voprosa v Belorusskoi Sotsialisticheskoi Respublike. Chast' 2. Rabota sredi natsional'nykh men'shinstv v BSSR (Minsk, 1927).

Presa Ukrains'koi RSR, 1918–1973. Naukovo-statystychnyi dovidnyk (Kharkov, 1974).

Prystaiko, Volodymyr, and Shapoval, Iurii, eds. *Mykhailo Hrushevs'kyi: Sprava "UNTs" i ostanni roky* (Kiev, 1999).

Prystaiko, Volodymyr, and Shapoval, Iurii, eds. *Sprava "Spilka Vyzvolennia Ukrainy". Nevidomi dokumenty i fakty* (Kiev, 1995).

Rakhin, A., and i Shauman, L. *Za chto zhiteli stanitsy Poltavskoi vyseliaiutsia s Kubani v severnye kraia* (Rostov-na-donu, 1932).

Ravich-Cherkasskii, M. *Istoriia kommunisticheskoi partii Ukrainy* (Kharkov, 1923).

Rubinshtein, L. *V bor'be za leninskuiu natsional'nuiu politiku* (Kazan, 1930).

S"ezdy sovetov soiuza SSR, soiuznykh i avtonomnykh Sovetskikh Sotsialisticheskikh Respublik. Sbornik dokumentov v trekh tomakh, 1917–1936 g., 3 vols. (Moscow, 1959–1960).

Shapoval, Iurii, and Prystaiko, Volodymyr, eds. *Mykhailo Hrushevskyi i HPU-NKVD. Trahichne desiatylittia, 1924–1934* (Kiev, 1996).

Shapoval, Iurii, Prystaiko, Volodymyr, and Zolotarov, Vadym, eds. *ChK-HPU-NKVD v Ukraini: osoby, fakty, dokumenty* (Kiev, 1997).

Shar, V. *Na karte Kubani novaia stanitsa krasnoarmeiskaia* (n.p., 1933).

Skrypnik, N. *Natsional'nyi vopros v programme kominterna* (Kharkov, 1929).

Skrypnyk, M. *Do rekonstruktsiinykh problem. Industriializatsiia, kolektyvizatsiia, nat-spytannia, samokrytyka. Dopovid' na 7 plenumi Kyivs'koho OPK KP/b/U. 27.II.1929* (Kharkov, 1929).

Skrypnyk, M. *Dzherela ta prychyny rozlamu v KPZU* (Kharkov, 1928).

Skrypnyk, M. O. *Do teorii borot'by dvokh kul'tur* (Kharkov, 1928).

Skrypnyk, M. O. *Narysy pidsumkiv ukrainizatsii ta obsluzhuvannia kul'turnykh potreb natsmenshostei USRR, zokrema rosiis'koi. Promova na zasidanni kolegii NKO USRR z 14.02.33 r.* (Kharkov, 1933).

Skrypnyk, M. *Neprymyrennym shliakhom. Dopovid' na okrpartkonferentsii v Odesi na 12-ho hrudnia 1928 roku* (Kharkov, 1929).

Skrypnyk, Mykola. *Stan ta perspektyvy kul'turnoho budivnytstva na Ukraini* (Kharkov, 1929).

Skrypnyk, Mykola. *Statti i promovy. Tom II. Chastyna persha. Natsional'ne pytannia* (Kharkov, 1929).

Skrypnyk, Mykola. *Statti i promovy. Natsional'ne pytannia. Tom II. Chastyna druha* (Kharkov, 1931).

Slomit' sabotazh seva i khlebozagotovok, organizovanye kulachestvom v raionakh Kubani (Moscow, 1932).

Stalin, I. *Marksizm i natsional'no-kolonial'nyi vopros* (Moscow, 1934).

Stalin, I. V. *Sochineniia*, 13 vols. (Moscow, 1953–1955).

Stalin, Joseph. *Marxism and the National Question. Selected Writings and Speeches* (New York, 1942).

Sultan-Galiev, Mirsaid. *Stat'i. Vystupleniia. Dokumenty* (Kazan, 1992).

Suprots kontrrevoliutsyinaha belaruskaha natsiianal-demokratyzmu (Minsk, 1931).

Vaganian, V. *Ne soglasen ni s odnim iz moikh opponentov. Otvet moim kritikam* (Moscow, 1927).

Vaganian, V. *O natsional'noi kul'ture* (Moscow, 1927).

Vsesoiuznaia perepis' naseleniia 1926 g., 66 Vols. (Moscow, 1926).

Vsesoiuznaia perepis' naseleniia 1937 g. Kratkie itogi (Moscow, 1991).

Vsesoiuznaia perepis' naseleniia 1939 goda. Osnovnye itogi (Moscow, 1992).

Zamch, I. *Partorganizatsiia na bor'bu za Ukrainizatsiiu* (Rostov-na-donu, 1932).

Zatonskyi, V. P. *Natsional'no-kul'turne budivnytstvo i borot'ba proty natsionalizmu* (Kiev, 1934).

Zinger, L., ed. *Natsional'nyi sostav proletariata v SSSR* (Moscow, 1934).

Ziuzkou, A. *Kryvavy shliakh belaruskai natsdemokratyi* (Minsk, 1931).

VI. SECONDARY SOURCES. BOOKS AND ARTICLES

Adamovich, Anthony. *Opposition to Sovietization in Belorussian Literature* (New York, 1958).

Anderson, Benedict. *Imagined Communities* (London, 1991).

Bahry, Donna. *Outside Moscow: Power, Politics and Budgetary Policy in the Soviet Republics* (New York, 1987).

Barkey, Karen, and Von Hagen, Mark, eds. *After Empire: Multiethnic Societies and Nation-Building. The Soviet Union and the Russian, Ottoman and Habsburg Empires* (Boulder, Colo., 1997).

Bauer, Otto. *Die Nationalitätenfrage und die Sozialdemokratie* (Vienna, 1907).

Beissinger, Mark. "The Persisting Ambiguity of Empire." *Post-Soviet Affairs* II (1995): 149–184.

Bennigsen, A. A., and Wimbush, S. E. *Muslim National Communism in the Soviet Union: A Revolutionary Strategy for the Colonial World* (Chicago, 1979).

Bilinsky, Yaroslav. *The Second Soviet Republic: The Ukraine after World War II* (New Brunswick, N.J., 1964).

Blank, Stephen. *The Sorcerer as Apprentice: Stalin as Commissar of Nationalities, 1917–1924* (Westport, Colo., 1994).

Blitstein, Peter. "Stalin's Nations: Soviet Nationality Policy between Planning and Primordialism, 1936–1953" (Ph.D. diss., University of California-Berkeley, 1999).

Borys, Jurij. *The Sovietization of Ukraine, 1917–1923* (Edmonton, 1980).

Brandenberger, David. "The 'Short Course' to Modernity: Stalinist History Textbooks, Mass Culture and the Formation of Popular Russian National Identity" (Ph.D. diss., Harvard University, 1999).

Brubaker, Rogers. *Nationalism Reframed: Nationhood and the National Question in the New Europe* (Oxford, 1996).

Buchsweiler, Meir. *Volksdeutsche in der Ukraine am Vorabend und Beginn des Zweiten Weltkriegs—ein Fall Doppelter Loyalität?* (Gerlingen, 1984).

Bugai, N. F. "20-40-e gody: deportatsiia naseleniia s territorii evropeiskoi Rossii." *Otechestvennaia istoriia*, no. 4 (1992): 37–40.

Bugai, N. F. *L. Beriia—I. Stalinu: "Soglasno vashemu ukazaniiu . . ."* (Moscow, 1995).

Bugai, Nikolai F. "'Koreiskii vopros' na Dal'nem Vostoke i deportatsiia 1937 goda." *Problemy Dal'nego Vostoka*, no. 4 (1992): 152–162.

Bugai, N. F., and Gonov, A. M. *Kavkaz: Narody v eshelonakh (20-e-60-e gody)* (Moscow, 1998).

Commission on the Ukraine Famine. *Oral History Project of the Commission on the Ukraine Famine*, ed. James E. Mace and Leonid Heretz. 3 vols. (Washington, D.C., 1990).

Connor, Walker. *The National Question in Marxist-Leninist Theory and Strategy* (Princeton, N.J., 1984).

Conquest, Robert. *The Great Terror: A Reassessment* (New York, 1990).

Conquest, Robert. *The Harvest of Sorrow: Soviet Collectivization and the Terror Famine* (New York, 1986).

Conquest, Robert. *The Nation Killers: The Soviet Deportation of Nationalities* (London, 1977).

Davies, R. W. *Crisis and Progress in the Soviet Economy, 1931–1933* (London, 1996).

Dawisha, Karen, and Bruce Parrot, eds. *The End of Empire? The Transformation of the USSR in Comparative Perspective* (Armonk, N.Y., 1997).

Demko, George J. *The Russian Colonization of Kazakhstan, 1896–1916* (Bloomington, Ind., 1969).

Dyck, Harvey. *Weimar Germany & Soviet Russia 1926–1933: A Study in Diplomatic Instability* (New York, 1966).

Edgar, Adrienne. "The Creation of Soviet Turkmenistan, 1924–1938" (Ph.D. diss., University of California-Berkeley, 1999).

Fairbanks, Charles H. Jr. "Clientelism and the Roots of Post-Soviet Disorder." In *Transcaucasia, Nationalism and Social Change: Essays in the History of Armenia, Azerbaijan, and Georgia*, ed. Ronald Grigor Suny (Ann Arbor, Mich., 1996): 341–376.

Fierman, William. *Language Planning and National Development: The Uzbek Experience* (Berlin, 1991).

Fitzpatrick, Sheila. "Ascribing Class: The Construction of Social Identity in Soviet Russia." *Journal of Modern History* 65 (December, 1993): 745–770.

Fitzpatrick, Sheila. *The Cultural Front: Power and Culture in Revolutionary Russia* (Ithaca, N.Y., 1992).

Fitzpatrick, Sheila, ed. *Cultural Revolution in Russia, 1928–1931* (Bloomington, Ind., 1978).

Fitzpatrick, Sheila. *Education and Social Mobility in the Soviet Union, 1921–1934* (Cambridge, 1979).

Galanter, Marc. *Competing Equalities: Law and the Backward Classes in India* (2nd ed., Delhi, 1991).

Gans, Herbert. "Symbolic Ethnicity: The Future of Ethnic Groups and Cultures in America." *Ethnic and Racial Studies* 2 (1979): 9–17.

Gelb, Michael. "An Early Soviet Ethnic Deportation: The Far-Eastern Koreans." *Russian Review* 54 (1995): 389–412.

Gelb, Michael. "'Karelian Fever': The Finnish Immigrant Community During Stalin's Purges." *Europe-Asia Studies* 45 (1993): 1091–1116.

Gelb, Michael. "The Western Finnic Minorities and the Origins of the Stalinist Nationalities Deportations." *Nationalities Papers* 24 (1996): 237–268.

Gellner, Ernest. *Nations and Nationalism* (Ithaca, N.Y., 1983).

Genis, V. L. "Deportatsiia russkikh iz Turkestana v 1921 godu ('Delo Safarova')." *Voprosy istorii*, no. 1 (1998): 44–58.

Getty, J. Arch. *Origins of the Great Purges* (Cambridge, 1985).

Getty, J. Arch, Rittersporn, Gabor, and Zemskov, Viktor. "Victims of the Soviet Penal System in the Pre-war Years: A First Approach on the Basis of Archival Evidence." *American Historical Review* 98 (1993).

Glazer, Nathan. *Affirmative Discrimination: Ethnic Inequality and Public Policy* (2nd ed., Cambridge, Mass., 1987).

Goldman, Wendy Z. *Women, The State and Revolution: Soviet Family Policy and Social Life, 1917–1936* (Cambridge, 1993).

Graziosi, Andrea. *Bol'sheviki i krest'iane na Ukraine, 1918–1919 gody. Ocherk o bol'shevizmakh, natsional-sotsializmakh i krest'ianskikh dvizheniiakh* (Moscow, 1997).

Graziosi, Andrea. "G. L. Piatakov (1890–1937): A Mirror of Soviet History." *Harvard Ukrainian Studies* 16 (1992): 102–166.

Gurr, Ted Robert, and Harff, Barbara. *Ethnic Conflict in World Politics* (Boulder, Colo., 1994).

Hagen, William. *Germans, Poles and Jews: The Nationality Conflict in the Prussian East* (Chicago, 1980).

Hardeman, Hilde. *Coming to Terms with the Soviet Regime: The "Changing Signposts" Movement among Russian Emigres in the Early 1920s* (DeKarlb, 1994).

Hayit, Baymirza. *"Basmatschi": Nationaler Kampf Turkestans in den Jahren 1917 bis 1934* (Köln, 1992).

Hirsch, Francine. "The Soviet Union as a Work-in-Progress: Ethnographers and the Category *Nationality* in the 1926, 1937 and 1939 Censuses." *Slavic Review* 56 (1997): 251–278.

Hirsch, Francine. "Empire of Nations: Colonial Technologies and the Making of the Soviet Union, 1917–1939" (Ph.D. diss., Princeton University, 1998).

Hirsch, Francine. "Toward an Empire of Nations: Border-Making and the Formation of Soviet National Identities." *Russian Review* 59 (2000): 201–26.

Hlevnjuk, Oleg. "Les mecanismes de la 'Grande Terreur' des annees 1937–1938 au Turkmenistan." *Cahiers du monde russe* 39 (1998): 197–208.

Holquist, Peter. "'Conduct Merciless Mass Terror': Decossackization on the Don, 1919." *Cahiers du monde russe* 38 (1997): 127–162.

Horowitz, Donald. *Ethnic Groups in Conflict* (Berkeley, Calif., 1985).

Hovannisian, Richard G. *The Republic of Armenia*, 4 vols. (Berkeley, Calif., 1971–1996).

Hroch, Miroslav. *Social Preconditions of National Revival in Europe* (Cambridge, 1985).

Hutchinson, John, and Smith, Anthony D., eds. *Ethnicity* (Oxford, 1996).

Inkeles, Alex, and Bauer, Raymond. *The Soviet Citizen: Daily Life in a Totalitarian Society* (Cambridge, Mass., 1961).

Isaev, M. I. *Iazykovoe stroitel'stvo v SSSR* (Moscow, 1979).

Ivnitskii, N. A. *Kollektivizatsiia i raskulachivanie (nachalo 30-kh godov)* (Moscow, 1996).

Iwanow, Mikolaj. *Pierwszy narod ukarany. Polacy v zviazku radzieckim, 1921–1939* (Warsaw, 1991).

Jacobson, Jon. *When the Soviet Union Entered World Politics* (Berkeley, Calif., 1994).

Kabuzan, V. *Russkie v mire* (St. Petersburg, 1996).

Kaiser, Robert J. *The Geography of Nationalism in Russia and the USSR* (Princeton, N.J., 1994).

Karklins, Rasma. *Ethnic Relations in the USSR: The Perspective from Below* (Boston, 1986).

Keller, Shoshana. "The Struggle Against Islam in Uzbekistan, 1921–1941: Policy, Bureaucracy, and Reality" (Ph.D. diss., Indiana University, 1995).

Khalid, Adeeb. *The Politics of Muslim Cultural Reform: Jadidism in Central Asia* (Berkeley, Calif., 1998).

Khlevniuk, O. V. *Politbiuro. Mekhanizmy politicheskoi vlasti v 1930—e gody* (Moscow, 1996).

Kirkwood, Michael, ed. *Language Planning in the Soviet Union* (New York, 1990).

Kondrashin, Viktor Viktorovich. "Golod 1932–1933 v derevne Povolzh'ia" (kand. diss., Moscow, 1991).

Kornai, Janos. *The Socialist System* (Princeton, N.J., 1992).

Kostyrchenko, Gennadi. *Out of the Red Shadows: Anti-Semitism in Stalin's Russia* (Amherst, N.Y., 1995).

Kotkin, Stephen. *Magnetic Mountain: Stalinism as a Civilization* (Berkeley, Calif., 1995).

Krawchenko, Bohdan. *Social Change and National Consciousness in Twentieth-Century Ukraine* (London, 1985).

Kuromiya, Hiroaki. *Freedom and Terror in the Donbas: A Ukrainian–Russian Borderland, 1870s–1990s* (Cambridge, 1998).

Kuromiya, Hiroaki. *Stalin's Industrial Revolution: Politics and Workers, 1928–1932* (Cambridge, 1988).

Laitin, David. *Ethnic Cleansing, Liberal Style*. MacArthur Foundation Program in Transnational Security. Working Paper Series, no. 4 (Cambridge, 1995).

Laitin, David. *Identity in Formation: The Russian-Speaking Populations in the Near Abroad* (Ithaca, N.Y., 1998).

Levin, Nora. *The Jews in the Soviet Union since 1917: Paradox of Survival*, 2 vols. (New York, 1988).

Lewin, Moshe. *Lenin's Last Struggle* (New York, 1968).

Liber, George O. *Soviet Nationality Policy, Urban Growth, and Identity Change in the Ukrainian SSR, 1923–1934* (Cambridge, 1992).

Lubin, Nancy. *Labour and Nationality in Soviet Central Asia* (Princeton, N.J., 1984).

Luckyj, George S. N. *Literary Politics in the Soviet Ukraine, 1917–1934* (rev. ed., Durham, N.C., 1990).

Macartney, C. A. *National States and National Minorities* (London, 1934).

Mace, James E. *Communism and the Dilemmas of National Liberation: National Communism in Soviet Ukraine, 1918–1933* (Cambridge, Mass, 1983).

Majstrenko, Iwan. *Borot'bism: A Chapter in the History of Ukrainian Communism* (New York, 1954).

Martin, Terry. "An Affirmative Action Empire: Ethnicity and the Soviet State" (Ph.D. diss., University of Chicago, 1996).

Martin, Terry. "Borders and Ethnic Conflict: The Soviet Experiment in Ethno-Territorial Proliferation." *Jahrbucher für Geschichte Osteuropas* 47 (1999): 538–555.

Martin, Terry. "The Empire's New Frontiers: New Russia's Path from Frontier to Okraina, 1774–1920." *Russian History* 19 (1992): 181–201.

Martin, Terry. "Interpreting the New Archival Signals: Nationalities Policy and the Nature of the Soviet Bureaucracy." *Cahiers du monde russe* 40 (1999): 113–124.

Martin, Terry. "Modernization or Neo-Traditionalism: Ascribed Nationality and Soviet Primordialism" In *Stalinism: New Approaches*, ed. Sheila Fitzpatrick (New York, 1999): 348–367.

Martin, Terry. "The Origins of Soviet Ethnic Cleansing." *Journal of Modern History* 70 (1998): 813–861.

Martin, Terry. "The Russification of the RSFSR." *Cahiers du monde russe* 39 (1998): 99–118.

Massell, Gregory J. *The Surrogate Proletariat: Moslem Women and Revolutionary Strategies in Soviet Central Asia, 1919–1929* (Princeton, N.J., 1974).

Matley, Ian M. "The Dispersal of the Ingrian Finns." *Slavic Review* 38 (March 1979): 1–16.

Matossian, Mary. *The Impact of Soviet Policies in Armenia* (Leiden, 1962).

Merl, Shtefan. "Golod 1932–1933 godov—genotsid ukraintsev dlia osushchestvleniia politiki rusifikatsii?" *Otechestvennaia istoriia*, no. 1 (1995): 49–61.

Moins, Nathalie. "Passeportisation, statistique des migrations et controle de l'identite sociale." *Cahiers du monde russe* 38 (1997): 587–600.

Moore, Barrington. *Social Origins of Dictatorship and Democracy: Lord and Peasant in the Making of the Modern World* (Boston, 1966).

Nahaylo, Bohdan, and Swoboda, Victor. *Soviet Disunion: A History of the Nationalities Problem in the USSR* (New York, 1990).

Naimark, Norman. *Fires of Hatred. Ethnic Cleansing in Twentieth-Century Europe* (Cambridge MA, 2000).

Nekrich, Aleksandr M. *The Punished Peoples: The Deportation and Fate of Soviet Minorities at the End of the Second World War* (New York, 1978).

Northrop, Douglas. "Uzbek Women and the Veil: Gender and Power in Stalinist Central Asia" (Ph.D. diss., Stanford University, 1999).

Nove, Alec, and Newth, J. A. *The Soviet Middle East: A Model for Development?* (London, 1967).

Olcott, Martha Brill. *The Kazakhs* (Stanford, Calif., 1987).

Okhotin, N., and Roginskii, A. "Iz istorii 'nemetskoi operatsii' NKVD 1937–1938 gg." in I. L. Shcherbakov ed., *Nakazannyi narod. Repressii protiv rossiiskikh nemtsev* (Moscow, 1999): 35–74.

Okhotin, N., and Roginskii, A. " 'Latyshskaia operatsiia' 1937–1938 godov. Arkhivnyi kommentarii." *30 Oktabria* no. 4 (2000): 5.

Omarov, M. *Rasstreliannaia step'* (Almaty, 1994).

Oskolkov, E. N. *Golod 1932/1933: Khlebozagotovki i golod 1932/1933 goda v Severo-Kavkazskom krae* (Rostov-na-donu, 1991).

Park, Alexander G. *Bolshevism in Turkestan, 1917–1927* (New York, 1957).

Payne, Matthew. "Turksib. The Building of the Turkestano-Siberian Railroad and the Politics of Production during the Cultural Revolution, 1926–1931" (Ph.D. diss, University of Chicago, 1995).

Penner, D'Ann R. "Stalin and the *Ital'ianka* of 1932–1933 in the Don Region." *Cahiers du monde russe* 39 (1998): 27–68.

Petrov, N. V., and Roginskii, A. B. " 'Pol'skaia operatsiia' NKVD 1937–1938 gg." in A. E. Gur'ianov ed., *Repressii protiv poliakov* (Moscow, 1997): 22–43.

Pipes, Richard. *The Formation of the Soviet Union: Communism and Nationalism* (rev. ed., Cambridge, Mass., 1964).

Pyrih, Ruslan. *Zhyttia Mykhaila Hrushevs'koho. Ostanne desiatylittia, 1924–1934* (Kiev, 1993).

Radziejowski, Janusz. *The Communist Party of Western Ukraine, 1919–1929* (Edmonton, 1983).

Represii protiv poliakov i pol'skikh grazhdan (Moscow, 1997).

Revesz, Laszlo. *Minderheitenschicksal in den Nachfolgestaaten der Donaumonarchie: Unter besonderer Beruecksichtigung der Magyarischen Minderheit* (Vienna, 1990).

Rublov, O. S., and Cherchenko, I. A. *Stalinshchyna i dolia zakhidnoukrains'koi intelihentsii. 20–50-ti roku XX st.* (Kiev, 1994).

Sabol, Steven. "The Creation of Soviet Central Asia: The 1924 National Delimitation." *Central Asian Survey* 14 (1995): 225–241.

Sakunov, Ksenofont. "Stalinist Terror in the Mari Republic: The Attack on 'Finno-Ugrian Bourgeois Nationalism.'" *Soviet and East European Review* 74 (1996): 658–682.

Sanborn, Joshua. "Family, Fraternity, and Nation-building in Russia, 1905–1925." In *A State of Nations: Empire and Nation-Building in the Age of Lenin and Stalin*, ed. Ronald Grigor Suny and Terry Martin (2001).

Schafer, Daniel. "Building Nations and Building States: The Tatar–Bashkir Question in Revolutionary Russia, 1917–1920" (Ph.D. diss., University of Michigan, 1995).

Serbyn, Roman, and Krawchenko, Bohdan, eds. *Famine in Ukraine, 1932–1933* (Edmonton, 1986).

Shapoval, I. I. *Liudyna i systema. Shtrykhy do portretu totalitarnoi doby v Ukraini* (Kiev, 1994).

Shapoval, I. I. *Ukraina 20–50-kh rokiv. Storinky nenapysanoi istorii* (Kiev, 1993).

Shearer, David R. "Crime and Social Disorder in Stalin's Russia: A Reassessment of the Great Retreat and the Origins of Mass Repression." *Cahiers du monde russe* 39 (1998): 119–148.

Shevelov, George Y. *The Ukrainian Language in the First Half of the Twentieth Century, 1900–1941: Its State and Status* (Cambridge, Mass., 1989).

Shimotomai, Nobuo. "A note on the Kuban Affair, 1932–1933." *Acta Slavica Iaponica* 1 (1983): 39–56.

Shkandrij, Myroslav. *Modernists, Marxists and the Nation: The Ukrainian Literary Discussion of the 1920s* (Edmonton, 1992).

Siegelbaum, Lewis H. *Stakhanovism and the Politics of Productivity in the USSR, 1935–1941* (Cambridge, 1988).

Simon, Gerhard. *Nationalism and Policy Toward the Nationalities in the Soviet Union* (Boulder, Colo., 1991).

Skocpol, Theda. *States and Social Revolutions* (Cambridge, 1979).

Slezkine, Yuri. *Arctic Mirrors: Russia and the Small Peoples of the North* (Ithaca, N.Y., 1994).

Slezkine, Yuri. "The USSR as a Communal Apartment, or How a Socialist State Promoted Ethnic Particularism." *Slavic Review* 53 (Summer, 1994): 414–452.

Smith, Jeremy. *The Bolsheviks and the National Question, 1917–1923* (London, 1999).

Smith, Michael. *Language and Power in the Creation of the USSR, 1917–1953* (Berlin, 1998).

Sovetskie kurdy. Vremia peremen (Moscow, 1993).

Solomon, Peter. *Soviet Criminal Justice under Stalin* (Cambridge, 1996).

Sowell, Thomas. *Preferential Policies: An International Perspective* (New York, 1990).

Suh, Daae-Sook, ed. *Koreans in the Soviet Union* (Honolulu, 1987).

Suny, Ronald Grigor. *The Making of the Georgian Nation* (Bloomington, Ind., 1988).

Suny, Ronald Grigor. *The Revenge of the Past: Nationalism, Revolution and the Collapse of the Soviet Union* (Stanford, Calif., 1993)

Szporluk, Roman. "Nationalities and the Russian Problem in the USSR: An Historical Outline." *Journal of International Affairs* 27 (1973): 22–40.

Tillett, Lowell. *The Great Friendship: Soviet Historians on the Non-Russian Nationalities* (Chapel Hill, N.C., 1969).

Tilly, Charles. *Coercion, Capital and European States, AD 990–1992* (Oxford, 1992).

Timasheff, Nicholas S. *The Great Retreat: The Growth and Decline of Communism in Russia* (New York, 1946).

Trimberger, Ellen Kay. *Revolution from Above: Military Bureaucrats and Development in Japan, Turkey, Egypt, and Peru* (New Brunswick, N.J., 1978).

Tucker, Robert C. *Political Culture and Leadership in Soviet Russia* (New York, 1987).

Tucker, Robert C. *Stalin in Power: The Revolution from Above, 1928–1941* (New York, 1990)

Vaksberg, Arkady. *Stalin Against the Jews* (New York, 1994).

Vihavainen, Timo, and Takala, Irina. *V sem'e edinoi*. *Natsional'naia politika partii bol'shevikov i ee osushchestvlenie na Severo-Zapade Rossii v 1920–1950-e* gody (Petrozavodsk, 1998).

Viola, Lynne. *Peasant Rebels under Stalin: Collectivization and the Culture of Peasant Resistance* (Oxford, 1996).

Walder, Andrew. *Communist Neo-Traditionalism: Work and Authority in Chinese Industry* (Berkeley, Calif., 1986).

Walt, Stephen M. *Revolution and War* (Ithaca, N.Y., 1996).

Wandruszka, Adam, and Urbanitsch, Peer, eds. *Die Habsburgermonarchie, 1848–1918. Band III. Die Völker des Reiches* (Vienna, 1980).

Zabrotski, Eduard. "Kalanizatsyina-perasialenchyia pratsesy u Belarusi u 20–30-ia hh." *Belaruski histarychny chasopis*, no. 4 (1993): 88–91.

Zagorovskii, P. V. *Sotsial'no-politichekaia istoriia Tsentral'no-Chernozemnoi oblasti, 1928–1934* (Voronezh, 1995).

Zaslavsky, Victor. *The Neo-Stalinist State: Class, Ethnicity, and Consensus in Soviet Society* (2nd ed., Amronk, N.Y., 1994).

Zemskov, V. N. "Spetsposelentsy (po dokumentatsii NKVD-MVD SSSR)." *Sotsiologicheskie issledovaniia*, no. 11 (1990).

Index

The *Wilder House Series in Politics, History, and Culture*

A series edited by

David D. Laitin
George Steinmetz